BUTTERWORTHS STUDENT STATUTES

Family Law

Second edition

ELIZABETH COOKE, MA, LL M, Solicitor

Lecturer in Law

Reading University

Butterworths

London, Edinburgh, Dublin

1999

United Kingdom	Butterworths, a Division of Reed Elsevier (UK) Ltd, Halsbury House, 35 Chancery Lane, LONDON WC2A 1EL and 4 Hill Street, EDINBURGH EH2 3JZ
Australia	Butterworths, a Division of Reed International Books Australia Pty Ltd, CHATSWOOD, New South Wales
Canada	Butterworths Canada Ltd, MARKHAM, Ontario
Hong Kong	Butterworths Asia (Hong Kong), HONG KONG
India	Butterworths India, NEW DELHI
Ireland	Butterworth (Ireland) Ltd, DUBLIN
Malaysia	Malayan Law Journal Sdn Bhd, KUALA LUMPUR
New Zealand	Butterworths of New Zealand Ltd, WELLINGTON
Singapore	Butterworths Asia, SINGAPORE
South Africa	Butterworths Publishers (Pty) Ltd, DURBAN
USA	Lexis Law Publishing, CHARLOTTESVILLE, Virginia

A CIP Catalogue record for this book is available from the British Library.

ISBN 0 406 92241 1

Printed by Hobbs the Printers Ltd, Totton, Hampshire

Visit us at our website: http://www.butterworths.co.uk

BUTTERWORTHS STUDENT STATUTES

FAMILY LAW

Preface

This edition both updates and expands the first edition of *Butterworths Student Statutes: Family Law*. It also provides a sad reflection on the progress of reform in the area of family law. A conspicuous feature of the first edition was the volume of material which was not yet implemented, but was reproduced alongside the current provisions. Since then we have seen the implementation of the sections of the Family Law Act 1996 dealing with domestic violence; however, even as the second edition goes to press the government has announced that it will not be bringing Part II of the 1996 Act into force in 2000, and it has not set an alternative date. So, sadly, the new divorce provisions remain inactive, and their implementation actually seems more remote than it did two years ago. Again, the two sets of provisions are reproduced so that the next development can be evaluated in the light of both.

Lizzie Cooke
Reading,
June 1999

Contents

Wills Act 1837

(c 26)

An Act for the amendment of the Laws with respect to Wills

[3 July 1837]

[18 Wills to be revoked by marriage, except in certain cases

(1)   Subject to subsections (2) to (4) below, a will shall be revoked by the testator's marriage.

(2)   A disposition in a will in exercise of a power of appointment shall take effect notwithstanding the testator's subsequent marriage unless the property so appointed would in default of appointment pass to his personal representatives.

(3)   Where it appears from a will that at the time it was made the testator was expecting to be married to a particular person and that he intended that the will should not be revoked by the marriage, the will shall not be revoked by his marriage to that person.

(4)   Where it appears from a will that at the time it was made the testator was expecting to be married to a particular person and that he intended that a disposition in the will should not be revoked by his marriage to that person,—
  (a) that disposition shall take effect notwithstanding the marriage; and
  (b) any other disposition in the will shall take effect also, unless it appears from the will that the testator intended the disposition to be revoked by the marriage.]

NOTES

Substituted with a saving by the Administration of Justice Act 1982, ss 18(1), 73(6).

[18A Effect of dissolution or annulment of marriage on wills

(1)   Where, after a testator has made a will, *a decree* of a court [of civil jurisdiction in England and Wales] dissolves or annuls his marriage [or his

marriage is dissolved or annulled and the divorce or annulment is entitled to recognition in England and Wales by virtue of Part II of the Family Law Act 1986],—

    [(a) provisions of the will appointing executors or trustees or conferring a power of appointment, if they appoint or confer the power on the former spouse, shall take effect as if the former spouse had died on the date on which the marriage is dissolved or annulled, and

    (b) any property which, or an interest in which, is devised or bequeathed to the former spouse shall pass as if the former spouse had died on that date,]

except in so far as a contrary intention appears by the will.

(2)   Subsection (1)(b) above is without prejudice to any right of the former spouse to apply for financial provision under the Inheritance (Provision for Family and Dependants) Act 1975.

(3)   . . .]

NOTES

Inserted with a saving by the Administration of Justice Act 1982, ss 18(2), 73(6).

Sub-s (1): words in first pair of square brackets substituted and words in second pair of square brackets inserted by the Family Law Act 1986, s 53; paras (a), (b) substituted by the Law Reform (Succession) Act 1995, s 3, with effect as respects a will made by a person dying on or after 1 January 1996 (regardless of the date of the will and the date of the dissolution or annulment); for the words in italics there are substituted the words "an order or decree" by the Family Law Act 1996, s 66(1), Sch 8, Pt I, para 1, subject to savings in s 66(2) of, and Sch 9, para 5 to, the 1996 Act, as from a day to be appointed.

Sub-s (3): repealed by the Law Reform (Succession) Act 1995, s 5, Schedule, with effect as respects a will made by a person dying on or after 1 January 1996 (regardless of the date of the will and the date of the dissolution or annulment).

Offences Against the Person Act 1861

(c 100)

An Act to consolidate and amend the Statute Law of England and Ireland relating to Offences against the Person

[6 August 1861]

Attempts to procure Abortion

58 Administering drugs or using instruments to procure abortion

Every woman, being with child, who, with intent to procure her own miscarriage, shall unlawfully administer to herself any poison or other noxious thing, or shall unlawfully use any instrument or other means whatsoever with the like intent, and whosoever, with intent to procure the miscarriage of any woman, whether she be or be not with child, shall unlawfully administer to her or cause to be taken by her any poison or other noxious thing, or shall unlawfully use any instrument or other means whatsoever with the like intent, shall be guilty of felony, and being convicted thereof shall be liable . . . to be kept in penal servitude for life . . .

NOTES

Words omitted repealed by the Statute Law Revision Act 1892 and the Statute Law Revision (No 2) Act 1893.

59 Procuring drugs, etc, to cause abortion

Whosoever shall unlawfully supply or procure any poison or other noxious thing, or any instrument or thing whatsoever, knowing that the same is intended to be unlawfully used or employed with intent to procure the miscarriage of any woman, whether she be or be not with child, shall be guilty of a misdemeanor, and being convicted thereof shall be liable . . . to be kept in penal servitude . . .

NOTES

Words omitted repealed by the Statute Law Revision Act 1892.

Married Women's Property Act 1882

(c 75)

An Act to consolidate and amend the Acts relating to the Property of Married Women

[18 August 1882]

17 Questions between husband and wife as to property to be decided in a summary way

In any question between husband and wife as to the title to or possession of property, either party, . . . may apply by summons or otherwise in a summary way [to the High Court or such county court as may be prescribed and the court may, on such an application (which may be heard in private), make such order with respect to the property as it thinks fit.

In this section "prescribed" means prescribed by rules of court and rules made for the purposes of this section may confer jurisdiction on county courts whatever the situation or value of the property in dispute.]

NOTES

Words omitted repealed by the Statute Law (Repeals) Act 1969; words in square brackets substituted by the Matrimonial and Family Proceedings Act 1984, s 43.

Law of Property Act 1925

(c 20)

An Act to consolidate the enactments relating to Conveyancing and the Law of Property in England and Wales

[9 April 1925]

PART I
GENERAL PRINCIPLES AS TO LEGAL ESTATES, EQUITABLE INTERESTS AND POWERS

[Trusts of land]

NOTES

Heading inserted by the Trusts of Land and Appointment of Trustees Act 1996, s 25(1), Sch 3, para 4(1), (7).

30 Powers of court where trustees for sale refuse to exercise powers

[(1)] If the trustees for sale refuse to sell or to exercise any of the powers conferred by either of the last two sections, or any requisite consent cannot be obtained, any person interested may apply to the court for a vesting or other order for giving effect to the proposed transaction or for an order directing the trustees for sale to give effect thereto, and the court may make such order as it thinks fit.

[(2)   The county court has jurisdiction under this section . . .]

NOTES

Repealed by the Trusts of Land and Appointment of Trustees Act 1996, s 25(2), Sch 4; the section is reproduced here for reasons of historical interest or in view of the savings contained in ss 3, 18(3), 25(5) of the 1996 Act.

Sub-s (1): numbered as such by the County Courts Act 1984, s 148(1), Sch 2, para 2.

Sub-s (2): added by the County Courts Act 1984, s 148(1), Sch 2, para 2; words omitted repealed by the High Court and County Courts Jurisdiction Order 1991, SI 1991/724, art 2(8), Schedule, Pt I.

Undivided Shares and Joint Ownership

37 Rights of husband and wife

A husband and wife shall, for all purposes of acquisition of any interest in property, under a disposition made or coming into operation after the commencement of this Act, be treated as two persons.

PART XI
MISCELLANEOUS

Miscellaneous

184 Presumption of survivorship in regard to claims to property

In all cases where, after the commencement of this Act, two or more persons have died in circumstances rendering it uncertain which of them survived the other or others, such deaths shall (subject to any order of the court), for all purposes affecting the title of property, be presumed to have occurred in order of seniority, and accordingly the younger shall be deemed to have survived the elder.

PART XII
CONSTRUCTION, JURISDICTION, AND GENERAL PROVISIONS

209 Short title, commencement, extent

(1)   This Act may be cited as the Law of Property Act 1925.

(2)   . . .

(3)   This Act extends to England and Wales only.

NOTES

Sub-s (2): repealed by the Statute Law Revision Act 1950.

Administration of Estates Act 1925

(c 23)

An Act to consolidate Enactments relating to the Administration of the Estates of Deceased Persons

[9 April 1925]

PART IV
DISTRIBUTION OF RESIDUARY ESTATE

46 Succession to real and personal estate on intestacy

(1)   The residuary estate of an intestate shall be distributed in the manner or be held on the trusts mentioned in this section, namely:—
    [(i) If the intestate leaves a husband or wife, then in accordance with the following Table:

TABLE

If the intestate—

(1) leaves—
    (a) no issue, and
    (b) no parent, or brother or sister
       or wife of the whole blood, or
       issue of a brother or sister
       of the whole blood

the residuary estate shall be held in trust for the surviving husband absolutely.

(2) leaves issue (whether or not persons mentioned in sub-paragraph (b) above also survive)

the surviving husband or wife shall take the personal chattels absolutely and, in addition, the residuary estate of the intestate (other than the personal chattels) shall stand charged with the payment of a [fixed net sum], free of death duties and costs, to the surviving husband or wife with interest thereon from the date of the death . . . [at such rate as the Lord Chancellor may specify by order] until paid or appropriated, and, subject to providing for that sum and the interest thereon, the residuary estate (other than the personal chattels) shall be held—

(a) as to one half upon trust for the surviving husband or wife during his or her life, and, subject to such life interest, on the statutory trusts for the issue of the intestate, and

(b) as to the other half, on the statutory trusts for the issue of the intestate.

(3) leaves one or more of the following, that is to say, a parent, a brother or sister of the whole blood, or issue of a brother or sister of the whole blood, but leaves no issue

the surviving husband or wife shall take the personal chattels absolutely and, in addition, the residuary estate of the intestate (other than the personal chattels) shall stand charged with the payment of a [fixed net sum], free of death duties and costs, to the surviving husband or wife with interest thereon from the date of the death . . . [at such rate as the Lord Chancellor may specify by order] until paid or appropriated, and, subject to providing for that sum and the interest thereon, the residuary estate (other than the personal chattels) shall be held—

(a) as to one half in trust for the surviving husband or wife absolutely, and

(b) as to the other half—

(i) where the intestate leaves one parent or both parents (whether or not brothers or sisters of the intestate or their issue also survive) in trust for the parent absolutely or, as the case may be, for the two parents in equal shares absolutely

(ii) where the intestate leaves no parent, on the statutory trusts for the brothers and sisters of the whole blood of the intestate.]

[The fixed net sums referred to in paragraphs (2) and (3) of this Table shall be of the amounts provided by or under section 1 of the Family Provision Act 1966]

(ii) If the intestate leaves issue but no husband or wife, the residuary estate of the intestate shall be held on the statutory trusts for the issue of the intestate;

(iii) If the intestate leaves [no husband or wife and] no issue but both parents, then . . . the residuary estate of the intestate shall be held in trust for the father and mother in equal shares absolutely;

(iv) If the intestate leaves [no husband or wife and] no issue but one parent, then . . . the residuary estate of the intestate shall be held in trust for the surviving father or mother absolutely;

(v) If the intestate leaves no [husband or wife and no issue and no] parent, then . . . the residuary estate of the intestate shall be held in trust for the following persons living at the death of the intestate, and in the following order and manner, namely:—

First, on the statutory trusts for the brothers and sisters of the whole blood of the intestate; but if no person takes an absolutely vested interest under such trusts; then

Secondly, on the statutory trusts for the brothers and sisters of the half blood of the intestate; but if no person takes an absolutely vested interest under such trusts; then

Thirdly, for the grandparents of the intestate and, if more than one survive the intestate, in equal shares; but if there is no member of this class; then

Fourthly, on the statutory trusts for the uncles and aunts of the intestate (being brothers or sisters of the whole blood of a parent of the intestate); but if no person takes an absolutely vested interest under such trusts; then

Fifthly, on the statutory trusts for the uncles and aunts of the intestate (being brothers or sisters of the half blood of a parent of the intestate) . . .

(vi) In default of any person taking an absolute interest under the foregoing provisions, the residuary estate of the intestate shall belong to the Crown or to the Duchy of Lancaster or to the Duke of Cornwall for the time being, as the case may be, as bona vacantia, and in lieu of any right to escheat.

The Crown or the said Duchy or the said Duke may (without prejudice to the powers reserved by section nine of the Civil List Act 1910, or any other powers), out of the whole or any part of the property devolving on them respectively, provide, in accordance with the existing practice, for dependents, whether kindred or not, of the intestate, and other persons for whom the intestate might reasonably have been expected to make provision.

[(1A) The power to make orders under subsection (1) above shall be exercisable by statutory instrument subject to annulment in pursuance of a resolution of either House of Parliament; and any such order may be varied or revoked by a subsequent order made under the power.]

(2) A husband and wife shall for all purposes of distribution or division under the foregoing provisions of this section be treated as two persons.

[(2A) Where the intestate's husband or wife survived the intestate but died before the end of the period of 28 days beginning with the day on which the intestate died, this section shall have effect as respects the intestate as if the husband or wife had not survived the intestate.]

[(3)   Where the intestate and the intestate's husband or wife have died in circumstances rendering it uncertain which of them survived the other and the intestate's husband or wife is by virtue of section one hundred and eighty-four of the Law of Property Act 1925, deemed to have survived the intestate, this section shall, nevertheless, have effect as respects the intestate as if the husband or wife had not survived the intestate.

(4)   The interest payable on [the fixed net sum] payable to a surviving husband or wife shall be primarily payable out of income.]

NOTES

Sub-s (1): para (i) substituted by the Intestates' Estates Act 1952, s 1, words in first and third pairs of square brackets substituted, and words at the end of the table added, by the Family Provision Act 1966, s 1, words in second and fourth pairs of square brackets substituted by the Administration of Justice Act 1977, s 28(1)(a) and words omitted repealed by the Statute Law (Repeals) Act 1981; words in square brackets in para (iii) inserted, and words omitted repealed, by the Intestates' Estates Act 1952, s 1; words in square brackets in para (iv) inserted, and words omitted repealed, by the Intestates' Estates Act 1952, s 1; words in square brackets in para (v) substituted, and words omitted repealed, by the Intestates' Estates Act 1952, s 1.

Sub-s (1A): inserted by the Administration of Justice Act 1977, s 28(1).

Sub-s (2A): inserted by the Law Reform (Succession) Act 1995, s 1(1), (3), with effect as respects an intestate dying on or after 1 January 1996.

Sub-s (3): added by the Intestates' Estates Act 1952, s 1(4).

Sub-s (4): added by the Intestates' Estates Act 1952, s 1(4); words in square brackets substituted by the Family Provision Act 1966, s 1.

47   Statutory trusts in favour of issue and other classes of relatives of intestate

(1)   Where under this Part of this Act the residuary estate of an intestate, or any part thereof, is directed to be held on the statutory trusts for the issue of the intestate, the same shall be held upon the following trusts, namely:—

(i)   In trust, in equal shares if more than one, for all or any the children or child of the intestate, living at the death of the intestate, who attain the age of [eighteen] years or marry under that age, and for all or any of the issue living at the death of the intestate who attain the age of [eighteen] years or marry under that age of any child of the intestate who predeceases the intestate, such issue to take through all degrees, according to their stocks, in equal shares if more than one, the share which their parent would have taken if living at the death of the intestate, and so that no issue shall take whose parent is living at the death of the intestate and so capable of taking;

(ii) The statutory power of advancement, and the statutory provisions which relate to maintenance and accumulation of surplus income, shall apply, but when an infant marries such infant shall be entitled to give valid receipts for the income of the infant's share or interest;

(iii) . . .

(iv) The personal representatives may permit any infant contingently interested to have the use and enjoyment of any personal chattels in such manner and subject to such conditions (if any) as the personal representatives may consider reasonable, and without being liable to account for any consequential loss.

(2)   If the trusts in favour of the issue of the intestate fail by reason of no child or other issue attaining an absolutely vested interest—

(a) the residuary estate of the intestate and the income thereof and all statutory accumulations, if any, of the income thereof, or so much thereof as may not have been paid or applied under any power affecting the same, shall go, devolve and be held under the provisions of this Part of this Act as if the intestate had died without leaving issue living at the death of the intestate;

(b) references in this Part of this Act to the intestate "leaving no issue" shall be construed as "leaving no issue who attain an absolutely vested interest";

(c) references in this Part of this Act to the intestate "leaving issue" or "leaving a child or other issue" shall be construed as "leaving issue who attain an absolutely vested interest."

(3)   Where under this Part of this Act the residuary estate of an intestate or any part thereof is directed to be held on the statutory trusts for any class of relatives of the intestate, other than issue of the intestate, the same shall be held on trusts corresponding to the statutory trusts for the issue of the intestate (other than the provision for bringing any money or property into account) as if such trusts (other than as aforesaid) were repeated with the substitution of references to the members or member of that class for references to the children or child of the intestate.

[(4)   References in paragraph (i) of subsection (1) of the last foregoing section to the intestate leaving, or not leaving, a member of the class consisting of brothers or sisters of the whole blood of the intestate and issue of brothers or sisters of the whole blood of the intestate shall be construed as references to the intestate leaving, or not leaving, a member of that class who attains an absolutely vested interest.

(5)   . . .]

NOTES

Sub-s (1): words in square brackets substituted, in relation to the estate of an intestate dying after 1 January 1970, by the Family Law Reform Act 1969, s 3(2); para (iii) repealed by the Law Reform (Succession) Act 1995, ss 1(2)(a), (3), 5, Schedule, with effect as respects an intestate dying on or after 1 January 1996.

Sub-s (4): added by the Intestates' Estates Act 1952, s 1(3)(c).

Sub-s (5): added by the Intestates' Estates Act 1952, s 1(3)(c); repealed by the Family Provision Act 1966, ss 9, 10, Sch 2.

[47A   Right of surviving spouse to have his own life interest redeemed

(1)   Where a surviving husband or wife is entitled to the interest in part of the residuary estate, and so elects, the personal representative shall purchase or redeem the life interest by paying the capital value thereof to the tenant for life, or the persons deriving title under the tenant for life, and the costs of the transaction; and thereupon the residuary estate of the intestate may be dealt with and distributed free from the life interest.

(2)   . . .

(3)   An election under this section shall only be exercisable if at the time of the election the whole of the said part of the residuary estate consists of property in possession, but, for the purposes of this section, a life interest in property partly in possession and partly not in possession shall be treated as consisting of two separate life interests in those respective parts of the property.

[(3A)   The capital value shall be reckoned in such manner as the Lord Chancellor may by order direct, and an order under this subsection may include transitional provisions.

(3B)   The power to make orders under subsection (3A) above shall be exercisable by statutory instrument subject to annulment in pursuance of a resolution of either House of Parliament; and any such order may be varied or revoked by a subsequent order made under the power.]

(4)   . . .

(5)   An election under this section shall be exercisable only within the period of twelve months from the date on which representation with respect to the estate of the intestate is first taken out:

Provided that if the surviving husband or wife satisfies the court that the limitation to the said period of twelve months will operate unfairly—
   (a) in consequence of the representation first taken out being probate of a will subsequently revoked on the ground that the will was invalid, or
   (b) in consequence of a question whether a person had an interest in the estate, or as to the nature of an interest in the estate, not having been determined at the time when representation was first taken out, or
   (c) in consequence of some other circumstances affecting the administration or distribution of the estate,

the court may extend the said period.

(6)   An election under this section shall be exercisable, except where the tenant for life is the sole personal representative, by notifying the personal representative (or, where there are two or more personal representatives of whom one is the tenant for life, all of them except the tenant for life) in writing; and a notification in writing under this subsection shall not be revocable except with the consent of the personal representative.

(7)   Where the tenant for life is the sole personal representative an election under this section shall not be effective unless written notice thereof is given to the [[Senior Registrar] of the Family Division of the High Court] within the period within which it must be made; and provision may be made by probate rules for keeping a record of such notices and making that record available to the public.

In this subsection the expression "probate rules" means rules [of court made under section 127 of the Supreme Court Act 1981].

(8)   An election under this section by a tenant for life who is an infant shall be as valid and binding as it would be if the tenant for life were of age; but the personal representative shall, instead of paying the capital value of the life interest to the tenant for life, deal with it in the same manner as with any other part of the residuary estate to which the tenant for life is absolutely entitled.

(9)   In considering for the purposes of the foregoing provisions of this section the question when representation was first taken out, a grant limited

to settled land or to trust property shall be left out of account and a grant limited to real estate or to personal estate shall be left out of account unless a grant limited to the remainder of the estate has previously been made or is made at the same time.]

NOTES

Inserted by the Intestates' Estates Act 1952, s 2.

Sub-ss (2), (4): repealed by the Administration of Justice Act 1977, ss 28(2), 32(4), Sch 5, Part VI.

Sub-ss (3A), (3B): inserted by the Administration of Justice Act 1977, s 28(3).

Sub-s (7): words in first (outer) pair of square brackets substituted by the Administration of Justice Act 1970, s 1(6), Sch 2, para 4; words in second (inner) pair of square brackets and words in third pair of square brackets substituted by the Supreme Court Act 1981, s 152(1), Sch 5.

48 Powers of personal representative in respect of interests of surviving spouse

(1) . . .

(2) The personal representatives may raise—

  (a) [the fixed net sum] or any part thereof and the interest thereon payable to the surviving husband or wife of the intestate on the security of the whole or any part of the residuary estate of the intestate (other than the personal chattels), so far as that estate may be sufficient for the purpose of the said sum and interest may not have been satisfied by an appropriation under the statutory power available in that behalf; and

  (b) in like manner the capital sum, if any, required for the purchase or redemption of the life interest of the surviving husband or wife of the intestate, or any part thereof not satisfied by the application for that purpose of any part of the residuary estate of the intestate;

and in either case the amount, if any, properly required for the payment of the costs of the transaction.

NOTES

Sub-s (1): repealed by the Intestates' Estates Act 1952, s 2.

Sub-s (2): words in square brackets substituted by the Family Provision Act 1966, s 1.

49 Application to cases of partial intestacy

[(1)] Where any person dies leaving a will effectively disposing of part of his property, this Part of this Act shall have effect as respects the part of his property not so disposed of subject to the provisions contained in the will and subject to the following modifications:—

[(aa) ...]

  (a) ...

  (b) The personal representative shall, subject to his rights and powers for the purposes of administration, be a trustee for the persons entitled under this Part of this Act in respect of the part of the estate not expressly disposed of unless it appears by the will that the personal representative is intended to take such part beneficially.

[(2), (3) ...]

[(4) The references in subsection (3) of section forty-seven A of this Act to property are references to property comprised in the residuary estate and, accordingly, where a will of the deceased creates a life interest in property in possession, and the remaining interest in that property forms part of the residuary estate, the said references are references to that remaining interest (which, until the life interest determines, is property not in possession).]

NOTES

Sub-s (1): numbered as such by the Intestates' Estates Act 1952, s 3; para (aa) inserted by the Intestates' Estates Act 1952, s 3, repealed by the Law Reform (Succession) Act 1995, ss 1(2)(b), (3), 5, Schedule, with effect as respects an intestate dying on or after 1 January 1996, words in square brackets substituted by the Family Provision Act 1966, s 1; para (a) repealed by the Law Reform (Succession) Act 1995, ss 1(2)(b), (3), 5, Schedule, with effect as respects an intestate dying on or after 1 January 1996, words in square brackets inserted by the Intestates' Estates Act 1952, s 3.

Sub-ss (2), (3): added by the Intestates' Estates Act 1952, s 3; repealed by the Law Reform (Succession) Act 1995, ss 1(2)(b), (3), 5, Schedule, with effect as respects an intestate dying on or after 1 January 1996.

Sub-s (4): added by the Intestates' Estates Act 1952, s 3.

PART V
SUPPLEMENTAL

58 Short title, commencement and extent

(1) This Act may be cited as the Administration of Estates Act 1925.

(2)   . . .

(3)   This Act extends to England and Wales only.

NOTES

Sub-s (2): repealed by the Statute Law Revision Act 1950.

Infant Life (Preservation) Act 1929

(c 34)

An Act to amend the law with regard to the destruction of children at or before birth

[10 May 1929]

1   Punishment for child destruction

(1)   Subject as hereinafter in this subsection provided, any person who, with intent to destroy the life of a child capable of being born alive, by any wilful act causes a child to die before it has an existence independent of its mother, shall be guilty of felony, to wit, of child destruction, and shall be liable on conviction thereof on indictment to penal servitude for life:

Provided that no person shall be found guilty of an offence under this section unless it is proved that the act which caused the death of the child was not done in good faith for the purpose only of preserving the life of the mother.

(2)   For the purposes of this Act, evidence that a woman had at any material time been pregnant for a period of twenty-eight weeks or more shall be prima facie proof that she was at that time pregnant of a child capable of being born alive.

2   Prosecution of offences

(1)   . . .

(2)   Where upon the trial of any person for the murder or manslaughter of any child, or for infanticide, or for an offence under

section fifty-eight of the Offences against the Person Act 1861 (which relates to administering drugs or using instruments to procure abortion), the jury are of opinion that the person charged is not guilty of murder, manslaughter or infanticide, or of an offence under the said section fifty-eight, as the case may be, but that he is shown by the evidence to be guilty of the felony of child destruction, the jury may find him guilty of that felony, and thereupon the person convicted shall be liable to be punished as if he had been convicted upon an indictment for child destruction.

(3)   Where upon the trial of any person for the felony of child destruction the jury are of opinion that the person charged is not guilty of that felony, but that he is shown by the evidence to be guilty of an offence under the said section fifty-eight of the Offences against the Person Act 1861, the jury may find him guilty of that offence, and thereupon the person convicted shall be liable to be punished as if he had been convicted upon an indictment under that section.

(4), (5)   . . .

NOTES

Sub-ss (1), (4): repealed by the Criminal Law Act 1967, s 10(2), Sch 3, Pt II.
Sub-s (5): repealed by the Police and Criminal Evidence Act 1984, s 119, Sch 7, Pt V.

3   Short title and extent

(1)   This Act may be cited as the Infant Life (Preservation) Act 1929.

(2)   This Act shall not extend to Scotland or Northern Ireland.

Children and Young Persons Act 1933

(c 12)

An Act to consolidate certain enactments relating to persons under the age of eighteen years

[13 April 1933]

PART I
PREVENTION OF CRUELTY AND EXPOSURE TO MORAL AND PHYSICAL DANGER

Offences

1 Cruelty to persons under sixteen

(1)   If any person who has attained the age of sixteen years and [has responsibility for] any child or young person under that age, wilfully assaults, ill-treats, neglects, abandons, or exposes him, or causes or procures him to be assaulted, ill-treated, neglected, abandoned, or exposed, in a manner likely to cause him unnecessary suffering or injury to health (including injury to or loss of sight, or hearing, or limb, or organ of the body, and any mental derangement), that person shall be guilty of a misdemeanour, and shall be liable—
  (a) on conviction on indictment, to a fine . . ., or alternatively, . . . or in addition thereto, to imprisonment for any term not exceeding [ten] years;
  (b) on summary conviction, to a fine not exceeding [the prescribed sum] or alternatively, . . . or in addition thereto, to imprisonment for any term not exceeding six months.

(2)   For the purposes of this section—
  (a) a parent or other person legally liable to maintain a child or young person[, or the legal guardian of a child or young person,] shall be deemed to have neglected him in a manner likely to cause injury to his health if he has failed to provide adequate food, clothing, medical aid or lodging for him, or if, having been unable otherwise to provide such food, clothing, medical aid or lodging, he has failed to take steps to procure it to be provided under [the enactments applicable in that behalf];
  (b) where it is proved that the death of an infant under three years of age was caused by suffocation (not being suffocation caused by disease or the presence of any foreign body in the throat or air passages of the infant) while the infant was in bed with some other person who has attained the age of sixteen years, that other person shall, if he was, when he went to bed, under the influence of drink, be deemed to have neglected the infant in a manner likely to cause injury to its health.

(3)   A person may be convicted of an offence under this section—

(a) notwithstanding that actual suffering or injury to health, or the likelihood of actual suffering or injury to health, was obviated by the action of another person;

(b) notwithstanding the death of the child or young person in question.

(4)–(6). . .

(7) Nothing in this section shall be construed as affecting the right of any parent, *teacher, or other person* having the lawful control or charge of a child or young person to administer punishment to him.

NOTES

Sub-s (1): words in first pair of square brackets substituted by the Children Act 1989, s 108(5), Sch 13, para 2; first words omitted repealed by the Children Act 1975, s 108(1)(b), Sch 4, Pt III; second and third words omitted repealed by the Children and Young Persons Act 1963, s 64(1), (3), Sch 3, para 1, Sch 5; word in second pair of square brackets substituted, in relation to the punishment for an offence committed on or after 29 September 1988, by the Criminal Justice Act 1988, s 45; words in third pair of square brackets substituted by virtue of by the Magistrates' Courts Act 1980, s 32(2).

Sub-s (2): words in first pair of square brackets inserted by the Children Act 1989, s 108(4), Sch 12, para 2; words in second pair of square brackets substituted by the National Assistance (Adaptation of Enactments) Regulations 1950, SI 1950/174.

Sub-s (4): repealed by the Criminal Law Act 1967, s 10, Sch 2, para 13(1), Sch 3, Pt III.

Sub-ss (5), (6): repealed by the Criminal Justice Act 1988, s 170(2), Sch 16.

Sub-s (7): for the words in italics there are substituted the words "or (subject to section 548 of the Education Act 1996) any other person," by the School Standards and Framework Act 1998, s 140(1), Sch 30, para 1, as from a day to be appointed.

Supplemental

[17 Interpretation of Part I

(1) For the purposes of this Part of this Act, the following shall be presumed to have responsibility for a child or young person—

(a) any person who—

(i) has parental responsibility for him (within the meaning of the Children Act 1989); or

(ii) is otherwise legally liable to maintain him; and

(b) any person who has care of him.

(2)   A person who is presumed to be responsible for a child or young person by virtue of subsection (1)(a) shall not be taken to have ceased to be responsible for him by reason only that he does not have care of him.]

NOTES

Substituted by the Children Act 1989, s 108(5), Sch 13, para 5.

PART III
PROTECTION OF CHILDREN AND YOUNG PERSONS IN RELATION TO
CRIMINAL AND SUMMARY PROCEEDINGS

Juvenile Offenders

[55   Power to order parent or guardian to pay fine, etc

(1)   Where—
   (a) a *child or* young person is convicted or found guilty of any offence for the commission of which a fine or costs may be imposed or a compensation order may be made under section 35 of the Powers of Criminal Courts Act 1973; and
   (b) the court is of opinion that the case would best be met by the imposition of a fine or costs or the making of such an order, whether with or without any other punishment,

it shall be the duty of the court to order that the fine, compensation or costs awarded be paid by the parent or guardian of *child or* young person instead of by the *child or* young person himself, unless the court is satisfied—
   (i) that the parent or guardian cannot be found; or
   (ii) that it would be unreasonable to make an order for payment, having regard to the circumstances of the case.

[(1A) Where but for this subsection—
   (a) a court would order a child or young person to pay a fine under [section 15(3)(a)] of the Children and Young Persons Act 1969 (failure to comply with requirement included in supervision order); or
   [(b) a court would impose a fine on a child or young person under section 19(3) of the Criminal Justice Act 1982 (breach of attendance centre order or attendance centre rules); or
   (bb) a court would impose a fine on a child or young person under paragraph 3(1)(a) or 4(1)(a) of Schedule 2 to the Criminal Justice Act

1991 (breach of requirement of a relevant order (within the meaning given by that Schedule) or of a combination order);]

[(c) a court would impose a fine on a child or young person under section 4(3) of the Criminal Justice and Public Order Act 1994 (breach of requirements of supervision under secure training order),][or

(d) a court would impose a fine on a child or young person under . . . paragraph 3 of Schedule 5 to that Act (breach of requirements of reparation order or action plan order),]

it shall be the duty of the court to order that the fine be paid by the parent or guardian of the child or young person instead of by the child or young person himself, unless the court is satisfied—

(i) that the parent or guardian cannot be found; or

(ii) that it would be unreasonable to make an order for payment, having regard to the circumstances of the case.]

[(1B) In the case of a young person who has attained the age of sixteen years, subsections (1) and (1A) above shall have effect as if, instead of imposing a duty, they conferred a power to make such an order as is mentioned in those subsections.]

(2) An order under this section may be made against a parent or guardian who, having been required to attend, has failed to do so, but, save as aforesaid, no such order shall be made without giving the parent or guardian an opportunity of being heard.

(3) A parent or guardian may appeal to the Crown Court against an order under this section made by a magistrates' court.

(4) A parent or guardian may appeal to the Court of Appeal against an order made under this section by the Crown Court, as if he had been convicted on indictment and the order were a sentence passed on his conviction.]

[(5) In relation to a child or young person for whom a local authority have parental responsibility and who—

(a) is in their care; or

(b) is provided with accommodation by them in the exercise of any functions (in particular those under the Children Act 1989) which stand referred to their social services committee under the Local Authority Social Services Act 1970,

references in this section to his parent or guardian shall be construed as references to that authority.

In this subsection "local authority" and "parental responsibility" have the same meanings as in the Children Act 1989.]

[(6)   In relation to any other child or young person, references in this section to his parent shall be construed in accordance with section 1 of the Family Law Reform Act 1987.]

NOTES

Substituted by the Criminal Justice Act 1982, s 26.

Sub-s (1): words in italics repealed by the Children and Young Persons Act 1969, ss 69(4)(c), (5), 72(4), as from a day to be appointed.

Sub-s (1A): inserted by the Criminal Justice Act 1988, s 127; words in square brackets in para (a) substituted, and paras (b), (bb) substituted for original para (b), by the Crime and Disorder Act 1998, s 106, Sch 7, para 1(1), (2); para (c) inserted by the Criminal Justice and Public Order Act 1994, s 168(2), Sch 10, para 4; para (d) added by the Crime and Disorder Act 1998, s 119, Sch 8, para 2, words omitted repealed by the Crime and Disorder Act 1998 (Commencement No 2 and Transitional Provisions) Order 1998, SI 1998/2372, art 2.

Sub-ss (1B), (5): inserted and added by the Criminal Justice Act 1991, s 57(1), (2).

Sub-s (6): added by the Crime and Disorder Act 1998, s 106, Sch 7, para 1(3).

PART VI
SUPPLEMENTAL

General

107   Interpretation

(1)   In this Act, unless the context otherwise requires, the following expressions have the meanings hereby respectively assigned to them, that is to say,—

. . . . .

"Child" means a person under the age of fourteen years;

"Guardian", in relation to a child or young person, includes any person who, in the opinion of the court having cognisance of any case in relation to the child or young person or in which the child or young person is concerned, has for the time being the [care of] the child or young person;

["Young person" means a person who has attained the age of fourteen and is under the age of eighteen years.]

(2)   . . .

NOTES

Sub-s (1): in definition "Guardian" words in square brackets substituted by the Children Act 1989, s 108(5), Sch 13, para 7; definition "Young person" substituted by the Criminal Justice Act 1991, s 68, Sch 8, para 1; definitions omitted outside the scope of this work.

Sub-s (2): repealed by the Children and Young Persons Act 1969, s 72(3), (4), Sch 5, para 12(3), Sch 6.

109   Short title, commencement, extent and repeals

(1)   This Act may be cited as the Children and Young Persons Act 1933.

(2)   . . .

(3)   Save as therein otherwise expressly provided, this Act shall not extend to Scotland or Northern Ireland.

(4)   . . .

NOTES

Sub-ss (2), (4): repealed by the Statute Law Revision Act 1950.

National Assistance Act 1948

(c 29)

An Act to terminate the existing poor law and to provide in lieu thereof for the assistance of persons in need by the National Assistance Board and by local authorities; to make further provisions for the welfare of disabled, sick, aged and other persons and for regulating homes for disabled and aged persons and charities for disabled persons; to amend the law relating to non-contributory old age pensions; to make provision as to the burial or cremation of deceased persons; and for purposes connected with the matters aforesaid

[13 May 1948]

PART III
LOCAL AUTHORITY SERVICES

Provision of Accommodation

21 Duty of local authorities to provide accommodation

(1)   [Subject to and in accordance with the provisions of this Part of this Act, a local authority may with the approval of the Secretary of State, and to such extent as he may direct shall, make arrangements for providing]—
   (a) residential accommodation for persons [aged eighteen or over] who by reason of age, [illness, disability] or any other circumstances are in need of care and attention which is not otherwise available to them; [and
 (aa) residential accommodation for expectant and nursing mothers who are in need of care and attention which is not otherwise available to them.]
   (b) . . .

(2)   In [making any such arrangements] a local authority shall have regard to the welfare of all persons for whom accommodation is provided, and in particular to the need for providing accommodation of different descriptions suited to different descriptions of such persons as are mentioned in the last foregoing subsection.

[(2A)   In determining for the purposes of paragraph (a) or (aa) of subsection (1) of this section whether care and attention are otherwise available to a person, a local authority shall disregard so much of the person's capital as does not exceed the capital limit for the purposes of section 22 of this Act.

(2B)   For the purposes of subsection (2A) of this section—
   (a) a person's capital shall be calculated in accordance with assessment regulations in the same way as if he were a person for whom accommodation is proposed to be provided as mentioned in subsection (3) of section 22 of this Act and whose ability to pay for the accommodation falls to be assessed for the purposes of that subsection; and
   (b) "the capital limit for the purposes of section 22 of this Act" means the amount for the time being prescribed in assessment regulations as the amount which a resident's capital (calculated in accordance with such regulations) must not exceed if he is to be assessed as unable to pay for his accommodation at the standard rate;

and in this subsection "assessment regulations" means regulations made for the purposes of section 22(5) of this Act.]

(3)   . . .

(4)   [Subject to the provisions of section 26 of this Act] accommodation provided by a local authority in the exercise of their [functions under this section] shall be provided in premises managed by the authority or, to such extent as may be [determined in accordance with the arrangements] under this section, in such premises managed by another local authority as may be agreed between the two authorities and on such terms, including terms as to the reimbursement of expenditure incurred by the said other authority, as may be so agreed.

(5)   References in this Act to accommodation provided under this Part thereof shall be construed as references to accommodation provided in accordance with this and the five next following sections, and as including references to board and other services, amenities and requisites provided in connection with the accommodation except where in the opinion of the authority managing the premises their provision is unnecessary.

(6)   References in this Act to a local authority providing accommodation shall be construed, in any case where a local authority agree with another local authority for the provision of accommodation in premises managed by the said other authority, as references to the first-mentioned local authority.

(7)   Without prejudice to the generality of the foregoing provisions of this section, a local authority may—
   (a) provide, in such cases as they may consider appropriate, for the conveyance of persons to and from premises in which accommodation is provided for them under this Part of the Act;
   [(b) make arrangements for the provision on the premises in which accommodation is being provided of such other services as appear to the authority to be required.]

. . . . .

(8)   . . . nothing in this section shall authorise or require a local authority to make any provision authorised or required to be made (whether by that or by any other authority) by or under any enactment not contained in this Part of this Act [or authorised or required to be provided under the National Health Service Act 1977].

NOTES

Sub-s (1): words in first pair of square brackets substituted by the Local Government Act 1972, s 195, Sch 23, para 2; words in second pair of square brackets inserted by the Children Act 1989, s 108(5), Sch 13, para 11(1); words in third pair of square brackets substituted, and words in fourth pair of square brackets inserted, by the National Health Service and Community Care Act 1990, s 42(1); para (b) repealed by the Housing (Homeless Persons) Act 1977, s 20(4), Schedule.

Sub-s (2): words in square brackets substituted by the Local Government Act 1972, s 195, Sch 23, para 2.

Sub-ss (2A), (2B): inserted by the Community Care (Residential Accommodation) Act 1998, s 1.

Sub-s (3): repealed by the Local Government Act 1972, ss 195, 272, Sch 23, para 2, Sch 30.

Sub-s (4): words in first pair of square brackets inserted by the National Health Service and Community Care Act 1990, s 66(1), Sch 9, para 5(1); words in other pairs of square brackets substituted by the Local Government Act 1972, s 195, Sch 23, para 2.

Sub-s (7): para (b) substituted, for paras (b), (c) as originally enacted, by the National Health Service and Community Care Act 1990, s 66(1), Sch 9, para 5(2); words omitted repealed by the National Health Service Reorganisation Act 1973, s 58, Sch 5.

Sub-s (8): words omitted repealed, and words in square brackets added, by the National Health Service and Community Care Act 1990, s 66(1), (2), Sch 9, para 5(3), Sch 10.

PART IV
GENERAL AND SUPPLEMENTARY

Recovery of Expenses

42 Liability to maintain wife or husband, and children

(1)   For the purposes of this Act—
  (a) a man shall be liable to maintain his wife and his children, and
  (b) a woman shall be liable to maintain her husband and her children.

[(2)   Any reference in subsection (1) of this section to a person's children shall be construed in accordance with section 1 of the Family Law Reform Act 1987.]

(3)   . . .

NOTES

Sub-s (2): substituted by the Family Law Reform Act 1987, s 33, Sch 2, para 5.
Sub-s (3): outside the scope of this work.

43 Recovery of cost of assistance from persons liable for maintenance

(1)   Where assistance is given or applied for by reference to the requirements of any person (in this section referred to as a person assisted), . . . the local authority concerned may make a complaint to the court against any other person who for the purposes of this Act is liable to maintain the person assisted.

(2)   On a complaint under this section the court shall have regard to all the circumstances and in particular to the resources of the defendant, and may order the defendant to pay such sum, weekly or otherwise, as the court may consider appropriate.

(3)   For the purposes of the application of the last foregoing subsection to payments in respect of assistance given before the complaint was made, a person shall not be treated as having at the time when the complaint is heard any greater resources than he had at the time when the assistance was given.

(4)   In this section the expression "assistance" means . . . the provision of accommodation under Part III of this Act (hereinafter referred to as "assistance under Part III of this Act"); and the expression "the court" means a court of summary jurisdiction [appointed for the commission area (within the meaning of [the Justices of the Peace Act 1997])] where the assistance was given or applied for.

(5)   Payments under subsection (2) of this section shall be made—
  (a) to . . . the local authority concerned, in respect of the cost of assistance, whether given before or after the making of the order, or
  (b) to the applicant for assistance or any other person being a person assisted, or
  (c) to such other person as appears to the court expedient in the interests of the person assisted,

or as to part in one such manner and as to part in another, as may be provided by the order.

[(6)   An order under this section shall be enforceable as a magistrates' court maintenance order within the meaning of section 150(1) of the Magistrates' Courts Act 1980.]

(7), (8)   . . .

Sub-ss (1), (5): words omitted repealed by the Supplementary Benefit Act 1966, s 39(3), Sch 8.

Sub-s (4): words omitted repealed by the Supplementary Benefit Act 1966, s 39(3), Sch 8; words in first (outer) pair of square brackets substituted by the Domestic Proceedings and Magistrates' Courts Act 1978, s 89(2), Sch 2, para 6, second words in (inner) pair of square brackets substituted by the Justices of the Peace Act 1997, s 73(2), Sch 5, para 5.

Sub-s (6): added by the Supplementary Benefits Act 1976, s 35(2), Sch 7, para 4; substituted by the Family Law Reform Act 1987, s 33(1), Sch 2, para 6.

Sub-ss (7), (8): outside the scope of this work.

68   Short title and commencement

(1)   This Act may be cited as the National Assistance Act 1948.

(2)   This Act shall come into operation on such day as the Minister of Health, or as respects Scotland the Secretary of State, may by order appoint, and different days may be appointed in relation to different provisions of this Act.

Marriage Act 1949

(c 76)

An Act to consolidate certain enactments relating to the solemnization and registration of marriages in England with such corrections and improvements as may be authorised under the Consolidation of Enactments (Procedure) Act 1949

[24 November 1949]

PART I
RESTRICTIONS ON MARRIAGE

1 Marriages within prohibited degrees

(1) A marriage solemnized between a man and any of the persons mentioned in the first column of Part I of the First Schedule to this Act, or between a woman and any of the persons mentioned in the second column of the said Part I, shall be void.

[(2) Subject to subsection (3) of this section, a marriage solemnized between a man and any of the persons mentioned in the first column of Part II of the First Schedule to this Act, or between a woman and any of the persons mentioned in the second column of the said Part II, shall be void.

(3) Any such marriage as is mentioned in subsection (2) of this section shall not be void by reason only of affinity if both the parties to the marriage have attained the age of twenty-one at the time of the marriage and the younger party has not at any time before attaining the age of eighteen been a child of the family in relation to the other party.

(4) Subject to subsection (5) of this section, a marriage solemnized between a man and any of the persons mentioned in the first column of Part III of the First Schedule to this Act or between a woman and any of the persons mentioned in the second column of the said Part III shall be void.

(5) Any such marriage as is mentioned in subsection (4) of this section shall not be void by reason only of affinity if both the parties to the marriage have attained the age of twenty-one at the time of the marriage and the marriage is solemnized—
  (a) in the case of a marriage between a man and the mother of a former wife of his, after the death of both the former wife and the father of the former wife;
  (b) in the case of a marriage between a man and the former wife of his son, after the death of both his son and the mother of his son;
  (c) in the case of a marriage between a woman and the father of a former husband of hers, after the death of both the former husband and the mother of the former husband;
  (d) in the case of a marriage between a woman and a former husband of her daughter, after the death of both her daughter and the father of her daughter.]

Sub-ss (2)–(5): added by the Marriage (Prohibited Degrees of Relationship) Act 1986, s 1(4), (8), Sch 1, para 2.

2 Marriages of persons under sixteen

A marriage solemnized between persons either of whom is under the age of sixteen shall be void.

3 Marriages of persons under twenty-one

(1)   Where the marriage of [a child], not being a widower or widow, is intended to be solemnized on the authority of a certificate issued by a superintendent registrar under Part III of this Act, whether by licence or without licence, the consent of the person or persons specified in [subsection (1A) of this section] shall be required [. . .]:

Provided that—
(a) if the superintendent registrar is satisfied that the consent of any person whose consent is so required cannot be obtained by reason of absence or inaccessibility or by reason of his being under any disability, the necessity for the consent of that person shall be dispensed with, if there is any other person whose consent is also required; and if the consent of no other person is required, the Registrar General may dispense with the necessity of obtaining any consent, or the court may, on application being made, consent to the marriage, and the consent of the court so given shall have the same effect as if it had been given by the person whose consent cannot be so obtained;
(b) if any person whose consent is required refuses his consent, the court may, on application being made, consent to the marriage, and the consent of the court so given shall have the same effect as if it had been given by the person whose consent is refused.

[(1A) The consents are—
(a) subject to paragraph (b) to (d) of this subsection, the consent of—
(i)   each parent (if any) of the child who has parental responsibility for him; and
(ii) each guardian (if any) of the child;
(b) where a residence order is in force with respect to the child, the consent of the person or persons with whom he lives, or is to live, as

a result of the order (in substitution for the consents mentioned in paragraph (a) of this subsection);

(c) where a care order is in force with respect to the child, the consent of the local authority designated in the order (in addition to the consents mentioned in paragraph (a) of this subsection);

(d) where neither paragraph (b) nor (c) of this subsection applies but a residence order was in force with respect to the child immediately before he reached the age of sixteen, the consent of the person or persons with whom he lived, or was to live, as a result of the order (in substitution for the consents mentioned in paragraph (a) of this subsection).

(1B) In this section "guardian of a child", "parental responsibility", "residence order" and "care order" have the same meaning as in the Children Act 1989.]

(2) The last foregoing subsection shall apply to marriages intended to be solemnized on the authority of a common licence, with the substitution of references to the ecclesiastical authority by whom the licence was granted for references to the superintendent registrar, and with the substitution of a reference to the Master of the Faculties for the reference to the Registrar General.

(3) Where the marriage of [a child], not being a widower or widow, is intended to be solemnized after the publication of banns of matrimony then, if any person whose consent to the marriage would have been required under this section in the case of a marriage intended to be solemnized otherwise than after the publication of the banns, openly and publicly declares or causes to be declared, in the church or chapel in which the banns are published, at the time of the publication, his dissent from the intended marriage, the publication of banns shall be void.

(4) A clergyman shall not be liable to ecclesiastical censure for solemnizing the marriage of [a child] after the publication of banns without the consent of the parents or guardians of [the child] unless he had notice of the dissent of any person who is entitled to give notice of dissent under the last foregoing subsection.

(5) For the purposes of this section, "the court" means the High Court, [the county court of the district in which any applicant or respondent resides] or a court of summary jurisdiction [[(appointed for the commission area (within the meaning of [the Justices of the Peace Act 1997])] in which any applicant or respondent resides] and rules of court may be made for enabling applications under this section—

(a) if made to the High Court, to be heard in chambers;

(b) if made to the county court, to be heard and determined by the registrar subject to appeal to the judge;

(c) if made to a court of summary jurisdiction, to be heard and determined otherwise than in open court,

and shall provide that, where an application is made in consequence of a refusal to give consent, notice of the application shall be served on the person who has refused consent.

(6)   Nothing in this section shall dispense with the necessity of obtaining the consent of the High Court to the marriage of a ward of court.

NOTES

Sub-s (1): words in first pair of square brackets substituted by the Family Law Reform Act 1987, s 33(1), Sch 2, para 9; words in second pair of square brackets substituted by the Children Act 1989, s 108(4), Sch 12, para 5(1); words omitted inserted by the Children Act 1975, s 108(1), Sch 3, para 7, repealed by the Children Act 1989, s 108(7), Sch 15.

Sub-ss (1A), (1B): inserted by the Children Act 1989, s 108(4), Sch 12, para 5(2).

Sub-ss (3), (4): words in square brackets substituted by the Family Law Reform Act 1987, s 33(1), Sch 2, para 9.

Sub-s (5): words in square brackets substituted or inserted by the Family Law Reform Act 1969, s 2(2), the Domestic Proceedings and Magistrates' Courts Act 1978, s 89(2), Sch 2, para 9, and the Justices of the Peace Act 1997, s 73(2), Sch 5, para 6.

4   Hours for solemnization of marriages

A marriage may be solemnized at any time between the hours of eight in the forenoon and six in the afternoon.

PART II
MARRIAGE ACCORDING TO RITES OF THE CHURCH OF ENGLAND

Preliminary

5   Methods of authorising marriages

A marriage according to the rites of the Church of England may be solemnized—

(a) after the publication of banns of matrimony;
(b) on the authority of a special licence of marriage granted by the Archbishop of Canterbury or any other person by virtue of the Ecclesiastical Licences Act 1533 (in this Act referred to as a "special licence");
(c) on the authority of a licence of marriage (other than a special licence) granted by an ecclesiastical authority having power to grant such a licence (in this Act referred to as a "common licence"); or
(d) on the authority of a certificate issued by a superintendent registrar under Part III of this Act;

[except that paragraph (a) of this section shall not apply in relation to the solemnization of any marriage mentioned in subsection (2) of section 1 of this Act].

NOTES

Words in square brackets added by the Marriage (Prohibited Degrees of Relationship) Act 1986, s 1(4), Sch 1, para 3.

[5A Marriages between certain persons related by affinity

No clergyman shall be obliged—
(a) to solemnize a marriage which, apart from the Marriage (Prohibited Degrees of Relationship) Act 1986, would have been void by reason of the relationship of the persons to be married; or
(b) to permit such a marriage to be solemnized in the church or chapel of which he is the minister.]

NOTES

Inserted by the Marriage (Prohibited Degrees of Relationship) Act 1986, s 3.

Miscellaneous Provisions

22 Witnesses

All marriages solemnized according to the rites of the Church of England shall be solemnized in the presence of two or more witnesses in addition to the clergyman by whom the marriage is solemnized.

25 Void marriages

If any persons knowingly and wilfully intermarry according to the rites of the Church of England (otherwise than by special licence)—

(a) [except in the case of a marriage in pursuance of section 26(1)(dd) of this Act] in any place other than a church or other building in which banns may be published;

(b) without banns having been duly published, a common licence having been obtained, or a certificate having been duly issued under Part III of this Act by a superintendent registrar to whom due notice of marriage has been given; or

(c) on the authority of a publication of banns which is void by virtue of subsection (3) of section three or subsection (2) of section twelve of this Act, on the authority of a common licence which is void by virtue of subsection (3) of section sixteen of this Act, or on the authority of a certificate of a superintendent registrar which is void by virtue of subsection (2) of section thirty-three of this Act;

(d) in the case of a marriage on the authority of a certificate of a superintendent registrar, in any place other than the church [building or other place specified in the notice of marriage and certificate as the place where the marriage is to be solemnized];

or if they knowingly and wilfully consent to or acquiesce in the solemnization of the marriage by any person who is not in Holy Orders, the marriage shall be void.

NOTES

Words in square brackets in paras (a), (d) substituted or inserted by the Marriage Act 1983, s 1(7), Sch 1, para 3.

PART III
MARRIAGE UNDER SUPERINTENDENT REGISTRAR'S CERTIFICATE

Issue of certificates

26 Marriages which may be solemnized on authority of superintendent registrar's certificate

(1) Subject to the provisions of this Part of this Act, the following marriages may be solemnized on the authority of a certificate of a superintendent registrar—

(a) a marriage in a registered building according to such form and ceremony as the persons to be married see fit to adopt;
(b) a marriage in the office of a superintendent registrar;
[(bb) a marriage on approved premises;]
(c) a marriage according to the usages of the Society of Friends (commonly called Quakers);
(d) a marriage between two persons professing the Jewish religion according to the usages of the Jews;
[(dd) the marriage (other than a marriage in pursuance of paragraph (c) or (d) above) of a person who is house-bound or is a detained person at the place where he or she usually resides;]
(e) a marriage according to the rites of the Church of England [in any church or chapel in which banns of matrimony may be published].

(2)   A marriage on the authority of a certificate of a superintendent registrar may be either by a licence issued by the superintendent registrar or without a licence:

Provided that a superintendent registrar shall not issue a licence [for a marriage intended to be solemnized at a person's residence in pursuance of subsection (1)(dd) of this section or] for a marriage in any church or chapel in which marriages may be solemnized according to the rites of the Church of England, or in any church or chapel belonging to the Church of England or licensed for the celebration of divine worship according to the rites and ceremonies of the Church of England.

NOTES

Sub-s (1): para (bb) inserted by the Marriage Act 1994, s 1(1); para (dd) inserted, and words in square brackets in para (e) added, by the Marriage Act 1983, s 1(7), Sch 1, para 4(a).
Sub-s (2): words in square brackets inserted by the Marriage Act 1983, s 1(7), Sch 1, para 4(b).

PART III
MARRIAGE UNDER SUPERINTENDENT REGISTRAR'S CERTIFICATE

Miscellaneous Provisions

49 Void marriages

If any persons knowingly and wilfully intermarry under the provisions of this Part of this Act—

   (a) without having given due notice of marriage to the superintendent registrar;

   (b) without a certificate for marriage having been duly issued by the superintendent registrar to whom notice of marriage was given;

   (c) without a licence having been so issued, in a case in which a licence is necessary;

   (d) on the authority of a certificate which is void by virtue of subsection (2) of section thirty-three of this Act;

   (e) in any place other than the church, chapel, registered building, office or other place specified in the notice of marriage and certificate of the superintendent registrar;

 [(ee) in the case of a marriage purporting to be in pursuance of section 26(1)(bb) of this Act, on any premises that at the time the marriage is solemnized are not approved premises;]

   (f) in the case of a marriage in a registered building (not being a marriage in the presence of an authorised person), in the absence of a registrar of the registration district in which the registered building is situated; . . .

   (g) in the case of a marriage in the office of a superintendent registrar, in the absence of the superintendent registrar or of a registrar of the registration district of that superintendent registrar; [. . .

 [(gg) in the case of a marriage on approved premises, in the absence of the superintendent registrar of the registration district in which the premises are situated or in the absence of a registrar of that district; or]

   (h) in the case of a marriage to which section 45A of this Act applies, in the absence of any superintendent registrar or registrar whose presence at that marriage is required by that section;]

the marriage shall be void.

NOTES

Paras (ee), (gg) inserted, and word omitted from para (f) repealed, by the Marriage Act 1994, s 1(3), Schedule, para 3; para (h) inserted by the Marriage Act 1983, s 1(7), Sch 1, para 13; word preceding para (gg) repealed by the Marriage Act 1994, s 1(3), Schedule, para 3.

PART VI
GENERAL

75 Offences relating to solemnization of marriages

(1)   Any person who knowingly and wilfully—

(a) solemnizes a marriage at any other time than between the hours of eight in the forenoon and six in the afternoon (not being a marriage by special licence, a marriage according to the usages of the Society of Friends or a marriage between two persons professing the Jewish religion according to the usages of the Jews);

(b) solemnizes a marriage according to the rites of the Church of England without banns of matrimony having been duly published (not being a marriage solemnized on the authority of a special licence, a common licence or a certificate of a superintendent registrar);

(c) solemnizes a marriage according to the said rites (not being a marriage by special licence [or a marriage in pursuance of section 26(1)(dd) of this Act]) in any place other than a church or other building in which banns may be published;

(d) solemnizes a marriage according to the said rites falsely pretending to be in Holy Orders;

shall be guilty of felony and shall be liable to imprisonment for a term not exceeding fourteen years.

(2) Any person who knowingly and wilfully—

(a) solemnizes a marriage (not being a marriage by special licence, a marriage according to the usages of the Society of Friends or a marriage between two persons professing the Jewish religion according to the usages of the Jews) in any place other than—
　　(i) a church or other building in which marriages may be solemnized according to the rites of the Church of England, or
　　(ii) the registered building [office[, approved premises] or person's residence specified as the place where the marriage was to be solemnized] in the notice of marriage and certificate required under Part III of this Act;

[(aa) solemnizes a marriage purporting to be in pursuance of section 26(1)(bb) of this Act on premises that are not approved premises;]

(b) solemnizes a marriage in any such registered building as aforesaid (not being a marriage in the presence of an authorised person) in the absence of a registrar of the district in which the registered building is situated;

[(bb) solemnizes a marriage in pursuance of section 26(1)(dd) of this Act, otherwise than according to the rites of the Church of England, in the absence of a registrar of the registration district in which the place where the marriage is solemnized is situated;]

(c) solemnizes a marriage in the office of a superintendent registrar in the absence of a registrar of the district in which the office is situated;

[(cc) solemnizes a marriage on approved premises in pursuance of section 26(1)(bb) of this Act in the absence of a registrar of the district in which the premises are situated;]

(d) solemnizes a marriage on the authority of a certificate of a superintendent registrar (not being a marriage by licence) within twenty-one days after the day on which the notice of marriage was entered in the marriage notice book; or

(e) solemnizes a marriage on the authority of a certificate of a superintendent registrar after the expiration of [the period which is, in relation to that marriage, the applicable period for the purposes of section 33 of this Act];

shall be guilty of felony and shall be liable to imprisonment for a term not exceeding five years.

(3) A superintendent registrar who knowingly and wilfully—

(a) issues any certificate for marriage (not being a marriage by licence) before the expiration of twenty-one days from the day on which the notice of marriage was entered in the marriage notice book, or issues a certificate for marriage by licence before the expiration of one whole day from the said day on which the notice was entered as aforesaid;

(b) issues any certificate or licence for marriage after the expiration of [the period which is, in relation to that marriage, the applicable period for the purposes of section 33 of this Act];

(c) issues any certificate the issue of which has been forbidden under section thirty of this Act by any person entitled to forbid the issue of such a certificate; or

(d) solemnizes or permits to be solemnized in his office [or, in the case of a marriage in pursuance of [section 26(1)(bb) or (dd)] of this Act, in any other place] any marriage which is void by virtue of any of the provisions of Part III of this Act;

shall be guilty of felony and shall be liable to imprisonment for a term not exceeding five years.

(4) No prosecution under this section shall be commenced after the expiration of three years from the commission of the offence.

(5) Any reference in subsection (2) of this section to a registered building shall be construed as including a reference to any chapel registered under section seventy of this Act.

NOTES

Sub-s (1): words in square brackets in para (c) inserted by the Marriage Act 1983, s 1(7), Sch 1, para 20(a).

Sub-s (2): words in first pair of square brackets in para (a) substituted by the Marriage Act 1983, s 1(7), Sch 1, para 20(b), words in square brackets therein inserted by the Marriage Act 1994, s 1(3), Schedule, para 7(a); paras (aa), (cc) inserted by the Marriage Act 1994, s 1(3), Schedule, para 7(b), (c); para (bb) inserted by the Marriage Act 1983, s 1(7), Sch 1, para 20(c); words in square brackets in para (e) substituted by the Deregulation (Validity of Civil Preliminaries to Marriage) Order 1997, SI 1997/986, art 2(4)(a).

Sub-s (3): words in square brackets in para (b) substituted by SI 1997/986, art 2(4)(b); words in first pair of square brackets in para (d) inserted by the Marriage Act 1983, s 1(7), Sch 1, para 20(d), words in square brackets therein substituted by the Marriage Act 1994, s 1(3), Schedule, para 7(d).

76 Offences relating to registration of marriages

(1)   Any person who refuses or without reasonable cause omits to register any marriage which he is required by this Act to register, and any person having the custody of a marriage register book or a certified copy of a marriage register book or part thereof who carelessly loses or injures the said book or copy or carelessly allows the said book or copy to be injured while in his keeping, shall be liable on summary conviction to a fine not exceeding [level 3 on the standard scale].

(2)   Where any person who is required under Part IV of this Act to make and deliver to a superintendent registrar a certified copy of entries made in the marriage register book kept by him, or a certificate that no entries have been made therein since the date of the last certified copy, refuses to deliver any such copy or certificate, or fails to deliver any such copy or certificate during any month in which he is required to do so, he shall be liable on summary conviction to a fine not exceeding [level 1 on the standard scale].

(3)   Any registrar who knowingly and wilfully registers any marriage which is void by virtue of any of the provisions of Part III of this Act shall be guilty of felony and shall be liable to imprisonment for a term not exceeding five years.

(4)   The balance of any sum paid or recovered on account of a fine imposed under subsection (1) or subsection (2) of this section, after making any such payments in respect of court or police fees as are mentioned in paragraphs (a), (b) and (c) of subsection (1) of section five of the Criminal Justice Administration Act 1914 shall be paid—
  (a) in the case of a fine imposed under subsection (1) of this section, into the Exchequer; and

(b) in the case of a fine imposed under subsection (2) of this section, to the Registrar General or such other person as may be appointed by the Treasury, for the use of His Majesty.

(5)   Subject as may be prescribed, a superintendent registrar may prosecute any person guilty of an offence under either of the said subsections committed within his district, and any costs incurred by the superintendent registrar in prosecuting such a person, being costs which are not otherwise provided for, shall be defrayed out of moneys provided by Parliament.

(6)   No prosecution under subsection (3) of this section shall be commenced after the expiration of three years from the commission of the offence.

NOTES

Sub-ss (1), (2): maximum fines increased and converted to a level on the standard scale by the Criminal Justice Act 1982, ss 37, 38, 46.

77 Offences by authorised persons

Any authorised person who refuses or fails to comply with the provisions of this Act or of any regulations made under section seventy-four thereof shall be guilty of an offence against this Act, and, unless the offence is one for which a specific penalty is provided under the foregoing provisions of this Part of this Act, shall be liable, on summary conviction, to a fine not exceeding [the prescribed sum] or, on conviction on indictment, to imprisonment for a term not exceeding two years or to a fine . . . and shall upon conviction cease to be an authorised person.

NOTES

Words in square brackets substituted by virtue of the Magistrates' Courts Act 1980, s 32(2); words omitted repealed by virtue of the Criminal Law Act 1977, s 32(1).

80 Short title, extent and commencement

(1)   This Act may be cited as the Marriage Act 1949.

(2)   Save as is otherwise expressly provided, this Act shall not extend to Scotland or to Northern Ireland.

(3)   . . .

(4)   This Act shall come into force on the first day of January, nineteen hundred and fifty.

Sub-s (3): outside the scope of this work.

FIRST SCHEDULE
KINDRED AND AFFINITY

PART I
PROHIBITED DEGREES OF RELATIONSHIP

Mother	Father
[Adoptive mother or former adoptive mother]	[Adoptive father or former adoptive father]
Daughter	Son
[Adoptive daughter or former adoptive daughter]	[Adoptive son or former adoptive son]
Father's mother	Father's father
Mother's mother	Mother's father
Son's daughter	Son's son
Daughter's daughter	Daughter's son
Sister	Brother
. . .	. . .
Father's sister	Father's brother
Mother's sister	Mother's brother
Brother's daughter	Brother's son
Sister's daughter	Sister's son

NOTES

Entries in square brackets inserted by the Children Act 1975, s 108(1)(a), Sch 3, para 8; words omitted repealed by the Marriage (Prohibited Degrees of Relationship) Act 1986, s 1(4), (6), (8), Sch 1, para 8.

[PART II
DEGREES OF AFFINITY REFERRED TO IN SECTION 1(2) AND (3)
OF THIS ACT

Daughter of former wife	Son of former husband
Former wife of father	Former husband of mother
Former wife of father's father	Former husband of father's mother
Former wife of mother's father	Former husband of mother's mother
Daughter of son of former wife	Son of son of former husband
Daughter of daughter of former wife	Son of daughter of former husband]

NOTES

Added by the Marriage (Prohibited Degrees of Relationship) Act 1986, s 1(4), (6), (8), Sch 1, para 8.

[PART III
DEGREES OF AFFINITY REFERRED TO IN SECTION 1(4) AND (5)
OF THIS ACT

Mother of former wife	Father of former husband
Former wife of son	Former husband of daughter]

NOTES

Added by the Marriage (Prohibited Degrees of Relationship) Act 1986, s 1(4), (6), (8), Sch 1, para 8.

Matrimonial Causes (Property and Maintenance) Act 1958

(c 35)

An Act to enable the power of the court in matrimonial proceedings to order alimony, maintenance or the securing of a sum of money to be exercised at any time after a decree; to provide for the setting aside of dispositions of property made for the purpose of reducing the assets available for satisfying such an order; to enable the court after the death of a party to a marriage which has been dissolved or annulled to make provision out of his estate in favour of the other party; and to extend the powers of the court under section seventeen of the Married Women's Property Act 1882

[7 July 1958]

7 Extension of s 17 of Married Women's Property Act 1882

(1) Any right of a wife, under section seventeen of the Married Women's Property Act 1882 to apply to a judge of the High Court or of a county court, in any question between husband and wife as to the title to or possession of property, shall include the right to make such an application where it is claimed by the wife that her husband has had in his possession or under his control—

    (a) money to which, or to a share of which, she was beneficially entitled (whether by reason that it represented the proceeds of property to which, or to an interest in which, she was beneficially entitled, or for any other reason), or

    (b) property (other than money) to which, or to an interest in which, she was beneficially entitled,

and that either that money or other property has ceased to be in his possession or under his control or that she does not know whether it is still in his possession or under his control.

(2) Where, on an application made to a judge of the High Court or of a county court under the said section seventeen, as extended by the preceding subsection, the judge is satisfied—

    (a) that the husband has had in his possession or under his control money or other property as mentioned in paragraph (a) or paragraph (b) of the preceding subsection, and

(b) that he has not made to the wife, in respect of that money or other property, such payment or disposition as would have been appropriate in the circumstances,

the power to make orders under that section shall be extended in accordance with the next following subsection.

(3)   Where the last preceding subsection applies, the power to make orders under the said section seventeen shall include power for the judge to order the husband to pay to the wife—

(a) in a case falling within paragraph (a) of subsection (1) of this section, such sum in respect of the money to which the application relates, or the wife's share thereof, as the case may be, or

(b) in a case falling within paragraph (b) of the said subsection (1), such sum in respect of the value of the property to which the application relates, or the wife's interest therein, as the case may be,

as the judge may consider appropriate.

(4)   Where on an application under the said section seventeen as extended by this section it appears to the judge that there is any property which—

(a) represents the whole or part of the money or property in question, and

(b) is property in respect of which an order could have been made under that section if an application had been made by the wife thereunder in a question as to the title to or possession of that property,

the judge (either in substitution for or in addition to the making of an order in accordance with the last preceding subsection) may make any order under that section in respect of that property which he could have made on such an application as is mentioned in paragraph (b) of this subsection.

(5)   The preceding provisions of this section shall have effect in relation to a husband as they have effect in relation to a wife, as if any reference to the husband were a reference to the wife and any reference to the wife were a reference to the husband.

[(6)   Any power of a judge which is exercisable on an application under the said section seventeen shall be exercisable in relation to an application made under that section as extended by this section.]

(7)   For the avoidance of doubt it is hereby declared that any power conferred by the said section seventeen to make orders with respect to any property includes power to order a sale of the property.

Sub-s (6): substituted by the Matrimonial and Family Proceedings Act 1984, s 46(1), Sch 1.

9 Short title, commencement and extent

(1)   This Act may be cited as the Matrimonial Causes (Property and Maintenance) Act 1958.

(2)   This Act shall come into operation on such day as may be appointed by the Lord Chancellor by an order made by statutory instrument.

(3)   This Act shall not extend to Scotland or to Northern Ireland.

Marriage (Enabling) Act 1960

(c 29)

An Act to enable a person to marry certain kin of a former spouse

[13 April 1960]

1 Certain marriages not to be void

(1)   No marriage hereafter contracted (whether in or out of Great Britain) between a man and a woman who is the sister, aunt or niece of a former wife of his (whether living or not), or was formerly the wife of his brother, uncle or nephew (whether living or not), shall by reason of that relationship be void or voidable under any enactment or rule of law applying in Great Britain as a marriage between persons within the prohibited degrees of affinity.

(2)   In the foregoing subsection words of kinship apply equally to kin of the whole and of the half blood.

(3)   This section does not validate a marriage, if either party to it is at the time of the marriage domiciled in a country outside Great Britain, and under the law of that country there cannot be a valid marriage between the parties.

(4)   . . .

NOTES

Sub-s (4): repealed by the Statute Law (Repeals) Act 1974.

2 Short title, citation and extent

(1)   This Act may be cited as the Marriage (Enabling) Act 1960, and this Act and the Marriage Acts 1949 to 1958 may be cited together as the Marriage Acts 1949 to 1960.

(2)   This Act shall not apply to Northern Ireland.

Law Reform (Husband and Wife) Act 1962

(c 48)

An Act to amend the law with respect to civil proceedings between husband and wife

[1 August 1962]

1 Actions in tort between husband and wife

(1)   Subject to the provisions of this section, each of the parties to a marriage shall have the like right of action in tort against the other as if they were not married.

(2)   Where an action in tort is brought by one of the parties to a marriage against the other during the subsistence of the marriage, the court may stay the action if it appears—
  (a) that no substantial benefit would accrue to either party from the continuation of the proceedings; or
  (b) that the question or questions in issue could more conveniently be disposed of on an application made under section seventeen of the Married Women's Property Act 1882 (determination of questions between husband and wife as to the title to or possession of property);

and without prejudice to paragraph (b) of this subsection the court may, in such an action, either exercise any power which could be exercised on an application under the said section seventeen, or give such directions as it thinks fit for the disposal under that section of any question arising in the proceedings.

(3), (4)   . . .

Sub-s (3): repealed by the Civil Procedure (Modification of Enactments) Order 1998, SI 1998/2940, art 4.

Sub-s (4): outside the scope of this work.

3   Short title, repeal, interpretation, saving and extent

(1)   This Act may be cited as the Law Reform (Husband and Wife) Act 1962.

(2)   . . .

(3)   The references in subsection (1) of section one and subsection (1) of section two of this Act to the parties to a marriage include references to the persons who were parties to a marriage which has been dissolved.

(4), (5)   . . .

Sub-s (2): repealed by the Statute Law (Repeals) Act 1974.

Sub-ss (4), (5): outside the scope of this work.

Married Women's Property Act 1964

(c 19)

An Act to amend the law relating to rights of property as between husband and wife

[25 March 1964]

1   Money and property derived from housekeeping allowance

If any question arises as to the right of a husband or wife to money derived from any allowance made by the husband for the expenses of the matrimonial home or for similar purposes, or to any property acquired out of such money, the money or property shall, in the absence of any agreement between them to the contrary, be treated as belonging to the husband and the wife in equal shares.

2 Short title and extent

(1)   This Act may be cited as the Married Women's Property Act 1964.

(2)   This Act does not extend to Northern Ireland.

Matrimonial Causes Act 1965

(c 72)

An Act to consolidate certain enactments relating to matrimonial causes, maintenance and declarations of legitimacy and British nationality, with corrections and improvements made under the Consolidation of Enactments (Procedure) Act 1949

[8 November 1965]

PART I
DIVORCE, NULLITY AND OTHER MATRIMONIAL SUITS

Divorce

8 Remarriage of divorced persons

(1)   . . .

(2)   No clergyman of the Church of England or the Church in Wales shall be compelled—
   (a) to solemnise the marriage of any person whose former marriage has been dissolved and whose former spouse is still living; or
   (b) to permit the marriage of such a person to be solemnised in the church or chapel of which he is the minister.

NOTES

Sub-s (1): repealed by the Matrimonial Causes Act 1973, ss 53, 54(1), Schs 1, 3.

46 Short title, interpretation, commencement and extent

(1)   This Act may be cited as the Matrimonial Causes Act 1965.

(2), (3)   . . .

(4)   . . . this Act does not extend to Scotland or Northern Ireland.

NOTES

Words omitted repealed by the Matrimonial Causes Act 1973, s 54(1), Sch 3.

Abortion Act 1967

(c 87)

*An Act to amend and clarify the law relating to termination of pregnancy
by registered medical practitioners*

[27 October 1967]

1   Medical termination of pregnancy

(1)   Subject to the provisions of this section, a person shall not be guilty
of an offence under the law relating to abortion when a pregnancy is
terminated by a registered medical practitioner if two registered medical
practitioners are of the opinion, formed in good faith—
  [(a) that the pregnancy has not exceeded its twenty-fourth week and
      that the continuance of the pregnancy would involve risk, greater
      than if the pregnancy were terminated, of injury to the physical or
      mental health of the pregnant woman or any existing children of
      her family; or
  (b) that the termination is necessary to prevent grave permanent
      injury to the physical or mental health of the pregnant woman;
      or
  (c) that the continuance of the pregnancy would involve risk to the life
      of the pregnant woman, greater than if the pregnancy were
      terminated; or
  (d) that there is a substantial risk that if the child were born it would
      suffer from such physical or mental abnormalities as to be seriously
      handicapped].

(2)   In determining whether the continuance of a pregnancy would involve
such risk of injury to health as is mentioned in paragraph (a) [or (b)] of
subsection (1) of this section, account may be taken of the pregnant woman's
actual or reasonably foreseeable environment.

(3)   Except as provided by subsection (4) of this section, any treatment for the termination of pregnancy must be carried out in a hospital vested in [the Secretary of State for the purposes of his functions under the National Health Service Act 1977 or the National Health Service (Scotland) Act 1978 [or in a hospital vested in a National Health Service trust] or in a place approved for the purposes of this section by the Secretary of State].

[(3A)   The power under subsection (3) of this section to approve a place includes power, in relation to treatment consisting primarily in the use of such medicines as may be specified in the approval and carried out in such manner as may be so specified, to approve a class of places.]

(4)   Subsection (3) of this section, and so much of subsection (1) as relates to the opinion of two registered medical practitioners, shall not apply to the termination of a pregnancy by a registered medical practitioner in a case where he is of the opinion, formed in good faith, that the termination is immediately necessary to save the life or to prevent grave permanent injury to the physical or mental health of the pregnant woman.

NOTES

Sub-s (1): paras (a)–(d) substituted for original paras (a), (b) by the Human Fertilisation and Embryology Act 1990, s 37(1).

Sub-s (2): words in square brackets inserted by the Human Fertilisation and Embryology Act 1990, s 37(2).

Sub-s (3): words in first (outer) pair of square brackets substituted by the Health Services Act 1980, Sch 1, para 17; words in second (inner) pair of square brackets inserted by the National Health Service and Community Care Act 1990, s 66(1), Sch 9, para 8.

Sub-s (3A): inserted by the Human Fertilisation and Embryology Act 1990, s 37(3).

2   Notification

(1)   The [Secretary of State] in respect of England and Wales, and the Secretary of State in respect of Scotland, shall by statutory instrument make regulations to provide—
  (a)   for requiring any such opinion as is referred to in section 1 of this Act to be certified by the practitioners or practitioner concerned in such form and at such time as may be prescribed by the regulations, and for requiring the preservation and disposal of certificates made for the purposes of the regulations;
  (b)   for requiring any registered medical practitioner who terminates a pregnancy to give notice of the termination and such other information relating to the termination as may be so prescribed;

(c) for prohibiting the disclosure, except to such persons or for such purposes as may be so prescribed, of notices given or information furnished pursuant to the regulations.

(2)   The information furnished in pursuance of regulations made by virtue of paragraph (b) of subsection (1) of this section shall be notified solely to the [Chief Medical Officer of the [Department of Health], or of the Welsh Office, or of the Scottish Home and Health Department].

(3)   Any person who wilfully contravenes or wilfully fails to comply with the requirements of regulations under subsection (1) of this section shall be liable on summary conviction to a fine not exceeding [level 5 on the standard scale].

(4)   Any statutory instrument made by virtue of this section shall be subject to annulment in pursuance of a resolution of either House of Parliament.

NOTES

Sub-s (1): words in square brackets substituted by virtue of the Secretary of State for Social Services Order 1968, SI 1968/1699, art 5(4).

Sub-s (2): words in first (outer) pair of square brackets substituted by the Transfer of Functions (Wales) Order 1969, SI 1969/388, art 2, Sch 1; words in in second (inner) pair of square brackets substituted by the Transfer of Functions (Health and Social Security) Order 1988, SI 1988/1843, art 5(4), Sch 3, para 3(a).

Sub-s (3): maximum fine increased by the Criminal Law Act 1977, s 31, Sch 6, and converted to a level on the standard scale by the Criminal Justice Act 1982, ss 37, 46.

4 Conscientious objection to participation in treatment

(1)   Subject to subsection (2) of this section, no person shall be under any duty, whether by contract or by any statutory or other legal requirement, to participate in any treatment authorised by this Act to which he has a conscientious objection:

Provided that in any legal proceedings the burden of proof of conscientious objection shall rest on the person claiming to rely on it.

(2)   Nothing in subsection (1) of this section shall affect any duty to participate in treatment which is necessary to save the life or to prevent grave permanent injury to the physical or mental health of a pregnant woman.

(3)   . . .

Sub-s (3): outside the scope of this work.

5 Supplementary provisions

[(1) No offence under the Infant Life (Preservation) Act 1929 shall be committed by a registered medical practitioner who terminates a pregnancy in accordance with the provisions of this Act.]

(2) For the purposes of the law relating to abortion, anything done with intent to procure [a woman's miscarriage (or, in the case of a woman carrying more than one foetus, her miscarriage of any foetus) is unlawfully done unless authorised by section 1 of this Act and, in the case of a woman carrying more than one foetus, anything done with intent to procure her miscarriage of any foetus is authorised by that section if—
   (a) the ground for termination of the pregnancy specified in subsection (1)(d) of that section applies in relation to any foetus and the thing is done for the purpose of procuring the miscarriage of that foetus, or
   (b) any of the other grounds for termination of the pregnancy specified in that section applies].

Sub-s (1): substituted by the Human Fertilisation and Embryology Act 1990, s 37(4).

Sub-s (2): words in square brackets substituted by the Human Fertilisation and Embryology Act 1990, s 37(5).

6 Interpretation

In this Act, the following expressions have meanings hereby assigned to them:—
   "the law relating to abortion" means sections 58 and 59 of the Offences against the Person Act 1861, and any rule of law relating to the procurement of abortion;

. . . . .

Definition omitted repealed by the Health Services Act 1980, s 25(4), Sch 7.

7 Short title, commencement and extent

(1)   This Act may be cited as the Abortion Act 1967.

(2)   This Act shall come into force on the expiration of the period of six months beginning with the date on which it is passed.

(3)   This Act does not extend to Northern Ireland.

Civil Evidence Act 1968

(C 64)

An Act to amend the law of evidence in relation to civil proceedings, and in respect of the privilege against self-incrimination to make corresponding amendments in relation to statutory powers of inspection or investigation
[25 October 1968]

PART II
MISCELLANEOUS AND GENERAL

Convictions, etc as evidence in civil proceedings

12 Findings of adultery and paternity as evidence in civil proceedings

(1)   In any civil proceedings—
  (a) the fact that a person has been found guilty of adultery in any matrimonial proceedings; and
  [(b) the fact that a person has been found to be the father of a child in relevant proceedings before any court in England and Wales [or Northern Ireland] or has been adjudged to be the father of a child in affiliation proceedings before any court in the United Kingdom;]

shall (subject to subsection (3) below) be admissible in evidence for the purpose of proving, where to do so is relevant to any issue in those civil proceedings, that he committed the adultery to which the finding relates or, as the case may be, is (or was) the father of that child, whether or not he offered any defence to the allegation of adultery or paternity and whether or not he is a party to the civil proceedings; but no finding or adjudication other than a subsisting one shall be admissible in evidence by virtue of this section.

(2)   In any civil proceedings in which by virtue of this section a person is proved to have been found guilty of adultery as mentioned in subsection (1)(a) above or [to have been found or adjudged] to be the father of a child as mentioned in subsection (1)(b) above—

   (a) he shall be taken to have committed the adultery to which the finding relates or, as the case may be, to be (or have been) the father of that child, unless the contrary is proved; and

   (b) without prejudice to the reception of any other admissible evidence for the purpose of identifying the facts on which the finding or adjudication was based, the contents of any document which was before the court, or which contains any pronouncement of the court, in the [other proceedings] in question shall be admissible in evidence for that purpose.

(3)   Nothing in this section shall prejudice the operation of any enactment whereby a finding of fact in any matrimonial or affiliation proceedings is for the purposes of any other proceedings made conclusive evidence of any fact.

(4)   Subsection (4) of section 11 of this Act shall apply for the purposes of this section as if the reference to subsection (2) were a reference to subsection (2) of this section.

(5)   In this section—

"matrimonial proceedings" means any matrimonial cause in the High Court or a county court in England and Wales or in the High Court in Northern Ireland, any consistorial action in Scotland, or any appeal arising out of any such cause or action;

["relevant proceedings" means—

   (a) proceedings on a complaint under section 42 of the National Assistance Act 1948 or section 26 of the Social Security Act 1986;

   (b) proceedings under the Children Act 1989;

   (c) proceedings which would have been relevant proceedings for the purposes of this section in the form in which it was in force before the passing of the Children Act 1989;

   [(d) section 27 of the Child Support Act 1991;]

   [(e) proceedings which are relevant proceedings as defined in section 8(5) of the Civil Evidence Act (Northern Ireland) 1971].]

"affiliation proceedings" means, in relation to Scotland, any action of affiliation and aliment;

and in this subsection "consistorial action" does not include an action of aliment only between husband and wife raised in the Court of Session or an action of interim aliment raised in the sheriff court.

NOTES

Sub-s (1): para (b) substituted by the Family Law Reform Act 1987, s 29(1), (2), words in square brackets therein inserted by the Children (Northern Ireland Consequential Amendments) Order 1995, SI 1995/756, art 6.

Sub-s (2): words in square brackets substituted by the Family Law Reform Act 1987, s 29(1), (3).

Sub-s (5): definition "relevant proceedings" originally inserted by the Family Law Reform Act 1987, s 29(1), (4), substituted by the Courts and Legal Services Act 1990, s 116, Sch 16, para 2(1); para (d) added by the Child Support Act 1991, s 27(5); para (e) added by SI 1995/756, art 6.

General

20 Short title, repeals, extent and commencement

(1)   This Act may be cited as the Civil Evidence Act 1968.

(2)   . . .

(3)   This Act shall not extend to Scotland or, . . . to Northern Ireland.

(4)   The following provisions of this Act, namely sections 13 to 19, this section (except subsection (2)) and the Schedule, shall come into force on the day this Act is passed, and the other provisions of this Act shall come into force on such day as the Lord Chancellor may by order made by statutory instrument appoint; and different days may be so appointed for different purposes of this Act or for the same purposes in relation to different courts or proceedings or otherwise in relation to different circumstances.

NOTES

Sub-s (2): outside the scope of   this work.

Sub-s (3): words omitted repealed by the Northern Ireland Constitution Act 1973, s 41(1), Sch 6, Pt I.

Family Law Reform Act 1969

(C 46)

An Act to amend the law relating to the age of majority, to persons who have not attained that age and to the time when a particular age is attained; to amend the law relating to the property rights of illegitimate children and of other persons whose relationship is traced through an illegitimate link; to make provision for the use of blood tests for the purpose of determining the paternity of any person in civil proceedings; to make provision with respect to the evidence required to rebut a presumption of legitimacy and illegitimacy; to make further provision, in connection with the registration of the birth of an illegitimate child, for entering the name of the father; and for connected purposes

[25 July 1969]

PART I
REDUCTION OF AGE OF MAJORITY AND RELATED PROVISIONS

1 Reduction of age of majority from 21 to 18

(1)   As from the date on which this section comes into force a person shall attain full age on attaining the age of eighteen instead of on attaining the age of twenty-one; and a person shall attain full age on that date if he has then already attained the age of eighteen but not the age of twenty-one.

(2)   The foregoing subsection applies for the purposes of any rule of law, and, in the absence of a definition or of any indication of a contrary intention, for the construction of "full age", "infant", "infancy", "minor", "minority" and similar expressions in—
   (a) any statutory provision, whether passed or made before, on or after the date on which this section comes into force; and
   (b) any deed, will or other instrument of whatever nature (not being a statutory provision) made on or after that date.

(3)   In the statutory provisions specified in Schedule 1 to this Act for any reference to the age of twenty-one years there shall be substituted a reference to the age of eighteen years; but the amendment by this subsection of the provisions specified in Part II of that Schedule shall be without prejudice to any power of amending or revoking those provisions.

(4)   This section does not affect the construction of any such expression as is referred to in subsection (2) of this section in any of the statutory

provisions described in Schedule 2 to this Act, and the transitional provisions and savings contained in Schedule 3 to this Act shall have effect in relation to this section.

(5)   The Lord Chancellor may by order made by statutory instrument amend any provision in any local enactment passed on or before the date on which this section comes into force (not being a provision described in paragraph 2 of Schedule 2 to this Act) by substituting a reference to the age of eighteen years for any reference therein to the age of twenty-one years; and any statutory instrument containing an order under this subsection shall be subject to annulment in pursuance of a resolution of either House of Parliament.

(6)   In this section "statutory provision" means any enactment (including, except where the context otherwise requires, this Act) and any order, rule, regulation, byelaw or other instrument made in the exercise of a power conferred by any enactment.

(7)   Notwithstanding any rule of law, a will or codicil executed before the date on which this section come into force shall not be treated for the purposes of this section as made on or after that date by reason only that the will or codicil is confirmed by a codicil executed on or after that date.

8   Consent by persons over 16 to surgical, medical and dental treatment

(1)   The consent of a minor who has attained the age of sixteen years to any surgical, medical or dental treatment which, in the absence of consent, would constitute a trespass to his person, shall be as effective as it would be if he were of full age; and where a minor has by virtue of this section given an effective consent to any treatment it shall not be necessary to obtain any consent for it from his parent or guardian.

(2)   In this section "surgical, medical or dental treatment" includes any procedure undertaken for the purposes of diagnosis, and this section applies to any procedure (including, in particular, the administration of an anaesthetic) which is ancillary to any treatment as it applies to that treatment.

(3)   Nothing in this section shall be construed as making ineffective any consent which would have been effective if this section had not been enacted.

9 Time at which a person attains a particular age

(1)   The time at which a person attains a particular age expressed in years shall be the commencement of the relevant anniversary of the date of his birth.

(2)   This section applies only where the relevant anniversary falls on a date after that on which this section comes into force, and, in relation to any enactment, deed, will or other instrument, has effect subject to any provision therein.

12 Persons under full age may be described as minors instead of infants

A person who is not of full age may be described as a minor instead of as an infant, and acordingly in this Act "minor" means such a person as aforesaid.

PART III
PROVISIONS FOR USE OF BLOOD TESTS IN DETERMINING PATERNITY

20 Power of court to require use of blood tests

(1)   In any civil proceedings in which the paternity of any person falls to be determined by the court hearing the proceedings, the court may, on an application by any party to the proceedings, give a direction for the use of blood tests to ascertain whether such tests show that a party to the proceedings is or is not thereby excluded from being the father of that person and for the taking, within a period to be specified in the direction, of blood samples from that person, the mother of that person and any party alleged to be the father of that person, the mother of that person and any party alleged to be the father of that person or from any, or any two, of those persons.

A court may at any time revoke or vary a direction previously given by it under this section.

[[(1A) An application for a direction under this section shall specify who is to carry out the tests.

(1B)   A direction under this section shall]—
    (a) specify, as the person who is to carry out the tests, the person specified in the application; or

(b) where the court considers that it would be inappropriate to specify that person (whether because to specify him would be incompatible with any provision made by or under regulations made under section 22 of this Act or for any other reason), decline to give the direction applied for.]

(2) *The person responsible for carrying out blood tests taken for the purpose of giving effect to a direction under this section shall make to the court by which the direction was given a report in which he shall state—*
  (a) *the results of the tests;*
  (b) *whether the party to whom the report relates is or is not excluded by the results from being the father of the person whose paternity is to be determined; and*
  (c) *if that party is not so excluded, the value, if any, of the results in determining whether that party is that person's father;*

and the report shall be received by the court as evidence in the proceedings of the matters stated therein.

(3) A report under subsection (2) of this section shall be in the form prescribed by regulations made under section 22 of this Act.

(4) Where a report has been made to a court under subsection (2) of this section, any party may, with the leave of the court, or shall, if the court so directs, obtain from the person who made the report a written statement explaining or amplifying any statement made in the report, and that statement shall be deemed for the purposes of this section (except subsection (3) thereof) to form part of the report made to the court.

(5) Where a direction is given under this section in any proceedings, a party to the proceedings, unless the court otherwise directs, shall not be entitled to call as a witness the person responsible for carrying out the tests taken for the purpose of giving effect to the direction, or any person by whom any thing necessary for the purpose of enabling those tests to be carried out was done, unless within fourteen days after receiving a copy of the report he serves notice on the other parties to the proceedings, or on such of them as the court may direct, of his intention to call that person; and where any such person is called as a witness the party who called him shall be entitled to cross-examine him.

(6) Where a direction is given under this section the party on whose application the direction is given shall pay the cost of taking and testing *blood samples* for the purpose of giving effect to the direction (including any expenses reasonably incurred by any person in taking any steps required

of him for the purpose), and of making a report to the court under this section, but the amount paid shall be treated as costs incurred by him in the proceedings.

NOTES

Sub-ss (1), (2): substituted by the Family Law Reform Act 1987, s 23(1), as from a day to be appointed, as follows—

"(1)   In any civil proceedings in which the parentage of any person falls to be determined, the court may, either of its own motion or on an application by any party to the proceedings, give a direction—

(a) for the use of scientific tests to ascertain whether such tests show that a party to the proceedings is or is not the father or mother of that person; and

(b) for the taking, within a period specified in the direction, of bodily samples from all or any of the following, namely, that person, any party who is alleged to be the father or mother of that person and any other party to the proceedings;

and the court may at any time revoke or vary a direction previously given by it under this subsection.

(2)   The person responsible for carrying out scientific tests in pursuance of a direction under subsection (1) above shall make to the court a report in which he shall state—

(a) the results of the tests;

(b) whether any party to whom the report relates is or is not excluded by the results from being the father or mother of the person whose parentage is to be determined; and

(c) in relation to any party who is not so excluded, the value, if any, of the results in determining whether that party is the father or mother of that person;

and the report shall be received by the court as evidence in the proceedings of the matters stated in it.

(2A)   Where the proceedings in which the parentage of any person falls to be determined are proceedings on an application under section 56 of the Family Law Act 1986, any reference in subsection (1) or (2) of this section to any party to the proceedings shall include a reference to any person named in the application.".

Sub-ss (1A), (1B): inserted by the Children Act 1989, s 89; words in square brackets substituted by the Courts and Legal Services Act 1990, s 116, Sch 16, Pt I, para 3.

Sub-s (6): for the words in italics there are substituted the words "bodily samples" by the Family Law Reform Act 1987, s 33(1), (2), Sch 2, para 21, Sch 3, para 1, subject to transitional provisions, as from a day to be appointed.

21   Consents, etc, required for taking of blood samples

(1)   Subject to the provisions of subsections (3) and (4) of this section, a *blood sample* which is required to be taken from any person for the purpose

of giving effect to a direction under section 20 of this Act shall not be taken from that person except with his consent.

(2)   The consent of a minor who has attained the age of sixteen years to the taking from himself of a *blood sample* shall be as effective as it would be if he were of full age; and where a minor has by virtue of this subsection given an effective consent to the taking of a *blood sample* it shall not be necessary to obtain any consent for it from any other person.

(3)   A *blood sample* may be taken from a person under the age of sixteen years, not being such a person as is referred to in subsection (4) of this section, if the person who has the care and control of him consents.

(4)   A *blood sample* may be taken from a person who is suffering from mental disorder within the meaning of [the Mental Health Act 1983] and is incapable of understanding the nature and purpose of *blood tests* if the person who has the care and control of him consents and the medical practitioner in whose care he is has certified that the taking of a *blood sample* from him will not be prejudicial to his proper care and treatment.

(5)   The foregoing provisions of this section are without prejudice to the provisions of section 23 of this Act.

NOTES

Words "blood sample" substituted in each place where they occur by the words "bodily sample" and words "blood tests" substituted by the words "scientific tests" by the Family Law Reform Act 1987, s 33(1), (2), Sch 2, para 22, Sch 3, para 1, subject to transitional provisions, as from a day to be appointed; words "the Mental Health Act 1983" in sub-s (4) substituted by the Mental Health Act 1983, s 148(1), Sch 4, para 25

22   Power to provide for manner of giving effect to direction for use of blood tests

(1)   The [Lord Chancellor] may by regulations make provision as to the manner of giving effect to directions under section 20 of this Act and, in particular, any such regulations may—
   (a)   provide that *blood samples* shall not be taken except by such medical practitioners as may be appointed by the [Lord Chancellor];
   [(aa)   prescribe the bodily samples to be taken;]
   (b)   regulate the taking, identification and transport of *blood samples*;

(c) require the production at the time when a *blood sample* is to be taken of such evidence of the identity of the person from whom it is to be taken as may be prescribed by the regulations;

(d) require any person from whom a *blood sample* is to be taken, or, in such cases as may be prescribed by the regulations, such other person as may be so prescribed, to state in writing whether he or the person from whom the sample is to be taken, as the case may be, has during such period as may be specified in the regulations suffered from any such illness [or condition or undergone any such treatment] as may be so specified or received a transfusion of blood;

(e) provide that *blood tests* shall not be carried out except by such persons, and at such places, as may be appointed by the [Lord Chancellor];

(f) prescribe the *blood tests* to be carried out and the manner in which they are to be carried out;

(g) regulate the charges that may be made for the taking and testing of *blood samples* and for the making of a report to a court under section 20 of this Act;

(h) make provision for securing that so far as practicable the *blood samples* to be tested for the purpose of giving effect to a direction under section 20 of this Act are tested by the same person;

(i) prescribe the form of the report to be made to a court under section 20 of this Act.

[(j) make different provision for different cases or for different descriptions of case.]

(2)   The power to make regulations under this section shall be exercisable by statutory instrument which shall be subject to annulment in pursuance of a resolution of either House of Parliament.

NOTES

Sub-s (1): references to the "Lord Chancellor" substituted by the Transfer of Functions (Magistrates' Courts and Family Law) Order 1992, SI 1992/709, art 3(2), Sch 2; words "blood samples", "blood sample" and "blood tests" substituted in each place where they occur by the words "bodily samples", "bodily sample" and "scientific tests" respectively, and paras (aa), (j) and words in square brackets in para (d) inserted, by the Family Law Reform Act 1987, s 33(1), (2), Sch 2, para 23, Sch 3, para 1, subject to transitional provisions, as from a day to be appointed.

23   Failure to comply with direction for taking blood tests

(1)   Where a court gives a direction under section 20 of this Act and any person fails to take any step required of him for the purpose of giving effect

to the direction, the court may draw such inferences, if any, from that fact as appear proper in the circumstances.

(2)   Where in any proceedings in which the *paternity* of any person falls to be determined by the court hearing the proceedings there is a presumption of law that that person is legitimate, then if—

(a)   a direction is given under section 20 of this Act in those proceedings, and

(b)   any party who is claiming any relief in the proceedings and who for the purpose of obtaining that relief is entitled to rely on the presumption fails to take any step required of him for the purpose of giving effect to the direction,

the court may adjourn the hearing for such period as it thinks fit to enable that party to take that step, and if at the end of that period he has failed without reasonable cause to take it the court may, without prejudice to subsection (1) of this section, dismiss his claim for relief notwithstanding the absence of evidence to rebut the presumption.

(3)   Where any person named in a direction under section 20 of this Act fails to consent to the taking of a *blood sample* from himself or from any person named in the direction of whom he has the care and control, he shall be deemed for the purposes of this section to have failed to take a step required of him for the purpose of giving effect to the direction.

NOTES

Word "paternity" substituted by the word "parentage" and words "blood sample" substituted by the words "bodily sample" by the Family Law Reform Act 1987, s 33(1), (2), Sch 2, para 24, Sch 3, para 1, subject to transitional provisions, as from a day to be appointed.

24   Penalty for personating another, etc, for purpose of providing *blood sample*

If for the purpose of providing a *blood sample* for a test required to give effect to a direction under section 20 of this Act any person personates another, or proffers a child knowing that it is not the child named in the direction, he shall be liable—

(a)   on conviction on indictment, to imprisonment for a term not exceeding two years, or

(b)   on summary conviction, to a fine not exceeding [the prescribed sum].

NOTES

Section heading: for the words in italics there are substituted the words "bodily sample" with savings by the Family Law Reform Act 1987, s 33(1), Sch 2, para 24, Sch 3, para 1, as from a day to be appointed.

For the words in italics there are substituted the words "bodily sample" with savings by the Family Law Reform Act 1987, s 33(1), Sch 2, para 25, Sch 3, para 1, as from a day to be appointed; words in second pair of square brackets substituted by virtue of the Magistrates' Courts Act 1980, s 32(2).

25 Interpretation of Part III

In this Part of this Act the following expressions have the meanings hereby respectively assigned to them, that is to say—

"blood samples" means blood taken for the purpose of blood tests;

"blood tests" means blood tests carried out under this Part of this Act and includes any test made with the object of ascertaining the inheritable characteristics of blood;

"excluded" means excluded subject to the occurrence of mutation [to section 27 of the Family Law Reform Act 1987 and to sections 27 to 29 of the Human Fertilisation and Embryology Act 1990].

["scientific tests" means scientific tests carried out under this Part of this Act and made with the object of ascertaining the inheritable characteristics of bodily fluids or bodily tissue.]

NOTES

Definitions in italics substituted as follows—

""bodily sample" means a sample of bodily fluid or bodily tissue taken for the purpose of scientific tests;"

and definition in square brackets added, by the Family Law Reform Act 1987, ss 23, 33(2), Sch 3, para 1, subject to transitional provisions, as from a day to be appointed; in definition "excluded" words in square brackets added by the Human Fertilisation and Embryology Act 1990, s 49(5), Sch 4, para 1.

PART IV
MISCELLANEOUS AND GENERAL

26 Rebuttal of presumption as to legitimacy and illegitimacy

Any presumption of law as to the legitimacy or illegitimacy of any person may in any civil proceedings be rebutted by evidence which shows that it is more probable than not that that person is illegitimate or legitimate, as the case may be, and it shall not be necessary to prove that fact beyond reasonable doubt in order to rebut the presumption.

28   Short title, interpretation, commencement and extent

(1)   This Act may be cited as the Family Law Reform Act 1969.

(2)   . . .

(3)   This Act shall come into force on such date as the Lord Chancellor may appoint by order made by statutory instrument, and different dates may be appointed for the coming into force of different provisions.

(4)   . . . save as aforesaid, this Act shall extend to England and Wales only.

NOTES

Sub-s (2): outside the scope of this work.
Sub-s (4): words omitted outside the scope of this work.

Law Reform (Miscellaneous Provisions) Act 1970

(c 33)

An Act to abolish actions for breach of promise of marriage and make provision with respect to the property of, and gifts between, persons who have been engaged to marry; to abolish the right of a husband to claim damages for adultery with his wife; to abolish actions for the enticement or harbouring of a spouse, or for the enticement, seduction or harbouring of a child; to make provision with respect to the maintenance of survivors of void marriages; and for purposes connected with the matters aforesaid
[29 May 1970]

Legal consequences of termination of contract to marry

1   Engagements to marry not enforceable at law

(1)   An agreement between two persons to marry one another shall not under the law of England and Wales have effect as a contract giving rise to

legal rights and no action shall lie in England and Wales for breach of such an agreement, whatever the law applicable to the agreement.

(2)   This section shall have effect in relation to agreements entered into before it comes into force, except that it shall not affect any action commenced before it comes into force.

2   Property of engaged couples

(1)   Where an agreement to marry is terminated, any rule of law relating to the rights of husbands and wives in relation to property in which either or both has or have a beneficial interest, including any such rule as explained by section 37 of the Matrimonial Proceedings and Property Act 1970, shall apply, in relation to any property in which either or both of the parties to the agreement had a beneficial interest while the agreement was in force, as it applies in relation to property in which a husband or wife has a beneficial interest.

(2)   Where an agreement to marry is terminated, section 17 of the Married Women's Property Act 1882 and section 7 of the Matrimonial Causes (Property and Maintenance) Act 1958 (which sections confer power on a judge of the High Court or a county court to settle disputes between husband and wife about property) shall apply, as if the parties were married, to any dispute between, or claim by, one of them in relation to property in which either or both had a beneficial interest while the agreement was in force; but an application made by virtue of this section to the judge under the said section 17, as originally enacted or as extended by the said section 7, shall be made within three years of the termination of the agreement.

3   Gifts between engaged couples

(1)   A party to an agreement to marry who makes a gift of property to the other party to the agreement on the condition (express or implied) that it shall be returned if the agreement is terminated shall not be prevented from recovering the property by reason only of his having terminated the agreement.

(2)   The gift of an engagement ring shall be presumed to be an absolute gift; this presumption may be rebutted by proving that the ring was given on the condition, express or implied, that it should be returned if the marriage did not take place for any reason.

Enticement of spouse, etc

5 Abolition of actions for enticement, seduction and harbouring of spouse or child

No person shall be liable in tort under the law of England and Wales—
  (a) to any other person on the ground only of his having induced the wife or husband of that other person to leave or remain apart from the other spouse;
  (b) to a parent (or person standing in the place of a parent) on the ground only of his having deprived the parent (or other person) of the services of his or her child by raping, seducing or enticing that child; or
  (c) to any other person for harbouring the wife or child of that other person,

except in the case of a cause of action accruing before this Act comes into force if an action in respect thereof has been begun before this Act comes into force.

Supplemental

7 Citation, repeal, commencement and extent

(1)   This Act may be cited as the Law Reform (Miscellaneous Provisions) Act 1970.

(2)   The enactments specified in the Schedule to this Act are hereby repealed to the extent specified in the third column of that Schedule, but the repeal of those enactments shall not affect any action commenced or petition presented before this Act comes into force or any claim made in any such action or on any such petition.

(3)   This Act shall come into force on 1st January 1971.

(4)   This Act does not extend to Scotland or Northern Ireland.

Matrimonial Proceedings and Property Act 1970

(C 45)

An Act to make fresh provision for empowering the court in matrimonial proceedings to make orders ordering either spouse to make financial provision for, or transfer property to, the other spouse or a child of the family, orders for the variation of ante-nuptial and post-nuptial settlements, orders for the custody and education of children and orders varying, discharging or suspending orders made in such proceedings; to make other amendments of the law relating to matrimonial proceedings; to abolish the right to claim restitution of conjugal rights; to declare what interest in property is acquired by a spouse who contributes to its improvement; to make provision as to a spouse's rights of occupation under section 1 of the Matrimonial Homes Act 1967 in certain cases; to extend section 17 of the Married Women's Property Act 1882 and section 7 of the Matrimonial Causes (Property and Maintenance) Act 1958; to amend the law about the property of a person whose marriage is the subject of a decree of judicial separation dying intestate; to abolish the agency of necessity of a wife; and for purposes connected with the matters aforesaid

[29 May 1970]

PART II
MISCELLANEOUS PROVISIONS

Provisions relating to property of married persons

37 Contributions by spouse in money or money's worth to the improvement of property

It is hereby declared that where a husband or wife contributes in money or money's worth to the improvement of real or personal property in which or in the proceeds of sale of which either or both of them has or have a beneficial interest, the husband or wife so contributing shall, if the contribution is of a substantial nature and subject to any agreement between them to the contrary express or implied, be treated as having then acquired by virtue of his or her contribution a share or an enlarged share, as the case may be, in that beneficial interest of such an extent as may have been then agreed or, in default of such agreement, as may seem in all the circumstances just to any court before which the question of the existence or extent of the beneficial interest of the husband or wife arises (whether in proceedings between them or in any other proceedings).

39 Extension of s 17 of Married Women's Property Act 1882

An application may be made to the High Court or a county court under section 17 of the Married Women's Property Act 1882 (powers of the court in disputes between husband and wife about property) (including that section as extended by section 7 of the Matrimonial Causes (Property and Maintenance) Act 1958) by either of the parties to a marriage notwithstanding that their marriage has been dissolved or annulled so long as the application is made within the period of three years beginning with the date on which the marriage was dissolved or annulled; and references in the said section 17 and the said section 7 to a husband or a wife shall be construed accordingly.

PART III
SUPPLEMENTARY

43 Citation, commencement and extent

(1) This Act may be cited as the Matrimonial Proceedings and Property Act 1970.

(2) . . .

(3) Any reference in any provision of this Act, or in any enactment amended by a provision of this Act, to the commencement of this Act shall be construed as a reference to the date on which that provision comes into force.

(4) . . . this Act does not extend to Scotland or Northern Ireland.

NOTES

Sub-s (2): repealed by the Matrimonial Causes Act 1973, s 54, Sch 3.
Sub-s (4): words omitted repealed by the Matrimonial Causes Act 1973, s 54, Sch 3, and by the Statute Law (Repeals) Act 1977.

Land Charges Act 1972

(C 61)

An Act to consolidate certain enactments relating to the registration of land charges and other instruments and matters affecting land

[9 August 1972]

Registration in register of land charges

2 The register of land charges

(1)   If a charge on or obligation affecting land falls into one of the classes described in this section, it may be registered in the register of land charges as a land charge of that class.

(2)–(6). . .

(7)   A Class F land charge is a charge affecting any land by virtue of the [Part IV of the Family Law Act 1996].

(8), (9)   . . .

NOTES

Sub-s (7): words in square brackets substituted by the Family Law Act 1996, s 66(1), Sch 8, Pt III, para 47.

Sub-ss (2)–(6), (8), (9): outside the scope of   this work.

Inheritance tax: except in relation to a liability to tax arising before 25 July 1986 capital transfer tax shall be known as inheritance tax and the Capital Transfer Tax Act 1984 may be cited as the Inheritance Tax Act 1984, by virtue of the Finance Act 1986, s 100. Accordingly references to capital transfer tax have been changed to references to inheritance tax throughout this Act.

Miscellaneous and supplementary

19 Short title, commencement and extent

(1)   This Act may be cited as the Land Charges Act 1972.

(2)   This Act shall come into force on such day as the Lord Chancellor may by order made by statutory instrument appoint; and different days may be so appointed for different purposes.

(3)   This Act extends to England and Wales only.

Matrimonial Causes Act 1973

(c 18)

An Act to consolidate certain enactments relating to matrimonial proceedings, maintenance agreements, and declarations of legitimacy, validity of marriage and British nationality, with amendments to give effect to recommendations of the Law Commission

[23 May 1973]

PART I
DIVORCE, NULLITY AND OTHER MATRIMONIAL SUITS

Divorce

1   Divorce on breakdown of marriage

(1)   Subject to section 3 below, a petition for divorce may be presented to the court by either party to a marriage on the ground that the marriage has broken down irretrievably.

(2)   The court hearing a petition for divorce shall not hold the marriage to have broken down irretrievably unless the petitioner satisfies the court of one or more of the following facts, that is to say—
  (a)   that the respondent has committed adultery and the petitioner finds it intolerable to live with the respondent;
  (b)   that the respondent has behaved in such a way that the petitioner cannot reasonably be expected to live with the respondent;
  (c)   that the respondent has deserted the petitioner for a continuous period of at least two years immediately preceding the presentation of the petition;
  (d)   that the parties of the marriage have lived apart for a continuous period of at least two years immediately preceding the presentation

of the petition (hereafter in this Act referred to as "two years' separation") and the respondent consents to a decree being granted;

(e) that the parties to the marriage have lived apart for a continuous period of at least five years immediately preceding the presentation of the petition (hereafter in this Act referred to as "five years' separation").

(3)   On a petition for divorce it shall be the duty of the court to inquire, so far as it reasonably can, into the facts alleged by the petitioner and into any facts alleged by the respondent.

(4)   If the court is satisfied on the evidence of any such fact as is mentioned in subsection (2) above, then, unless it is satisfied on all the evidence that the marriage has not broken down irretrievably, it shall, subject to [section 5] below, grant a decree of divorce.

(5)   Every decree of divorce shall in the first instance be a decree nisi and shall not be made absolute before the expiration of six months from its grant unless the High Court by general order from time to time fixes a shorter period, or unless in any particular case the court in which the proceedings are for the time being pending from time to time by special order fixes a shorter period than the period otherwise applicable for the time being by virtue of this subsection.

NOTES

Sub-s (4): words in square brackets substituted by the Matrimonial and Family Proceedings Act 1984, s 46(1), Sch 1, para 10.

Repealed, together with ss 2–7, 9, 10, 17, 18, 20, 22 of this Act, by the Family Law Act 1996, s 66(3), Sch 10, subject to savings in s 66(2) of, and Sch 9, para 5 to, the 1996 Act, as from a day to be appointed.

2   Supplemental provisions as to facts raising presumption of breakdown

(1)   One party to a marriage shall not be entitled to rely for the purposes of section 1(2)(a) above on adultery committed by the other if, after it became known to him that the other had committed that adultery, the parties have lived with each other for a period exceeding, or periods together exceeding, six months.

(2)   Where the parties to a marriage have lived with each other after it became known to one party that the other had committed adultery, but

subsection (1) above does not apply, in any proceedings for divorce in which the petitioner relies on that adultery the fact that the parties have lived with each other after that time shall be disregarded in determining for the purposes of section 1(2)(a) above whether the petitioner finds it intolerable to live with the respondent.

(3)   Where in any proceedings for divorce the petitioner alleges that the respondent has behaved in such a way that the petitioner cannot reasonably be expected to live with him, but the parties to the marriage have lived with each other for a period or periods after the date of the occurrence of the final incident relied on by the petitioner and held by the court to support his allegation, that fact shall be disregarded in determining for the purposes of section 1(2)(b) above whether the petitioner cannot reasonably be expected to live with the respondent if the length of that period or of those periods together was six months or less.

(4)   For the purposes of section 1(2)(c) above the court may treat a period of desertion as having continued at a time when the deserting party was incapable of continuing the necessary intention if the evidence before the court is such that, had that party not been so incapable, the court would have inferred that his desertion continued at that time.

(5)   In considering for the purposes of section 1(2) above whether the period for which the respondent has deserted the petitioner or the period for which the parties to a marriage have lived apart has been continuous, no account shall be taken of any one period (not exceeding six months) or of any two or more periods (not exceeding six months in all) during which the parties resumed living with each other, but no period during which the parties lived with each other shall count as part of the period of desertion or of the period for which the parties to the marriage lived apart, as the case may be.

(6)   For the purposes of section 1(2)(d) and (e) above and this section a husband and wife shall be treated as living apart unless they are living with each other in the same household, and references in this section to the parties to a marriage living with each other shall be construed as references to their living with each other in the same household.

(7)   Provision shall be made by rules of court for the purpose of ensuring that where in pursuance of section 1(2)(d) above the petitioner alleges that the respondent consents to a decree being granted the respondent has been given such information as will enable him to understand the consequences to him of his consenting to a decree being granted and the steps which he must take to indicate that he consents to the grant of a decree.

Repealed as noted to s 1.

[3 Bar on petitions for divorce within one year of marriage

(1)   No petition for divorce shall be presented to the court before the expiration of the period of one year from the date of the marriage.

(2)   Nothing in this section shall prohibit the presentation of a petition based on matters which occurred before the expiration of that period.]

Substituted by the Matrimonial and Family Proceedings Act 1984, s 1.
Repealed as noted to s 1.

4   Divorce not precluded by previous judicial separation

(1)   A person shall not be prevented from presenting a petition for divorce, or the court from granting a decree of divorce, by reason only that the petitioner or respondent has at any time, on the same facts or substantially the same facts as those proved in support of the petition, been granted a decree of judicial separation or an order under, or having effect as if made under, the Matrimonial Proceedings (Magistrates' Courts) Act 1960 [or Part I of the Domestic Proceedings and Magistrates' Courts Act 1978] or any corresponding enactments in force in Northern Ireland, the Isle of Man or any of the Channel Islands.

(2)   On a petition for divorce in such a case as is mentioned in subsection (1) above, the court may treat the decree or order as sufficient proof of any adultery, desertion or other fact by reference to which it was granted, but shall not grant a decree of divorce without receiving evidence from the petitioner.

(3)   Where a petition for divorce in such a case follows a decree of judicial separation or [(subject to subsection (5) below)] an order containing a provision exempting one party to the marriage from the obligation to cohabit with the other, for the purposes of that petition a period of desertion immediately preceding the institution of the proceedings for the decree or order shall, if the parties have not resumed cohabitation and the decree or order has been continuously in force since

*it was granted, be deemed immediately to precede the presentation of
the petition.*

*[(4)   For the purposes of section 1(2)(c) above the court may treat as a
period during which the respondent has deserted the petitioner any of the
following periods, that is to say—*

    *(a) any period during which there is in force an injunction granted by
the High Court or a county court which excludes the respondent
from the matrimonial home;*

    *(b) any period during which there is in force an order made by the
High Court or a county court under [section 1 or 9 of the
Matrimonial Homes Act 1983] which prohibits the exercise by the
respondent of the right to occupy a dwelling-house in which the
applicant and the respondent have or at any time have had a
matrimonial home;*

    *(c) any period during which there is in force an order made by a
magistrates' court under section 16(3) of the Domestic Proceedings
and Magistrates' Courts Act 1978 which requires the respondent to
leave the matrimonial home or prohibits the respondent from entering
the matrimonial home.*

(5)   Where—

    *(a) a petition for divorce is presented after the date on which Part I of
the Domestic Proceedings and Magistrates' Courts Act 1978 comes
into force, and*

    *(b) an order made under the Matrimonial Proceedings (Magistrates'
Courts) Act 1960 containing a provision exempting the petitioner from
the obligation to cohabit with the respondent is in force on that date,*

*then, for the purpose of section 1(2)(c) above, the court may treat a period
during which such a provision was included in that order (whether before
or after that date) as a period during which the respondent has deserted the
petitioner.]*

<hr>

NOTES

Sub-ss (1), (3): words in square brackets inserted by the Domestic Proceedings
and Magistrates' Courts Act 1978, ss 62, 89(2)(a), Sch 2, para 38.

Sub-s (4): inserted by the Domestic Proceedings and Magistrates' Courts Act
1978, s 62; words in square brackets substituted by the Matrimonial Homes Act
1983, s 12, Sch 2.

Sub-s (5): added by the Domestic Proceedings and Magistrates' Courts Act 1978,
s 62.

Repealed as noted to s 1.

5 Refusal of decree in five year separation cases on grounds of grave hardship to respondent

(1)   The respondent to a petition for divorce in which the petitioner alleges five years' separation may oppose the grant of a decree on the ground that the dissolution of the marriage will result in grave financial or other hardship to him and that it would in all the circumstances be wrong to dissolve the marriage.

(2)   Where the grant of a decree is opposed by virtue of this section, then—
   (a) if the court finds that the petitioner is entitled to rely in support of his petition on the fact of five years' separation and makes no such finding as to any other fact mentioned in section 1(2) above, and
   (b) if apart from this section the court would grant a decree on the petition,

the court shall consider all the circumstances, including the conduct of the parties to the marriage and the interests of those parties and of any children or other persons concerned, and if of opinion that the dissolution of the marriage will result in grave financial or other hardship to the respondent and that it would in all the circumstances be wrong to dissolve the marriage it shall dismiss the petition.

(3)   For the purposes of this section hardship shall include the loss of the chance of acquiring any benefit which the respondent might acquire if the marriage were not dissolved.

NOTES

Repealed as noted to s 1.

6 Attempts at reconciliation of parties to marriage

(1)   Provision shall be made by rules of court for requiring the solicitor acting for a petitioner for divorce to certify whether he has discussed with the petitioner the possibility of a reconciliation and given him the names and addresses of persons qualified to help effect a reconciliation between parties to a marriage who have becomes estranged.

(2)   If at any stage of proceedings for divorce it appears to the court that there is a reasonable possibility of a reconciliation between the parties to the marriage, the court may adjourn the proceedings for such period as it thinks fit to enable attempts to be made to effect such a reconciliation.

The power conferred by the foregoing provision is additional to any other power of the court to adjourn proceedings.

NOTES

Repealed as noted to s 1.

7 Consideration by the court of certain agreements or arrangements

Provision may be made by rules of court for enabling the parties to a marriage, or either of them, on application made either before or after the presentation of a petition for divorce, to refer to the court any agreement or arrangement made or proposed to be made between them, being an agreement or arrangement which relates to, arises out of, or is connected with, the proceedings for divorce which are contemplated or, as the case may be, have begun, and for enabling the court to express an opinion, should it think it desirable to do so, as to the reasonableness of the agreement or arrangement and to give such directions, if any, in the matter as it thinks fit.

NOTES

Repealed as noted to s 1,

8 Intervention of Queen's Proctor

(1)   In the case of a petition for divorce—
  (a) the court may, if it thinks fit, direct all necessary papers in the matter to be sent to the Queen's Proctor, who shall under the directions of the Attorney-General instruct counsel to argue before the court any question in relation to the matter which the court considers it necessary or expedient to have fully argued;
  (b) any person may at any time during the progress of the proceedings *or before the decree nisi is made absolute* give information to the Queen's Proctor on any matter material to the due decision of the case, and the Queen's Proctor may thereupon take such steps as the Attorney-General considers necessary or expedient.

(2)   Where the Queen's Proctor intervenes or shows cause against *a decree nisi in any proceedings for divorce*, the court may make such order

as may be just as to the payment by other parties to the proceedings of the costs incurred by him in so doing or as to the payment by him of any costs incurred by any of those parties by reason of his so doing.

(3)   . . .

NOTES

Sub-s (1): for the first words in italics there are substituted the words "proceedings for a divorce order", and words in italics in para (b) repealed, by the Family Law Act 1996, s 66(1), (3), Sch 8, Pt I, paras 4, 5(a), (b), Sch 10, subject to savings in s 66(2) of, and Sch 9, para 5 to, the 1996 Act, as from a day to be appointed.

Sub-s (2): for the words in italics there are substituted the words "the making of a divorce order" by the Family Law Act 1996, s 66(1), Sch 8, Pt I, paras 4, 5(c), subject to savings in s 66(2) of, and Sch 9, para 5 to, the 1996 Act, as from a day to be appointed.

Sub-s (3): outside the scope of this work.

9 Proceedings after decree nisi: general powers of court

(1)   Where a decree of divorce has been granted but not made absolute, then, without prejudice to section 8 above, any person (excluding a party to the proceedings other than the Queen's Proctor) may show cause why the decree should not be made absolute by reason of material facts not having been brought before the court; and in such a case the court may—

(a) notwithstanding anything in section 1(5) above (but subject to sections 10(2) to (4) and 41 below) make the decree absolute; or

(b) rescind the decree; or

(c) require further inquiry; or

(d) otherwise deal with the case as it thinks fit.

(2)   Where a decree of divorce has been granted and no application for it to be made absolute has been made by the party to whom it was granted, then, at any time after the expiration of three months from the earliest date on which that party could have made such an application, the party against whom it was granted may make an application to the court, and on that application the court may exercise any of the powers mentioned in paragraphs (a) to (d) of subsection (1) above.

NOTES

Repealed as noted to s 1.

10 Proceedings after decree nisi: special protection for respondent in separation cases

(1)   Where in any case the court has granted a decree of divorce on the basis of a finding that the petitioner was entitled to rely in support of his petition on the fact of two years' separation coupled with the respondent's consent to a decree being granted and has made no such finding as to any other fact mentioned in section 1(2) above, the court may, on an application made by the respondent at any time before the decree is made absolute, rescind the decree if it is satisfied that the petitioner misled the respondent (whether intentionally or unintentionally) about any matter which the respondent took into account in deciding to give his consent.

(2)   The following provisions of this section apply where—
(a)   the respondent to a petition for divorce in which the petitioner alleged two years' or five years' separation coupled, in the former case, with the respondent's consent to a decree being granted, has applied to the court for consideration under subsection (3) below of his financial position after the divorce; and
(b)   the court has granted a decree on the petition on the basis of a finding that the petitioner was entitled to rely in support of his petition on the fact of two years' or five years' separation (as the case may be) and has made no such finding as to any other fact mentioned in section 1(2) above.

(3)   The court hearing an application by the respondent under subsection (2) above shall consider all the circumstances, including the age, health, conduct, earning capacity, financial resources and financial obligations of each of the parties, and the financial position of the respondent as, having regard to the divorce, it is likely to be after the death of the petitioner should the petitioner die first; and, subject to subsection (4) below, the court shall not make the decree absolute unless it is satisfied—
(a)   that the petitioner should not be required to make any financial provision for the respondent, or
(b)   that the financial provision made by the petitioner for the respondent is reasonable and fair or the best that can be made in the circumstances.

(4)   The court may if it thinks fit make the decree absolute notwithstanding the requirements of subsection (3) above if—
(a)   it appears that there are circumstances making it desirable that the decree should be made absolute without delay, and

(b) the court has obtained a satisfactory undertaking from the petitioner that he will make such financial provision for the respondent as the court may approve.

Repealed as noted to s 1.

Nullity

11 Grounds on which a marriage is void

A marriage celebrated after 31st July 1971 shall be void on the following grounds only, that is to say—
  (a) that it is not a valid marriage under the provisions of [the [Marriage Acts 1949 to 1986]] (that is to say where—
    (i) the parties are within the prohibited degrees of relationship;
    (ii) either party is under the age of sixteen; or
    (iii) the parties have intermarried in disregard of certain requirements as to the formation of marriage);
  (b) that at the time of the marriage either party was already lawfully married;
  (c) that the parties are not respectively male and female;
  (d) in the case of a polygamous marriage entered into outside England and Wales, that either party was at the time of the marriage domiciled in England and Wales.

For the purposes of paragraph (d) of this subsection a marriage [is not polygamous if] at its inception neither party has any spouse additional to the other.

Words in first (outer) pair of square brackets in para (a) substituted by the Marriage Act 1983, s 2(4); words in second (inner) pair of square brackets substituted by the Marriage (Prohibited Degrees of Relationship) Act 1986, s 6(4); words in third pair of square brackets substituted by the Private International Law (Miscellaneous Provisions) Act 1995, s 8(2), Sch, para 2(2).

12 Grounds on which a marriage is voidable

A marriage celebrated after 31st July 1971 shall be voidable on the following grounds only, that is to say—

   (a)   that the marriage has not been consummated owing to the incapacity of either party to consummate it;

   (b)   that the marriage has not been consummated owing to the wilful refusal of the respondent to consummate it;

   (c)   that either party to the marriage did not validly consent to it, whether in consequence of duress, mistake, unsoundness of mind or otherwise;

   (d)   that at the time of the marriage either party, though capable of giving a valid consent, was suffering (whether continuously or intermittently) from mental disorder within the meaning of [the Mental Health Act 1983] of such a kind or to such an extent as to be unfitted for marriage;

   (e)   that at the time of the marriage the respondent was suffering from venereal disease in a communicable form;

   (f)   that at the time of the marriage the respondent was pregnant by some person other than the petitioner.

NOTES

Words in square brackets in para (d) substituted by the Mental Health Act 1983, s 148, Sch 4, para 34.

13   Bars to relief where marriage is voidable

(1)   The court shall not, in proceedings instituted after 31st July 1971, grant a decree of nullity on the ground that a marriage is voidable if the respondent satisfies the court—

   (a)   that the petitioner, with knowledge that it was open to him to have the marriage avoided, so conducted himself in relation to the respondent as to lead the respondent reasonably to believe that he would not seek to do so; and

   (b)   that it would be unjust to the respondent to grant the decree.

[(2)   Without prejudice to subsection (1) above, the court shall not grant a decree of nullity by virtue of section 12 above on the grounds mentioned in paragraph (c), (d), (e) or (f) of that section unless—

   (a)   it is satisfied that proceedings were instituted within the period of three years from the date of the marriage, or

   (b)   leave for the institution of proceedings after the expiration of that period has been granted under subsection (4) below.]

(3)   Without prejudice to subsections (1) and (2) above, the court shall not grant a decree of nullity by virtue of section 12 above on the grounds

mentioned in paragraph (e) or (f) of that section unless it is satisfied that the petitioner was at the time of the marriage ignorant of the facts alleged.

[(4)   In the case of proceedings for the grant of a decree of nullity by virtue of section 12 above on the grounds mentioned in paragraph (c), (d), (e) or (f) of that section, a judge of the court may, on an application made to him, grant leave for the institution of proceedings after the expiration of the period of three years from the date of the marriage if—

(a)   he is satisfied that the petitioner has at some time during that period suffered from mental disorder within the meaning of the Mental Health Act 1983, and

(b)   he considers that in all the circumstances of the case it would be just to grant leave for the institution of proceedings.

(5)   An application for leave under subsection (4) above may be made after the expiration of the period of three years from the date of the marriage.]

NOTES

Sub-s (2): substituted by the Matrimonial and Family Proceedings Act 1984, s 2.

Sub-ss (4), (5): added by the Matrimonial and Family Proceedings Act 1984, s 2.

14   Marriages governed by foreign law or celebrated abroad under English law

(1)   Where, apart from this Act, any matter affecting the validity of a marriage would fall to be determined (in accordance with the rules of private international law) by reference to the law of a country outside England and Wales, nothing in section 11, 12 or 13(1) above shall—

(a)   preclude the determination of that matter as aforesaid; or

(b)   require the application to the marriage of the grounds or bar there mentioned except so far as applicable in accordance with those rules.

(2)   In the case of a marriage which purports to have been celebrated under the Foreign Marriage Acts 1892 to 1947 or has taken place outside England and Wales and purports to be a marriage under common law, section 11 above is without prejudice to any ground on which the marriage may be void under those Acts or, as the case may be, by virtue of the rules governing the celebration of marriages outside England and Wales under common law.

15 Application of ss 1(5), 8 and 9 to nullity proceedings

Sections 1(5), 8 and 9 above shall apply in relation to proceedings for nullity of marriage as if for any reference in those provisions to divorce there were substituted a reference to nullity of marriage.

NOTES

Substituted, together with new ss 15A, 15B, for s 15 as originally enacted, by the Family Law Act 1996, s 66(1), Sch 8, Pt I, paras 4, 6, subject to savings in s 66(2) of, and Sch 9, para 5 to, the 1996 Act, as from a day to be appointed, as follows—

"**15   Decrees of nullity to be decrees nisi**
Every decree of nullity of marriage shall in the first instance be a decree nisi and shall not be made absolute before the end of six weeks from its grant unless—
(a) the High Court by general order from time to time fixes a shorter period; or
(b) in any particular case, the court in which the proceedings are for the time being pending from time to time by special order fixes a shorter period than the period otherwise applicable for the time being by virtue of this section.

15A   Intervention of Queen's Proctor
(1)   In the case of a petition for nullity of marriage—
(a) the court may, if it thinks fit, direct all necessary papers in the matter to be sent to the Queen's Proctor, who shall under the directions of the Attorney-General instruct counsel to argue before the court any question in relation to the matter which the court considers it necessary or expedient to have fully argued;
(b) any person may at any time during the progress of the proceedings or before the decree nisi is made absolute give information to the Queen's Proctor on any matter material to the due decision of the case, and the Queen's Proctor may thereupon take such steps as the Attorney-General considers necessary or expedient.
(2)   If the Queen's Proctor intervenes or shows cause against a decree nisi in any proceedings for nullity of marriage, the court may make such order as may be just as to the payment by other parties to the proceedings of the costs incurred by him in so doing or as to the payment by him of any costs incurred by any of those parties by reason of his so doing.
(3)   Subsection (3) of section 8 above applies in relation to this section as it applies in relation to that section.

15B   Proceedings after decree nisi: general powers of court
(1)   Where a decree of nullity of marriage has been granted under this Act but not made absolute, then, without prejudice to section 15A above, any person (excluding a party to the proceedings other than the Queen's Proctor) may show cause why the

decree should not be made absolute by reason of material facts not having been brought before the court; and in such a case the court may—

(a) notwithstanding anything in section 15 above (but subject to section 41 below) make the decree absolute; or

(b) rescind the decree; or

(c) require further inquiry; or

(d) otherwise deal with the case as it thinks fit.

(2) Where a decree of nullity of marriage has been granted under this Act and no application for it to be made absolute has been made by the party to whom it was granted, then, at any time after the expiration of three months from the earliest date on which that party could have made such an application, the party against whom it was granted may make an application to the court, and on that application the court may exercise any of the powers mentioned in paragraphs (a) to (d) of subsection (1) above.".

16 Effect of decree of nullity in case of voidable marriage

A decree of nullity granted after 31st July 1971 in respect of a voidable marriage shall operate to annul the marriage only as respects any time after the decree has been made absolute, and the marriage shall, notwithstanding the decree, be treated as if it had existed up to that time.

Other matrimonial suits

17 Judicial separation

(1)   A petition for judicial separation may be presented to the court by either party to a marriage on the ground that any such fact as is mentioned in section 1(2) above exists, and the provisions of section 2 above shall apply accordingly for the purposes of a petition for judicial separation alleging any such fact, as they apply in relation to a petition for divorce alleging that fact.

(2)   On a petition for judicial separation it shall be the duty of the court to inquire, so far as it reasonably can, into the facts alleged by the petitioner and into any facts alleged by the respondent, but the court shall not be concerned to consider whether the marriage has broken down irretrievably, and if it is satisfied on the evidence of any such fact as is mentioned in section 1(2) above it shall, subject to section 41 below, grant a decree of judicial separation.

(3)   *Sections 6 and 7 above shall apply for the purpose of encouraging the reconciliation of parties to proceedings for judicial separation and of enabling the parties to a marriage to refer to the court for its opinion an agreement or arrangement relevant to actual or contemplated proceedings for judicial separation, as they apply in relation to proceedings for divorce.*

NOTES

Repealed as noted to s 1.

18   Effects of judicial separation

(1)   *Where the court grants a decree of judicial separation it shall no longer be obligatory for the petitioner to cohabit with the respondent.*

(2)   *If while a decree of judicial separation is in force and the separation is continuing either of the parties to the marriage dies intestate as respects all or any of his or her real or personal property, the property as respects which he or she died intestate shall devolve as if the other party to the marriage had then been dead.*

(3)   *Notwithstanding anything in section 2(1)(a) of the Matrimonial Proceedings (Magistrates' Courts) Act 1960, a provision in force under an order made, or having effect as if made, under that section exempting one party to a marriage from the obligation to cohabit with the other shall not have effect as a decree of judicial separation for the purposes of subsection (2) above.*

NOTES

Repealed as noted to s 1.

19   Presumption of death and dissolution of marriage

(1)   Any married person who alleges that reasonable grounds exist for supposing that the other party to the marriage is dead may . . . present a petition to the court to have it presumed that the other party is dead and to have the marriage dissolved, and the court may, if satisfied that such reasonable grounds exist, grant a decree of presumption of death and dissolution of the marriage.

(2)   . . .

(3)   In any proceedings under this section the fact that for a period of seven years or more the other party to the marriage has been continually absent from the petitioner and the petitioner has no reason to believe that the other party has been living within that time shall be evidence that the other party is dead until the contrary is proved.

(4)   Sections *1(5), 8 and 9* above shall apply to a petition and a decree under this section as they apply to a petition for *divorce* and a decree of *divorce* respectively.

(5)   . . .

(6)   It is hereby declared that neither collusion nor any other conduct on the part of the petitioner which has at any time been a bar to relief in matrimonial proceedings constitutes a bar to the grant of a decree under this section.

NOTES

Sub-s (1): words omitted repealed by the Domicile and Matrimonial Proceedings Act 1973, ss 6(4), 17(2), Sch 6.

Sub-ss (2), (5): repealed by the Domicile and Matrimonial Proceedings Act 1973, ss 6(4), 17(2), Sch 6.

Sub-s (4): for the first words in italics there are substituted the words "15, 15A and 15B" and for the second and final words in italics there are substituted the words "nullity of marriage" by the Family Law Act 1996, s 66(1), Sch 8, Pt I, paras 4, 7, subject to savings in s 66(2) of, and Sch 9, para 5 to, the 1996 Act, as from a day to be appointed.

General

20   Relief for respondent in divorce proceedings

If in any proceedings for divorce the respondent alleges and proves any such fact as is mentioned in subsection (2) of section 1 above (treating the respondent as the petitioner and the petitioner as the respondent for the purposes of that subsection) the court may give to the respondent the relief to which he would have been entitled if he had presented a petition seeking that relief.

NOTES

Repealed as noted to s 1.

PART II
FINANCIAL RELIEF FOR PARTIES TO MARRIAGE AND CHILDREN OF FAMILY

Financial provision and property adjustment orders

21 Financial provision and property adjustment orders

*(1)   The financial provision orders for the purposes of this Act are the orders
for periodical or lump sum provision available (subject to the provisions of
this Act) under section 23 below for the purpose of adjusting the financial
position of the parties to a marriage and any children of the family in connection
with proceedings for divorce, nullity of marriage or judicial separation and
under section 27(6) below on proof of neglect by one party to a marriage to
provide, or to make a proper contribution towards, reasonable maintenance
for the other or a child of the family, that is to say—*

(a)   *any order for periodical payments in favour of a party to a marriage
under section 23(1)(a) or 27(6)(a) or in favour of a child of the family
under section 23(1)(d), (2) or (4) or 27(6)(d);*

(b)   *any order for secured periodical payments in favour of a party to a
marriage under section 23(1)(b) or 27(6)(b) or in favour of a child of
the family under section 23(1)(e), (2) or (4) or 27(6)(e); and*

(c)   *any order for lump sum provision in favour of a party to a marriage
under section 23(1)(c) or 27(6)(c) or in favour of a child of the family
under section 23(1)(f), (2) or (4) or 27(6)(f);*

*and references in this Act (except in paragraphs 17(1) and 23 of Schedule 1
below) to periodical payments orders, secured periodical payments orders,
and orders for the payment of a lump sum are references to all or some of
the financial provision orders requiring the sort of financial provision in
question according as the context of each reference may require.*

*(2)   The property adjustment orders for the purposes of this Act are the
orders dealing with property rights available (subject to the provisions of
this Act) under section 24 below for the purpose of adjusting the financial
position of the parties to a marriage and any children of the family on or
after the grant of a decree of divorce, nullity of marriage or judicial
separation, that is to say—*

(a)   *any order under subsection (1)(a) of that section for a transfer of property;*

(b)   *any order under subsection (1)(b) of that section for a settlement of
property; and*

(c)   *any order under subsection (1)(c) or (d) of that section for a variation
of settlement.*

NOTES

Substituted by the Family Law Act 1996, s 15(1), (3), Sch 2, paras 1, 2, subject to savings in s 66(2) of, and Sch 9, para 5 to, the 1996 Act, as from a day to be appointed, as follows—

"21   Financial provision and property adjustment orders

(1)   For the purposes of this Act, a financial provision order is—

(a)   an order that a party must make in favour of another person such periodical payments, for such term, as may be specified (a "periodical payments order");

(b)   an order that a party must, to the satisfaction of the court, secure in favour of another person such periodical payments, for such term, as may be specified (a "secured periodical payments order");

(c)   an order that a party must make a payment in favour of another person of such lump sum or sums as may be specified (an "order for the payment of a lump sum").

(2)   For the purposes of this Act, a property adjustment order is—

(a)   an order that a party must transfer such of his or her property as may be specified in favour of the other party or a child of the family;

(b)   an order that a settlement of such property of a party as may be specified must be made, to the satisfaction of the court, for the benefit of the other party and of the children of the family, or either or any of them;

(c)   an order varying, for the benefit of the parties and of the children of the family, or either or any of them, any marriage settlement;

(d)   an order extinguishing or reducing the interest of either of the parties under any marriage settlement.

(3)   Subject to section 40 below, where an order of the court under this Part of this Act requires a party to make or secure a payment in favour of another person or to transfer property in favour of any person, that payment must be made or secured or that property transferred—

(a)   if that other person is the other party to the marriage, to that other party; and

(b)   if that other person is a child of the family, according to the terms of the order—

(i)   to the child; or

(ii)   to such other person as may be specified, for the benefit of that child.

(4)   References in this section to the property of a party are references to any property to which that party is entitled either in possession or in reversion.

(5)   Any power of the court under this Part of this Act to make such an order as is mentioned in subsection (2)(b) to (d) above is exercisable even though there are no children of the family.

(6)   In this section—

"marriage settlement" means an ante-nuptial or post-nuptial settlement made on the parties (including one made by will or codicil);

"party" means a party to a marriage; and

"specified" means specified in the order in question.".

Ancillary relief in connection with divorce proceedings, etc

22 Maintenance pending suit

On a petition for divorce, nullity of marriage or judicial separation, the court may make an order for maintenance pending suit, that is to say, an order requiring either party to the marriage to make to the other such periodical payments for his or her maintenance and for such term, being a term beginning not earlier than the date of the presentation of the petition and ending with the date of the determination of the suit, as the court thinks reasonable.

NOTES

Repealed as noted to s 1.

[22A Financial provision orders: divorce and separation

(1)   On an application made under this section, the court may at the appropriate time make one or more financial provision orders in favour of—
  (a) a party to the marriage to which the application relates; or
  (b) any of the children of the family.

(2)   The "appropriate time" is any time—
  (a) after a statement of marital breakdown has been received by the court and before any application for a divorce order or for a separation order is made to the court by reference to that statement;
  (b) when an application for a divorce order or separation order has been made under section 3 of the 1996 Act and has not been withdrawn;
  (c) when an application for a divorce order has been made under section 4 of the 1996 Act and has not been withdrawn;
  (d) after a divorce order has been made;
  (e) when a separation order is in force.

(3)   The court may make—
  (a) a combined order against the parties on one occasion,
  (b) separate orders on different occasions,
  (c) different orders in favour of different children,
  (d) different orders from time to time in favour of the same child,

but may not make, in favour of the same party, more than one periodical payments order, or more than one order for payment of a lump sum, in relation to any marital proceedings, whether in the course of the proceedings or by reference to a divorce order or separation order made in the proceedings.

(4)   If it would not otherwise be in a position to make a financial provision order in favour of a party or child of the family, the court may make an interim periodical payments order, an interim order for the payment of a lump sum or a series of such orders, in favour of that party or child.

(5)   Any order for the payment of a lump sum made under this section may—
    (a) provide for the payment of the lump sum by instalments of such amounts as may be specified in the order; and
    (b) require the payment of the instalments to be secured to the satisfaction of the court.

(6)   Nothing in subsection (5) above affects—
    (a) the power of the court under this section to make an order for the payment of a lump sum; or
    (b) the provisions of this Part of this Act as to the beginning of the term specified in any periodical payments order or secured periodical payments order.

(7)   Subsection (8) below applies where the court—
    (a) makes an order under this section ("the main order") for the payment of a lump sum; and
    (b) directs—
        (i) that payment of that sum, or any part of it, is to be deferred; or
        (ii) that that sum, or any part of it, is to be paid by instalments.

(8)   In such a case, the court may, on or at any time after making the main order, make an order ("the order for interest") for the amount deferred, or the instalments, to carry interest (at such rate as may be specified in the order for interest)—
    (a) from such date, not earlier than the date of the main order, as may be so specified;
    (b) until the date when the payment is due.

(9)   This section is to be read subject to any restrictions imposed by this Act and to section 19 of the 1996 Act.]

NOTES
Commencement: to be appointed.
Inserted, together with s 22B, by the Family Law Act 1996, s 15(1), (3), Sch 2, paras 1, 3, subject to savings in s 66(2) of, and Sch 9, para 5 to, the 1996 Act.

[22B   Restrictions affecting section 22A

(1)   No financial provision order, other than an interim order, may be made under section 22A above so as to take effect before the making of a divorce order or separation order in relation to the marriage, unless the court is satisfied—
   (a) that the circumstances of the case are exceptional; and
   (b) that it would be just and reasonable for the order to be so made.

(2)   Except in the case of an interim periodical payments order, the court may not make a financial provision order under section 22A above at any time while the period for reflection and consideration is interrupted under section 7(8) of the 1996 Act.

(3)   No financial provision order may be made under section 22A above by reference to the making of a statement of marital breakdown if, by virtue of section 5(3) or 7(9) of the 1996 Act (lapse of divorce or separation process), it has ceased to be possible—
   (a) for an application to be made by reference to that statement; or
   (b) for an order to be made on such an application.

(4)   No financial provision order may be made under section 22A after a divorce order has been made, or while a separation order is in force, except—
   (a) in response to an application made before the divorce order or separation order was made; or
   (b) on a subsequent application made with the leave of the court.

(5)   In this section, "period for reflection and consideration" means the period fixed by section 7 of the 1996 Act.]

NOTES
Commencement: to be appointed.
Inserted as noted to s 22A.

23 Financial provision orders in connection with divorce proceedings, etc

(1)   On granting a decree of divorce, a decree of nullity of marriage or a decree of judicial separation or at any time thereafter (whether, in the case of a decree of divorce or of nullity of marriage, before or after the decree is made absolute), the court may make any one or more of the following orders, that is to say—

    (a) an order that either party to the marriage shall make to the other such periodical payments, for such term, as may be specified in the order;

    (b) an order that either party to the marriage shall secure to the other to the satisfaction of the court such periodical payments, for such term, as may be so specified;

    (c) an order that either party to the marriage shall pay to the other such lump sum or sums as may be so specified;

    (d) an order that a party to the marriage shall make to such person as may be specified in the order for the benefit of a child of the family, or to such a child, such periodical payments, for such term, as may be so specified;

    (e) an order that a party to the marriage shall secure to such person as may be so specified for the benefit of such a child, or to such a child, to the satisfaction of the court, such periodical payments, for such term, as may be so specified;

    (f) an order that a party to the marriage shall pay to such person as may be so specified for the benefit of such a child, or to such a child, such lump sum as may be so specified;

subject, however, in the case of an order under paragraph (d), (e) or (f) above, to the restrictions imposed by section 29(1) and (3) below on the making of financial provision orders in favour of children who have attained the age of eighteen.

(2)   The court may also, subject to those restrictions, make any one or more of the orders mentioned in subsection (1)(d), (e) and (f) above—

    (a) in any proceedings for divorce, nullity of marriage or judicial separation, before granting a decree; and

    (b) where any such proceedings are dismissed after the beginning of the trial, either forthwith or within a reasonable period after the dismissal.

(3)   Without prejudice to the generality of subsection (1)(c) or (f) above—

    (a) an order under this section that a party to a marriage shall pay a lump sum to the other party may be made for the purpose of enabling

that other party to meet any liabilities or expenses reasonably incurred by him or her in maintaining himself or herself or any child of the family before making an application for an order under this section in his or her favour;

(b) an order under this section for the payment of a lump sum to or for the benefit of a child of the family may be made for the purpose of enabling any liabilities or expenses reasonably incurred by or for the benefit of that child before the making of an application for an order under this section in his favour to be met; and

(c) an order under this section for the payment of a lump sum may provide for the payment of that sum by instalments of such amount as may be specified in the order and may require the payment of the instalments to be secured to the satisfaction of the court.

(4)   The power of the court under subsection (1) or (2)(a) above to make an order in favour of a child of the family shall be exercisable from time to time; and where the court makes an order in favour of a child under subsection (2)(b) above, it may from time to time, subject to the restrictions mentioned in subsection (1) above, make a further order in his favour of any of the kinds mentioned in subsection (1)(d), (e) or (f) above.

(5)   Without prejudice to the power to give a direction under section 30 below for the settlement of an instrument by conveyancing counsel, where an order is made under subsection (1)(a), (b) or (c) above on or after granting a decree of divorce or nullity of marriage, neither the order nor any settlement made in pursuance of the order shall take effect unless the decree has been made absolute.

[(6)   Where the court—
  (a) makes an order under this section for the payment of a lump of sum; and
  (b) directs—
    (i)   that payment of that sum or any part of it shall be deferred; or
    (ii) that that sum or any part of it shall be paid by instalments,

the court may order that the amount deferred or the instalments shall carry interest at such rate as may be specified by the order from such date, not earlier than the date of the order, as may be so specified, until the date when payment of it is due.]

NOTES

Sub-s (6): added by the Administration of Justice Act 1982, s 16.

Substituted by the Family Law 1996, s 15(1), (3), Sch 2, paras 1, 4, subject to savings in s 66(2) of, and Sch 9, para 5 to, the 1996 Act, as from a day to be appointed.

[23A Property adjustment orders: divorce and separation

(1)   On an application made under this section, the court may, at any time mentioned in section 22A(2) above, make one or more property adjustment orders.

(2)   If the court makes, in favour of the same party to the marriage, more than one property adjustment order in relation to any marital proceedings, whether in the course of the proceedings or by reference to a divorce order or separation order made in the proceedings, each order must fall within a different paragraph of section 21(2) above.

(3)   The court shall exercise its powers under this section, so far as is practicable, by making on one occasion all such provision as can be made by way of one or more property adjustment orders in relation to the marriage as it thinks fit.

(4)   Subsection (3) above does not affect section 31 or 31A below.

(5)   This section is to be read subject to any restrictions imposed by this Act and to section 19 of the 1996 Act.]

NOTES

Commencement: to be appointed.
Inserted, together with s 23B by the Family Law Act 1996, s 15(1), (3), Sch 2, paras 1, 5, subject to savings in s 66(2) of, and Sch 9, para 5 to, the 1996 Act as from a day to be appointed.

[23B Restrictions affecting section 23A

(1)   No property adjustment order may be made under section 23A above so as to take effect before the making of a divorce order or separation order in relation to the marriage unless the court is satisfied—
    (a) that the circumstances of the case are exceptional; and
    (b) that it would be just and reasonable for the order to be so made.

(2)   The court may not make a property adjustment order under section 23A above at any time while the period for reflection and consideration is interrupted under section 7(8) of the 1996 Act.

(3)   No property adjustment order may be made under section 23A above by virtue of the making of a statement of marital breakdown if, by virtue of section 5(3) or 7(5) of the 1996 Act (lapse of divorce or separation process), it has ceased to be possible—
   (a) for an application to be made by reference to that statement; or
   (b) for an order to be made on such an application.

(4)   No property adjustment order may be made under section 23A above after a divorce order has been made, or while a separation order is in force, except—
   (a) in response to an application made before the divorce order or separation order was made; or
   (b) on a subsequent application made with the leave of the court.

(5)   In this section, "period for reflection and consideration" means the period fixed by section 7 of the 1996 Act.]

NOTES

Commencement: to be appointed.
Inserted as noted to s 23A.

24   Property adjustment orders in connection with divorce proceedings, etc

(1)   On granting a decree of divorce, a decree of nullity of marriage or a decree of judicial separation or at any time thereafter (whether, in the case of a decree of divorce or of nullity of marriage, before or after the decree is made absolute), the court may make any one or more of the following orders, that is to say—
   (a) an order that a party to the marriage shall transfer to the other party, to any child of the family or to such person as may be specified in the order for the benefit of such a child such property as may be so specified, being property to which the first- mentioned party is entitled, either in possession or reversion;
   (b) an order that a settlement of such property as may be so specified, being property to which a party to the marriage is so entitled, be made to the satisfaction of the court for the benefit of the other

party to the marriage and of the children of the family or either or any of them;

    (c) an order varying for the benefit of the parties to the marriage and of the children of the family or either or any of them any ante-nuptial or post-nuptial settlement (including such a settlement made by will or codicil) made on the parties to the marriage;

    (d) an order extinguishing or reducing the interest of either of the parties to the marriage under any such settlement;

subject, however, in the case of an order under paragraph (a) above, to the restrictions imposed by section 29(1) and (3) below on the making of orders for a transfer of property in favour of children who have attained the age of eighteen.

(2)   The court may make an order under subsection (1)(c) above notwithstanding that there are no children of the family.

(3)   Without prejudice to the power to give a direction under section 30 below for the settlement of an instrument by conveyancing counsel, where an order is made under this section on or after granting a decree of divorce or nullity of marriage, neither the order nor any settlement made in pursuance of the order shall take effect unless the decree has been made absolute.

NOTES

Substituted by the Family Law Act 1996, s 15(1), (3), Sch 2, paras 1, 6, subject to savings in s 66(2) of, and Sch 9, para 5 to, the 1996 Act, as from a day to be appointed.

[24A Orders for sale of property

(1)   Where the court makes under *section 23 or 24 of this Act* a secured periodical payments order, an order for the payment of a lump sum or a property adjustment order, then, on making that order or at any time thereafter, the court may make a further order for the sale of such property as may be specified in the order, being property in which or in the proceeds of sale of which either or both of the parties to the marriage has or have a beneficial interest, either in possession or reversion.

(2)   Any order made under subsection (1) above may contain such consequential or supplementary provisions as the court thinks fit and, without prejudice to the generality of the foregoing provision, may include—

(a) provision requiring the making of a payment out of the proceeds of sale of the property to which the order relates, and

(b) provision requiring any such property to be offered for sale to a person, or class of persons, specified in the order.

(3) Where an order is made under subsection (1) above on or after the grant of a decree of *divorce or* nullity of marriage, the order shall not take effect unless the decree has been made absolute.

(4) Where an order is made under subsection (1) above, the court may direct that the order, or such provision thereof as the court may specify, shall not take effect until the occurrence of an event specified by the court or the expiration of a period so specified.

(5) Where an order under subsection (1) above contains a provision requiring the proceeds of sale of the property to which the order relates to be used to secure periodical payments to a party to the marriage, the order shall cease to have effect on the death or re-marriage of that person.

[(6) Where a party to a marriage has a beneficial interest in any property, or in the proceeds of sale thereof, and some other person who is not a party to the marriage also has a beneficial interest in that property or in the proceeds of sale thereof, then, before deciding whether to make an order under this section in relation to that property, it shall be the duty of the court to give that other person an opportunity to make representations with respect to the order; and any representations made by that other person shall be included among the circumstances to which the court is required to have regard under section 25(1) below.]]

<table>
NOTES
</table>

Inserted by the Matrimonial Homes and Property Act 1981, s 7.

Sub-s (1): for the words in italics there are substituted the words "any of sections 22A to 24 above" by the Family Law Act 1996, s 66(1), Sch 8, Pt I, paras 4, 8, subject to savings in s 66(2) of, and Sch 9, para 5 to, the 1996 Act, as from a day to be appointed.

Sub-s (3): words in italics repealed by the Family Law Act 1996, s 66(3), Sch 10, subject to savings in s 66(2) of, and Sch 9, para 5 to, the 1996 Act, as from a day to be appointed.

Sub-s (6): added by the Matrimonial and Family Proceedings Act 1984, s 46(1), Sch 1.

[25 Matters to which court is to have regard in deciding how to exercise its powers under ss 23, 24 and 24A

(1)   It shall be the duty of the court in deciding whether to exercise its powers under *section 23, 24 or 24A* above and, if so, in what manner, to have regard to all the circumstances of the case, first consideration being given to the welfare while a minor of any child of the family who has not attained the age of eighteen.

(2)   As regards the exercise of the powers of the court under *section 23(1)(a), (b) or (c),* 24 or 24A above in relation to a party to the marriage, the court shall in particular have regard to the following matters—
    (a) the income, earning capacity, property and other financial resources which each of the parties to the marriage has or is likely to have in the foreseeable future, including in the case of earning capacity any increase in that capacity which it would in the opinion of the court be reasonable to expect a party to the marriage to take steps to acquire;
    (b) the financial needs, obligations and responsibilities which each of the parties to the marriage has or is likely to have in the foreseeable future;
    (c) the standard of living enjoyed by the family before the breakdown of the marriage;
    (d) the age of each party to the marriage and the duration of the marriage;
    (e) any physical or mental disability of either of the parties to the marriage;
    (f) the contributions which each of the parties has made or is likely in the foreseeable future to make to the welfare of the family, including any contribution by looking after the home or caring for the family;
    (g) the conduct of each of the parties[, whatever the nature of the conduct and whether it occurred during the marriage or after the separation of the parties or (as the case may be) dissolution or annulment of the marriage,], if that conduct is such that it would in the opinion of the court be inequitable to disregard it;
    (h) *in the case of proceedings for divorce or nullity of marriage,* the value to each of the parties to the marriage of any benefit *(for example, a pension)* which, by reason of the dissolution or annulment of the marriage, that party will lose the chance of acquiring.

(3)   As regards the exercise of the powers of the court under *section 23(1)(d), (e) or (f), (2) or (4)* 24 or 24A above in relation to a child of the family, the court shall in particular have regard to the following matters—
    (a) the financial needs of the child;

   (b) the income, earning capacity (if any), property and other financial resources of the child;

   (c) any physical or mental disability of the child;

   (d) the manner in which he was being and in which the parties to the marriage expected him to be educated or trained;

   (e) the considerations mentioned in relation to the parties to the marriage in paragraphs (a), (b), (c) and (e) of subsection (2) above.

(4)   As regards the exercise of the powers of the court under *section 23(1)(d), (e) or (f), (2) or (4), 24 or 24A* above against a party to a marriage in favour of a child of the family who is not the child of that party, the court shall also have regard—

   (a) to whether that party assumed any responsibility for the child's maintenance, and, if so, to the extent to which, and the basis upon which, that party assumed such responsibility and to the length of time for which that party discharged such responsibility;

   (b) to whether in assuming and discharging such responsibility that party did so knowing that the child was not his or her own;

   (c) to the liability of any other person to maintain the child.

[(5)   In relation to any power of the court to make an interim periodical payments order or an interim order for the payment of a lump sum, the preceding provisions of this section, in imposing any obligation on the court with respect to the matters to which it is to have regard, shall not require the court to do anything which would cause such a delay as would, in the opinion of the court, be inappropriate having regard—

   (a) to any immediate need for an interim order;

   (b) to the matters in relation to which it is practicable for the court to inquire before making an interim order; and

   (c) to the ability of the court to have regard to any matter and to make appropriate adjustments when subsequently making a financial provision order which is not interim.]]

   Commencement: to be appointed (sub-s (5)); 12 October 1984 (sub-ss (1)–(4)).

   Substituted by the Matrimonial and Family Proceedings Act 1984, s 3.

   Sub-s (1): for the words in italics there are substituted the words "any of sections 22A to 24A" by the Family Law Act 1996, s 66(1), Sch 8, Pt I, paras 4, 9(1), (2), subject to savings in s 66(2) of, and Sch 9, para 5 to, the 1996 Act, as from a day to be appointed.

   Sub-s (2): for the first words in italics there are substituted the words "section 22A or 23 above to make a financial provision order in favour of a party to a marriage or the exercise of its powers under section 23A,", words in square brackets in para (g) inserted, and first words in italics in para (h) repealed, by the Family Law Act 1996, s 66(1), (3), Sch 8, Pt I, paras 4, 9(1), (3), Sch 10, subject to savings in s 66(2) of, and Sch 9, para 5 to, the 1996 Act, as from a day to be appointed; second words in italics in para (h) repealed by the Pensions Act 1995, s 166(2), subject to savings in the Pensions Act (Commencement) (No 5) Order 1996, SI 1996/1675, arts 4, 5.

Sub-s (3): for the words in italics there are substituted the words "section 22A or 23 above to make a financial provision order in favour of a child of the family or the exercise of its powers under section 23A," by the Family Law Act 1996, s 66(1), Sch 8, Pt I, paras 4, 9(1), (4), subject to savings in s 66(2) of, and Sch 9, para 5 to, the 1996 Act, as from a day to be appointed.

Sub-s (4): for the words in italics there are substituted the words "any of sections 22A to 24A" by the Family Law Act 1996, s 66(1), Sch 8, Pt I, paras 4, 9(1), (5), subject to savings in s 66(2) of, and Sch 9, para 5 to, the 1996 Act, as from a day to be appointed.

Sub-s (5): added by the Family Law Act 1996, s 66(1), Sch 8, Pt I, paras 4, 9(1), (6), subject to savings in s 66(2) of, and Sch 9, para 5 to, the 1996 Act, as from a day to be appointed.

[25A   Exercise of court's powers in favour of party to marriage on decree of divorce or nullity of marriage

(1)   Where on or after the grant of a decree of divorce or nullity of marriage the court decides to exercise its powers under section 23(1)(a), (b) or (c), 24 or 24A above in favour of a party to the marriage, it shall be the duty of the court to consider whether it would be appropriate so to exercise those powers that the financial obligations of each party towards the other will be terminated as soon after the grant of the decree as the court considers just and reasonable.

(2)   Where the court decides in such a case to make a periodical payments or secured periodical payments order in favour of a party to the marriage, the court shall in particular consider whether it would be appropriate to require those payments to be made or secured only for such term as would in the opinion of the court be sufficient to enable the party in whose favour the order is made to adjust without undue hardship to the termination of his or her financial dependence on the other party.

(3)   Where on or after the grant of a decree of divorce or nullity of marriage an application is made by a party to the marriage for a periodical payments or secured periodical payments order in his or her favour, then, if the court considers that no continuing obligation should be imposed on either party to make or secure periodical payments in favour of the other, the court may dismiss the application with a direction that the applicant shall not be entitled

*to make any future application in relation to that marriage for an order
under section 23(1)(a) or (b) above.]*

NOTES

Inserted by the Matrimonial and Family Proceedings Act 1984, s 3.

Sub-s (1): words in italics in first place substituted by the words "If the court
decides to exercise any of its powers under any of sections 22A to 24A above in
favour of a party to a marriage (other than its power to make an interim periodical
payments order or an interim order for the payment of a lump sum)" and words in
italics in second place substituted by the words "a divorce order or decree of nullity"
by the Family Law Act 1996, s 66(1), Sch 8, Pt I, paras 4, 10(1)–(3), subject to
savings in s 66(2) of, and Sch 9, para 5 to, the 1996 Act, as from a day to be
appointed.

Sub-s (3): substituted by the Family Law Act 1996, s 66(1), Sch 8, Pt I, paras 4,
10(1), (4), subject to savings in s 66(2) of, and Sch 9, para 5 to, the 1996 Act, as from
a day to be appointed, as follows—

"(3) If the court—
(a) would have power under section 22A or 23 above to make a financial provision
order in favour of a party to a marriage ("the first party"), but
(b) considers that no continuing obligation should be imposed on the other party
to the marriage ("the second party") to make or secure periodical payments
in favour of the first party,

it may direct that the first party may not at any time after the direction takes
effect, apply to the court for the making against the second party of any periodical
payments order or secured periodical payments order and, if the first party has
already applied to the court for the making of such an order, it may dismiss the
application.

(3A) If the court—
(a) exercises, or has exercised, its power under section 22A at any time before
making a divorce order, and
(b) gives a direction under subsection (3) above in respect of a periodical payments
order or a secured periodical payments order,

it shall provide for the direction not to take effect until a divorce order is
made.".

[25B Pensions

(1)   The matters to which the court is to have regard under section 25(2)
above include—
(a) in the case of paragraph (a), any benefits under a pension scheme
which a party to the marriage has or is likely to have, and
(b) in the case of paragraph (h), any benefits under a pension scheme
which, by reason of the dissolution or annulment of the marriage, a
party to the marriage will lose the chance of acquiring,

and, accordingly, in relation to benefits under a pension scheme, section 25(2)(a) above shall have effect as if "in the foreseeable future" were omitted.

(2)   In any proceedings for a financial provision order under *section 23* above in a case where a party to the marriage has, or is likely to have, any benefit under a pension scheme, the court shall, in addition to considering any other matter which it is required to consider apart from this subsection, consider—

   (a) whether, having regard to any matter to which it is required to have regard in the proceedings by virtue of subsection (1) above, such an order (whether deferred or not) should be made, and

   (b) where the court determines to make such an order, how the terms of the order should be affected, having regard to any such matter;

   [(c) in particular, where the court determines to make such an order, whether the order should provide for the accrued rights of the party with pension rights ("the pension rights") to be divided between that party and the other party in such a way as to reduce the pension rights of the party with those rights and to create pension rights for the other party.]

(3)   The following provisions apply where, having regard to any benefits under a pension scheme, the court determines to make an order under *section 23* above.

(4)   To the extent to which the order is made having regard to any benefits under a pension scheme, the order may require the trustees or managers of the pension scheme in question, if at any time any payment in respect of any benefits under the scheme becomes due to the party with pension rights, to make a payment for the benefit of the other party.

(5)   The amount of any payment which, by virtue of subsection (4) above, the trustees or managers are required to make under the order at any time shall not exceed the amount of the payment which is due at that time to the party with pension rights.

(6)   Any such payment by the trustees or managers—

   (a) shall discharge so much of the trustees or managers liability to the party with pension rights as corresponds to the amount of the payment, and

   (b) shall be treated for all purposes as a payment made by the party with pension rights in or towards the discharge of his liability under the order.

(7)   Where the party with pension rights may require any benefits which he has or is likely to have under the scheme to be commuted, the order may require him to commute the whole or part of those benefits; and this section applies to the payment of any amount commuted in pursuance of the order as it applies to other payments in respect of benefits under the scheme.]

[(8)   If a pensions adjustment order under subsection (2)(c) above is made, the pension rights shall be reduced and pension rights of the other party shall be created in the prescribed manner with benefits payable on prescribed conditions, except that the court shall not have the power—

(a) to require the trustees or managers of the scheme to provide benefits under their own scheme if they are able and willing to create the rights for the other party by making a transfer payment to another scheme and the trustees and managers of that other scheme are able and willing to accept such a payment and to create those rights; or

(b) to require the trustees or managers of the scheme to make a transfer to another scheme—

  (i)   if the scheme is an unfunded scheme (unless the trustees or managers are able and willing to make such a transfer payment); or

  (ii) in prescribed circumstances.

(9)   No pensions adjustment order may be made under subsection (2)(c) above—

(a) if the scheme is a scheme of a prescribed type, or

(b) in prescribed circumstances, or

(c) insofar as it would affect benefits of a prescribed type.]

NOTES

Commencement: 1 August 1996.

Inserted by the Pensions Act 1995, s 166(1), subject to savings in the Pensions Act 1995 (Commencement) (No 5) Order 1996, SI 1996/1675, arts 4, 5.

Sub-s (2): for the words in italics there are substituted the words "section 22A or 23", and para (c) inserted, by the Family Law Act 1996, ss 16(1), (2), 66(1), Sch 8, Pt I, paras 4, 11, subject to savings in s 66(2) of, and Sch 9, para 5 to, the 1996 Act, as from a day to be appointed.

Sub-s (3): for the words in italics there are substituted the words "section 22A or 23" by the Family Law Act 1996, s 66(1), Sch 8, Pt I, paras 4, 11, subject to savings in s 66(2) of, and Sch 9, para 5 to, the 1996 Act, as from a day to be appointed.

Sub-ss (8), (9): added by the Family Law Act 1996, s 16(1), (3), subject to savings in s 66(2) of, and Sch 9, para 5 to, the 1996 Act, as from a day to be appointed.

[25C Pensions: lump sums

(1)   The power of the court under *section 23* above to order a party to a marriage to pay a lump sum to the other party includes, where the benefits which the party with pension rights has or is likely to have under a pension scheme include any lump sum payable in respect of his death, power to make any of the following provision by the order.

(2)   The court may—
   (a) if the trustees or managers of the pension scheme in question have power to determine the person to whom the sum, or any part of it, is to be paid, require them to pay the whole or part of that sum, when it becomes due, to the other party,
   (b) if the party with pension rights has power to nominate the person to whom the sum, or any part of it, is to be paid, require the party with pension rights to nominate the other party in respect of the whole or part of that sum,
   (c) in any other case, require the trustees or managers of the pension scheme in question to pay the whole or part of that sum, when it becomes due, for the benefit of the other party instead of to the person to whom, apart from the order, it would be paid.

(3)   Any payment by the trustees or managers under an order made under *section 23* above by virtue of this section shall discharge so much of the trustees, or managers, liability in respect of the party with pension rights as corresponds to the amount of the payment.]

NOTES

Commencement: 1 August 1996.
Inserted by the Pensions Act 1995, s 166(1), subject to savings in the Pensions Act 1995 (Commencement) (No 5) Order 1996, SI 1996/1675, arts 4, 5.
Sub-ss (1), (3): for the words in italics there are substituted the words "section 22A or 23" by the Family Law Act 1996, s 66(1), Sch 8, Pt I, paras 4, 11, subject to savings in s 66(2) of, and Sch 9, para 5 to, the 1996 Act, as from a day to be appointed.

[25D Pensions: supplementary

(1)   Where—

(a) an order made under *section 23* above by virtue of section 25B or
25C above imposes any requirement on the trustees or managers of
a pension scheme ("the first scheme") and the party with pension
rights acquires transfer credits under another pension scheme ("the
new scheme") which are derived (directly or indirectly) from a transfer
from the first scheme of all his accrued rights under that scheme
(including transfer credits allowed by that scheme), and

(b) the trustees or managers of the new scheme have been given notice
in accordance with regulations,

the order shall have effect as if it has been made instead in respect of the
trustees or managers of the new scheme; and in this subsection "transfer
credits" has the same meaning as in the Pension Schemes Act 1993.

(2) Regulations may—

(a) in relation to any provision of sections 25B or 25C above which
authorises the court making an order under *section 23* above to
require the trustees or managers of a pension scheme to make a
payment for the benefit of the other party, make provision as to the
person to whom, and the terms on which, the payment is to be
made [or prescribe the rights of the other party under the pension
scheme,]

[(aa) make such consequential modifications of any enactment or
subordinate legislation as appear to the Lord Chancellor necessary
or expedient to give effect to the provisions of section 25B; and an
order under this paragraph may make provision applying generally
in relation to enactments and subordinate legislation of a description
specified in the order,]

(b) require notices to be given in respect of changes of circumstances
relevant to such orders which include provision made by virtue of
sections 25B and 25C above,

(c) make provision for the trustees or managers of any pension
scheme to provide, for the purposes of orders under *section 23*
above, information as to the value of any benefits under the
scheme,

(d) make provision for the recovery of the administrative expenses of—

(i) complying with such orders, so far as they include provision
made by virtue of sections 25B and 25C above, and

(ii) providing such information,

from the party with pension rights or the other party,

(e) make provision for the value of any benefits under a pension scheme
to be calculated and verified, for the purposes of orders under *section
23* above, in a prescribed manner,

and regulations made by virtue of paragraph (e) above may provide for that value to be calculated and verified in accordance with guidance which is prepared and from time to time revised by a prescribed person and approved by the Secretary of State.

(3)   In this section and sections 25B and 25C above—
    (a)   references to a pension scheme include—
       (i)   a retirement annuity contract, or
      (ii)   an annuity, or insurance policy, purchased or transferred for the purpose of giving effect to rights under a pension scheme,
    (b)   in relation to such a contract or annuity, references to the trustees or managers shall be read as references to the provider of the annuity,
    (c)   in relation to such a policy, references to the trustees or managers shall be read as references to the insurer,

and in section 25B(1) and (2) above, references to benefits under a pension scheme include any benefits by way of pension, whether under a pension scheme or not.

(4)   In this section and sections 25B and 25C above—
    ["funded scheme" means a scheme under which the benefits are provided for by setting aside resources related to the value of the members' rights as they accrue (and 'unfunded scheme' shall be construed accordingly);]
    "the party with pension rights" means the party to the marriage who has or is likely to have benefits under a pension scheme and "the other party" means the other party to the marriage,
    "pension scheme" means an occupational pension scheme or a personal pension scheme (applying the definitions in section 1 of the Pension Schemes Act 1993, but as if the reference to employed earners in the definition of "personal pension scheme" were to any earners),
    "prescribed" means prescribed by regulations, and
    "regulations" means regulations made by the Lord Chancellor;
    ["subordinate legislation" has the same meaning as in the Interpretation Act 1978;]

and the power to make regulations under this section shall be exercisable by statutory instrument, which shall be subject to annulment in pursuance of a resolution of either House of Parliament.

[(4A)   Other expressions used in section 25B above shall be construed in accordance with section 124 (interpretation of Part I) of the Pensions Act 1995.]]

Inserted with savings by the Pensions Act 1995, s 166(1); for savings see SI 1996/1675, art 5.

Sub-s (1): for the words in italics in para (a) there are substituted the words "section 22A or 23" with savings by the Family Law Act 1996, s 66(1), Sch 8, para 11, as from a day to be appointed; for savings see s 66(2), Sch 9, para 5 thereof.

Sub-s (2): for the words in italics in paras (a), (c) and (e) there are substituted in each place the words "section 22A or 23" with savings, words in final pair of square brackets in para (a) and whole of para (aa) inserted with savings, by the Family Law Act 1996, ss 16(4)(a), 66(1), Sch 8, para 11, as from a day to be appointed; for savings see s 66(2), Sch 9, para 5 thereof.

Sub-s (4): definitions "funded scheme" and "subordinate legislation" inserted with savings by the Family Law Act 1996, s 16(4)(b), as from a day to be appointed; for savings see s 66(2), Sch 9, para 5 thereof.

Sub-s (4A): inserted with savings by the Family Law Act 1996, s 16(4)(c), as from a day to be appointed; for savings see s 66(2), Sch 9, para 5 thereof.

26 Commencement of proceedings for ancillary relief, etc

(1) Where a petition for divorce, nullity of marriage or judicial separation has been presented, then, subject to subsection (2) below, proceedings for maintenance pending suit under section 22 above, for a financial provision order under section 23 above, or for a property adjustment order may be begun, subject to and in accordance with rules of court, at any time after the presentation of the petition.

(2) Rules of court may provide, in such cases as may be prescribed by the rules—
  (a) that applications for any such relief as is mentioned in subsection (1) above shall be made in the petition or answer; and
  (b) that applications for any such relief which are not so made, or are not made until after the expiration of such period following the presentation of the petition or filing of the answer as may be so prescribed, shall be made only with the leave of the court.

Sub-s (1): for the words in italics there are substituted the words "(1) If a petition for nullity of marriage has been presented, then, subject to subsection (2) below, proceedings", by the Family Law Act 1996, s 66(1), Sch 8, Pt I, paras 4, 12, subject to savings in s 66(2) of, and Sch 9, para 5 to, the 1996 Act, as from a day to be appointed.

27 Financial provision orders, etc, in case of neglect by party to marriage to maintain other party or child of the family

[(1) Either party to a marriage may apply to the court for an order under this section on the ground that the other party to the marriage (in this section referred to as the respondent)—
  (a) has failed to provide reasonable maintenance for the applicant, or
  (b) has failed to provide, or to make a proper contribution towards, reasonable maintenance for any child of the family.]

(2) The court shall not entertain an application under this section [unless—
  (a) the applicant or the respondent is domiciled in England and Wales on the date of the application; or
  (b) the applicant has been habitually resident there throughout the period of one year ending with that date; or
  (c) the respondent is resident there on that date].

[(3) Where an application under this section is made on the ground mentioned in subsection (1)(a) above, then, in deciding—
  (a) whether the respondent has failed to provide reasonable maintenance for the applicant, and
  (b) what order, if any, to make under this section in favour of the applicant,

the court shall have regard to all the circumstances of the case including the matters mentioned in section 25(2) above, and where an application is also made under this section in respect of a child of the family who has not attained the age of eighteen, first consideration shall be given to the welfare of the child while a minor.]

[(3A) Where an application under this section is made on the ground mentioned in subsection (1)(b) above then, in deciding—
  (a) whether the respondent has failed to provide, or to make a proper contribution towards, reasonable maintenance for the child of the family to whom the application relates, and
  (b) what order, if any, to make under this section in favour of the child,

the court shall have regard to all the circumstances of the case including the matters mentioned in [section 25(3)(a) to (e)] above, and where the child of the family to whom the application relates is not the child of the respondent, including also the matters mentioned in [section 25(4)] above.

(3B) In relation to an application under this section on the ground mentioned in subsection (1)(a) above, [section 25(2)(c) above] shall have effect as if for the reference therein to the breakdown of the marriage there were substituted a reference to the failure to provide reasonable maintenance for the applicant, and in relation to an application under this section on the ground mentioned in subsection (1)(b) above, [section 25(2)(c) above (as it applies by virtue of section 25(3)(e) above)] shall have effect as if for the reference therein to the breakdown of the marriage there were substituted a reference to the failure to provide, or to make a proper contribution towards, reasonable maintenance for the child of the family to whom the application relates.]

(5) Where on an application under this section it appears to the court that the applicant or any child of the family to whom the application relates is in immediate need of financial assistance, but it is not yet possible to determine what order, if any, should be made on the application, the court may make an interim order for maintenance, that is to say, an order requiring the respondent[—

(a)] to make to the applicant until the determination of the application such periodical payments as the court thinks reasonable[, or

(b) to pay to the applicant such lump sum or sums as the court thinks reasonable.]

(6) *Where on an application under this section the applicant satisfies the court of any ground mentioned in subsection (1) above, the court may make [any one or more of the following orders], that is to say—*

(a) an order that the respondent shall make to the applicant such periodical payments, for such term, as may be specified in the order;

(b) an order that the respondent shall secure to the applicant, to the satisfaction of the court, such periodical payments, for such term, as may be so specified;

(c) an order that the respondent shall pay to the applicant such lump sum as may be so specified;

(d) an order that the respondent shall make to such person as may be specified in the order for the benefit of the child to whom the application relates, or to that child, such periodical payments, for such term, as may be so specified;

(e) an order that the respondent shall secure to such person as may be so specified for the benefit of that child, or to that child, to the

satisfaction of the court, such periodical payments, for such term, as may be so specified;

   (f) *an order that the respondent shall pay to such person as may be so specified for the benefit of that child, or to that child, such lump sum as may be so specified;*

subject, however, in the case of an order under paragraph (d), (e) or (f) above, to the restrictions imposed by section 29(1) and (3) below on the making of financial provision orders in favour of children who have attained the age of eighteen.

[(6A) An application for the variation under section 31 of this Act of a periodical payments order or secured periodical payments order made under this section in favour of a child may, if the child has attained the age of sixteen, be made by the child himself.]

[(6B) Where a periodical payments order made in favour of a child under this section ceases to have effect on the date on which the child attains the age of sixteen or at any time after that date but before or on the date on which he attains the age of eighteen, then if, on an application made to the court for an order under this subsection, it appears to the court that—

   (a) the child is, will be or (if an order were made under this subsection) would be receiving instruction at an educational establishment or undergoing training for a trade, profession or vocation, whether or not he also is, will be or would be in gainful employment; or

   (b) there are special circumstances which justify the making of an order under this subsection,

the court shall have power by order to revive the first mentioned order from such date as the court may specify, not being earlier than the date of the making of the application, and to exercise its power under section 31 of this Act in relation to any order so revived.]

(7)   Without prejudice to the generality of subsection *(6)(c) or (f)* above, an order under this section for the payment of a lump sum—

   (a) may be made for the purpose of enabling any liabilities or expenses reasonably incurred in maintaining the applicant or any child of the family to whom the application relates before the making of the application to be met;

   (b) may provide for the payment of that sum by instalments of such amount as may be specified in the order and may require the payment of the instalments to be secured to the satisfaction of the court.

(8) ...

NOTES

Sub-s (1): substituted by the Domestic Proceedings and Magistrates' Courts Act 1978, s 63(1).

Sub-s (2): words in square brackets substituted by the Domicile and Matrimonial Proceedings Act 1973, s 6(1).

Sub-s (3): substituted by the Matrimonial and Family Proceedings Act 1984, s 4.

Sub-ss (3A), (3B): substituted by the Domestic Proceedings and Magistrates' Courts Act 1978, s 63(2); words in square brackets substituted by the Matrimonial and Family Proceedings Act 1984, s 46(1), Sch 1, para 13.

Sub-s (5): figure in square brackets inserted, and words in square brackets added, by the Family Law Act 1996, s 66(1), Sch 8, Pt I, paras 4, 13(1), (2), subject to savings in s 66(2) of, and Sch 9, para 5 to, the 1996 Act, as from a day to be appointed.

Sub-s (6): words in square brackets substituted by the Domestic Proceedings and Magistrates' Courts Act 1978, s 63(3); whole subsection substituted by the Family Law Act 1996, s 66(1), Sch 8, Pt I, paras 4, 13(1), (3), subject to savings in s 66(2) of, and Sch 9, para 5 to, the 1996 Act, as from a day to be appointed, as follows—

"(6) Subject to the restrictions imposed by the following provisions of this Act, if on an application under this section the applicant satisfies the court of any ground mentioned in subsection (1) above, the court may make one or more financial provision orders against the respondent in favour of the applicant or a child of the family.".

Sub-s (6A): inserted by the Domestic Proceedings and Magistrates' Courts Act 1978, s 63(4).

Sub-s (6B): inserted by the Domestic Proceedings and Magistrates' Courts Act 1978, s 63(4); substituted by the Family Law Reform Act 1987, s 33(1), Sch 2, para 52.

Sub-s (7): for the words in italics there are substituted the number "(6)" by the Family Law Act 1996, s 66(1), Sch 8, Pt I, paras 4, 13(1), (4), subject to savings in s 66(2) of, and Sch 9, para 5 to, the 1996 Act, as from a day to be appointed.

Sub-s (8): repealed by the Domestic Proceedings and Magistrates' Courts Act 1978, ss 63(5), 89(2)(b), Sch 3.

*Additional provisions with respect to financial provision and
property adjustment orders*

28 Duration of continuing financial provision orders in favour of party to marriage, and effect of remarriage

(1) [Subject *in the case of an order made on or after the grant of a decree of a divorce or nullity of marriage* to the provisions of sections 25A(2) above

and 31(7) below, the term to be specified in a periodical payments or secured periodical payments order in favour of a party to a marriage shall be such term as the court thinks fit, except that the term shall not begin before or extend beyond the following limits], that is to say—

(a) *in the case of a periodical payments order, the term shall begin not earlier than the date of the making of an application for the order, and shall be so defined as not to extend beyond the death of either of the parties to the marriage or, where the order is made on or after the grant of a decree of divorce or nullity of marriage, the remarriage of the party in whose favour the order is made; and*

(b) *in the case of a secured periodical payments order, the term shall begin not earlier than the date of the making of an application for the order, and shall be so defined as not to extend beyond the death or, where the order is made on or after the grant of such a decree, the remarriage of the party in whose favour the order is made.*

[(1A) *Where a periodical payments or secured periodical payments order in favour of a party to a marriage is made on or after the grant of a decree of divorce or nullity of marriage*, the court may direct that that party shall not be entitled to apply under section 31 below for the extension of the term specified in the order].

[(1B) If the court—

(a) exercises, or has exercised, its power under section 22A at any time before making a divorce order, and

(b) gives a direction under subsection (1A) above in respect of a periodical payments order or a secured periodical payments order,

it shall provide for the direction not to take effect until a divorce order is made.]

(2) Where a periodical payments or secured periodical payments order in favour of a party to a marriage is made otherwise than *on or after the grant of a decree of divorce or nullity of marriage*, and the marriage in question is subsequently dissolved or annulled but the order continues in force, the order shall, notwithstanding anything in it, cease to have effect on the remarriage of that party, except in relation to any arrears due under it on the date of the remarriage.

(3) If after the grant of *a decree* dissolving or annulling a marriage either party to that marriage remarries [whether at any time before or after the commencement of this Act], that party shall not be entitled to apply, by

reference to the grant of *that decree*, for a financial provision order in his or her favour, or for a property adjustment order, against the other party to that marriage.

Sub-s (1): words in first pair of square brackets substituted by the Matrimonial and Family Proceedings Act 1984, s 5; words in italics therein repealed by the Family Law Act 1996, s 66(3), Sch 10, subject to savings in s 66(2) of, and Sch 9, para 5 to, the 1996 Act, as from a day to be appointed; paras (a), (b) substituted by the Family Law Act 1996, s 15(1), (3), Sch 2, paras 1, 7(1), subject to savings in s 66(2) of, and Sch 9, para 5 to, the 1996 Act, as from a day to be appointed, as follows—

"(a) a term specified in the order which is to begin before the making of the order shall begin no earlier—

  (i) where the order is made by virtue of section 22A(2)(a) or (b) above, unless sub- paragraph (ii) below applies, than the beginning of the day on which the statement of marital breakdown in question was received by the court;

  (ii) where the order is made by virtue of section 22A(2)(b) above and the application for the divorce order was made following cancellation of an order preventing divorce under section 10 of the 1996 Act, than the date of the making of that application;

  (iii) where the order is made by virtue of section 22A(2)(c) above, than the date of the making of the application for the divorce order; or

  (iv) in any other case, than the date of the making of the application on which the order is made;

(b) a term specified in a periodical payments order or secured periodical payments order shall be so defined as not to extend beyond—

  (i) in the case of a periodical payments order, the death of the party by whom the payments are to be made; or

  (ii) in either case, the death of the party in whose favour the order was made or the remarriage of that party following the making of a divorce order or decree of nullity.".

Sub-s (1A): inserted by the Matrimonial and Family Proceedings Act 1984, s 5; words in italics substituted by the Family Law Act 1996, s 66(1), Sch 8, Pt I, paras 4, 14(1), (2), subject to savings in s 66(2) of, and Sch 9, para 5 to, the 1996 Act, as from a day to be appointed, as follows—

"(1A) At any time when—

(a) the court exercises, or has exercised, its power under section 22A or 23 above to make a financial provision order in favour of a party to a marriage,

(b) but for having exercised that power, the court would have power under one of those sections to make such an order, and

(c) an application for a divorce order or a petition for a decree of nullity of marriage is outstanding or has been granted in relation to the marriage,".

Sub-s (1B): inserted by the Family Law Act 1996, s 66(1), Sch 8, Pt I, para 14(1), (3), subject to savings in s 66(2) of, and Sch 9, para 5 to, the 1996 Act, as from a day to be appointed.

Sub-s (2): for the words in italics there are substituted the words "at such a time as is mentioned in subsection (1A)(c) above" by the Family Law Act 1996, s 66(1), Sch 8, Pt I, paras 4, 14(1), (4), subject to savings in s 66(2) of, and para 5 of Sch 9 to, the 1996 Act, as from a day to be appointed.

Sub-s (3): for the first words in italics there are substituted the words "an order or decree" and for the second words in italics there are substituted the words "that order or decree", by the Family Law Act 1996, s 66(1), Sch 8, Pt I, paras 4, 14(1), (5), subject to savings in s 66(2) of, and Sch 9, para 5 to, the 1996 Act, as from a day to be appointed; words in square brackets inserted by the Matrimonial and Family Proceedings Act 1984, s 5.

29 Duration of continuing financial provision orders in favour of children, and age limit on making certain orders in their favour

(1)   Subject to subsection (3) below, no financial provision order and no order for a transfer of property under *section 24(1)(a)* above shall be made in favour of a child who has attained the age of eighteen.

[(1A)   The term specified in a periodical payments order or secured periodical payments order made in favour of a child shall be such term as the court thinks fit.

(1B)   If that term is to begin before the making of the order, it may do so no earlier than—
  (a) in the case of an order made by virtue of section 22A(2)(a) or (b) above, except where paragraph (b) below applies, the beginning of the day on which the statement of marital breakdown in question was received by the court;
  (b) in the case of an order made by virtue of section 22A(2)(b) above where the application for the divorce order was made following cancellation of an order preventing divorce under section 10 of the 1996 Act, the date of the making of that application;
  (c) in the case of an order made by virtue of section 22A(2)(c) above, the date of the making of the application for the divorce order; or
  (d) in any other case, the date of the making of the application on which the order is made.]

(2)   The term to be specified in a periodical payments or secured periodical payments order in favour of a child may begin with the date of the making

of an application for the order in question or any later date [or a date ascertained in accordance with subsection (5) or (6) below] but—

(a) shall not in the first instance extend beyond the date of the birthday of the child next following his attaining the upper limit of the compulsory school age *(that is to say, the age that is for the time being that limit by virtue of section 35 of the Education Act 1944 together with any Order in Council made under that section)* [unless the court considers that in the circumstances of the case the welfare of the child requires that it should extend to a later date]; and

(b) shall not in any event, subject to subsection (3) below, extend beyond the date of the child's eighteenth birthday.

(3)   Subsection (1) above, and paragraph (b) of subsection (2), shall not apply in the case of a child, if it appears to the court that—

(a) the child is, or will be, or if an order were made without complying with either or both of those provisions would be, receiving instruction at an educational establishment or undergoing training for a trade, profession or vocation, whether or not he is also, or will also be, in gainful employment; or

(b) there are special circumstances which justify the making of an order without complying with either or both of those provisions.

(4)   Any periodical payments order in favour of a child shall, notwithstanding anything in the order, cease to have effect on the death of the person liable to make payments under the order, except in relation to any arrears due under the order on the date of the death.

[(5)   Where—

(a) a maintenance assessment ("the current assessment") is in force with respect to a child; and

(b) an application is made under Part II of this Act for a periodical payments or secured periodical payments order in favour of that child—

   (i)   in accordance with section 8 of the Child Support Act 1991, and

   (ii) before the end of the period of 6 months beginning with the making of the current assessment

the term to be specified in any such order made on that application may be expressed to begin on, or at any time after, the earliest permitted date.

(6)   For the purposes of subsection (5) above, "the earliest permitted date" is whichever is the later of—

(a) the date 6 months before the application is made; or

(b) the date on which the current assessment took effect or, where successive maintenance assessments have been continuously in force with respect to a child, on which the first of those assessments took effect.

(7) Where—

(a) a maintenance assessment ceases to have effect or is cancelled by or under any provision of the Child Support Act 1991; and

(b) an application is made, before the end of the period of 6 months beginning with the relevant date, for a periodical payments or secured periodical payments order in favour of a child with respect to whom that maintenance assessment was in force immediately before it ceased to have effect or was cancelled,

the term to be specified in any such order made on that application may begin with the date on which that maintenance assessment ceased to have effect or, as the case may be, the date with effect from which it was cancelled, or any later date.

(8) In subsection (7)(b) above—

(a) where the maintenance assessment ceased to have effect, the relevant date is the date on which it so ceased; and

(b) where the maintenance assessment was cancelled, the relevant date is the later of—

(i) the date on which the person who cancelled it did so, and

(ii) the date from which the cancellation first had effect.]

NOTES

Commencement: to be appointed (sub-ss (1A), (1B)); 5 April 1993 (sub-ss (5)–(8)); 1 January 1974 (sub-ss (1), (2)–(4)).

Sub-s (1): for the words in italics there are substituted the words "such as is mentioned in section 21(2)(a)" by the Family Law Act 1996, s 66(1), Sch 8, Pt I, paras 4, 15, subject to savings in s 66(2) of, and Sch 9, para 5 to, the 1996 Act, as from a day to be appointed.

Sub-ss (1A), (1B): inserted by the Family Law Act 1996, s 15(1), (3), Sch 2, paras 1, 7(2), subject to savings in s 66(2) of, and Sch 9, para 5 to, the 1996 Act, as from a day to be appointed.

Sub-s (2): first words in italics repealed by the Family Law Act 1996, s 66(3), Sch 10, subject to savings in s 66(2) of, and Sch 9, para 5 to, the 1996 Act, as from a day to be appointed; words in first pair of square brackets inserted by the Maintenance Orders (Backdating) Order 1993, SI 1993/623, art 2, Sch 1, para 1; words in italics in para (a) substituted by the words "(construed in accordance with section 8 of the Education Act 1996)" by the Education Act

1996, s 582(1), Sch 37, para 136, as from a day to be appointed, words in final pair of square brackets inserted by the Matrimonial and Family Proceedings Act 1984, s 5.

Sub-ss (5)–(8): added by Maintenance Orders (Backdating) Order 1993, SI 1993/623, art 2, Sch 1, para 2.

30 Direction for settlement of instrument for securing payments or effecting property adjustment

Where the court decides to make a financial provision order requiring any payments to be secured or a property adjustment order—
  (a) it may direct that the matter be referred to one of the conveyancing counsel of the court for him to settle a proper instrument to be executed by all necessary parties; and
  (b) where the order is to be made in proceedings for *divorce*, nullity of marriage *or judicial separation* it may, if it thinks fit, defer the grant of the decree in question until the instrument has been duly executed.

NOTES

Words in italics repealed by the Family Law Act 1996, s 66(3), Sch 10, subject to savings in s 66(2) of, and Sch 9, para 5 to, the 1996 Act, as from a day to be appointed.

Variation, discharge and enforcement of certain orders, etc

31 Variation, discharge, etc, of certain orders for financial relief

(1)   Where the court has made an order to which this section applies, then, subject to the provisions of this section [and of section 28(1A) above], the court shall have power to vary or discharge the order or to suspend any provision thereof temporarily and to revive the operation of any provision so suspended.

(2)   This section applies to the following orders [under this Part of this Act], that is to say—
  (a) any order for maintenance pending suit and any interim order for maintenance;
  (b) any periodical payments order;

(c)   any secured periodical payments order;

(d)   any order made by virtue of section 23(3)(c) or 27(7)(b) above (provision for payment of a lump sum by instalments);

[(dd) any deferred order made by virtue of section *23(1)(c)* (lump sums) which includes provision made by virtue of—

    (i)   section 25B(4), or

    (ii) section 25C,

(provision in respect of pension rights);]

[(de) any other order for the payment of a lump sum, if it is made at a time when no divorce order has been made, and no separation order is in force, in relation to the marriage;]

(e)   any order for a settlement of property under section 24(1)(b) or for a variation of settlement under section 24(1)(c) or (d) above, being an order made on or after the grant of a decree of judicial separation;

[(f)   any order made under section 24A(1) above for the sale of property].

[(2A) Where the court has made an order referred to in subsection (2)(a), (b) or (c) above, then, subject to the provisions of this section, the court shall have power to remit the payment of any arrears due under the order or of any part thereof.]

[(2B) Where the court has made an order referred to in subsection (2)(dd)(ii) above, this section shall cease to apply to the order on the death of either of the parties to the marriage.]

(3)   The powers exercisable by the court under this section in relation to an order shall be exercisable also in relation to any instrument executed in pursuance of the order.

(4)   The court shall not exercise the powers conferred by this section in relation to an order *for a settlement under section 24(1)(b) or for a variation of settlement under section 24(1)(c) or (d)* above except on an application made in proceedings—

(a)   for the rescission of the decree of judicial separation by reference to which the order was made, or

(b)   for the dissolution of the marriage in question.

[(4A) In relation to an order which falls within subsection (2)(de) or (ea) above ("the subsection (2) order")—

(a)   the powers conferred by this section may be exercised—

(i) only on an application made before the subsection (2) order has or, but for paragraph (b) below, would have taken effect; and

(ii) only if, at the time when the application is made, no divorce order has been made in relation to the marriage and no separation order has been so made since the subsection (2) order was made; and

(b) an application made in accordance with paragraph (a) above prevents the subsection (2) order from taking effect before the application has been dealt with.

(4B) No variation—

(a) of a financial provision order made under section 22A above, other than an interim order, or

(b) of a property adjustment order made under section 23A above,

shall be made so as to take effect before the making of a divorce order or separation order in relation to the marriage, unless the court is satisfied that the circumstances of the case are exceptional, and that it would be just and reasonable for the variation to be so made.]

(5) [Subject to subsections (7A) to (7F) below and without prejudice to any power exercisable by virtue of subsection (2)(d), (dd) or (e) above or otherwise than by virtue of this section,] no property adjustment order shall be made on an application for the variation of a periodical payments or secured periodical payments order made (whether in favour of a party to a marriage or in favour of a child of the family) under *section 23* above, and no order for the payment of a lump sum shall be made on an application for the variation of a periodical payments or secured periodical payments order in favour of a party to a marriage (whether made under *section 23* or under section 27 above).

(6) Where the person liable to make payments under a secured periodical payments order has died, an application under this section relating to that order [(and to any order made under section 24A(1) above which requires the proceeds of sale of property to be used for securing those payments) may be made by the person entitled to payments under the periodical payments order] or by the personal representatives of the deceased person, but no such application shall, except with the permission of the court, be made after the end of the period of six months from the date on which representation in regard to the estate of that person is first taken out.

[(7) In exercising the powers conferred by this section the court shall have regard to all the circumstances of the case, first consideration being given to the welfare while a minor of any child of the family who has not attained the age of eighteen, and the circumstances of the case shall include any change in any of the matters to which the court was required to have regard when making the order to which the application relates, and—

(a) in the case of a periodical payments or secured periodical payments order made *on or after the grant of a decree of divorce or nullity of marriage, the court shall consider* whether in all the circumstances and after having regard to any such change it would be appropriate to vary the order so that payments under the order are required to be made or secured only for such further period as will in the opinion of the court be sufficient [(in the light of any proposed exercise by the court, where the marriage has been dissolved, of its powers under subsection (7B) below)] to enable the party in whose favour the order was made to adjust without undue hardship to the termination of those payments;

(b) in a case where the party against whom the order was made has died, the circumstances of the case shall also include the changed circumstances resulting from his or her death.]

[(7A) Subsection (7B) below applies where, after the dissolution of a marriage, the court—

(a) discharges a periodical payments order or secured periodical payments order made in favour of a party to the marriage; or

(b) varies such an order so that payments under the order are required to be made or secured only for such further period as is determined by the court.

(7B) The court has power, in addition to any power it has apart from this subsection, to make supplemental provision consisting of any of—

(a) an order for the payment of a lump sum in favour of a party to the marriage;

(b) one or more property adjustment orders in favour of a party to the marriage;

(c) a direction that the party in whose favour the original order discharged or varied was made is not entitled to make any further application for—

(i) a periodical payments or secured periodical payments order, or

(ii) an extension of the period to which the original order is limited by any variation made by the court.

(7C) An order for the payment of a lump sum made under subsection (7B) above may—

(a) provide for the payment of that sum by instalments of such amount as may be specified in the order; and

(b) require the payment of the instalments to be secured to the satisfaction of the court.

(7D) [Section 23(6)] above apply where the court makes an order for the payment of a lump sum under [section 23] above as they apply where it makes such an order under section 22A above.

(7E) If under subsection (7B) above the court makes more than one property adjustment order in favour of the same party to the marriage, each of those orders must fall within a different paragraph of section 21(2) above.

(7F) Sections 24A and 30 above apply where the court makes a property adjustment order under subsection (7B) above as they apply where it makes such an order under [section 24] above.]

(8) The personal representatives of a deceased person against whom a secured periodical payments order was made shall not be liable for having distributed any part of the estate of the deceased after the expiration of the period of six months referred to in subsection (6) above on the ground that they ought to have taken into account the possibility that the court might permit an application under this section to be made after that period by the person entitled to payments under the order; but this subsection shall not prejudice any power to recover any part of the estate so distributed arising by virtue of the making of an order in pursuance of this section.

(9) In considering for the purposes of subsection (6) above the question when representation was first taken out, a grant limited to settled land or to trust property shall be left out of account and a grant limited to real estate or to personal estate shall be left out of account unless a grant limited to the remainder of the estate has previously been made or is made at the same time.

[(10) Where the court, in exercise of its powers under this section, decides to vary or discharge a periodical payments or secured periodical payments order, then, subject to section 28(1) and (2) above, the court shall have power to direct that the variation or discharge shall not take effect until the expiration of such period as may be specified in the order.]

[(11) Where—
   (a) a periodical payments or secured periodical payments order in favour of more than one child ("the order") is in force;

(b) the order requires payments specified in it to be made to or for the benefit of more than one child without apportioning those payments between them;

(c) a maintenance assessment ("the assessment") is made with respect to one or more, but not all, of the children with respect to whom those payments are to be made; and

(d) an application is made, before the end of the period of 6 months beginning with the date on which the assessment was made, for the variation or discharge of the order,

the court may, in exercise of its powers under this section to vary or discharge the order, direct that the variation or discharge shall take effect from the date on which the assessment took effect or any later date.

(12) Where—

(a) an order ("the child order") of a kind prescribed for the purposes of section 10(1) of the Child Support Act 1991 is affected by a maintenance assessment;

(b) on the date on which the child order became so affected there was in force a periodical payments or secured periodical payments order ("the spousal order") in favour of a party to a marriage having the care of the child in whose favour the child order was made; and

(c) an application is made, before the end of the period of 6 months beginning with the date on which the maintenance assessment was made, for the spousal order to be varied or discharged,

the court may, in exercise of its powers under this section to vary or discharge the spousal order, direct that the variation or discharge shall take effect from the date on which the child order became so affected or any later date.

(13) For the purposes of subsection (12) above, an order is affected if it ceases to have effect or is modified by or under section 10 of the Child Support Act 1991.

(14) Subsections (11) and (12) above are without prejudice to any other power of the court to direct that the variation of discharge of an order under this section shall take effect from a date earlier than that on which the order for variation or discharge was made.]

NOTES

Commencement: to be appointed (sub-ss (7A)–(7F)); 1 August 1996 (sub-s (2B)); 5 April 1993 (sub-ss (11)–(14)); 12 October 1984 (sub-ss (7), (10)); 1 January 1983 (sub-s (2A)); 1 January 1974 (sub-ss (1), (2), (3)–(6), (8), (9)).

Sub-s (1): words in square brackets inserted by the Matrimonial and Family Proceedings Act 1984, s 6.

Sub-s (2): words in first pair of square brackets inserted, words in italics in para (a) repealed, and para (d) is substituted, by the Family Law Act 1996, s 66(1), (3), Sch 8, Pt I, paras 4, 16(1), (2)(a), (b), Sch 10, subject to savings in s 66(2), of, and Sch 9, para 5 to, the 1996 Act, as from a day to be appointed, as follows—

"(d) an order for the payment of a lump sum in a case in which the payment is to be by instalments;";

para (dd) inserted by the Pensions Act 1995, s 166(3)(a), subject to savings in the Pensions Act 1995 (Commencement) (No 5) Order 1996, SI 1996/1675, arts 4, 5; number in italics in para (dd) substituted by the number "21(1)(c)", para (de) inserted, and para (e) substituted by paras (e), (ea), by the Family Law Act 1996, s 66(1), Sch 8, Pt I, paras 4, 16(1), (2)(c)–(e), subject to savings in s 66(2) of, and Sch 9, para 5 to, the 1996 Act, as from a day to be appointed, as follows—

"(e) any order under section 23A of a kind referred to in section 21(2)(b),(c) or (d) which is made on or after the making of a separation order;

(ea) any order under section 23A which is made at a time when no divorce order has been made, and no separation order is in force, in relation to the marriage;";

and para (f) added by the Matrimonial Homes and Property Act 1981, s 8(2)(a).

Sub-s (2A): inserted by the Administration of Justice Act 1982, s 5.

Sub-s (2B): inserted by the Pensions Act 1995, s 166(3)(b), subject to savings in SI 1996/1675, arts 4, 5.

Sub-s (4): first words in italics substituted by the words "referred to in subsection (2)(e)", and paras (a), (b) substituted by the words "on an application for a divorce order in relation to the marriage", by the Family Law Act 1996, s 66(1), Sch 8, Pt I, paras 4, 16(1), (3), subject to savings in s 66(2) of, and Sch 9, para 5 to, the 1996 Act, as from a day to be appointed.

Sub-ss (4A), (4B): inserted by the Family Law Act 1996, s 66(1), Sch 8, Pt I, paras 4, 16(1), (4), subject to savings in s 66(2) of, and Sch 9, para 5 to, the 1996 Act, as from a day to be appointed.

Sub-s (5): words in first pair of square brackets inserted by the Family Law Act 1996, s 66(1), Sch 8, para 16(5)(a), subject to savings in s 66(2) of, and Sch 9, para 5 to, the 1996 Act, and words in italics substituted by the words "section 22A or 23", by the Family Law Act 1996, s 66(1), Sch 8, Pt I, paras 4, 16(1), (5), subject to savings in s 66(2) of, and Sch 9, para 5 to, the 1996 Act, as from a day to be appointed.

Sub-s (6): words in square brackets substituted by the Matrimonial Homes and Property Act 1981, s 8(2)(b).

Sub-s (7): substituted by the Matrimonial and Family Proceedings Act 1984, s 6; words in italics in para (a) substituted by the words "in favour of a party to a marriage, the court shall, if the marriage has been dissolved or annulled, consider", as from a day to be appointed, and words in final pair of square brackets inserted, by the Family Law Act 1996, s 66(1), Sch 8, Pt I, paras 4, 16(1), (6), and applies to orders made before the commencement of the amendment; see s 66(2) of, and Sch 9, para 6(2) to, that Act.

Sub-ss (7A)–(7C), (7E): inserted by the Family Law Act 1996, s 66(1), Sch 8, Pt I, paras 4, 16(1), (7), and applies to orders made before the commencement of the insertion; see s 66(2), Sch 9, para 6(2) thereof.

Sub-ss (7D), (7F): inserted by the Family Law Act 1996, s 66(1), Sch 8, Pt I, paras 4, 16(1), (7), and applies to orders made before the commencement of the insertion; see s 66(2), Sch 9, para 6(2) thereof; words in square brackets substituted by the Family Law Act 1996 (Commencement) (No 3) Order 1998, SI 1998/2572, art 4.

Sub-s (10): inserted by the Matrimonial and Family Proceedings Act 1984, s 6.

Sub-ss (11)–(14): added by the Maintenance Orders (Backdating) Order 1993, SI 1993/623, art 2, Sch 1, para 3.

[31A   Variation etc following reconciliations

(1)   Where, at a time before the making of a divorce order—

(a)   an order ("a paragraph (a) order") for the payment of a lump sum has been made under section 22A above in favour of a party,

(b)   such an order has been made in favour of a child of the family but the payment has not yet been made, or

(c)   a property adjustment order ("a paragraph (c) order") has been made under section 23A above,

the court may, on an application made jointly by the parties to the marriage, vary or discharge the order.

(2)   Where the court varies or discharges a paragraph (a) order, it may order the repayment of an amount equal to the whole or any part of the lump sum.

(3)   Where the court varies or discharges a paragraph (c) order, it may (if the order has taken effect)—

(a)   order any person to whom property was transferred in pursuance of the paragraph (c) order to transfer—

(i)   the whole or any part of that property, or

(ii)   the whole or any part of any property appearing to the court to represent that property,

in favour of a party to the marriage or a child of the family; or

(b)   vary any settlement to which the order relates in favour of any person or extinguish or reduce any person's interest under that settlement.

(4)   Where the court acts under subsection (3) it may make such supplemental provision (including a further property adjustment order or an order for the payment of a lump sum) as it thinks appropriate in

consequence of any transfer, variation, extinguishment or reduction to be made under paragraph (a) or (b) of that subsection.

(5)   Sections 24A and 30 above apply for the purposes of this section as they apply where the court makes a property adjustment order under section 23A or 24 above.

(6)   The court shall not make an order under subsection (2), (3) or (4) above unless it appears to it that there has been a reconciliation between the parties to the marriage.

(7)   The court shall also not make an order under subsection (3) or (4) above unless it appears to it that the order will not prejudice the interests of—
  (a)   any child of the family; or
  (b)   any person who has acquired any right or interest in consequence of the paragraph (c) order and is not a party to the marriage or a child of the family.]

NOTES

Commencement: to be appointed.
Inserted by the Family Law Act 1996, s 15(1), (3), Sch 2, paras 1, 8, subject to savings in s 66(2) of, and Sch 9, para 5 to, the 1996 Act, as from a day to be appointed.

32 Payment of certain arrears unenforceable without the leave of the court

(1)   A person shall not be entitled to enforce through the High Court or any county court the payment of any arrears due under *an order for maintenance pending suit, an interim order for maintenance or any financial provision order* without the leave of that court if those arrears became due more than twelve months before proceedings to enforce the payment of them are begun.

(2)   The court hearing an application for the grant of leave under this section may refuse leave, or may grant leave subject to such restrictions and conditions (including conditions as to the allowing of time for payment or the making of payment by instalments) as that court thinks proper, or may remit the payment of the arrears or of any part thereof.

(3)   An application for the grant of leave under this section shall be made in such manner as may be prescribed by rules of court.

NOTES

Sub-s (1): words in italics substituted by the words "any financial provision order under this Part of this Act or any interim order for maintenance" by the Family Law Act 1996, s 66(1), Sch 8, Pt I, paras 4, 17, subject to savings in s 66(2) of, and Sch 9, para 5 to, the 1996 Act, as from a day to be appointed.

33 Orders for repayment in certain cases of sums paid under certain orders

(1)   Where on an application made under this section in relation to an order to which this section applies it appears to the court that by reason of—
- (a) a change in the circumstances of the person entitled to, or liable to make, payments under the order since the order was made, or
- (b) the changed circumstances resulting from the death of the person so liable,

the amount received by the person entitled to payments under the order in respect of a period after those circumstances changed or after the death of the person liable to make payments under the order, as the case may be, exceeds the amount which the person so liable or his or her personal representatives should have been required to pay, the court may order the respondent to the application to pay to the applicant such sum, not exceeding the amount of the excess, as the court thinks just.

(2)   *This section applies to the following orders, that is to say—*
- *(a) any order for maintenance pending suit and any interim order for maintenance;*
- *(b) any periodical payments order; and*
- *(c) any secured periodical payments order.*

(3)   An application under this section may be made by the person liable to make payments under an order to which this section applies or his or her personal representatives and may be made against the person entitled to payments under the order or her or his personal representatives.

(4)   An application under this section may be made in proceedings in the High Court or a county court for—
- (a) the variation or discharge of the order to which this section applies, or
- (b) leave to enforce, or the enforcement of, the payment of arrears under that order;

but when not made in such proceedings shall be made to a county court, and accordingly references in this section to the court are references to the High Court or a county court, as the circumstances require.

(5)   The jurisdiction conferred on a county court by this section shall be exercisable notwithstanding that by reason of the amount claimed in the application the jurisdiction would not but for this subsection be exercisable by a county court.

(6)   An order under this section for the payment of any sum may provide for the payment of that sum by instalments of such amount as may be specified in the order.

NOTES

Sub-s (2): substituted by the Family Law Act 1996, s 66(1), Sch 8, Pt I, paras 4, 18, subject to savings in s 66(2) of, and Sch 9, para 5 to, the 1996 Act, as from a day to be appointed, as follows—
"(2) This section applies to the following orders under this Part of this Act—
(a) any periodical payments order;
(b) any secured periodical payments order; and
(c) any interim order for maintenance, so far as it requires the making of periodical payments.".

Consent orders

[33A   Consent orders for financial provision on property adjustment

(1)   Notwithstanding anything in the preceding provisions of this Part of this Act, on an application for a consent order for financial relief the court may, unless it has reason to think that there are other circumstances into which it ought to inquire, make an order in the terms agreed on the basis only of the prescribed information furnished with the application.

(2)   Subsection (1) above applies [(subject, in the case of the powers of the court under section 31A above, to subsections (6) and (7) of that section)] to an application for a consent order varying or discharging an order for financial relief as it applies to an application for an order for financial relief.

(3)   In this section—
    "consent order", in relation to an application for an order, means an order in the terms applied for to which the respondent agrees;

"order for financial relief" means an order under any of sections 23, 24, 24A or 27 above; and

"prescribed" means prescribed by rules of court.]

NOTES

Inserted by the Matrimonial and Family Proceedings Act 1984, s 7.

Sub-s (2): words in square brackets inserted by the Family Law Act 1996, s 66(1), Sch 8, Pt I, paras 4, 19(1), (2), subject to savings in s 66(2) of, and Sch 9, para 5 to, the 1996 Act, as from a day to be appointed.

Sub-s (3): words in italics substituted by the words "any of the following orders under this Part of this Act, that is to say, any financial provision order, any property adjustment order, any order for the sale of property or any interim order for maintenance" by the Family Law Act 1996, s 66(1), Sch 8, Pt I, paras 4, 19(1), (3), subject to savings in s 66(2) of, and Sch 9, para 5 to, the 1996 Act, as from a day to be appointed.

Maintenance agreements

34 Validity of maintenance agreements

(1)   If a maintenance agreement includes a provision purporting to restrict any right to apply to a court for an order containing financial arrangements, then—

(a) that provision shall be void; but

(b) any other financial arrangements contained in the agreement shall not thereby be rendered void or unenforceable and shall, unless they are void or unenforceable for any other reason (and subject to sections 35 and 36 below), be binding on the parties to the agreement.

(2)   In this section and in section 35 below—

"maintenance agreement" means any agreement in writing made, whether before or after the commencement of this Act, between the parties to a marriage, being—

(a) an agreement containing financial arrangements, whether made during the continuance or after the dissolution or annulment of the marriage; or

(b) a separation agreement which contains no financial arrangements in a case where no other agreement in writing between the same parties contains such arrangements;

"financial arrangements" means provisions governing the rights and liabilities towards one another when living separately of the parties to a marriage (including a marriage which has been dissolved or annulled) in respect of the making or securing of payments or the disposition or use of any property, including such rights and liabilities with respect to the maintenance or education of any child, whether or not a child of the family.

35 Alteration of agreements by court during lives of parties

(1)   Where a maintenance agreement is for the time being subsisting and each of the parties to the agreement is for the time being either domiciled or resident in England and Wales, then, subject to subsection (3) below, either party may apply to the court or to a magistrates' court for an order under this section.

(2)   If the court to which the application is made is satisfied either—
  (a) that by reason of a change in the circumstances in the light of which any financial arrangements contained in the agreement were made or, as the case may be, financial arrangements were omitted from it (including a change foreseen by the parties when making the agreement), the agreement should be altered so as to make different, or, as the case may be, so as to contain, financial arrangements, or
  (b) that the agreement does not contain proper financial arrangements with respect to any child of the family,

then subject to subsections (3), (4) and (5) below, that court may by order make such alterations in the agreement—
  (i) by varying or revoking any financial arrangements contained in it, or
  (ii) by inserting in it financial arrangements for the benefit of one of the parties to the agreement or of a child of the family,

as may appear to that court to be just having regard to all the circumstances, including, if relevant, the matters mentioned in [section 25(4)] above; and the agreement shall have effect thereafter as if any alteration made by the order had been made by agreement between the parties and for valuable consideration.

(3)   A magistrates' court shall not entertain an application under subsection (1) above unless both the parties to the agreement are resident in England and Wales and at least one of the parties is resident [within the commission area (within the meaning of [the Justices of the Peace Act 1997]) for which the court is appointed], and shall not have power to make any order on such an application except—

(a) in a case where the agreement includes no provision for periodical payments by either of the parties, an order inserting provision for the making by one of the parties of periodical payments for the maintenance of the other party or for the maintenance of any child of the family;

(b) in a case where the agreement includes provision for the making by one of the parties of periodical payments, an order increasing or reducing the rate of, or terminating, any of those payments.

(4) Where a court decides to alter, by order under this section, an agreement by inserting provision for the making or securing by one of the parties to the agreement of periodical payments for the maintenance of the other party or by increasing the rate of the periodical payments which the agreement provides shall be made by one of the parties for the maintenance of the other, the term for which the payments or, as the case may be, the additional payments attributable to the increase are to be made under the agreement as altered by the order shall be such term as the court may specify, subject to the following limits, that is to say—

(a) where the payments will not be secured, the term shall be so defined as not to extend beyond the death of either of the parties to the agreement or the remarriage of the party to whom the payments are to be made;

(b) where the payments will be secured, the term shall be so defined as not to extend beyond the death or remarriage of that party.

(5) Where a court decides to alter, by order under this section, an agreement by inserting provision for the making or securing by one of the parties to the agreement of periodical payments for the maintenance of a child of the family or by increasing the rate of the periodical payments which the agreement provides shall be made or secured by one of the parties for the maintenance of such a child, then, in deciding the term for which under the agreement as altered by the order the payments, or as the case may be, the additional payments attributable to the increase are to be made or secured for the benefit of the child, the court shall apply the provisions of section 29(2) and (3) above as to age limits as if the order in question were a periodical payments or secured periodical payments order in favour of the child.

(6) For the avoidance of doubt it is hereby declared that nothing in this section or in section 34 above affects any power of a court before which any proceedings between the parties to a maintenance agreement are brought under any other enactment (including a provision of this Act) to make an order containing financial arrangements or any right of either party to apply for such an order in such proceedings.

[(7) Subject to subsection (5) above, references in this Act to any such order as is mentioned in section 21 above shall not include references to any order under this section.]

Commencement: to be appointed (sub-s (7)); 1 January 1974 (sub-ss (1)–(6)).

Sub-s (2): words in square brackets substituted by the Matrimonial and Family Proceedings Act 1984, s 46(1), Sch 1, para 13.

Sub-s (3): words in first (outer) pair of square brackets substituted by the Matrimonial and Family Proceedings Act 1984, s 46(1), Sch 1, para 13; words in second (inner) pair of square brackets substituted by the Justices of the Peace Act 1997, s 73(2), Sch 5, para 14.

Sub-s (7): added by the Family Law Act 1996, s 66(1), Sch 8, Pt I, paras 4, 20, subject to savings in s 66(2) of, and Sch 9, para 5 to, the 1996 Act, as from a day to be appointed.

36 Alteration of agreements by court after death of one party

(1) Where a maintenance agreement within the meaning of section 34 above provides for the continuation of payments under the agreement after the death of one of the parties and that party dies domiciled in England and Wales, the surviving party or the personal representatives of the deceased party may, subject to subsections (2) and (3) below, apply to the High Court or a county court for an order under section 35 above.

(2) An application under this section shall not, except with the permission of the High Court or a county court, be made after the end of the period of six months from the date on which representation in regard to the estate of the deceased is first taken out.

(3) A county court shall not entertain an application under this section, or an application for permission to make an application under this section, unless it would have jurisdiction by virtue of [section 22 of the Inheritance (Provision for Family and Dependants) Act 1975] (which confers jurisdiction on county courts in proceedings under [that Act if the value of the property mentioned in that section] does not exceed £5,000 or such larger sum as may be fixed by order of the Lord Chancellor) to hear and determine proceedings for an order under [section 2 of that Act] in relation to the deceased's estate.

(4) If a maintenance agreement is altered by a court on an application made in pursuance of subsection (1) above, the like consequences shall ensue as if the alteration had been made immediately before the death by agreement between the parties and for valuable consideration.

(5)   The provisions of this section shall not render the personal representatives of the deceased liable for having distributed any part of the estate of the deceased after the expiration of the period of six months referred to in subsection (2) above on the ground that they ought to have taken into account the possibility that a court might permit an application by virtue of this section to be made by the surviving party after that period; but this subsection shall not prejudice any power to recover any part of the estate so distributed arising by virtue of the making of an order in pursuance of this section.

(6)   Section 31(9) above shall apply for the purposes of subsection (2) above as it applies for the purposes of subsection (6) of section 31.

(7)   Subsection (3) of [section 22 of the Inheritance (Provision for Family and Dependants) Act 1975 (which enables rules of court to provide for the transfer from a county court to the High Court or from the High court to a county court of proceedings for an order under section 2 of that Act) and paragraphs (a) and (b) of subsection (4)] of that section (provisions relating to proceedings commenced in county court before coming into force of order of the Lord Chancellor under that section) shall apply in relation to proceedings consisting of any such application as is referred to in subsection (3) above as they apply in relation to [proceedings for an order under section 2 of that Act].

NOTES

Sub-ss (3), (7): words in square brackets substituted by the Inheritance (Provision for Family and Dependants) Act 1975, s 26(1).

Miscellaneous and supplemental

37   Avoidance of transactions intended to prevent or reduce financial relief

(1)   For the purposes of this section "financial relief" means relief under any of the provisions of sections *22, 23, 24, 27, 31 (except subsection (6))* and 35 above, and any reference in this section to defeating a person's claim for financial relief is a reference to preventing financial relief from being granted to that person, or to that person for the benefit of a child of the family, or reducing the amount of any financial relief which might be so granted, or frustrating or impeding the enforcement of any order which might be or has been made at his instance under any of those provisions.

(2)   Where proceedings for financial relief are brought by one person against another, the court may, on the application of the first-mentioned person—

    (a) if it is satisfied that the other party to the proceedings is, with the intention of defeating the claim for financial relief, about to make any disposition or to transfer out of the jurisdiction or otherwise deal with any property, make such order as it thinks fit for restraining the other party from so doing or otherwise for protecting the claim;

    (b) if it is satisfied that the other party has, with that intention, made a reviewable disposition and that if the disposition were set aside financial relief or different financial relief would be granted to the applicant, make an order setting aside the disposition;

    (c) if it is satisfied, in a case where an order has been obtained under any of the provisions mentioned in subsection (1) above by the applicant against the other party, that the other party has, with that intention, made a reviewable disposition, make an order setting aside the disposition;

and an application for the purposes of paragraph (b) above shall be made in the proceedings for the financial relief in question.

(3)   Where the court makes an order under subsection (2)(b) or (c) above setting aside a disposition it shall give such consequential directions as it thinks fit for giving effect to the order (including directions requiring the making of any payments or the disposal of any property).

(4)   Any disposition made by the other party to the proceedings for financial relief in question (whether before or after the commencement of those proceedings) is a reviewable disposition for the purposes of subsection (2)(b) and (c) above unless it was made for valuable consideration (other than marriage) to a person who, at the time of the disposition, acted in relation to it in good faith and without notice of any intention on the part of the other party to defeat the applicant's claim for financial relief.

(5)   Where an application is made under this section with respect to a disposition which took place less than three years before the date of the application or with respect to a disposition or other dealing with property which is about to take place and the court is satisfied—

    (a) in a case falling within subsection (2)(a) or (b) above, that the disposition or other dealing would (apart from this section) have the consequence, or

    (b) in a case falling within subsection (2)(c) above, that the disposition has had the consequence, of defeating the applicant's claim for financial relief, it shall be presumed, unless the contrary is shown, that the person who disposed of or is about to dispose of or deal with the property did so or, as the case may be, is about to do so, with the intention of defeating the applicant's claim for financial relief.

(6)   In this section "disposition" does not include any provision contained in a will or codicil but, with that exception, includes any conveyance, assurance or gift of property of any description, whether made by an instrument or otherwise.

(7)   This section does not apply to a disposition made before 1st January 1968.

NOTES

Sub-s (1): words in italics substituted by the words "22A to 24, 27, 31 (except subsection (6)), 31A" by the Family Law Act 1996, s 66(1), Sch 8, Pt I, paras 4, 21, subject to savings in s 66(2) of, and Sch 9, para 5 to, the 1996 Act, as from a day to be appointed.

38   Orders for repayment in certain cases of sums paid after cessation of order by reason of remarriage

(1)   Where—
   (a)   a periodical payments or secured periodical payments order in favour of a party to a marriage (hereafter in this section referred to as "a payments order") has ceased to have effect by reason of the remarriage of that party, and
   (b)   the person liable to make payments under the order or his or her personal representatives made payments in accordance with it in respect of a period after the date of the remarriage in the mistaken belief that the order was still subsisting,

the person so liable or his or her personal representatives shall not be entitled to bring proceedings in respect of a cause of action arising out of the   circumstances mentioned in paragraphs (a) and (b) above against the person entitled to payments under the order or her or his personal representatives, but may instead make an application against that person or her or his personal representatives under this section.

(2)   On an application under this section the court may order the respondent to pay to the applicant a sum equal to the amount of the payments made in respect of the period mentioned in subsection (1)(b)

above or, if it appears to the court that it would be unjust to make that order, it may either order the respondent to pay to the applicant such lesser sum as it thinks fit or dismiss the application.

(3)   An application under this section may be made in proceedings in the High Court or a county court for leave to enforce, or the enforcement of, payment of arrears under the order in question, but when not made in such proceedings shall be made to a county court; and accordingly references in this section to the court are references to the High Court or a county court, as the circumstances require.

(4)   The jurisdiction conferred on a county court by this section shall be exercisable notwithstanding that by reason of the amount claimed in the application the jurisdiction would not but for this subsection be exercisable by a county court.

(5)   An order under this section for the payment of any sum may provide for the payment of that sum by instalments of such amount as may be specified in the order.

(6)   The clerk of a magistrates' court to whom any payments under a payments order are required to be made, and the collecting officer under an attachment of earnings order made to secure payments under a payments order, shall not be liable—
  (a) in the case of the clerk, for any act done by him in pursuance of the payments order after the date on which that order ceased to have effect by reason of the remarriage of the person entitled to payments under it, and
  (b) in the case of the collecting officer, for any act done by him after that date in accordance with any enactment or rule of court specifying how payments made to him in compliance with the attachment of earnings order are to be dealt with,

if, but only if, the act was one which he would have been under a duty to do had the payments order not so ceased to have effect and the act was done before notice in writing of the fact that the person so entitled had remarried was given to him by or on behalf of that person, the person liable to make payments under the payments order or the personal representatives of either of those persons.

(7)   In this section "collecting officer", in relation to an attachment of earnings order, means the officer of the High Court, the registrar of a county court or the clerk of a magistrates' court to whom a person makes payments in compliance with the order.

39 Settlement, etc, made in compliance with a property adjustment order may be avoided on bankruptcy of settlor

The fact that a settlement or transfer of property had to be made in order to comply with a property adjustment order shall not prevent that settlement or transfer from being [a transaction in respect of which an order may be made under [section 339 or 340 of the Insolvency Act 1986] (transfers at an undervalue and preferences)].

NOTES

Words in first (outer) pair of square brackets substituted by the Insolvency Act 1985, s 235, Sch 8, para 23; words in second (inner) pair of square brackets substituted by the Insolvency Act 1986, s 439(2), Sch 14.

40 Payments, etc, under order made in favour of person suffering from mental disorder

Where the court makes an order under this Part of this Act requiring payments (including a lump sum payment) to be made, or property to be transferred, to a party to a marriage and the court is satisfied that the person in whose favour the order is made is incapable, by reason of mental disorder within the meaning of the Mental Health Act 1959, of managing and administering his or her property and affairs then, subject to any order, direction or authority made or given in relation to that person under Part VIII of that Act, the court may order the payments to be made, or as the case may be, the property to be transferred, to such persons having charge of that person as the court may direct.

PART III
PROTECTION, CUSTODY, ETC, OF CHILDREN

[41 Restrictions on decrees for dissolution, annulment or separation affecting children

(1)   In any proceedings for a decree of *divorce or* nullity of marriage, *or a decree of judicial separation*, the court shall consider—
  (a) whether there are any children of the family to whom this section applies; and
  (b) where there are any such children, whether (in the light of the arrangements which have been, or are proposed to be, made for

their upbringing and welfare) it should exercise any of its powers under the Children Act 1989 with respect to any of them.

(2)   Where, in any case to which this section applies, it appears to the court that—

(a) the circumstances of the case require it, or are likely to require it, to exercise any of its powers under the Act of 1989 with respect to any such child;

(b) it is not in a position to exercise the power or (as the case may be) those powers without giving further consideration to the case; and

(c) there are exceptional circumstances which make it desirable in the interests of the child that the court should give a direction under this section,

it may direct that the decree of *divorce or* nullity is not to be made absolute, *or that the decree of judicial separation is not to be granted*, until the court orders otherwise.

(3)   This section applies to—

(a) any child of the family who has not reached the age of sixteen at the date when the court considers the case in accordance with the requirements of this section; and

(b) any child of the family who has reached that age at that date and in relation to whom the court directs that this section shall apply.]

NOTES

Substituted by the Children Act 1989, s 108(4), Sch 12, para 31.

Sub-ss (1), (2): words in italics repealed by the Family Law Act 1996, s 66(3), Sch 10, subject to savings in s 66(2) of, and Sch 9, para 5 to, the 1996 Act, as from a day to be appointed.

PART IV
MISCELLANEOUS AND SUPPLEMENTAL

47 Matrimonial relief and declarations of validity in respect of polygamous marriages

(1)   A court in England and Wales shall not be precluded from granting matrimonial relief or making a declaration concerning the validity of a marriage by reason only that [either party to the marriage is, or has during the subsistence of the marriage been, married to more than one person].

(2)   In this section "matrimonial relief" means—
- (a)   any [divorce order, any separation order under the 1996 Act or any] decree under Part I of this Act;
- (b)   a financial provision order under section 27 above;
- (c)   an order under section 35 above altering a maintenance agreement;
- (d)   an order under any provision of this Act [or the 1996 Act] which confers a power exercisable in connection with, or in connection with proceedings for, *such decree or order* as is mentioned in paragraphs (a) to (c) above;
- [(dd) an order under Part III of the Matrimonial and Family Proceedings Act 1984;]
- (e)   an order under [Part I of the Domestic Proceedings and Magistrates' Courts Act 1978].

[(3)   In this section "a declaration concerning the validity of a marriage" means any declaration under Part III of the Family Law Act 1986 involving a determination as to the validity of a marriage.]

[(4)   Provision may be made by rules of court—
- (a)   for requiring notice of proceedings brought by virtue of this section to be served on any additional spouse of a party to the marriage in question; and
- (b)   for conferring on any such additional spouse the right to be heard in the proceedings,

in such cases as may be specified in the rules.]

NOTES

Commencement: 8 January 1996 (sub-s (4)); 4 April 1988 (sub-s (3)); 1 January 1974 (remainder).

Sub-s (1): words in square brackets substituted by the Private International Law (Miscellaneous Provisions) Act 1995, s 8(2), Schedule, para 2(3)(a).

Sub-s (2): words in square brackets in para (a) and words in first pair of square brackets in para (d) inserted, and words in italics in para (d) substituted by the words "a statement of marital breakdown or any such order or decree", by the Family Law Act 1996, s 66(1), Sch 8, Pt I, paras 4, 22, subject to savings in s 66(2) of, and Sch 9, para 5 to, the 1996 Act, as from a day to be appointed; para (dd) inserted by the Matrimonial and Family Proceedings Act 1984, s 46(1), Sch 1; words in square brackets in para (e) substituted by the Domestic Proceedings and Magistrates' Courts Act 1978, s 89(2)(a), Sch 2, para 39.

Sub-s (3): substituted by the Family Law Act 1986, s 68(1), Sch 1, para 14.

Sub-s (4): substituted by the Private International Law (Miscellaneous Provisions) Act 1995, s 8(2), Schedule, para 2(3)(b).

48   Evidence

(1)   The evidence of a husband or wife shall be admissible in any proceedings to prove that marital intercourse did or did not take place between them during any period.

(2)   In any proceedings for nullity of marriage, evidence on the question of sexual capacity shall be heard in camera unless in any case the judge is satisfied that in the interests of justice any such evidence ought to be heard in open court.

52   Interpretation

(1)   In this Act—
    ["the 1996 Act" means the Family Law Act 1996;]

. . . . .

    "child", in relation to one or both of the parties to a marriage, includes an illegitimate ... child of that party or, as the case may be, of both parties;
    "child of the family", in relation to the parties to a marriage, means—
        (a) a child of both of those parties; and
        (b) any other child, not being a child who [is placed with those parties as foster parents] by a local authority or voluntary organisation, who has been treated by both of those parties as a child of their family;
    "the court" (except where the context otherwise requires) means the High Court or, where a county court has jurisdiction by virtue of [Part V of the Matrimonial and Family Proceedings Act 1984], a county court;

. . . . .

    "education" includes training.
    ["maintenance assessment" has the same meaning as it has in the Child Support Act 1991 by virtue of section 54 of that Act as read with any regulations in force under that section.]
    ["statement of marital breakdown" has the same meaning as in the Family Law Act 1996.]

(2)   In this Act—
    (a) references to financial provision orders, periodical payments and secured periodical payments orders and orders for the payment of a

lump sum, and references to property adjustment orders, shall be construed in accordance *with section 21 above*; and

(b) references *to orders for maintenance pending suit and* to interim orders for maintenance shall be construed *respectively* in accordance with *section 22 and* section 27(5) above.

(3) For the avoidance of doubt it is hereby declared that references in this Act to remarriage include references to a marriage which is by law void or voidable.

(4) Except where the contrary intention is indicated, references in this Act to any enactment include references to that enactment as amended, extended or applied by or under any subsequent enactment, including this Act.

NOTES

Sub-s (1): definitions "the 1996 Act" inserted and "statement of marital breakdown" added by the Family Law Act 1996, s 66(1), Sch 8, Pt I, paras 4, 24, subject to savings in s 66(2) of, and Sch 9, para 5 to, the 1996 Act, as from a day to be appointed; definition "adopted" and words omitted from definition "child" repealed by the Children Act 1975, s 108(1)(b), Sch 4, Pt I; in definition "child of the family" words in square brackets substituted by the Children Act 1989, s 108(4), Sch 12, para 33; definition "the court" substituted by the Matrimonial and Family Proceedings Act 1984, s 46(1), Sch 1; final definition omitted repealed by the Children Act 1989, s 108(7), Sch 15; definition "maintenance assessment" inserted by the Maintenance Orders (Backdating) Order 1993, SI 1993/623, art 2, Sch 1, para 4.

Sub-s (2): words in italics in para (a) substituted by the Family Law Act 1996, s 66(1), Sch 8, Pt I, paras 4, 25, subject to savings in s 66(2) of, and Sch 9, para 5 to, the 1996 Act, as from a day to be appointed, as follows—

"(subject to section 35(7) above) with section 21 above and—

(i) in the case of a financial provision order or periodical payments order, as including (except where the context otherwise requires) references to an interim periodical payments order under section 22A or 23 above; and

(ii) in the case of a financial provision order or order for the payment of a lump sum, as including (except where the context otherwise requires) references to an interim order for the payment of a lump sum under section 22A or 23 above;";

words in italics in para (b) repealed by s 66(3) of, and Sch 10 to, the 1996 Act, subject to savings in s 66(2) of, and Sch 9, para 5 to, the 1996 Act, as from a day to be appointed.

55 Citation, commencement and extent

(1) This Act may be cited as the Matrimonial Causes Act 1973.

(2)   This Act shall come into force on such day as the Lord Chancellor may appoint by order made by statutory instrument.

(3)   Subject to the provisions of paragraphs 3(2) . . . of Schedule 2 below, this Act does not extend to Scotland or Northern Ireland.

NOTES

Sub-s (3): words omitted repealed by the Statute Law (Repeals) Act 1977.

Domicile and Matrimonial Proceedings Act 1973

(c 45)

An Act to amend the law relating to the domicile of married women and persons not of full age, to matters connected with domicile and to jurisdiction in matrimonial proceedings including actions for reduction of consistorial decrees; to make further provision about the recognition of divorces and legal separations; and for purposes connected therewith

[25 July 1973]

PART I
DOMICILE

Husband and wife

1   Abolition of wife's dependent domicile

(1)   Subject to subsection (2) below, the domicile of a married woman as at any time after the coming into force of this section shall, instead of being the same as her husband's by virtue only of marriage, be ascertained by reference to the same factors as in the case of any other individual capable of having an independent domicile.

(2)   Where immediately before this section came into force a woman was married and then had her husband's domicile by dependence, she is to be treated as retaining that domicile (as a domicile of choice, if it is not also

her domicile of origin) unless and until it is changed by acquisition or revival of another domicile either on or after the coming into force of this section.

(3)   This section extends to England and Wales, Scotland and Northern Ireland.

Minors and pupils

3   Age at which independent domicile can be acquired

(1)   The time at which a person first becomes capable of having an independent domicile shall be when he attains the age of sixteen or marries under that age; and in the case of a person who immediately before 1st January 1974 was incapable of having an independent domicile, but had then attained the age of sixteen or been married, it shall be that date.

(2)   This section extends to England and Wales and Northern Ireland (but not to Scotland).

4   Dependent domicile of child not living with his father

(1)   Subsection (2) of this section shall have effect with respect to the dependent domicile of a child as at any time after the coming into force of this section when his father and mother are alive but living apart.

(2)   The child's domicile as at that time shall be that of his mother if—
   (a) he then has his home with her and has no home with his father; or
   (b) he has at any time had her domicile by virtue of paragraph (a) above and has not since had a home with his father.

(3)   As at any time after the coming into force of this section, the domicile of a child whose mother is dead shall be that which she last had before she died if at her death he had her domicile by virtue of subsection (2) above and he has not since had a home with his father.

(4)   Nothing in this section prejudices any existing rule of law as to the cases in which a child's domicile is regarded as being, by dependence, that of his mother.

(5)   In this section, "child" means a person incapable of having an independent domicile; . . .

(6)   This section extends to England and Wales, Scotland and Northern Ireland.

NOTES

Sub-s (5): words omitted repealed by the Children Act 1975, s 108(1)(b), Sch 4, Pt I.

PART II
JURISDICTION IN MATRIMONIAL PROCEEDINGS (ENGLAND AND WALES)

5   Jurisdiction of High Court and county courts

(1)   Subsections (2) to (5) below shall have effect, *subject to section 6(3) and (4) of this Act*, with respect to the jurisdiction of the court to entertain—
   (a) proceedings for *divorce, judicial separation or* nullity of marriage; and
   (b) proceedings for death to be presumed and a marriage to be dissolved in pursuance of section 19 of the Matrimonial Causes Act 1973;

and in this Part of this Act "the court" means the High Court and a divorce county court within the meaning of [Part V of the Matrimonial and Family Proceedings Act 1984].

(2)   *The court shall have jurisdiction to entertain proceedings for divorce or judicial separation if (and only if) either of the parties to the marriage—*
   (a) is domiciled in England and Wales on the date when the proceedings are begun; or
   (b) was habitually resident in England and Wales throughout the period of one year ending with that date.

(3)   The court shall have jurisdiction to entertain proceedings for nullity of marriage if (and only if) either of the parties to the marriage—
   (a) is domiciled in England and Wales on the date when the proceedings are begun; or
   (b) was habitually resident in England and Wales throughout the period of one year ending with that date; or
   (c) died before that date and either—
      (i) was at death domiciled in England and Wales, or
      (ii) had been habitually resident in England and Wales throughout the period of one year ending with the date of death.

(4)   The court shall have jurisdiction to entertain proceedings for death to be presumed and a marriage to be dissolved if (and only if) the petitioner—
   (a) is domiciled in England and Wales on the date when the proceedings are begun; or
   (b) was habitually resident in England and Wales throughout the period of one year ending with that date.

(5), (6)   . . .

Sub-s (1): words in italics repealed by the Family Law Act 1996, s 66(3), Sch 10, subject to savings in s 66(2) of, and Sch 9, para 5 to, the 1996 Act, as from a day to be appointed; words in square brackets substituted by the Matrimonial and Family Proceedings Act 1984, s 46(1), Sch 1.

Sub-s (2): repealed by the Family Law Act 1996, s 66(3), Sch 10, subject to savings in s 66(2) of, and Sch 9, para 5 to, the 1996 Act, as from a day to be appointed.

Sub-ss (5), (6): outside the scope of this work.

PART V
MISCELLANEOUS AND GENERAL

17 Citation, etc

(1)   This Act may be cited as the Domicile and Matrimonial Proceedings Act 1973.

(2)   Subject to sections 6(4), 12(6) and 14(3) of this Act, the enactments specified in Schedule 6 to this Act (including certain enactments of the Parliament of Northern Ireland) are hereby repealed to the extent specified in the third column of that Schedule.

(3)   . . .

(4)   Part II of this Act extends to England and Wales only; Part III extends to Scotland only; . . . ; and this Part extends to the whole of the United Kingdom.

(5)   This Act shall come into force on 1st January 1974.

Sub-s (3): repealed by the Zimbabwe Act 1979, s 6(3), Sch 3.

Sub-s (4): words omitted repealed by the Matrimonial Causes (Northern Ireland) Order 1978, SI 1978/1045, art 63(b), Sch 5.

Inheritance (Provision for Family and Dependants) Act 1975

(c 63)

An Act to make fresh provisions for empowering the court to make orders for the making out of the estate of a deceased person of provision for the spouse, former spouse, child, child of the family or dependant of that person; and for matters connected therewith

[12 November 1975]

NOTES

Capital transfer tax: except in relation to a liability to tax arising before 25 July 1986 capital transfer tax shall be known as inheritance tax and the Capital Transfer Tax Act 1984 may be cited as the Inheritance Tax Act 1984, by virtue of the Finance Act 1986, s 100.

Powers of court to order financial provision from deceased's estate

1 Application for financial provision from deceased's estate

(1)   Where after the commencement of this Act a person dies domiciled in England and Wales and is survived by any of the following persons—
   (a) the wife or husband of the deceased;
   (b) a former wife or former husband of the deceased who has not remarried;
 [(ba) any person (not being a person included in paragraph (a) or (b) above) to whom subsection (1A) below applies;]
   (c) a child of the deceased;
   (d) any person (not being a child of the deceased) who, in the case of any marriage to which the deceased was at any time a party, was treated by the deceased as a child of the family in relation to that marriage;
   (e) any person (not being a person included in the foregoing paragraphs of this subsection) who immediately before the death of the deceased was being maintained, either wholly or partly, by the deceased;

that person may apply to the court for an order under section 2 of this Act on the ground that the disposition of the deceased's estate effected by his will or the law relating to intestacy, or the combination of his will and that law, is not such as to make reasonable financial provision for the applicant.

[(1A) This subsection applies to a person if the deceased died on or after 1st January 1996 and, during the whole of the period of two years ending immediately before the date when the deceased died, the person was living—
(a) in the same household as the deceased, and
(b) as the husband or wife of the deceased.]

(2)   In this Act "reasonable financial provision"—
(a) in the case of an application made by virtue of subsection (1)(a) above by the husband or wife of the deceased (except where *the marriage with the deceased was the subject of a decree of judicial separation and at the date of death the decree was in force* and the separation was continuing), means such financial provision as it would be reasonable in all the circumstances of the case for a husband or wife to receive, whether or not that provision is required for his or her maintenance;
(b) in the case of any other application made by virtue of subsection (1) above, means such financial provision as it would be reasonable in all the circumstances of the case for the applicant to receive for his maintenance.

(3)   For the purposes of subsection (1)(e) above, a person shall be treated as being maintained by the deceased, either wholly or partly, as the case may be, if the deceased, otherwise than for full valuable consideration, was making a substantial contribution in money or money's worth towards the reasonable needs of that person.

NOTES

Sub-s (1): para (ba) inserted by the Law Reform (Succession) Act 1995, s 2(1), (2).

Sub-s (1A): inserted by the Law Reform (Succession) Act 1995, s 2(1), (3).

Sub-s (2): words in italics in para (a) substituted by the words ", at the date of death, a separation order under the Family Law Act 1996 was in force in relation to the marriage" by the Family Law Act 1996, s 66(1), Sch 8, Pt I, para 27(1), (2), subject to savings in s 66(2) of, and Sch 9, para 5 to, the 1996 Act, as from a day to be appointed.

2 Powers of court to make orders

(1)   Subject to the provisions of this Act, where an application is made for an order under this section, the court may, if it is satisfied that the disposition of the deceased's estate effected by his will or the law relating to intestacy, or the combination of his will and that law, is not such as to make reasonable financial provision for the applicant, make any one or more of the following orders—

(a) an order for the making to the applicant out of the net estate of the deceased of such periodical payments and for such term as may be specified in the order;

(b) an order for the payment to the applicant out of that estate of a lump sum of such amount as may be so specified;

(c) an order for the transfer to the applicant of such property comprised in that estate as may be so specified;

(d) an order for the settlement for the benefit of the applicant of such property comprised in that estate as may be so specified;

(e) an order for the acquisition out of property comprised in that estate of such property as may be so specified and for the transfer of the property so acquired to the applicant or for the settlement thereof for his benefit;

(f) an order varying any ante-nuptial or post-nuptial settlement (including such a settlement made by will) made on the parties to a marriage to which the deceased was one of the parties, the variation being for the benefit of the surviving party to that marriage, or any child of that marriage, or any person who was treated by the deceased as a child of the family in relation to that marriage.

(2)   An order under subsection (1)(a) above providing for the making out of the net estate of the deceased of periodical payments may provide for—

(a) payments of such amount as may be specified in the order,

(b) payments equal to the whole of the income of the net estate or of such portion thereof as may be so specified,

(c) payments equal to the whole of the income of such part of the net estate as the court may direct to be set aside or appropriated for the making out of the income thereof of payments under this section,

or may provide for the amount of the payments or any of them to be determined in any other way the court thinks fit.

(3)   Where an order under subsection (1)(a) above provides for the making of payments of an amount specified in the order, the order may direct that such part of the net estate as may be so specified shall be set aside or

appropriated for the making out of the income thereof of those payments; but no larger part of the net estate shall be so set aside or appropriated than is sufficient, at the date of the order, to produce by the income thereof the amount required for the making of those payments.

(4)   An order under this section may contain such consequential and supplemental provisions as the court thinks necessary or expedient for the purpose of giving effect to the order or for the purpose of securing that the order operates fairly as between one beneficiary of the estate of the deceased and another and may, in particular, but without prejudice to the generality of this subsection—

(a) order any person who holds any property which forms part of the net estate of the deceased to make such payment or transfer such property as may be specified in the order;

(b) varying the disposition of the deceased's estate effected by the will or the law relating to intestacy, or by both the will and the law relating to intestacy, in such manner as the court thinks fair and reasonable having regard to the provisions of the order and all the circumstances of the case;

(c) confer on the trustees of any property which is the subject of an order under this section such powers as appear to the court to be necessary or expedient.

3   Matters to which court is to have regard in exercising powers under s 2

(1)   Where an application is made for an order under section 2 of this Act, the court shall, in determining whether the disposition of the deceased's estate effected by his will or the law relating to intestacy, or the combination of his will and that law, is such as to make reasonable financial provision for the applicant and, if the court considers that reasonable financial provision has not been made, in determining whether and in what manner it shall exercise its powers under that section, have regard to the following matters, that is to say—

(a) the financial resources and financial needs which the applicant has or is likely to have in the foreseeable future;

(b) the financial resources and financial needs which any other applicant for an order under section 2 of this Act has or is likely to have in the foreseeable future;

(c) the financial resources and financial needs which any beneficiary of the estate of the deceased has or is likely to have in the foreseeable future;

   (d) any obligations and responsibilities which the deceased had towards any applicant for an order under the said section 2 or towards any beneficiary of the estate of the deceased;

   (e) the size and nature of the net estate of the deceased;

   (f) any physical or mental disability of any applicant for an order under the said section 2 or any beneficiary of the estate of the deceased;

   (g) any other matter, including the conduct of the applicant or any other person, which in the circumstances of the case the court may consider relevant.

(2)   Without prejudice to the generality of paragraph (g) of subsection (1) above, where an application for an order under section 2 of this Act is made by virtue of section 1(1)(a) or 1(1)(b) of this Act, the court shall, in addition to the matters specifically mentioned in paragraphs (a) to (f) of that subsection, have regard to—

   (a) the age of the applicant and the duration of the marriage;

   (b) the contribution made by the applicant to the welfare of the family of the deceased, including any contribution made by looking after the home or caring for the family;

and, in the case of an application by the wife or husband of the deceased, the court shall also, unless at the date of death a *decree of judicial separation* was in force and the separation was continuing, have regard to the provision which the applicant might reasonably have expected to receive if on the day on which the deceased died the marriage, instead of being terminated by death, had been terminated by a *decree of divorce*.

[(2A) Without prejudice to the generality of paragraph (g) of subsection (1) above, where an application for an order under section 2 of this Act is made by virtue of section 1(1)(ba) of this Act, the court shall, in addition to the matters specifically mentioned in paragraphs (a) to (f) of that subsection, have regard to—

   (a) the age of the applicant and the length of the period during which the applicant lived as the husband or wife of the deceased and in the same household as the deceased;

   (b) the contribution made by the applicant to the welfare of the family of the deceased, including any contribution made by looking after the home or caring for the family.]

(3)   Without prejudice to the generality of paragraph (g) of subsection (1) above, where an application for an order under section 2 of this Act is made by virtue of section 1(1)(c) or 1(1)(d) of this Act, the court shall, in addition to the matters specifically mentioned in paragraphs (a) to (f) of

that subsection, have regard to the manner in which the applicant was being or in which he might expect to be educated or trained, and where the application is made by virtue of section 1(1)(d) the court shall also have regard—

(a) to whether the deceased had assumed any responsibility for the applicant's maintenance and, if so, to the extent to which and the basis upon which the deceased assumed that responsibility and to the length of time for which the deceased discharged that responsibility;

(b) to whether in assuming and discharging that responsibility the deceased did so knowing that the applicant was not his own child;

(c) to the liability of any other person to maintain the applicant.

(4)   Without prejudice to the generality of paragraph (g) of subsection (1) above, where an application for an order under section 2 of this Act is made by virtue of section 1(1)(e) of this Act, the court shall, in addition to the matters specifically mentioned in paragraphs (a) to (f) of that subsection, have regard to the extent to which and the basis upon which the deceased assumed responsibility for the maintenance of the applicant, and to the length of time for which the deceased discharged that responsibility.

(5)   In considering the matters to which the court is required to have regard under this section, the court shall take into account the facts as known to the court at the date of the hearing.

(6)   In considering the financial resources of any person for the purposes of this section the court shall take into account his earning capacity and in considering the financial needs of any person for the purposes of this section the court shall take into account his financial obligations and responsibilities.

NOTES

Sub-s (2): first words in italics substituted by the words "separation order under the Family Law Act 1996" and second words in italics substituted by the words "a divorce order" by the Family Law Act 1996, s 66(1), Sch 8, Pt I, para 27(1), (3), subject to savings in s 66(2) of, and Sch 9, para 5 to, the 1996 Act, as from a day to be appointed.

Sub-s (2A): inserted by the Law Reform (Succession) Act 1995, s 2(1), (4).

4   Time-limit for applications

An application for an order under section 2 of this Act shall not, except with the permission of the court, be made after the end of the period of six months from the date on which representation with respect to the estate of the deceased is first taken out.

5   Interim orders

(1)   Where an application for an order under section 3 of this Act it appears to the court—
  (a) that the applicant is in immediate need of financial assistance, but it is not yet possible to determine what order (if any) should be made under that section; and
  (b) that property forming part of the net estate of the deceased is or can be made available to meet the need of the applicant;

the court may order that, subject to such conditions or restrictions, if any, as the court may impose and to any further order of the court, there shall be paid to the applicant out of the net estate of the deceased such sum or sums and (if more than one) at such intervals as the court thinks reasonable; and the court may order that, subject to the provisions of this Act, such payments are to be made until such date as the court may specify, not being later than the date on which the court either makes an order under the said section 2 or decides not to exercise its powers under that section.

(2)   Subsections (2), (3) and (4) of section 2 of this Act shall apply in relation to an order under this section as they apply in relation to an order under that section.

(3)   In determining what order, if any, should be made under this section the court shall, so far as the urgency of the case admits, have regard to the same matters as those to which the court is required to have regard under section 3 of this Act.

(4)   An order made under section 2 of this Act may provide that any sum paid to the applicant by virtue of this section shall be treated to such an extent and in such manner as may be provided by that order as having been paid on account of any payment provided for by that order.

6   Variation, discharge, etc of orders for periodical payments

(1)   Subject to the provisions of this Act, where the court has made an order under section 2(1)(a) of this Act (in this section referred to as "the original order") for the making of periodical payments to any person (in

this section referred to as "the original recipient"), the court, on an application under this section, shall have power by order to vary or discharge the original order or to suspend any provision of it temporarily and to revive the operation of any provision so suspended.

(2)   Without prejudice to the generality of subsection (1) above, an order made on an application for the variation of the original order may—
  (a) provide for the making out of any relevant property of such periodical payments and for such term as may be specified in the order to any person who has applied, or would but for section 4 of this Act be entitled to apply, for an order under section 2 of this Act (whether or not, in the case of any application, an order was made in favour of the applicant);
  (b) provide for the payment out of any relevant property of a lump sum of such amount as may be so specified to the original recipient or to any such person as is mentioned in paragraph (a) above;
  (c) provide for the transfer of the relevant property, or such part thereof as may be so specified, to the original recipient or to any such person as is so mentioned.

(3)   Where the original order provides that any periodical payments payable thereunder to the original recipient are to cease on the occurrence of an event specified in the order (other than the remarriage of a former wife or former husband) or on the expiration of a period so specified, then, if, before the end of the period of six months from the date of the occurrence of that event or of the expiration of that period, an application is made for an order under this section, the court shall have power to make any order which it would have had power to make if the application had been made before the date (whether in favour of the original recipient or any such person as is mentioned in subsection (2)(a) above and whether having effect from that date or from such later date as the court may specify).

(4)   Any reference in this section to the original order shall include a reference to an order made under this section and any reference in this section to the original recipient shall include a reference to any person to whom periodical payments are required to be made by virtue of an order under this section.

(5)   An application under this section may be made by any of the following persons, that is to say—
  (a) any person who by virtue of section 1(1) of this Act has applied, or would but for section 4 of this Act be entitled to apply, for an order under section 2 of this Act,

(b) the personal representatives of the deceased,

(c) the trustees of any relevant property, and

(d) any beneficiary of the estate of the deceased.

(6) An order under this section may only affect—

(a) property the income of which is at the date of the order applicable wholly or in part for the making of periodical payments to any person who has applied for an order under this Act, or

(b) in the case of an application under subsection (3) above in respect of payments which have ceased to be payable on the occurrence of an event or the expiration of a period, property the income of which was so applicable immediately before the occurrence of that event or the expiration of that period, as the case may be,

and any such property as is mentioned in paragraph (a) or (b) above is in subsections (2) and (5) above referred to as "relevant property".

(7) In exercising the powers conferred by this section the court shall have regard to all circumstances of the case, including any change in any of the matters to which the court was required to have regard when making the order to which the application relates.

(8) Where the court makes an order under this section, it may give such consequential directions as it thinks necessary or expedient having regard to the provisions of the order.

(9) No such order as is mentioned in section 2(1)(d), (e) or (f), 9, 10 or 11 of this Act shall be made on an application under this section.

(10) For the avoidance of doubt it is hereby declared that, in relation to an order which provides for the making of periodical payments which are to cease on the occurrence of an event specified in the order (other than the remarriage of a former wife or former husband) or on the expiration of a period so specified, the power to vary an order includes power to provide for the making of periodical payments after the expiration of that period or the occurrence of that event.

7 Payment of lump sums by instalments

(1) An order under section 2(1)(b) or 6(2)(b) of this Act for the payment of a lump sum may provide for the payment of that sum by instalments of such amount as may be specified in the order.

(2)   Where an order is made by virtue of subsection (1) above, the court shall have power, on an application made by the person to whom the lump sum is payable, by the personal representatives of the deceased or by the trustees of the property out of which the lump sum is payable, to vary that order by varying the number of instalments payable, the amount of any instalment and the date on which any instalment becomes payable.

Property available for financial provision

8   Property treated as part of "net estate"

(1)   Where a deceased person has in accordance with the provisions of any enactment nominated any person to receive any sum of money or other property on his death and that nomination is in force at the time of his death, that sum of money, after deducting therefrom any [inheritance tax] payable in respect thereof, or that other property, to the extent of the value thereof at the date of the death of the deceased after deducting therefrom any [inheritance tax] so payable, shall be treated for the purposes of this Act as part of the net estate of the deceased; but this subsection shall not render any person liable for having paid that sum or transferred that other property to the person named in the nomination in accordance with the directions given in the nomination.

(2)   Where any sum of money or other property is received by any person as a donatio mortis causa made by a deceased person, that sum of money, after deducting therefrom any [inheritance tax] payable thereon, or that other property, to the extent of the value thereof at the date of the death of the deceased after deducting therefrom any [inheritance tax] so payable, shall be treated for the purposes of this Act as part of the net estate of the deceased; but this subsection shall not render any person liable for having paid that sum or transferred that other property in order to give effect to that donatio mortis causa.

(3)   The amount of [inheritance tax] to be deducted for the purposes of this section shall not exceed the amount of that tax which has been borne by the person nominated by the deceased or, as the case may be, the person who has received a sum of money or other property as a donatio mortis causa.

9 Property held on a joint tenancy

(1)   Where a deceased person was immediately before his death beneficially entitled to a joint tenancy of any property, then, if, before the end of the period of six months from the date on which representation with respect to the estate of the deceased was first taken out, an application is made for an order under section 2 of this Act, the court for the purpose of facilitating the making of financial provision for the applicant under this Act may order that the deceased's severable share of that property, at the value thereof immediately before his death, shall, to such extent as appears to the court to be just in all the circumstances of the case, be treated for the purposes of this Act as part of the net estate of the deceased.

(2)   In determining the extent to which any severable share is to be treated as part of the net estate of the deceased by virtue of an order under subsection (1) above, the court shall have regard to any [inheritance tax] payable in respect of that severable share.

(3)   Where an order is made under subsection (1) above, the provisions of this section shall not render any person liable for anything done by him before the order was made.

(4)   For the avoidance of doubt it is hereby declared that for the purposes of this section there may be a joint tenancy of a chose in action.

Powers of court in relation to transactions intended to defeat applications for financial provision

10 Dispositions intended to defeat applications for financial provision

(1)   Where an application is made to the court for an order under section 2 of this Act, the applicant may, in the proceedings on that application, apply to the court for an order under subsection (2) below.

(2)   Where on an application under subsection (1) above the court is satisfied—
  (a) that, less than six years before the date of the death of the deceased, the deceased with the intention of defeating an application for financial provision under this Act made a disposition, and

(b) that full valuable consideration for that disposition was not given by the person to whom or for the benefit of whom the disposition was made (in this section referred to as "the donee") or by any other person, and

(c) that the exercise of the powers conferred by this section would facilitate the making of financial provision for the applicant under this Act,

then, subject to the provisions of this section and of sections 12 and 13 of this Act, the court may order the donee (whether or not at the date of the order he holds any interest in the property disposed of to him or for his benefit by the deceased) to provide, for the purpose of the making of that financial provision, such sum of money or other property as may be specified in the order.

(3)   Where an order is made under subsection (2) above as respects any disposition made by the deceased which consisted of the payment of money to or for the benefit of the donee, the amount of any sum of money or the value of any property ordered to be provided under that subsection shall not exceed the amount of the payment made by the deceased after deducting therefrom any [inheritance tax] borne by the donee in respect of that payment.

(4)   Where an order is made under subsection (2) above as respects any disposition made by the deceased which consisted of the transfer of property (other than a sum of money) to or for the benefit of the donee, the amount of any sum of money or the value of any property ordered to be provided under that subsection shall not exceed the value at the date of the death of the deceased of the property disposed of by him to or for the benefit of the donee (or if that property has been disposed of by the person to whom it was transferred by the deceased, the value at the date of that disposal thereof) after deducting therefrom any capital transfer tax borne by the donee in respect of the transfer of that property by the deceased.

(5)   Where an application (in this subsection referred to as "the original application") is made for an order under subsection (2) above in relation to any disposition, then, if on an application under this subsection by the donee or by any applicant for an order under section 2 of this Act the court is satisfied—

(a) that, less than six years before the date of the death of the deceased, the deceased with the intention of defeating an application for financial provision under this Act made a disposition other than the disposition which is the subject of the original application, and

   (b) that full valuable consideration for that other disposition was not given by the person to whom or for the benefit of whom that other disposition was made or by any other person,

the court may exercise in relation to the person to whom or for the benefit of whom that other disposition was made the powers which the court would have had under subsection (2) above if the original application had been made in respect of that other disposition and the court had been satisfied as to the matters set out in paragraphs (a), (b) and (c) of that subsection; and where any application is made under this subsection, any reference in this section (except in subsection (2)(b)) to the donee shall include a reference to the person to whom or for the benefit of whom that other disposition was made.

(6)   In determining whether and in what manner to exercise its powers under this section, the court shall have regard to the circumstances in which any disposition was made and any valuable consideration which was given therefor, the relationship, if any, of the donee to the deceased, the conduct and financial resources of the donee and all the other circumstances of the case.

(7)   In this section "disposition" does not include—
   (a) any provision in a will, any such nomination as is mentioned in section 8(1) of this Act or any donatio mortis causa, or
   (b) any appointment of property made, otherwise than by will, in the exercise of a special power of appointment,

but, subject to these exceptions, includes any payment of money (including the payment of a premium under a policy of assurance) and any conveyance, assurance, appointment or gift of property of any description, whether made by an instrument or otherwise.

(8)   The provisions of this section do not apply to any disposition made before the commencement of this Act.

11 Contracts to leave property by will

(1)   Where an application is made to a court for an order under section 2 of this Act, the applicant may, in the proceedings on that application, apply to the court for an order under this section.

(2)   Where on an application under subsection (1) above the court is satisfied—

(a) that the deceased made a contract by which he agreed to leave by his will a sum of money or other property to any person or by which he agreed that a sum of money or other property would be paid or transferred to any person out of his estate, and

(b) that the deceased made that contract with the intention of defeating an application for financial provision under this Act, and

(c) that when the contract was made full valuable consideration for that contract was not given or promised by the person with whom or for the benefit of whom the contract was made (in this section referred to as "the donee") or by any other person, and

(d) that the exercise of the powers conferred by this section would facilitate the making of financial provision for the applicant under this Act,

then, subject to the provisions of this section and of sections 12 and 13 of this Act, the court may make any one or more of the following orders, that is to say—

(i) if any money has been paid or any other property has been transferred to or for the benefit of the donee in accordance with the contract, an order directing the donee to provide, for the purpose of the making of that financial provision, such sum of money or other property as may be specified in the order;

(ii) if the money or all the money has not been paid or the property or all the property has not been transferred in accordance with the contract, an order directing the personal representatives not to make any payment or transfer any property, or not to make any further payment or transfer any further property, as the case may be, in accordance therewith or directing the personal representatives only to make such payment or transfer such property as may be specified in the order.

(3) Notwithstanding anything in subsection (2) above, the court may exercise its powers thereunder in relation to any contract made by the deceased only to the extent that the court considers that the amount of any sum of money paid or to be paid or the value of any property transferred or to be transferred in accordance with the contract exceeds the value of any valuable consideration given or to be given for that contract, and for this purpose the court shall have regard to the value of property at the date of the hearing.

(4) In determining whether and in what manner to exercise its powers under this section, the court shall have regard to the circumstances in which the contract was made, the relationship, if any, of the donee to the

deceased, the conduct and financial resources of the donee and all the other circumstances of the case.

(5)   Where an order has been made under subsection (2) above in relation to any contract the rights of any person to enforce that contract or to recover damages or to obtain other relief for the breach thereof shall be subject to any adjustment made by the court under section 12(3) of this Act and shall survive to such extent only as is consistent with giving effect to the terms of that order.

(6)   The provisions of this section do not apply to a contract made before the commencement of this Act.

12   Provisions supplementary to ss 10 and 11

(1)   Where the exercise of any of the powers conferred by section 10 or 11 of this Act is conditional on the court being satisfied that a disposition or contract was made by a deceased person with the intention of defeating an application for financial provision under this Act, that condition shall be fulfilled if the court is of the opinion that, on a balance of probabilities, the intention of the deceased (though not necessarily his sole intention) in making the disposition or contract was to prevent an order for financial provision being made under this Act or to reduce the amount of the provision which might otherwise be granted by an order thereunder.

(2)   Where an application is made under section 11 of this Act with respect to any contract made by the deceased and no valuable consideration was given or promised by any person for that contract then, notwithstanding anything in subsection (1) above, it shall be presumed, unless the contrary is shown, that the deceased made that contract with the intention of defeating an application for financial provision under this Act.

(3)   Where the court makes an order under section 10 or 11 of this Act it may give such consequential directions as it thinks fit (including directions requiring the making of any payment or the transfer of any property) for giving effect to the order or for securing a fair adjustment of the rights of the persons affected thereby.

(4)   Any power conferred on the court by the said section 10 or 11 to order the donee, in relation to any disposition or contract, to provide any sum of money or other property shall be exercisable in like manner in relation to the personal representative of the donee, and—

(a) any reference in section 10(4) to the disposal of property by the donee shall include a reference to disposal by the personal representative of the donee, and

(b) any reference in section 10(5) to an application by the donee under that subsection shall include a reference to an application by the personal representative of the donee;

but the court shall not have power under the said section 10 or 11 to make an order in respect of any property forming part of the estate of the donee which has been distributed by the personal representative; and the personal representative shall not be liable for having distributed any such property before he has notice of the making of an application under the said section 10 or 11 on the ground that he ought to have taken into account the possibility that such an application would be made.

13 Provisions as to trustees in relation to ss 10 and 11

(1) Where an application is made for—
 (a) an order under section 10 of this Act in respect of a disposition made by the deceased to any person as a trustee, or
 (b) an order under section 11 of this Act in respect of any payment made or property transferred, in accordance with a contract made by the deceased, to any person as a trustee,

the powers of the court under the said section 10 or 11 to order that trustee to provide a sum of money or other property shall be subject to the following limitation (in addition, in a case of an application under section 10, to any provision regarding the deduction of [inheritance tax]) namely, that the amount of any sum of money or the value of any property ordered to be provided—
 (i) in the case of an application in respect of a disposition which consisted of the payment of money or an application in respect of the payment of money in accordance with a contract, shall not exceed the aggregate of so much of that money as is at the date of the order in the hands of the trustee and the value at that date of any property which represents that money or is derived therefrom and is at that date in the hands of the trustee;
 (ii) in the case of an application in respect of a disposition which consisted of the transfer of property (other than a sum of money) or an application in respect of the transfer of property (other than a sum of money) in accordance with a contract, shall not exceed the aggregate of the value at the date of the order of so much of that

property as is at that date in the hands of the trustee and the value at that date of any property which represents the first mentioned property or is derived therefrom and is at that date in the hands of the trustee.

(2)   Where any such application is made in respect of a disposition made to any person as a trustee or in respect of any payment made or property transferred in pursuance of a contract to any person as a trustee, the trustee shall not be liable for having distributed any money or other property on the ground that he ought to have taken into account the possibility that such an application would be made.

(3)   Where any such application is made in respect of a disposition made to any person as a trustee or in respect of any payment made or property transferred in accordance with a contract to any person as a trustee, any reference in the said section 10 or 11 to the donee shall be construed as including a reference to the trustee or trustees for the time being of the trust in question and any reference in subsection (1) or (2) above to a trustee shall be construed in the same way.

Special provisions relating to cases of divorce, separation, etc

14   Provision as to cases where no financial relief was granted in divorce proceedings, etc

(1)   Where, within twelve months from the date on which a decree of divorce or nullity of marriage has been made absolute or a decree of judicial separation has been granted, a party to the marriage dies and—
 (a) an application for a financial provision order under *section 23* of the Matrimonial Causes Act 1973 or a property adjustment order under *section 24* of that Act has not been made by the other party to that marriage, or
 (b) such an application has been made but the proceedings thereon have not been determined at the time of the death of the deceased,

then, if an application for an order under section 2 of this Act is made by that other party, the court shall, notwithstanding anything in section 1 or section 3 of this Act, have power, if it thinks it just to do so, to treat that party for the purposes of that application as if *the decree of divorce or nullity of marriage had not been made absolute or the decree of judicial separation had not been granted, as the case may be.*

(2)   This section shall not apply in relation to a *decree of judicial separation* unless at the date of the death of the deceased *the decree* was in force and the separation was continuing.

Sub-s (1): first words in italics substituted by the words "a divorce order or separation order has been made under the Family Law Act 1996 in relation to a marriage or a decree of nullity of marriage has been made absolute", second words in italics substituted by the words "section 22A or 23", third words in italics substituted by the words "section 23A or 24", and words in italics after para (b) substituted by the words ", as the case may be, the divorce order or separation order had not been made or the decree of nullity had not been made absolute", by the Family Law Act 1996, s 66(1), Sch 8, Pt I, para 27(1), (4)(a)–(c), subject to savings in s 66(2) of, and Sch 9, para 5 to, the 1996 Act, as from a day to be appointed.

Sub-s (2): first words in italics substituted by the words "separation order" and second words in italics substituted by the words "the order" by the Family Law Act 1996, s 66(1), Sch 8, Pt I, para 27(1), (4)(d), subject to savings in s 66(2) of, and Sch 9, para 5 to, the 1996 Act, as from a day to be appointed.

15   Restriction imposed in divorce proceedings, etc on application under this Act

[(1)   On the grant of a decree of divorce, a decree of nullity of marriage or a decree of judicial separation or at any time thereafter the court, if it considers it just to do so, may, on the application of either party to the marriage, order that the other party to the marriage shall not on the death of the applicant be entitled to apply for an order under section 2 of this Act.

In this subsection "the court" means the High Court or, where a county court has jurisdiction by virtue of Part V of the Matrimonial and Family Proceedings Act 1984, a county court.]

(2)   *In the case of a decree of divorce or nullity of marriage an order may be made under subsection (1) above before or after the decree is made absolute, but if it is made before the decree is made absolute it shall not take effect unless the decree is made absolute.*

(3)   *Where an order made under subsection (1) above on the grant of a decree of divorce or nullity of marriage has come into force with respect to a party to a marriage, then, on the death of the other party to that marriage, the court shall not entertain any application for an order under section 2 of this Act made by the first-mentioned party.*

*(4)   Where an order made under subsection (1) above on the grant of a
decree of judicial separation has come into force with respect to any party
to a marriage, then, if the other party to that marriage dies while the decree
is in force and the separation is continuing, the court shall not entertain
any application for an order under section 2 of this Act made by the first-
mentioned party.*

NOTES

Sub-s (1): substituted by the Matrimonial and Family Proceedings Act 1984,
s 8; words in italics substituted by the Family Law Act 1996, s 66(1), Sch 8, Pt I,
para 27(1), (5), subject to savings in s 66(2) of, and Sch 9, para 5 to, the 1996 Act,
as from a day to be appointed, as follows—

"At any time when the court—
(a) has jurisdiction under section 23A or 24 of the Matrimonial Causes Act
     1973 to make a property adjustment order in relation to a marriage; or
(b) would have such jurisdiction if either the jurisdiction had not already been
     exercised or an application for such an order were made with the leave of the
     court,".

Sub-ss (2)–(4): substituted by the Family Law Act 1996, s 66(1), Sch 8, Pt I,
para 27(1), (6), subject to savings in s 66(2) of, and Sch 9, para 5 to, the 1996 Act,
as follows—

"(2) An order made under subsection (1) above with respect to any party to a
marriage has effect in accordance with subsection (3) below at any time—
(a) after the marriage has been dissolved;
(b) after a decree of nullity has been made absolute in relation to the marriage;
     and
(c) while a separation order under the Family Law Act 1996 is in force in relation
     to the marriage and the separation is continuing.
(3) If at any time when an order made under subsection (1) above with respect
to any party to a marriage has effect the other party to the marriage dies, the court
shall not entertain any application made by the surviving party to the marriage for
an order under section 2 of this Act.".

[15A   Restriction imposed in proceedings under Matrimonial and Family Proceedings Act 1984 on application under this Act

(1)   On making an order under section 17 of the Matrimonial and
Family Proceedings Act 1984 (orders for financial provision and property
adjustment following overseas divorces, etc) the court, if it considers
it just to do so, may, on the application of either party to the marriage,
order that the other party to the marriage shall not on the death of
the applicant be entitled to apply for an order under section 2 of this
Act.

In this subsection "the court" means the High Court or, where a county court has jurisdiction by virtue of Part V of the Matrimonial and Family Proceedings Act 1984, a county court.

(2)   Where an order under subsection (1) above has been made with respect to a party to a marriage which has been dissolved or annulled, then, on the death of the other party to that marriage, the court shall not entertain an application under section 2 of this Act made by the first-mentioned party.

(3)   Where an order under subsection (1) above has been made with respect to a party to a marriage the parties to which have been legally separated, then, if the other party to the marriage dies while the legal separation is in force, the court shall not entertain an application under section 2 of this Act made by the first-mentioned party.]

NOTES

Inserted by the Matrimonial and Family Proceedings Act 1984, s 25.

16 Variation and discharge of secured periodical payments orders made under Matrimonial Causes Act 1973

(1)   Where an application for an order under section 2 of this Act is made to the court by any person who was at the time of the death of the deceased entitled to payments from the deceased under a secured periodical payments order made under the Matrimonial Causes Act 1973, then, in the proceedings on that application, the court shall have power, if an application is made under this section by that person or by the personal representative of the deceased, to vary or discharge that periodical payments order or to revive the operation of any provision thereof which has been suspended under section 31 of that Act.

(2)   In exercising the powers conferred by this section the court shall have regard to all the circumstances of the case, including any order which the court proposes to make under section 2 or section 5 of this Act and any change (whether resulting from the death of the deceased or otherwise) in any of the matters to which the court was required to have regard when making the secured periodical payments order.

(3)   The powers exercisable by the court under this section in relation to an order shall be exercisable also in relation to any instrument executed in pursuance of the order.

17 Variation and revocation of maintenance agreements

(1)   Where an application for an order under section 2 of this Act is made to the court by any person who was at the time of the death of the deceased entitled to payments from the deceased under a maintenance agreement which provided for the continuation of payments under the agreement after the death of the deceased, then, in the proceedings on that application, the court shall have power, if an application is made under this section by that person or by the personal representative of the deceased, to vary or revoke that agreement.

(2)   In exercising the powers conferred by this section the court shall have regard to all the circumstances of the case, including any order which the court proposes to make under section 2 or section 5 of this Act and any change (whether resulting from the death of the deceased or otherwise) in any of the circumstances in the light of which the agreement was made.

(3)   If a maintenance agreement is varied by the court under this section the like consequences shall ensue as if the variation had been made immediately before the death of the deceased by agreement between the parties and for valuable consideration.

(4)   In this section "maintenance agreement", in relation to a deceased person, means any agreement made, whether in writing or not and whether before or after the commencement of this Act, by the deceased with any person with whom he entered into a marriage, being an agreement which contained provisions governing the rights and liabilities towards one another when living separately of the parties to that marriage (whether or not the marriage has been dissolved or annulled) in respect of the making or securing of payments or the disposition or use of any property, including such rights and liabilities with respect to the maintenance or education of any child, whether or not a child of the deceased or a person who was treated by the deceased as a child of the family in relation to that marriage.

18 Availability of court's powers under this Act in applications under ss 31 and 36 of the Matrimonial Causes Act 1973

(1)   Where—
  (a) a person against whom a secured periodical payments order was made under the Matrimonial Causes Act 1973 has died and an application is made under section 31(6) of that Act for the variation or discharge of that order or for the revival of the operation of any provision thereof which has been suspended, or

(b) a party to a maintenance agreement within the meaning of section 34 of that Act has died, the agreement being one which provides for the continuation of payments thereunder after the death of one of the parties, and an application is made under section 36(1) of that Act for the alteration of the agreement under section 35 thereof.

the court shall have power to direct that the application made under the said section 31(6) or 36(1) shall be deemed to have been accompanied by an application for an order under section 2 of this Act.

(2)   Where the court gives a direction under subsection (1) above it shall have power, in the proceedings on the application under the said section 31(6) or 36(1), to make any order which the court would have had power to make under the provisions of this Act if the application under the said section 31(6) or 36(1), as the case may be, had been made jointly with an application for an order under the said section 2; and the court shall have power to give such consequential directions as may be necessary for enabling the court to exercise any of the powers available to the court under this Act in the case of an application for an order under section 2.

(3)   Where an order made under section 15(1) of this Act is in force with respect to a party to a marriage, the court shall not give a direction under subsection (1) above with respect to any application made under the said section 31(6) or 36(1) by that party on the death of the other party.

Miscellaneous and supplementary provisions

19   Effect, duration and form of orders

(1)   Where an order is made under section 2 of this Act then for all purposes, including the purposes of the enactments relating to [inheritance tax], the will or the law relating to intestacy, or both the will and the law relating to intestacy, as the case may be, shall have effect and be deemed to have had effect as from the deceased's death subject to the provisions of the order.

(2)   Any order made under section 2 or 5 of this Act in favour of—
   (a) an applicant who was the former husband or former wife of the deceased, or
   (b) an applicant who was the husband or wife of the deceased in a case where the marriage with the deceased was the subject of a decree of

judicial separation and at the date of death the decree was in force and the separation was continuing,

shall, in so far as it provides for the making of periodical payments, cease to have effect on the remarriage of the applicant, except in relation to any arrears due under the order on the date of the remarriage.

(3)　A copy of every order made under this Act [other than an order made under section 15(1) of this Act] shall be sent to the principal registry of the Family Division for entry and filing, and a memorandum of the order shall be endorsed on, or permanently annexed to, the probate or letters of administration under which the estate is being administered.

NOTES

Sub-s (2): words in italics in para (b) substituted by the words ", at the date of death, a separation order under the Family Law Act 1996 was in force in relation to the marriage with the deceased" by the Family Law Act 1996, s 66(1), Sch 8, Pt I, para 27(1), (7), subject to savings in s 66(2) of, and Sch 9, para 5 to, the 1996 Act, as from a day to be appointed.

Sub-s (3): words in square brackets inserted by the Administration of Justice Act 1982, s 52.

20　Provisions as to personal representatives

(1)　The provisions of this Act shall not render the personal representative of a deceased person liable for having distributed any part of the estate of the deceased, after the end of the period of six months from the date on which representation with respect to the estate of the deceased is first taken out, on the ground that he ought to have taken into account the possibility—

(a) that the court might permit the making of an application for an order under section 2 of this Act after the end of that period, or

(b) that, where an order has been made under the said section 2, the court might exercise in relation thereto the powers conferred on it by section 6 of this Act,

but this subsection shall not prejudice any power to recover, by reason of the making of an order under this Act, any part of the estate so distributed.

(2)　Where the personal representative of a deceased person pays any sum directed by an order under section 5 of this Act to be paid out of the deceased's net estate, he shall not be under any liability by reason of that estate not being sufficient to make the payment, unless at the time of making the payment he has reasonable cause to believe that the estate is not sufficient.

(3) Where a deceased person entered into a contract by which he agreed to leave by his will any sum of money or other property to any person or by which he agreed that a sum of money or other property would be paid or transferred to any person out of his estate, then, if the personal representative of the deceased has reason to believe that the deceased entered into the contract with the intention of defeating an application for financial provision under this Act, he may, notwithstanding anything in that contract, postpone the payment of that sum of money or the transfer of that property until the expiration of the period of six months from the date on which representation with respect to the estate of the deceased is first taken out or, if during that period an application is made for an order under section 2 of this Act, until the determination of the proceedings on that application.

23 Determination of date on which representation was first taken out

In considering for the purposes of this Act when representation with respect to the estate of a deceased person was first taken out, a grant limited to settled land or to trust property shall be left out of account, and a grant limited to real estate or to personal estate shall be left out of account unless a grant limited to the remainder of the estate has previously been made or is made at the same time.

24 Effect of this Act on s 46(1)(vi) of Administration of Estates Act 1925

Section 46(1)(vi) of the Administration of Estates Act 1925, in so far as it provides for the devolution of property on the Crown, the Duchy of Lancaster or the Duke of Cornwall as bona vacantia, shall have effect subject to the provisions of this Act.

25 Interpretation

(1) In this Act—
  "beneficiary", in relation to the estate of a deceased person, means—

(a) a person who under the will of the deceased or under the law relating to intestacy is beneficially interested in the estate or would be so interested if an order had not been made under this Act, and

(b) a person who has received any sum of money or other property which by virtue of section 8(1) or 8(2) of this Act is treated as part of the net estate of the deceased or would have received that sum or other property if an order had not been made under this Act;

"child" includes an illegitimate child and a child en ventre sa mere at the death of the deceased;

"the court" [unless the context otherwise requires] means the High Court, or where a county court has jurisdiction by virtue of section 22 of this Act, a county court;

["former wife" or "former husband" means a person whose marriage with the deceased was during the lifetime of the deceased either—

(a) dissolved or annulled by *a decree* of divorce or a decree of nullity of marriage granted under the law of any part of the British Islands, or

(b) dissolved or annulled in any country or territory outside the British Islands by a divorce or annulment which is entitled to be recognised as valid by the law of England and Wales;]

"net estate", in relation to a deceased person, means—

(a) all property of which the deceased had power to dispose by his will (otherwise than by virtue of a special power of appointment) less the amount of his funeral, testamentary and administration expenses, debts and liabilities, including any [inheritance tax] payable out of his estate on his death;

(b) any property in respect of which the deceased held a general power of appointment (not being a power exercisable by will) which has not been exercised;

(c) any sum of money or other property which is treated for the purposes of this Act as part of the net estate of the deceased by virtue of section 8(1) or (2) of this Act;

(d) any property which is treated for the purposes of this Act as part of the net estate of the deceased by virtue of an order made under section 9 of the Act;

(e) any sum of money or other property which is, by reason of a disposition or contract made by the deceased, ordered under section 10 or 11 of this Act to be provided for the purpose of the making of financial provision under this Act;

"property" includes any chose in action;

"reasonable financial provision" has the meaning assigned to it by section 1 of this Act;

"valuable consideration" does not include marriage or a promise of marriage;

"will" includes codicil.

(2) For the purposes of paragraph (a) of the definition of "net estate" in subsection (1) above a person who is not of full age and capacity shall be treated as having power to dispose by will of all property of which he would have had power to dispose by will if he had been of full age and capacity.

(3) Any reference in this Act to provision out of the net estate of a deceased person includes a reference to provision extending to the whole of that estate.

(4) For the purposes of this Act any reference to a wife or husband shall be treated as including a reference to a person who in good faith entered into a void marriage with the deceased unless either—

    (a) the marriage of the deceased and that person was dissolved or annulled during the lifetime of the deceased and the dissolution or annulment is recognised by the law of England and Wales, or

    (b) that person has during the lifetime of the deceased entered into a later marriage.

(5) Any reference in this Act to remarriage or to a person who has remarried includes a reference to a marriage which is by law void or voidable or to a person who has entered into such a marriage, as the case may be, and a marriage shall be treated for the purposes of this Act as a remarriage, in relation to any party thereto, notwithstanding that the previous marriage of that party was void or voidable.

(6) Any reference in this Act to an order or decree made under the Matrimonial Causes Act 1973 or under any section of that Act shall be construed as including a reference to an order or decree which is deemed to have been made under that Act or under that section thereof, as the case may be.

(7) Any reference in this Act to any enactment is a reference to that enactment as amended by or under any subsequent enactment.

NOTES

Sub-s (1): in definition "court" words in square brackets inserted by the Matrimonial and Family Proceedings Act 1984, s 8; definitions "former wife" and "former husband" substituted by the Matrimonial and Family Proceedings Act 1984, s 25, words in italics therein substituted by the words "an order or decree" by the Family Law Act 1996, s 66(1), Sch 8, Pt I, para 27(1), (8), subject to savings in s 66(2) of, and Sch 9, para 5 to, the 1996 Act, as from a day to be appointed.

27 Short title, commencement and extent

(1)   This Act may be cited as the Inheritance (Provision for Family and Dependants) Act 1975.

(2)   This Act does not extend to Scotland or Northern Ireland.

(3)   This Act shall come into force on 1st April 1976.

Congenital Disabilities (Civil Liability) Act 1976

(c 28)

An Act to make provision as to civil liability in the case of children born disabled in consequence of some person's fault; and to extend the Nuclear Installations Act 1965, so that children so born in consequence of a breach of duty under that Act may claim compensation

[22 July 1976]

1 Civil liability to child born disabled

(1)   If a child is born disabled as the result of such an occurrence before its birth as is mentioned in subsection (2) below, and a person (other than the child's own mother) is under this section answerable to the child in respect of the occurrence, the child's disabilities are to be regarded as damage resulting from the wrongful act of that person and actionable accordingly at the suit of the child.

(2)   An occurrence to which this section applies is one which—
   (a) affected either parent of the child in his or her ability to have a normal, healthy child; or
   (b) affected the mother during her pregnancy, or affected her or the child in the course of its birth, so that the child is born with disabilities which would not otherwise have been present.

(3)   Subject to the following subsections, a person (here referred to as "the defendant") is answerable to the child if he was liable in tort to the parent or would, if sued in due time, have been so; and it is no answer that there could not have been such liability because the parent suffered no actionable injury, if there was a breach of legal duty which, accompanied by injury, would have given rise to the liability.

(4)   In the case of an occurrence preceding the time of conception, the defendant is not answerable to the child if at that time either or both of the parents knew the risk of their child being born disabled (that is to say, the particular risk created by the occurrence); but should it be the child's father who is the defendant, this subsection does not apply if he knew of the risk and the mother did not.

(5)   The defendant is not answerable to the child, for anything he did or omitted to do when responsible in a professional capacity for treating or advising the parent, if he took reasonable care having due regard to then received professional opinion applicable to the particular class of case; but this does not mean that he is answerable only because he departed from received opinion.

(6)   Liability to the child under this section may be treated as having been excluded or limited by contract made with the parent affected, to the same extent and subject to the same restrictions as liability in the parent's own case; and a contract term which could have been set up by the defendant in an action by the parent, so as to exclude or limit his liability to him or her, operates in the defendant's favour to the same, but no greater, extent in an action under this section by the child.

(7)   If in the child's action under this section it is shown that the parent affected shared the responsibility for the child being born disabled, the damages are to be reduced to such extent as the court thinks just and equitable having regard to the extent of the parent's responsibility.

[1A   Extension of section 1 to cover infertility treatments

(1)   In any case where—
  (a) a child carried by a woman as the result of the placing in her of an embryo or of sperm and eggs or her artificial insemination is born disabled,
  (b) the disability results from an act or omission in the course of the selection, or the keeping or use outside the body, of the embryo

carried by her or of the gametes used to bring about the creation of the embryo, and

(c) a person is under this section answerable to the child in respect of the act or omission,

the child's disabilities are to be regarded as damage resulting from the wrongful act of that person and actionable accordingly at the suit of the child.

(2) Subject to subsection (3) below and the applied provisions of section 1 of this Act, a person (here referred to as "the defendant") is answerable to the child if he was liable in tort to one or both of the parents (here referred to as "the parent or parents concerned") or would, if sued in due time, have been so; and it is no answer that there could not have been such liability because the parent or parents concerned suffered no actionable injury, if there was a breach of legal duty which, accompanied by injury, would have given rise to the liability.

(3) The defendant is not under this section answerable to the child if at the time the embryo, or the sperm and eggs, are placed in the woman or the time of her insemination (as the case may be) either or both of the parents knew the risk of their child being born disabled (that is to say, the particular risk created by the act or omission).

(4) Subsections (5) to (7) of section 1 of this Act apply for the purposes of this section as they apply for the purposes of that but as if references to the parent or the parent affected were references to the parent or parents concerned.]

NOTES

Inserted by the Human Fertilisation and Embryology Act 1990, s 44.

2 Liability of woman driving when pregnant

A woman driving a motor vehicle when she knows (or ought reasonably to know) herself to be pregnant is to be regarded as being under the same duty to take care for the safety of her unborn child as the law imposes on her with respect to the safety of other people; and if in consequence of her breach of that duty her child is born with disabilities which would not otherwise have been present, those disabilities are to be regarded as damage resulting from her wrongful act and actionable accordingly at the suit of the child.

4 Interpretation and other supplementary provisions

(1)   References in this Act to a child being born disabled or with disabilities are to its being born with any deformity, disease or abnormality, including predisposition (whether or not susceptible of immediate prognosis) to physical or mental defect in the future.

(2)   In this Act—
  (a) "born" means born alive (the moment of a child's birth being when it first has a life separate from its mother), and "birth" has a corresponding meaning; and
  (b) "motor vehicle" means a mechanically propelled vehicle intended or adapted for use on roads

[and references to embryos shall be construed in accordance with section 1 of the Human Fertilisation and Embryology Act 1990].

(3)   Liability to a child under section 1 [1A] or 2 of this Act is to be regarded—
  (a) as respects all its incidents and any matters arising or to arise out of it; and
  (b) subject to any contrary context or intention, for the purpose of construing references in enactments and documents to personal or bodily injuries and cognate matters,

as liability for personal injuries sustained by the child immediately after its birth.

(4)   No damages shall be recoverable under [any] of those sections in respect of any loss of expectation of life, nor shall any such loss be taken into account in the compensation payable in respect of a child under the Nuclear Installations Act 1965 as extended by section 3, unless (in either case) the child lives for at least 48 hours.

[(4A) In any case where a child carried by a woman as the result of the placing in her of an embryo or of sperm and eggs or her artificial insemination is born disabled, any reference in section 1 of this Act to a parent includes a reference to a person who would be a parent but for sections 27 to 29 of the Human Fertilisation and Embryology Act 1990.]

(5)   This Act applies in respect of births after (but not before) its passing, and in respect of any such birth it replaces any law in force before its passing, whereby a person could be liable to a child in respect of disabilities

with which it might be born; but in section 1(3) of this Act the expression "liable in tort" does not include any reference to liability by virtue of this Act, or to liability by virtue of any such law.

(6) . . .

Sub-s (2): words in square brackets added or inserted by the Human Fertilisation and Embryology Act 1990, s 44(2).

Sub-s (3): figure in square brackets inserted by the Human Fertilisation and Embryology Act 1990, s 44(2).

Sub-s (4): word in square brackets substituted by the Human Fertilisation and Embryology Act 1990, s 44(2).

Sub-s (4A): inserted by the Human Fertilisation and Embryology Act 1990, s 35(4).

Sub-s (6): outside the scope of this work.

5 Crown application

This Act binds the Crown.

6 Citation and extent

(1)   This Act may be cited as the Congenital Disabilities (Civil Liability) Act 1976.

(2)   This Act extends to Northern Ireland but not to Scotland.

Fatal Accidents Act 1976

(c 30)

An Act to consolidate the Fatal Accidents Acts

[22 July 1976]

[1 Right of action for wrongful act causing death

(1)   If death is caused by any wrongful act, neglect or default which is such as would (if death had not ensued) have entitled the person injured to maintain an action and recover damages in respect thereof, the person

who would have been liable if death had not ensued shall be liable to an action for damages, notwithstanding the death of the person injured.

(2)   Subject to section 1A(2) below, every such action shall be for the benefit of the dependants of the person ("the deceased") whose death has been so caused.

(3)   In this Act "dependant" means—
  (a) the wife or husband or former wife or husband of the deceased;
  (b) any person who—
     (i)   was living with the deceased in the same household immediately before the date of the death; and
     (ii) had been living with the deceased in the same household for at least two years before that date; and
     (iii) was living during the whole of that period as the husband or wife of the deceased;
  (c) any parent or other ascendant of the deceased;
  (d) any person who was treated by the deceased as his parent;
  (e) any child or other descendant of the deceased;
  (f) any person (not being a child of the deceased) who, in the case of any marriage to which the deceased was at any time a party, was treated by the deceased as a child of the family in relation to that marriage;
  (g) any person who is, or is the issue of, a brother, sister, uncle or aunt of the deceased.

(4)   The reference to the former wife or husband of the deceased in subsection (3)(a) above includes a reference to a person whose marriage to the deceased has been annulled or declared void as well as a person whose marriage to the deceased has been dissolved.

(5)   In deducing any relationship for the purposes of subsection (3) above—
  (a) any relationship of affinity shall be treated as a relationship by consanguinity, any relationship of the half blood as a relationship of the whole blood, and the stepchild of any person as his child, and
  (b) an illegitimate person shall be treated as the legitimate child of his mother and reputed father.

(6)   Any reference in this Act to injury includes any disease and any impairment of a person's physical or mental condition.]

NOTES

Substituted, together with ss 1A, 2–4, for original ss 1–4, by the Administration of Justice Act 1982, s 3.

[1A Bereavement

(1)   An action under this Act may consist of or include a claim for damages for bereavement.

(2)   A claim for damages for bereavement shall only be for the benefit—
    (a) of the wife or husband of the deceased; and
    (b) where the deceased was a minor who was never married—
        (i)   of his parents, if he was legitimate; and
        (ii) of his mother, if he was illegitimate.

(3)   Subject to subject (5) below, the sum to be awarded as damages under this section shall be [£7,500].

(4)   Where there is a claim for damages under this section for the benefit of both the parents of the deceased, the sum awarded shall be divided equally between them (subject to any deduction falling to be made in respect of costs not recovered from the defendant).

(5)   The Lord Chancellor may by order made by statutory instrument, subject to annulment in pursuance of a resolution of either House of Parliament, amend this section by varying the sum for the time being specified in subsection (3) above.]

NOTES

Substituted as noted to s 1 at **[173]**.
Sub-s (3): sum in square brackets substituted by the Damages for Bereavement (Variation of Sum) (England and Wales) Order 1990, SI 1990/2575, art 2.

[2 Persons entitled to bring the action

(1)   The action shall be brought by and in the name of the executor or administrator of the deceased.

(2)   If—
    (a) there is no executor or administrator of the deceased, or
    (b) no action is brought within six months after the death by and in the name of an executor or administrator of the deceased,

the action may be brought by and in the name of all or any of the persons for whose benefit an executor or administrator could have brought it.

(3)   Not more than one action shall lie for and in respect of the same subject matter of complaint.

(4)   The plaintiff in the action shall be required to deliver to the defendant or his solicitor full particulars of the persons for whom and on whose behalf the action is brought and of the nature of the claim in respect of which damages are sought to be recovered.]

NOTES

Substituted as noted to s 1.

[3   Assessment of damages

(1)   In the action such damages, other than damages for bereavement, may be awarded as are proportioned to the injury resulting   from the death to the dependants respectively.

(2)   After deducting the costs not recovered from the defendant any amount recovered otherwise than as damages for bereavement shall be divided among the dependants in such shares as may be directed.

(3)   In an action under this Act where there fall to be assessed damages payable to a widow in respect of the death of her husband there shall not be taken account the re- marriage of the widow or her prospects of re-marriage.

(4)   In an action under this Act where there fall to be assessed damages payable to a person who is a dependant by virtue of section 1(3)(b) above in respect of the death of the person with whom the dependant was living as husband   or wife there shall be taken into account (together with any other matter that appears to the court to be relevant to the action) the fact that the dependant had no enforceable right to financial support by the deceased as a result of their living together.

(5)   If the dependants have incurred funeral expenses in respect of the deceased, damages may be awarded in respect of those expenses.

(6)   Money paid into court in satisfaction of a cause of action under this Act may be in one sum without specifying any person's share.]

NOTES

Substituted as noted to s 1.

[4 Assessment of damages: disregard of benefits

In assessing damages in respect of a person's death in an action under this Act, benefits which have accrued or will or may accrue to any person from his estate or otherwise as a result of his death shall be disregarded.]

NOTES

Substituted as noted to s 1.

5 Contributory negligence

Where any person dies as the result partly of his own fault and partly of the fault of any other person or persons, and accordingly if an action were brought for the benefit of the estate under the Law Reform (Miscellaneous Provisions) Act 1934 the damages recoverable would be reduced under section 1(1) of the Law Reform (Contributory Negligence) Act 1945, any damages recoverable in an action . . . under this Act shall be reduced to a proportionate extent.

NOTES

Words omitted repealed by the Administration of Justice Act 1982, s 3(2), s 75, Sch 9, Pt I.

7 Short title, etc

(1)   This Act may be cited as the Fatal Accidents Act 1976.

(2)   This Act shall come into force on 1st September 1976, but shall not apply to any cause of action arising on a death before it comes into force.

(3)   This Act shall not extend to Scotland or Northern Ireland.

Legitimacy Act 1976

(C 31)

An Act to consolidate certain enactments relating to legitimacy
[22 July 1976]

1 Legitimacy of children of certain void marriages

(1)   The child of a void marriage, whenever born, shall, subject to subsection (2) below and Schedule 1 to this Act, be treated as the legitimate child of his parents if at the time of [the insemination resulting in the birth, or where there was no such insemination, the child's conception] (or at the time of the celebration of the marriage if later) both or either of the parties reasonably believed that the marriage was valid.

(2)   This section only applies where the father of the child was domiciled in England and Wales at the time of the birth or, if he died before the birth, was so domiciled immediately before his death.

[(3)   It is hereby declared for the avoidance of doubt that subsection (1) above applies notwithstanding that the belief that the marriage was valid was due to a mistake as to law.

(4)   In relation to a child born after the coming into force of section 28 of the Family Law Reform Act 1987, it shall be presumed for the purposes of subsection (1) above, unless the contrary is shown, that one of the parties to the void marriage reasonably believed at the time of the insemination resulting in the birth or, where there was no such insemination, the child's conception (or at the time of the celebration of the marriage if later) that the marriage was valid.]

NOTES

Sub-s (1): words in square brackets substituted by the Family Law Reform Act 1987, s 28(1), Sch 3, para 1.

Sub-ss (3), (4): added by the Family Law Reform Act 1987, s 28(2), Sch 3, para 1.

2 Legitimation by subsequent marriage of parents

Subject to the following provisions of this Act, where the parents of an illegitimate person marry one another, the marriage shall, if the father of the illegitimate person is at the date of marriage domiciled in England and Wales, render that person, if living, legitimate from the date of the marriage.

3 Legitimation by extraneous law

Subject to the following provisions of this Act, where the parents of an illegitimate person marry one another and the father of the illegitimate person is not at the time of the marriage domiciled in England and Wales but is domiciled in a country by the law of which the illegitimate person became legitimated by virtue of such subsequent marriage, that person, if living, shall in England and Wales be recognised as having been so legitimated from the date of the marriage notwithstanding that, at the time of his birth, his father was domiciled in a country the law of which did not permit legitimation by subsequent marriage.

4   Legitimation of adopted child

(1)   [Section 39 of the Adoption Act 1976] does not prevent an adopted child being legitimated under section 2 or 3 above if either natural parent is the sole adoptive parent.

(2)   Where an adopted child (with a sole adoptive parent) is legitimated—
  (a) [subsection (2) of the said section 39] shall not apply after the legitimation to the natural relationship with the other natural parent, and
  (b) revocation of the adoption order in consequence of the legitimation shall not affect [section 39, 41 or 42 of the Adoption Act 1976] as it applies to any instrument made before the date of legitimation.

NOTES

Words in square brackets substituted by the Adoption Act 1976, s 73(2), Sch 3, para 23.

5   Rights of legitimated persons and others to take interests in property

(1)   Subject to any contrary indication, the rules of construction contained in this section apply to any instrument other than an existing instrument, so far as the instrument contains a disposition of property.

(2)   For the purposes of this section, provisions of the law of intestate succession applicable to the estate of a deceased person shall be treated as if contained in an instrument executed by him (while of full capacity) immediately before his death.

(3)   A legitimated person, and any other person, shall be entitled to take any interest as if the legitimated person had been born legitimate.

(4)   A disposition which depends on the date of birth of a child or children of the parent or parents shall be construed as if—

    (a) a legitimated child had been born on the date of legitimation,

    (b) two or more legitimated children legitimated on the same date had been born on that date in the order of their actual births,

but this does not affect any reference to the age of a child.

(5)   Examples of phrases in wills on which subsection (4) above can operate are—

    1. Children of A "living at my death or born afterwards".

    2. Children of A "living at my death or born afterwards before any one of such children for the time being in existence attains a vested interest, and who attain the age of 21 years".

    3. As in example 1 or 2, but referring to grandchildren of A, instead of children of A.

    4. A for life "until he has a child" and then to his child or children.

Note. Subsection (4) above will not affect the reference to the age of 21 years in example 2.

(6)   If an illegitimate person or a person adopted by one of his natural parents dies, or has died before the commencement of this Act, and—

    (a) after his death his parents marry or have married; and

    (b) the deceased would, if living at the time of the marriage, have become a legitimated person,

this section shall apply for the construction of the instrument so far as it relates to the taking of interests by, or in succession to, his spouse, children and remoter issue as if he had been legitimated by virtue of the marriage.

(7)   In this section "instrument" includes a private Act settling property, but not any other enactment.

6   Dispositions depending on date of birth

(1)   Where a disposition depends on the date of birth of a child who was born illegitimate and who is legitimated (or, if deceased, is treated as legitimated), section 5(4) above does not affect entitlement under Part II of the Family Law Reform Act 1969 (illegitimate children).

(2)   Where a disposition depends on the date of birth of an adopted child who is legitimated (or, if deceased, is treated as legitimated) section 5(4)

above does not affect entitlement by virtue of [section 42(2) of the Adoption Act 1976].

(3)   This section applies for example where—
   (a) a testator dies in 1976 bequeathing a legacy to his eldest grandchild living at a specified time,
   (b) a daughter has an illegitimate child in 1977 who is the first grandchild,
   (c) his married son has a child in 1978,
   (d) subsequently the illegitimate child is legitimated,

and in all those cases the daughter's child remains the eldest grandchild of the testator throughout.

NOTES

Sub-s (2): words in square brackets substituted by the Adoption Act 1976, s 73(2), Sch 3, para 24.

7   Protection of trustees and personal representatives

(1)   A trustee or personal representative is not under a duty, by virtue of the law relating to trusts or the administration of estates, to enquire, before conveying or distributing any property, whether any person is illegitimate or has been adopted by one of his natural parents, and could be legitimated (or if deceased be treated as legitimated), if that fact could affect entitlement to the property.

(2)   A trustee or personal representative shall not be liable to any person by reason of a conveyance or distribution of the property made without regard to any such fact if he has not received notice of the fact before the conveyance or distribution.

(3)   This section does not prejudice the right of a person to follow the property, or any property representing it, into the hands of another person, other than a purchaser, who has received it.

8   Personal rights and obligations

A legitimated person shall have the same rights, and shall be under the same obligations in respect of the maintenance and support of himself or of any other person as if he had been born legitimate, and, subject to the provisions of this Act, the provisions of any Act relating to claims for damages, compensation, allowance, benefit or otherwise by or in respect of a legitimate child shall apply in like manner in the case of a legitimated person.

9 Re-registration of birth of legitimated persons

(1) It shall be the duty of the parents of a legitimated person or, in cases where re-registration can be effected on information furnished by one parent and one of the parents is dead, of the surviving parent to furnish to the Registrar General information with a view to obtaining the re-registration of the birth of that person within 3 months after the date of the marriage by virtue of which he was legitimated.

(2) The failure of the parents of either of them to furnish information as required by subsection (1) above in respect of any legitimated person shall not affect the legitimation of that person.

(3) This section does not apply in relation to a person who was legitimated otherwise than by virtue of the subsequent marriage of his parents.

(4) Any parent who fails to give information as required by this section shall be liable on summary conviction to a fine not exceeding [level 1 on the standard scale].

NOTES

Sub-s (4): maximum fine increased and converted to a level on the standard scale by the Criminal Justice Act 1982, ss 37, 38, 46.

10 Interpretation

(1) In this Act, except where the context otherwise requires,—
   "disposition" includes the conferring of a power of appointment and any other disposition of an interest in or right over property;
   "existing", in relation to an instrument, means one made before 1st January 1976;
   "legitimated person" means a person legitimated or recognised as legitimated—
      (a) under section 2 or 3 above; or
      (b) under section 1 or 8 of the Legitimacy Act 1926; or
      (c) except in section 8, by a legitimation (whether or not by virtue of the subsequent marriage of his parents) recognised by the

law of England and Wales and effected under the law of any other country;

and cognate expressions shall be construed accordingly;

"power of appointment" includes any discretionary power to transfer a beneficial interest in property without the furnishing of valuable consideration;

"void marriage" means a marriage, not being voidable only, in respect of which the High Court has or had jurisdiction to grant a decree of nullity, or would have or would have had such jurisdiction if the parties were domiciled in England and Wales.

(2)   For the purposes of this Act "legitimated person" includes, where the context admits, a person legitimated, or recognised as legitimated, before the passing of the Children Act 1975.

(3)   For the purpose of this Act, except where the context otherwise requires,—
   (a) the death of the testator is the date at which a will or codicil is to be regarded as made;
   (b) an oral disposition of property shall be deemed to be contained in an instrument made when the disposition was made.

(4)   . . .

(5)   Except in so far as the context otherwise requires, any reference in this Act to an enactment shall be construed as a reference to that enactment as amended by or under any other enactment, including this Act.

NOTES

Sub-s (4): repealed by the Trusts of Land and Appointment of Trustees Act 1996, s 25(2), Sch 4, subject to savings in s 25(4), (5) thereof.

12   Short title, commencement and extent

(1)   This Act may be cited as the Legitimacy Act 1976.

(2)   This Act shall come into force at the end of the period of one month beginning with the date on which it is passed.

(3)   This Act does not extend to Scotland or to Northern Ireland.

Adoption Act 1976

(C 36)

An Act to consolidate the enactments having effect in England and Wales in relation to adoption

[22 July 1976]

PART I
THE ADOPTION SERVICE

The Adoption Service

1 Establishment of Adoption Service

(1)   It is the duty of every local authority to establish and maintain within their area a service designed to meet the needs, in relation to adoption, of—

(a) children who have been or may be adopted,

(b) parents and guardians of such children, and

(c) persons who have adopted or may adopt a child,

and for that purpose to provide the requisite facilities, or secure that they are provided by approved adoption societies.

(2)   The facilities to be provided as part of the service maintained under subsection (1) include—

(a) temporary board and lodging where needed by pregnant women, mothers or children;

(b) arrangements for assessing children and prospective adopters, and placing children for adoption;

(c) counselling for persons with problems relating to adoption.

(3)   The facilities of the service maintained under subsection (1) shall be provided in conjunction with the local authority's other social services and with approved adoption societies in their area, so that help may be given in a co-ordinated manner without duplication, omission or avoidable delay.

(4)   The services maintained by local authorities under subsection (1) may be collectively referred to as "the Adoption Service", and a local authority or approved adoption society may be referred to as an adoption agency.

2 Local authorities' social services

The social services referred to in section 1(3) are the functions of a local authority which stand referred to the authority's social services committee, including, in particular but without prejudice to the generality of the foregoing, a local authority's functions—

[(a) under the Children Act 1989, relating to family assistance orders, local authority support for children and families, care and supervision and emergency protection of children, community homes, voluntary homes and organisations, registered children's homes, private arrangements for fostering children, child minding and day care for young children and children accommodated by [Health Authorities, Special Health Authorities,] [National Health Service trusts] and local education authorities or in residential care, nursing or mental nursing homes or in independent schools; and

(b) under the National Health Service Act 1977, relating to the provision of care for expectant and nursing mothers.]

NOTES

Paras (a), (b) substituted by the Children Act 1989, s 88, Sch 10, para 1; words in first pair of square brackets in para (a) substituted by the Health Authorities Act 1995, s 2(1), Sch 1, para 101; words in second pair of square brackets inserted by the National Health Service and Community Care Act 1990, s 66(1), Sch 9, para 17.

Adoption societies

3 Approval of adoption societies

(1)   Subject to regulations under section 9(1), a body [which is a voluntary organisation and desires] to act as an adoption society or, if it is already an adoption society, [desires] to continue to act as such may, in the manner specified by regulations made by the Secretary of State, apply to the Secretary of State for his approval to its doing so.

(2)   On an application under subsection (1), the Secretary of State shall take into account the matters relating to the applicant specified in subsections (3) to (5) and any other relevant considerations, and if, but only if, he is satisfied that the applicant is likely to make, or, if the applicant is an approved adoption society, is making, an effective contribution to the Adoption Service he shall by notice to the applicant give his approval, which

shall be operative from a date specified in the notice or, in the case of a renewal of approval, from the date of the notice.

(3)   In considering the application, the Secretary of State shall have regard, in relation to the period for which approval is sought, to the following—
    (a) the applicant's adoption programme, including, in particular, its ability to make provision for children who are free for adoption
    (b) the number and qualifications of its staff,
    (c) its financial resources, and
    (d) the organisation and control of its operations.

(4)   Where it appears to the Secretary of State that the applicant is likely to operate extensively within the area of a particular local authority he shall ask the authority whether they support the application, and shall take account of any views about it put to him by the authority.

(5)   Where the applicant is already an approved adoption society or, whether before or after the passing of this Act, previously acted as an adoption society, the Secretary of State, in considering the application, shall also have regard to the record and reputation of the applicant in the adoption field, and the areas within which and the scale on which it is currently operating or has operated in the past.

(6)   If after considering the application the Secretary of State is not satisfied that the applicant is likely to make or, as the case may be, is making an effective contribution to the Adoption Service, the Secretary of State shall, subject to section 5(1) and (2), by notice inform the applicant that its application is refused.

(7)   If not withdrawn earlier under section 4, approval given under this section shall last for a period of three years from the date on which it becomes operative, and shall then expire or, in the case of an approved adoption society whose further application for approval is pending at that time, shall expire on the date that application is granted or, as the case may be, refused.

NOTES

Sub-s (1): words in square brackets substituted by the Health and Social Services and Social Security Adjudications Act 1983, s 9, Sch 2, para 29.

Welfare of children

6 Duty to promote welfare of children

In reaching any decision relating to the adoption of a child a court or adoption agency shall have regard to all the circumstances, first consideration being given to the need to safeguard and promote, the welfare of the child throughout his childhood; and shall so far as practicable ascertain the wishes and feelings of the child regarding the decision and give due consideration to them, having regard to his age and understanding.

7 Religious upbringing of adopted child

An adoption agency shall in placing a child for adoption have regard (so far as is practicable) to any wishes of a child's parents and guardians as to the religious upbringing of the child.

Supplemental

11 Restriction on arranging adoptions and placing of children

(1)   A person other than an adoption agency shall not make arrangements for the adoption of a child, or place a child for adoption, unless—
   (a) the proposed adopter is a relative of the child, or
   (b) he is acting in pursuance of an order of the High Court.

[(2)   An adoption society which is—
   (a) approved as respects Scotland under section 3 of the Adoption (Scotland) Act 1978; or
   (b) registered as respects Northern Ireland under Article 4 of the Adoption (Northern Ireland) Order 1987,

but which is not approved under section 3 of this Act, shall not act as an adoption society in England and Wales except to the extent that the society considers it necessary to do so in the interests of a person mentioned in section 1 of the Act of 1978 or Article 3 of the Order of 1987.]

(3)   A person who—
   (a) takes part in the management or control of a body of persons which exists wholly or partly for the purpose of making arrangements for the adoption of children and which is not an adoption agency; or

(b) contravenes subsection (1) or

(c) receives a child placed with him in contravention of subsection (1),

shall be guilty of an offence and liable on summary conviction to imprisonment for a term not exceeding 3 months or to a fine not exceeding [level 5 on the standard scale] or to both.

(4)   In any proceedings for an offence under paragraph (a) of subsection (3), proof of things done or of words written, spoken or published (whether or not in the presence of any party to the proceedings) by any person taking part in the management or control of a body of persons, or in making arrangements for the adoption of children on behalf of the body, shall be admissible as evidence of the purpose for which that body exists.

(5)   . . .

NOTES

Sub-s (2): substituted by the Children Act 1989, s 88, Sch 10, para 2.

Sub-s (3): maximum fine increased and converted to a level on the standard scale by the Criminal Justice Act 1982, ss 37, 38, 46.

Sub-s (5): repealed by the Children Act 1989, s 108(7), Sch 15.

PART II
ADOPTION ORDERS

The making of adoption orders

12 Adoption orders

(1)   An adoption order is an order [giving parental responsibility for a child to] the adopters, made on their application by an authorised court.

(2)   The order does not affect [parental responsibility so far as it relates] to any period before the making of the order.

(3)   The making of an adoption order operates to extinguish—
   [(a) the parental responsibility which any person has for the child immediately before the making of the order;
   (aa) any order under the Children Act 1989]; and
   (b) any duty arising by virtue of an agreement or the order of a court to make payments, so far as the payments are in respect of the

child's maintenance [or upbringing for any period after the making of the order.]

(4)   Subsection (3)(b) does not apply to a duty arising by virtue of an agreement—
(a) which constitutes a trust, or
(b) which expressly provides that the duty is not to be extinguished by the making of an adoption order.

(5)   An adoption order may not be made in relation to a child who is or has been married.

(6)   An adoption order may contain such terms and conditions as the court thinks fit.

(7)   An adoption order may be made notwithstanding that the child is already an adopted child.

NOTES

Sub-ss (1)–(3): words in square brackets substituted by the Children Act 1989, s 88, Sch 10, para 3.

13   Child to live with adopters before order is made

(1)   Where—
(a) the applicant, or one of the applicants, is a parent, step-parent or relative of the child, or
(b) the child was placed with the applicants by an adoption agency or in pursuance of an order of the High Court,

an adoption order shall not be made unless the child is at least 19 weeks old and at all times during the preceding 13 weeks had his home with the applicants or one of them.

(2)   Where subsection (1) does not apply, an adoption order shall not be made unless the child is at least 12 months old and at all times during the preceding 12 months had his home with the applicants or one of them.

(3)   An adoption order shall not be made unless the court is satisfied that sufficient opportunities to see the child with the applicant or, in the case of an application by a married couple, both applicants together in the home environment have been afforded—

    (a) where the child was placed with the applicant by an adoption agency, to that agency, or

    (b) in any other case, to the local authority within whose area the home is.

14 Adoption by married couple

[(1)   An adoption order shall not be made on the application of more than one person except in the circumstances specified in subsections (1A) and (1B).

(1A)   An adoption order may be made on the application of a married couple where both the husband and the wife have attained the age of 21 years.

(1B)   An adoption order may be made on the application of a married couple where—

    (a) the husband or the wife—

       (i) is the father or mother of the child; and

      (ii) has attained the age of 18 years;

and

    (b) his or her spouse has attained the age of 21 years.]

(2)   An adoption order shall not be made on the application of a married couple unless—

    (a) at least one of them is domiciled in a part of the United Kingdom, or in the Channel Islands or the Isle of Man, or

    (b) the application is for a Convention adoption order and section 17 is complied with.

(3)   . . .

NOTES

Sub-ss (1), (1A), (1B): substituted, for sub-s (1) as originally enacted, by the Children Act 1989, s 88, Sch 10, para 4.

Sub-s (3): repealed by the Children Act 1989, s 108(7), Sch 15.

15 Adoption by one person

(1)   . . . an adoption order may be made on the application of one person where he has attained the age of 21 years and—

(a) is not married, or
(b) is married and the court is satisfied that—
    (i) his spouse cannot be found, or
    (ii) the spouses have separated and are living apart, and the separation is likely to be permanent, or
    (iii) his spouse is by reason of ill-health, whether physical or mental, incapable of making an application for an adoption order.

(2) An adoption order shall not be made on the application of one person unless—
(a) he is domiciled in a part of the United Kingdom, or in the Channel Islands or the Isle of Man, or
(b) the application is for a Convention adoption order and section 17 is complied with.

(3) An adoption order shall not be made on the application of the mother or father of the child alone unless the court is satisfied that—
(a) the other natural parent is dead or cannot be found [or, by virtue of section 28 of the Human Fertilisation and Embryology Act 1990, there is no other parent], or
(b) there is some other reason justifying the exclusion of the other natural parent,

and where such an order is made the reason justifying the exclusion of the other natural parent shall be recorded by the court.

(4) . . .

NOTES

Sub-s (1): words omitted repealed by the Children Act 1989, s 108(7), Sch 15.
Sub-s (3): words in square brackets inserted by the Human Fertilisation and Embryology Act 1990, s 49, Sch 4, para 4.
Sub-s (4): repealed by the Children Act 1989, s 108(7), Sch 15.

16 Parental agreement

(1) An adoption order shall not be made unless—
(a) the child is free for adoption by virtue of an order made—
    [(i) in England and Wales, under section 18;
    (ii) in Scotland, under section 18 of the Adoption (Scotland) Act 1978; or
    (iii) in Northern Ireland, under Article 17(1) or 18(1) of the Adoption (Northern Ireland) Order 1987]; or

(b) in the case of each parent or guardian of the child the court is satisfied that—

    (i) he freely, and with full understanding of what is involved, agrees unconditionally to the making of an adoption order (whether or not he knows the identity of the applicants), or

    (ii) his agreement to the making of the adoption order should be dispensed with on a ground specified in subsection (2).

(2)   The grounds mentioned in subsection (1)(b)(ii) are that the parent or guardian—

(a) cannot be found or is incapable of giving agreement;

(b) is withholding his agreement unreasonably;

(c) has persistently failed without reasonable cause to discharge [his parental responsibility for] the child;

(d) has abandoned or neglected the child;

(e) has persistently ill-treated the child;

(f) has seriously ill-treated the child (subject to subsection (5)).

(3)   Subsection (1) does not apply in any case where the child is not a United Kingdom national and the application for the adoption order is for a Convention adoption order.

(4)   Agreement is ineffective for the purposes of subsection (1)(b)(i) if given by the mother less than six weeks after the child's birth.

(5)   Subsection (2)(f) does not apply unless (because of the ill-treatment or for other reasons) the rehabilitation of the child within the household of the parent or guardian is unlikely.

NOTES

Sub-ss (1), (2): words in square brackets substituted by the Children Act 1989, s 88, Sch 10, para 5.

17 Convention adoption orders

(1)   An adoption order shall be made as a Convention adoption order if the application is for a Convention adoption order and the following conditions are satisfied both at the time of the application and when the order is made.

(2)   The child—

(a) must be a United Kingdom national or a national of a Convention country, and

    (b) must habitually reside in British territory or a Convention country.

(3)   The applicant or applicants and the child must not all be United Kingdom nationals living in British territory.

(4)   If the application is by a married couple, either—
    (a) each must be a United Kingdom national or a national of a Convention country, and both must habitually reside in Great Britain, or
    (b) both must be United Kingdom nationals, and each must habitually reside in British territory or a Convention country,

and if the applicants are nationals of the same Convention country the adoption must not be prohibited by a specified provision (as defined in subsection (8)) of the internal law of that country.

(5)   If the application is by one person, either—
    (a) he must be a national of a Convention country, and must habitually reside in Great Britain, or
    (b) he must be a United Kingdom national and must habitually reside in British territory or a Convention country,

and if he is a national of a Convention country the adoption must not be prohibited by a specified provision (as defined in subsection (8)) of the internal law of that country.

(6)   If the child is not a United Kingdom national the order shall not be made—
    (a) except in accordance with the provisions, if any, relating to consents and consultations of the internal law relating to adoption of the Convention country of which the child is a national, and
    (b) unless the court is satisfied that each person who consents to the order in accordance with that internal law does so with full understanding of what is involved.

(7)   The reference to consents and consultations in subsection (6) does not include a reference to consent by and consultation with the applicant and members of the applicant's family (including his or her spouse), and for the purposes of subsection (6) consents may be proved in the manner prescribed by rules and the court shall be treated as the authority by whom, under the law mentioned in subsection (6), consents may be dispensed with and the adoption in question may be effected; and where the provisions there mentioned require the attendance before that authority of any person who does not reside in Great Britain, that requirement shall be treated as satisfied for the purposes of subsection (6) if—

    (a) that person has been given a reasonable opportunity of communicating his opinion on the adoption in question to the proper officer or clerk of the court, or to an appropriate authority of the country in question, for transmission to the court; and

    (b) where he has availed himself of that opportunity, his opinion has been transmitted to the court.

(8)   In subsections (4) and (5) "specified provision" means a provision specified in an order of the Secretary of State as one notified to the Government of the United Kingdom in pursuance of the provisions of the Convention which relate to prohibitions on an adoption contained in the national law of the Convention country in question.

Freeing for adoption

18 Freeing child for adoption

(1)   Where, on an application by an adoption agency, an authorised court is satisfied in the case of each parent or guardian of the child that—

    (a) he freely, and with full understanding of what is involved, agrees generally and unconditionally to the making of an adoption order, or

    (b) his agreement to the making of an adoption order should be dispensed with on a ground specified in section 16(2),

the court shall make an order declaring the child free for adoption.

(2)   No application shall be made under subsection (1) unless—

    (a) it is made with the consent of a parent or guardian of a child, or

    (b) the adoption agency is applying for dispensation under subsection (1)(b) of the agreement of each parent or guardian of the child, and the child is in the care of the adoption agency.

[(2A) For the purposes of subsection (2) a child is in the care of an adoption agency if the adoption agency is a local authority and he is in their care.]

(3)   No agreement required under subsection (1)(a) shall be dispensed with under subsection (1)(b) unless the child is already placed for adoption or the court is satisfied that it is likely that the child will be placed for adoption.

(4)   An agreement by the mother of the child is ineffective for the purposes of this section if given less than 6 weeks after the child's birth.

(5)   On the making of an order under this section, [parental responsibility for the child is given to] the adoption agency, and subsections (2) [to (4)] of section 12 apply as if the order were an adoption order and the agency were the adopters.

(6)   Before making an order under this section, the court shall satisfy itself, in relation to each parent or guardian [of the child who can be found], that he has been given an opportunity of making, if he so wishes, a declaration that he prefers not to be involved in future questions concerning the adoption of the child; and any such declaration shall be recorded by the court.

[(7)   Before making an order under this section in the case of a child whose father does not have parental responsibility for him, the court shall satisfy itself in relation to any person claiming to be the father that—
   (a) he has no intention of applying for—
      (i) an order under section 4(1) of the Children Act 1989, or
      (ii) a residence order under section 10 of that Act, or
   (b) if he did make any such application, it would be likely to be refused.]

[(8)   Subsections (5) and (7) of section 12 apply in relation to the making of an order under this section as they apply in relation to the making of an order under that section.]

    Sub-s (2A): inserted by the Children Act 1989, s 88, Sch 10, para 6(1).
    Sub-s (5): words in square brackets substituted by the Children Act 1989, s 88, Sch 10, para 6(2).
    Sub-s (6): words in square brackets substituted by the Health and Social Services and Social Security Adjudications Act 1983, s 9, Sch 2, para 31.
    Sub-s (7): substituted by the Children Act 1989, s 88, Sch 10, para 6(3).
    Sub-s (8): added by the Family Law Reform Act 1987, s 33(1), Sch 2, para 67; substituted by the Children Act 1989, s 88, Sch 10, para 6(3).

19 Progress reports to former parents

(1)   This section and section 20 apply to any person ("the former parent"), who was required to be given an opportunity of making a declaration under section 18(6) but did not do so.

(2)   Within the 14 days following the date 12 months after the making of the order under section 18 the adoption agency [to which parental responsibility was given] on the making of the order, unless it has previously

by notice to the former parent informed him that an adoption order has been made in respect of the child, shall by notice to the former parent inform him—

    (a) whether an adoption order has been made in respect of the child, and (if not)

    (b) whether the child has his home with a person with whom he has been placed for adoption.

(3)   If at the time when the former parent is given notice under subsection (2) an adoption order has not been made in respect of the child, it is thereafter the duty of the adoption agency to give notice to the former parent of the making of an adoption order (if and when made), and meanwhile to give the former parent notice whenever the child is placed for adoption or ceases to have his home with a person with whom he has been placed for adoption.

(4)   If at any time the former parent by notice makes a declaration to the adoption agency that he prefers not to be involved in future questions concerning the adoption of the child—

    (a) the agency shall secure that the declaration is recorded by the court which made the order under section 18, and

    (b) the agency is released from the duty of complying further with subsection (3) as respects that former parent.

NOTES

Sub-s (2): words in square brackets substituted by the Children Act 1989, s 88, Sch 10, para 7.

20   Revocation of s 18 order

(1)   The former parent, at any time more than 12 months after the making of the order under section 18 when—

    (a) no adoption order has been made in respect of the child, and

    (b) the child does not have his home with a person with whom he has been placed for adoption,

may apply to the court which made the order for a further order revoking it on the ground that he wishes to resume [parental responsibility].

(2)   While the application is pending the adoption agency having [parental responsibility] shall not place the child for adoption without the leave of the court.

[(3)   The revocation of an order under section 18 ("a section 18 order") operates—

(a) to extinguish the parental responsibility given to the adoption agency under the section 18 order;

(b) to give parental responsibility for the child to—

(i)   the child's mother; and

(ii) where the child's father and mother were married to each other at the time of his birth, the father; and

(c) to revive—

(i)   any parental responsibility agreement,

(ii)   any order under section 4(1) of the Children Act 1989, and

(iii) any appointment of a guardian in respect of the child (whether made by a court or otherwise),

extinguished by the making of the section 18 order.

(3A)   Subject to subsection (3)(c), the revocation does not—

(a) operate to revive—

(i)   any order under the Children Act 1989, or

(ii) any duty referred to in section 12(3)(b),

extinguished by the making of the section 18 order; or

(b) affect any person's parental responsibility so far as it relates to the period between the making of the section 18 order and the date of revocation of that order.]

(4)   Subject to subsection (5), if the application is dismissed on the ground that to allow it would contravene the principle embodied in section 6—

(a) the former parent who made the application shall not be entitled to make any further application under subsection (1) in respect of the child, and

(b) the adoption agency is released from the duty of complying further with section 19(3) as respects that parent.

(5)   Subsection (4)(a) shall not apply where the court which dismissed the application gives leave to the former parent to make a further application under subsection (1), but such leave shall not be given unless it appears to the court that because of a change in circumstances or for any other reason it is proper to allow the application to be made.

NOTES

Sub-ss (1), (2): words in square brackets substituted by the Children Act 1989, s 88, Sch 10, para 8(1).

Sub-ss (3), (3A): substituted, for sub-s (3) as originally enacted, by the Children Act 1989, s 88, Sch 10, para 8(2).

[21 Variation of section 18 order so as to substitute one adoption agency for another

(1)   On an application to which this section applies, an authorised court may vary an order under section 18 so as to give parental responsibility for the child to another adoption agency ("the substitute agency") in place of the agency for the time being having parental responsibility for the child under the order ("the existing agency").

(2)   This section applies to any application made jointly by—
  (a) the existing agency; and
  (b) the would-be substitute agency.

(3)   Where an order under section 18 is varied under this section, section 19 shall apply as if the substitute agency had been given responsibility for the child on the making of the order.]

NOTES

Substituted by the Children Act 1989, s 88, Sch 10, para 9.

Supplemental

22 Notification to local authority of adoption application

(1)   An adoption order shall not be made in respect of a child who was not placed with the applicant by an adoption agency unless the applicant has, at least 3 months before the date of the order, given notice to the local authority within whose area he has his home of his intention to apply for the adoption order.

[(1A) An application for such an adoption order shall not be made unless the person wishing to make the application has, within the period of two years preceding the making of the application, given notice as mentioned in subsection (1).

(1B)   In subsections (1) and (1A) the references to the area in which the applicant or person has his home are references to the area in which he has his home at the time of giving the notice.]

(2)   On receipt of such a notice the local authority shall investigate the matter and submit to the court a report of their investigation.

(3)   Under subsection (2), the local authority shall in particular investigate,—
  (a) so far as is practicable, the suitability of the applicant, and any other matters relevant to the operation of section 6 in relation to the application; and
  (b) whether the child was placed with the applicant in contravention of section 11.

(4)   A local authority which [receive] notice under subsection (1) in respect of a child whom the authority know to be [looked after by] another local authority shall, not more than 7 days after the receipt of the notice, inform that other local authority in writing, that they have received the notice.

NOTES

Sub-ss (1A), (1B): inserted by the Children Act 1989, s 88, Sch 10, para 10(1).
Sub-s (4): words in square brackets substituted by the Children Act 1989, s 88, Sch 10, para 10(2).

23   Reports where child placed by agency

Where an application for an adoption order relates to a child placed by an adoption agency, the agency shall submit to the court a report on the suitability of the applicants and any other matters relevant to the operation of section 6, and shall assist the court in any manner the court may direct.

24   Restrictions on making adoption orders

(1)   The court shall not proceed to hear an application for an adoption order in relation to a child where a previous application for a British adoption order made in relation to the child by the same persons was refused by any court unless—
  (a) in refusing the previous application the court directed that this subsection should not apply or
  (b) it appears to the court that because of a change in circumstances or for any other reason it is proper to proceed with the application.

(2)   The court shall not make an adoption order in relation to a child unless it is satisfied that the applicants have not, as respects the child, [contravened] section 57.

Sub-s (2): words in square brackets substituted by the Health and Social Services and Social Security Adjudications Act 1983, s 9, Sch 2, para 32.

25 Interim orders

(1)   Where on an application for an adoption order the requirements of sections 16(1) and 22(1) are complied with, the court may postpone the determination of the application and make an order [giving parental responsibility for the child to] the applicants for a probationary period not exceeding 2 years upon such terms for the maintenance of the child and otherwise as the court thinks fit.

(2)   Where the probationary period specified in an order under subsection (1) is less than 2 years, the court may by a further order extend the period to a duration not exceeding 2 years in all.

NOTES

Sub-s (1): words in square brackets substituted by the Children Act 1989, s 88, Sch 10, para 11.

PART III
CARE AND PROTECTION OF CHILDREN AWAITING ADOPTION

Restrictions on removal of children

27 Restrictions on removal where adoption agreed or application made under s 18

(1)   While an application for an adoption is pending in a case where a parent or guardian of the child has agreed to the making of the adoption order, (whether or not he knows the identity of the applicant), the parent or guardian is not entitled, against the will of the person with whom the child has his home, to remove the child from the [home] of that person except with the leave of the court.

(2)   While an application is pending for an order freeing a child for adoption and—

  (a)   the child is in the care of the adoption agency making the application, and

(b) the application was not made with the consent of each parent or guardian of the child,

no parent or guardian of the child is entitled, against the will of the person with whom the child has his home, to remove the child from the [home] of that person except with the leave of the court.

[(2A) For the purposes of subsection (2) a child is in the care of an adoption agency if the adoption agency is a local authority and he is in their care.]

(3) Any person who contravenes subsection (1) or (2) shall be guilty of an offence and liable on summary conviction to imprisonment for a term not exceeding 3 months or a fine not exceeding [level 5 on the standard scale] or both.

(4), (5)   . . .

NOTES

Sub-ss (1), (2): words in square brackets substituted by the Children Act 1989, s 88, Sch 10, para 12.

Sub-s (2A): inserted by the Children Act 1989, s 88, Sch 10, para 13.

Sub-s (3): maximum fine increased and converted to a level on the standard scale by the Criminal Justice Act 1982, ss 37, 38, 46.

Sub-ss (4), (5): repealed by the Health and Social Services and Social Security Adjudications Act 1983, s 30, Sch 10, Pt I.

28 Restrictions on removal where applicant has provided home for 5 years

(1) While an application for an adoption order in respect of a child made by the person with whom the child has had his home for the 5 years preceding the application is pending, no person is entitled, against the will of the applicant, to remove the child from the applicant's [home] except with the leave of the court or under authority conferred by any enactment or on the arrest of the child.

(2) Where a person ("the prospective adopter") gives notice to the local authority within whose area he has his home that he intends to apply for an adoption order in respect of a child who for the preceding 5 years has had his home with the prospective adopter, no person is entitled, against the will of the prospective adopter, to remove the child from the prospective adopter's [home], except with the leave of a court or under authority conferred by any enactment or on the arrest of the child, before—

(a) the prospective adopter applies for the adoption order, or

(b) the period of 3 months from the receipt of the notice by the local authority expires,

whichever occurs first.

[(2A) The reference in subsections (1) and (2) to any enactment does not include a reference to section 20(8) of the Children Act 1989.]

[(3)   In any case where subsection (1) or (2) applies and—

(a) the child was being looked after by a local authority before he began to have his home with the applicant or, as the case may be, the prospective adopter, and

(b) the child is still being looked after by a local authority,

the authority which are looking after the child shall not remove him from the home of the applicant or the prospective adopter except in accordance with section 30 or 31 or with the leave of a court.]

(4)   In subsections (2) and (3) "a court" means a court with jurisdiction to make adoption orders.

(5)   A local authority which [receive] such notice as is mentioned in subsection (2) in respect of a child whom the authority know to be [looked after by another local authority] shall, not more than 7 days after the receipt of the notice, inform that other authority . . . , in writing, that they have received the notice.

(6)   Subsection (2) does not apply to any further notice served by the prospective adopter on any local authority in respect of the same child during the period referred to in paragraph (b) of that subsection or within 28 days after its expiry.

(7)   Any person who contravenes subsection (1) or (2) shall be guilty of an offence and liable on summary conviction to imprisonment for a term not exceeding 3 months or a fine not exceeding [level 5 on the standard scale] or both.

(8), (9)   . . .

(10)   The Secretary of State may by order amend subsection (1) or (2) to substitute a different period for the period of 5 years mentioned in that subsection (or the period which, by a previous order under this subsection, was substituted for that period).

Sub-ss (1), (2): word in square brackets substituted by the Children Act 1989, s 88, Sch 10, para 12.

Sub-s (2A): inserted by the Children Act 1989, s 88, Sch 10, para 14(1).

Sub-s (3): substituted by the Children Act 1989, s 88, Sch 10, para 14(2).

Sub-s (5): words in square brackets substituted, and words omitted repealed, by the Children Act 1989, ss 88, 108(7), Sch 10, para 14(3), Sch 15.

Sub-s (7): maximum fine increased and converted to levels on the standard scale by the Criminal Justice Act 1982, ss 37, 38, 46.

Sub-ss (8), (9): repealed by the Health and Social Services and Social Security Adjudications Act 1983, s 30, Sch 10, Pt I.

29 Return of child taken away in breach of s 27 or 28

[(1)   An authorised court may, on the application of a person from whose home a child has been removed in breach of—

(a) section 27 or 28,

(b) section 27 or 28 of the Adoption (Scotland) Act 1978, or

(c) Article 28 or 29 of the Adoption (Northern Ireland) Order 1987,

order the person who has so removed the child to return the child to the applicant.

(2)   An authorised court may, on the application of a person who has reasonable grounds for believing that another person is intending to remove a child from his home in breach of—

(a) section 27 or 28,

(b) section 27 or 28 of the Adoption (Scotland) Act 1978, or

(c) Article 28 or 29 of the Adoption (Northern Ireland) Order 1987,

by order direct that other person not to remove the child from the applicant's home in breach of any of those provisions.]

(3)   If, in the case of an order made by the High Court under subsection (1), the High Court or, in the case of an order made by a county court under subsection (1), a county court is satisfied that the child has not been returned to the applicant, the court may make an order authorising an officer of the court to search such premises as may be specified in the order for the child and, if the officer finds the child, to return the child to the applicant.

(4)   If a justice of the peace is satisfied by information on oath that there are reasonable grounds for believing that a child to whom an order under subsection (1) relates is in premises specified in the information, he may

issue a search warrant authorising a constable to search the premises for the child; and if a constable acting in pursuance of a warrant under this section finds the child, he shall return the child to the person on whose application the order under subsection (1) was made.

(5)   An order under subsection (3) may be enforced in like manner as a warrant for committal.

NOTES

Sub-ss (1), (2): substituted by the Children Act 1989, s 88, Sch 10, para 15.

30   Return of children placed for adoption by adoption agencies

(1)   Subject to subsection (2), at any time after a child has been [placed with] any person in pursuance of arrangements made by an adoption agency for the adoption of the child by that person, and before an adoption order has been made on the application of that person in respect of the child,—
  (a) that person may give notice to the agency of his intention not to [give the child a home]; or
  (b) the agency may cause notice to be given to that person of their intention not to allow the child to remain in his [home].

(2)   No notice under paragraph (b) of subsection (1) shall be given in respect of a child in relation to whom an application has been made for an adoption order except with the leave of the court to which the application has been made.

(3)   Where a notice is given to an adoption agency by any person or by an adoption agency to any person under subsection (1), or where an application for an adoption order made by any person in respect of a child placed [with him] by an adoption agency is refused by the court or withdrawn, that person shall, within 7 days after the date on which notice was given or the application refused or withdrawn, as the case may be, cause the child to be returned to the agency, who shall receive the child.

(4)   Where the period specified in an interim order made under section 25 (whether as originally made or as extended under subsection (2) of that section) expires without an adoption order having been made in respect of the child, subsection (3) shall apply as if the application for an adoption order upon which the interim order was made, had been refused at the expiration of that period.

(5)   It shall be sufficient compliance with the requirements of subsection (3) if the child is delivered to, and is received by, a suitable person nominated for the purpose by the adoption agency.

(6)   Where an application for an adoption order is refused the court may, if it thinks fit at any time before the expiry of the period of 7 days mentioned in subsection (3), order that period to be extended to a duration, not exceeding 6 weeks, specified in the order.

(7)   Any person who contravenes the provisions of this section shall be guilty of an offence and liable on summary conviction to imprisonment for a term not exceeding 3 months or to a fine not exceeding [level 5 on the standard scale] or to both; and the court by which the offender is convicted may order the child in respect of whom the offence is committed to be returned to his parent or guardian or to the adoption agency which made the arrangements referred to in subsection (1).

NOTES

Sub-s (1): words in square brackets substituted by the Children Act 1989, s 88, Sch 10, para 16(1).

Sub-s (3): words in square brackets substituted by the Children Act 1989, s 88, Sch 10, para 16(2).

Sub-s (7): maximum fine increased and converted to a level on the standard scale by the Criminal Justice Act 1982, ss 37, 38, 46.

31   Application of s 30 where child not placed for adoption

(1)   Where a person gives notice in pursuance of section 22 (1) to the local authority within whose area he has his home of his intention to apply for an adoption order in respect of a [child—
  (a) who is (when the notice is given) being looked after by a local authority; but
  (b) who was placed with that person otherwise than in pursuance of such arrangements as are mentioned in section 30(1),

that section shall apply as if the child had been placed in pursuance of such arrangements] except that where the application is refused by the court or withdrawn the child need not be returned to the local authority in whose care he is unless that authority so require.

(2)   Where notice of intention is given as aforesaid in respect of any child who is [(when the notice is given) being looked after by] a local

authority then, until the application for an adoption order has been made and disposed of, any right of the local authority to require the child to be returned to them otherwise than in pursuance of section 30 shall be suspended.

(3) While the child [has his home with] the person by whom the notice is given no contribution shall be payable (whether under a contribution order or otherwise) in respect of the child by any person liable under [Part III of Schedule 2 to the Children Act 1989] to make contributions in respect of him (but without prejudice to the recovery of any sum due at the time the notice is given), unless 12 weeks have elapsed since the giving of the notice without the application being made or the application has been refused by the court or withdrawn.

[(4) Nothing in this section affects the right of any person who has parental responsibility for a child to remove him under section 20(8) of the Children Act 1989.]

NOTES

Sub-ss (1), (2): words in square brackets substituted by the Children Act 1989, s 88, Sch 10, para 17(1), (2).

Sub-s (3): words in square brackets substituted by the Children Act 1989, s 88, Sch 10, para 17(3).

Sub-s (4): added by the Children Act 1989, s 88, Sch 10, para 17(4).

Protected children

32 Meaning of "protected child"

(1) Where a person gives notice in pursuance of section 22 (1) to the local authority within whose area he lives of his intention to apply for an adoption order in respect of a child, the child is for the purposes of this Part a protected child while he has his home with that person.

(2) A child shall be deemed to be a protected child for the purposes of this Part if he is a protected child within the meaning of—
   [(a) section 32 of the Adoption (Scotland) Act 1978; or
   (b) Article 33 of the Adoption (Northern Ireland) Order 1987].

(3) A child is not a protected child by reason of any such notice as is mentioned in subsection (1) while—

[(a) he is in the care of any person—
   (i)   in any community home, voluntary home or registered children's home;
  (ii)   in any school in which he is receiving full-time education;
 (iii)   in any health service hospital]; or
[(b) he is—
   (i)   suffering from mental disorder within the meaning of the Mental Health Act 1983; and
  (ii)   resident in a residential care home, within the meaning of Part I of Schedule 4 to the Health and Social Services and Social Security Adjudications Act 1983;] or
(c) he is liable to be detained or subject to guardianship under [the Mental Health Act 1983]
[(d) he is in the care of any person in any home or institution not specified in this subsection but provided, equipped and maintained by the Secretary of State].

[(3A) In subsection (3) "community home", "voluntary home", "registered children's home", "school" and "health service hospital" have the same meaning as in the Children Act 1989.]

[(4)   A protected child ceases to be a protected child—
  (a) on the grant or refusal of the application for an adoption order;
  (b) on the notification to the local authority for the area where the child has his home that the application for an adoption order has been withdrawn;
  (c) in a case where no application is made for an adoption order, on the expiry of the period of two years from the giving of the notice;
  (d) on the making of a residence order, a care order or a supervision order under the Children Act 1989 in respect of the child;
  (e) on the appointment of a guardian for him under that Act;
  (f) on his attaining the age of 18 years; or
  (g) on his marriage,

whichever first occurs.

(5)   In subsection (4)(d) the references to a care order and a supervision order do not include references to an interim care order or interim supervision order.]

NOTES

Sub-s (2): words in square brackets substituted by the Children Act 1989, s 88, Sch 10, para 18(1).

Sub-s (3): para (a) substituted by the Children Act 1989, s 88, Sch 10, para 18(2); para (b) substituted by the Health and Social Services and Social Security Adjudications Act 1983, s 29, Sch 9, para 19; words in square brackets in para (c) substituted by the Mental Health Act 1983, s 148, Sch 4, para 45; para (d) added by the Children Act 1989, s 88, Sch 10, para 18(2).

Sub-s (3A): inserted by the Children Act 1989, s 88, Sch 10, para 18(3).

Sub-ss (4), (5): substituted for original sub-s (4) by the Children Act 1989, s 88, Sch 10, para 18(4).

33 Duty of local authorities to secure well-being of protected children

(1)   It shall be the duty of every local authority to secure that protected children within their area are visited from time to time by officers of the authority, who shall satisfy themselves as to the well-being of the children and give such advice as to their care and maintenance as may appear to be needed.

(2)   Any officer of a local authority authorised to visit protected children may, after producing, if asked to do so, some duly authenticated document showing that he is so authorised, inspect any premises in the area of the authority in which such children are to be or are being kept.

35 Notices and information to be given to local authorities

(1)   Where a person [with whom a protected child has his home] changes his permanent address he shall, not less than 2 weeks before the change, or, if the change is made in an emergency, not later than one week after the change, give notice specifying the new address to the local authority in whose area his permanent address is before the change, and if the new address is in the area of another local authority, the authority to whom the notice is given shall inform that other local authority and give them such of the following particulars as are known to them, that is to say—
  (a) the name, sex and date and place of birth of the child;
  (b) the name and address of every person who is a parent or guardian or acts as a guardian of the child or from whom the child was received.

(2)   If a protected child dies, the person [with whom he had his home] at his death shall within 48 hours give notice of the child's death to the local authority.

Sub-ss (1), (2): words in square brackets substituted by the Children Act 1989, s 88, Sch 10, para 19.

36 Offences relating to protected children

(1)   A person shall be guilty of an offence if—
  (a) being required, under section 35 to give any notice or information, he fails to give the notice within the time specified in that provision or fails to give the information within a reasonable time, or knowingly makes or causes or procures another person to make any false or misleading statement in the notice of information;
  (b) he refuses to allow the visiting of a protected child by a duly authorised officer of a local authority or the inspection, under the power conferred by section 33(2) of any premises;
  (c) . . .

(2)   A person guilty of an offence under this section shall be liable on summary conviction to imprisonment for a term not exceeding 3 months or a fine not exceeding [level 5 on the standard scale] or both.

Sub-s (1): para (c) repealed by the Children Act 1989, s 108(7), Sch 15.
Sub-s (2): maximum fine increased and converted to a level on the standard scale by the Criminal Justice Act 1982, ss 37, 38, 46.

37 Miscellaneous provisions relating to protected children

(1)   . . .

(2)   A person who maintains a protected child shall be deemed for the purposes of the Life Assurance Act 1774 to have no interest in the life of the child.

(3), (4)   . . .

Sub-ss (1), (3), (4): repealed by the Children Act 1989, s 108(7), Sch 15.

PART IV
STATUS OF ADOPTED CHILDREN

38 Meaning of "adoption" in Part IV

(1)   In this Part "adoption" means adoption—
  (a) by an adoption order;
  (b) by an order made under the Children Act 1975, the Adoption Act 1958, the Adoption Act 1950 or any enactment repealed by the Adoption Act 1950;
  (c) by an order made in Scotland, Northern Ireland, the Isle of Man or in any of the Channel Islands;
  (d) which is an overseas adoption; or
  (e) which is an adoption recognised by the law of England and Wales and effected under the law of any other country,

and cognate expressions shall be construed accordingly.

(2)   The definition of adoption includes, where the context admits, an adoption effected before the passing of the Children Act 1975, and the date of an adoption effected by an order is the date of the making of the order.

39 Status conferred by adoption

(1)   An adopted child shall be treated in law—
  (a) where the adopters are a married couple, as if he had been born as a child of the marriage (whether or not he was in fact born after the marriage was solemnized);
  (b) in any other case, as if he had been born to the adopter in wedlock (but not as a child of any actual marriage of the adopter).

(2)   An adopted child shall, subject to subsection (3), be treated in law as if he were not the child of any person other than the adopters or adopter.

(3)   In the case of a child adopted by one of its natural parents as sole adoptive parent, subsection (2) has no effect as respects entitlement to property depending on relationship to that parent, or as respects anything else depending on that relationship.

(4)   It is hereby declared that this section prevents an adopted child from being illegitimate.

(5)   This section has effect—
  (a) in the case of an adoption before 1st January 1976, from that date, and
  (b) in the case of any other adoption, from the date of the adoption.

(6)   Subject to the provisions of this Part, this section—
  (a) applies for the construction of enactments or instruments passed or made before the adoption or later, and so applies subject to any contrary indication; and
  (b) has effect as respects things done, or events occurring, after the adoption, or after 31st December 1975, whichever is the later.

41   Adoptive relatives

(1)   A relationship existing by virtue of section 39 may be referred to as an adoptive relationship, and—
  (a) a male adopter may be referred to as the adoptive father;
  (b) a female adopter may be referred to as the adoptive mother;
  (c) any other relative of any degree under an adoptive relationship may be referred to as an adoptive relative of that degree,

but this section does not prevent the term "parent", or any other term not qualified by the word "adoptive" being treated as including an adoptive relative.

42   Rules of construction for instruments concerning property

(1)   Subject to any contrary indication, the rules of construction contained in this section apply to any instrument, other than an existing instrument, so far as it contains a disposition of property.

(2)   In applying section 39(1) to a disposition which depends on the date of birth of a child or children of the adoptive parent or parents, the disposition shall be construed as if—
  (a) the adopted child had been born on the date of adoption,
  (b) two or more children adopted on the same date had been born on that date in the order of their actual births,

but this does not affect any reference to the age of a child.

(3)   Examples of phrases in wills on which subsection (2) can operate are—

1. Children of A "living at my death or born afterwards".
2. Children of A "living at my death or born afterwards before any one of such children for the time being in existence attains a vested interest and who attain the age of 21 years".
3. As in example 1 or 2, but referring to grandchildren of A instead of children of A.
4. A for life "until he has a child", and then to his child or children.

Note. Subsection (2) will not affect the reference to the age of 21 years in example 2.

(4)   Section 39(2) does not prejudice any interest vested in possession in the adopted child before the adoption, or any interest expectant (whether immediately or not) upon an interest so vested.

(5)   Where it is necessary to determine for the purposes of a disposition of property effected by an instrument whether a woman can have a child, it shall be presumed that once a woman has attained the age of 55 years she will not adopt a child after execution of the instrument, and, notwithstanding section 39, if she does so that child shall not be treated as her child or as the child of her spouse (if any) for the purposes of the instrument.

(6)   In this section, "instrument" includes a private Act settling property, but not any other enactment.

43   Dispositions depending on date of birth

(1)   Where a disposition depends on the date of birth of a child who was born illegitimate and who is adopted by one of the natural parents as sole adoptive parent, section 42 (2) does not affect entitlement under Part II of the Family Law Reform Act 1969 (illegitimate children).

(2)   Subsection (1) applies for example where—
  (a) a testator dies in 1976 bequeathing a legacy to his eldest grandchild living at a specified time,
  (b) his daughter has an illegitimate child in 1977 who is the first grandchild,
  (c) his married son has a child in 1978,
  (d) subsequently the illegitimate child is adopted by the mother as sole adoptive parent,

and in all those cases the daughter's child remains the eldest grandchild of the testator throughout.

44 Property devolving with peerages etc

(1)   An adoption does not affect the descent of any peerage or dignity or title of honour.

(2)   An adoption shall not affect the devolution of any property limited (expressly or not) to devolve (as nearly as the law permits) along with any peerage or dignity or title of honour.

(3)   Subsection (2) applies only if and so far as a contrary intention is not expressed in the instrument, and shall have effect subject to the terms of the instrument.

45 Protection of trustees and personal representatives

(1)   A trustee or personal representative is not under a duty, by virtue of the law relating to trusts or the administration of estates, to enquire, before conveying or distributing any property, whether any adoption has been effected or revoked if that fact could affect entitlement to the property.

(2)   A trustee or personal representative shall not be liable to any person by reason of a conveyance or distribution of the property made without regard to any such fact if he has not received notice of the fact before the conveyance or distribution.

(3)   This section does not prejudice the right of a person to follow the property, or any property representing it, into the hands of another person, other than a purchaser, who has received it.

46 Meaning of "disposition"

(1)   In this Part, unless the context otherwise requires,—
   "disposition" includes the conferring of a power of appointment and any other disposition of an interest in or right over property;
   "power of appointment" includes any discretionary power to transfer a beneficial interest in property without the furnishing of valuable consideration.

(2)   This Part applies to an oral disposition as if contained in an instrument made when the disposition was made.

(3)   For the purposes of this Part, the death of the testator is the date at which a will or codicil is to be regarded as made.

(4)   For the purposes of this Part, provisions of the law of intestate succession applicable to the estate of a deceased person shall be treated as if contained in an instrument executed by him (while of full capacity) immediately before his death.

(5)   . . .

47 Miscellaneous enactments

(1)   Section 39 does not apply for the purposes of the table of kindred and affinity in Schedule 1 to the Marriage Act 1949 or sections 10 and 11 (incest) of the Sexual Offences Act 1956.

(2)   . . . , section 39 does not apply for the purposes of any provision of—
  (a) [the British Nationality Act 1981],
  (b) the Immigration Act 1971,
  (c) any instrument having effect under an enactment within paragraph (a) or (b), or
  (d) any other provision of the law for the time being in force which determines [British citizenship, British Dependent Territories citizenship[, the status of a British National (Overseas)] or British Overseas citizenship].

(3)–(5) . . .

48 Pensions

Section 39(2) does not affect entitlement to a pension which is payable to or for the benefit of a child and is in payment at the time of his adoption.

49 Insurance

Where a child is adopted whose natural parent has effected an insurance with a friendly society or a collecting society or an industrial insurance company for the payment on the death of the child of money for funeral expenses, the rights and liabilities under the policy shall by virtue of the adoption be transferred to the adoptive parents who shall for the purposes of the enactments relating to such societies and companies be treated as the person who took out the policy.

PART V
REGISTRATION AND REVOCATION OF ADOPTION ORDERS AND
CONVENTION ADOPTIONS

50 Adopted Children Register

(1)   The Registrar General shall maintain at the General Register Office a register, to be called the Adopted Children Register, in which shall be made such entries as may be directed to be made therein by adoption orders, but no other entries.

(2)   A certified copy of an entry in the Adopted Children Register, if purporting to be sealed or stamped with the seal of the General Register Office, shall, without any further or other proof of that entry, be received as evidence of the adoption to which it relates and, where the entry contains a record of the date of the birth or the country or the district and sub-district of the birth of the adopted person, shall also be received as aforesaid as evidence of that date or country or district and sub-district in all respects as if the copy were a certified copy of an entry in the Registers of Births.

(3)   The Registrar General shall cause an index of the Adopted Children Register to be made and kept in the General Register Office; and every person shall be entitled to search that index and to have a certified copy of any entry in the Adopted Children Register in all respects upon and subject to the same terms, conditions and regulations as to payment of fees and

otherwise as are applicable under the Births and Deaths Registration Act 1953, and the Registration Service Act 1953, in respect of searches in other indexes kept in the General Register Office and in respect of the supply from that office or certified copies of entries in the certified copies of the Registers of Births and Deaths.

(4)   The Registrar General shall, in addition to the Adopted Children Register and the index thereof, keep such other registers and books, and make such entries therein, as may be necessary to record and make traceable the connection between any entry in the Registers of Births which has been marked "Adopted" and any corresponding entry in the Adopted Children Register.

(5)   The registers and books kept under subsection (4) shall not be, nor shall any index thereof be, open to public inspection or search, and the Registrar General shall not furnish any person with any information contained in or with any copy or extract from any such registers or books except in accordance with section 51 or under an order of any of the following courts, that is to say—
  (a) the High Court;
  (b) the Westminster County Court or such other county court as may be prescribed; and
  (c) the court by which an adoption order was made in respect of the person to whom the information, copy or extract relates.

(6)   In relation to an adoption order made by a magistrates' court, the reference in paragraph (c) of subsection (5) to the court by which the order was made includes a reference to a court acting for the same petty sessions area.

(7)   Schedule 1 to this Act, which, among other things, provides for the registration of adoptions and the amendment of adoption orders, shall have effect.

51   Disclosure of birth records of adopted children

(1)   Subject to [what follows], the Registrar General shall on an application made in the prescribed manner by an adopted person a record of whose birth is kept by the Registrar General and who has attained the age of 18 years supply to that person on payment of the prescribed fee (if any) such information as is necessary to enable that person to obtain a certified copy of the record of his birth.

(2)   On an application made in the prescribed manner by an adopted person under the age of 18 years, a record of whose birth is kept by the Registrar General and who is intending to be married in England or Wales, and on payment of the prescribed fee (if any), the Registrar General shall inform the applicant whether or not it appears from information contained in the registers of live births or other records that the applicant and the person whom he intends to marry may be within the prohibited degrees of relationship for the purposes of the Marriage Act 1949.

[(3)   Before supplying any information to an applicant under subsection (1), the Registrar General shall inform the applicant that counselling services are available to him—
  (a) if he is in England and Wales—
    (i)   at the General Register Office;
    (ii)   from the local authority in whose area he is living;
    (iii) where the adoption order relating to him was made in England and Wales, from the local authority in whose area the court which made the order sat; or
    (iv)   from any other local authority;
  (b) if he is in Scotland—
    (i)   from the regional or islands council in whose area he is living;
    (ii)   where the adoption order relating to him was made in Scotland, from the council in whose area the court which made the order sat; or
    (iii) from any other regional or islands council;
  (c) if he is in Northern Ireland—
    (i)   from the Board in whose area he is living;
    (ii)   where the adoption order relating to him was made in Northern Ireland, from the Board in whose area the court which made the order sat; or
    (iii) from any other Board;
  (d) if he is in the United Kingdom and his adoption was arranged by an adoption society—
    (i)   approved under section 3,
    (ii)   approved under section 3 of the Adoption (Scotland) Act 1978,
    (iii) registered under Article 4 of the Adoption (Northern Ireland) Order 1987,

from that society.

(4)   Where an adopted person who is in England and Wales—
  (a) applies for information under—

    (i) subsection (1), or

    (ii) Article 54 of the Adoption (Northern Ireland) Order 1987, or

  (b) is supplied with information under section 45 of the Adoption (Scotland) Act 1978,

it shall be the duty of the persons and bodies mentioned in subsection (5) to provide counselling for him if asked by him to do so.

(5)   The persons and bodies are—

  (a) the Registrar General;

  (b) any local authority falling within subsection (3)(a)(ii) to (iv);

  (c) any adoption society falling within subsection (3)(d) in so far as it is acting as an adoption society in England and Wales.

(6)   If the applicant chooses to receive counselling from a person or body falling within subsection (3), the Registrar General shall send to the person or body the information to which the applicant is entitled under subsection (1).

(7)   Where a person—

  (a) was adopted before 12th November 1975, and

  (b) applies for information under subsection (1),

the Registrar General shall not supply the information to him unless he has attended an interview with a counsellor arranged by a person or body from whom counselling services are available as mentioned in subsection (3).

(8)   Where the Registrar General is prevented by subsection (7) from supplying information to a person who is not living in the United Kingdom, he may supply the information to any body which—

  (a) the Registrar General is satisfied is suitable to provide counselling to that person, and

  (b) has notified the Registrar General that it is prepared to provide such counselling.

(9)   In this section—

"a Board" means a Health and Social Services Board established under Article 16 of the Health and Personal Social Services (Northern Ireland) Order 1972; and

"prescribed" means prescribed by regulations made by the Registrar General.]

NOTES

Sub-s (1): words in square brackets substituted by the Children Act 1989, s 88, Sch 10, para 20.

Sub-ss (3)–(9): substituted, for sub-ss (3)–(7) as originally enacted, by the Children Act 1989, s 88, Sch 10, para 20.

[51A   Adoption Contact Register

(1)   The Registrar General shall maintain at the General Register Office a register to be called the Adoption Contact Register.

(2)   The register shall be in two parts—
  (a) Part I: Adopted Persons; and
  (b) Part II: Relatives.

(3)   The Registrar General shall, on payment of such fee as may be prescribed, enter in Part I of the register the name and address of any adopted person who fulfils the conditions in subsection (4) and who gives notice that he wishes to contact any relative of his.

(4)   The conditions are that—
  (a) a record of the adopted person's birth is kept by the Registrar General; and
  (b) the adopted person has attained the age of 18 years and—
    (i)   has been supplied by the Registrar General with information under section 51; or
    (ii) has satisfied the Registrar General that he has such information as is necessary to enable him to obtain a certified copy of the record of his birth.

(5)   The Registrar General shall, on payment of such fee as may be prescribed, enter in Part II of the register the name and address of any person who fulfils the conditions in subsection (6) and who gives notice that he wishes to contact an adopted person.

(6)   The conditions are that—
  (a) a record of the adopted person's birth is kept by the Registrar General; and
  (b) the person giving notice under subsection (5) has attained the age of 18 years and has satisfied the Registrar General that—
    (i)   he is a relative of the adopted person; and
    (ii) he has such information as is necessary to enable him to obtain a certified copy of the record of the adopted person's birth.

(7)   The Registrar General shall, on receiving notice from any person named in an entry in the register that he wishes the entry to be cancelled, cancel the entry.

(8)   Any notice given under this section must be in such form as may be determined by the Registrar General.

(9)   The Registrar General shall transmit to an adopted person whose name is entered in Part I of the register the name and address of any relative in respect of whom there is an entry in Part II of the register.

(10)   Any entry cancelled under subsection (7) ceases from the time of cancellation to be an entry for the purposes of subsection (9).

(11)   The register shall not be open to public inspection or search and the Registrar General shall not supply any person with information entered in the register (whether in an uncancelled or a cancelled entry) except in accordance with this section.

(12)   The register may be kept by means of a computer.

(13)   In this section—
    (a) "relative" means any person (other than an adoptive relative) who is related to the adopted person by blood (including half-blood) or marriage;
    (b) "address" includes any address at or through which the person concerned may be contacted; and
    (c) "prescribed" means prescribed by the Secretary of State.]

NOTES

Inserted by the Children Act 1989, s 88, Sch 10, para 21.

52   Revocation of adoptions on legitimation

(1)   Where any person adopted by his father or mother alone has subsequently become a legitimated person on the marriage of his father and mother, the court by which the adoption order was made may, on the application of any of the parties concerned, revoke that order.

(2)   Where any person legitimated by virtue of section 1 of the Legitimacy Act 1959, had been adopted by his father and mother before the commencement of that Act, the court by which the adoption order was made may, on the application of any of the parties concerned, revoke that order.

(3)   Where a person adopted by his father or mother alone by virtue of a regulated adoption has subsequently become a legitimated person on the marriage of his father and mother, the High Court may, upon an application under this subsection by the parties concerned, by order revoke the adoption.

(4)   In relation to an adoption order made by a magistrates' court, the reference in subsections (1) and (2) to the court by which the order was made includes a reference to a court acting for the same petty sessions area.

53   Annulment etc of overseas adoptions

(1)   The High Court may, upon an application under this subsection, by order annul a regulated adoption [or an adoption effected by a Convention adoption order]—
  (a) on the ground that at the relevant time the adoption was prohibited by a notified provision, if under the internal law then in force in the country of which the adopter was then a national or the adopters were then nationals the adoption could have been impugned on that ground;
  (b) on the ground that at the relevant time the adoption contravened provisions relating to consents of the internal law relating to adoption of the country of which the adopted person was then a national, if under that law the adoption could then have been impugned on that ground;
  (c) on any other ground on which the adoption can be impugned under the law for the time being in force in the country in which the adoption was effected.

(2)   The High Court may, upon an application under this subsection—
  (a) order that an overseas adoption or a determination shall cease to be valid in Great Britain on the ground that the adoption or determination is contrary to public policy or that the authority which purported to authorise the adoption or make the determination was not competent to entertain the case;
  (b) decide the extent, if any, to which a determination has been affected by a subsequent determination.

(3)   Any court in Great Britain may, in any proceedings in that court, decide that an overseas adoption or a determination shall, for the purposes of those proceedings, be treated as invalid in Great Britain on either of the grounds mentioned in subsection (2).

(4)   An order or decision of the Court of Session on an application under subsection (3) of section 6 of the Adoption Act 1968 shall be recognised and have effect as if it were an order or decision of the High Court on an application under subsection (3) of this section.

(5)   Except as provided by this section and section 52(3) the validity of an overseas adoption or a determination shall not be impugned in England and Wales in proceedings in any court.

NOTES

Sub-s (1): words in square brackets inserted by the Domestic Proceedings and Magistrates' Courts Act 1978, s 74(2).

54   Provisions supplementary to ss 52(3) and 53

(1)   Any application for an order under section 52(3) or 53 or a decision under section 53(3) shall be made in the prescribed manner and within such period, if any, as may be prescribed.

(2)   No application shall be made under section 52(3) or section 53(1) in respect of an adoption unless immediately before the application is made the person adopted or the adopter habitually resides in England and Wales or, as the case may be, both adopters habitually reside there.

(3)   In deciding in pursuance of section 53 whether such an authority as is mentioned in section 59 was competent to entertain a particular case, a court shall be bound by any finding of fact made by the authority and stated by the authority to be so made for the purpose of determining whether the authority was competent to entertain the case.

(4)   In section 53—
  "determination" means such a determination as is mentioned in section 59 of this Act;
  "notified provision" means a provision specified in an order of the Secretary of State as one in respect of which a notification to or by the Government of the United Kingdom was in force at the relevant time in pursuance of the provisions of the Convention relating to prohibitions contained in the national law of the adopter; and
  "relevant time" means the time when the adoption in question purported to take effect under the law of the country in which it purports to have been effected.

PART VI

MISCELLANEOUS AND SUPPLEMENTAL

55 Adoption of children abroad

(1)   Where on an application made in relation to a child by a person who is not domiciled in England and Wales or Scotland [or Northern Ireland] an authorised court is satisfied that he intends to adopt the child under the law of or within the country in which the applicant is domiciled, the court may, subject to the following provisions of this section, make an order [giving him parental responsibility for the child].

(2)   The provisions of Part II relating to adoption orders, except sections 12(1), 14(2), 15(2), 17 to 21 and 25, shall apply in relation to orders under this section as they apply in relation to adoption orders subject to the modification that in section 13(1) for "19" and "13" there are substituted "32" and "26" respectively.

(3)   Sections 50 and 51 and paragraphs 1 and 2(1) of Schedule 1 shall apply in relation to an order under this section as they apply in relation to an adoption order except that any entry in the Registers of Births, or the Adopted Children Register which is required to be marked in consequence of the making of an order under this section shall, in lieu of being marked with the word "Adopted" or "Re-adopted" (with or without the addition of the [words "Scotland)" or "(Northern Ireland)"]), be marked with the words "Proposed foreign adoption" or "Proposed foreign re- adoption", as the case may require.

(4)   . . . .

NOTES

Sub-ss (1), (3): words in square brackets substituted by the Children Act 1989, s 88, Sch 10, para 22.

Sub-s (4): repealed by the Children Act 1989, s 108(7), Sch 15.

56 Restriction on removal of children for adoption outside Great Britain

(1)   Except under the authority of an order under section 55, [section 49 of the Adoption (Scotland) Act 1978 or Article 57 of the Adoption (Northern Ireland) Order 1987] it shall not be lawful for any person to take or send a

child who is a British subject or a citizen of the Republic of Ireland out of Great Britain to any place outside the [United Kingdom, the Channel Islands and the Isle of Man] with a view to the adoption of the child by any person not being a parent or guardian or relative of the child; and any person who takes or sends a child out of Great Britain to any place in contravention of this subsection, or makes or takes part in any arrangements for [placing a child with] any person for that purpose, shall be guilty of an offence and liable on summary conviction to imprisonment for a term not exceeding 3 months or to a fine not exceeding [level 5 on the standard scale] or to both.

(2)   In any proceedings under this section, a report by a British consular officer of a deposition made before a British consular officer and authenticated under the signature of that officer shall, upon proof that the officer or the deponent cannot be found in the United Kingdom, be admissible as evidence of the matters stated therein, and it shall not be necessary to prove the signature or official character of the person who appears to have signed any such report or deposition.

(3)   A person shall be deemed to take part in arrangements for [placing a child with] a person for the purpose referred to in subsection (1) if—
    (a) he facilitates the placing of the child [with] that person; or
    (b) he initiates or takes part in any negotiations of which the purpose or effect is the conclusion of any agreement or the making of any arrangement therefor, and if he causes another person to do so.

NOTES

Sub-s (1): maximum fine increased and converted to a level on the standard scale by the Criminal Justice Act 1982, ss 37, 38, 46; other words in square brackets substituted by the Children Act 1989, s 88, Sch 10, para 23.

Sub-s (3): words in square brackets substituted by the Children Act 1989, s 88, Sch 10, para 23(1).

57 Prohibition on certain payments

(1)   Subject to the provisions of this section, it shall not be lawful to make or give to any person any payment or reward for or in consideration of—
    (a) the adoption by that person of a child;
    (b) the grant by that person of any agreement or consent required in connection with the adoption of a child;

(c) the [handing over of a child by that person] with a view to the adoption of the child; or

(d) the making by that person of any arrangements for the adoption of a child.

(2) Any person who makes or gives, or agrees or offers to make or give, any payment or reward prohibited by this section, or who receives or agrees to receive or attempts to obtain any such payment or reward, shall be guilty of an offence and liable on summary conviction to imprisonment for a term not exceeding 3 months or to a fine not exceeding [level 5 on the standard scale] or to both; . . .

(3) This section does not apply to any payment made to an adoption agency by a parent or guardian of a child or by a person who adopts or proposes to adopt a child, being a payment in respect of expenses reasonably incurred by the agency in connection with the adoption of the child, or to any payment or reward authorised by the court to which an application for an adoption order in respect of a child is made.

[(3A) This section does not apply to—
  (a) any payment made by an adoption agency to a person who has applied or proposes to apply to a court for an adoption order or an order under section 55 (adoption of children abroad), being a payment of or towards any legal or medical expenses incurred or to be incurred by that person in connection with the application; or
  (b) any payment made by an adoption agency to another adoption agency in consideration of the placing of a child [with] any person with a view to the child's adoption; or
  (c) any payment made by an adoption agency to a voluntary organisation for the time being approved for the purposes of this paragraph by the Secretary of State as a fee for the services of that organisation in putting that adoption agency into contact with another adoption agency with a view to the making of arrangements between the adoption agencies for the adoption of a child.

In paragraph (c) "voluntary organisation" means a body, other than a public or local authority, the activities of which are not carried on for profit.]

(4)–(10)   . . .

NOTES

Sub-s (1): words in square brackets in para (c) substituted by the Children Act 1989, s 88, Sch 10, para 24(1).

Sub-s (2): maximum fine increased and converted to a level on the standard scale by the Criminal Justice Act 1982, ss 37, 38, 46; words omitted repealed by the Children Act 1989, s 108(7), Sch 15.

Sub-s (3A): inserted by the Criminal Law Act 1977, s 65, Sch 12; words in square brackets substituted by the Children Act 1989, s 88, Sch 10, para 24(2).

Sub-ss (4)–(6), (8)–(10): repealed by the Children Act 1989, s 108(7), Sch 15.

Sub-s (7): repealed by the Adoption Allowance Schemes Order 1989, SI 1989/166, art 2, and the Children Act 1989, s 108(7), Sch 15.

[57A Permitted allowances

(1)   The Secretary of State may make regulations for the purpose of enabling adoption agencies to pay allowances to persons who have adopted, or intend to adopt, children in pursuance of arrangements made by the agencies.

(2)   Section 57(1) shall not apply to any payment made by an adoption agency in accordance with the regulations.

(3)   The regulations may, in particular, make provision as to—
  (a) the procedure to be followed by any agency in determining whether a person should be paid an allowance;
  (b) the circumstances in which an allowance may be paid;
  (c) the factors to be taken into account in determining the amount of an allowance;
  (d) the procedure for review, variation and termination of allowances; and
  (e) the information about allowances to be supplied by any agency to any person who is intending to adopt a child.

(4)   Any scheme approved under section 57(4) shall be revoked as from the coming into force of this section.

(5)   Section 57(1) shall not apply in relation to any payment made—
  (a) in accordance with a scheme revoked under subsection (4) or section 57(5)(b); and
  (b) to a person to whom such payments were made before the revocation of the scheme.

(6)   Subsection (5) shall not apply where any person to whom any payments may lawfully be made by virtue of subsection (5) agrees to receive (instead of such payments) payments complying with regulations made under this section.]

Inserted by the Children Act 1989, s 88, Sch 10, para 25.

58   Restriction on advertisements

(1)   It shall not be lawful for any advertisement to be published indicating—
   (a) that the parent or guardian of a child desires to cause a child to be adopted; or
   (b) that a person desires to adopt a child; or
   (c) that any person (not being an adoption agency) is willing to make arrangements for the adoption of a child.

(2)   Any person who causes to be published or knowingly publishes an advertisement in contravention of the provisions of this section shall be guilty of an offence and liable on summary conviction to a fine not exceeding [level 5 on the standard scale].

Sub-s (2): maximum fine increased and converted to a level on the standard scale by the Criminal Justice Act 1982, ss 37, 38, 46.

61   Evidence of agreement and consent

(1)   Any agreement or consent which is required by this Act to be given to the making of an order or application for an order (other than an order to which section 17(6) applies) may be given in writing, and, if the document signifying the agreement or consent is witnessed in accordance with rules, it shall be admissible in evidence without further proof of the signature of the person by whom it was executed.

(2)   A document signifying such agreement or consent which purports to be witnessed in accordance with rules shall be presumed to be so witnessed, and to have been executed and witnessed on the date and at the place specified in the document, unless the contrary is proved.

62   Courts

(1)   In this Act, "authorised court", as respects an application for an order relating to a child, shall be construed as follows.

(2)   Subject to subsections (4) to (6), if the child is in England or Wales when the application is made, the following are authorised courts—

(a) the High Court;

(b) . . .

(c) any other county court prescribed by rules made under *[section 75 of the County Courts Act 1984]*;

(d) a magistrates' court within whose area the child is, and, in the case of an application for an order freeing the child for adoption, a magistrates' court within whose area a parent or guardian of the child is.

(3)   If, in the case of an application for an adoption order or for an order freeing a child for adoption, the child is not in Great Britain when the application is made, the High Court is the authorised court.

(4)   In the case of an application for a Convention adoption order, paragraphs (b), (c) and (d) of subsection (2) do not apply.

(5)   Subsection (2) does not apply in the case of an application under section 29 but for the purposes of such an application the following are authorised courts—

(a) if there is pending in respect of the child an application for an adoption order or an order freeing him for adoption, the court in which that application is pending;

(b) if paragraph (a) does not apply and there is no application for an order under—

[(i) section 12 or 18 of the Adoption (Scotland) Act 1978; or

(ii) Article 12, 17 or 18 of the Adoption (Northern Ireland) Order 1987],

the High Court, the county court within whose district the applicant lives and the magistrates' court within whose area the applicant lives.

(6)   In the case of an order under section 55, paragraph (d) of subsection (2) does not apply.

[(7)   Any court to which the proceedings on an application are transferred under any enactment is, as regards the transferred proceedings, an authorised court if it is not an authorised court under the preceding provisions of this section.]

NOTES

Sub-s (2): para (b) repealed by the Children (Allocation of Proceedings) (Amendment) (No 2) Order 1994, SI 1994/3138, art 6; words in square brackets in italics in para (c) substituted by the County Courts Act 1984, s 148(1), Sch 2, para 58; further substituted by the words "section 66(1) of this Act" by the Matrimonial and Family Proceedings Act 1984, s 46(1), Sch 1, para 20(a), as from a day to be appointed.

Sub-s (5): words in square brackets substituted by the Children Act 1989, s 88, Sch 10, para 28.

Sub-s (7): added by the Matrimonial and Family Proceedings Act 1984, s 46(1), Sch 1, para 20(b).

63   Appeals etc

(1)   . . .

(2)   Subject to subsections (3) . . . , where on an application to a magistrates' court under this Act the court makes or refuses to make an order, an appeal shall lie to the High Court.

(3)   . . . where an application is made to a magistrates' court under this Act, and the court considers that the matter is one which would more conveniently be dealt with by the High Court, the magistrates' court shall refuse to make an order, and in that case no appeal shall lie to the High Court.

(4)   [No appeal shall lie to the High Court] against an order made under section 34.

NOTES

Sub-s (1): repealed by the Matrimonial and Family Proceedings Act 1984, s 46(3), Sch 3.

Sub-ss (2), (3): words omitted repealed by the Health and Social Services and Social Security Adjudications Act 1983, s 30, Sch 10, Pt I.

Sub-s (4): words in square brackets substituted by the Health and Social Services and Social Security Adjudications Act 1983, s 9, Sch 2, para 36.

64   Proceedings to be in private

Proceedings under [this Act]—
   (a) in the High Court, may be disposed of in chambers;
   (b) in a county court, shall be heard and determined in camera;
   (c) . . .

NOTES

Words in square brackets substituted, and para (c) repealed, by the Domestic Proceedings and Magistrates' Courts Act 1978, ss 73(2), 89(2)(b), Sch 3.

65 Guardians ad litem and reporting officers

(1)   For the purpose of any application for an adoption order or an order freeing a child for adoption or an order under section 20 or 55 rules shall provide for the appointment, in such cases as are prescribed—

   (a) of a person to act as guardian ad litem of the child upon the hearing of the application, with the duty of safeguarding the interests of the child in the prescribed manner;

   (b) of a person to act as reporting officer for the purpose of witnessing agreements to adoption and performing such other duties as the rules may prescribe.

(2)   A person who is employed—

   (a) in the case of an application for an adoption order, by the adoption agency by whom the child was placed; or

   (b) in the case of an application for an order freeing a child for adoption, by the adoption agency by whom the application was made; or

   (c) in the case of an application under section 20, by the adoption agency with the parental rights and duties relating to the child,

shall not be appointed to act as guardian ad litem or reporting officer for the purposes of the application but, subject to that, the same person may if the court thinks fit be both guardian ad litem and reporting officer.

[65A   Panels for selection of guardians ad litem and reporting officers

(1)   The Secretary of State may by regulations provide for the establishment of panels of persons from whom guardians ad litem and reporting officers appointed under rules made under section 65 must be selected.

(2)   The regulations may, in particular, make provision—

   (a) as to the constitution, administration and procedures of panels;

   (b) requiring two or more specified local authorities to make arrangements for the joint management of a panel;

   (c) for the defrayment by local authorities of expenses incurred by members of panels;

(d) for the payment by local authorities of fees and allowances for members of panels;

(e) as to the qualifications for membership of a panel;

(f) as to the training to be given to members of panels;

(g) as to the co-operation required of specified local authorities in the provision of panels in specified areas; and

(h) for monitoring the work of guardians ad litem and reporting officers.

(3) Rules of court may make provision as to the assistance which any guardian ad litem or reporting officer may be required by the court to give to it.]

[(4) The Secretary of State may, with the consent of the Treasury, make such grants with respect to expenditure of any local authority—

(a) in connection with the establishment and administration of guardian ad litem and reporting officer panels in accordance with section 65;

(b) in paying expenses, fees, allowances and in the provision of training for members of such panels,

as he considers appropriate.]

NOTES

Inserted by the Children Act 1989, s 88, Sch 10, para 29.

Sub-s (4): added by the Courts and Legal Services Act 1990, s 116, Sch 16, para 7.

72 Interpretation

(1) In this Act, unless the context otherwise requires—

"adoption agency" in sections 11, 13, 18 to 23 and 27 to 31 includes an adoption agency within the meaning of[—

(a) section 1 of the Adoption (Scotland) Act 1978; and

(b) Article 3 of the Adoption (Northern Ireland) Order 1987];

["adoption order"—

(a) means an order under section 12(1); and

(b) in sections 12(3) and (4), 18 to 20, 27, 28 and 30 to 32 and in the definition of "British adoption order" in this subsection includes an order under section 12 of the Adoption (Scotland) Act 1978 and Article 12 of the Adoption (Northern Ireland) Order 1987 (adoption orders in Scotland and Northern Ireland respectively); and

    (c) in sections 27, 28 and 30 to 32 includes an order under section 55, section 49 of the Adoption (Scotland) Act 1978 and Article 57 of the Adoption (Northern Ireland) Order 1987 (orders in relation to children being adopted abroad)];

"adoption society" means a body of persons whose functions consist of or include the making of arrangements for the adoption of children;

"approved adoption society" means an adoption society approved under Part I;

"authorised court" shall be construed in accordance with section 62;

"body of persons" means any body of persons, whether incorporated or unincorporated;

["British adoption order" means—

    (a) an adoption order as defined in this subsection, and

    (b) an order under any provision for the adoption of a child effected under the law of any British territory outside the United Kingdom];

"British territory" means, for the purposes of any provision of this Act, any of the following countries, that is to say, Great Britain, Northern Ireland, the Channel Islands, the Isle of Man and a colony, being a country designated for the purposes of that provision by order of the Secretary of State or, if no country is so designated, any of those countries;

"child", except where used to express a relationship, means a person who has not attained the age of 18 years;

"the Convention" means the Convention relating to the adoption of children concluded at the Hague on 15th November 1965 and signed on behalf of the United Kingdom on that date;

"Convention adoption order" means an adoption order made in accordance with section 17(1);

"Convention country" means any country outside British territory, being a country for the time being designated by an order of the Secretary of State as a country in which, in his opinion, the Convention is in force;

"existing", in relation to an enactment or other instrument, means one passed or made at any time before 1st January 1976;

["guardian" has the same meaning as in the Children Act 1989];

"internal law" has the meaning assigned by section 71;

"local authority" means the council of a county (other than a metropolitan county), a metropolitan district, a London borough or the Common Council of the City of London [but, in relation to Wales, means the council of a county or county borough] . . . ;

"notice" means a notice in writing;

"order freeing a child for adoption" means an order under section 18 [and in [sections 27(2) and 59 includes an order under—

(a) section 18 of the Adoption (Scotland) Act 1978; and

(b) Article 17 or 18 of the Adoption (Northern Ireland) Order 1987]];

"overseas adoption" has the meaning assigned by subsection (2);

["parent" means in relation to a child, any parent who has parental responsibility for the child under the Children Act 1989;

"parental responsibility" and "parental responsibility agreement" have the same meaning as in the Children Act 1989;]

. . . . .

"prescribed" means prescribed by rules;

"regulated adoption" means an overseas adoption of a description designated by an order under subsection (2) as that of an adoption regulated by the Convention;

"relative" in relation to a child means a grandparent, brother, sister, uncle or aunt, whether of the full blood or half-blood or by affinity and includes, where the child is illegitimate, the father of the child and any person who would be a relative within the meaning of this definition if the child were the legitimate child of his mother and father;

"rules" means rules made under section 66(1) or made by virtue of section 66(2) under [section 144 of the Magistrates' Courts Act 1980];

"specified order" means any provision for the adoption of a child effected under enactments similar to section 12(1) and 17 in force in . . . any British territory outside the United Kingdom;

"United Kingdom national" means, for the purposes of any provision of this Act, a citizen of the United Kingdom and colonies satisfying such conditions, if any, as the Secretary of State may by order specify for the purposes of that provision;

["upbringing" has the same meaning as in the Children Act 1989];

"voluntary organisation" means a body other than a public or local authority the activities of which are not carried on for profit.

[(1A) In this Act, in determining with what person, or where, a child has his home, any absence of the child at a hospital or boarding school and any other temporary absence shall be disregarded.

(1B) In this Act, references to a child who is in the care of or looked after by a local authority have the same meaning as in the Children Act 1989.]

(2) In this Act "overseas adoption" means an adoption of such a description as the Secretary of State may by order specify, being a description of adoptions of children appearing to him to be effected under the law of any country outside Great Britain; and an order under this subsection may contain provision as to the manner in which evidence of an overseas adoption may be given.

(3)　　For the purposes of this Act, a person shall be deemed to make arrangements for the adoption of a child if he enters into or makes any agreement or arrangement for, or for facilitating, the adoption of the child by any other person, whether the adoption is effected, or is intended to be effected, in Great Britain or elsewhere, or if he initiates or takes part in any negotiations of which the purpose or effect is the conclusion of any agreement or the making of any arrangement therefor, and if he causes another person to do so.

(4)　　Except so far as the context otherwise requires, any reference in this Act to an enactment shall be construed as a reference to that enactment as amended by or under any other enactment, including this Act.

(5)　　In this Act, except where otherwise indicated—
　　(a)　a reference to a numbered Part, section or Schedule is a reference to the Part or section of, or the Schedule to, this Act so numbered, and
　　(b)　a reference in a section to a numbered subsection is a reference to the subsection of that section so numbered, and
　　(c)　a reference in a section, subsection or Schedule to a numbered paragraph is a reference to the paragraph of that section, subsection or Schedule so numbered.

NOTES

Sub-s (1): in definition "adoption agency" words in square brackets substituted by the Children Act 1989, s 88, Sch 10, para 30; definition "adoption order" substituted by the Children Act 1989, s 88, Sch 10, para 30; definition "British adoption order" substituted by the Children Act 1989, s 88, Sch 10, para 30; definition "guardian" substituted by the Children Act 1989, s 88, Sch 10, para 30; in definition "local authority" words in square brackets inserted by the Local Government (Wales) Act 1994, s 22(4), Sch 10, para 9, words omitted repealed by the Children Act 1989, s 108(7), Sch 15; in definition "order freeing a child for adoption" words in first pair of square brackets substituted by the Health and Social Services and Social Security Adjudications Act 1983, s 9, Sch 2, para 37, words in square brackets therein substituted by the Children Act 1989, s 88, Sch 10, para 30; definitions "parent", "parental responsibility", "parental responsibility agreement" and "upbringing" inserted by the Children Act 1989, s 88, Sch 10, para 30, definition omitted repealed by the Children Act 1989, s 108(7), Sch 15; in definition "rules" words in square brackets substituted by the Magistrates' Courts Act 1980, s 154, Sch 7, para 142; in definition "specified order" words omitted repealed by the Children Act 1989, s 108(7), Sch 15.

Sub-ss (1A), (1B): substituted for sub-s (1A), as inserted by the Family Law Reform Act 1987, s 33(1), Sch 2, para 68, by the Children Act 1989, s 88, Sch 10, para 30(9).

74 Short title, commencement and extent

(1)   This Act may be cited as the Adoption Act 1976.

(2)   This Act shall come into force on such date as the Secretary of State may by order appoint and different dates may be appointed for different provisions.

[(3)   This Act extends to England and Wales only.]

NOTES

Sub-s (3): substituted, for sub-ss (3), (4) as originally enacted, by the Children Act 1989, s 88, Sch 10, para 31.

Rent Act 1977

(c 42)

An Act to consolidate the Rent Act 1968, Parts III, IV and VIII of the Housing Finance Act 1972, the Rent Act 1974, sections 7 to 10 of the Housing Rents and Subsidies Act 1975, and certain related enactments, with amendments to give effect to recommendations of the Law Commission

[29 July 1977]

PART I
PRELIMINARY

Protected and statutory tenancies

1 Protected tenants and tenancies

Subject to this Part of this Act, a tenancy under which a dwelling-house (which may be a house or part of a house) is let as a separate dwelling is a protected tenancy for the purposes of this Act.

Any reference in this Act to a protected tenant shall be construed accordingly.

2 Statutory tenants and tenancies

(1)   Subject to this Part of this Act—
    (a) after the termination of a protected tenancy of a dwelling-house the person who, immediately before that termination, was the protected tenant of the dwelling-house shall, if and so long as he occupies the dwelling-house as his residence, be the statutory tenant of it; and
    (b) Part I of Schedule 1 to this Act shall have effect for determining what person (if any) is the statutory tenant of a dwelling-house [or, as the case may be, is entitled to an assured tenancy of a dwelling-house by succession] at any time after the death of a person who, immediately before his death, was either a protected tenant of the dwelling-house or the statutory tenant of it by virtue of paragraph (a) above.

(2)–(5) . . .

NOTES

Sub-s (1): words in square brackets in para (b) inserted by the Housing Act 1988, s 39(1).
Sub-ss (2)–(5): outside the scope of this work.

3 Terms and conditions of statutory tenancies

(1)   So long as he retains possession, a statutory tenant shall observe and be entitled to the benefit of all the terms and conditions of the original contract of tenancy, so far as they are consistent with the provisions of this Act.

(2)–(5) . . .

NOTES
Sub-ss (2)–(5): outside the scope of this work.

156 Short title, commencement and extent

(1)   This Act may be cited as the Rent Act 1977.

(2)   This Act shall come into force on the expiry of the period of one month beginning with the date on which it is passed.

(3)   This Act does not extend to Scotland or Northern Ireland.

SCHEDULE 1
STATUTORY TENANCIES

Sections 2, 3

PART I
STATUTORY TENANTS BY SUCCESSION

1.   Paragraph 2 . . . below shall have effect, subject to section 2(3) of this Act, for the purpose of determining who is the statutory tenant of a dwelling-house by succession after the death of the person (in this Part of this Schedule referred to as "the original tenant") who, immediately before his death, was a protected tenant of the dwelling-house or the statutory tenant of it by virtue of his previous protected tenancy.

[2.   The surviving spouse (if any) of the original tenant, if residing in the dwelling-house immediately before the death of the original tenant, shall after the death be the statutory tenant if and so long as he or she occupies the dwelling-house as his or her residence.

[(2)   For the purposes of this paragraph, a person who was living with the original tenant as his or her wife or husband shall be treated as the spouse of the original tenant.

(3)   If, immediately after the death of the original tenant, there is, by virtue of sub-paragraph (2) above, more than one person who fulfils the conditions in sub-paragraph (1) above, such one of them as may be decided by agreement or, in default of agreement, by the county court shall be treated as the surviving spouse for the purposes of this paragraph.]]

3.   Where paragraph 2 above does not apply, but a person who was a member of the original tenant's family was residing with him [in the dwelling-house] at the time of and for the [period of 2 years] immediately before his death then, after his death, that person or if there is more than one such person such one of them as may be decided by agreement, or in default of agreement by the county court, shall be [entitled to an assured tenancy of the dwelling-house by succession].

[(2)   If the original tenant died within the period of 18 months beginning on the operative date, then, for the purposes of this paragraph, a person who was residing in the dwelling-house with the original tenant at the time of his death and for the period which began 6 months before the operative date and ended at the time of his death shall be taken to have been residing with the original tenant for the period of 2 years immediately before his death.]

4.   A person who becomes the statutory tenant of a dwelling-house by virtue of paragraph 2 . . . above is in this Part of this Schedule referred to as "the first successor".

5.   If, immediately before his death, the first successor was still a statutory tenant, paragraph 6 [below shall have effect], for the purpose of determining who is [entitled to an assured tenancy of the dwelling-house by succession].

[6.—(1)   Where a person who–
- (a) was a member of the original tenant's family immediately before that tenant's death, and
- (b) was a member of the first successor's family immediately before the first successor's death,

was residing in the dwelling-house with the first successor at the time of, and for the period of 2 years immediately before, the first successor's death, that person or, if there is more than one such person, such one of them as may be decided by agreement or, in default of agreement, by the county court shall be entitled to an assured tenancy of the dwelling-house by succession.

(2)   If the first successor died within the period of 18 months beginning on the operative date, then, for the purposes of this paragraph, a person who was residing in the dwelling- house with the first successor at the time of his death and for the period which began 6 months before the operative date and ended at the time of his death shall be taken to have been residing with the first successor for the period of 2 years immediately before his death.]

7.–11. . . .

NOTES

Paras 1, 4: words omitted repealed by the Housing Act 1988, ss 39, 140, Sch 4, Pt I, paras 1, 4, Sch 18, in cases where the original tenant dies on or after 15 January 1989.

Para 2: substituted, in relation to deaths occurring after 28 November 1980, by the Housing Act 1980, s 76; sub-paras (2), (3) added by the Housing Act 1988, s 39, Sch 4, Pt I, para 2, in cases where the original tenant dies on or after 15 January 1989.

Para 3: words in square brackets added or substituted by the Housing Act 1988, s 39, Sch 4, Pt I, para 3, in cases where the original tenant dies on or after 15 January 1989.

Para 5: words in square brackets substituted by the Housing Act 1988, s 39, Sch 4, Pt I, para 5, in cases where the original tenant dies on or after 15 January 1989, and in cases where the original tenant died before 15 January 1989 and the first successor dies on or after that date.

Para 6: substituted by the Housing Act 1988, s 39, Sch 4, Pt I, para 6, in cases where the original tenant dies on or after 15 January 1989, and in cases where the original tenant died before 15 January 1989 and the first successor dies on or after that date.

Para 7: repealed by the Housing Act 1988, ss 39, 140, Sch 4, Pt I, para 7, Sch 18, in cases where the original tenant dies on or after 15 January 1989, and in cases where the original tenant died before 15 January 1989 and the first successor dies on or after that date.

Para 8–11: outside the scope of this work.

Domestic Proceedings and Magistrates' Courts Act 1978

(C 22)

An Act to make fresh provision for matrimonial proceedings in magistrates' courts; to amend enactments relating to other proceedings so as to eliminate certain differences between the law relating to those proceedings and the law relating to matrimonial proceedings in magistrates' courts; to extend section 15 of the Justices of the Peace Act 1949; to amend Part II of the Magistrates' Courts Act 1952; to amend section 2 of the Administration of Justice Act 1964; to amend the Maintenance Orders (Reciprocal Enforcement) Act 1972; to amend certain enactments relating to adoption; and for purposes connected with those matters

[30 June 1978]

PART I
MATRIMONIAL PROCEEDINGS IN MAGISTRATES' COURTS

Powers of court to make orders for financial provision for parties to a marriage and children of the family

1   Grounds of application for financial provision

Either party to a marriage may apply to a magistrates' court for an order under section 2 of this Act on the ground that the other party to the marriage

. . . —

(a) has failed to provide reasonable maintenance for the applicant; or
(b) has failed to provide, or to make a proper contribution towards, reasonable maintenance for any child of the family; *or*
(c) *has behaved in such a way that the applicant cannot reasonably be expected to live with the respondent; or*
(d) has deserted the applicant.

NOTES

First words omitted repealed by the Matrimonial and Family Proceedings Act 1984, s 46(1), Sch 1; paras (c), (d) repealed by the Family Law Act 1996, ss 18(1), 66(3), Sch 10, subject to savings in s 66(2) of, and Sch 9, para 5 to, the 1996 Act, as from a day to be appointed.

2   Powers of court to make orders for financial provision

(1)   Where on an application for an order under this section the applicant satisfies the court of any ground mentioned in section 1 of this Act, the court may, subject to the provisions of this Part of this Act, make any one or more of the following orders, that is to say—

(a) an order that the respondent shall make to the applicant such periodical payments, and for such term, as may be specified in the order;
(b) an order that the respondent shall pay to the applicant such lump sum as may be so specified;
(c) an order that the respondent shall make to the applicant for the benefit of a child of the family to whom the application relates, or to such a child, such periodical payments, and for such term, as may be so specified;
(d) an order that the respondent shall pay to the applicant for the benefit of a child of the family to whom the application relates, or to such a child, such lump sum as may be so specified.

(2)   Without prejudice to the generality of subsection (1)(b) or (d) above, an order under this section for the payment of a lump sum may be made for the purpose of enabling any liability or expenses reasonably incurred in maintaining the applicant, or any child of the family to whom the application relates, before the making of the order to be met.

(3)   The amount of any lump sum required to be paid by an order under this section shall not exceed £500 or such larger amount as the [Lord Chancellor] may from time to time by order fix for the purposes of this subsection.

Any order made by the [Lord Chancellor] under this subsection shall be made by statutory instrument and shall be subject to annulment in pursuance of a resolution of either House of Parliament.

NOTES

Sub-s (3): words in square brackets substituted by the Transfer of Functions (Magistrates' Courts and Family Law) Order 1992, SI 1992/709, art 3(2), Sch 2.

[3 Matters to which court is to have regard in exercising its powers under s 2

(1)   Where an application is made for an order under section 2 of this Act, it shall be the duty of the court, in deciding whether to exercise its powers under that section and, if so, in what manner, to have regard to all the circumstances of the case, first consideration being given to the welfare while a minor of any child of the family who has not attained the age of eighteen.

(2)   As regards the exercise of its powers under subsection (1)(a) or (b) of section 2, the court shall in particular have regard to the following matters—
  (a) the income, earning capacity, property and other financial resources which each of the parties to the marriage has or is likely to have in the foreseeable future, including in the case of earning capacity any increase in that capacity which it would in the opinion of the court be reasonable to expect a party to the marriage to take steps to acquire;
  (b) the financial needs, obligations and responsibilities which each of the parties to the marriage has or is likely to have in the foreseeable future;
  (c) the standard of living enjoyed by the parties to the marriage before the occurrence of the conduct which is alleged as the ground of the application;
  (d) the age of each party to the marriage and the duration of the marriage;
  (e) any physical or mental disability of either of the parties to the marriage;
  (f) the contributions which each of the parties has made or is likely in the foreseeable future to make to the welfare of the family, including any contribution by looking after the home or caring for the family;
  (g) the conduct of each of the parties, if that conduct is such that it would in the opinion of the court be inequitable to disregard it.

(3)   As regards the exercise of its power under subsection (1)(c) or (d) of section 2, the court shall in particular have regard to the following matters—

(a) the financial needs of the child;

(b) the income, earning capacity (if any), property and other financial resources of the child;

(c) any physical or mental disability of the child;

(d) the standard of living enjoyed by the family before the occurrence of the conduct which is alleged as the ground of the application;

(e) the manner in which the child was being and in which the parties to the marriage expected him to be educated or trained;

(f) the matters mentioned in relation to the parties to the marriage in paragraphs (a) and (b) of subsection (2) above.

(4)   As regards the exercise of its power under section 2 in favour of a child of the family who is not the child of the respondent, the court shall also have regard—

(a) to whether the respondent has assumed any responsibility for the child's maintenance and, if he did, to the extent to which, and the basis on which, he assumed that responsibility and to the length of time during which he discharged that responsibility;

(b) to whether in assuming and discharging that responsibility the respondent did so knowing that the child was not his own child;

(c) to the liability of any other person to maintain the child.]

NOTES

Substituted by the Matrimonial and Family Proceedings Act 1984, s 9.

4   Duration of orders for financial provision for a party to a marriage

(1)   The term to be specified in any order made under section 2(1)(a) of this Act shall be such term as the court thinks fit except that the term shall not begin earlier than the date of the making of the application for the order and shall not extend beyond the death of either of the parties to the marriage.

(2)   Where an order is made under the said section 2(1)(a) and the marriage of the parties affected by the order is subsequently dissolved or annulled but the order continues in force, the order shall, notwithstanding anything in it, cease to have effect on the remarriage of the party in whose favour it was made, except in relation to any arrears due under the order on the date of the remarriage.

5   Age limit on making orders for financial provision for children and duration of such orders

(1)   Subject to subsection (3) below, no order shall be made under section 2(1)(c) or (d) of this Act in favour of a child who has attained the age of eighteen.

(2)   The term to be specified in an order made under section 2(1)(c) of this Act in favour of a child may begin with the date of the making of an application for the order in question or any later date [or a date ascertained in accordance with subsection (5) or (6) below] but—

(a)   shall not in the first instance extend beyond the date of the birthday of the child next following his attaining the upper limit of the compulsory school age *(that is to say, the age that is for the time being that limit by virtue of section 35 of the Education Act 1944 together with any Order in Council made under that section)* [unless the court considers that in the circumstances of the case the welfare of the child requires that it should extend to a later date]; and

(b)   shall not in any event, subject to subsection (3) below, extend beyond the date of the child's eighteenth birthday.

(3)   The court—

(a)   may make an order under section 2(1)(c) or (d) of this Act in favour of a child who has attained the age of eighteen, and

(b)   may include in an order made under section 2(1)(c) of this Act in relation to a child who has not attained that age a provision for extending beyond the date when the child will attain that age the term for which by virtue of the order any payments are to be made to or for the benefit of that child,

if it appears to the court—

(i)   that the child is, or will be, or if such an order or provision were made would be, receiving instruction at an educational establishment or undergoing training for a trade, profession or vocation, whether or not he is also, or will also be, in gainful employment; or

(ii)   that there are special circumstances which justify the making of the order or provision.

(4)   Any order made under section 2(1)(c) of this Act in favour of a child shall, notwithstanding anything in the order, cease to have effect on the death of the person liable to make payments under the order.

[(5)   Where—
  (a) a maintenance assessment ("the current assessment") is in force with respect to a child; and
  (b) an application is made for an order under section 2(1)(c) of this Act—
      (i)   in accordance with section 8 of the Child Support Act 1991; and
      (ii) before the end of the period of 6 months beginning with the making of the current assessment,

the term to be specified in any such order made on that application may be expressed to begin on, or at any time after, the earliest permitted date.

(6)   For the purposes of subsection (5) above, "the earliest permitted date" is whichever is the later of—
  (a) the date 6 months before the application is made; or
  (b) the date on which the current assessment took effect or, where successive maintenance assessments have been continuously in force with respect to a child, on which the first of those assessments took effect.

(7)   Where—
  (a) a maintenance assessment ceases to have effect or is cancelled by or under any provision of the Child Support Act 1991; and
  (b) an application is made, before the end of the period of 6 months beginning with the relevant date, for an order under section 2(1)(c) of this Act in relation to a child with respect to whom that maintenance assessment was in force immediately before it ceased to have effect or was cancelled,

the term to be specified in any such order, or in any interim order under section 19 of this Act, made on that application, may begin with the date on which that maintenance assessment ceased to have effect or, as the case may be, the date with effect from which it was cancelled, or any later date.

(8)   In subsection (7)(b) above—
  (a) where the maintenance assessment ceased to have effect, the relevant date is the date on which it so ceased; and
  (b) where the maintenance assessment was cancelled, the relevant date is the later of—
      (i)   the date on which the person who cancelled it did so, and
      (ii) the date from which the cancellation first had effect.]

NOTES

Sub-s (2): words in first pair of square brackets inserted by the Maintenance Orders (Backdating) Order 1993, SI 1993/623, art 2, Sch 1, para 4; words in italics in para (a) substituted by the words "(construed in accordance with section 8 of the Education Act 1996)" by the Education Act 1996, s 582(1), Sch 37, para 138, as from a day to be appointed; final words in square brackets substituted by the Matrimonial and Family Proceedings Act 1984, s 9.

Sub-ss (5)–(8): added by the Maintenance Orders (Backdating) Order 1993, SI 1993/623, art 2, Sch 1, para 5.

[6   Orders for payments which have been agreed by the parties

(1)   Either party to a marriage may apply to a magistrates' court for an order under this section on the ground that either the party making the application or the other party to the marriage has agreed to make such financial provision as may be specified in the application and, subject to subsection (3) below, the court on such an application may, if—

  (a) it is satisfied that the applicant or the respondent, as the case may be, has agreed to make that provision, and
  (b) it has no reason to think that it would be contrary to the interests of justice to exercise its powers hereunder,

order that the applicant or the respondent, as the case may be, shall make the financial provision specified in the application.

(2)   In this section "financial provision" means the provision mentioned in any one or more of the following paragraphs, that is to say—

  (a) the making of periodical payments by one party to the other,
  (b) the payment of a lump sum by one party to the other,
  (c) the making of periodical payments by one party to a child of the family or to the other party for the benefit of such a child,
  (d) the payment by one party of a lump sum to a child of the family or to the other party for the benefit of such a child,

and any reference in this section to the financial provision specified in an application made under subsection (1) above or specified by the court under subsection (5) below is a reference to the type of provision specified in the application or by the court, as the case may be, to the amount so specified as the amount of any payment to be made thereunder and, in the case of periodical payments, to the term so specified as the term for which the payments are to be made.

(3)   Where the financial provision specified in an application under subsection (1) above includes or consists of provision in respect of a child of the family, the court shall not make an order under that subsection unless it considers that the provision which the applicant or the respondent, as the case may be, has agreed to make in respect of

that child provides for, or makes a proper contribution towards, the financial needs of the child.

(4)   A party to a marriage who has applied for an order under section 2 of this Act shall not be precluded at any time before the determination of that application from applying for an order under this section; but if an order is made under this section on the application of either party and either of them has also made an application for an order under section 2 of this Act, the application made for the order under section 2 shall be treated as if it had been withdrawn.

(5)   Where on an application under subsection (1) above the court decides—
  (a)   that it would be contrary to the interests of justice to make an order for the making of the financial provision specified in the application, or
  (b)   that any financial provision which the applicant or the respondent, as the case may be, has agreed to make in respect of a child of the family does not provide for, or make a proper contribution towards, the financial needs of that child,

  but is of the opinion—
  (i)   that it would not be contrary to the interests of justice to make an order for the making of some other financial provision specified by the court, and
  (ii)   that, in so far as that other financial provision contains any provision for a child of the family, it provides for, or makes a proper contribution towards, the financial needs of that child,

then if both the parties agree, the court may order that the applicant or the respondent, as the case may be, shall make that other financial provision.

(6)   Subject to subsection (8) below, the provisions of section 4 of this Act shall apply in relation to an order under this section which requires periodical payments to be made to a party to a marriage for his own benefit as they apply in relation to an order under section 2(1)(a) of this Act.

(7)   Subject to subsection (8) below, the provisions of section 5 of this Act shall apply in relation to an order under this section for the making of financial provision in respect of a child of the family as they apply in relation to an order under section 2(1)(c) or (d) of this Act.

(8)   Where the court makes an order under this section which contains provision for the making of periodical payments and, by virtue of

subsection (4) above, an application for an order under section 2 of this Act is treated as if it had been withdrawn, then the term which may be specified as the term for which the payments are to be made may begin with the date of the making of the application for the order under section 2 or any later date.

(9)   Where the respondent is not present or represented by counsel or solicitor at the hearing of an application for an order under subsection (1) above, the court shall not make an order under this section unless there is produced to the court such evidence as may be prescribed by rules of—

  (a) the consent of the respondent to the making of the order,
  (b) the financial resources of the respondent, and
  (c) in a case where the financial provision specified in the application includes or consists of provision in respect of a child of the family to be made by the applicant to the respondent for the benefit of the child or to the child, the financial resources of the child.]

NOTES

Substituted by the Matrimonial and Family Proceedings Act 1984, s 10.

7   Powers of court where parties are living apart by agreement

(1)   Where the parties to a marriage have been living apart for a continuous period exceeding three months, *neither party having deserted the other*, and one of the parties has been making periodical payments for the benefit of the other party or of a child of the family, that other party may apply to a magistrates' court for an order under this section, and any application made under this subsection shall specify the aggregate amount of the payments so made during the period of three months immediately preceding the date of the making of the application.

(2)   Where on an application for an order under this section the court is satisfied that the respondent has made the payments specified in the application, the court may, subject to the provisions of this Part of this Act, make one or both of the following orders, that is to say—

  (a) an order that the respondent shall make to the applicant such periodical payments, and for such term, as may be specified in the order;
  (b) an order that the respondent shall make to the applicant for the benefit of a child of the family to whom the application relates, or to such a child, such periodical payments, and for such term, as may be so specified.

(3)   The court in the exercise of its powers under this section—
- (a) shall not require the respondent to make payments which exceed in aggregate during any period of three months the aggregate amount paid by him for the benefit of the applicant or a child of the family during the period of three months immediately preceding the date of the making of the application;
- (b) shall not require the respondent to make payments to or for the benefit of any person which exceed in amount the payments which the court considers that it would have required the respondent to make to or for the benefit of that person on an application under section 1 of this Act;
- (c) shall not require payments to be made to or for the benefit of a child of the family who is not a child of the respondent unless the court considers that it would have made an order in favour of that child on an application under section 1 of this Act.

(4)   Where on an application under this section the court considers that the orders which it has the power to make under this section—
- (a) would not provide reasonable maintenance for the applicant, or
- (b) if the application relates to a child of the family, would not provide, or make a proper contribution towards reasonable maintenance for that child,

the court shall refuse to make an order under this section, but the court may treat the application as if it were an application for an order under section 2 of this Act.

(5)   The provisions of section 3 of this Act shall apply in relation to an application for an order under this section as they apply in relation to an application for an order under section 2 of this Act subject to the modification that for the reference in [subsection (2)(c)] of the said section 3 to the occurrence of the conduct which is alleged as the ground of the application there shall be substituted a reference to the living apart of the parties to the marriage.

(6)   The provisions of section 4 of this Act shall apply in relation to an order under this section which requires periodical payments to be made to the applicant for his own benefit as they apply in relation to an order under section 2(1)(a) of this Act.

(7)   The provisions of section 5 of this Act shall apply in relation to an order under this section for the making of periodical payments in respect of a child of the family as they apply in relation to an order under section 2(1)(c) of this Act.

NOTES

Sub-s (1): words in italics repealed by the Family Law Act 1996, ss 18(2), 66(3), Sch 10, subject to savings in s 66(2) of, and para 5 of Sch 9 to, the 1996 Act, as from a day to be appointed.

Sub-s (5): words in square brackets substituted by the Matrimonial and Family Proceedings Act 1984, s 46(1), Sch 1, para 22.

Powers of court as to the custody etc of children

[8 Restrictions on making of orders under this Act: welfare of children

Where an application is made by a party to a marriage for an order under section 2, 6 or 7 of this Act, then, if there is a child of the family who is under the age of eighteen, the court shall not dismiss or make a final order on the application until it has decided whether to exercise any of its powers under the Children Act 1989 with respect to the child.]

NOTES

Substituted by the Children Act 1989, s 108(5), Sch 13, para 36.

Interim orders

19 Interim orders

(1)   Where an application is made for an order under section 2, 6 or 7 of this Act—

 (a) the magistrates' court at any time before making a final order on, or dismissing, the application or on refusing to make an order on the application by virtue of section 27 of this Act, and

 (b) the High Court on ordering the application to be reheard by a magistrates' court (either after the refusal of an order under section 27 of this Act or on an appeal under section 29 of this Act),

shall, subject to the provisions of this Part of this Act, have the . . . —

 (i) power to make an order (in this Part of this Act referred to as an "interim maintenance order") which requires the respondent to make to the applicant or to any child of the family who is under the age of eighteen, or to the applicant for the benefit of such a child, such periodical payments as the court thinks reasonable;

(ii) . . .

(2) . . .

(3)   An interim maintenance order may provide for payments to be made from such date as the court may specify, [except that, subject to section 5(5) and (6) of this Act, the date shall not be] earlier than the date of the making of the application for an order under section 2, 6 or 7 of this Act; and where such an order made by the High Court on an appeal under section 29 of this Act provides for payments to be made from a date earlier than the date of the making of the order, the interim order may provide that payments made by the respondent under an order made by a magistrates' court shall, to such extent and in such manner as may be provided by the interim order, be treated as having been paid on account of any payment provided for by the interim order.

[(3A)   Where an application is made for an order under section 6 of this Act by the party to the marriage who has agreed to make the financial provision specified in the application—
   (a)   subsection (1) shall apply as if the reference in paragraph (i) to the respondent were a reference to the applicant and the references to the applicant were references to the respondent; and
   (b)   [subsection] (3) shall apply accordingly.]

(4)   . . .

(5)   Subject to subsection (6) below, an interim order made on an application for an order under section 2, 6 or 7 of this Act shall cease to have effect on whichever of the following dates occurs first, that is to say—
   (a)   the date, if any, specified for the purpose in the interim order;
   (b)   the date of the expiration of the period of three months beginning with the date of the making of the interim order;
   (c)   the date on which a magistrates' court either makes a final order on or dismisses the application.

(6)   Where an interim order made under subsection (1) above would, but for this subsection, cease to have effect by virtue of subsection (5)(a) or (b) above, the magistrates' court which made the order or, in the case of an interim order made by the High Court, the magistrates' court by which the application for an order under section 2, 6 or 7 of this Act is to be reheard, shall have power by order to provide that the interim order shall continue in force for a further period, and any order continued in force under this subsection shall cease to have effect on whichever of the following dates occurs first, that is to say—

   (a) the date, if any, specified for the purpose in the order made under this subsection;

   (b) the date of the expiration of the period of three months beginning with the date of the making of the order under this subsection or, if more than one order has been made under this subsection with respect to the application, beginning with the date of the making of the first of those orders;

   (c) the date on which the court either makes a final order on, or dismisses, the application.

(7)   Not more than one interim maintenance order . . . may be made with respect to any application for an order under section 2, 6 or 7 of this Act, but without prejudice to the powers of a court under this section on any further such application.

(8)   No appeal shall lie from the making of or refusal to make, the variation of or refusal to vary, or the revocation of or refusal to revoke, an interim maintenance order.

(9)   An interim order made by the High Court under this section on ordering that an application be reheard by a magistrates' court shall for the purpose of its enforcement and for the purposes of section 20 . . . of this Act, be treated as if it were an order of that magistrates' court and not of the High Court.

NOTES

Words omitted from sub-ss (1), (7), (9) and whole of sub-ss (2), (4) repealed by the Children Act 1989, s 108(7), Sch 15.

Sub-s (3): words in square brackets substituted by the Maintenance Orders (Backdating) Order 1993, SI 1993/623, art 2, Sch 1, para 6.

Sub-s (3A): inserted by the Matrimonial and Family Proceedings Act 1984, s 46(1), Sch 1; word in square brackets in para (b) substituted by the Children Act 1989, s 108(5), Sch 13, para 37.

Variation, revocation and cessation of orders etc

20 Variation, revival and revocation of orders for periodical payments

(1)   Where a magistrates' court has made an order under section 2(1)(a) or (c) of this Act for the making of periodical payments the court shall have

power, on an application made under this section, to vary or revoke that order and also to make an order under section 2(1)(b) or (d) of this Act.

[(2)   Where a magistrates' court has made an order under section 6 of this Act for the making of periodical payments by a party to a marriage the court shall have power, on an application made under this section, to vary or revoke that order and also to make an order for the payment of a lump sum by that party either—

(a) to the other party to the marriage, or

(b) to a child of the family or to that other party for the benefit of that child.]

(3)   Where a magistrates' court has made an order under section 7 of this Act for the making of periodical payments, the court shall have power, on an application made under this section, to vary or revoke that order.

(4)   . . .

(5)   Where a magistrates' court has made an interim maintenance order under section 19 of this Act, the court, on an application made under this section, shall have power to vary or revoke that order, except that the court shall not by virtue of this subsection extend the period for which the order is in force.

(6)   The power of the court under this section to vary an order for the making of periodical payments shall include power to suspend any provision thereof temporarily and to revive any provision so suspended.

(7)   Where the court has power by virtue of this section to make an order for the payment of a lump sum, the amount of the lump sum shall not exceed the maximum amount that may at that time be required to be paid under section 2(3) of this Act, but the court may make an order for the payment of a lump sum not exceeding that amount notwithstanding that the person required to pay the lump sum was required to pay a lump sum by a previous order under this Part of this Act.

(8)   Where the court has power by virtue of subsection (2) above to make an order for the payment of a lump sum and the respondent [or the applicant, as the case may be,] has agreed to pay a lump sum of an amount exceeding the maximum amount that may at that time be required to be paid under section 2(3) of this Act, the court may, notwithstanding anything in subsection (7) above, make an order for the payment of a lump sum of that amount.

(9)   An order made by virtue of this section which varies an order for the making of periodical payments may, . . . , provide that the payments as so varied shall be made from such date as the court may specify, [except that, subject to subsections (9A) and (9B) below, the date shall not be] earlier than the date of the making of the application under this section.

[(9A) Where—
  (a) there is in force an order ("the order")—
    (i)   under section 2(1)(c) of this Act,
    (ii) under section 6(1) of this Act making provision of a kind mentioned in paragraph (c) of section 6(2) of this Act (regardless of whether it makes provision of any other kind mentioned in that paragraph),
    (iii) under section 7(2)(b) of this Act, or
    (iv) which is an interim maintenance order under which the payments are to be made to a child or to the applicant for the benefit of a child;
  (b) the order requires payments specified in it to be made to or for the benefit of more than one child without apportioning those payments between them;
  (c) a maintenance assessment ("the assessment") is made with respect to one or more, but not all, of the children with respect to whom those payments are to be made; and
  (d) an application is made, before the end of the period of 6 months beginning with the date on which the assessment was made, for the variation or revocation of the order,

the court may, in exercise of its powers under this section to vary or revoke the order, direct that the variation or revocation shall take effect from the date on which the assessment took effect or any later date.

(9B) Where—
  (a) an order ("the child order") of a kind prescribed for the purposes of section 10(1) of the Child Support Act 1991 is affected by a maintenance assessment;
  (b) on the date on which the child order became so affected there was in force an order ("the spousal order")—
    (i)   under section 2(1)(a) of this Act,
    (ii) under section 6(1) of this Act making provision of a kind mentioned in section 6(2)(a) of this Act (regardless of whether it makes provision of any other kind mentioned in that paragraph),
    (iii) under section 7(2)(a) of this Act, or

(iv) which is an interim maintenance order under which the payments are to be made to the applicant (otherwise than for the benefit of a child); and

(c) an application is made, before the end of the period of 6 months beginning with the date on which the maintenance assessment was made, for the spousal order to be varied or revoked,

the court may, in exercise of its powers under this section to vary or revoke the spousal order, direct that the variation or revocation shall take effect from the date on which the child order became so affected or any later date.

(9C) For the purposes of subsection (9B) above, an order is affected if it ceases to have effect or is modified by or under section 10 of the Child Support Act 1991.]

(10) . . .

(11) In exercising the powers conferred by this section the court shall, so far as it appears to the court just to do so, give effect to any agreement which has been reached between the parties in relation to the application and, if there is no such agreement or if the court decides not to give effect to the agreement, the court shall have regard to all the circumstances of the case, [first consideration being given to the welfare while a minor of any child of the family who has not attained the age of eighteen, and the circumstances of the case shall include any change] in any of the matters to which the court was required to have regard when making the order to which the application relates or, in the case of an application for the variation or revocation of an order made under section 6 of this Act or on an appeal under section 29 of this Act, to which the court would have been required to have regard if that order had been made under section 2 of this Act.

[(12) An application under this section may be made—

(a) where it is for the variation or revocation of an order under section 2, 6, 7 or 19 of this Act for periodical payments, by either party to the marriage in question; and

(b) where it is for the variation of an order under section 2(1)(c), 6 or 7 of this Act for periodical payments to or in respect of a child, also by the child himself, if he has attained the age of sixteen.]

(13) . . .

NOTES

Sub-s (2): substituted by the Matrimonial and Family Proceedings Act 1984, s 11.

Sub-s (4): repealed by the Children Act 1989, s 108(7), Sch 15.

Sub-s (8): words in square brackets inserted by the Matrimonial and Family Proceedings Act 1984, s 46(1), Sch 1, para 25.

Sub-s (9): words omitted repealed by the Children Act 1989, s 108(7), Sch 15; words in square brackets substituted by the Maintenance Orders (Backdating) Order 1993, SI 1993/623, art 2, Sch 1, para 7.

Sub-ss (9A)–(9C): inserted by SI 1993/623, art 2, Sch 1, para 8.

Sub-ss (10), (13): repealed by the Family Law Reform Act 1987, s 33(4), Sch 4.

Sub-s (11): words in square brackets substituted by the Matrimonial and Family Proceedings Act 1984, s 9.

Sub-s (12): substituted by the Children Act 1989, s 108(5), Sch 13, para 38.

[20ZA Variation of orders for periodical payments: further provisions

(1)   Subject to subsections (7) and (8) below, the power of the court under section 20 of this Act to vary an order for the making of periodical payments shall include power, if the court is satisfied that payment has not been made in accordance with the order, to exercise one of its powers under paragraphs (a) to (d) of section 59(3) of the Magistrates' Courts Act 1980.

(2)   In any case where—
    (a) a magistrates' court has made an order under this Part of this Act for the making of periodical payments, and
    (b) payments under the order are required to be made by any method of payment falling within section 59(6) of the Magistrates' Courts Act 1980 (standing order, etc),

an application may be made under this subsection to the clerk to the justices for the petty sessions area for which the court is acting for the order to be varied as mentioned in subsection (3) below.

(3)   Subject to subsection (5) below, where an application is made under subsection (2) above, the clerk, after giving written notice (by post or otherwise) of the application to the respondent and allowing the respondent, within the period of 14 days beginning with the date of the giving of that notice, an opportunity to make written representations, may vary the order to provide that payments under the order shall be made to the clerk.

(4)   The clerk may proceed with an application under subsection (2) above notwithstanding that the respondent has not received written notice of the application.

(5)   Where an application has been made under subsection (2) above, the clerk may, if he considers it inappropriate to exercise his power under subsection (3) above, refer the matter to the court which, subject to subsections (7) and (8) below, may vary the order by exercising one of its powers under paragraphs (a) to (d) of section 59(3) of the Magistrates' Courts Act 1980.

(6)   Subsection (4) of section 59 of the Magistrates' Courts Act 1980 (power of court to order that account be opened) shall apply for the purposes of subsections (1) and (5) above as it applies for the purposes of that section.

(7)   Before varying the order by exercising one of its powers under paragraphs (a) to (d) of section 59(3) of the Magistrates' Courts Act 1980, the court shall have regard to any representations made by the parties to the application.

(8)   If the court does not propose to exercise its power [under paragraph (c), (cc) or (d)] of subsection (3) of section 59 of the Magistrates' Courts Act 1980, the court shall, unless upon representations expressly made in that behalf by the person to whom payments under the order are required to be made it is satisfied that it is undesirable to do so, exercise its power under paragraph (b) of that subsection.

(9)   Subsection (12) of section 20 of this Act shall have effect for the purposes of applications under subsection (2) above as it has effect for the purposes of applications under that section.

(10)   None of the powers of the court, or of the clerk to the justices, conferred by this section shall be exercisable in relation to an order under this Part of this Act for the making of periodical payments which is not a qualifying maintenance order (within the meaning of section 59 of the Magistrates' Courts Act 1980).]

Inserted by the Maintenance Enforcement Act 1991, s 5.

Sub-s (8): words in square brackets substituted by the Child Support Act 1991 (Consequential Amendments) Order 1994, SI 1994/731, art 2.

[20A   Revival of orders for periodical payments

(1)   Where an order made by a magistrates' court under this Part of this Act for the making of periodical payments to or in respect of a child (other than an interim maintenance order) ceases to have effect—

(a) on the date on which the child attains the age of sixteen, or

(b) at any time after that date but before or on the date on which he attains the age of eighteen,

the child may apply to the court which made the order for an order for its revival.

(2)   If on such an application it appears to the court that—

(a) the child is, will be or (if an order were made under this subsection) would be receiving instruction at an educational establishment or undergoing training for a trade, profession or vocation, whether or not while in gainful employment, or

(b) there are special circumstances which justify the making of an order under this subsection,

the court shall have power by order to revive the order from such date as the court may specify, not being earlier than the date of the making of the application.

(3)   Any order revived under this section may be varied or revoked under section 20 in the same way as it could have been varied or revoked had it continued in being.]

NOTES

Inserted by the Family Law Reform Act 1987, s 33(1), Sch 2, para 69; substituted by the Children Act 1989, s 108(5), Sch 13, para 39.

22   Variation of instalments of lump sum

Where in the exercise of its powers under [section 75 of the Magistrates' Courts Act 1980] a magistrates' court orders that a lump sum required to be paid under this Part of this Act shall be paid by instalments, the court, on an application made by either the person liable to pay or the person entitled to receive that sum, shall have power to vary that order by varying the number of instalments payable, the amount of any instalment payable and the date on which any instalment becomes payable.

NOTES

Words in square brackets substituted by the Magistrates' Courts Act 1980, s 154, Sch 7, para 160.

23 Supplementary provisions with respect to variation and revocation of orders

(1) . . .

(2) The powers of a magistrates' court to revoke, revive or vary an order for the periodical payment of money [and the power of the clerk of a magistrates' court to vary such an order] under [section 60 of the Magistrates' Courts Act 1980] and [the power of a magistrates' court] to suspend or rescind certain other orders under [section 63(2) of that Act] shall not apply in relation to an order made under this Part of this Act.

NOTES

Sub-s (1): repealed by the Courts and Legal Services Act 1990, s 125(7), Sch 20.

Sub-s (2): words in first and third pairs of square brackets inserted by the Maintenance Enforcement Act 1991, s 11(1), Sch 2, para 2; words in second and final pairs of square brackets substituted by the Magistrates' Courts Act 1980, s 154, Sch 7, para 161.

25 Effect on certain orders of parties living together

(1) Where—
    (a) periodical payments are required to be made to one of the parties to a marriage (whether for his own benefit or for the benefit of a child of the family) by an order made under section 2, [or 6] of this Act or by an interim maintenance order made under section 19 of this Act (otherwise than on an application under section 7 of this Act), . . .
    (b) . . .

the order shall be enforceable notwithstanding that the parties to the marriage are living with each other at the date of the making of the order or that, although they are not living with each other at that date, they subsequently resume living with each other; but the order shall cease to have effect if after that date the parties continue to live with each other, or resume living with each other, for a continuous period exceeding six months.

(2) Where any of the following orders is made under this Part of this Act, that is to say—
    (a) an order under section 2, [or 6] of this Act which requires periodical payments to be made to a child of the family, [or]

(b) an interim maintenance order under section 19 of this Act (otherwise than on an application under section 7 of this Act) which requires periodical payments to be made to a child of the family,

(c), (d) . . .

then, unless the court otherwise directs, the order shall continue to have effect and be enforceable notwithstanding that the parties to the marriage in question are living with each other at the date of the making of the order or that, although they are not living with each other at that date, they subsequently resume living with each other.

(3) Any order made under section 7 of this Act, and any interim maintenance order made on an application for an order under that section, shall cease to have effect if the parties to the marriage resume living with each other.

(4) Where an order made under this Part of this Act ceases to have effect by virtue of subsection (1) or (3) above or by virtue of a direction given under subsection (2) above, a magistrates' court may, on an application made by either party to the marriage, make an order declaring that the first mentioned order ceased to have effect from such date as the court may specify.

NOTES

Sub-ss (1), (2): words omitted repealed and words in square brackets substituted, inserted or added by the Children Act 1989, s 108(5), (7), Sch 13, para 41, Sch 15.

Reconciliation

26 Reconciliation

(1) Where an application is made for an order under section 2 of this Act the court, before deciding whether to exercise its powers under that section, shall consider whether there is any possibility of reconciliation between the parties to the marriage in question; and if at any stage of the proceedings on that application it appears to the court that there is a reasonable possibility of such a reconciliation, the court may adjourn the proceedings for such period as it thinks fit to enable attempts to be made to effect a reconciliation.

(2) Where the court adjourns any proceedings under subsection (1) above, it may request a probation officer or any other person to attempt to effect

a reconciliation between the parties to the marriage, and where any such request is made, the probation officer or that other person shall report in writing to the court whether the attempt has been successful or not, but shall not include in that report any other information.

32   Enforcement etc of orders for payment of money

[(1)   An order for the payment of money made by a magistrates' court under this Part of this Act shall be enforceable as a magistrates' court maintenance order.]

(2)   Without prejudice to [section 59 of the Magistrates' Courts Act 1980] (which relates to the power of a magistrates' court to direct periodical payments to be made through the clerk of a magistrates' court), a magistrates' court making an order under this Part of this Act for the making of a periodical payment by one person to another may direct that it shall be made to some third party on that other person's behalf instead of directly to that other person; and, for the purposes of any order made under this Part of this Act, [the said section 59] shall have effect as if, in [subsection (7)] thereof, for the words ["the person who applied for the maintenance order"] there were substituted the words "the person to whom the payments under the order fall to be made".

(3)   Any person for the time being under an obligation to make payments in pursuance of any order for the payment of money made under this Part of this Act shall give notice of any change of address to such person, if any, as may be specified in the order; and any person who without reasonable excuse fails to give such a notice shall be liable on summary conviction to a fine not exceeding [level 2 on the standard scale].

(4)   A person shall not be entitled to enforce through the High Court or any county court the payment of any arrears due under an order made by virtue of this Part of this Act without the leave of that court if those arrears became due more than twelve months before proceedings to enforce the payment of them are begun.

(5)   The court hearing an application for the grant of leave under subsection (4) above may refuse leave, or may grant leave subject to such restrictions and conditions (including conditions as to the allowing of time

for payment or the making of payment by instalments) as that court thinks proper, or may remit the payment of such arrears or any part thereof.

(6)   An application for the grant of leave under subsection (4) above shall be made in such manner as may be prescribed by rules.

Sub-s (1): substituted by the Family Law Reform Act 1987, s 33(1), Sch 2, para 70.

Sub-s (2): words in first and second pairs of square brackets substituted by the Magistrates' Courts Act 1980, s 154, Sch 7, para 164; words in final pair of square brackets substituted by the Maintenance Enforcement Act 1991, s 11(1), Sch 2, para 3.

Sub-s (3): maximum fine converted to a level on the standard scale by the Criminal Justice Act 1982, ss 37, 46.

PART V
SUPPLEMENTARY PROVISIONS

88   Interpretation

(1)   In this Act—
. . . . .
"child", in relation to one or both of the parties to a marriage, includes [a child whose father and mother were not married to each other at the time of his birth];
"child of the family", in relation to the parties to a marriage, means—
(a)   a child of both of those parties; and
(b)   any other child, not being a child who is [placed with those parties as foster parents] by a local authority or voluntary organisation, who has been treated by both of those parties as a child of their family;
"commission area" has the same meaning as in [the Justices of the Peace Act 1997];
["family proceedings"] has the meaning assigned to it by [section 65 of the Magistrates' Courts Act 1980];
"local authority" means the council of a county (other than a metropolitan county), of a metropolitan district or of a London borough, or the Common Council of the City of London;
["magistrates' court maintenance order" has the same meaning as in section 150(1) of the Magistrates' Courts Act 1980;]

["maintenance assessment" has the same meaning as it has in the Child Support Act 1991 by virtue of section 54 of that Act as read with any regulations in force under that section.]

["petty sessions area" has the same meaning as in the Justices of the Peace Act 1997;]

"rules" means rules made under [section 144 of the Magistrates' Courts Act 1980].

(2)   References in this Act to the parties to a marriage living with each other shall be construed as references to their living with each other in the same household.

(3)   For the avoidance of doubt it is hereby declared that references in this Act to remarriage include references to a marriage which is by law void or voidable.

(4), (5)   . . .

NOTES

Sub-s (1): definition omitted repealed by the Children Act 1989, s 108(7), Sch 15; in definition "commission area" words in square brackets and whole of definition "petty sessions area" substituted by the Justices of the Peace Act 1997, s 73(2), Sch 5, para 18; in definitions "child" and "child of the Family", words in square brackets substituted by the Children Act 1989, s 108(5), Sch 13, para 43; in definition "family proceedings" words in first pair of square brackets substituted by the Children Act 1989, s 92, Sch 11, para 6, words in second pair of square brackets substituted by the Magistrates' Courts Act 1980, s 154, Sch 7, para 167; definition "magistrates' court maintenance order" inserted by the Family Law Reform Act 1987, s 33(1), Sch 2, para 71; definition "maintenance assessment" inserted by the Maintenance Orders (Backdating) Order 1993, SI 1993/623, art 2, Sch 1, para 9; in definition "rules" words in square brackets substituted by the Magistrates' Courts Act 1980, s 154, Sch 7, para 167.

Sub-ss (4), (5): outside the scope of this work.

90   Short title and extent

(1)   This Act may be cited as the Domestic Proceedings and Magistrates' Courts Act 1978.

(2)   . . .

(3)   Except for the following provisions, that is to say—
    (a) sections 54, 59, 74 (5), 88 (5), 89 (2), (3) and (4) and this section, and
    (b) [paragraphs 12, 13, 14 and 33] of Schedule 2 and Schedule 3,

this Act does not extend to Northern Ireland, and in section 88 (5) of this Act any reference to an enactment includes a reference to an enactment contained in an Act of the Parliament of Northern Ireland or a Measure of the Northern Ireland Assembly.

NOTES

Sub-s (2): outside the scope of this work.

Sub-s (3): words in square brackets substituted by the Maintenance Orders (Reciprocal Enforcement) Act 1992, s 2(1), Sch 2, para 1.

Supreme Court Act 1981

(c 54)

An Act to consolidate with amendments the Supreme Court of Judicature (Consolidation) Act 1925 and other enactments relating to the Supreme Court in England and Wales and the administration of justice therein; to repeal certain obsolete or unnecessary enactments so relating; to amend Part VIII of the Mental Health Act 1959, the Courts-Martial (Appeals) Act 1968, the Arbitration Act 1979 and the law relating to county courts; and for connected purposes

[28 July 1981]

41 Wards of court

(1)   Subject to the provisions of this section, no minor shall be made a ward of court except by virtue of an order to that effect made by the High Court.

(2)   Where an application is made for such an order in respect of a minor, the minor shall become a ward of court on the making of the application, but shall cease to be a ward of court at the end of such period as may be prescribed unless within that period an order has been made in accordance with the application.

[(2A)   Subsection (2) does not apply with respect to a child who is the subject of a care order (as defined by section 105 of the Children Act 1989).]

(3)   The High Court may, either upon an application in that behalf or without such an application, order that any minor who is for the time being a ward of court shall cease to be a ward of court.

Sub-s (2A): inserted by the Children Act 1989, s 108(5), (6), Sch 13, para 45(2), Sch 14, para 1.

Child Abduction Act 1984

(c 37)

An Act to amend the criminal law relating to the abduction of children
[12 July 1984]

PART I
OFFENCES UNDER LAW OF ENGLAND AND WALES

1 Offence of abduction of child by parent, etc

(1)   Subject to subsections (5) and (8) below, a person connected with a child under the age of sixteen commits an offence if he takes or sends the child out of the United Kingdom without the appropriate consent.

[(2)   A person is connected with a child for the purposes of this section if—
  (a) he is a parent of the child; or
  (b) in the case of a child whose parents were not married to each other at the time of his birth, there are reasonable grounds for believing that he is the father of the child; or
  (c) he is a guardian of the child; or
  (d) he is a person in whose favour a residence order is in force with respect to the child; or
  (e) he has custody of the child.

(3)   In this section "the appropriate consent", in relation to a child means—
  (a) the consent of each of the following—
    (i)   the child's mother;
    (ii) the child's father, if he has parental responsibility for him;
    (iii) any guardian of the child;
    (iv) any person in whose favour a residence order is in force with respect to the child;
    (v)   any person who has custody of the child; or
  (b) the leave of the court granted under or by virtue of any provision of Part II of the Children Act 1989; or

(c) if any person has custody of the child, the leave of the court which awarded custody to him.

(4)   A person does not commit an offence under this section by taking or sending a child out of the United Kingdom without obtaining the appropriate consent if—
  (a) he is a person in whose favour there is a residence order in force with respect to the child, and
  (b) he takes or sends him out of the United Kingdom for a period of less than one month.

(4A)   Subsection (4) above does not apply if the person taking or sending the child out of the United Kingdom does so in breach of an order under Part II of the Children Act 1989.]

(5)   A person does not commit an offence under this section by doing anything without the consent of another person whose consent is required under the foregoing provisions if—
  (a) he does it in the belief that the other person—
      (i)   has consented; or
      (ii) would consent if he was aware of all the relevant circumstances; or
  (b) he has taken all reasonable steps to communicate with the other person but has been unable to communicate with him; or
  (c) the other person has unreasonably refused to consent,

      . . . . .

[(5A) Subsection (5)(c) above does not apply if—
  (a) the person who refused to consent is a person—
      (i)   in whose favour there is a residence order in force with respect to the child; or
      (ii) who has custody of the child; or
  (b) the person taking or sending the child out of the United Kingdom is, by so acting, in breach of an order made by a court in the United Kingdom.]

(6)   Where, in proceedings for an offence under this section, there is sufficient evidence to raise an issue as to the application of subsection (5) above, it shall be for the prosecution to prove that that subsection does not apply.

[(7)   For the purposes of this section—
  (a) "guardian of a child", "residence order" and "parental responsibility" have the same meaning as in the Children Act 1989; and

(b) a person shall be treated as having custody of a child if there is in force an order of a court in the United Kingdom awarding him (whether solely or jointly with another person) custody, legal custody or care and control of the child.]

(8)   This section shall have effect subject to the provisions of the Schedule to this Act in relation to a child who is in the care of a local authority [detained in a place of safety, remanded to a local authority accommodation or the subject of] proceedings or an order relating to adoption.

NOTES

Sub-ss (2)–(4A): substituted, for sub-ss (2)–(4) as originally enacted, by the Children Act 1989, s 108(4), (6), Sch 12, para 37(2), Sch 14, para 1.

Sub-s (5A): substituted for part of original wording in sub-s (5) by the Children Act 1989, s 108(4), (6), Sch 12, para 37(3), Sch 14, para 1.

Sub-s (7): substituted by the Children Act 1989, s 108(4), (6), Sch 12, para 37(4), Sch 14, para 1.

Sub-s (8): words in square brackets substituted by the Children Act 1989, s 108(4), (6), Sch 12, para 37(5), Sch 14, para 1.

2   Offence of abduction of child by other persons

(1)   [Subject to subsection (3) below, a person, other than one mentioned in subsection (2) below,] commits an offence if, without lawful authority or reasonable excuse, he takes or detains a child under the age of sixteen—
   (a) so as to remove him from the lawful control of any person having lawful control of the child; or
   (b) so as to keep him out of the lawful control of any person entitled to lawful control of the child.

[(2)   The persons are—
   (a) where the father and mother of the child in question were married to each other at the time of his birth, the child's father and mother;
   (b) where the father and mother of the child in question were not married to each other at the time of his birth, the child's mother; and
   (c) any other person mentioned in section 1(2)(c) to (e) above.

(3)   In proceedings against any person for an offence under this section, it shall be a defence for that person to prove—
   (a) where the father and mother of the child in question were not married to each other at the time of his birth—
      (i) that he is the child's father; or

  (ii) that, at the time of the alleged offence, he believed, on reasonable grounds, that he was the child's father; or
  (b) that, at the time of the alleged offence, he believed that the child had attained the age of sixteen.]

NOTES

Sub-s (1): words in square brackets substituted by the Children Act 1989, s 108(4), (6), Sch 12, para 38(1), Sch 14, para 1.

Sub-ss (2), (3): substituted, for sub-s (2) as originally enacted, by the Children Act 1989, s 108(4), (6), Sch 12, para 38(2), Sch 14, para 1.

3 Construction of references to taking, sending and detaining

For the purposes of this Part of this Act—
  (a) a person shall be regarded as taking a child if he causes or induces the child to accompany him or any other person or causes the child to be taken;
  (b) a person shall be regarded as sending a child if he causes the child to be sent; . . .
  (c) a person shall be regarded as detaining a child if he causes the child to be detained or induces the child to remain with him or any other person [and
  (d) references to a child's parents and to a child whose parents were (or were not) married to each other at the time of his birth shall be construed in accordance with section 1 of the Family Law Reform Act 1987 (which extends their meaning).]

NOTES

Word omitted from para (b) repealed, and para (d) and the word "and" immediately preceding it added, by the Children Act 1989, s 108(4), (6), (7), Sch 12, para 39, Sch 14, paras 1, 27, Sch 15.

4 Penalties and prosecutions

(1) A person guilty of an offence under this Part of this Act shall be liable—
  (a) on summary conviction, to imprisonment for a term not exceeding six months or to a fine not exceeding the statutory maximum, . . ., or to both such imprisonment and fine;
  (b) on conviction on indictment, to imprisonment for a term not exceeding seven years.

(2)   No prosecution for an offence under section 1 above shall be instituted except by or with the consent of the Director of Public Prosecutions.

Sub-s (1): words omitted repealed by the Statute Law (Repeals) Act 1993.

5   Restriction on prosecutions for offence of kidnapping

Except by or with the consent of the Director of Public Prosecutions no prosecution shall be instituted for an offence of kidnapping if it was committed—
  (a) against a child under the age of sixteen; and
  (b) by a person connected with the child, within the meaning of section 1 above.

PART II
OFFENCE UNDER LAW OF SCOTLAND

6   Offence in Scotland of parent, etc taking or sending child out of United Kingdom

(1)   Subject to subsections (4) and (5) below, a person connected with a child under the age of sixteen years commits an offence if he takes or sends the child out of the United Kingdom—
  (a) without the appropriate consent if there is in respect of the child—
      (i)   an order of a court in the United Kingdom awarding custody of the child to any person [or naming any person as the person with whom the child is to live]; or
      (ii) an order of a court in England, Wales or Northern Ireland making the child a ward of court;
  (b) if there is in respect of the child an order of a court in the United Kingdom prohibiting the removal of the child from the United Kingdom or any part of it.

(2)   A person is connected with a child for the purposes of this section if—
  (a) he is a parent or guardian of the child; or
  (b) there is in force an order of a court in the United Kingdom awarding custody of the child to him [or naming him as the person with whom the child is to live] (whether solely or jointly with any other person); or

(c) in the case of [a child whose parents are not and have never been married to one another], there are reasonable grounds for believing that he is the father of the child.

(3)   In this section, the "appropriate consent" means—
  (a) in relation to a child to whom subsection (1)(a)(i) above applies—
    (i) the consent of each person
      (a) who is a parent or guardian of the child; or
      (b) to whom custody of the child has been awarded [or who is named as the person with whom the child is to live (whether the award is made, or the person so named is named] solely or jointly with any other person) by an order of a court in the United Kingdom; or
    (ii) the leave of that court;
  (b) in relation to a child to whom subsection (1)(a)(ii) above applies, the leave of the court which made the child a ward of court;

Provided that, in relation to a child to whom more than one order referred to in subsection (1)(a) above applies, the appropriate consent may be that of any court which has granted an order as referred to in the said subsection (1)(a); and where one of these orders is an order referred to in the said subsection (1)(a)(ii) no other person as referred to in paragraph (a)(i) above shall be entitled to give the appropriate consent.

(4)   In relation to a child to whom subsection (1)(a)(i) above applies, a person does not commit an offence by doing anything without the appropriate consent if—
  (a) he does it in the belief that each person referred to in subsection (3)(a)(i) above—
    (i) has consented; or
    (ii) would consent if he was aware of all the relevant circumstances; or
  (b) he has taken all reasonable steps to communicate with such other person but has been unable to communicate with him.

(5)   In proceedings against any person for an offence under this section it shall be a defence for that person to show that at the time of the alleged offence he had no reason to believe that there was in existence an order referred to in subsection (1) above.

(6)   For the purposes of this section—
  (a) a person shall be regarded as taking a child if he causes or induces the child to accompany him or any other person, or causes the child to be taken; and

(b) a person shall be regarded as sending a child if he causes the child to be sent.

(7)   In this section "guardian" means [...] a person appointed by deed or will or by order of a court of competent jurisdiction to be the guardian of a child.

NOTES

Sub-s (1): words in square brackets in para (a) inserted by the Children (Scotland) Act 1995, s 105(4), Sch 4, para 34(a).

Sub-s (2): words in square brackets in para (b) inserted by the Children (Scotland) Act 1995, s 105(4), Sch 4, para 34(b); words in square brackets in para (c) substituted by the Law Reform (Parent and Child) (Scotland) Act 1986, s 10(1), Sch 1, para 20(a).

Sub-s (3): words in square brackets in para (a) substituted by the Children (Scotland) Act 1995, s 105(4), Sch 4, para 34(c).

Sub-s (7): words in square brackets omitted inserted by the Law Reform (Parent and Child) (Scotland) Act 1986, s 10(1), Sch 1, para 20(b), repealed by the Age of Legal Capacity (Scotland) Act 1991, s 10, Sch 2.

PART III
SUPPLEMENTARY

13 Short title, commencement and extent

(1)   This Act may be cited as the Child Abduction Act 1984.

(2)   This Act shall come into force at the end of the period of three months beginning with the day on which it is passed.

(3)   Part I of this Act extends to England and Wales only, Part II extends to Scotland only and in Part III section 11(1) and (5)(a) and section 12 do not extend to Scotland and section 11(1), (2) and (5)(a) and (c) does not extend to Northern Ireland.

SCHEDULE
MODIFICATIONS OF SECTION I FOR CHILDREN IN CERTAIN CASES
Section 1(8)

Children in care of local authorities and voluntary organisations

1.—(1) This paragraph applies in the case of a child who is in the care of a local authority [within the meaning of the Children Act 1989] in England or Wales.

(2)   Where this paragraph applies, section 1 of this Act shall have effect as if—
  (a) the reference in subsection (1) to the appropriate consent were a reference to the consent of the local authority . . . in whose care the child is; and
  (b) subsections (3) to (6) were omitted.

Children in places of safety

2.—[(1) This paragraph applies in the case of a child who is—
  (a) detained in a place of safety under section 16(3) of the Children and Young Persons Act 1969; or
  (b) remanded to local authority accommodation under section 23 of that Act.]

(2)   Where this paragraph applies, section 1 of this Act shall have effect as if—
  (a) the reference in subsection (1) to the appropriate consent were a reference to the leave of any magistrates' court acting for the area in which the place of safety is; and
  (b) subsections (3) to (6) were omitted.

Adoption and custodianship

3.—(1) This paragraph applies in the case of a child—
  (a) who is the subject of an order under [section 18 of the Adoption Act 1976] freeing him for adoption; or
  (b) who is the subject of a pending application for such an order; or
  (c) who is the subject of a pending application for an adoption order; or
  (d) who is the subject of an order under [section 55 of the Adoption Act 1976] relating to adoption abroad or of a pending application for such an order; or
  (e) . . .

(2)   Where this paragraph applies, section 1 of this Act shall have effect as if—
  (a) the reference in subsection (1) to the appropriate consent were a reference—
    (i) in a case within sub-paragraph (1)(a) above, to the consent of the adoption agency which made the application for the [section 18

order or, if the section 18 order has been varied under section 21 of that Act so as to give parental responsibility to another agency], to the consent of that other agency;

   (ii) in a case within sub-paragraph (1)(b), [or (c)] above, to the leave of the court to which the application was made; and

   (iii) in a case within sub-paragraph (1)(d) above, to the leave of the court which made the order or, as the case may be, to which the application was made; and

(b) subsections (3) to (6) were omitted.

[(3) Sub-paragraph (2) above shall be construed as if the references to the court included, in any case where the court is a magistrates' court, a reference to any magistrates' court acting for the same area as that court.]

Cases within paragraphs 1 and 3

4.   In the case of a child falling within both paragraph 1 and paragraph 3 above, the provisions of paragraph 3 shall apply to the exclusion of those in paragraph 1.

Interpretation

[5.   In this Schedule—

   (a) "adoption agency" and "adoption order" have the same meaning as in the Adoption Act 1976; and

   (b) "area", in relation to a magistrates' court, means the petty sessions area (within the meaning of [the Justices of the Peace Act 1997]) for which the court is appointed.]

NOTES

Paras 1–3: words omitted repealed, and words in square brackets substituted, inserted or added, by the Children Act 1989, s 108(4), (6), Sch 12, para 40, Sch 14, paras 1, 27, Sch 15.

Para 5: substituted by the Children Act 1989, s 108(4), (6), Sch 12, para 40, Sch 14, para 1; words in square brackets substituted by the Justices of the Peace Act 1997, s 73(2), Sch 5, para 20.

Surrogacy Arrangements Act 1985

(c 49)

An Act to regulate certain activities in connection with arrangements made with a view to women carrying children as surrogate mothers

[16 July 1985]

1 Meaning of "surrogate mother", "surrogacy arrangement" and other terms

(1)   The following provisions shall have effect for the interpretation of this Act.

(2)   "Surrogate mother" means a woman who carries a child in pursuance of an arrangement—

    (a) made before she began to carry the child, and

    (b) made with a view to any child carried in pursuance of it being handed over to, and [parental responsibility being met] (so far as practicable) by, another person or other persons.

(3)   An arrangement is a surrogacy arrangement if, were a woman to whom the arrangement relates to carry a child in pursuance of it, she would be a surrogate mother.

(4)   In determining whether an arrangement is made with such a view as is mentioned in subsection (2) above regard may be had to the circumstances as a whole (and, in particular, where there is a promise or understanding that any payment will or may be made to the woman or for her benefit in respect of the carrying of any child in pursuance of the arrangement, to that promise or understanding).

(5)   An arrangement may be regarded as made with such a view though subject to conditions relating to the handing over of any child.

(6)   A woman who carries a child is to be treated for the purposes of subsection (2)(a) above as beginning to carry it at the time of the insemination [or of the placing in her of an embryo, of an egg in the process of fertilisation or of sperm and eggs, as the case may be,] that results in her carrying the child.

(7)   "Body of persons" means a body of persons corporate or unincorporate.

(8)   "Payment" means payment in money or money's worth.

(9)   This Act applies to arrangements whether or not they are lawful ...

[1A   Surrogacy arrangements unenforceable

No surrogacy arrangement is enforceable by or against any of the persons making it.]

2   Negotiating surrogacy arrangements on a commercial basis, etc

(1)   No person shall on a commercial basis do any of the following acts in the United Kingdom, that is—
  (a) initiate or take part in any negotiations with a view to the making of a surrogacy arrangement,
  (b) offer or agree to negotiate the making of a surrogacy arrangement, or
  (c) compile any information with a view to its use in making, or negotiating the making of, surrogacy arrangements;

and no person shall in the United Kingdom knowingly cause another to do any of those acts on a commercial basis.

(2)   A person who contravenes subsection (1) above is guilty of an offence; but it is not a contravention of that subsection—

(a) for a woman, with a view to becoming a surrogate mother herself, to do any act mentioned in that subsection or to cause such an act to be done, or

(b) for any person, with a view to a surrogate mother carrying a child for him, to do such an act or to cause such an act to be done.

(3) For the purposes of this section, a person does an act on a commercial basis (subject to subsection (4) below) if—

(a) any payment is at any time received by himself or another in respect of it, or

(b) he does it with a view to any payment being received by himself or another in respect of making, or negotiating or facilitating the making of, any surrogacy arrangement.

In this subsection "payment" does not include payment to or for the benefit of a surrogate mother or prospective surrogate mother.

(4) In proceedings against a person for an offence under subsection (1) above, he is not to be treated as doing an act on a commercial basis by reason of any payment received by another in respect of the act if it is proved that—

(a) in a case where the payment was received before he did the act, he did not do the act knowing or having reasonable cause to suspect that any payment had been received in respect of the act; and

(b) in any other case, he did not do the act with a view to any payment being received in respect of it.

(5) Where—

(a) a person acting on behalf of a body of persons takes any part in negotiating or facilitating the making of a surrogacy arrangement in the United Kingdom, and

(b) negotiating or facilitating the making of surrogacy arrangements is an activity of the body,

then, if the body at any time receives any payment made by or on behalf of—

    (i) a woman who carries a child in pursuance of the arrangement,

    (ii) the person or persons for whom she carries it, or

    (iii) any person connected with the woman or with that person or those persons,

the body is guilt of an offence.

For the purposes of this subsection, a payment received by a person connected with a body is to be treated as received by the body.

(6)   In proceedings against a body for an offence under subsection (5) above, it is a defence to prove that the payment concerned was not made in respect of the arrangement mentioned in paragraph (a) of that subsection.

(7)   A person who in the United Kingdom takes part in the management or control—

(a) of any body of persons, or

(b) of any of the activities of any body of persons,

is guilty of an offence if the activity described in subsection (8) below is an activity of the body concerned.

(8)   The activity referred to in subsection (7) above is negotiating or facilitating the making of surrogacy arrangements in the United Kingdom, being—

(a) arrangements the making of which is negotiated or facilitated on a commercial basis, or

(b) arrangements in the case of which payments are received (or treated for the purposes of subsection (5) above as received) by the body concerned in contravention of subsection (5) above.

(9)   In proceedings against a person for an offence under subsection (7) above, it is a defence to prove that he neither knew nor had reasonable cause to suspect that the activity described in subsection (8) above was an activity of the body concerned; and for the purposes of such proceedings any arrangement falling within subsection (8)(b) above shall be disregarded if it is proved that the payment concerned was not made in respect of the arrangement.

3   Advertisements about surrogacy

(1)   This section applies to any advertisement containing an indication (however expressed)—

(a) that any person is or may be willing to enter into a surrogacy arrangement or to negotiate or facilitate the making of a surrogacy arrangement, or

(b) that any person is looking for a woman willing to become a surrogate mother or for persons wanting a woman to carry a child as a surrogate mother.

(2)   Where a newspaper or periodical containing an advertisement to which this section applies is published in the United Kingdom, any proprietor, editor or publisher of the newspaper or periodical is guilty of an offence.

(3)   Where an advertisement to which this section applies is conveyed by means of a telecommunication system so as to be seen or heard (or both) in the United Kingdom, any person who in the United Kingdom causes it to be so conveyed knowing it to contain such an indication as is mentioned in subsection (1) above is guilty of an offence.

(4)   A person who publishes or causes to be published in the United Kingdom an advertisement to which this section applies (not being an advertisement contained in a newspaper or periodical or conveyed by means of a telecommunication system) is guilty of an offence.

(5)   A person who distributes or causes to be distributed in the United Kingdom an advertisement to which this section applies (not being an advertisement contained in a newspaper or periodical published outside the United Kingdom or an advertisement conveyed by means of a telecommunication system) knowing it to contain such an indication as is mentioned in subsection (1) above is guilty of an offence.

(6)   In this section "telecommunication system" has the same meaning as in the Telecommunications Act 1984.

4   Offences

(1)   A person guilty of an offence under this Act shall be liable on summary conviction—
   (a) in the case of an offence under section 2 to a fine not exceeding level 5 on the standard scale or to imprisonment for a term not exceeding 3 months or both,
   (b) in the case of an offence under section 3 to a fine not exceeding level 5 on the standard scale.

. . . . .

In this subsection "the standard scale" has the meaning given by section 75 of the Criminal Justice Act 1982.

(2)   No proceedings for an offence under this Act shall be instituted—
   (a) in England and Wales, except by or with the consent of the Director of Public Prosecutions; and
   (b) in Northern Ireland, except by or with the consent of the Director of Public Prosecutions for Northern Ireland.

(3)   Where an offence under this Act committed by a body corporate is proved to have been committed with the consent or connivance of, or to be

attributable to any neglect on the part of, any director, manager, secretary or other similar officer of the body corporate or any person who was purporting to act in any such capacity, he as well as the body corporate is guilty of the offence and is liable to be proceeded against and punished accordingly.

(4)   Where the affairs of a body corporate are managed by its members, subsection (3) above shall apply in relation to the acts and defaults of a member in connection with his functions of management as if he were a director of the body corporate.

(5)   In any proceedings for an offence under section 2 of this Act, proof of things done or of words written, spoken or published (whether or not in the presence of any party to the proceedings) by any person taking part in the management or control of a body of persons or of any of the activities of the body, or by any person doing any of the acts mentioned in subsection (1)(a) to (c) of that section on behalf of the body, shall be admissible as evidence of the activities of the body.

(6)   In relation to an offence under this Act, section 127(1) of the Magistrates' Courts Act 1980 (information must be laid within six months of commission of offence), [section 136(1) of the Criminal Procedure (Scotland) Act 1995] (proceedings must be commenced within that time) and Article 19(1) of the Magistrates' Courts (Northern Ireland) Order 1981 (complaint must be made within that time) shall have effect as if for the reference to six months there were substituted a reference to two years.

NOTES

Sub-s (1): words omitted repealed by the Statute Law (Repeals) Act 1993.
Sub-s (6): words in square brackets substituted by the Criminal Procedure (Consequential Provisions) (Scotland) Act 1995, s 5, Sch 4, para 57.

5   Short title and extent

(1)   This Act may be cited as the Surrogacy Arrangements Act 1985.

(2)   This Act extends to Northern Ireland.

Child Abduction and Custody Act 1985

(c 60)

An Act to enable the United Kingdom to ratify two international Conventions relating respectively to the civil aspects of international child abduction and to the recognition of custody decisions

[25 July 1985]

PART I
INTERNATIONAL CHILD ABDUCTION

1 The Hague Convention

(1)   In this Part of this Act "the Convention" means the Convention on the Civil Aspects of International Child Abduction which was signed at The Hague on 25th October 1980.

(2)   Subject to the provisions of this Part of this Act, the provisions of that Convention set out in Schedule 1 to this Act shall have the force of law in the United Kingdom.

PART II
RECOGNITION AND ENFORCEMENT OF CUSTODY DECISIONS

12 The European Convention

(1)   In this Part of this Act "the Convention" means the European Convention on Recognition and Enforcement of Decisions concerning Custody of Children and on the Restoration of Custody of Children which was signed in Luxembourg on 20th May 1980.

(2)   Subject to the provisions of this Part of this Act, the provisions of that Convention set out in Schedule 2 to this Act (which includes Articles 9 and 10 as they have effect in consequence of a reservation made by the United Kingdom under Article 17) shall have the force of law in the United Kingdom.

PART III
SUPPLEMENTARY

29   Short title, commencement and extent

(1)   This Act may be cited as the Child Abduction and Custody Act 1985.

(2)   This Act shall come into force on such day as may be appointed by an order made by statutory instrument by the Lord Chancellor and the Lord Advocate; and different days may be so appointed for different provisions.

(3)   This Act extends to Northern Ireland.

SCHEDULE I
CONVENTION ON THE CIVIL ASPECTS OF INTERNATIONAL CHILD
ABDUCTION

Section 1(2)

CHAPTER I
SCOPE OF THE CONVENTION

Article 3

The removal or the retention of a child is to be considered wrongful where—
  (a) it is in breach of rights of custody attributed to a person, an institution or any other body, either jointly or alone, under the law of the State in which the child was habitually resident immediately before the removal or retention; and
  (b) at the time of removal or retention those rights were actually exercised, either jointly or alone, or would have been so exercised but for the removal or retention.

The rights of custody mentioned in sub-paragraph (a) above may arise in particular by operation of law or by reason of a judicial or administrative decision, or by reason of an agreement having legal effect under the law of that State

Article 4

The Convention shall apply to any child who was habitually resident in a Contracting State immediately before any breach of custody or access rights. The Convention shall cease to apply when the child attains the age of sixteen years.

Article 5

For the purposes of this Convention—
- (a) "rights of custody" shall include rights relating to the care of the person of the child and, in particular, the right to determine the child's place of residence;
- (b) "rights of access" shall include the right to take a child for a limited period of time to a place other than the child's habitual residence.

CHAPTER II
CENTRAL AUTHORITIES

Article 7

Central Authorities shall co-operate with each other and promote co-operation amongst the competent authorities in their respective States to secure the prompt return of children and to achieve the other objects of this Convention.

In particular, either directly or through any intermediary, they shall take all appropriate measures—
- (a) to discover the whereabouts of a child who has been wrongfully removed or retained;
- (b) to prevent further harm to the child or prejudice to interested parties by taking or causing to be taken provisional measures;
- (c) to secure the voluntary return of the child or to bring about an amicable resolution of the issues;
- (d) to exchange, where desirable, information relating to the social background of the child;
- (e) to provide information of a general character as to the law of their State in connection with the application of the Convention;
- (f) to initiate or facilitate the institution of judicial or administrative proceedings with a view to obtaining the return of the child and, in a proper case, to make arrangements for organizing or securing the effective exercise of rights of access;
- (g) where the circumstances so require, to provide or facilitate the provision of legal aid and advice, including the participation of legal counsel and advisers;

(h) to provide such administrative arrangements as may be necessary and appropriate to secure the safe return of the child;

(i) to keep each other informed with respect to the operation of this Convention and, as far as possible, to eliminate any obstacles to its application.

CHAPTER III
RETURN OF CHILDREN

Article 8

Any person, institution or other body claiming that a child has been removed or retained in breach of custody rights may apply either to the Central Authority of the child's habitual residence or to the Central Authority of any other Contracting State for assistance in securing the return of the child.

The application shall contain—

(a) information concerning the identity of the applicant, of the child and of the person alleged to have removed or retained the child;

(b) where available, the date of birth of the child;

(c) the grounds on which the applicant's claim for return of the child is based;

(d) all available information relating to the whereabouts of the child and the identity of the person with whom the child is presumed to be.

The application may be accompanied or supplemented by—

(e) an authenticated copy of any relevant decision or agreement;

(f) a certificate or an affidavit emanating from a Central Authority, or other competent authority of the State of the child's habitual residence, or from a qualified person, concerning the relevant law of that State;

(g) any other relevant document.

Article 9

If the Central Authority which receives an application referred to in Article 8 has reason to believe that the child is in another Contracting State, it shall directly and without delay transmit the application to the Central Authority of that Contracting State and inform the requesting Central Authority, or the applicant, as the case may be.

Article 10

The Central Authority of the State where the child is shall take or cause to be taken all appropriate measures in order to obtain the voluntary return of the child.

Article 11

The judicial or administrative authorities of Contracting States shall act expeditiously in proceedings for the return of children.

If the judicial or administrative authority concerned has not reached a decision within six weeks from the date of commencement of the proceedings, the applicant or the Central Authority of the requested State, on its own initiative or if asked by the Central Authority of the requesting State, shall have the right to request a statement of the reasons for the delay. If a reply is received by the Central Authority of the requested State, that Authority shall transmit the reply to the Central Authority of the requesting State, or to the applicant, as the case may be.

Article 12

Where a child has been wrongfully removed or retained in terms of Article 3 and, at the date of the commencement of the proceedings before the judicial or administrative authority of the Contracting State where the child is, a period of less than one year has elapsed from the date of the wrongful removal or retention, the authority concerned shall order the return of the child forthwith.

The judicial or administrative authority, even where the proceedings have been commenced after the expiration of the period of one year referred to in the preceding paragraph, shall also order the return of the child, unless it is demonstrated that the child is now settled in its new environment.

Where the judicial or administrative authority in the requested state has reason to believe that the child has been taken to another State, it may stay the proceedings or dismiss the application for the return of the child.

Article 13

Notwithstanding the provisions of the preceding Article, the judicial or administrative authority of the requested State is not bound to order the return of the child if the person, institution or other body which opposes its return establishes that—

(a) the person, institution or other body having the care of the person of the child was not actually exercising the custody rights at the time of removal or retention, or had consented to or subsequently acquiesced in the removal or retention; or

(b) there is a grave risk that his or her return would expose the child to physical or psychological harm or otherwise place the child in an intolerable situation.

The judicial or administrative authority may also refuse to order the return of the child if it finds that the child objects to being returned and has attained an age and degree of maturity at which it is appropriate to take account of its views.

In considering the circumstances referred to in this Article, the judicial and administrative authorities shall take into account the information relating to the social background of the child provided by the Central Authority or other competent authority of the child's habitual residence.

Article 14

In ascertaining whether there has been a wrongful removal or retention within the meaning of Article 3, the judicial or administrative authorities of the requested State may take notice directly of the law of, and of judicial or administrative decisions, formally recognised or not in the State of the habitual residence of the child, without recourse to the specific procedures for the proof of that law or for the recognition of foreign decisions which would otherwise be applicable.

Article 15

The judicial or administrative authorities of a Contracting State may, prior to the making of an order for the return of the child, request that the applicant obtain from the authorities of the State of the habitual residence of the child a decision or other determination that the removal or retention was wrongful within the meaning of Article 3 of the Convention, where such a decision or determination may be obtained in that State. The Central Authorities of the Contracting States shall so far as practicable assist applicants to obtain such a decision or determination.

Article 16

After receiving notice of a wrongful removal or retention of a child in the sense of Article 3, the judicial or administrative authorities of the Contracting State to which the child has been removed or in which it has been retained shall not decide on the merits of rights of custody until it has been determined that the child is not to be returned under this Convention or unless an application under this Convention is not lodged within a reasonable time following receipt of the notice.

Article 17

The sole fact that a decision relating to custody has been given in or is entitled to recognition in the requested State shall not be a ground for refusing to return a child under this Convention, but the judicial or administrative authorities of the requested State may take account of the reasons for that decision in applying this Convention.

Article 18

The provisions of this Chapter do not limit the power of a judicial or administrative authority to order the return of the child at any time.

Article 19

A decision under this Convention concerning the return of the child shall not be taken to be a determination on the merits of any custody issue.

CHAPTER IV
RIGHTS OF ACCESS

Article 21

An application to make arrangements for organising or securing the effective exercise of rights of access may be presented to the Central Authorities of the Contracting States in the same way as an application for the return of a child.

The Central Authorities are bound by the obligations of co-operation which are set forth in Article 7 to promote the peaceful enjoyment of access rights and the fulfilment of any conditions to which the exercise of those rights may be subject. The Central Authorities shall take steps to remove, as far as possible, all obstacles to the exercise of such rights. The Central Authorities, either directly or through intermediaries, may initiate or assist in the institution of proceedings with a view to organising or protecting these rights and securing respect for the conditions to which the exercise of these rights may be subject.

CHAPTER V
GENERAL PROVISIONS

Article 22

No security , bond or deposit, however described, shall be required to guarantee the payment of costs and expenses in the judicial or administrative proceedings falling within the scope of this Convention.

Article 24

Any application, communication or other document sent to the Central Authority of the requested State shall be in the original language, and shall be accompanied by a translation into the official language or one of the official languages of the requested State or, where that is not feasible, a translation into French or English.

Article 26

Each Central Authority shall bear its own costs in applying this Convention.

Central Authorities and other public services of Contracting States shall not impose any charges in relation to applications submitted under this Convention. In particular, they may not require any payment from the applicant towards the costs and expenses of the proceedings or, where applicable, those arising from the participation of legal counsel or advisers. However, they may require the payment of the expenses incurred or to be incurred in implementing the return of the child.

However, a Contracting State may, by making a reservation in accordance with Article 42, declare that it shall not be bound to assume any costs referred to in the preceding paragraph resulting from the participation of legal counsel or advisers or from court proceedings, except insofar as those costs may be covered by its system of legal aid and advice.

Upon ordering the return of a child or issuing an order concerning rights of access under this Convention, the judicial or administrative authorities may, where appropriate, direct the person who removed or retained the child, or who prevented the exercise of rights of access, to pay necessary expenses incurred by or on behalf of the applicant, including travel expenses, any costs incurred or payments made for locating the child, the costs of legal representation of the applicant, and those of returning the child.

Article 27

When it is manifest that the requirements of this Convention are not fulfilled or that the application is otherwise not well founded, a Central Authority is not bound to accept the application. In that case, the Central Authority shall forthwith inform the applicant or the Central Authority through which the application was submitted, as the case may be, of its reasons.

Article 28

A Central Authority may require that the application be accompanied by a written authorisation empowering it to act on behalf of the applicant, or to designate a representative so to act.

Article 29

This Convention shall not preclude any person, institution or body who claims that there has been a breach of custody or access rights within the meaning of Article 3 or 21 from applying directly to the judicial or administrative authorities of a Contracting State, whether or not under the provisions of this Convention.

Article 30

Any application submitted to the Central Authorities or directly to the judicial or administrative authorities of a Contracting State in accordance with the terms of this Convention, together with documents and any other information appended thereto or provided by a Central Authority, shall be admissible in the courts or administrative authorities of the Contracting States.

Article 31

In relation to a State which in matters of custody of children has two or more systems of law applicable in different territorial units—
  (a) any reference to habitual residence in that State shall be construed as referring to habitual residence in a territorial unit of that State;
  (b) any reference to the law of the State of habitual residence shall be construed as referring to the law of the territorial unit in that State where the child habitually resides.

Article 32

In relation to a State which in matters of custody of children has two or more systems of law applicable to different categories of persons, any reference to the law of that State shall be construed as referring to the legal system specified by the law of that State.

SCHEDULE 2
EUROPEAN CONVENTION ON RECOGNITION AND ENFORCEMENT OF DECISIONS CONCERNING CUSTODY OF CHILDREN

Article 1

For the purposes of this Convention:
  (a) "child" means a person of any nationality, so long as he is under 16 years of age and has not the right to decide on his own place of residence under the law of his habitual residence, the law of his nationality or the internal law of the State addressed;
  (b) "authority" means a judicial or administrative authority;
  (c) "decision relating to custody" means a decision of an authority in so far as it relates to the care of the person of the child, including the right to decide on the place of his residence, or to the right of access to him;
  (d) "improper removal" means the removal of a child across an international frontier in breach of a decision relating to his custody which has been given in a Contracting State and which is enforceable in such a State; "improper removal" also includes:
    (i) the failure to return a child across an international frontier at the end of a period of the exercise of the right of access to this child or at the end of any other temporary stay in a territory other than that where the custody is exercised;

(ii) a removal which is subsequently declared unlawful within the meaning of Article 12.

Article 4

(1)   Any person who has obtained in a Contracting State a decision relating to the custody of a child and who wishes to have that decision recognised or enforced in another Contracting State may submit an application for this purpose to the central authority in any Contracting State.

(2)   The application shall be accompanied by the documents mentioned in Article 13.

(3)   The central authority receiving the application, if it is not the central authority in the State addressed, shall send the documents directly and without delay to that central authority.

(4)   The central authority receiving the application may refuse to intervene where it is manifestly clear that the conditions laid down by this Convention are not satisfied.

(5)   The central authority receiving the application shall keep the applicant informed without delay of the progress of his application.

Article 5

(1)   The central authority in the State addressed shall take or cause to be taken without delay all steps which it considers to be appropriate, if necessary by instituting proceedings before its competent authorities, in order:
  (a) to discover the whereabouts of the child;
  (b) to avoid, in particular by any necessary provisional measures, prejudice to the interests of the child or of the applicant;
  (c) to secure the recognition or enforcement of the decision;
  (d) to secure the delivery of the child to the applicant where enforcement is granted;
  (e) to inform the requesting authority of the measures taken and their results.

(2)   Where the central authority in the State addressed has reason to believe that the child is in the territory of another Contracting State it

shall send the documents directly and without delay to the central authority of that State.

(3)   With the exception of the cost of repatriation, each Contracting State undertakes not to claim any payment from an applicant in respect of any measures taken under paragraph (1) of this Article by the central authority of that State on the applicant's behalf, including the costs of proceedings and, where applicable, the costs incurred by the assistance of a lawyer.

(4)   If recognition or enforcement is refused, and if the central authority of the State addressed considers that it should comply with a request by the applicant to bring in that State proceedings concerning the substance of the case, that authority shall use its best endeavours to secure the representation of the applicant in the proceedings under conditions no less favourable than those available to a person who is resident in and a national of that State and for this purpose it may, in particular, institute proceedings before its competent authorities.

Article 7

A decision relating to custody given in a Contracting State shall be recognised and, where it is enforceable in the State of origin, made enforceable in every other Contracting State.

Article 9

(1)   (*Recognition and enforcement may be refused*) if:
  (a)   in the case of a decision given in the absence of the defendant or his legal representative, the defendant was not duly served with the document which instituted the proceedings or an equivalent document in sufficient time to enable him to arrange his defence; but such a failure to effect service cannot constitute a ground for refusing recognition or enforcement where service was not effected because the defendant had concealed his whereabouts from the person who instituted the proceedings in the State of origin;
  (b)   in the case of a decision given in the absence of the defendant or his legal representative, the competence of the authority giving the decision was not founded:
    (i)   on the habitual residence of the defendant; or
    (ii) on the last common habitual residence of the child's parents, at least one parent being still habitually resident there, or
    (iii) on the habitual residence of the child;

(c) the decision is incompatible with a decision relating to custody which became enforceable in the State addressed before the removal of the child, unless the child has had his habitual residence in the territory of the requesting State for one year before his removal.

(3)   In no circumstances may the foreign decision be reviewed as to its substance.

Article 10

(1)   (*Recognition and enforcement may also be refused*) on any of the following grounds:
  (a) if it is found that the effects of the decision are manifestly incompatible with the fundamental principles of the law relating to the family and children in the State addressed;
  (b) if it is found that by reason of a change in the circumstances including the passage of time but not including a mere change in the residence of the child after an improper removal, the effects of the original decision are manifestly no longer in accordance with the welfare of the child;
  (c) if at the time when the proceedings were instituted in the State of origin:
    (i) the child was a national of the State addressed or was habitually resident there and no such connection existed with the State of origin;
    (ii) the child was a national both of the State of origin and of the State addressed and was habitually resident in the State addressed;
  (d) if the decision is incompatible with a decision given in the State addressed or enforceable in that State after being given in a third State, pursuant to proceedings begun before the submission of the request for recognition or enforcement, and if the refusal is in accordance with the welfare of the child.

(2)   Proceedings for recognition or enforcement may be adjourned on any of the following grounds:
  (a) if an ordinary form of review of the original decision has been commenced;
  (b) if proceedings relating to the custody of the child, commenced before the proceedings in the State of origin were instituted, are pending in the State addressed;
  (c) if another decision concerning the custody of the child is the subject of proceedings for enforcement or of any other proceedings concerning the recognition of the decision.

Article 11

(1)   Decisions on rights of access and provisions of decisions relating to custody which deal with the rights of access shall be recognised and enforced subject to the same conditions as other decisions relating to custody.

(2)   However, the competent authority of the State addressed may fix the conditions for the implementation and exercise of the right of access taking into account, in particular, undertakings given by the parties on this matter.

(3)   Where no decision on the right of access has been taken or where recognition or enforcement of the decision relating to custody is refused, the central authority of the State addressed may apply to its competent authorities for a decision on the right of access if the person claiming a right of access so requests.

Article 12

Where, at the time of the removal of a child across an international frontier, there is no enforceable decision given in a Contracting State relating to his custody, the provisions of this Convention shall apply to any subsequent decision, relating to the custody of that child and declaring the removal to be unlawful, given in a Contracting State at the request of any interested person.

Article 13

(1)   A request for recognition or enforcement in another Contracting State of a decision relating to custody shall be accompanied by:
  (a) a document authorising the central authority of the State addressed to act on behalf of the applicant or to designate another representative for that purpose;
  (b) a copy of the decision which satisfies the necessary conditions of authenticity;
  (c) in the case of a decision given in the absence of the defendant or his legal representative, a document which establishes that the defendant was duly served with the document which instituted the proceedings or an equivalent document;
  (d) if applicable, any document which establishes that, in accordance with the law of the State of origin, the decision is enforceable;
  (e) if possible, a statement indicating the whereabouts or likely whereabouts of the child in the State addressed;
  (f) proposals as to how the custody of the child should be restored.

Article 15

(1)   Before reaching a decision under paragraph (1)(b) of Article 10, the authority concerned in the State addressed:
   (a) shall ascertain the child's views unless this is impracticable having regard in particular to his age and understanding; and
   (b) may request that any appropriate enquiries be carried out.

(2)   The cost of enquiries in any Contracting State shall be met by the authorities of the State where they are carried out.

Requests for enquiries and the results of enquiries may be sent to the authority concerned through the central authorities.

Article 26

(1)   In relation to a State which has in matters of custody two or more systems of law of territorial application:
   (a) reference to the law of a person's habitual residence or to the law of a person's nationality shall be construed as referring to the system of law determined by the rules in force in that State or, if there are no such rules, to the system of law with which the person concerned is most closely connected;
   (b) reference to the State of origin or to the State addressed shall be construed as referring, as the case may be, to the territorial unit where the decision was given or to the territorial unit where recognition or enforcement of the decision or restoration of custody is requested.

(2)   Paragraph (1)(a) of this Article also applies *mutatis mutandis* to States which have in matters of custody two or more systems of law of personal application.

Housing Act 1985

(c 68)

An Act to consolidate the Housing Acts (except those provisions consolidated in the Housing Associations Act 1985 and the Landlord and Tenant Act 1985), and certain related provisions, with amendments to give effect to recommendations of the Law Commission

[30 October 1985]

PART IV
SECURE TENANCIES AND RIGHTS OF SECURE TENANTS

Security of tenure

79   Secure tenancies

(1)   A tenancy under which a dwelling-house is let as a separate dwelling is a secure tenancy at any time when the conditions described in sections 80 and 81 as the landlord condition and the tenant condition are satisfied.

(2)–(4) . . .

80   The landlord condition

(1)   The landlord condition is that the interest of the landlord belongs to one of the following authorities or bodies—
   a local authority,
   a new town corporation,
   [a housing action trust]
   an urban development corporation,
                    .....
                    .....
   a . . . housing co-operative to which this section applies.

(2)–(4) . . .

81 The tenant condition

The tenant condition is that the tenant is an individual and occupies the dwelling- house as his only or principal home; or, where the tenancy is a joint tenancy, that each of the joint tenants is an individual and at least one of them occupies the dwelling-house as his only or principal home.

Succession on death of tenant

87 Persons qualified to succeed secure tenant

A person is qualified to succeed the tenant under a secure tenancy if he occupies the dwelling-house as his only or principal home at the time of the tenant's death and either—
  (a) he is the tenant's spouse, or
  (b) he is another member of the tenant's family and has resided with the tenant throughout the period of twelve months ending with the tenant's death;

unless, in either case, the tenant was himself a successor, as defined in section 88.

Supplementary provisions

113 Members of a person's family

(1) A person is a member of another's family within the meaning of this Part if—
  (a) he is the spouse of that person, or he and that person live together as husband and wife, or
  (b) he is that person's parent, grandparent, child, grandchild, brother, sister, uncle, aunt, nephew or niece.

(2) For the purpose of subsection (1)(b)—
  (a) a relationship by marriage shall be treated as a relationship by blood,
  (b) a relationship of the half-blood shall be treated as a relationship of the whole blood,
  (c) the stepchild of a person shall be treated as his child, and

(d)   an illegitimate child shall be treated as the legitimate child of his mother and reputed father.

PART XVIII
MISCELLANEOUS AND GENERAL PROVISIONS

Final provisions

625   Short title, commencement and extent

(1)   This Act may be cited as the Housing Act 1985.

(2)   This Act comes into force on 1st April 1986.

(3)   This Act extends to England and Wales only.

Marriage (Prohibited Degrees of Relationship) Act 1986

(c 16)

An Act to make further provision with regard to the marriage of persons related by affinity

[20 May 1986]

1   Marriage between certain persons related by affinity not to be void

(1)   A marriage solemnized after the commencement of this Act between a man and a woman who is the daughter or grand-daughter of a former spouse of his (whether the former spouse is living or not) or who is the former spouse of his father or grand-father (whether his father or grandfather is living or not) shall not be void by reason only of that relationship if both the parties have attained the age of twenty-one at the time of the marriage and the younger party has not at any time before attaining the age of eighteen been a child of the family in relation to the other party.

(2)   A marriage solemnized after the commencement of this Act between a man and a woman who is the grandmother of a former spouse of his (whether the former spouse is living or not) or is a former spouse of his grandson (whether his grandson is living or not) shall not be void by reason only of that relationship.

(3)   A marriage solemnized after the commencement of this Act between a man and a woman who is the mother of a former spouse of his shall not be void by reason only of that relationship if the marriage is solemnized after the death of both that spouse and the father of that spouse and after both the parties to the marriage have attained the age of twenty-one.

(4)   A marriage solemnized after the commencement of this Act between a man and a woman who is a former spouse of his son shall not be void by reason only of that relationship if the marriage is solemnized after the death of both his son and the mother of his son and after both the parties to the marriage have attained the age of twenty-one.

(5)   In this section "child of the family" in relation to any person, means a child who has lived in the same household as that person and been treated by that person as a child of his family.

(6)   The Marriage Act 1949 shall have effect subject to the amendments specified in the Schedule to this Act, being amendments consequential on the preceding provisions of this section.

(7)   Where, apart from this Act, any matter affecting the validity of a marriage would fall to be determined (in accordance with the rules of private international law) by reference to the law of a country outside England and Wales nothing in this Act shall preclude the determination of that matter in accordance with that law.

(8)   Nothing in this section shall affect any marriage solemnized before the commencement of this Act.

6   Short title, citation, commencement and extent

(1)   This Act may be cited as the Marriage (Prohibited Degrees of Relationship) Act 1986.

(2)   This Act so far as it extends to England and Wales may be cited with the Marriage Acts 1949 to 1983 and the Marriage (Wales) Act 1986 as the Marriage Acts 1949 to 1986.

(3)–(6) . . .

NOTES

Sub-ss (3)–(6): outside the scope of this work.

Insolvency Act 1986

(1986 c 45)

An Act to consolidate the enactments relating to company insolvency and winding up (including the winding up of companies that are not insolvent, and of unregistered companies); enactments relating to the insolvency and bankruptcy of individuals; and other enactments bearing on those two subject matters, including the functions and qualification of insolvency practitioners, the public administration of insolvency, the penalisation and redress of malpractice and wrongdoing, and the avoidance of certain transactions at an undervalue

[25 July 1986]

CHAPTER V
EFFECT OF BANKRUPTCY ON CERTAIN RIGHTS, TRANSACTIONS, ETC

Rights of occupation

336 Rights of occupation etc of bankrupt's spouse

(1)   Nothing occurring in the initial period of the bankruptcy (that is to say, the period beginning with the day of the presentation of the petition for the bankruptcy order and ending with the vesting of the bankrupt's estate in a trustee) is to be taken as having given rise to any [matrimonial home rights under Part IV of the Family Law Act 1996] in relation to a dwelling house comprised in the bankrupt's estate.

(2)   Where a spouse's [matrimonial home rights under the Act of 1996] are a charge on the estate or interest of the other spouse, or of trustees for the other spouse, and the other spouse is adjudged bankrupt—

(a)   the charge continues to subsist notwithstanding the bankruptcy and, subject to the provisions of that Act, binds the trustee of the bankrupt's estate and persons deriving title under that trustee, and

(b) any application for an order [under section 33 of that Act] shall be made to the court having jurisdiction in relation to the bankruptcy.

(3) Where a person and his spouse or former spouse are trustees for sale of a dwelling house and that person is adjudged bankrupt, any application by the trustee of the bankrupt's estate for an order under section 30 of the Law of Property Act 1925 (powers of court where trustees for sale refuse to act) shall be made to the court having jurisdiction in relation to the bankruptcy.

(4) On such an application as is mentioned in subsection (2) *or (3)* the court shall make such order under [section 33 of the Act of 1996] *or section 30 of the Act of 1925* as it thinks just and reasonable having regard to—
(a) the interests of the bankrupt's creditors,
(b) the conduct of the spouse or former spouse, so far as contributing to the bankruptcy,
(c) the needs and financial resources of the spouse or former spouse,
(d) the needs of any children, and
(e) all the circumstances of the case other than the needs of the bankrupt.

(5) Where such an application is made after the end of the period of one year beginning with the first vesting under Chapter IV of this Part of the bankrupt's estate in a trustee, the court shall assume, unless the circumstances of the case are exceptional, that the interests of the bankrupt's creditors outweigh all other considerations.

NOTES

Sub-ss (1), (2): words in square brackets substituted by the Family Law Act 1996, s 66(1), Sch 8, Pt III, para 57(1)–(3).
Sub-s (3): repealed by the Trusts of Land and Appointment of Trustees Act 1996, s 25(2), Sch 4, subject to savings in s 25(4), (5) of the 1996 Act.
Sub-s (4): words in italics repealed by the Trusts of Land and Appointment of Trustees Act 1996, s 25(2), Sch 4, subject to savings in s 25(4), (5) of the 1996 Act; words in square brackets substituted by the Family Law Act 1996, s 66(1), Sch 8, Pt III, para 57(1), (4), as from a day to be appointed.

337 Rights of occupation of bankrupt

(1) This section applies where—
(a) a person who is entitled to occupy a dwelling house by virtue of a beneficial estate or interest is adjudged bankrupt, and
(b) any persons under the age of 18 with whom that person had at some time occupied that dwelling house had their home with that person

at the time when the bankruptcy petition was presented and at the commencement of the bankruptcy.

(2)   Whether or not the bankrupt's spouse (if any) has [matrimonial home rights under Part IV of the Family Law Act 1996]—
  (a) the bankrupt has the following rights as against the trustee of his estate—
       (i) if in occupation, a right not to be evicted or excluded from the dwelling house or any part of it, except with the leave of the court,
       (ii) if not in occupation, a right with the leave of the court to enter into and occupy the dwelling house, and
  (b) the bankrupt's rights are a charge, having the like priority as an equitable interest created immediately before the commencement of the bankruptcy, on so much of his estate or interest in the dwelling house as vests in the trustee.

[(3)   The Act of 1996 has effect, with the necessary modifications, as if—
  (a) the rights conferred by paragraph (a) of subsection (2) were matrimonial home rights under that Act,
  (b) any application for such leave as is mentioned in that paragraph were an application for an order under section 33 of that Act, and
  (c) any charge under paragraph (b) of that subsection on the estate or interest of the trustee were a charge under that Act on the estate or interest of a spouse.]

(4)   Any application for leave such as is mentioned in subsection (2)(a) or otherwise by virtue of this section for an order under [section 33 of the Act of 1996] shall be made to the court having jurisdiction in relation to the bankruptcy.

(5)   On such an application the court shall make such order under [section 33 of the Act of 1996] as it thinks just and reasonable having regard to the interests of the creditors, to the bankrupt's financial resources, to the needs of the children and to all the circumstances of the case other than the needs of the bankrupt.

(6)   Where such an application is made after the end of the period of one year beginning with the vesting (under Chapter IV of this Part) of the bankrupt's estate in a trustee, the court shall assume, unless the circumstances of the case are exceptional, that the interests of the bankrupt's creditors outweigh all other considerations.

NOTES

Sub-ss (2), (4), (5): words in square brackets substituted by the Family Law Act 1996, s 66(1), Sch 8, Pt III, para 58(1), (2), (4).

Sub-s (3): substituted by the Family Law Act 1996, s 66(1), Sch 8, Pt III, para 58(1), (3)

338 Payments in respect of premises occupied by bankrupt

Where any premises comprised in a bankrupt's estate are occupied by him (whether by virtue of the preceding section or otherwise) on condition that he makes payments towards satisfying any liability arising under a mortgage of the premises or otherwise towards the outgoings of the premises, the bankrupt does not, by virtue of those payments, acquire any interest in the premises.

Adjustment of prior transactions, etc

339 Transactions at an undervalue

(1)   Subject as follows in this section and sections 341 and 342, where an individual is adjudged bankrupt and he has at a relevant time (defined in section 341) entered into a transaction with any person at an undervalue, the trustee of the bankrupt's estate may apply to the court for an order under this section.

(2)   The court shall, on such an application, make such order as it thinks fit for restoring the position to what it would have been if that individual had not entered into that transaction.

(3)   For the purposes of this section and sections 341 and 342, an individual enters into a transaction with a person at an undervalue if—
   (a) he makes a gift to that person or he otherwise enters into a transaction with that person on terms that provide for him to receive no consideration,
   (b) he enters into a transaction with that person in consideration of marriage, or
   (c) he enters into a transaction with that person for a consideration the value of which, in money or money's worth, is significantly less than the value, in money or money's worth, of the consideration provided by the individual.

340 Preferences

(1) Subject as follows in this and the next two sections, where an individual is adjudged bankrupt and he has at a relevant time (defined in section 341) given a preference to any person, the trustee of the bankrupt's estate may apply to the court for an order under this section.

(2) The court shall, on such an application, make such order as it thinks fit for restoring the position to what it would have been if that individual had not given that preference.

(3) For the purposes of this and the next two sections, an individual gives a preference to a person if—
   (a) that person is one of the individual's creditors or a surety or guarantor for any of his debts or other liabilities, and
   (b) the individual does anything or suffers anything to be done which (in either case) has the effect of putting that person into a position which, in the event of the individual's bankruptcy, will be better than the position he would have been in if that thing had not been done.

(4) The court shall not make an order under this section in respect of a preference given to any person unless the individual who gave the preference was influenced in deciding to give it by a desire to produce in relation to that person the effect mentioned in subsection (3)(b) above.

(5) An individual who has given a preference to a person who, at the time the preference was given, was an associate of his (otherwise than by reason only of being his employee) is presumed, unless the contrary is shown, to have been influenced in deciding to give it by such a desire as is mentioned in subsection (4).

(6) The fact that something has been done in pursuance of the order of a court does not, without more, prevent the doing or suffering of that thing from constituting the giving of a preference.

341 "Relevant time" under ss 339, 340

(1) Subject as follows, the time at which an individual enters into a transaction at an undervalue or gives a preference is a relevant time if the transaction is entered into or the preference given—
   (a) in the case of a transaction at an undervalue, at a time in the period of 5 years ending with the day of the presentation of the bankruptcy petition on which the individual is adjudged bankrupt,

(b) in the case of a preference which is not a transaction at an undervalue and is given to a person who is an associate of the individual (otherwise than by reason only of being his employee), at a time in the period of 2 years ending with that day, and

(c) in any other case of a preference which is not a transaction at an undervalue, at a time in the period of 6 months ending with that day.

(2) Where an individual enters into a transaction at an undervalue or gives a preference at a time mentioned in paragraph (a), (b) or (c) of subsection (1) (not being, in the case of a transaction at an undervalue, a time less than 2 years before the end of the period mentioned in paragraph (a)), that time is not a relevant time for the purposes of sections 339 and 340 unless the individual—

(a) is insolvent at that time, or

(b) becomes insolvent in consequence of the transaction or preference;

but the requirements of this subsection are presumed to be satisfied, unless the contrary is shown, in relation to any transaction at an undervalue which is entered into by an individual with a person who is an associate of his (otherwise than by reason only of being his employee).

(3) For the purposes of subsection (2), an individual is insolvent if—

(a) he is unable to pay his debts as they fall due, or

(b) the value of his assets is less than the amount of his liabilities, taking into account his contingent and prospective liabilities.

(4) A transaction entered into or preference given by a person who is subsequently adjudged bankrupt on a petition under section 264(1)(d) (criminal bankruptcy) is to be treated as having been entered into or given at a relevant time for the purposes of sections 339 and 340 if it was entered into or given at any time on or after the date specified for the purposes of this subsection in the criminal bankruptcy order on which the petition was based.

(5) No order shall be made under section 339 or 340 by virtue of subsection (4) of this section where an appeal is pending (within the meaning of section 277) against the individual's conviction of any offence by virtue of which the criminal bankruptcy order was made.

NOTES

Sub-ss (4), (5): repealed by the Criminal Justice Act 1988, s 170(2), Sch 16, as from a day to be appointed.

342 Orders under ss 339, 340

(1)   Without prejudice to the generality of section 339(2) or 340(2), an order under either of those sections with respect to a transaction or preference entered into or given by an individual who is subsequently adjudged bankrupt may (subject as follows)—

(a) require any property transferred as part of the transaction, or in connection with the giving of the preference, to be vested in the trustee of the bankrupt's estate as part of that estate;

(b) require any property to be so vested if it represents in any person's hands the application either of the proceeds of sale of property so transferred or of money so transferred;

(c) release or discharge (in whole or in part) any security given by the individual;

(d) require any person to pay, in respect of benefits received by him from the individual, such sums to the trustee of his estate as the court may direct;

(e) provide for any surety or guarantor whose obligations to any person were released or discharged (in whole or in part) under the transaction or by the giving of the preference to be under such new or revived obligations to that person as the court thinks appropriate;

(f) provide for security to be provided for the discharge of any obligation imposed by or arising under the order, and for such an obligation to be charged on any property and for the security or charge to have the same priority as a security or charge released or discharged (in whole or in part) under the transaction or by the giving of the preference; and

(g) provide for the extent to which any person whose property is vested by the order in the trustee of the bankrupt's estate, or on whom obligations are imposed by the order, is to be able to prove in the bankruptcy for debts or other liabilities which arose from, or were released or discharged (in whole or in part) under or by, the transaction or the giving of the preference.

(2)   An order under section 339 or 340 may affect the property of, or impose any obligation on, any person whether or not he is the person with whom the individual in question entered into the transaction or, as the case may be, the person to whom the preference was given; but such an order—

(a) shall not prejudice any interest in property which was acquired from a person other than that individual and was acquired [in good faith and for value], or prejudice any interest deriving from such an interest, and

(b) shall not require a person who received a benefit from the transaction or preference [in good faith and for value] to pay a sum to the trustee of the bankrupt's estate, except where he was a party to the transaction or the payment is to be in respect of a preference given to that person at a time when he was a creditor of that individual.

[(2A) Where a person has acquired an interest in property from a person other than the individual in question, or has received a benefit from the transaction or preference, and at the time of that acquisition or receipt—
  (a) he had notice of the relevant surrounding circumstances and of the relevant proceedings, or
  (b) he was an associate of, or was connected with, either the individual in question or the person with whom that individual entered into the transaction or to whom that individual gave the preference,

then, unless the contrary is shown, it shall be presumed for the purposes of paragraph (a) or (as the case may be) paragraph (b) of subsection (2) that the interest was acquired or the benefit was received otherwise than in good faith.]

(3)   Any sums required to be paid to the trustee in accordance with an order under section 339 or 340 shall be comprised in the bankrupt's estate.

[(4)   For the purposes of subsection (2A)(a), the relevant surrounding circumstances are (as the case may require)—
  (a) the fact that the individual in question entered into the transaction at an undervalue; or
  (b) the circumstances which amounted to the giving of the preference by the individual in question.

(5)   For the purposes of subsection (2A)(a), a person has notice of the relevant proceedings if he has notice—
  (a) of the fact that the petition on which the individual in question is adjudged bankrupt has been presented; or
  (b) of the fact that the individual in question has been adjudged bankrupt.

(6)   Section 249 in Part VII of this Act shall apply for the purposes of subsection (2A)(b) as it applies for the purposes of the first Group of Parts.]

NOTES

Sub-s (2): words in square brackets in paras (a), (b) substituted by the Insolvency (No 2) Act 1994, s 2(1), in relation to interests acquired and benefits received after 26 July 1994.

Sub-s (2A): inserted by the Insolvency (No 2) Act 1994, s 2(2), in relation to interests acquired and benefits received after 26 July 1994.

Sub-ss (4)–(6): substituted for sub-s (4) as originally enacted by the Insolvency (No 2) Act 1994, s 2(3), in relation to interests acquired and benefits received after 26 July 1994.

PART XIX
FINAL PROVISIONS

444   Citation

This Act may be cited as the Insolvency Act 1986.

Family Law Act 1986

(c 55)

An Act to amend the law relating to the jurisdiction of courts in the United Kingdom to make orders with regard to the custody of children; to make provision as to the recognition and enforcement of such orders throughout the United Kingdom; to make further provision as to the imposition, effect and enforcement of restrictions on the removal of children from the United Kingdom or from any part of the United Kingdom; to amend the law relating to the jurisdiction of courts in Scotland as to tutory and curatory; to amend the law relating to the recognition of divorces, annulments and legal separations; to make further provision with respect to the effect of divorces and annulments on wills; to amend the law relating to the powers of courts to make declarations relating to the status of a person; to abolish the right to petition for jactitation of marriage; to repeal the Greek Marriages Act 1884; to make further provision with respect to family proceedings rules; to amend the Child Abduction Act 1984, the Child Abduction (Northern Ireland) Order 1985 and the Child Abduction and Custody Act 1985; and for connected purposes

[7 November 1986]

PART I
CHILD CUSTODY

CHAPTER I
PRELIMINARY

I   Orders to which Part I applies

(1)   Subject to the following provisions of this section, in this Part ["Part I order"] means—

[(a) a section 8 order made by a court in England and Wales under the Children Act 1989, other than an order varying or discharging such an order;]

  (b) an order made by a court of civil jurisdiction in Scotland under any enactment or rule of law with respect to the [residence, custody, care or control of a child, contact with or], access to a child or the education or upbringing of a child, excluding—

     (i) an order committing the care of a child to a local authority or placing a child under the supervision of a local authority;

    (ii) an adoption order as defined in section 12(1) of the Adoption (Scotland) Act 1978;

   (iii) an order freeing a child for adoption made under section 18 of the said Act of 1978;

   (iv) an order [giving parental responsibilities and parental rights in relation to] a child made in the course of proceedings for the adoption of the child (other than an order made following the making of a direction under section 53(1) of the Children Act 1975);

    (v) an order made under the Education (Scotland) Act 1980;

   (vi) an order made under Part II or III of the Social Work (Scotland) Act 1968;

   (vii) an order made under the Child Abduction and Custody Act 1985;

  (viii) an order for the delivery of a child or other order for the enforcement of a [Part I order];

   (ix) an order relating to the [guardianship] of a child;

[(c) an Article 8 order made by a court in Northern Ireland under the Children (Northern Ireland) Order 1995, other than an order varying or discharging such an order;]

[(d) an order made by a court in England and Wales in the exercise of the inherent jurisdiction of the High Court with respect to children—

     (i) so far as it gives care of a child to any person or provides for contact with, or the education of, a child; but

    (ii) excluding an order varying or revoking such an order;

[(e) an order made by the High Court in Northern Ireland in the exercise of its inherent jurisdiction with respect to children—

     (i) so far as it gives care of a child to any person or provides for contact with, or the education of, a child; but

    (ii) excluding an order varying or discharging such an order;]]

(2)   In this Part ["Part I order"] does not include—

  (a)–(c)   . . .

[(3)   In this Part, "Part I order"—

  (a) includes any order which would have been a custody order by virtue of this section in any form in which it was in force at any time before its amendment by the Children Act 1989 [or the Children (Northern Ireland) Order 1995, as the case may be]; and

(b) (subject to sections 32 and 40 of this Act) excludes any order which would have been excluded from being a custody order by virtue of this section in any such form.]

(6)   Provision may be made by act of sederunt prescribing, in relation to orders within subsection (1)(b) above, what constitutes an application for the purposes of this Part.

NOTES

Sub-s (1): para (a) substituted, and paras (d), (e) substituted for para (d) as originally enacted, by the Children Act 1989, s 108(5), Sch 13, para 63; words in first and second pairs of square brackets in para (b) substituted by the Children (Scotland) Act 1995, s 105(4), Sch 4, para 41(2); words in third and final pairs of square brackets substituted by the Age of Legal Capacity (Scotland) Act 1991, s 10, Sch 1, para 44; para (c) substituted by the Children (Northern Ireland Consequential Amendments) Order 1995, SI 1995/756, art 12(1), (2)(a)(i); para (e) further substituted by SI 1995/756, art 12(1), (2)(a)(ii).

Sub-s (2): words in square brackets substituted, and para (b) repealed, by the Children Act 1989, s 108(5), (7), Sch 13, para 63(2), Sch 15; paras (a), (c) repealed by SI 1995/756, art 15, Schedule.

Sub-s (3): substituted, for sub-ss (3)–(5) as originally enacted, by the Children Act 1989, s 108(5), Sch 13, para 63(3); words in square brackets inserted by SI 1995/756, art 12(1), (2)(b).

CHAPTER II
JURISDICTION OF COURTS IN ENGLAND AND WALES

[2   Jurisdiction: general

(1)   A court in England and Wales shall not have jurisdiction to make a section 1(1)(a) order with respect to a child in or in connection with matrimonial proceedings in England and Wales unless the condition in section 2A of this Act is satisfied.

(2)   A court in England and Wales shall not have jurisdiction to make a section 1(1)(a) order in a non-matrimonial case (that is to say, where the condition in section 2A of this Act is not satisfied) unless the condition in section 3 of this Act is satisfied.

(3)   A court in England and Wales shall not have jurisdiction to make a section 1(1)(d) order unless—
    (a)   the condition in section 3 of this Act is satisfied, or

(b)   the child concerned is present in England and Wales on the relevant
date and the court considers that the immediate exercise of its powers
is necessary for his protection.]

NOTES

Substituted, together with s 2A, for s 2 as originally enacted by the Children Act
1989, s 108(5), Sch 13, para 64.

Sub-ss (1), (2): substituted by the Family Law Act 1996, s 66(1), Sch 8, para
37(1), (2), subject to savings in s 66(2) of, and Sch 9, para 5 to, the 1996 Act, as from
a day to be appointed, as follows—

"(1) A court in England and Wales shall not have jurisdiction to make a section
1(1)(a) order with respect to a child unless—

(a) the case falls within section 2A below; or
(b) in any other case, the condition in section 3 below is satisfied.".

[2A   Jurisdiction in or in connection with matrimonial proceedings

*(1)   The condition referred to in section 2(1) of this Act is that the
matrimonial proceedings are proceedings in respect of the marriage of the
parents of the child concerned and—*

(a)   the proceedings—
  (i)   are proceedings for divorce or nullity of marriage, and
  (ii) are continuing;
(b)   the proceedings—
  (i)   are proceedings for judicial separation,
  (ii) are continuing,

and the jurisdiction of the court is not excluded by subsection (2) below; or
*(c)   the proceedings have been dismissed after the beginning of the trial
but—*
  (i)   the section 1(1)(a) order is being made forthwith, or
  (ii) the application for the order was made on or before the dismissal.

(2)   For the purposes of subsection (1)(b) above, the jurisdiction of the
court is excluded if, after the grant of a decree of judicial separation, on the
relevant date, proceedings for divorce or nullity in respect of the marriage
are continuing in Scotland or Northern Ireland.

(3)   Subsection (2) above shall not apply if the court *in which the other
proceedings there referred to* are continuing has made—

(a) an order under section 13(6) or [19A(4)] of this Act (not being an
order made by virtue of section 13(6)(a)(i)), or

    (b)   an order under section 14(2) or 22(2) of this Act which is recorded as being made for the purpose of enabling Part I proceedings to be taken in England and Wales with respect to the child concerned.

(4)   Where a court—
    (a)   has jurisdiction to make a section 1(1)(a) order *in or in connection with matrimonial proceedings*, but
    (b)   considers that it would be more appropriate for Part I matters relating to the child to be determined outside England and Wales,

the court may by order direct that, while the order under this subsection is in force, no section 1(1)(a) order shall be made by any court *in or in connection with those proceedings* [by virtue of section 2(1)(a) of this Act].]

NOTES

Substituted as noted to s 2.

Sub-s (1): substituted by the Family Law Act 1996, s 66(1), Sch 8, para 37(1), (3), subject to savings in s 66(2) of, and Sch 9, para 5 to, the 1996 Act, as from a day to be appointed, as follows—

"(1)   Subject to subsections (2) to (4) below, a case falls within this section for the purposes of the making of a section 1(1)(a) order if that order is made—

    (a) at a time when—
        (i) a statement of marital breakdown under section 5 of the Family Law Act 1996 with respect to the marriage of the parents of the child concerned has been received by the court; and
        (ii) it is or may become possible for an application for a divorce order or for a separation order to be made by reference to that statement; or
    (b) at a time when an application in relation to that marriage for a divorce order, or for a separation order under the Act of 1996, has been made and not withdrawn.

(1A)   A case also falls within this section for the purposes of the making of a section 1(1)(a) order if that order is made in or in connection with any proceedings for the nullity of the marriage of the parents of the child concerned and—

    (a) those proceedings are continuing; or
    (b) the order is made—
        (i) immediately on the dismissal, after the beginning of the trial, of the proceedings; and
        (ii) on an application made before the dismissal.".

Sub-s (2): words in italics substituted by the words "A case does not fall within this section if a separation order under the Family Law Act 1996 is in force in relation to the marriage of the parents of the child concerned if," by the Family Law Act 1996, s 66(1), Sch 8, para 37(1), (4), subject to savings in s 66(2) of, and Sch 9, para 5 to, the 1996 Act, as from a day to be appointed.

Sub-s (3): first words in italics substituted by the words "in Scotland, Northern Ireland or a specified dependent territory in which the proceedings for divorce or nullity" by the Family Law Act 1996, s 66(1), Sch 8, para 37(1), (5), subject to savings in s 66(2) of, and Sch 9, para 5 to, the 1996 Act, as from a day to be appointed; number in square brackets in para (a) substituted by the Children (Northern Ireland Consequential Amendments) Order 1995, SI 1995/756, art 12(1), (5)(a).

Sub-s (4): words in italics substituted by the words "by virtue of the case falling within this section" by the Family Law Act 1996, s 66(1), Sch 8, para 37(1), (6), subject to savings in s 66(2) of, and Sch 9, para 5 to, the 1996 Act, as from a day to be appointed.

3 Habitual residence or presence of child

(1)   The condition referred to in *[section 2(2)]* of this Act is that on the relevant date the child concerned—
  (a) is habitually resident in England and Wales, or
  (b) is present in England and Wales and is not habitually resident in any part of the United Kingdom,

and, in either case, the jurisdiction of the court is not excluded by subsection (2) below.

(2)   For the purposes of subsection (1) above, the jurisdiction of the court is excluded if, on the relevant date, [matrimonial proceedings] are continuing in a court in Scotland or Northern Ireland in respect of the marriage of the parents of the child concerned.

(3)   Subsection (2) above shall not apply if the court in which the other proceedings there referred to are continuing has made—
  (a) an order under section 13(6) or [19A(4)] of this Act (not being an order made by virtue of section 13(6)(a)(i), or
  (b) an order under section 14(2) or 22(2) of this Act which is recorded as made for the purpose of enabling [Part I proceedings with respect to] the child concerned to be taken in England and Wales,

and that order is in force.

(4)–(6) . . .

Sub-s (1): words in first pair of square brackets in italics originally substituted by the Children Act 1989, s 108(5), Sch 13, paras 62, 65, further substituted by the words "section 2(1)(b)" by the Family Law Act 1996, s 66(1), Sch 8, para 37(1), (7), subject to savings in s 66(2) of, and Sch 9, para 5 to, the 1996 Act, as from a day to be appointed.

Sub-s (3): number in square brackets in para (a) substituted by the Children (Northern Ireland Consequential Amendments) Order 1995, SI 1995/756, art 12(1), (5)(b); words in square brackets in para (b) substituted by the Children Act 1989, s 108(5), Sch 13, paras 62, 65.

Sub-ss (4)–(6): repealed by the Children Act 1989, s 108(7), Sch 15.

5 Power of court to refuse application or stay proceedings

(1)   A court in England and Wales which has jurisdiction to make a [Part I order] may refuse an application for the order in any case where the matter in question has already been determined in proceedings outside England and Wales.

(2)   Where, at any stage of the proceedings on an application made to a court in England and Wales for a [Part I order], or for the variation of a [Part I order], it appears to the court—

(a) that proceedings with respect to the matters to which the application relates are continuing outside England and Wales, or

(b) that it would be more appropriate for those matters to be determined in proceedings to be taken outside England and Wales,

the court may stay the proceedings on the application.

(3)   The court may remove a stay granted in accordance with subsection (2) above if it appears to the court that there has been unreasonable delay in the taking or prosecution of the other proceedings referred to in that subsection, or that those proceedings are stayed, sisted or concluded.

(4)   Nothing in this section shall affect any power exercisable apart from this section to refuse an application or to grant or remove a stay.

NOTES

Sub-ss (1), (2): words in square brackets substituted by the Children Act 1989, s 108(5), Sch 13, para 62.

6 Duration and variation of [Part I orders]

(1)   If a [Part I order] made by a court in Scotland or Northern Ireland (or a variation of such an order) comes into force with respect to a child at a time when a [Part I order] made by a court in England and Wales has effect with respect to him, the latter order shall cease to have effect so far as it makes provision for any matter for which the same or different provision

is made by (or by the variation of) the order made by the court in Scotland or Northern Ireland.

(2)   Where by virtue of subsection (1) above a [Part I order] has ceased to have effect so far as it makes provision for any matter, a court in England and Wales shall not have jurisdiction to vary that order so as to make provision for that matter.

[(3)   A court in England and Wales shall not have jurisdiction to vary a Part I order if, on the relevant date, matrimonial proceedings are continuing in Scotland or Northern Ireland in respect of the marriage of the parents of the child concerned.

(3A)   Subsection (3) above shall not apply if—
 (a) the Part I order was made in or in connection with proceedings for divorce or nullity in England and Wales in respect of the marriage of the parents of the child concerned; and
 (b) those proceedings are continuing.

(3B)   Subsection (3) above shall not apply if—
 (a) the Part I order was made in or in connection with proceedings for judicial separation in England and Wales;
 (b) those proceedings are continuing; and
 (c) the decree of judicial separation has not yet been granted.]

(4)   Subsection (3) above shall not apply if the court in which the proceedings there referred to are continuing has made—
 (a) an order under section 13(6) or [19A(4)] of this Act (not being an order made by virtue of section 13(6)(a)(i)), or
 (b) an order under section 14(2) or 22(2) of this Act which is recorded as made for the purpose of enabling proceedings with respect to the custody of the child concerned to be taken in England and Wales,

and that order is in force.

(5)   Subsection (3) above shall not apply in the case of a [variation of a section 1(1)(d) order if the child concerned] is present in England and Wales on the relevant date and the court considers that the immediate exercise of its powers is necessary for his protection.

[(6)   Subsection (7) below applies where a Part I order which is—
 (a) a residence order (within the meaning of the Children Act 1989) in favour of a person with respect to a child,

(b) an order made in the exercise of the High Court's inherent jurisdiction with respect to children by virtue of which a person has care of a child, or

(c) an order—

(i) of a kind mentioned in section 1(3)(a) of this Act,

(ii) under which a person is entitled to the actual possession of a child,

ceases to have effect in relation to that person by virtue of subsection (1) above.

(7) Where this subsection applies, any family assistance order made under section 16 of the Children Act 1989 with respect to the child shall also cease to have effect.

(8) For the purposes of subsection (7) above the reference to a family assistance order under section 16 of the Children Act 1989 shall be deemed to include a reference to an order for the supervision of a child made under—

(a) section 7(4) of the Family Law Reform Act 1969,

(b) section 44 of the Matrimonial Causes Act 1973,

(c) section 2(2)(a) of the Guardianship Act 1973,

(d) section 34(5) or 36(3)(b) of the Children Act 1975, or

(e) section 9 of the Domestic Proceedings and Magistrates' Courts Act 1978;

but this subsection shall cease to have effect once all such orders for the supervision of children have ceased to have effect in accordance with Schedule 14 to the Children Act 1989.]

NOTES

Section-heading: words in square brackets substituted by the Children Act 1989, s 108(5), Sch 13, para 62.

Sub-ss (1), (2), (5): words in square brackets substituted by the Children Act 1989, s 108(5), Sch 13, paras 62, 66.

Sub-ss (3)–(3B): substituted, for sub-s (3) as originally enacted, by the Children Act 1989, s 108(5), Sch 13, para 66; sub-s (3A) further substituted for existing sub-ss (3A), (3B) by the Family Law Act 1996, s 66(1), Sch 8, para 37(1), (8), subject to savings in s 66(2) of, and Sch 9, para 5 to, the 1996 Act, as from a day to be appointed, as follows—

"(3A) Subsection (3) above does not apply if the Part I order was made in a case falling within section 2A of this Act.".

Sub-s (4): number in square brackets in para (a) substituted by the Children (Northern Ireland Consequential Amendments) Order 1995, SI 1995/756, art 12(1), (5)(c).

Sub-ss (6)–(8): substituted for sub-ss (6), (7) as originally enacted by the Children Act 1989, s 108(5), Sch 13, para 66.

[7   Interpretation of Chapter II

In this Chapter—

    (a) "child" means a person who has not attained the age of eighteen;

    (b) "matrimonial proceedings" means proceedings for divorce, nullity of marriage or judicial separation;

    (c) "the relevant date" means, in relation to the making or variation of an order—

        (i) where an application is made for an order to be made or varied, the date of the application (or first application, if two or more are determined together), and

        (ii) where no such application is made, the date on which the court is considering whether to make or, as the case may be, vary the order; and

    (d) "section 1(1)(a) order" and "section 1(1)(d) order" mean orders falling within section 1(1)(a) and (d) of this Act respectively.]

NOTES

Substituted by the Children Act 1989, s 108(5), Sch 13, para 67.

CHAPTER V

RECOGNITION AND ENFORCEMENT

25   Recognition of [Part I orders]: general

(1)   Where a [Part I order] made by a court in any part of the United Kingdom is in force with respect to a child who has not attained the age of sixteen, then, subject to subsection (2) below, the order shall be recognised in any other part of the United Kingdom as having the same effect in that other part as if it had been made by the appropriate court in that other part and as if that court had had jurisdiction to make it.

(2)   Where a [Part I order] includes provision as to the means by which rights conferred by the order are to be enforced, subsection (1) above shall not apply to that provision.

(3)   A court in a part of the United Kingdom in which a [Part I order] is recognised in accordance with subsection (1) above shall not enforce the order unless it has been registered in that part of the United Kingdom under section 27 of this Act and proceedings for enforcement are taken in accordance with section 29 of this Act.

Words in square brackets substituted by the Children Act 1989, s 108(5), Sch 13, para 62.

27 Registration

(1)   Any person on whom any rights are conferred by a [Part I order] may apply to the court which made it for the order to be registered in another part of the United Kingdom under this section.

(2)   An application under this section shall be made in the prescribed manner and shall contain the prescribed information and be accompanied by such documents as may be prescribed.

(3)   On receiving an application under this section the court which made the [Part I order] shall, unless it appears to the court that the order is no longer in force, cause the following documents to be sent to the appropriate court in the part of the United Kingdom specified in the application, namely—
(a) a certified copy of the order, and
(b) where the order has been varied, prescribed particulars of any variation which is in force, and
(c) a copy of the application and of any accompanying documents.

(4)   Where the prescribed officer of the appropriate court receives a certified copy of a [Part I order] under subsection (3) above, he shall forthwith cause the order, together with particulars of any variation, to be registered in that court in the prescribed manner.

(5)   An order shall not be registered under this section in respect of a child who has attained the age of sixteen, and the registration of an order in respect of a child who has not attained the age of sixteen shall cease to have effect on the attainment by the child of that age.

Sub-ss (1), (3), (4): words in square brackets substituted by the Children Act 1989, s 108(5), Sch 13, para 62.

28 Cancellation and variation of registration

(1)   A court which revokes, recalls or varies an order registered under section 27 of this Act shall cause notice of the revocation, recall or

variation to be given in the prescribed manner to the prescribed officer of the court in which it is registered and, on receiving the notice, the prescribed officer—

(a) in the case of the revocation or recall of the order, shall cancel the registration, and

(b) in the case of the variation of the order, shall cause particulars of the variation to be registered in the prescribed manner.

(2) Where—

(a) an order registered under section 27 of this Act ceases (in whole or in part) to have effect in the part of the United Kingdom in which it was made, otherwise than because of its revocation, recall or variation, or

(b) an order registered under section 27 of this Act in Scotland ceases (in whole or in part) to have effect there as a result of the making of an order in proceedings outside the United Kingdom,

the court in which the order is registered may, of its own motion or on the application of any person who appears to the court to have an interest in the matter, cancel the registration (or, if the order has ceased to have effect in part, cancel the registration so far as it relates to the provisions which have ceased to have effect).

29 Enforcement

(1) Where a [Part I order] has been registered under section 27 of this Act, the court in which it is registered shall have the same powers for the purpose of enforcing the order as it would have if it had itself made the order and had jurisdiction to make it; and proceedings for or with respect to enforcement may be taken accordingly.

(2) Where an application has been made to any court for the enforcement of an order registered in that court under section 27 of this Act, the court may, at any time before the application is determined, give such interim directions as it thinks fit for the purpose of securing the welfare of the child concerned or of preventing changes in the circumstances relevant to the determination of the application.

(3) The references in subsection (1) above to a [Part I order] do not include references to any provision of the order as to the means by which rights conferred by the order are to be enforced.

NOTES

Sub-ss (1), (3): words in square brackets substituted by the Children Act 1989, s 108(5), Sch 13, para 62.

30 Staying or sisting of enforcement proceedings

(1)   Where in accordance with section 29 of this Act proceedings are taken in any court for the enforcement of an order registered in that court, any person who appears to the court to have an interest in the matter may apply for the proceedings to be stayed or sisted on the ground that he has taken or intends to take other proceedings (in the United Kingdom or elsewhere) as a result of which the order may cease to have effect, or may have a different effect, in the part of the United Kingdom in which it is registered.

(2)   If after considering an application under subsection (1) above the court considers that the proceedings for enforcement should be stayed or sisted in order that other proceedings may be taken or concluded, it shall stay or sist the proceedings for enforcement accordingly.

(3)   The court may remove a stay or recall a sist granted in accordance with subsection (2) above if it appears to the court—
  (a) that there has been unreasonable delay in the taking or prosecution of the other proceedings referred to in that subsection, or
  (b) that those other proceedings are concluded and that the registered order, or a relevant part of it, is still in force.

(4)   Nothing in this section shall affect any power exercisable apart from this section to grant, remove or recall a stay or sist.

31 Dismissal of enforcement proceedings

(1)   Where in accordance with section 29 of this Act proceedings are taken in any court for the enforcement of an order registered in that court, any person who appears to the court to have an interest in the matter may apply for those proceedings to be dismissed on the ground that the order has (in whole or in part) ceased to have effect in the part of the United Kingdom in which it was made.

(2)   Where in accordance with section 29 of this Act proceedings are taken in the Court of Session for the enforcement of an order registered in that court, any person who appears to the court to have an interest in the

matter may apply for those proceedings to be dismissed on the ground that the order has (in whole or in part) ceased to have effect in Scotland as a result of the making of an order in proceedings outside the United Kingdom.

(3)   If, after considering an application under subsection (1) or (2) above, the court is satisfied that the registered order has ceased to have effect, it shall dismiss the proceedings for enforcement (or, if it is satisfied that the order has ceased to have effect in part, it shall dismiss the proceedings so far as they relate to the enforcement of provisions which have ceased to have effect).

32   Interpretation of Chapter V

(1)   In this Chapter—
   "the appropriate court", in relation to England and Wales or Northern Ireland, means the High Court and, in relation to Scotland, means the Court of Session;
   ["Part I order"] includes (except where the context otherwise requires) any order within section 1(3) of this Act which, on the assumptions mentioned in subsection (3) below—
      (a) could have been made notwithstanding the provisions of this Part;
      (b) would have been a [Part I order] for the purposes of this Part; and
      (c) would not have ceased to have effect by virtue of section 6, 15 or 23 of this Act.

(2)   In the application of this Chapter to Scotland, ["Part I order"] also includes (except where the context otherwise requires) any order within section 1(3) of this Act which, on the assumptions mentioned in subsection (3) below—
      (a) would have been a [Part I order] for the purposes of this Part; and
      (b) would not have ceased to have effect by virtue of section 6 or 23 of this Act,

and which, but for the provisions of this Part, would be recognised in Scotland under any rule of law.

(3)   The said assumptions are—
      (a) that this Part had been in force at all material times; and
      (b) that any reference in section 1 of this Act to any enactment included a reference to any corresponding enactment previously in force.

Sub-ss (1), (2): words in square brackets substituted by the Children Act 1989, s 108(5), Sch 13, para 62.

CHAPTER VI
MISCELLANEOUS AND SUPPLEMENTAL

33 Power to order disclosure of child's whereabouts

(1)   Where in proceedings for or relating to a [Part I order] in respect of a child there is not available to the court adequate information as to where the child is, the court may order any person who it has reason to believe may have relevant information to disclose it to the court.

(2)   A person shall not be excused from complying with an order under subsection (1) above by reason that to do so may incriminate him or his spouse of an offence; but a statement or admission made in compliance with such an order shall not be admissible in evidence against either of them in proceedings for any offence other than perjury.

(3)   A court in Scotland before which proceedings are pending for the enforcement of an order [relating to parental responsibilities or parental rights in relation to] a child made outside the United Kingdom which is recognised in Scotland shall have the same powers as it would have under subsection (1) above if the order were its own.

Sub-s (1): words in square brackets substituted by the Children Act 1989, s 108(5), Sch 13, para 62.

Sub-s (3): words in square brackets substituted by the Children (Scotland) Act 1995, s 105(4), Sch 4, para 41(7).

34 Power to order recovery of child

(1)   Where—
   (a) a person is required by a [Part I order], or an order for the enforcement of a [Part I order], to give up a child to another person ("the person concerned"), and
   (b) the court which made the order imposing the requirement is satisfied that the child has not been given up in accordance with the order,

the court may make an order authorising an officer of the court or a constable to take charge of the child and deliver him to the person concerned.

(2)   The authority conferred by subsection (1) above includes authority—
    (a) to enter and search any premises where the person acting in pursuance of the order has reason to believe the child may be found, and
    (b) to use such force as may be necessary to give effect to the purpose of the order.

(3)   Where by virtue of—
    [(a) section 14 of the Children Act 1989,] or
    [(b) Article 14 (enforcement of residence orders) of the Children (Northern Ireland) Order 1995,]

a [Part I order] (or a provision of a [Part I order]) may be enforced as if it were an order requiring a person to give up a child to another person, subsection (1) above shall apply as if the [Part I order] had included such a requirement.

(4)   This section is without prejudice to any power conferred on a court by or under any other enactment or rule of law.

NOTES

Sub-s (1): words in square brackets substituted by the Children Act 1989, s 108(5), Sch 13, paras 62, 70.

Sub-s (3): words in first, third, fourth and final pairs of square brackets substituted by the Children Act 1989, s 108(5), Sch 13, paras 62, 70; para (b) substituted by the Children (Northern Ireland Consequential Amendments) Order 1995, SI 1995/756, art 12(1), (3).

35 Powers to restrict removal of child from jurisdiction

(1), (2)   . . .

(3)   A court in Scotland—
    (a) at any time after the commencement of proceedings in connection with which the court would have jurisdiction to make a [Part I order], or
    (b) in any proceedings in which it would be competent for the court to grant an interdict prohibiting the removal of a child from its jurisdiction,

may, on an application by any of the persons mentioned in subsection (4) below, grant interdict or interim interdict prohibiting the removal of the child from the United Kingdom or any part of the United Kingdom, or out of the control of the person in [whose care] the child is.

(4)　　The said persons are—
   (a)　any party to the proceedings,
   (b)　the [guardian] of the child concerned, and
   (c)　any other person who has or wishes to obtain the *custody or* care of the child.

(5)　　In subsection (3) above "the court" means the Court of Session or the sheriff; and for the purposes of subsection (3)(a) above, proceedings shall be held to commence—
   (a)　in the Court of Session, when a summons is signeted or a petition is presented;
   (b)　in the sheriff court, when the warrant of citation is signed.

NOTES

Sub-s (1): repealed by the Children Act 1989, s 108(7), Sch 15.

Sub-s (2): repealed by the Children (Northern Ireland) Order 1995, SI 1995/755, art 185(2), Sch 10, subject to savings in Sch 8 thereto.

Sub-s (3): words in first pair of square brackets substituted by the Children Act 1989, s 108(5), Sch 13, para 62; words in final pair of square brackets substituted by the Children (Scotland) Act 1995, s 105(4), Sch 4, para 41(8).

Sub-s (4): words in square brackets in para (b) substituted by the Age of Legal Capacity (Scotland) Act 1991, s 10, Sch 1, para 47; words "custody or" in para (c) repealed, in relation to Scotland, by the Children (Scotland) Act 1995, s 105(5), Sch 5.

36　Effect of orders restricting removal

(1)　　This section applies to any order made by a court in the United Kingdom prohibiting the removal of a child from the United Kingdom or from any specified part of it.

(2)　　An order to which this section applies shall have effect in each part of the United Kingdom other than the part in which it was made—
   (a)　as if it had been made by the appropriate court in that other part, and
   (b)　in the case of an order which has the effect of prohibiting the child's removal to that other part, as if it had included a prohibition on his

further removal to any place except one to which he could be removed consistently with the order.

(3)   The references in subsections (1) and (2) above to prohibitions on a child's removal include references to prohibitions subject to exceptions; and in a case where removal is prohibited except with the consent of the court, nothing in subsection (2) above shall be construed as affecting the identity of the court whose consent is required.

(4)   In this section "child" means a person who has not attained the age of sixteen; and this section shall cease to apply to an order relating to a child when he attains the age of sixteen.

37   Surrender of passports

(1)   Where there is in force an order prohibiting or otherwise restricting the removal of a child from the United Kingdom or from any specified part of it, the court by which the order was in fact made, or by which it is treated under section 36 of this Act as having been made, may require any person to surrender any United Kingdom passport which has been issued to, or contains particulars of, the child.

(2)   In this section "United Kingdom passport" means a current passport issued by the Government of the United Kingdom.

38   Automatic restriction on removal of wards of court

(1)   The rule of law which (without any order of the court) restricts the removal of a ward of court from the jurisdiction of the court shall, in a case to which this section applies, have effect subject to the modifications in subsection (3) below.

(2)   This section applies in relation to a ward of court if—
  (a) proceedings for divorce, nullity or judicial separation in respect of the marriage of his parents are continuing in a court in another part of the United Kingdom (that is to say, in a part of the United Kingdom outside the jurisdiction of the court of which he is a ward), or
  (b) he is habitually resident in another part of the United Kingdom,

except where that other part is Scotland and he has attained the age of sixteen.

(3)   Where this section applies, the rule referred to in subsection (1) above shall not prevent—

(a) the removal of the ward of court, without the consent of any court, to the other part of the United Kingdom mentioned in subsection (2) above, or

(b) his removal to any other place with the consent of either the appropriate court in that other part of the United Kingdom or the court mentioned in subsection (2)(a) above.

[(4)   The reference in subsection (2) above to a time when proceedings for divorce or judicial separation are continuing in respect of a marriage in another part of the United Kingdom includes, in relation to any case in which England and Wales would be another part of the United Kingdom, any time when—

(a) a statement of marital breakdown under section 5 of the Family Law Act 1996 with respect to that marriage has been received by the court and it is or may become possible for an application for a divorce order or for a separation order to be made by reference to that statement; or

(b) an application in relation to that marriage for a divorce order, or for a separation order under the Act of 1996, has been made and not withdrawn.]

NOTES

Commencement: 4 April 1988 (sub-ss (1)–(3)); to be appointed (remainder).

Sub-s (4): added by the Family Law Act 1996, s 66(1), Sch 8, para 37(1), (9), subject to savings in s 66(2) of, and Sch 9 para 5 to, the 1996 Act, as from a day to be appointed.

39   Duty to furnish particulars of other proceedings

Parties to proceedings for or relating to a [Part I order] shall, to such extent and in such manner as may be prescribed, give particulars of other proceedings known to them which relate to the child concerned (including proceedings instituted abroad and proceedings which are no longer continuing).

NOTES

Words in square brackets substituted by the Children Act 1989, s 108(5), (6), Sch 13, para 62, Sch 14, para 1.

40 Interpretation of Chapter VI

(1)   In this Chapter—
   "the appropriate court" has the same meaning as in Chapter V;
   ["Part I order"] includes (except where the context otherwise requires)
      any such order as is mentioned in section 32(1) of this Act.

(2)   In the application of this Chapter to Scotland, ["Part I order"] also
includes (except where the context otherwise requires) any such order as
is mentioned in section 32(2) of this Act.

NOTES

Words in square brackets substituted by the Children Act 1989, s 108(5),
Sch 13, para 62.

41   Habitual residence after removal without consent, etc

(1)   Where a child who—
   (a) has not attained the age of sixteen, and
   (b) is habitually resident in a part of the United Kingdom,

becomes habitually resident outside that part of the United Kingdom in
consequence of circumstances of the kind specified in subsection (2) below,
he shall be treated for the purposes of this Part as continuing to be habitually
resident in that part of the United Kingdom for the period of one year
beginning with the date on which those circumstances arise.

(2)   The circumstances referred to in subsection (1) above exist where
the child is removed from or retained outside, or himself leaves or remains
outside, the part of the United Kingdom in which he was habitually resident
before his change of residence—
   (a) without the agreement of the person or all the persons having, under
        the law of that part of the United Kingdom, the right to determine
        where he is to reside, or
   (b) in contravention of an order made by a court in any part of the
        United Kingdom.

(3)   A child shall cease to be treated by virtue of subsection (1) above as
habitually resident in a part of the United Kingdom if, during the period
there mentioned—
   (a) he attains the age of sixteen, or

(b) he becomes habitually resident outside that part of the United Kingdom with the agreement of the person or persons mentioned in subsection (2)(a) above and not in contravention of an order made by a court in any part of the United Kingdom.

42 General interpretation of Part I

(1) In this Part—

"certified copy", in relation to an order of any court, means a copy certified by the prescribed officer of the court to be a true copy of the order or of the official record of the order;

["parental responsibilities" and "parental rights" have the meanings respectively given by sections 1(3) and 2(4) of the Children (Scotland) Act 1995;]

"part of the United Kingdom" means England and Wales, Scotland or Northern Ireland;

"prescribed" means prescribed by rules of court or act of sederunt.

(2) For the purposes of this Part proceedings in England and Wales or in Northern Ireland for divorce, nullity or judicial separation in respect of the marriage of the parents of a child shall, *unless they have been dismissed, be treated as continuing until the child concerned attains the age of eighteen (whether or not a decree has been granted and whether or not, in the case of a decree of divorce or nullity of marriage, that decree has been made absolute).*

(3) For the purposes of this Part, matrimonial proceedings in a court in Scotland which has jurisdiction in those proceedings to make a [Part I order] with respect to a child shall, unless they have been dismissed or decree of absolvitor has been granted therein, be treated as continuing until the child concerned attains the age of sixteen.

(4) Any reference in this Part to proceedings in respect of the marriage of the parents of a child shall, in relation to a child who, although not a child of both parties to the marriage, is a child of the family of those parties, be construed as a reference to proceedings in respect of that marriage; and for this purpose "child of the family"—

(a) if the proceedings are in England and Wales, means any child who has been treated by both parties as a child of their family, except a child who [is placed with those parties as foster parents] by a local authority or a voluntary organisation;

(b) if the proceedings are in Scotland, means any child [who has been treated by both parties as a child of their family, except a child who has been placed with those parties as foster parents by a local authority or a voluntary organisation;]

(c) if the proceedings are in Northern Ireland, means any child who has been treated by both parties as a child of their family, except a child who [is placed with those parties as foster parents by an authority within the meaning of the Children (Northern Ireland) Order 1995] or a voluntary organisation.

(5)　References in this Part to [Part I orders] include (except where the context otherwise requires) references to [Part I orders] as varied.

(6)　For the purposes of this Part each of the following orders shall be treated as varying the [Part I order] to which it relates—

(a) an order which provides for a person [to be allowed contact with or] to be given access to a child who is the subject of a [Part I order], or which makes provision for the education of such a child,

(b)–(d) . . .

. . .

[(7)　In this Part—

(a) references to Part I proceedings in respect of a child are references to any proceedings for a Part I order or an order corresponding to a Part I order and include, in relation to proceedings outside the United Kingdom, references to proceedings before a tribunal or other authority having power under the law having effect there to determine Part I matters; and

(b) references to Part I matters are references to matters that might be determined by a Part I order or an order corresponding to a Part I order.]

NOTES

Sub-s (1): definition "parental responsibilities" inserted by the Children (Scotland) Act 1995, s 105(4), Sch 4, para 41(9)(a).

Sub-s (2): words in italics substituted by the Family Law Act 1996, s 66(1), Sch 8, para 37(1), (10), subject to savings in s 66(2) of, and Sch 9, para 5 to, the 1996 Act, as from a day to be appointed, as follows—

"be treated as continuing (irrespective of whether a divorce order, separation order or decree of nullity has been made)—

(a) from the time when a statement of marital breakdown under section 5 of the Family Law Act 1996 with respect to the marriage is received by the court in England and Wales until such time as the court may designate or, if earlier, until the time when—

(i) the child concerned attains the age of eighteen; or

(ii) it ceases, by virtue of section 5(3) or 7(9) of that Act (lapse of divorce or separation process) to be possible for an application for a divorce order, or for a separation order, to be made by reference to that statement; and

(b) from the time when a petition for nullity is presented in relation to the marriage in England and Wales or a petition for divorce, judicial separation or nullity is presented in relation to the marriage in Northern Ireland or a specified dependent territory, until the time when—

(i) the child concerned attains the age of eighteen; or

(ii) if earlier, proceedings on the petition are dismissed.".

Sub-s (3): words in square brackets substituted by the Children Act 1989, s 108(5), Sch 13, para 62.

Sub-s (4): words in first pair of square brackets substituted by the Children Act 1989, s 108(5), (7), Sch 13, para 71, Sch 15; words in square brackets in para (b) substituted by the Children (Scotland) Act 1995, s 105(4), Sch 4, para 41(9)(b); words in square brackets in para (c) substituted by the Children (Northern Ireland Consequential Amendments) Order 1995, SI 1995/756, art 12(1), (4).

Sub-s (5): words in square brackets substituted by the Children Act 1989, s 108(5), Sch 13, para 62.

Sub-s (6): words in first and third pairs of square brackets substituted, words in second pair of square brackets inserted by the Children Act 1989, s 108(5), (7), Sch 13, paras 62, 71, Sch 15, and words omitted repealed by SI 1995/756, art 15, Schedule.

Sub-s (7): substituted by the Children Act 1989, s 108(5), Sch 13, para 62(3).

PART III
DECLARATIONS OF STATUS

55 Declarations as to marital status

(1)   Subject to the following provisions of this section, any person may apply to the court for one or more of the following declarations in relation to a marriage specified in the application, that is to say—

(a) a declaration that the marriage was at its inception a valid marriage;

(b) a declaration that the marriage subsisted on a date specified in the application;

(c) a declaration that the marriage did not subsist on a date so specified;

(d) a declaration that the validity of a divorce, annulment or legal separation obtained in any country outside England and Wales in respect of the marriage is entitled to recognition in England and Wales;

(e) a declaration that the validity of a divorce, annulment or legal separation so obtained in respect of the marriage is not entitled to recognition in England and Wales.

(2)   A court shall have jurisdiction to entertain an application under subsection (1) above if, and only if, either of the parties to the marriage to which the application relates—
  (a) is domiciled in England and Wales on the date of the application, or
  (b) has been habitually resident in England and Wales throughout the period of one year ending with that date, or
  (c) died before that date and either—
    (i)   was at death domiciled in England and Wales, or
    (ii) had been habitually resident in England and Wales throughout the period of one year ending with the date of death.

(3)   Where an application under subsection (1) above is made by any person other than a party to the marriage to which the application relates, the court shall refuse to hear the application if it considers that the applicant does not have a sufficient interest in the determination of that application.

[56   Declarations of parentage, legitimacy or legitimation

(1)   Any person may apply to the court for a declaration—
  (a) that a person named in the application is or was his parent; or
  (b) that he is the legitimate child of his parents.

(2)   Any person may apply to the court for one (or for one or, in the alternative, the other) of the following declarations, that is to say—
  (a) a declaration that he has become a legitimated person;
  (b) a declaration that he has not become a legitimated person.

(3)   A court shall have jurisdiction to entertain an application under this section if, the applicant—
  (a) is domiciled in England and Wales on the date of the application; or
  (b) has been habitually resident in England and Wales throughout the period of one year ending with that date.

(4)   Where a declaration is made on an application under subsection (1) above, the prescribed officer of the court shall notify the Registrar General, in such a manner and within such period as may be prescribed, of the making of that declaration.

(5)   In this section "legitimated person" means a person legitimated or recognised as legitimated—
  (a) under section 2 or 3 of the Legitimacy Act 1976;
  (b) under section 1 or 8 of the Legitimacy Act 1926; or

(c) by a legitimation (whether or not by virtue of the subsequent marriage of his parents) recognised by the law of England and Wales and effected under the law of another country.]

NOTES

Substituted by the Family Law Reform Act 1987, s 22.

57 Declarations as to adoptions effected overseas

(1) Any person whose status as an adopted child of any person depends on whether he has been adopted by that person by either—
  (a) an overseas adoption as defined by section 72(2) of the Adoption Act 1976, or
  (b) an adoption recognised by the law of England and Wales and effected under the law of any country outside the British Islands,

may apply to the court for one (or for one or, in the alternative, the other) of the declarations mentioned in subsection (2) below.

(2) The said declarations are—
  (a) a declaration that the applicant is for the purposes of section 39 of the Adoption Act 1976 the adopted child of that person;
  (b) a declaration that the applicant is not for the purposes of that section the adopted child of that person.

(3) A court shall have jurisdiction to entertain an application under subsection (1) above if, and only if, the applicant—
  (a) is domiciled in England and Wales on the date of the application, or
  (b) has been habitually resident in England and Wales throughout the period of one year ending with that date.

(4) . . .

NOTES

Sub-s (4): spent.

58 General provisions as to the making and effect of declarations

(1) Where on an application for a declaration under this Part the truth of the proposition to be declared is proved to the satisfaction of the court,

the court shall make that declaration unless to do so would manifestly be contrary to public policy.

(2)   Any declaration made under this Part shall be binding on Her Majesty and all other persons.

(3)   The court, on the dismissal of an application for a declaration under this Part, shall not have power to make any declaration for which an application has not been made.

(4)   No declaration which may be applied for under this Part may be made otherwise than under this Part by any court.

(5)   No declaration may be made by any court, whether under this Part or otherwise—
   (a) that a marriage was at its inception void;
   (b) that any person is or was illegitimate.

(6)   Nothing in this section shall affect the powers of any court to grant a decree of nullity of marriage.

PART IV
MISCELLANEOUS AND GENERAL

69   Short title, commencement and extent

(1)   This Act may be cited as the Family Law Act 1986.

(2)–(7) . . .

NOTES

Sub-ss (2)–(7): outside the scope of this work.

Family Law Reform Act 1987

(c 42)

An Act to reform the law relating to the consequences of birth outside marriage; to make further provision with respect to the rights and duties of parents and the determination of parentage; and for connected purposes
[15 May 1987]

PART I
GENERAL PRINCIPLE

I   General principle

(1)   In this Act and enactments passed and instruments made after the coming into force of this section, references (however expressed) to any relationship between two persons shall, unless the contrary intention appears, be construed without regard to whether or not the father and mother of either of them, or the father and mother of any person through whom the relationship is deduced, have or had been married to each other at any time.

(2)   In this Act and enactments passed after the coming into force of this section, unless the contrary intention appears—
   (a) references to a person whose father and mother were married to each other at the time of his birth include; and
   (b) references to a person whose father and mother were not married to each other at the time of his birth do not include,

references to any person whom subsection (3) below applies, and cognate references shall be construed accordingly.

(3)   This subsection applies to any person who—
   (a) is treated as legitimate by virtue of section 1 of the Legitimacy Act 1976;
   (b) is a legitimated person within the meaning of section 10 of that Act;
   (c) is an adopted child within the meaning of Part IV of that Act 1976; or
   (d) is otherwise treated in law as legitimate.

(4)   For the purpose of construing references falling within subsection (2) above, the time of a person's birth shall be taken to include any time during the period beginning with—
   (a) the insemination resulting in his birth; or
   (b) where there was no such insemination, his conception,

and (in either case) ending with his birth.

2   Construction of enactments relating to parental rights and duties

(1)   In the following enactments, namely—
   (a) section 42(1) of the National Assistance Act 1948;

(b) section 6 of the Family Law Reform Act 1969;

(c) the Guardianship of Minors Act 1971 (in this Act referred to as "the 1971 Act");

(d) Part I of the Guardianship Act 1973 (in this Act referred to as "the 1973 Act");

(e) Part II of the Children Act 1975;

(f) the Child Care Act 1980 except Part I and sections 13, 24, 64 and 65;

(g) . . .

references (however expressed) to any relationship between two persons shall be construed in accordance with section 1 above.

(2) . . .

NOTES

Sub-s (1): para (g) repealed by the Social Security (Consequential Provisions) Act 1992, s 3, Sch 1.

Sub-s (2): amends the Guardianship Act 1973, s 1(7).

PART III
PROPERTY RIGHTS

18 Succession on intestacy

(1) In Part IV of the Administration of Estates Act 1925 (which deals with the distribution of the estate of an intestate), references (however expressed) to any relationship between two persons shall be construed in accordance with section 1 above.

(2) For the purposes of subsection (1) above and that Part of that Act, a person whose father and mother were not married to each other at the time of his birth shall be presumed not to have been survived by his father, or by any person related to him only through his father, unless the contrary is shown.

(3) In section 50(1) of that Act (which relates to the construction of documents), the reference to Part IV of that Act, or to the foregoing provisions of that Part, shall in relation to an instrument inter vivos made, or a will or codicil coming into operation, after the coming into force of this section (but not in relation to instruments inter vivos made or wills or codicils coming into operation earlier) be construed as including references to this section.

(4)   This section does not affect any rights under the intestacy of a person dying before the coming into force of this section.

19   Dispositions of property

(1)   In the following dispositions, namely—
  (a) dispositions inter vivos made on or after the date on which this section comes into force; and
  (b) dispositions by will or codicil where the will or codicil is made on or after that date,

references (whether express or implied) to any relationship between two persons shall be construed in accordance with section 1 above.

(2)   It is hereby declared that the use, without more, of the word "heir" or "heirs" or any expression [purporting to create] an entailed interest in real or personal property does not show a contrary intention for the purposes of section 1 as applied by subsection (1) above.

(3)   In relation to the dispositions mentioned in subsection (1) above, section 33 of the Trustee Act 1925 (which specifies the trust implied by a direction that income is to be held on protective trusts for the benefit of any person) shall have effect as if any reference (however expressed) to any relationship between two persons were constructed in accordance with section 1 above.

(4)   Where under any disposition of real or personal property, any interest in such property is limited (whether subject to any preceding limitation or charge or not) in such a way that it would, apart from this section, devolve (as nearly as the law permits) along with a dignity or title of honour, then—
  (a) whether or not the disposition contains an express reference to the dignity or title of honour; and
  (b) whether or not the property or some interest in the property may in some event become severed from it,

nothing in this section shall operate to sever the property or any interest in it from the dignity or title, but the property or interest shall devolve in all respects as if this section had not been enacted.

(5)   This section is without prejudice to section 42 of the Adoption Act 1976 (construction of dispositions in cases of adoption).

Sub-s (2): words in square brackets substituted by the Trusts of Land and Appointment of Trustees Act 1996, s 25(1), Sch 3, para 25.

(6)   In this section "disposition" means a disposition, including an oral disposition, of real or personal property whether inter vivos or by will or codicil.

(7)   Notwithstanding any rule of law, a disposition made by will or codicil executed before the date on which this section comes into force shall not be treated for the purposes of this section as made on or after that date by reason only that the will or codicil is confirmed by a codicil executed on or after that date.

PART VI
MISCELLANEOUS AND SUPPLEMENTAL

Miscellaneous

27 Artificial insemination

(1)   Where after the coming into force of this section a child is born in England and Wales as the result of the artificial insemination of a woman who—
  (a) was at the time of the insemination a party to a marriage (being a marriage which had not at that time been dissolved or annulled); and
  (b) was artificially inseminated with the semen of some person other than the other party to that marriage,

then, unless it is proved to the satisfaction of any court by which the matter has to be determined that the other party to that marriage did not consent to the insemination, the child shall be treated in law as the child of the parties to that marriage and shall not be treated as the child of any person other than the parties to that marriage.

(2)   Any reference in this section to a marriage includes a reference to a void marriage if at the time of the insemination resulting in the birth of the child both or either of the parties reasonably believed that the marriage was valid; and for the purposes of this section it shall be presumed, unless the contrary is shown, that one of the parties so believed at that time that the marriage was valid.

(3)   Nothing in this section shall affect the succession to any dignity or title of honour or render any person capable of succeeding to or transmitting a right to succeed to any such dignity or title.

34   Short title, commencement and extent

(1)   This Act may be cited as the Family Law Reform Act 1987.

(2)   This Act shall come into force on such day as the Lord Chancellor may by order made by statutory instrument appoint; and different days may be so appointed for different provisions or different purposes.

(3), (4)   . . .

(5)   Subject to subsection (4) above, this Act extends to England and Wales only.

NOTES

Sub-ss (3), (4): outside the scope of   this work.

Housing Act 1988

(c 50)

An Act to make further provision with respect to dwelling-houses let on tenancies or occupied under licences; to amend the Rent Act 1977 and Rent (Agriculture) Act 1976; to establish a body, Housing for Wales, having functions relating to housing associations; to amend the Housing Associations Act 1985 and to repeal and re-enact with amendments certain provisions of Part II of that Act; to make provision for the establishment of housing action trusts for areas designated by the Secretary of State; to confer on persons approved for the purpose the right to acquire from public sector landlords certain dwelling-houses occupied by secure tenants; to make further provision about rent officers, the administration of housing benefit and rent allowance subsidy, the right to buy, repair notices and certain disposals of land and the application of capital money arising thereon; to make provision consequential upon the Housing (Scotland) Act 1988; and for connected purposes

[15 November 1988]

PART I
RENTED ACCOMMODATION

CHAPTER I
ASSURED TENANCIES

Miscellaneous

17 Succession to assured periodic tenancy by spouse

(1)   In any case where—
  (a) the sole tenant under an assured periodic tenancy dies, and
  (b) immediately before the death, the tenant's spouse was occupying the dwelling-house as his or her only or principal home, and
  (c) the tenant was not himself a successor, as defined in subsection (2) or subsection (3) below,

then, on the death, the tenancy vests by virtue of this section in the spouse (and, accordingly, does not devolve under the tenant's will or intestacy).

(2)   For the purposes of this section, a tenant is a successor in relation to a tenancy if—
  (a) the tenancy became vested in him either by virtue of this section or under the will or intestacy of a previous tenant; or
  (b) at some time before the tenant's death the tenancy was a joint tenancy held by himself and one or more other persons and, prior to his death, he became the sole tenant by survivorship; or
  (c) he became entitled to the tenancy as mentioned in section 39(5) below.

(3)   For the purposes of this section, a tenant is also a successor in relation to a tenancy (in this subsection referred to as "the new tenancy") which was granted to him (alone or jointly with others) if—
  (a) at some time before the grant of the new tenancy, he was, by virtue of subsection (2) above, a successor in relation to an earlier tenancy of the same or substantially the same dwelling-house as is let under the new tenancy; and
  (b) at all times since he became such a successor he has been a tenant (alone or jointly with others) of the dwelling-house which is let under the new tenancy or of a dwelling-house which is substantially the same as that dwelling-house.

(4)   For the purposes of this section, a person who was living with the tenant as his or her wife or husband shall be treated as the tenant's spouse.

(5)   If, on the death of the tenant, there is, by virtue of subsection (4) above, more than one person who fulfils the condition in subsection (1)(b) above, such one of them as may be decided by agreement or, in default of agreement, by the county court shall be treated as the tenant's spouse for the purposes of this section.

PART V
MISCELLANEOUS AND GENERAL

Supplementary

141   Short title, commencement and extent

(1)   This Act may be cited as the Housing Act 1988.

(2)–(5) . . .

(6)   This Act does not extend to Northern Ireland.

NOTES

Sub-ss (2)–(5): outside the scope of this work.

Children Act 1989

(c 41)

An Act to reform the law relating to children; to provide for local authority services for children in need and others; to amend the law with respect to children's homes, community homes, voluntary homes and voluntary organisations; to make provision with respect to fostering, child minding and day care for young children and adoption; and for connected purposes

[16 November 1989]

PART I
INTRODUCTORY

1 Welfare of the child

(1)   When a court determines any question with respect to—
  (a) the upbringing of a child; or
  (b) the administration of a child's property or the application of any
       income arising from it,

the child's welfare shall be the court's paramount consideration.

(2)   In any proceedings in which any question with respect to the
upbringing of a child arises, the court shall have regard to the general
principle that any delay in determining the question is likely to prejudice
the welfare of the child.

(3)   In the circumstances mentioned in subsection (4), a court shall have
regard in particular to—
  (a) the ascertainable wishes and feelings of the child concerned
       (considered in the light of his age and understanding);
  (b) his physical, emotional and educational needs;
  (c) the likely effect on him of any change in his circumstances;
  (d) his age, sex, background and any characteristics of his which the
       court considers relevant;
  (e) any harm which he has suffered or is at risk of suffering;
  (f) how capable each of his parents, and any other person in relation to
       whom the court considers the question to be relevant, is of meeting
       his needs;
  (g) the range of powers available to the court under this Act in the
       proceedings in question.

(4)   The circumstances are that—
  (a) the court is considering whether to make, vary or discharge a section
       8 order, and the making, variation or discharge of the order is opposed
       by any party to the proceedings; or
  (b) the court is considering whether to make, vary or discharge an order
       under Part IV.

(5)   Where a court is considering whether or not to make one or more
orders under this Act with respect to a child, it shall not make the order or
any of the orders unless it considers that doing so would be better for the
child than making no order at all.

2   Parental responsibility for children

(1)   Where a child's father and mother were married to each other at the time of his birth, they shall each have parental responsibility for the child.

(2)   Where a child's father and mother were not married to each other at the time of his birth—
  (a) the mother shall have parental responsibility for the child;
  (b) the father shall not have parental responsibility for the child, unless he acquires it in accordance with the provisions of this Act.

(3)   References in this Act to a child whose father and mother were, or (as the case may be) were not, married to each other at the time of his birth must be read with section 1 of the Family Law Reform Act 1987 (which extends their meaning).

(4)   The rule of law that a father is the natural guardian of his legitimate child is abolished.

(5)   More than one person may have parental responsibility for the same child at the same time.

(6)   A person who has parental responsibility for a child at any time shall not cease to have that responsibility solely because some other person subsequently acquires parental responsibility for the child.

(7)   Where more than one person has parental responsibility for a child, each of them may act alone and without the other (or others) in meeting that responsibility; but nothing in this Part shall be taken to affect the operation of any enactment which requires the consent of more than one person in a matter affecting the child.

(8)   The fact that a person has parental responsibility for a child shall not entitle him to act in any way which would be incompatible with any order made with respect to the child under this Act.

(9)   A person who has parental responsibility for a child may not surrender or transfer any part of that responsibility to another but may arrange for some or all of it to be met by one or more persons acting on his behalf.

(10)   The person with whom any such arrangement is made may himself be a person who already has parental responsibility for the child concerned.

(11)   The making of any such arrangement shall not affect any liability of the person making it which may arise from any failure to meet any part of his parental responsibility for the child concerned.

3   Meaning of "parental responsibility"

(1)   In this Act "parental responsibility" means all the rights, duties, powers, responsibilities and authority which by law a parent of a child has in relation to the child and his property.

(2)   It also includes the rights, powers and duties which a guardian of the child's estate (appointed, before the commencement of section 5, to act generally) would have had in relation to the child and his property.

(3)   The rights referred to in subsection (2) include, in particular, the right of the guardian to receive or recover in his own name, for the benefit of the child, property of whatever description and wherever situated which the child is entitled to receive or recover.

(4)   The fact that a person has, or does not have, parental responsibility for a child shall not affect—
  (a) any obligation which he may have in relation to the child (such as a statutory duty to maintain the child); or
  (b) any rights which, in the event of the child's death, he (or any other person) may have in relation to the child's property.

(5)   A person who—
  (a) does not have parental responsibility for a particular child; but
  (b) has care of the child,

may (subject to the provisions of this Act) do what is reasonable in all the circumstances of the case for the purpose of safeguarding or promoting the child's welfare.

4   Acquisition of parental responsibility by father

(1)   Where a child's father and mother were not married to each other at the time of his birth—
  (a) the court may, on the application of the father, order that he shall have parental responsibility for the child; or

(b) the father and mother may by agreement ("a parental responsibility agreement") provide for the father to have parental responsibility for the child.

(2)   No parental responsibility agreement shall have effect for the purposes of this Act unless—
(a) it is made in the form prescribed by regulations made by the Lord Chancellor; and
(b) where regulations are made by the Lord Chancellor prescribing the manner in which such agreements must be recorded, it is recorded in the prescribed manner.

(3)   Subject to section 12(4), an order under subsection (1)(a), or a parental responsibility agreement, may only be brought to an end by an order of the court made on the application—
(a) of any person who has parental responsibility for the child; or
(b) with leave of the court, of the child himself.

(4)   The court may only grant leave under subsection (3)(b) if it is satisfied that the child has sufficient understanding to make the proposed application.

5   Appointment of guardians

(1)   Where an application with respect to a child is made to the court by any individual, the court may by order appoint that individual to be the child's guardian if—
(a) the child has no parent with parental responsibility for him; or
(b) a residence order has been made with respect to the child in favour of a parent or guardian of his who has died while the order was in force.

(2)   The power conferred by subsection (1) may also be exercised in any family proceedings if the court considers that the order should be made even though no application has been made for it.

(3)   A parent who has parental responsibility for his child may appoint another individual to be the child's guardian in the event of his death.

(4)   A guardian of a child may appoint another individual to take his place as the child's guardian in the event of his death.

(5)   An appointment under subsection (3) or (4) shall not have effect unless it is made in writing, is dated and is signed by the person making the appointment or—

(a) in the case of an appointment made by a will which is not signed by the testator, is signed at the direction of the testator in accordance with the requirements of section 9 of the Wills Act 1837; or

(b) in any other case, is signed at the direction of the person making the appointment, in his presence and in the presence of two witnesses who each attest the signature.

(6) A person appointed as a child's guardian under this section shall have parental responsibility for the child concerned.

(7) Where—
(a) on the death of any person making an appointment under subsection (3) or (4), the child concerned has no parent with parental responsibility for him; or

(b) immediately before the death of any person making such an appointment, a residence order in his favour was in force with respect to the child,

the appointment shall take effect on the death of that person.

(8) Where, on the death of any person making an appointment under subsection (3) or (4)—
(a) the child concerned has a parent with parental responsibility for him; and

(b) subsection (7)(b) does not apply,

the appointment shall take effect when the child no longer has a parent who has parental responsibility for him.

(9) Subsections (1) and (7) do not apply if the residence order referred to in paragraph (b) of those subsections was also made in favour of a surviving parent of the child.

(10) Nothing in this section shall be taken to prevent an appointment under subsection (3) or (4) being made by two or more persons acting jointly.

(11) Subject to any provision made by rules of court, no court shall exercise the High Court's inherent jurisdiction to appoint a guardian of the estate of any child.

(12) Where rules of court are made under subsection (11) they may prescribe the circumstances in which, and conditions subject to which, an appointment of such a guardian may be made.

(13)   A guardian of a child may only be appointed in accordance with the provisions of this section.

6   Guardians: revocation and disclaimer

(1)   An appointment under section 5(3) or (4) revokes an earlier such appointment (including one made in an unrevoked will or codicil) made by the same person in respect of the same child, unless it is clear (whether as the result of an express provision in the later appointment or by any necessary implication) that the purpose of the later appointment is to appoint an additional guardian.

(2)   An appointment under section 5(3) or (4) (including one made in an unrevoked will or codicil) is revoked if the person who made the appointment revokes it by a written and dated instrument which is signed—
    (a) by him; or
    (b) at his direction, in his presence and in the presence of two witnesses who each attest the signature.

(3)   An appointment under section 5(3) or (4) (other than one made in a will or codicil) is revoked if, with the intention of revoking the appointment, the person who made it—
    (a) destroys the instrument by which it was made; or
    (b) has some other person destroy that instrument in his presence.

[(3A)   An appointment under section 5(3) or (4) (including one made in an unrevoked will or codicil) is revoked if the person appointed is the spouse of the person who made the appointment and either—
    (a) a decree of a court of civil jurisdiction in England and Wales dissolves or annuls the marriage, or
    (b) the marriage is dissolved or annulled and the divorce or annulment is entitled to recognition in England and Wales by virtue of Part II of the Family Law Act 1986,

unless a contrary intention appears by the appointment.]

(4)   For the avoidance of doubt, an appointment under section 5(3) or (4) made in a will or codicil is revoked if the will or codicil is revoked.

(5)   A person who is appointed as a guardian under section 5(3) or (4) may disclaim his appointment by an instrument in writing signed by him and made within a reasonable time of his first knowing that the appointment has taken effect.

(6)   Where regulations are made by the Lord Chancellor prescribing the manner in which such disclaimers must be recorded, no such disclaimer shall have effect unless it is recorded in the prescribed manner.

(7)   Any appointment of a guardian under section 5 may be brought to an end at any time by order of the court—
   (a) on the application of any person who has parental responsibility for the child;
   (b) on the application of the child concerned, with leave of the court; or
   (c) in any family proceedings, if the court considers that it should be brought to an end even though no application has been made.

NOTES

Commencement: 8 November 1995 (sub-s (3A)); 14 October 1991 (remainder).

Sub-s (3A): inserted by the Law Reform (Succession) Act 1995, s 4; para (a) substituted by the Family Law Act 1996, s 66(1), Sch 8, Pt I, para 41(1), (2), subject to savings in s 66(2) of, and Sch 9, para 5 to, the 1996 Act, as from a day to be appointed, as follows—

   "(a) a court of civil jurisdiction in England and Wales by order dissolves, or by decree annuls, a marriage, or".

7   Welfare reports

(1)   A court considering any question with respect to a child under this Act may—
   (a) ask a probation officer; or
   (b) ask a local authority to arrange for—
      (i)   an officer of the authority; or
      (ii) such other person (other than a probation officer) as the authority considers appropriate,

to report to the court on such matters relating to the welfare of that child as are required to be dealt with in the report.

(2)   The Lord Chancellor may make regulations specifying matters which, unless the court orders otherwise, must be dealt with in any report under this section.

(3)   The report may be made in writing, or orally, as the court requires.

(4)   Regardless of any enactment or rule of law which would otherwise prevent it from doing so, the court may take account of—
   (a) any statement contained in the report; and

(b) any evidence given in respect of the matters referred to in the report,

in so far as the statement or evidence is, in the opinion of the court, relevant to the question which it is considering.

(5) It shall be the duty of the authority or probation officer to comply with any request for a report under this section.

PART II

ORDERS WITH RESPECT TO CHILDREN IN FAMILY PROCEEDINGS

General

8 Residence, contact and other orders with respect to children

(1) In this Act—
"a contact order" means an order requiring the person with whom a child lives, or is to live, to allow the child to visit or stay with the person named in the order, or for that person and the child otherwise to have contact with each other;
"a prohibited steps order" means an order that no step which could be taken by a parent in meeting his parental responsibility for a child, and which is of a kind specified in the order, shall be taken by any person without the consent of the court;
"a residence order" means an order settling the arrangements to be made as to the person with whom a child is to live; and
"a specific issue order" means an order giving directions for the purpose of determining a specific question which has arisen, or which may arise, in connection with any aspect of parental responsibility for a child.

(2) In this Act "a section 8 order" means any of the orders mentioned in subsection (1) and any order varying or discharging such an order.

(3) For the purposes of this Act "family proceedings" means [(subject to subsection (5))] any proceedings—
(a) under the inherent jurisdiction of the High Court in relation to children; and
(b) under the enactments mentioned in subsection (4),

but does not include proceedings on an application for leave under section 100(3).

(4)   The enactments are—
(a) Parts I, II and IV of this Act;
(b) the Matrimonial Causes Act 1973;
(c) . . .
(d) the Adoption Act 1976;
(e) the Domestic Proceedings and Magistrates' Courts Act 1978;
(f) . . .
(g) Part III of the Matrimonial and Family Proceedings Act 1984.
[(h) the Family Law Act 1996.]
[(i) sections 11 and 12 of the Crime and Disorder Act 1998.]

[(5)   For the purposes of any reference in this Act to family proceedings powers which under this Act are exercisable in family proceedings shall also be exercisable in relation to a child, without any such proceedings having been commenced or any application having been made to the court under this Act, if—
(a) a statement of marital breakdown under section 5 of the Family Law Act 1996 with respect to the marriage in relation to which that child is a child of the family has been received by the court; and
(b) it may, in due course, become possible for an application for a divorce order or for a separation order to be made by reference to that statement.]

NOTES

Commencement: 14 October 1991 (sub-ss (1)–(4)); to be appointed (remainder).

Sub-s (3): words in square brackets inserted by the Family Law Act 1996, s 66(1), Sch 8, Pt I, para 41(1), (3), subject to savings in s 66(2) of, and Sch 9, para 5 to, the 1996 Act, as from a day to be appointed.

Sub-s (4): paras (c) and (f) repealed, and para (h) added, by the Family Law Act 1996, s 66(1), (3), Sch 8, Pt III, para 60(1), Sch 10, subject to savings in s 66(2) of, and Sch 9, paras 5, 8–10 to, the 1996 Act; para (i) added by the Crime and Disorder Act 1998, s 119, Sch 8, para 68.

Sub-s (5): added by the Family Law Act 1996, s 66(1), Sch 8, Pt I, para 41(1), (4), subject to savings in s 66(2) of, and Sch 9, paras 5, 8–10 to, the 1996 Act, as from a day to be appointed.

9   Restrictions on making section 8 orders

(1)   No court shall make any section 8 order, other than a residence order, with respect to a child who is in the care of a local authority.

(2)   No application may be made by a local authority for a residence order or contact order and no court shall make such an order in favour of a local authority.

(3)   A person who is, or was at any time within the last six months, a local authority foster parent of a child may not apply for leave to apply for a section 8 order with respect to the child unless—

(a) he has the consent of the authority;

(b) he is a relative of the child; or

(c) the child has lived with him for at least three years preceding the application.

(4)   The period of three years mentioned in subsection (3)(c) need not be continuous but must have begun not more than five years before the making of the application.

(5)   No court shall exercise its powers to make a specific issue order or prohibited steps order—

(a) with a view to achieving a result which could be achieved by making a residence or contact order; or

(b) in any way which is denied to the High Court (by section 100(2)) in the exercise of its inherent jurisdiction with respect to children.

(6)   No court shall make any section 8 order which is to have effect for a period which will end after the child has reached the age of sixteen unless it is satisfied that the circumstances of the case are exceptional.

(7)   No court shall make any section 8 order, other than one varying or discharging such an order, with respect to a child who has reached the age of sixteen unless it is satisfied that the circumstances of the case are exceptional.

10   Power of court to make section 8 orders

(1)   In any family proceedings in which a question arises with respect to the welfare of any child, the court may make a section 8 order with respect to the child if—

(a) an application for the order has been made by a person who—

(i)   is entitled to apply for a section 8 order with respect to the child; or

(ii) has obtained the leave of the court to make the application; or

(b) the court considers that the order should be made even though no such application has been made.

(2)   The court may also make a section 8 order with respect to any child on the application of a person who—

(a) is entitled to apply for a section 8 order with respect to the child; or

(b) has obtained the leave of the court to make the application.

(3)   This section is subject to the restrictions imposed by section 9.

(4)   The following persons are entitled to apply to the court for any section 8 order with respect to a child—

(a) any parent or guardian of the child;

(b) any person in whose favour a residence order is in force with respect to the child.

(5)   The following persons are entitled to apply for a residence or contact order with respect to a child—

(a) any party to a marriage (whether or not subsisting) in relation to whom the child is a child of the family;

(b) any person with whom the child has lived for a period of at least three years;

(c) any person—

(i) in any case where a residence order is in force with respect to the child, has the consent of each of the persons in whose favour the order was made;

(ii) in any case where the child is in the care of a local authority, has the consent of that authority; or

(iii) in any other case, has the consent of each of those (if any) who have parental responsibility for the child.

(6)   A person who would not otherwise be entitled (under the previous provisions of this section) to apply for the variation or discharge of a section 8 order shall be entitled to do so if—

(a) the order was made on his application; or

(b) in the case of a contact order, he is named in the order.

(7)   Any person who falls within a category of person prescribed by rules of court is entitled to apply for any such section 8 order as may be prescribed in relation to that category of person.

(8)   Where the person applying for leave to make an application for a section 8 order is the child concerned, the court may only grant leave if it is satisfied that he has sufficient understanding to make the proposed application for the section 8 order.

(9)   Where the person applying for leave to make an application for a section 8 order is not the child concerned, the court shall, in deciding whether or not to grant leave, have particular regard to—

(a) the nature of the proposed application for the section 8 order;
(b) the applicant's connection with the child;
(c) any risk there might be of that proposed application disrupting the child's life to such an extent that he would be harmed by it; and
(d) where the child is being looked after by a local authority—
(i)   the authority's plans for the child's future; and
(ii) the wishes and feelings of the child's parents.

(10)   The period of three years mentioned in subsection (5)(b) need not be continuous but must not have begun more than five years before, or ended more than three months before, the making of the application.

11   General principles and supplementary provisions

(1)   In proceedings in which any question of making a section 8 order, or any other question with respect to such an order, arises, the court shall (in the light of any rules made by virtue of subsection (2))—
(a) draw up a timetable with a view to determining the question without delay; and
(b) give such directions as it considers appropriate for the purpose of ensuring, so far as is reasonably practicable, that that timetable is adhered to.

(2)   Rules of court may—
(a) specify periods within which specified steps must be taken in relation to proceedings in which such questions arise; and
(b) make other provision with respect to such proceedings for the purpose of ensuring, so far as is reasonably practicable, that such questions are determined without delay.

(3)   Where a court has power to make a section 8 order, it may do so at any time during the course of the proceedings in question even though it is not in a position to dispose finally of those proceedings.

(4)   Where a residence order is made in favour of two or more persons who do not themselves all live together, the order may specify the periods during which the child is to live in the different households concerned.

(5)   Where—
(a) a residence order has been made with respect to a child; and
(b) as a result of the order the child lives, or is to live, with one of two parents who each have parental responsibility for him,

the residence order shall cease to have effect if the parents live together for a continuous period of more than six months.

(6)   A contact order which requires the parent with whom a child lives to allow the child to visit, or otherwise have contact with, his other parent shall cease to have effect if the parents live together for a continuous period of more than six months.

(7)   A section 8 order may—
   (a) contain directions about how it is to be carried into effect;
   (b) impose conditions which must be complied with by any person—
     (i)   in whose favour the order is made;
     (ii) who is a parent of the child concerned;
    (iii) who is not a parent of his but who has parental responsibility for him; or
    (iv) with whom the child is living,

and to whom the conditions are expressed to apply;
   (c) be made to have effect for a specified period, or contain provisions which are to have effect for a specified period;
   (d) make such incidental, supplemental or consequential provision as the court thinks fit.

12   Residence orders and parental responsibility

(1)   Where the court makes a residence order in favour of the father of a child it shall, if the father would not otherwise have parental responsibility for the child, also make an order under section 4 giving him that responsibility.

(2)   Where the court makes a residence order in favour of any person who is not the parent or guardian of the child concerned that person shall have parental responsibility for the child while the residence order remains in force.

(3)   Where a person has parental responsibility for a child as a result of subsection (2), he shall not have the right—
   (a) to consent, or refuse to consent, to the making of an application with respect to the child under section 18 of the Adoption Act 1976;
   (b) to agree, or refuse to agree, to the making of an adoption order, or an order under section 55 of the Act of 1976, with respect to the child; or
   (c) to appoint a guardian for the child.

(4)   Where subsection (1) requires the court to make an order under section 4 in respect of the father of a child, the court shall not bring that order to an end at any time while the residence order concerned remains in force.

13   Change of child's name or removal from jurisdiction

(1)   Where a residence order is in force with respect to a child, no person may—

(a) cause the child to be known by a new surname; or

(b) remove him from the United Kingdom;

without either the written consent of every person who has parental responsibility for the child or the leave of the court.

(2)   Subsection (1)(b) does not prevent the removal of a child, for a period of less than one month, by the person in whose favour the residence order is made.

(3)   In making a residence order with respect to a child the court may grant the leave required by subsection (1)(b), either generally or for specified purposes.

14   Enforcement of residence orders

(1)   Where—

(a) a residence order is in force with respect to a child in favour of any person; and

(b) any other person (including one in whose favour the order is also in force) is in breach of the arrangements settled by that order,

the person mentioned in paragraph (a) may, as soon as the requirement in subsection (2) is complied with, enforce the order under section 63(3) of the Magistrates' Courts Act 1980 as if it were an order requiring the other person to produce the child to him.

(2)   The requirement is that a copy of the residence order has been served on the other person.

(3)   Subsection (1) is without prejudice to any other remedy open to the person in whose favour the residence order is in force.

Financial relief

15   Orders for financial relief with respect to children

(1)   Schedule 1 (which consists primarily of the re-enactment, with consequential amendments and minor modifications, of provisions of [section 6 of the Family Law Reform Act 1969] the Guardianship of Minors Acts 1971 and 1973, the Children Act 1975 and of sections 15 and 16 of the Family Law Reform Act 1987) makes provision in relation to financial relief for children.

(2)   The powers of a magistrates' court under section 60 of the Magistrates' Courts Act 1980 to revoke, revive or vary an order for the periodical payment of money [and the power of the clerk of a magistrates' court to vary such an order] shall not apply in relation to an order made under Schedule 1.

NOTES

Sub-s (1): words in square brackets inserted by the Courts and Legal Services Act 1990, s 116, Sch 16, para 10.

Sub-s (2): words in square brackets inserted by the Maintenance Enforcement Act 1991, s 11(1), Sch 2, para 10.

Family assistance orders

16   Family assistance orders

(1)   Where, in any family proceedings, the court has power to make an order under this Part with respect to any child, it may (whether or not it makes such an order) make an order requiring—
   (a) a probation officer to be made available; or
   (b) a local authority to make an officer of the authority available,

to advise, assist and (where appropriate) befriend any person named in the order.

(2)   The persons who may be named in an order under this section ("a family assistance order") are—
   (a) any parent or guardian of the child;

    (b) any person with whom the child is living or in whose favour a contact order is in force with respect to the child;

    (c) the child himself.

(3)   No court may make a family assistance order unless—

    (a) it is satisfied that the circumstances of the case are exceptional; and

    (b) it has obtained the consent of every person to be named in the order other than the child.

(4)   A family assistance order may direct—

    (a) the person named in the order; or

    (b) such of the persons named in the order as may be specified in the order,

to take such steps as may be so specified with a view to enabling the officer concerned to be kept informed of the address of any person named in the order and to be allowed to visit any such person.

(5)   Unless it specifies a shorter period, a family assistance order shall have effect for a period of six months beginning with the day on which it is made.

(6)   Where—

    (a) a family assistance order is in force with respect to a child; and

    (b) a section 8 order is also in force with respect to the child,

the officer concerned may refer to the court the question whether the section 8 order should be varied or discharged.

(7)   A family assistance order shall not be made so as to require a local authority to make an officer of theirs available unless—

    (a) the authority agree; or

    (b) the child concerned lives or will live within their area.

(8)   Where a family assistance order requires a probation officer to be made available, the officer shall be selected in accordance with arrangements made by the probation committee for the area in which the child lives or will live.

(9)   If the selected probation officer is unable to carry out his duties, or dies, another probation officer shall be selected in the same manner.

PART III
LOCAL AUTHORITY SUPPORT FOR CHILDREN
AND FAMILIES

Provision of services for children and their families

17 Provision of services for children in need, their families and others

(1)   It shall be the general duty of every local authority (in addition to the other duties imposed on them by this Part)—
  (a) to safeguard and promote the welfare of children within their area who are in need; and
  (b) so far as is consistent with that duty, to promote the upbringing of such children by their families,

by providing a range and level of services appropriate to those children's needs.

(2)   For the purpose principally of facilitating the discharge of their general duty under this section, every local authority shall have the specific duties and powers set out in Part I of Schedule 2.

(3)   Any service provided by an authority in the exercise of functions conferred on them by this section may be provided for the family of a particular child in need or for any member of his family, if it is provided with a view to safeguarding or promoting the child's welfare.

(4)   The Secretary of State may by order amend any provision of Part I of Schedule 2 or add any further duty or power to those for the time being mentioned there.

(5)   Every local authority—
  (a) shall facilitate the provision by others (including in particular voluntary organisations) of services which the authority have power to provide by virtue of this section, or section 18, 20, 23 or 24; and
  (b) may make such arrangements as they see fit for any person to act on their behalf in the provision of any such service.

(6)   The services provided by a local authority in the exercise of functions conferred on them by this section may include giving assistance in kind or, in exceptional circumstances, in cash.

(7)   Assistance may be unconditional or subject to conditions as to the repayment of the assistance or of its value (in whole or in part).

(8)   Before giving any assistance or imposing any conditions, a local authority shall have regard to the means of the child concerned and of each of his parents.

(9)   No person shall be liable to make any repayment of assistance or of its value at any time when he is in receipt of income support[, family credit or disability working allowance] under the [Part VII of the Social Security Contributions and Benefits Act 1992] [or of an income-based jobseeker's allowance].

(10)   For the purposes of this Part a child shall be taken to be in need if—
  (a) he is unlikely to achieve or maintain, or to have the opportunity of achieving or maintaining, a reasonable standard of health or development without the provision for him of services by a local authority under this Part;
  (b) his health or development is likely to be significantly impaired, or further impaired, without the provision for him of such services; or
  (c) he is disabled,

and "family", in relation to such a child, includes any person who has parental responsibility for the child and any other person with whom he has been living.

(11)   For the purposes of this Part, a child is disabled if he is blind, deaf or dumb or suffers from mental disorder of any kind or is substantially and permanently handicapped by illness, injury or congenital deformity or such other disability as may be prescribed; and in this Part—
  "development" means physical, intellectual, emotional, social or behavioural development; and
  "health" means physical or mental health.

NOTES

Sub-s (9): words in first pair of square brackets substituted by the Disability Living Allowance and Disability Working Allowance Act 1991, s 7, Sch 3, Pt II, para 13; words in second pair of square brackets substituted by the Social Security (Consequential Provisions) Act 1992, s 4, Sch 2, para 108(a); words in third pair of square brackets added by the Jobseekers Act 1995, s 41(4), Sch 2, para 19(2).

18 Day care for pre-school and other children

(1)   Every local authority shall provide such day care for children in need within their area who are—
    (a) aged five or under; and
    (b) not yet attending schools,

as is appropriate.

(2)   A local authority may provide day care for children within their area who satisfy the conditions mentioned in subsection (1)(a) and (b) even though they are not in need.

(3)   A local authority may provide facilities (including training, advice, guidance and counselling) for those—
    (a) caring for children in day care; or
    (b) who at any time accompany such children while they are in day care.

(4)   In this section "day care" means any form of care or supervised activity provided for children during the day (whether or not it is provided on a regular basis).

(5)   Every local authority shall provide for children in need within their area who are attending any school such care or supervised activities as is appropriate—
    (a) outside school hours; or
    (b) during school holidays.

(6)   A local authority may provide such care or supervised activities for children within their area who are attending any school even though those children are not in need.

(7)   In this section "supervised activity" means an activity supervised by a responsible person.

19 Review of provision for day care, child minding etc

(1)   Every local authority in England and Wales shall review—
    (a) the provision which they make under section 18;
    (b) the extent to which the services of child minders are available within their area with respect to children under the age of eight; and

(c) the provision for day care within their area made for children under the age of eight by persons other, than the authority, required to register under section 71(1)(b).

(2) A review under subsection (1) shall be conducted—
(a) together with the appropriate local education authority; and
(b) at least once in every review period.

(3) Every local authority in Scotland shall, at least once in every review period, review—
(a) the provision for day care within their area made for children under the age of eight by the local authority and by persons required to register under section 71(1)(b); and
(b) the extent to which the services of child minders are available within their area with respect to children under the age of eight.

(4) In conducting any such review, the two authorities or, in Scotland, the authority shall have regard to the provision made with respect to children under the age of eight in relevant establishments within their area.

(5) In this section—
"relevant establishment" means any establishment which is mentioned in paragraphs 3 and 4 of Schedule 9 (hospitals, schools and other establishments exempt from the registration requirements which apply in relation to the provision of day care); and
"review period" means the period of one year beginning with the commencement of this section and each subsequent period of three years beginning with an anniversary of that commencement.

(6) Where a local authority have conducted a review under this section they shall publish the result of the review—
(a) as soon as is reasonably practicable;
(b) in such form as they consider appropriate; and
(c) together with any proposals they may have with respect to the matters reviewed.

(7) The authorities conducting any review under this section shall have regard to—
(a) any representations made to any one of them by any relevant [Health Authority, Special Health Authority] or health board; and
(b) any other representations which they consider to be relevant.

(8) In the application of this section to Scotland, "day care" has the same meaning as in section 79 and "health board" has the same meaning as in the National Health Service (Scotland) Act 1978.

Sub-s (7): words in square brackets substituted by the Health Authorities Act 1995, s 2(1), Sch 1, para 118(2).

Provision of accommodation for children

20 Provision of accommodation for children: general

(1)　Every local authority shall provide accommodation for any child in need within their area who appears to them to require accommodation as a result of—
  (a) there being no person who has parental responsibility for him;
  (b) his being lost or having been abandoned; or
  (c) the person who has been caring for him being prevented (whether or not permanently, and for whatever reason) from providing him with suitable accommodation or care.

(2)　Where a local authority provide accommodation under subsection (1) for a child who is ordinarily resident in the area of another local authority, that other local authority may take over the provision of accommodation for the child within—
  (a) three months of being notified in writing that the child is being provided with accommodation; or
  (b) such other longer period as may be prescribed.

(3)　Every local authority shall provide accommodation for any child in need within their area who has reached the age of sixteen and whose welfare the authority consider is likely to be seriously prejudiced if they do not provide him with accommodation.

(4)　A local authority may provide accommodation for any child within their area (even though a person who has parental responsibility for him is able to provide him with accommodation) if they consider that to do so would safeguard or promote the child's welfare.

(5)　A local authority may provide accommodation for any person who has reached the age of sixteen but is under twenty-one in any community home which takes children who have reached the age of sixteen if they consider that to do so would safeguard or promote his welfare.

(6)　Before providing accommodation under this section, a local authority shall, so far as is reasonably practicable and consistent with the child's welfare—

(a) ascertain the child's wishes regarding the provision of accommodation; and

(b) give due consideration (having regard to his age and understanding) to such wishes of the child as they have been able to ascertain.

(7) A local authority may not provide accommodation under this section for any child if any person who—

(a) has parental responsibility for him; and

(b) is willing and able to—

(i) provide accommodation for him; or

(ii) arrange for accommodation to be provided for him,

objects.

(8) Any person who has parental responsibility for a child may at any time remove the child from accommodation provided by or on behalf of the local authority under this section.

(9) Subsections (7) and (8) do not apply while any person—

(a) in whose favour a residence order is in force with respect to the child; or

(b) who has care of the child by virtue of an order made in the exercise of the High Court's inherent jurisdiction with respect to children,

agrees to the child being looked after in accommodation provided by or on behalf of the local authority.

(10) Where there is more than one such person as is mentioned in subsection (9), all of them must agree.

(11) Subsections (7) and (8) do not apply where a child who has reached the age of sixteen agrees to being provided with accommodation under this section.

21 Provision for accommodation for children in police protection or detention or on remand, etc

(1) Every local authority shall make provision for the reception and accommodation of children who are removed or kept away from home under Part V.

(2) Every local authority shall receive, and provide accommodation for, children—

(a) in police protection whom they are requested to receive under section 46(3)(f);

(b) whom they are requested to receive under section 38(6) of the Police and Criminal Evidence Act 1984;

(c) who are—
   (i) on remand [(within the meaning of the section)] under section [16(3A) or] 23(1) of the Children and Young Persons Act 1969; or
   (ii) the subject of a supervision order imposing a residence requirement under section 12AA of that Act,

and with respect to whom they are the designated authority.

(3) Where a child has been—
(a) removed under Part V; or
(b) detained under section 38 of the Police and Criminal Evidence Act 1984,

and he is not being provided with accommodation by a local authority or in a hospital vested in the Secretary of State [or otherwise made available pursuant to arrangements made by a [Health Authority]], any reasonable expenses of accommodating him shall be recoverable from the local authority in whose area he is ordinarily resident.

NOTES

Sub-s (2): words in first pair of square brackets in para (c) inserted by the Criminal Justice and Public Order Act 1994, s 168(1), Sch 9, para 38, as from a day to be appointed, words in final pair of square brackets inserted by the Courts and Legal Services Act 1990, s 116, Sch 16, para 11.

Sub-s (3): words in outer pair of square brackets inserted by the National Health Service and Community Care Act 1990, s 66(1), Sch 9, para 36(1), words in square brackets therein substituted by the Health Authorities Act 1995, s 2(1), Sch 1, para 118(3).

Duties of local authorities in relation to children looked after by them

22 General duty of local authority in relation to children looked after by them

(1) In this Act, any reference to a child who is looked after by a local authority is a reference to a child who is—
(a) in their care; or
(b) provided with accommodation by the authority in the exercise of any functions (in particular those under this Act) which stand referred

to their social services committee under the Local Authority Social Services Act 1970.

(2)   In subsection (1) "accommodation" means accommodation which is provided for a continuous period of more than 24 hours.

(3)   It shall be the duty of a local authority looking after any child—
   (a) to safeguard and promote his welfare; and
   (b) to make such use of services available for children cared for by their own parents as appears to the authority reasonable in his case.

(4)   Before making any decision with respect to a child whom they are looking after, or proposing to look after, a local authority shall, so far as is reasonably practicable, ascertain the wishes and feelings of—
   (a) the child;
   (b) his parents;
   (c) any person who is not a parent of his but who has parental responsibility for him; and
   (d) any other person whose wishes and feelings the authority consider to be relevant,

regarding the matter to be decided.

(5)   In making any such decision a local authority shall give due consideration—
   (a) having regard to his age and understanding, to such wishes and feelings of the child as they have been able to ascertain;
   (b) to such wishes and feelings of any person mentioned in subsection (4)(b) to (d) as they have been able to ascertain; and
   (c) to the child's religious persuasion, racial origin and cultural and linguistic background.

(6)   If it appears to a local authority that it is necessary, for the purpose of protecting members of the public from serious injury, to exercise their powers with respect to a child whom they are looking after in a manner which may not be consistent with their duties under this section, they may do so.

(7)   If the Secretary of State considers it necessary, for the purpose of protecting members of the public from serious injury, to give directions to a local authority with respect to the exercise of their powers with respect to a child whom they are looking after, he may give such directions to the authority.

(8)   Where any such directions are given to an authority they shall comply with them even though doing so is inconsistent with their duties under this section.

23   Provision of accommodation and maintenance by local authority for children whom they are looking after

(1)   It shall be the duty of any local authority looking after a child—
  (a) when he is in their care, to provide accommodation for him; and
  (b) to maintain him in other respects apart from providing accommodation for him.

(2)   A local authority shall provide accommodation and maintenance for any child whom they are looking after by—
  (a) placing him (subject to subsection (5) and any regulations made by the Secretary of State) with—
       (i)   a family;
       (ii) a relative of his; or
       (iii) any other suitable person,

on such terms as to payment by the authority and otherwise as the authority may determine;
  (b) maintaining him in a community home;
  (c) maintaining him in a voluntary home;
  (d) maintaining him in a registered children's home;
  (e) maintaining him in a home provided [in accordance with arrangements made] by the Secretary of State under section 82(5) on such terms as the Secretary of State may from time to time determine; or
  (f) making such other arrangements as—
       (i) seem appropriate to them; and
       (ii) comply with any regulations made by the Secretary of State.

(3)   Any person with whom a child has been placed under subsection (2)(a) is referred to in this Act as a local authority foster parent unless he falls within subsection (4).

(4)   A person falls within this subsection if he is—
  (a) a parent of the child;
  (b) a person who is not a parent of the child but who has parental responsibility for him; or

(c) where the child is in care and there was a residence order in force with respect to him immediately before the care order was made, a person in whose favour the residence order was made.

(5) Where a child is in the care of a local authority, the authority may only allow him to live with a person who falls within subsection (4) in accordance with regulations made by the Secretary of State.

[(5A) For the purposes of subsection (5) a child shall be regarded as living with a person if he stays with that person for a continuous period of more than 24 hours].

(6) Subject to any regulations made by the Secretary of State for the purposes of this subsection, any local authority looking after a child shall make arrangements to enable him to live with—
(a) a person falling within subsection (4); or
(b) a relative, friend or other person connected with him,

unless that would not be reasonably practicable or consistent with his welfare.

(7) Where a local authority provide accommodation for a child whom they are looking after, they shall, subject to the provisions of this Part and so far as is reasonably practicable and consistent with his welfare, secure that—
(a) the accommodation is near his home; and
(b) where the authority are also providing accommodation for a sibling of his, they are accommodated together.

(8) Where a local authority provide accommodation for a child whom they are looking after and who is disabled, they shall, so far as is reasonably practicable, secure that the accommodation is not unsuitable to his particular needs.

(9) Part II of Schedule 2 shall have effect for the purposes of making further provision as to children looked after by local authorities and in particular as to the regulations that may be made under subsections (2)(a) and (f) and (5).

NOTES

Sub-s (2): words in square brackets in para (e) inserted by the Courts and Legal Services Act 1990, s 116, Sch 16, para 12.

Sub-s (5A): inserted by the Courts and Legal Services Act 1990, s 116, Sch 16, para 12.

Advice and assistance for certain children

24 Advice and assistance for certain children

(1) Where a child is being looked after by a local authority, it shall be the duty of the authority to advise, assist and befriend him with a view to promoting his welfare when he ceases to be looked after by them.

(2) In this Part "a person qualifying for advice and assistance" means a person within the area of the authority who is under twenty-one and who was, at any time after reaching the age of sixteen but while still a child—
   (a) looked after by a local authority;
   (b) accommodated by or on behalf of a voluntary organisation;
   (c) accommodated in a registered children's home;
   (d) accommodated—
      (i) by any [Health Authority, Special Health Authority] or local education authority; or
      (ii) in any residential care home, nursing home or mental nursing home [or in any accommodation provided by a National Health Service trust],

   for a consecutive period of at least three months; or
   (e) privately fostered,

but who is no longer so looked after, accommodated or fostered.

(3) Subsection (2)(d) applies even if the period of three months mentioned there began before the child reached the age of sixteen.

(4) Where—
   (a) a local authority know that there is within their area a person qualifying for advice and assistance;
   (b) the conditions in subsection (5) are satisfied; and
   (c) that person has asked them for help of a kind which they can give under this section,

they shall (if he was being looked after by a local authority or was accommodated by or on behalf of a voluntary organisation) and may (in any other case) advise and befriend him.

(5) The conditions are that—
   (a) it appears to the authority that the person concerned is in need of advice and being befriended;

(b) where that person was not being looked after by the authority, they are satisfied that the person by whom he was being looked after does not have the necessary facilities for advising or befriending him.

(6) Where as a result of this section a local authority are under a duty, or are empowered, to advise and befriend a person, they may also give him assistance.

(7) Assistance given under subsections (1) to (6) may be in kind or, in exceptional circumstances, in cash.

(8) A local authority may give assistance to any person who qualifies for advice and assistance by virtue of subsection (2)(a) by—
(a) contributing to expenses incurred by him in living near the place where he is, or will be—
(i) employed or seeking employment; or
(ii) receiving education or training; or
(b) making a grant to enable him to meet expenses connected with his education or training.

(9) Where a local authority are assisting the person under subsection (8) by making a contribution or grant with respect to a course of education or training, they may—
(a) continue to do so even though he reaches the age of twenty-one before completing the course; and
(b) disregard any interruption in his attendance on the course if he resumes it as soon as is reasonably practicable.

(10) Subsections (7) to (9) of section 17 shall apply in relation to assistance given under this section (otherwise than under subsection (8)) as they apply in relation to assistance given under that section.

(11) Where it appears to a local authority that a person whom they have been advising and befriending under this section, as a person qualifying for advice and assistance, proposes to live, or is living, in the area of another local authority, they shall inform that other local authority.

(12) Where a child who is accommodated—
(a) by a voluntary organisation or in a registered children's home;
(b) by any [Health Authority, Special Health Authority] or local education authority; or
(c) in any residential care home, nursing home or mental nursing home [or any accommodation provided by a National Health Service trust],

ceases to be so accommodated, after reaching the age of sixteen, the organisation, authority or (as the case may be) person carrying on the home shall inform the local authority within whose area the child proposes to live.

(13)   Subsection (12) only applies, by virtue of paragraph (b) or (c), if the accommodation has been provided for a consecutive period of at least three months.

[(14)   Every local authority shall establish a procedure for considering any representations (including any complaint) made to them by a person qualifying for advice and assistance about the discharge of their functions under this Part in relation to him.

(15)   In carrying out any consideration of representations under subsection (14), a local authority shall comply with any regulations made by the Secretary of State for the purposes of this subsection.]

NOTES

Sub-ss (2), (12): words in square brackets substituted by the Health Authorities Act 1995, s 2(1), Sch 1, para 118(4); words in final pair of square brackets inserted by the National Health Service and Community Care Act 1990, s 66(1), Sch 9, para 36(2).

Sub-ss (14), (15): added by the Courts and Legal Services Act 1990, s 116, Sch 16, para 13.

Secure accommodation

25   Use of accommodation for restricting liberty

(1)   Subject to the following provisions of this section, a child who is being looked after by a local authority may not be placed, and, if placed, may not be kept, in accommodation provided for the purpose of restricting liberty ("secure accommodation") unless it appears—
  (a) that—
    (i) he has a history of absconding and is likely to abscond from any other description of accommodation; and
    (ii) if he absconds, he is likely to suffer significant harm; or
  (b) that if he is kept in any other description of accommodation he is likely to injure himself or other persons.

(2)   The Secretary of State may by regulations—
  (a)   specify a maximum period—
     (i)   beyond which a child may not be kept in secure accommodation without the authority of the court; and
     (ii) for which the court may authorise a child to be kept in secure accommodation;
  (b)   empower the court from time to time to authorise a child to be kept in secure accommodation for such further period as the regulations may specify; and
  (c)   provide that applications to the court under this section shall be made only by local authorities.

(3)   It shall be the duty of a court hearing an application under this section to determine whether any relevant criteria for keeping a child in secure accommodation are satisfied in his case.

(4)   If a court determines that any such criteria are satisfied, it shall make an order authorising the child to be kept in secure accommodation and specifying the maximum period for which he may be so kept.

(5)   On any adjournment of the hearing of an application under this section, a court may make an interim order permitting the child to be kept during the period of the adjournment in secure accommodation.

(6)   No court shall exercise the powers conferred by this section in respect of a child who is not legally represented in that court unless, having been informed of his right to apply for legal aid and having had the opportunity to do so, he refused or failed to apply.

(7)   The Secretary of State may by regulations provide that—
  (a)   this section shall or shall not apply to any description of children specified in the regulations;
  (b)   this section shall have effect in relation to children of a description specified in the regulations subject to such modifications as may be so specified;
  (c)   such other provisions as may be so specified shall have effect for the purpose of determining whether a child of a description specified in the regulations may be placed or kept in secure accommodation.

(8)   The giving of an authorisation under this section shall not prejudice any power of any court in England and Wales or Scotland to give directions relating to the child to whom the authorisation relates.

(9)   This section is subject to section 20(8).

26 Review of cases and inquiries into representations

(1)   The Secretary of State may make regulations requiring the case of each child who is being looked after by a local authority to be reviewed in accordance with the provisions of the regulations.

(2)   The regulations may, in particular, make provision—
   - (a) as to the manner in which each case is to be reviewed;
   - (b) as to the considerations to which the local authority are to have regard in reviewing each case;
   - (c) as to the time when each case is first to be reviewed and the frequency of subsequent reviews;
   - (d) requiring the authority, before conducting any review, to seek the views of—
      - (i) the child;
      - (ii) his parents;
      - (iii) any person who is not a parent of his but who has parental responsibility for him; and
      - (iv) any other person whose views the authority consider to be relevant,

including, in particular, the views of those persons in relation to any particular matter which is to be considered in the course of the review;
   - (e) requiring the authority to consider, in the case of a child who is in their care, whether an application should be made to discharge the care order;
   - (f) requiring the authority to consider, in the case of a child in accommodation provided by the authority, whether the accommodation accords with the requirements of this Part;
   - (g) requiring the authority to inform the child, so far as is reasonably practicable, of any steps he may take under this Act;
   - (h) requiring the authority to make arrangements, including arrangements with such other bodies providing services as it considers appropriate, to implement any decision which they propose to make in the course, or as a result, of the review;
   - (i) requiring the authority to notify details of the result of the review and of any decision taken by them in consequence of the review to—
      - (i) the child;
      - (ii) his parents;

(iii) any person who is not a parent of his but who has parental responsibility for him; and

(iv) any other person whom they consider ought to be notified;

(j) requiring the authority to monitor the arrangements which they have made with a view to ensuring that they comply with the regulations.

(3) Every local authority shall establish a procedure for considering any representations (including any complaint) made to them by—

(a) any child who is being looked after by them or who is not being looked after by them but is in need;

(b) a parent of his;

(c) any person who is not a parent of his but who has parental responsibility for him;

(d) any local authority foster parent;

(e) such other person as the authority consider has a sufficient interest in the child's welfare to warrant his representations being considered by them,

about the discharge by the authority of any of their functions under this Part in relation to the child.

(4) The procedure shall ensure that at least one person who is not a member or officer of the authority takes part in—

(a) the consideration; and

(b) any discussions which are held by the authority about the action (if any) to be taken in relation to the child in the light of the consideration.

(5) In carrying out any consideration of representations under this section a local authority shall comply with any regulations made by the Secretary of State for the purpose of regulating the procedure to be followed.

(6) The Secretary of State may make regulations requiring local authorities to monitor the arrangements that they have made with a view to ensuring that they comply with any regulations made for the purposes of subsection (5).

(7) Where any representation has been considered under the procedure established by a local authority under this section, the authority shall—

(a) have due regard to the findings of those considering the representation; and

(b) take such steps as are reasonably practicable to notify (in writing)—

(i) the person making the representation;

(ii) the child (if the authority consider that he has sufficient understanding); and

(iii) such other persons (if any) as appear to the authority to be likely to be affected,

of the authority's decision in the matter and their reasons for taking that decision and of any action which they have taken, or propose to take.

(8)   Every local authority shall give such publicity to their procedure for considering representations under this section as they consider appropriate.

27   Co-operation between authorities

(1)   Where it appears to a local authority that any authority . . . mentioned in subsection (3) could, by taking any specified action, help in the exercise of any of their functions under this Part, they may request the help of that other authority . . ., specifying the action in question.

(2)   An authority whose help is so requested shall comply with the request if it is compatible with their own statutory or other duties and obligations and does not unduly prejudice the discharge of any of their functions.

(3)   The [authorities] are—
  (a) any local authority;
  (b) any local education authority;
  (c) any local housing authority;
  (d) any [Health Authority, Special Health Authority] [or National Health Service trust]; and
  (e) any person authorised by the Secretary of State for the purposes of this section.

(4)   . . .

NOTES

Sub-s (1): words omitted repealed by the Courts and Legal Services Act 1990, ss 116, 125(7), Sch 16, para 14, Sch 20.

Sub-s (3): word in first pair of square brackets substituted, and words in final pair of square brackets in para (d) inserted, by the Courts and Legal Services Act 1990, s 116, Sch 16, para 14; words in second pair of square brackets in para (d) substituted by the Health Authorities Act 1995, s 2(1), Sch 1, para 118(5).

Sub-s (4): repealed by the Education Act 1993, s 307(1), (3), Sch 19, para 147, Sch 21, Pt II.

28 Consultation with local education authorities

(1)   Where—
   (a) a child is being looked after by a local authority; and
   (b) the authority propose to provide accommodation for him in an establishment at which education is provided for children who are accommodated there,

they shall, so far as is reasonably practicable, consult the appropriate local education authority before doing so.

(2)   Where any such proposal is carried out, the local authority shall, as soon as is reasonably practicable, inform the appropriate local education authority of the arrangements that have been made for the child's accommodation.

(3)   Where the child ceases to be accommodated as mentioned in subsection (1)(b), the local authority shall inform the appropriate local education authority.

(4)   In this section "the appropriate local education authority" means—
   (a) the local education authority within whose area the local authority's area falls; or,
   (b) where the child has special educational needs and a statement of his needs is maintained under [Part IV of the Education Act 1996], the local education authority who maintain the statement.

NOTES

   Sub-s (4): words in square brackets in para (b) substituted by the Education Act 1996, s 582(1), Sch 37, Pt I, para 84.

29 Recoupment of cost of providing services etc

(1)   Where a local authority provide any service under section 17 or 18, other than advice, guidance or counselling, they may recover from a person specified in subsection (4) such charge for the service as they consider reasonable.

(2)   Where the authority are satisfied that that person's means are insufficient for it to be reasonably practicable for him to pay the charge, they shall not require him to pay more than he can reasonably be expected to pay.

(3)　No person shall be liable to pay any charge under subsection (1) at any time when he is in receipt of income support[, family credit or disability working allowance] under the [Part VII of the Social Security Contributions and Benefits Act 1992] [or of an income-based jobseeker's allowance].

(4)　The persons are—
- (a)　where the service is provided for a child under sixteen, each of his parents;
- (b)　where it is provided for a child who has reached the age of sixteen, the child himself; and
- (c)　where it is provided for a member of the child's family, that member.

(5)　Any charge under subsection (1) may, without prejudice to any other method of recovery, be recovered summarily as a civil debt.

(6)　Part III of Schedule 2 makes provision in connection with contributions towards the maintenance of children who are being looked after by local authorities and consists of the re-enactment with modifications of provisions in Part V of the Child Care Act 1980.

(7)　Where a local authority provide any accommodation under section 20(1) for a child who was (immediately before they began to look after him) ordinarily resident within the area of another local authority, they may recover from that other authority any reasonable expenses incurred by them in providing the accommodation and maintaining him.

(8)　Where a local authority provide accommodation under section 21(1) or (2)(a) or (b) for a child who is ordinarily resident within the area of another local authority and they are not maintaining him in—
- (a)　a community home provided by them;
- (b)　a controlled community home; or
- (c)　a hospital vested in the Secretary of State, [or any other hospital made available pursuant to arrangements made by a [Health Authority]]

they may recover from that other authority any reasonable expenses incurred by them in providing the accommodation and maintaining him.

(9)　Where a local authority comply with any request under section 27(2) in relation to a child or other person who is not ordinarily resident within their area, they may recover from the local authority in whose area the child or person is ordinarily resident any [reasonable expenses] incurred by them in respect of that person.

Sub-s (3): words in first pair of square brackets substituted by the Disability Living Allowance and Disability Working Allowance Act 1991, s 7, Sch 3, Pt II, para 14; words in second pair of square brackets substituted by the Social Security (Consequential Provisions) Act 1992, s 4, Sch 2, para 108(b); words in third pair of square brackets added by the Jobseekers Act 1995, s 41(4), Sch 2, para 19(3).

Sub-s (8): words in outer pair of square brackets in para (c) inserted by the National Health Service and Community Care Act 1990, s 66(1), Sch 9, para 36(3), words in square brackets therein substituted by the Health Authorities Act 1995, s 2(1), Sch 1, para 118(6).

Sub-s (9): words in square brackets substituted by the Courts and Legal Services Act 1990, s 116, Sch 16, para 15.

30 Miscellaneous

(1)   Nothing in this Part shall affect any duty imposed on a local authority by or under any other enactment.

(2)   Any question arising under section 20(2), 21(3) or 29(7) to (9) as to the ordinary residence of a child shall be determined by agreement between the local authorities concerned or, in default of agreement, by the Secretary of State.

(3)   Where the functions conferred on a local authority by this Part and the functions of a local education authority are concurrent, the Secretary of State may by regulations provide by which authority the functions are to be exercised.

(4)   The Secretary of State may make regulations for determining, as respects any local education authority functions specified in the regulations, whether a child who is being looked after by a local authority is to be treated, for purposes so specified, as a child of parents of sufficient resources or as a child of parents without resources.

PART IV
CARE AND SUPERVISION

General

31 Care and supervision orders

(1)   On the application of any local authority or authorised person, the court may make an order—

(a) placing the child with respect to whom the application is made in the care of a designated local authority; or

(b) putting him under the supervision of a designated local authority or of a probation officer.

(2)   A court may only make a care order or supervision order if it is satisfied—

(a) that the child concerned is suffering, or is likely to suffer, significant harm; and

(b) that the harm, or likelihood of harm, is attributable to—

(i)   the care given to the child, or likely to be given to him if the order were not made, not being what it would be reasonable to expect a parent to give to him; or

(ii) the child's being beyond parental control.

(3)   No care order or supervision order may be made with respect to a child who has reached the age of seventeen (or sixteen, in the case of a child who is married).

(4)   An application under this section may be made on its own or in any other family proceedings.

(5)   The court may—

(a) on an application for a care order, make a supervision order;

(b) on an application for a supervision order, make a care order.

(6)   Where an authorised person proposes to make an application under this section he shall—

(a) if it is reasonably practicable to do so; and

(b) before making the application,

consult the local authority appearing to him to be the authority in whose area the child concerned is ordinarily resident.

(7)   An application made by an authorised person shall not be entertained by the court if, at the time when it is made, the child concerned is—

(a) the subject of an earlier application for a care order, or supervision order, which has not been disposed of; or

(b) subject to—

(i)   a care order or supervision order;

(ii) an order under section 7(7)(b) of the Children and Young Persons Act 1969; or

(iii) a supervision requirement within the meaning of [Part II of the Children (Scotland) Act 1995].

(8)   The local authority designated in a care order must be—
  (a) the authority within whose area the child is ordinarily resident; or
  (b) where the child does not reside in the area of a local authority, the authority within whose area any circumstances arose in consequence of which the order is being made.

(9)   In this section—
  "authorised person" means—
    (a) the National Society for the Prevention of Cruelty to Children and any of its officers; and
    (b) any person authorised by order of the Secretary of State to bring proceedings under this section and any officer of a body which is so authorised;
  "harm" means ill-treatment or the impairment of health or development;
  "development" means physical, intellectual, emotional, social or behavioural development;
  "health" means physical or mental health; and
  "ill-treatment" includes sexual abuse and forms of ill-treatment which are not physical.

(10)   Where the question of whether harm suffered by a child is significant turns on the child's health or development, his health or development shall be compared with that which could reasonably be expected of a similar child.

(11)   In this Act—
  "a care order" means (subject to section 105(1)) an order under subsection (1)(a) and (except where express provision to the contrary is made) includes an interim care order made under section 38; and
  "a supervision order" means an order under subsection (1)(b) and (except where express provision to the contrary is made) includes an interim supervision order made under section 38.

NOTES

Sub-s (7): words in square brackets in para (b) substituted by the Children (Scotland) Act 1995, s 105(4), Sch 4, para 48(2).

32 Period within which application for order under this Part must be disposed of

(1)   A court hearing an application for an order under this Part shall (in the light of any rules made by virtue of subsection (2))—

    (a) draw up a timetable with a view to disposing of the application without delay; and

    (b) give such directions as it considers appropriate for the purpose of ensuring, so far as is reasonably practicable, that that timetable is adhered to.

(2)   Rules of court may—

    (a) specify periods within which specified steps must be taken in relation to such proceedings; and

    (b) make other provisions with respect to such proceedings for the purpose of ensuring, so far as is reasonably practicable, that they are disposed of without delay.

Care orders

33 Effect of care order

(1)   Where a care order is made with respect to a child it shall be the duty of the local authority designated by the order to receive the child into their care and to keep him in their care while the order remains in force.

(2)   Where—

    (a) a care order has been made with respect to a child on the application of an authorised person; but

    (b) the local authority designated by the order was not informed that that person proposed to make the application,

the child may be kept in the care of that person until received into the care of the authority.

(3)   While a care order is in force with respect to a child, the local authority designated by the order shall—

    (a) have parental responsibility for the child; and

    (b) have the power (subject to the following provisions of this section) to determine the extent to which a parent or guardian of the child may meet his parental responsibility for him.

(4)   The authority may not exercise the power in subsection (3)(b) unless they are satisfied that it is necessary to do so in order to safeguard or promote the child's welfare.

(5)   Nothing in subsection (3)(b) shall prevent a parent or guardian of the child who has care of him from doing what is reasonable in all the circumstances of the case for the purpose of safeguarding or promoting his welfare.

(6)   While a care order is in force with respect to a child, the local authority designated by the order shall not—
  (a) cause the child to be brought up in any religious persuasion other than that in which he would have been brought up if the order had not been made; or
  (b) have the right—
    (i)   to consent or refuse to consent to the making of an application with respect to the child under section 18 of the Adoption Act 1976;
    (ii) to agree or refuse to agree to the making of an adoption order, or an order under section 55 of the Act of 1976, with respect to the child; or
    (iii) to appoint a guardian for the child.

(7)   While a care order is in force with respect to a child, no person may—
  (a) cause the child to be known by a new surname; or
  (b) remove him from the United Kingdom,

without either the written consent of every person who has parental responsibility for the child or the leave of the court.

(8)   Subsection (7)(b) does not—
  (a) prevent the removal of such a child, for a period of less than one month, by the authority in whose care he is; or
  (b) apply to arrangements for such a child to live outside England and Wales (which are governed by paragraph 19 of Schedule 2).

(9)   The power in subsection (3)(b) is subject (in addition to being subject to the provisions of this section) to any right, duty, power, responsibility or authority which a parent or guardian of the child has in relation to the child and his property by virtue of any other enactment.

34   Parental contact etc with children in care

(1)   Where a child is in the care of a local authority, the authority shall (subject to the provisions of this section) allow the child reasonable contact with—

(a) his parents;

(b) any guardian of his;

(c) where there was a residence order in force with respect to the child immediately before the care order was made, the person in whose favour the order was made; and

(d) where, immediately before the care order was made a person had care of the child by virtue of an order made in the exercise of the High Court's inherent jurisdiction with respect to children, that person.

(2)   On an application made by the authority or the child, the court may make such order as it considers appropriate with respect to the contact which is to be allowed between the child and any named person.

(3)   On an application made by—

(a) any person mentioned in paragraphs (a) to (d) of subsection (1); or

(b) any person who has obtained the leave of the court to make the application,

the court may make such order as it considers appropriate with respect to the contact which is to be allowed between the child and that person.

(4)   On an application made by the authority or the child, the court may make an order authorising the authority to refuse to allow contact between the child and any person who is mentioned in paragraphs (a) to (d) of subsection (1) and named in the order.

(5)   When making a care order with respect to a child, or in any family proceedings in connection with a child who is in the care of a local authority, the court may make an order under this section, even though no application for such an order has been made with respect to the child, if it considers that the order should be made.

(6)   An authority may refuse to allow the contact that would otherwise be required by virtue of subsection (1) or an order under this section if—

(a) they are satisfied that it is necessary to do so in order to safeguard or promote the child's welfare; and

(b) the refusal—

(i)   is decided upon as a matter of urgency; and

(ii) does not last for more than seven days.

(7)   An order under this section may impose such conditions as the court considers appropriate.

(8)   The Secretary of State may by regulations make provision as to—
   (a) the steps to be taken by a local authority who have exercised their powers under subsection (6);
   (b) the circumstances in which, and conditions subject to which, the terms of any order under this section may be departed from by agreement between the local authority and the person in relation to whom the order is made;
   (c) notification by a local authority of any variation or suspension of arrangements made (otherwise than under an order under this section) with a view to affording any person contact with a child to whom this section applies.

(9)   The court may vary or discharge any order made under this section on the application of the authority, the child concerned or the person named in the order.

(10)   An order under this section may be made either at the same time as the care order itself or later.

(11)   Before making a care order with respect to any child the court shall—
   (a) consider the arrangements which the authority have made, or propose to make, for affording any person contact with a child to whom this section applies; and
   (b) invite the parties to the proceedings to comment on those arrangements.

Supervision orders

35   Supervision orders

(1)   While a supervision order is in force it shall be the duty of the supervisor—
   (a) to advise, assist and befriend the supervised child;
   (b) to take such steps as are reasonably necessary to give effect to the order; and
   (c) where—
      (i) the order is not wholly complied with; or
      (ii) the supervisor considers that the order may no longer be necessary,

to consider whether or not to apply to the court for its variation or discharge.

(2)   Parts I and II of Schedule 3 make further provision with respect to supervision orders.

36   Education supervision orders

(1)   On the application of any local education authority, the court may make an order putting the child with respect to whom the application is made under the supervision of a designated local education authority.

(2)   In this Act "an education supervision order" means an order under subsection (1).

(3)   A court may only make an education supervision order if it is satisfied that the child concerned is of compulsory school age and is not being properly educated.

(4)   For the purposes of this section, a child is being properly educated only if he is receiving efficient full-time education suitable to his age, ability and aptitude and any special educational needs he may have.

(5)   Where a child is—
  (a) the subject of a school attendance order which is in force under [section 437 of the Education Act 1996] and which has not been complied with; or
  (b) a registered pupil at a school which he is not attending regularly within the meaning of [section 444] of that Act,

then, unless it is proved that he is being properly educated, it shall be assumed that he is not.

(6)   An education supervision order may not be made with respect to a child who is in the care of a local authority.

(7)   The local education authority designated in an education supervision order must be—
  (a) the authority within whose area the child concerned is living or will live; or
  (b) where—
    (i)   the child is a registered pupil at a school; and
    (ii) the authority mentioned in paragraph (a) and the authority within whose area the school is situated agree,

the latter authority.

(8)   Where a local education authority propose to make an application for an education supervision order they shall, before making the application, consult the . . . appropriate local authority.

(9)   The appropriate local authority is—
   (a) in the case of a child who is being provided with accommodation by, or on behalf of, a local authority, that authority; and
   (b) in any other case, the local authority within whose area the child concerned lives, or will live.

(10)   Part III of Schedule 3 makes further provision with respect to education supervision orders.

Powers of court

37   Powers of court in certain family proceedings

(1)   Where, in any family proceedings in which a question arises with respect to the welfare of any child, it appears to the court that it may be appropriate for a care or supervision order to be made with respect to him, the court may direct the appropriate authority to undertake an investigation of the child's circumstances.

(2)   Where the court gives a direction under this section the local authority concerned shall, when undertaking the investigation, consider whether they should—
   (a) apply for a care order or for a supervision order with respect to the child;
   (b) provide services or assistance for the child or his family; or
   (c) take any other action with respect to the child.

(3)   Where a local authority undertake an investigation under this section, and decide not to apply for a care order or supervision order with respect to the child concerned, they shall inform the court of—
   (a) their reasons for so deciding;

(b) any service or assistance which they have provided, or intend to provide, for the child and his family; and

(c) any other action which they have taken, or propose to take, with respect to the child.

(4)   The information shall be given to the court before the end of the period of eight weeks beginning with the date of the direction, unless the court otherwise directs.

(5)   The local authority named in a direction under subsection (1) must be—

(a) the authority in whose area the child is ordinarily resident; or

(b) where the child [is not ordinarily resident] in the area of a local authority, the authority within whose area any circumstances arose in consequence of which the direction is being given.

(6)   If, on the conclusion of any investigation or review under this section, the authority decide not to apply for a care order or supervision order with respect to the child—

(a) they shall consider whether it would be appropriate to review the case at a later date; and

(b) if they decide that it would be, they shall determine the date on which that review is to begin.

NOTES

Sub-s (5): words in square brackets substituted by the Courts and Legal Services Act 1990, s 116, Sch 16, para 16.

38   Interim orders

(1)   Where—

(a) in any proceedings on an application for a care order or supervision order, the proceedings are adjourned; or

(b) the court gives a direction under section 37(1),

the court may make an interim care order or an interim supervision order with respect to the child concerned.

(2)   A court shall not make an interim care order or interim supervision order under this section unless it is satisfied that there are reasonable grounds for believing that the circumstances with respect to the child are as mentioned in section 31(2).

(3)   Where, in any proceedings on an application for a care order or supervision order, a court makes a residence order with respect to the child concerned, it shall also make an interim supervision order with respect to him unless satisfied that his welfare will be satisfactorily safeguarded without an interim order being made.

(4)   An interim order made under or by virtue of this section shall have effect for such period as may be specified in the order, but shall in any event cease to have effect on whichever of the following events first occurs—

(a) the expiry of the period of eight weeks beginning with the date on which the order is made;

(b) if the order is the second or subsequent such order made with respect to the same child in the same proceedings, the expiry of the relevant period;

(c) in a case which falls within subsection (1)(a), the disposal of the application;

(d) in a case which falls within subsection (1)(b), the disposal of an application for a care order or supervision order made by the authority with respect to the child;

(e) in a case which falls within subsection (1)(b) and in which—

(i)   the court has given a direction under section 37(4), but

(ii) no application for a care order or supervision order has been made with respect to the child,

the expiry of the period fixed by that direction.

(5)   In subsection (4)(b) "the relevant period" means—

(a) the period of four weeks beginning with the date on which the order in question is made; or

(b) the period of eight weeks beginning with the date on which the first order was made if that period ends later than the period mentioned in paragraph (a).

(6)   Where the court makes an interim care order, or interim supervision order, it may give such directions (if any) as it considers appropriate with regard to the medical or psychiatric examination or other assessment of the child; but if the child is of sufficient understanding to make an informed decision he may refuse to submit to the examination or other assessment.

(7)   A direction under subsection (6) may be to the effect that there is to be—

(a) no such examination or assessment; or

(b) no such examination or assessment unless the court directs otherwise.

(8)   A direction under subsection (6) may be—
  (a) given when the interim order is made or at any time while it is in force; and
  (b) varied at any time on the application of any person falling within any class of person prescribed by rules of court for the purposes of this subsection.

(9)   Paragraphs 4 and 5 of Schedule 3 shall not apply in relation to an interim supervision order.

(10)   Where a court makes an order under or by virtue of this section it shall, in determining the period for which the order is to be in force, consider whether any party who was, or might have been, opposed to the making of the order was in a position to argue his case against the order in full.

[38A   Power to include exclusion requirement in interim care order

(1)   Where—
  (a) on being satisfied that there are reasonable grounds for believing that the circumstances with respect to a child are as mentioned in section 31(2)(a) and (b)(i), the court makes an interim care order with respect to a child, and
  (b) the conditions mentioned in subsection (2) are satisfied,

the court may include an exclusion requirement in the interim care order.

(2)   The conditions are—
  (a) that there is reasonable cause to believe that, if a person ("the relevant person") is excluded from a dwelling-house in which the child lives, the child will cease to suffer, or cease to be likely to suffer, significant harm, and
  (b) that another person living in the dwelling-house (whether a parent of the child or some other person)—
    (i) is able and willing to give to the child the care which it would be reasonable to expect a parent to give him, and
    (ii) consents to the inclusion of the exclusion requirement.

(3)   For the purposes of this section an exclusion requirement is any one or more of the following—
  (a) a provision requiring the relevant person to leave a dwelling-house in which he is living with the child,
  (b) a provision prohibiting the relevant person from entering a dwelling-house in which the child lives, and

(c)   a provision excluding the relevant person from a defined area in which a dwelling-house in which the child lives is situated.

(4)   The court may provide that the exclusion requirement is to have effect for a shorter period than the other provisions of the interim care order.

(5)   Where the court makes an interim care order containing an exclusion requirement, the court may attach a power of arrest to the exclusion requirement.

(6)   Where the court attaches a power of arrest to an exclusion requirement of an interim care order, it may provide that the power of arrest is to have effect for a shorter period than the exclusion requirement.

(7)   Any period specified for the purposes of subsection (4) or (6) may be extended by the court (on one or more occasions) on an application to vary or discharge the interim care order.

(8)   Where a power of arrest is attached to an exclusion requirement of an interim care order by virtue of subsection (5), a constable may arrest without warrant any person whom he has reasonable cause to believe to be in breach of the requirement.

(9)   Sections 47(7), (11) and (12) and 48 of, and Schedule 5 to, the Family Law Act 1996 shall have effect in relation to a person arrested under subsection (8) of this section as they have effect in relation to a person arrested under section 47(6) of that Act.

(10)   If, while an interim care order containing an exclusion requirement is in force, the local authority have removed the child from the dwelling-house from which the relevant person is excluded to other accommodation for a continuous period of more than 24 hours, the interim care order shall cease to have effect in so far as it imposes the exclusion requirement.]

NOTES

Commencement: to be appointed.
Inserted, together with s 38B, by the Family Law Act 1996, s 52, Sch 6, para 1, as from a day to be appointed.

[38B Undertakings relating to interim care orders

(1)   In any case where the court has power to include an exclusion requirement in an interim care order, the court may accept an undertaking from the relevant person.

(2)   No power of arrest may be attached to any undertaking given under subsection (1).

(3)   An undertaking given to a court under subsection (1)—
    (a) shall be enforceable as if it were an order of the court, and
    (b) shall cease to have effect if, while it is in force, the local authority have removed the child from the dwelling house from which the relevant person is excluded to other accommodation for a continuous period of more than 24 hours.

(4)   This section has effect without prejudice to the powers of the High Court and county court apart from this section.

(5)   In this section "exclusion requirement" and "relevant person" have the same meaning as in section 38A.]

NOTES

Commencement: to be appointed.
Inserted as noted to s 38A.

39   Discharge and variation etc of care orders and supervision orders

(1)   A care order may be discharged by the court on the application of—
    (a) any person who has parental responsibility for the child;
    (b) the child himself; or
    (c) the local authority designated by the order.

(2)   A supervision order may be varied or discharged by the court on the application of—
    (a) any person who has parental responsibility for the child;
    (b) the child himself; or
    (c) the supervisor.

(3)   On the application of a person who is not entitled to apply for the order to be discharged, but who is a person with whom the child is living,

a supervision order may be varied by the court in so far as it imposes a requirement which affects that person.

[(3A)   On the application of a person who is not entitled to apply for the order to be discharged, but who is a person to whom an exclusion requirement contained in the order applies, an interim care order may be varied or discharged by the court in so far as it imposes the exclusion requirement.

(3B)   Where a power of arrest has been attached to an exclusion requirement of an interim care order, the court may, on the application of any person entitled to apply for the discharge of the order so far as it imposes the exclusion requirement, vary or discharge the order in so far as it confers a power of arrest (whether or not any application has been made to vary or discharge any other provision of the order).]

(4)   Where a care order is in force with respect to a child the court may, on the application of any person entitled to apply for the order to be discharged, substitute a supervision order for the care order.

(5)   When a court is considering whether to substitute one order for another under subsection (4) any provision of this Act which would otherwise require section 31(2) to be satisfied at the time when the proposed order is substituted or made shall be disregarded.

NOTES

Commencement: 14 October 1991 (sub-ss (1)–(3), (4), (5)); to be appointed (remainder).

Sub-ss (3A), (3B): inserted by the Family Law Act 1996, s 52, Sch 6, para 2, as from a day to be appointed.

40   Orders pending appeals in cases about care or supervision orders

(1)   Where—
  (a) a court dismisses an application for a care order; and
  (b) at the time when the court dismisses the application, the child concerned is the subject of an interim care order,

the court may make a care order with respect to the child to have effect subject to such directions (if any) as the court may see fit to include in the order.

(2)   Where—
    (a)   a court dismisses an application for a care order, or an application for a supervision order; and
    (b)   at the time when the court dismisses the application, the child concerned is the subject of an interim supervision order,

the court may make a supervision order with respect to the child to have effect subject to such directions (if any) as the court may see fit to include in the order.

(3)   Where a court grants an application to discharge a care order or supervision order, it may order that—
    (a)   its decision is not to have effect; or
    (b)   the care order, or supervision order, is to continue to have effect but subject to such directions as the court sees fit to include in the order.

(4)   An order made under this section shall only have effect for such period, not exceeding the appeal period, as may be specified in the order.

(5)   Where—
    (a)   an appeal is made against any decision of a court under this section; or
    (b)   any application is made to the appellate court in connection with a proposed appeal against that decision.

the appellate court may extend the period for which the order in question is to have effect, but not so as to extend it beyond the end of the appeal period.

(6)   In this section "the appeal period" means—
    (a)   where an appeal is made against the decision in question, the period between the making of that decision and the determination of the appeal; and
    (b)   otherwise, the period during which an appeal may be made against the decision.

Guardians ad litem

41   Representation of child and of his interests in certain proceedings

(1)   For the purpose of any specified proceedings, the court shall appoint a guardian ad litem for the child concerned unless satisfied that it is not necessary to do so in order to safeguard his interests.

(2)   The guardian ad litem shall—
   (a)   be appointed in accordance with the rules of court; and
   (b)   be under a duty to safeguard the interests of the child in the manner prescribed by such rules.

(3)   Where—
   (a)   the child concerned is not represented by a solicitor; and
   (b)   any of the conditions mentioned in subsection (4) is satisfied,

the court may appoint a solicitor to represent him.

(4)   The conditions are that—
   (a)   no guardian ad litem has been appointed for the child;
   (b)   the child has sufficient understanding to instruct a solicitor and wishes to do so;
   (c)   it appears to the court that it would be in the child's best interests for him to be represented by a solicitor.

(5)   Any solicitor appointed under or by virtue of this section shall be appointed, and shall represent the child, in accordance with rules of court.

(6)   In this section "specified proceedings" means any proceedings—
   (a)   on an application for a care order or supervision order;
   (b)   in which the court has given a direction under section 37(1) and has made, or is considering whether to make, an interim care order;
   (c)   on an application for the discharge of a care order or the variation or discharge of a supervision order;
   (d)   on an application under section 39(4);
   (e)   in which the court is considering whether to make a residence order with respect to a child who is the subject of a care order;
   (f)   with respect to contact between a child who is the subject of a care order and any other person;
   (g)   under Part V;
   (h)   on an appeal against—
      (i)   the making of, or refusal to make, a care order, supervision order or any order under section 34;
      (ii)   the making of, or refusal to make, a residence order with respect to a child who is the subject of a care order; or
      (iii) the variation or discharge, or refusal of an application to vary or discharge, an order of a kind mentioned in sub-paragraph (i) or (ii);
      (iv)   the refusal of an application under section 39(4); or
      (v)   the making of, or refusal to make, an order under Part V; or

(i) which are specified for the time being, for the purposes of this section, by rules of court.

(7) The Secretary of State may by regulations provide for the establishment of panels of persons from whom guardians ad litem appointed under this section must be selected.

(8) Subsection (7) shall not be taken to prejudice the power of the Lord Chancellor to confer or impose duties on the Official Solicitor under section 90(3) of the Supreme Court Act 1981.

(9) The regulations may, in particular, make provision—
 (a) as to the constitution, administration and procedures of panels;
 (b) requiring two or more specified local authorities to make arrangements for the joint management of a panel;
 (c) for the defrayment by local authorities of expenses incurred by members of panels;
 (d) for the payment by local authorities of fees and allowances for members of panels;
 (e) as to the qualifications for membership of a panel;
 (f) as to the training to be given to members of panels;
 (g) as to the co-operation required of specified local authorities in the provision of panels in specified areas; and
 (h) for monitoring the work of guardians ad litem.

(10) Rules of court may make provision as to—
 (a) the assistance which any guardian ad litem may be required by the court to give to it;
 (b) the consideration to be given by any guardian ad litem, where an order of a specified kind has been made in the proceedings in question, as to whether to apply for the variation or discharge of the order;
 (c) the participation of guardians ad litem in reviews, of a kind specified in the rules, which are conducted by the court.

(11) Regardless of any enactment or rule of law which would otherwise prevent it from doing so, the court may take account of—
 (a) any statement contained in a report made by a guardian ad litem who is appointed under this section for the purpose of the proceedings in question; and
 (b) any evidence given in respect of the matters referred to in the report,

in so far as the statement or evidence is, in the opinion of the court, relevant to the question which the court is considering.

[(12) The Secretary of State may, with the consent of the Treasury, make such grants with respect to expenditure of any local authority—

    (a) in connection with the establishment and administration of guardian ad litem panels in accordance with this section;

    (b) in paying expenses, fees, allowances and in the provision of training for members of such panels,

as he considers appropriate.]

NOTES

    Sub-s (12): added by the Courts and Legal Services Act 1990, s 116, Sch 16, para 17.

42 Right of guardian ad litem to have access to local authority records

(1) Where a person has been appointed as a guardian ad litem under this Act he shall have the right at all reasonable times to examine and take copies of—

    (a) any records of, or held by, a local authority [or an authorised person] which were compiled in connection with the making, or proposed making, by any person of any application under this Act with respect to the child concerned; . . .

    (b) any . . . records of, or held by, a local authority which were compiled in connection with any functions which stand referred to their social services committee under the Local Authority Social Services Act 1970, so far as those records relate to that child [; or

    (c) any records of, or held by, an authorised person which were compiled in connection with the activities of that person, so far as those records relate to that child].

(2) Where a guardian ad litem takes a copy of any record which he is entitled to examine under this section, that copy or any part of it shall be admissible as evidence of any matter referred to in any—

    (a) report which he makes to the court in the proceedings in question; or

    (b) evidence which he gives in those proceedings.

(3) Subsection (2) has effect regardless of any enactment or rule of law which would otherwise prevent the record in question being admissible in evidence.

[(4) In this section "authorised person" has the same meaning as in section 31.]

Sub-s (1): words omitted repealed, and words in square brackets inserted, by the Courts and Legal Services Act 1990, ss 116, 125(7), Sch 16, para 18, Sch 20.

Sub-s (4): added by the Courts and Legal Services Act 1990, s 116, Sch 16, para 18.

PART V
PROTECTION OF CHILDREN

43 Child assessment orders

(1)   On the application of a local authority or authorised person for an order to be made under this section with respect to a child, the court may make the order if, but only if, it is satisfied that—

   (a) the applicant has reasonable cause to suspect that the child is suffering, or is likely to suffer, significant harm;

   (b) an assessment of the state of the child's health or development, or of the way in which he has been treated, is required to enable the applicant to determine whether or not the child is suffering, or is likely to suffer, significant harm; and

   (c) it is unlikely that such an assessment will be made, or be satisfactory, in the absence of an order under this section.

(2)   In this Act "a child assessment order" means an order under this section.

(3)   A court may treat an application under this section as an application for an emergency protection order.

(4)   No court shall make a child assessment order if it is satisfied—

   (a) that there are grounds for making an emergency protection order with respect to the child; and

   (b) that it ought to make such an order rather than a child assessment order.

(5)   A child assessment order shall—

   (a) specify the date by which the assessment is to begin; and

   (b) have effect for such period, not exceeding 7 days beginning with that date, as may be specified in the order.

(6)   Where a child assessment order is in force with respect to a child it shall be the duty of any person who is in a position to produce the child—

(a) to produce him to such person as may be named in the order; and
(b) to comply with such directions relating to the assessment of the child as the court thinks fit to specify in the order.

(7)   A child assessment order authorises any person carrying out the assessment, or any part of the assessment, to do so in accordance with the terms of the order.

(8)   Regardless of subsection (7), if the child is of sufficient understanding to make an informed decision he may refuse to submit to a medical or psychiatric examination or other assessment.

(9)   The child may only be kept away from home—
(a) in accordance with directions specified in the order;
(b) if it is necessary for the purposes of the assessment; and
(c) for such period or periods as may be specified in the order.

(10)   Where the child is to be kept away from home, the order shall contain such directions as the court thinks fit with regard to the contact that he must be allowed to have with other persons while away from home.

(11)   Any person making an application for a child assessment order shall take such steps as are reasonably practicable to ensure that notice of the application is given to—
(a) the child's parents;
(b) any person who is not a parent of his but who has parental responsibility for him;
(c) any other person caring for the child;
(d) any person in whose favour a contact order is in force with respect to the child;
(e) any person who is allowed to have contact with the child by virtue of an order under section 34; and
(f) the child,

before the hearing of the application.

(12)   Rules of court may make provision as to the circumstances in which—
(a) any of the persons mentioned in subsection (11); or
(b) such other person as may be specified in the rules,

may apply to the court for a child assessment order to be varied or discharged.

(13)   In this section "authorised person" means a person who is an authorised person for the purposes of section 31.

44 Orders for emergency protection of children

(1)   Where any person ("the applicant") applies to the court for an order to be made under this section with respect to a child, the court may make the order if, but only if, it is satisfied that—
  (a) there is reasonable cause to believe that the child is likely to suffer significant harm if—
    (i) he is not removed to accommodation provided by or on behalf of the applicant; or
    (ii) he does not remain in the place in which he is then being accommodated;
  (b) in the case of an application made by a local authority—
    (i) enquiries are being made with respect to the child under section 47(1)(b); and
    (ii) those enquiries are being frustrated by access to the child being unreasonably refused to a person authorised to seek access and that the applicant has reasonable cause to believe that access to the child is required as a matter of urgency; or
  (c) in the case of an application made by an authorised person—
    (i) the applicant has reasonable cause to suspect that a child is suffering, or is likely to suffer, significant harm;
    (ii) the applicant is making enquiries with respect to the child's welfare; and
    (iii) those enquiries are being frustrated by access to the child being unreasonably refused to a person authorised to seek access and the applicant has reasonable cause to believe that access to the child is required as a matter of urgency.

(2)   In this section—
  (a) "authorised person" means a person who is an authorised person for the purposes of section 31; and
  (b) "a person authorised to seek access" means—
    (i) in the case of an application by a local authority, an officer of the local authority or a person authorised by the authority to act on their behalf in connection with the enquiries; or
    (ii) in the case of an application by an authorised person, that person.

(3)   Any person—
  (a) seeking access to a child in connection with enquiries of a kind mentioned in subsection (1); and
  (b) purporting to be a person authorised to do so,

shall, on being asked to do so, produce some duly authenticated document as evidence that he is such a person.

(4)   While an order under this section ("an emergency protection order") is in force it—

   (a) operates as a direction to any person who is in a position to do so to comply with any request to produce the child to the applicant;

   (b) authorises—

      (i) the removal of the child at any time to accommodation provided by or on behalf of the applicant and his being kept there; or

     (ii) the prevention of the child's removal from any hospital, or other place, in which he was being accommodated immediately before the making of the order; and

   (c) gives the applicant parental responsibility for the child.

(5)   Where an emergency protection order is in force with respect to a child, the applicant—

   (a) shall only exercise the power given by virtue of subsection (4)(b) in order to safeguard the welfare of the child;

   (b) shall take, and shall only take, such action in meeting his parental responsibility for the child as is reasonably required to safeguard or promote the welfare of the child (having regard in particular to the duration of the order); and

   (c) shall comply with the requirements of any regulations made by the Secretary of State for the purposes of this subsection.

(6)   Where the court makes an emergency protection order, it may give such directions (if any) as it considers appropriate with respect to—

   (a) the contact which is, or is not, to be allowed between the child and any named person;

   (b) the medical or psychiatric examination or other assessment of the child.

(7)   Where any direction is given under subsection (6)(b), the child may, if he is of sufficient understanding to make an informed decision, refuse to submit to the examination or other assessment.

(8)   A direction under subsection (6)(a) may impose conditions and one under subsection (6)(b) may be to the effect that there is to be—

   (a) no such examination or assessment; or

   (b) no such examination or assessment unless the court directs otherwise.

(9)   A direction under subsection (6) may be—

   (a) given when the emergency protection order is made or at any time while it is in force; and

(b) varied at any time on the application of any person falling within any class of person prescribed by rules of court for the purposes of this subsection.

(10) Where an emergency protection order is in force with respect to a child and—
 (a) the applicant has exercised the power given by subsection (4)(b)(i) but it appears to him that it is safe for the child to be returned; or
 (b) the applicant has exercised the power given by subsection (4)(b)(ii) but it appears to him that it is safe for the child to be allowed to be removed from the place in question,

he shall return the child or (as the case may be) allow him to be removed.

(11) Where he is required by subsection (10) to return the child the applicant shall—
 (a) return him to the care of the person from whose care he was removed; or
 (b) if that is not reasonably practicable, return him to the care of—
  (i) a parent of his;
  (ii) any person who is not a parent of his but who has parental responsibility for him; or
  (iii) such other person as the applicant (with the agreement of the court) considers appropriate.

(12) Where the applicant has been required by subsection (10) to return the child, or to allow him to be removed, he may again exercise his powers with respect to the child (at any time while the emergency protection order remains in force) if it appears to him that a change in the circumstances of the case makes it necessary for him to do so.

(13) Where an emergency protection order has been made with respect to a child, the applicant shall, subject to any direction given under subsection (6), allow the child reasonable contact with—
 (a) his parents;
 (b) any person who is not a parent of his but who has parental responsibility for him;
 (c) any person with whom he was living immediately before the making of the order;
 (d) any person in whose favour a contact order is in force with respect to him;
 (e) any person who is allowed to have contact with the child by virtue of an order under section 34; and
 (f) any person acting on behalf of any of those persons.

(14)　Wherever it is reasonably practicable to do so, an emergency protection order shall name the child; and where it does not name him it shall describe him as clearly as possible.

(15)　A person shall be guilty of an offence if he intentionally obstructs any person exercising the power under subsection (4)(b) to remove, or prevent the removal of, a child.

(16)　A person guilty of an offence under subsection (15) shall be liable on summary conviction to a fine not exceeding level 3 on the standard scale.

[44A　Power to include exclusion requirement in emergency protection order

(1)　Where—
- (a) on being satisfied as mentioned in section 44(1)(a), (b) emergency or (c), the court makes an emergency protection order with respect to a child, and
- (b) the conditions mentioned in subsection (2) are satisfied,

the court may include an exclusion requirement in the emergency protection order.

(2)　The conditions are—
- (a) that there is reasonable cause to believe that, if a person ("the relevant person") is excluded from a dwelling-house in which the child lives, then—
  - (i) in the case of an order made on the ground mentioned in section 44(1)(a), the child will not be likely to suffer significant harm, even though the child is not removed as mentioned in section 44(1)(a)(i) or does not remain as mentioned in section 44(1)(a)(ii), or
  - (ii) in the case of an order made on the ground mentioned in paragraph (b) or (c) of section 44(1), the enquiries referred to in that paragraph will cease to be frustrated, and
- (b) that another person living in the dwelling-house (whether a parent of the child or some other person)—
  - (i) is able and willing to give to the child the care which it would be reasonable to expect a parent to give him, and
  - (ii) consents to the inclusion of the exclusion requirement.

(3)　For the purposes of this section an exclusion requirement is any one or more of the following—

(a) a provision requiring the relevant person to leave a dwelling-house in which he is living with the child,

(b) a provision prohibiting the relevant person from entering a dwelling-house in which the child lives, and

(c) a provision excluding the relevant person from a defined area in which a dwelling-house in which the child lives is situated.

(4) The court may provide that the exclusion requirement is to have effect for a shorter period than the other provisions of the order.

(5) Where the court makes an emergency protection order containing an exclusion requirement, the court may attach a power of arrest to the exclusion requirement.

(6) Where the court attaches a power of arrest to an exclusion requirement of an emergency protection order, it may provide that the power of arrest is to have effect for a shorter period than the exclusion requirement.

(7) Any period specified for the purposes of subsection (4) or (6) may be extended by the court (on one or more occasions) on an application to vary or discharge the emergency protection order.

(8) Where a power of arrest is attached to an exclusion requirement of an emergency protection order by virtue of subsection (5), a constable may arrest without warrant any person whom he has reasonable cause to believe to be in breach of the requirement.

(9) Sections 47(7), (11) and (12) and 48 of, and Schedule 5 to, the Family Law Act 1996 shall have effect in relation to a person arrested under subsection (8) of this section as they have effect in relation to a person arrested under section 47(6) of that Act.

(10) If, while an emergency protection order containing an exclusion requirement is in force, the applicant has removed the child from the dwelling-house from which the relevant person is excluded to other accommodation for a continuous period of more than 24 hours, the order shall cease to have effect in so far as it imposes the exclusion requirement.]

NOTES

Commencement: to be appointed.

Inserted, together with s 44B, by the Family Law Act 1996, s 52, Sch 6, para 3, as from a day to be appointed.

[44B   Undertakings relating to emergency protection orders

(1)   In any case where the court has power to include an exclusion requirement in an emergency protection order, the court may accept an undertaking from the relevant person.

(2)   No power of arrest may be attached to any undertaking given under subsection (1).

(3)   An undertaking given to a court under subsection (1)—
   (a) shall be enforceable as if it were an order of the court, and
   (b) shall cease to have effect if, while it is in force, the applicant has removed the child from the dwelling-house from which the relevant person is excluded to other accommodation for a continuous period of more than 24 hours.

(4)   This section has effect without prejudice to the powers of the High Court and county court apart from this section.

(5)   In this section "exclusion requirement" and "relevant person" have the same meaning as in section 44A.]

NOTES
Commencement: to be appointed.
Inserted as noted to s 44A.

45   Duration of emergency protection orders and other supplemental provisions

(1)   An emergency protection order shall have effect for such period, not exceeding eight days, as may be specified in the order.

(2)   Where—
   (a) the court making an emergency protection order would, but for this subsection, specify a period of eight days as the period for which the order is to have effect; but
   (b) the last of those eight days is a public holiday (that is to say, Christmas Day, Good Friday, a bank holiday or a Sunday),

the court may specify a period which ends at noon on the first later day which is not such a holiday.

(3)   Where an emergency protection order is made on an application under section 46(7), the period of eight days mentioned in subsection (1) shall begin with the first day on which the child was taken into police protection under section 46.

(4)   Any person who—
  (a) has parental responsibility for a child as the result of an emergency protection order; and
  (b) is entitled to apply for a care order with respect to the child,

may apply to the court for the period during which the emergency protection order is to have effect to be extended.

(5)   On an application under subsection (4) the court may extend the period during which the order is to have effect by such period, not exceeding seven days, as it thinks fit, but may do so only if it has reasonable cause to believe that the child concerned is likely to suffer significant harm if the order is not extended.

(6)   An emergency protection order may only be extended once.

(7)   Regardless of any enactment or rule of law which would otherwise prevent it from doing so, a court hearing an application for, or with respect to, an emergency protection order may take account of—
  (a) any statement contained in any report made to the court in the course of, or in connection with, the hearing; or
  (b) any evidence given during the hearing,

which is, in the opinion of the court, relevant to the application.

(8)   Any of the following may apply to the court for an emergency protection order to be discharged—
  (a) the child;
  (b) a parent of his;
  (c) any person who is not a parent of his but who has parental responsibility for him; or
  (d) any person with whom he was living immediately before the making of the order.

[(8A) On the application of a person who is not entitled to apply for the order to be discharged, but who is a person to whom an exclusion requirement contained in the order applies, an emergency protection order may be varied or discharged by the court in so far as it imposes the exclusion requirement.

(8B) Where a power of arrest has been attached to an exclusion requirement of an emergency protection order, the court may, on the application of any person entitled to apply for the discharge of the order so far as it imposes the exclusion requirement, vary or discharge the order in so far as it confers a power of arrest (whether or not any application has been made to vary or discharge any other provision of the order).]

(9) No application for the discharge of an emergency protection order shall be heard by the court before the expiry of the period of 72 hours beginning with the making of the order.

[(10) No appeal may be made against—
  (a) the making of, or refusal to make, an emergency protection order;
  (b) the extension of, or refusal to extend, the period during which such an order is to have effect;
  (c) the discharge of, or refusal to discharge, such an order; or
  (d) the giving of, or refusal to give, any direction in connection with such an order.]

(11) Subsection (8) does not apply—
  (a) where the person who would otherwise be entitled to apply for the emergency protection order to be discharged—
    (i) was given notice (in accordance with rules of court) of the hearing at which the order was made; and
    (ii) was present at that hearing; or
  (b) to any emergency protection order the effective period of which has been extended under subsection (5).

(12) A court making an emergency protection order may direct that the applicant may in exercising any powers which he has by virtue of the order, be accompanied by a registered medical practitioner, registered nurse or registered health visitor, if he so chooses.

NOTES

Commencement: 14 October 1991 (sub-ss (1)–(8), (9)–(12)); to be appointed (remainder).

Sub-ss (8A), (8B): inserted by the Family Law Act 1996, s 52, Sch 6, para 4, as from a day to be appointed.

Sub-s (10): substituted by the Courts and Legal Services Act 1990, s 116, Sch 16, para 19.

46 Removal and accommodation of children by police in cases of emergency

(1)   Where a constable has reasonable cause to believe that a child would otherwise be likely to suffer significant harm, he may—
  (a) remove the child to suitable accommodation and keep him there; or
  (b) take such steps as are reasonable to ensure that the child's removal from any hospital, or other place, in which he is then being accommodated is prevented.

(2)   For the purposes of this Act, a child with respect to whom a constable has exercised his powers under this section is referred to as having been taken into police protection.

(3)   As soon as is reasonably practicable after taking a child into police protection, the constable concerned shall—
  (a) inform the local authority within whose area the child was found of the steps that have been, and are proposed to be, taken with respect to the child under this section and the reasons for taking them;
  (b) give details to the authority within whose area the child is ordinarily resident ("the appropriate authority") of the place at which the child is being accommodated;
  (c) inform the child (if he appears capable of understanding)—
     (i) of the steps that have been taken with respect to him under this section and of the reasons for taking them; and
     (ii) of the further steps that may be taken with respect to him under this section;
  (d) take such steps as are reasonably practicable to discover the wishes and feelings of the child;
  (e) secure that the case is inquired into by an officer designated for the purposes of this section by the chief officer of the police area concerned; and
  (f) where the child was taken into police protection by being removed to accommodation which is not provided—
     (i) by or on behalf of a local authority; or
     (ii) as a refuge, in compliance with the requirements of section 51,

secure that he is moved to accommodation which is so provided.

(4)   As soon as is reasonably practicable after taking a child into police protection, the constable concerned shall take such steps as are reasonably practicable to inform—
  (a) the child's parents;

(b) every person who is not a parent of his but who has parental responsibility for him; and

(c) any other person with whom the child was living immediately before being taken into police protection,

of the steps that he has taken under this section with respect to the child, the reasons for taking them and the further steps that may be taken with respect to him under this section.

(5)   On completing any inquiry under subsection (3)(e), the officer conducting it shall release the child from police protection unless he considers that there is still reasonable cause for believing that the child would be likely to suffer significant harm if released.

(6)   No child may be kept in police protection for more than 72 hours.

(7)   While a child is being kept in police protection, the designated officer may apply on behalf of the appropriate authority for an emergency protection order to be made under section 44 with respect to the child.

(8)   An application may be made under subsection (7) whether or not the authority know of it or agree to its being made.

(9)   While a child is being kept in police protection—

(a) neither the constable concerned nor the designated officer shall have parental responsibility for him; but

(b) the designated officer shall do what is reasonable in all the circumstances of the case for the purpose of safeguarding or promoting the child's welfare (having regard in particular to the length of the period during which the child will be so protected).

(10)   Where a child has been taken into police protection, the designated officer shall allow—

(a) the child's parents;

(b) any person who is not a parent of the child but who has parental responsibility for him;

(c) any person with whom the child was living immediately before he was taken into police protection;

(d) any person in whose favour a contact order is in force with respect to the child;

(e) any person who is allowed to have contact with the child by virtue of an order under section 34; and

(f) any person acting on behalf of any of those persons,

to have such contact (if any) with the child as, in the opinion of the designated officer, is both reasonable and in the child's best interests.

(11) Where a child who has been taken into police protection is in accommodation provided by, or on behalf of, the appropriate authority, subsection (10) shall have effect as if it referred to the authority rather than to the designated officer.

47 Local authority's duty to investigate

(1) Where a local authority—
  (a) are informed that a child who lives, or is found, in their area—
    (i) is the subject of an emergency protection order; or
    (ii) is in police protection; or
    [(iii) has contravened a ban imposed by a curfew notice within the meaning of Chapter I of Part I of the Crime and Disorder Act 1998; or]
  (b) have reasonable cause to suspect that a child who lives, or is found, in their area is suffering, or is likely to suffer, significant harm,

the authority shall make, or cause to be made, such enquiries as they consider necessary to enable them to decide whether they should take any action to safeguard or promote the child's welfare. [In the case of a child falling within paragraph (a)(iii) above, the enquiries shall be commenced as soon as practicable, and, in any event, within 48 hours of the authority receiving the information.]

(2) Where a local authority have obtained an emergency protection order with respect to a child, they shall make, or cause to be made, such enquiries as they consider necessary to enable them to decide what action they should take to safeguard or promote the child's welfare.

(3) The enquiries shall, in particular, be directed towards establishing—
  (a) whether the authority should make any application to the court, or exercise any of their other powers under this Act [or section 11 of the Crime and Disorder Act 1998 (child safety orders)], with respect to the child;
  (b) whether, in the case of a child—
    (i) with respect to whom an emergency protection order has been made; and
    (ii) who is not in accommodation provided by or on behalf of the authority,

it would be in the child's best interests (while an emergency protection order remains in force) for him to be in such accommodation; and

    (c) whether, in the case of a child who has been taken into police protection, it would be in the child's best interests for the authority to ask for an application to be made under section 46(7).

(4)   Where enquiries are being made under subsection (1) with respect to a child, the local authority concerned shall (with a view to enabling them to determine what action, if any, to take with respect to him) take such steps as are reasonably practicable—

    (a) to obtain access to him; or

    (b) to ensure that access to him is obtained, on their behalf, by a person authorised by them for the purpose,

unless they are satisfied that they already have sufficient information with respect to him.

(5)   Where, as a result of any such enquiries, it appears to the authority that there are matters connected with the child's education which should be investigated, they shall consult the relevant local education authority.

(6)   Where, in the course of enquiries made under this section—

    (a) any officer of the local authority concerned; or

    (b) any person authorised by the authority to act on their behalf in connection with those enquiries—

        (i) is refused access to the child concerned; or

        (ii) is denied information as to his whereabouts,

the authority shall apply for an emergency protection order, a child assessment order, a care order or a supervision order with respect to the child unless they are satisfied that his welfare can be satisfactorily safeguarded without their doing so.

(7)   If, on the conclusion of any enquiries or review made under this section, the authority decide not to apply for an emergency protection order, a child assessment order, a care order or a supervision order they shall—

    (a) consider whether it would be appropriate to review the case at a later date; and

    (b) if they decide that it would be, determine the date on which that review is to begin.

(8)   Where, as a result of complying with this section, a local authority conclude that they should take action to safeguard or promote the child's welfare they shall take that action (so far as it is both within their power and reasonably practicable for them to do so).

(9)   Where a local authority are conducting enquiries under this section, it shall be the duty of any person mentioned in subsection (11) to assist them with those enquiries (in particular by providing relevant information and advice) if called upon by the authority to do so.

(10)   Subsection (9) does not oblige any person to assist a local authority where doing so would be unreasonable in all the circumstances of the case.

(11)   The persons are—
   (a) any local authority;
   (b) any local education authority;
   (c) any local housing authority;
   (d) any [Health Authority, Special Health Authority] [or National Health Service Trust]; and
   (e) any person authorised by the Secretary of State for the purposes of this section.

(12)   Where a local authority are making enquiries under this section with respect to a child who appears to them to be ordinarily resident within the area of another authority, they shall consult that other authority, who may undertake the necessary enquiries in their place.

NOTES

Sub-ss (1), (3): words in square brackets inserted by the Crime and Disorder Act 1998, ss 15, 119, Sch 8, para 69.

Sub-s (11): words in first pair of square brackets in para (d) substituted by the Health Authorities Act 1995, s 2(1), Sch 1, para 118(7), words in second pair of square brackets inserted by the Courts and Legal Services Act 1990, s 116, Sch 16, para 20.

48   Powers to assist in discovery of children who may be in need of emergency protection

(1)   Where it appears to a court making an emergency protection order that adequate information as to the child's whereabouts—
   (a) is not available to the applicant for the order; but
   (b) is available to another person,

it may include in the order a provision requiring that other person to disclose, if asked to do so by the applicant, any information that he may have as to the child's whereabouts.

(2)   No person shall be excused from complying with such a requirement on the ground that complying might incriminate him or his spouse of an

offence; but a statement or admission made in complying shall not be admissible in evidence against either of them in proceedings for any offence other than perjury.

(3)   An emergency protection order may authorise the applicant to enter premises specified by the order and search for the child with respect to whom the order is made.

(4)   Where the court is satisfied that there is reasonable cause to believe that there may be another child on those premises with respect to whom an emergency protection order ought to be made, it may make an order authorising the applicant to search for that other child on those premises.

(5)   Where—
  (a) an order has been made under subsection (4);
  (b) the child concerned has been found on the premises; and
  (c) the applicant is satisfied that the grounds for making an emergency protection order exist with respect to him,

the order shall have effect as if it were an emergency protection order.

(6)   Where an order has been made under subsection (4), the applicant shall notify the court of its effect.

(7)   A person shall be guilty of an offence if he intentionally obstructs any person exercising the power of entry and search under subsection (3) or (4).

(8)   A person guilty of an offence under subsection (7) shall be liable on summary conviction to a fine not exceeding level 3 on the standard scale.

(9)   Where, on an application made by any person for a warrant under this section, it appears to the court—
  (a) that a person attempting to exercise powers under an emergency protection order has been prevented from doing so by being refused entry to the premises concerned or access to the child concerned; or
  (b) that any such person is likely to be so prevented from exercising any such powers,

it may issue a warrant authorising any constable to assist the person mentioned in paragraph (a) or (b) in the exercise of those powers, using reasonable force if necessary.

(10)   Every warrant issued under this section shall be addressed to, and executed by, a constable who shall be accompanied by the person applying for the warrant if—

(a) that person so desires; and

(b) the court by whom the warrant is issued does not direct otherwise.

(11)   A court granting an application for a warrant under this section may direct that the constable concerned may, in executing the warrant, be accompanied by a registered medical practitioner, registered nurse or registered health visitor if he so chooses.

(12)   An application for a warrant under this section shall be made in the manner and form prescribed by rules of court.

(13)   Wherever it is reasonably practicable to do so, an order under subsection (4), an application for a warrant under this section and any such warrant shall name the child; and where it does not name him it shall describe him as clearly as possible.

49   Abduction of children in care etc

(1)   A person shall be guilty of an offence if, knowingly and without lawful authority or reasonable excuse, he—

(a) takes a child to whom this section applies away from the responsible person;

(b) keeps such a child away from the responsible person; or

(c) induces, assists or incites such a child to run away or stay away from the responsible person.

(2)   This section applies in relation to a child who is—

(a) in care;

(b) the subject of an emergency protection order; or

(c) in police protection,

and in this section "the responsible person" means any person who for the time being has care of him by virtue of the care order, the emergency protection order, or section 46, as the case may be.

(3)   A person guilty of an offence under this section shall be liable on summary conviction to imprisonment for a term not exceeding six months, or to a fine not exceeding level 5 on the standard scale, or to both.

50   Recovery of abducted children etc

(1)   Where it appears to the court that there is reason to believe that a child to whom this section applies—
   (a) has been unlawfully taken away or is being unlawfully kept away from the responsible person;
   (b) has run away or is staying away from the responsible person; or
   (c) is missing,

the court may make an order under this section ("a recovery order").

(2)   This section applies to the same children to whom section 49 applies and in this section "the responsible person" has the same meaning as in section 49.

(3)   A recovery order—
   (a) operates as a direction to any person who is in a position to do so to produce the child on request to any authorised person;
   (b) authorises the removal of the child by any authorised person;
   (c) requires any person who has information as to the child's whereabouts to disclose that information, if asked to do so, to a constable or an officer of the court;
   (d) authorises a constable to enter any premises specified in the order and search for the child, using reasonable force if necessary.

(4)   The court may make a recovery order only on the application of—
   (a) any person who has parental responsibility for the child by virtue of a care order or emergency protection order; or
   (b) where the child is in police protection, the designated officer.

(5)   A recovery order shall name the child and—
   (a) any person who has parental responsibility for the child by virtue of a care order or emergency protection order; or
   (b) where the child is in police protection, the designated officer.

(6)   Premises may only be specified under subsection (3)(d) if it appears to the court that there are reasonable grounds for believing the child to be on them.

(7)   In this section—
   "an authorised person" means—
      (a) any person specified by the court;
      (b) any constable;
      (c) any person who is authorised—

> (i) after the recovery order is made; and
>
> (ii) by a person who has parental responsibility for the child by virtue of a care order or an emergency protection order,

to exercise any power under a recovery order; and

"the designated officer" means the officer designated for the purposes of section 46.

(8) Where a person is authorised as mentioned in subsection (7)(c)—

(a) the authorisation shall identify the recovery order; and

(b) any person claiming to be so authorised shall, if asked to do so, produce some duly authenticated document showing that he is so authorised.

(9) A person shall be guilty of an offence if he intentionally obstructs an authorised person exercising the power under subsection (3)(b) to remove a child.

(10) A person guilty of an offence under this section shall be liable on summary conviction to a fine not exceeding level 3 on the standard scale.

(11) No person shall be excused from complying with any request made under subsection (3)(c) on the ground that complying with it might incriminate him or his spouse of an offence; but a statement or admission made in complying shall not be admissible in evidence against either of them in proceedings for an offence other than perjury.

(12) Where a child is made the subject of a recovery order whilst being looked after by a local authority, any reasonable expenses incurred by an authorised person in giving effect to the order shall be recoverable from the authority.

(13) A recovery order shall have effect in Scotland as if it had been made by the Court of Session and as if that court had had jurisdiction to make it.

(14) In this section "the court", in relation to Northern Ireland, means a magistrates' court within the meaning of the Magistrates' Courts (Northern Ireland) Order 1981.

51 Refuges for children at risk

(1) Where it is proposed to use a voluntary home or registered children's home to provide a refuge for children who appear to be at risk of harm, the

Secretary of State may issue a certificate under this section with respect to that home.

(2)   Where a local authority or voluntary organisation arrange for a foster parent to provide such a refuge, the Secretary of State may issue a certificate under this section with respect to that foster parent.

(3)   In subsection (2) "foster parent" means a person who is, or who from time to time is, a local authority foster parent or a foster parent with whom children are placed by a voluntary organisation.

(4)   The Secretary of State may by regulations—
  (a)   make provision as to the manner in which certificates may be issued;
  (b)   impose requirements which must be complied with while any certificate is in force; and
  (c)   provide for the withdrawal of certificates in prescribed circumstances.

(5)   Where a certificate is in force with respect to a home, none of the provisions mentioned in subsection (7) shall apply in relation to any person providing a refuge for any child in that home.

(6)   Where a certificate is in force with respect to a foster parent, none of those provisions shall apply in relation to the provision by him of a refuge for any child in accordance with arrangements made by the local authority or voluntary organisation.

(7)   The provisions are—
  (a)   section 49;
  [(b)   sections 82 (recovery of certain fugitive children) and 83 (harbouring) of the Children (Scotland) Act 1995, so far as they apply in relation to anything done in England and Wales;]
  (c)   section 32(3) of the Children and Young Persons Act 1969 (compelling, persuading, inciting or assisting any person to be absent from detention, etc.), so far as it applies in relation to anything done in England and Wales;
  (d)   section 2 of the Child Abduction Act 1984.

NOTES

Sub-s (7): para (b) substituted by the Children (Scotland) Act 1995, s 105(4), Sch 4, para 48(3).

52 Rules and regulations

(1)   Without prejudice to section 93 or any other power to make such rules, rules of court may be made with respect to the procedure to be followed in connection with proceedings under this Part.

(2)   The rules may, in particular make provision—
  (a) as to the form in which any application is to be made or direction is to be given;
  (b) prescribing the persons who are to be notified of—
    (i)   the making, or extension, of an emergency protection order; or
    (ii)   the making of an application under section 45(4) or (8) or 46(7); and
  (c) as to the content of any such notification and the manner in which, and person by whom, it is to be given.

(3)   The Secretary of State may by regulations provide that, where—
  (a) an emergency protection order has been made with respect to a child;
  (b) the applicant for the order was not the local authority within whose area the child is ordinarily resident; and
  (c) that local authority are of the opinion that it would be in the child's best interests for the applicant's responsibilities under the order to be transferred to them,

that authority shall (subject to their having complied with any requirements imposed by the regulations) be treated, for the purposes of this Act, as though they and not the original applicant had applied for, and been granted, the order.

(4)   Regulations made under subsection (3) may, in particular, make provision as to—
  (a) the considerations to which the local authority shall have regard in forming an opinion as mentioned in subsection (3)(c); and
  (b) the time at which responsibility under any emergency protection order is to be treated as having been transferred to a local authority.

PART VI
COMMUNITY HOMES

53 Provision of community homes by local authorities

(1)   Every local authority shall make such arrangements as they consider appropriate for securing that homes ("community homes") are available—

(a) for the care and accommodation of children looked after by them; and

(b) for purposes connected with the welfare of children (whether or not looked after by them),

and may do so jointly with one or more other local authorities.

(2) In making such arrangements, a local authority shall have regard to the need for ensuring the availability of accommodation—
(a) of different descriptions; and
(b) which is suitable for different purposes and the requirements of different descriptions of children.

(3) A community home may be a home—
(a) provided, [equipped, maintained and (subject to subsection (3A)) managed] by a local authority; or
(b) provided by a voluntary organisation but in respect of which a local authority and the organisation—
(i) propose that, in accordance with an instrument of management, the [equipment, maintenance and (subject to subsection (3B)) management] of the home shall be the responsibility of the local authority; or
(ii) so propose that the management, equipment and maintenance of the home shall be the responsibility of the voluntary organisation.

[(3A) A local authority may make arrangements for the management by another person of accommodation provided by the local authority for the purpose of restricting the liberty of children.

(3B) Where a local authority are to be responsible for the management of a community home provided by a voluntary organisation, the local authority may, with the consent of the body of managers constituted by the instrument of management for the home, make arrangements for the management by another person of accommodation provided for the purpose of restricting the liberty of children.]

(4) Where a local authority are to be responsible for the management of a community home provided by a voluntary organisation, the authority shall designate the home as a controlled community home.

(5) Where a voluntary organisation are to be responsible for the management of a community home provided by the organisation, the local authority shall designate the home as an assisted community home.

(6)   Schedule 4 shall have effect for the purpose of supplementing the provisions of this Part.

NOTES

Commencement: 8 March 1996 (sub-ss (3A), (3B)); 14 October 1991 (remainder).

Sub-s (3): words in square brackets substituted by the Criminal Justice and Public Order Act 1994, s 22(1), (2)(a).

Sub-ss (3A), (3B): inserted by the Criminal Justice and Public Order Act 1994, s 22(1), (2)(b).

PART VII
VOLUNTARY HOMES AND VOLUNTARY ORGANISATIONS
(*Outside the scope of this work.*)

PART VIII
REGISTERED CHILDREN'S HOMES
(*Outside the scope of this work.*)

PART IX
PRIVATE ARRANGEMENTS FOR FOSTERING CHILDREN
(*Outside the scope of this work.*)

PART X
CHILD MINDING AND DAY CARE FOR YOUNG CHILDREN
(*Outside the scope of this work.*)

PART XI
SECRETARY OF STATE'S SUPERVISORY FUNCTIONS
AND RESPONSIBILITIES

81   Inquiries

(1)   The Secretary of State may cause an inquiry to be held into any matter connected with—

(a) the functions of the social services committee of a local authority, in so far as those functions relate to children;

(b) the functions of an adoption agency;

(c) the functions of a voluntary organisation, in so far as those functions relate to children;

(d) a . . . children's home or voluntary home;

(e) a residential care home, nursing home or mental nursing home, so far as it provides accommodation for children;

(f) a home provided [in accordance with arrangements made] by the Secretary of State under section 82(5);

(g) the detention of a child under section 53 of the Children and Young Persons Act 1933.

(2) Before an inquiry is begun, the Secretary of State may direct that it shall be held in private.

(3) Where no direction has been given, the person holding the inquiry may if he thinks fit hold it, or any part of it, in private.

(4) Subsections (2) to (5) of section 250 of the Local Government Act 1972 (powers in relation to local inquiries) shall apply in relation to an inquiry under this section as they apply in relation to a local inquiry under that section.

(5) In this section "functions" includes powers and duties which a person has otherwise than by virtue of any enactment.

NOTES

Sub-s (1): word omitted from para (d) repealed, and words in square brackets in para (f) inserted, by the Courts and Legal Services Act 1990, ss 116, 125(7), Sch 16, para 21, Sch 20.

82 Financial support by Secretary of State

(1) The Secretary of State may (with the consent of the Treasury) defray or contribute towards—

(a) any fees or expenses incurred by any person undergoing approved child care training;

(b) any fees charged, or expenses incurred, by any person providing approved child care training or preparing material for use in connection with such training; or

(c) the cost of maintaining any person undergoing such training.

(2) The Secretary of State may make grants to local authorities in respect of expenditure incurred by them in providing secure accommodation in community homes other than assisted community homes.

(3)   Where—
   (a) a grant has been made under subsection (2) with respect to any secure accommodation; but
   (b) the grant is not used for the purpose for which it was made or the accommodation is not used as, or ceases to be used as, secure accommodation,

the Secretary of State may (with the consent of the Treasury) require the authority concerned to repay the grant, in whole or in part.

(4)   The Secretary of State may make grants to voluntary organisations towards—
   (a) expenditure incurred by them in connection with the establishment, maintenance or improvement of voluntary homes which, at the time when the expenditure was incurred—
      (i) were assisted community homes; or
      (ii) were designated as such; or
   (b) expenses incurred in respect of the borrowing of money to defray any such expenditure.

(5)   The Secretary of State may arrange for the provision, equipment and maintenance of homes for the accommodation of children who are in need of particular facilities and services which—
   (a) are or will be provided in those homes; and
   (b) in the opinion of the Secretary of State, are unlikely to be readily available in community homes.

(6)   In this Part—
   "child care training" means training undergone by any person with a view to, or in the course of—
      (a) his employment for the purposes of any of the functions mentioned in section 83(9) or in connection with the adoption of children or with the accommodation of children in a residential care home, nursing home or mental nursing home; or
      (b) his employment by a voluntary organisation for similar purposes;
   "approved child care training" means child care training which is approved by the Secretary of State; and
   "secure accommodation" means accommodation provided for the purpose of restricting the liberty of children.

(7)   Any grant made under this section shall be of such amount, and shall be subject to such conditions, as the Secretary of State may (with the consent of the Treasury) determine.

PART XI
SECRETARY OF STATE'S SUPERVISORY
FUNCTIONS AND RESPONSIBILITIES

83 Research and returns of information

(1)   The Secretary of State may conduct, or assist other persons in conducting, research into any matter connected with—
  (a) his functions, or the functions of local authorities, under the enactments mentioned in subsection (9);
  (b) the adoption of children; or
  (c) the accommodation of children in a residential care home, nursing home or mental nursing home.

(2)   Any local authority may conduct, or assist other persons in conducting, research into any matter connected with—
  (a) their functions under the enactments mentioned in subsection (9);
  (b) the adoption of children; or
  (c) the accommodation of children in a residential care home, nursing home or mental nursing home.

(3)   Every local authority shall, at such times and in such form as the Secretary of State may direct, transmit to him such particulars as he may require with respect to—
  (a) the performance by the local authority of all or any of their functions—
    (i)   under the enactments mentioned in subsection (9); or
    (ii) in connection with the accommodation of children in a residential care home, nursing home or mental nursing home; and
  (b) the children in relation to whom the authority have exercised those functions.

(4)   Every voluntary organisation shall, at such times and in such form as the Secretary of State may direct, transmit to him such particulars as he may require with respect to children accommodated by them or on their behalf.

(5)   The Secretary of State may direct the clerk of each magistrates' court to which the direction is expressed to relate to transmit—
  (a) to such person as may be specified in the direction; and
  (b) at such times and in such form as he may direct;
such particulars as he may require with respect to proceedings of the court which relate to children.

(6)   The Secretary of State shall in each year lay before Parliament a consolidated and classified abstract of the information transmitted to him under subsections (3) to (5).

(7)   The Secretary of State may institute research designed to provide information on which requests for information under this section may be based.

(8)   The Secretary of State shall keep under review the adequacy of the provision of child care training and for that purpose shall receive and consider any information from or representations made by—
  (a) the Central Council for Education and Training in Social Work;
  (b) such representatives of local authorities as appear to him to be appropriate; or
  (c) such other persons or organisations as appear to him to be appropriate,

concerning the provision of such training.

(9)   The enactments are—
  (a) this Act;
  (b) the Children and Young Persons Acts 1933 to 1969;
  (c) section 116 of the Mental Health Act 1983 (so far as it relates to children looked after by local authorities);
  (d) section 10 of the Mental Health (Scotland) Act 1984 (so far as it relates to children for whom local authorities have responsibility).

84   Local authority failure to comply with statutory duty: default power of Secretary of State

(1)   If the Secretary of State is satisfied that any local authority has failed, without reasonable excuse, to comply with any of the duties imposed on them by or under this Act he may make an order declaring that authority to be in default with respect to that duty.

(2)   An order under subsection (1) shall give the Secretary of State's reasons for making it.

(3)   An order under subsection (1) may contain such directions for the purpose of ensuring that the duty is complied with, within such period as may be specified in the order, as appears to the Secretary of State to be necessary.

(4)   Any such direction shall, on the application of the Secretary of State, be enforceable by mandamus.

PART XII
MISCELLANEOUS AND GENERAL

Effect and duration of orders etc

91 Effect and duration of orders etc

(1)   The making of a residence order with respect to a child who is the subject of a care order discharges the care order.

(2)   The making of a care order with respect to a child who is the subject of any section 8 order discharges that order.

(3)   The making of a care order with respect to a child who is the subject of a supervision order discharges that other order.

(4)   The making of a care order with respect to a child who is a ward of court brings that wardship to an end.

(5)   The making of a care order with respect to a child who is the subject of a school attendance order made under [section 437 of the Education Act 1996] discharges the school attendance order.

(6)   Where an emergency protection order is made with respect to a child who is in care, the care order shall have effect subject to the emergency protection order.

(7)   Any order made under section 4(1) or 5(1) shall continue in force until the child reaches the age of eighteen, unless it is brought to an end earlier.

(8)   Any—
    (a) agreement under section 4; or
    (b) appointment under section 5(3) or (4),

shall continue in force until the child reaches the age of eighteen, unless it is brought to an end earlier.

(9)   An order under Schedule 1 has effect as specified in that Schedule.

(10)   A section 8 order shall, if it would otherwise still be in force, cease to have effect when the child reaches the age of sixteen, unless it is to have effect beyond that age by virtue of section 9(6).

(11)   Where a section 8 order has effect with respect to a child who has reached the age of sixteen, it shall, if it would otherwise still be in force, cease to have effect when he reaches the age of eighteen.

(12)   Any care order, other than an interim care order, shall continue in force until the child reaches the age of eighteen, unless it is brought to an end earlier.

(13)   Any order made under any other provision of this Act in relation to a child shall, if it would otherwise still be in force, cease to have effect when he reaches the age of eighteen.

(14)   On disposing of any application for an order under this Act, the court may (whether or not it makes any other order in response to the application) order that no application for an order under this Act of any specified kind may be made with respect to the child concerned by any person named in the order without leave of the court.

(15)   Where an application ("the previous application") has been made for—
  (a) the discharge of a care order;
  (b) the discharge of a supervision order;
  (c) the discharge of an education supervision order;
  (d) the substitution of a supervision order for a care order; or
  (e) a child assessment order,

no further application of a kind mentioned in paragraphs (*a*) to (*e*) may be made with respect to the child concerned, without leave of the court, unless the period between the disposal of the previous application and the making of the further application exceeds six months.

(16)   Subsection (15) does not apply to applications made in relation to interim orders.

(17)   Where—
  (a) a person has made an application for an order under section 34;
  (b) the application has been refused; and
  (c) a period of less than six months has elapsed since the refusal,

that person may not make a further application for such an order with respect to the same child, unless he has obtained the leave of the court.

NOTES

   Sub-s (5): words in square brackets substituted by the Education Act 1996, s 582(1), Sch 37, Pt I, para 90.

92 Jurisdiction of courts

(1)   The name "domestic proceedings", given to certain proceedings in magistrates' courts, is hereby changed to "family proceedings" and the names "domestic court" and "domestic court panel" are hereby changed to "family proceedings court" and "family panel", respectively.

(2)   Proceedings under this Act shall be treated as family proceedings in relation to magistrates' courts.

(3)   Subsection (2) is subject to the provisions of section 65(1) and (2) of the Magistrates' Courts Act 1980 (proceedings which may be treated as not being family proceedings), as amended by this Act.

(4)   A magistrates' court shall not be competent to entertain any application, or make any order, involving the administration or application of—
   (a) any property belonging to or held in trust for a child; or
   (b) the income of any such property.

(5)   The powers of a magistrates' court under section 63(2) of the Act of 1980 to suspend or rescind orders shall not apply in relation to any order made under this Act.

(6)   Part I of Schedule 11 makes provision, including provision for the Lord Chancellor to make orders, with respect to the jurisdiction of courts and justices of the peace in relation to—
   (a) proceedings under this Act; and
   (b) proceedings under certain other enactments.

(7)   For the purposes of this Act "the court" means the High Court, a county court or a magistrates' court.

(8)   Subsection (7) is subject to the provision made by or under Part I of Schedule 11 and to any express provision as to the jurisdiction of any court made by any other provision of this Act.

(9)   The Lord Chancellor may by order make provision for the principal registry of the Family Division of the High Court to be treated as if it were a county court for such purposes of this Act, or of any provision made under this Act, as may be specified in the order.

(10)　Any order under subsection (9) may make such provision as the Lord Chancellor thinks expedient for the purpose of applying (with or without modifications) provisions which apply in relation to the procedure in county courts to the principal registry when it acts as if it were a county court.

(11)　Part II of Schedule 11 makes amendments consequential on this section.

94　Appeals

(1)　[Subject to any express provisions to the contrary made by or under this Act, an] appeal shall lie to the High Court against—
    (a)　the making by a magistrates' court of any order under this Act; or
    (b)　any refusal by a magistrates' court to make such an order.

(2)　Where a magistrates' court has power, in relation to any proceedings under this Act, to decline jurisdiction because it considers that the case can more conveniently be dealt with by another court, no appeal shall lie against any exercise by that magistrates' court of that power.

(3)　Subsection (1) does not apply in relation to an interim order for periodical payments made under Schedule 1.

(4)　On an appeal under this section, the High Court may make such orders as may be necessary to give effect to its determination of the appeal.

(5)　Where an order is made under subsection (4) the High Court may also make such incidental or consequential orders as appear to it to be just.

(6)　Where an appeal from a magistrates' court relates to an order for the making of periodical payments, the High Court may order that its determination of the appeal shall have effect from such date as it thinks fit to specify in the order.

(7)　The date so specified must not be earlier than the earliest date allowed in accordance with rules of court made for the purposes of this section.

(8)　Where, on an appeal under this section in respect of an order requiring a person to make periodical payments, the High Court reduces the amount of those payments or discharges the order—
    (a)　it may order the person entitled to the payments to pay to the person making them such sum in respect of payments already made as the High Court thinks fit; and

(b) if any arrears are due under the order for periodical payments, it may remit payment of the whole, or part, of those arrears.

(9)   Any order of the High Court made on an appeal under this section (other than one directing that an application be re-heard by a magistrates' court) shall, for the purposes—

(a) of the enforcement of the order; and

(b) of any power to vary, revive or discharge orders,

be treated as if it were an order of the magistrates' court from which the appeal was brought and not an order of the High Court.

(10)   The Lord Chancellor may by order make provision as to the circumstances in which appeals may be made against decisions taken by courts on questions arising in connection with the transfer, or proposed transfer, of proceedings by virtue of any order under paragraph 2 of Schedule 11.

(11)   Except to the extent provided for in any order made under subsection (10), no appeal may be made against any decision of a kind mentioned in that subsection.

NOTES

Sub-s (1): words in square brackets substituted by the Courts and Legal Services Act 1990, s 116, Sch16, para 23.

95   Attendance of child at hearing under Part IV or V

(1)   In any proceedings in which a court is hearing an application for an order under Part IV or V, or is considering whether to make any such order, the court may order the child concerned to attend such stage or stages of the proceedings as may be specified in the order.

(2)   The power conferred by subsection (1) shall be exercised in accordance with rules of court.

(3)   Subsections (4) to (6) apply where—

(a) an order under subsection (1) has not been complied with; or

(b) the court has reasonable cause to believe that it will not be complied with.

(4)   The court may make an order authorising a constable, or such person as may be specified in the order—

(a) to take charge of the child and to bring him to the court; and

(b) to enter and search any premises specified in the order if he has reasonable cause to believe that the child may be found on the premises.

(5)   The court may order any person who is in a position to do so to bring the child to the court.

(6)   Where the court has reason to believe that a person has information about the whereabouts of the child it may order him to disclose it to the court.

96 Evidence given by, or with respect to, children

(1)   Subsection (2) applies where a child who is called as a witness in any civil proceedings does not, in the opinion of the court, understand the nature of an oath.

(2)   The child's evidence may be heard by the court if, in its opinion—
  (a) he understands that it is his duty to speak the truth; and
  (b) he has sufficient understanding to justify his evidence being heard.

(3)   The Lord Chancellor may by order make provision for the admissibility of evidence which would otherwise be inadmissible under any rule of law relating to hearsay.

(4)   An order under subsection (3) may only be made with respect to—
  (a) civil proceedings in general or such civil proceedings, or class of civil proceedings, as may be prescribed; and
  (b) evidence in connection with the upbringing, maintenance or welfare of a child.

(5)   An order under subsection (3)—
  (a) may, in particular, provide for the admissibility of statements which are made orally or in a prescribed form or which are recorded by any prescribed method of recording;
  (b) may make different provision for different purposes and in relation to different descriptions of court; and
  (c) may make such amendments and repeals in any enactment relating to evidence (other than in this Act) as the Lord Chancellor considers necessary or expedient in consequence of the provision made by the order.

(6)   Subsection (5)(b) is without prejudice to section 104(4).

(7)   In this section—
["civil proceedings" means civil proceedings, before any tribunal, in
relation to which the strict rules of evidence apply, whether as a
matter of law or by agreement of the parties, and references to "the
court" shall be construed accordingly;] and
"prescribed" means prescribed by an order under subsection (3).

NOTES

Sub-s (7): definition "civil proceedings" substituted by the Civil Evidence Act
1995, s 15(1), Sch 1, para 16.

97   Privacy for children involved in certain proceedings

(1)   Rules made under section 144 of the Magistrates' Courts Act 1980
may make provision for a magistrates' court to sit in private in proceedings
in which any powers under this Act may be exercised by the court with
respect to any child.

(2)   No person shall publish any material which is intended, or likely, to
identify—
  (a) any child as being involved in any proceedings before a magistrates'
       court in which any power under this Act may be exercised by the
       court with respect to that or any other child; or
  (b) an address or school as being that of a child involved in any such
       proceedings.

(3)   In any proceedings for an offence under this section it shall be a defence
for the accused to prove that he did not know, and had no reason to suspect,
that the published material was intended, or likely, to identify the child.

(4)   The court or the [Lord Chancellor] may, if satisfied that the welfare
of the child requires it, by order dispense with the requirements of
subsection (2) to such extent as may be specified in the order.

(5)   For the purposes of this section—
  "publish" includes—
    [(a) include a programme service (within the meaning of the
         Broadcasting Act 1990);] or
    (b) cause to be published; and
  "material" includes any picture or representation.

(6)   Any person who contravenes this section shall be guilty of an offence and liable, on summary conviction, to a fine not exceeding level 4 on the standard scale.

(7)   Subsection (1) is without prejudice to—
  (a) the generality of the rule making power in section 144 of the Act of 1980; or
  (b) any other power of a magistrates' court to sit in private.

(8)   [Sections 69 (sittings of magistrates' courts for family proceedings) and 71 (newspaper reports of certain proceedings) of the Act of 1980] shall apply in relation to any proceedings to which this section applies subject to the provisions of this section.

NOTES

Sub-s (4): words in square brackets substituted by the Transfer of Functions (Magistrates' Courts and Family Law) Order 1992, SI 1992/709, art 3(2), Sch 2.

Sub-s (5): in definition "publish" words in square brackets substituted by the Broadcasting Act 1990, s203(1), Sch 20, para 53.

Sub-s (8): words in square brackets substituted by the Courts and Legal Services Act 1990, s 116, Sch16, para 24.

98 Self-incrimination

(1)   In any proceedings in which a court is hearing an application for an order under Part IV or V, no person shall be excused from—
  (a) giving evidence on any matter; or
  (b) answering any question put to him in the course of his giving evidence,

on the ground that doing so might incriminate him or his spouse of an offence.

(2)   A statement or admission made in such proceedings shall not be admissible in evidence against the person making it or his spouse in proceedings for an offence other than perjury.

100 Restrictions on use of wardship jurisdiction

(1)   . . .

(2)   No court shall exercise the High Court's inherent jurisdiction with respect to children—

(a) so as to require a child to be placed in the care, or put under the supervision, of a local authority;

(b) so as to require a child to be accommodated by or on behalf of a local authority;

(c) so as to make a child who is the subject of a care order a ward of court; or

(d) for the purpose of conferring on any local authority power to determine any question which has arisen, or which may arise, in connection with any aspect of parental responsibility for a child.

(3)   No application for any exercise of the court's inherent jurisdiction with respect to children may be made by a local authority unless the authority have obtained the leave of the court.

(4)   The court may only grant leave if it is satisfied that—

(a) the result which the authority wish to achieve could not be achieved through the making of any order of a kind to which subsection (5) applies; and

(b) there is reasonable cause to believe that if the court's inherent jurisdiction is not exercised with respect to the child he is likely to suffer significant harm.

(5)   This subsection applies to any order—

(a) made otherwise than in the exercise of the court's inherent jurisdiction; and

(b) which the local authority is entitled to apply for (assuming, in the case of any application which may only be made with leave, that leave is granted).

NOTES

Sub-s (1): repeals the Family Law Reform Act 1969, s 7.

Search warrants

102 Power of constable to assist in exercise of certain powers to search for children or inspect premises

(1)   Where, on an application made by any person for a warrant under this section, it appears to the court—

(a) that a person attempting to exercise powers under any enactment mentioned in subsection (6) has been prevented from doing so by being refused entry to the premises concerned or refused access to the child concerned; or

(b) that any such person is likely to be so prevented from exercising any such powers,

it may issue a warrant authorising any constable to assist that person in the exercise of those powers, using reasonable force if necessary.

(2)   Every warrant issued under this section shall be addressed to, and executed by, a constable who shall be accompanied by the person applying for the warrant if—

(a) that person so desires; and

(b) the court by whom the warrant is issued does not direct otherwise.

(3)   A court granting an application for a warrant under this section may direct that the constable concerned may, in executing the warrant, be accompanied by a registered medical practitioner, registered nurse or registered health visitor if he so chooses.

(4)   An application for a warrant under this section shall be made in the manner and form prescribed by rules of court.

(5)   Where—

(a) an application for a warrant under this section relates to a particular child; and

(b) it is reasonably practicable to do so,

the application and any warrant granted on the application shall name the child; and where it does not name him it shall describe him as clearly as possible.

(6)   The enactments are—

(a) sections 62, 64, 67, 76, 80, 86 and 87;

(b) paragraph 8(1)(b) and (2)(b) of Schedule 3;

(c) section 33 of the Adoption Act 1976 (duty of local authority to secure that protected children are visited from time to time).

General

103 Offences by bodies corporate

(1)   This section applies where any offence under this Act is committed by a body corporate.

(2)   If the offence is proved to have been committed with the consent or connivance of or to be attributable to any neglect on the part of any director, manager, secretary or other similar officer of the body corporate, or any person who was purporting to act in any such capacity he (as well as the body corporate) shall be guilty of the offence and shall be liable to be proceeded against and punished accordingly.

105   Interpretation

(1)   In this Act—
   "adoption agency" means a body which may be referred to as an adoption agency by virtue of section 1 of the Adoption Act 1976;
   "bank holiday" means a day which is a bank holiday under the Banking and Financial Dealings Act 1971;
   "care order" has the meaning given by section 31(11) and also includes any order which by or under any enactment has the effect of, or is deemed to be, a care order for the purposes of this Act; and any reference to a child who is in the care of an authority is a reference to a child who is in their care by virtue of a care order;
   "child" means, subject to paragraph 16 of Schedule 1, a person under the age of eighteen;
   "child assessment order" has the meaning given by section 43(2);
   "child minder" has the meaning given by section 71;
   "child of the family", in relation to the parties to a marriage, means—
      (a)   a child of both of those parties;
      (b)   any other child, not being a child who is placed with those parties as foster parents by a local authority or voluntary organisation, who has been treated by both of those parties as a child of their family;
   "children's home" has the same meaning as in section 63;
   "community home" has the meaning given by section 53;
   "contact order" has the meaning given by section 8(1);
   "day care" has the same meaning as in section 18;
   "disabled", in relation to a child, has the same meaning as in section 17(11);
                                             . . . . .
   "domestic premises" has the meaning given by section 71(12);
   ["dwelling-house" includes—
      (a)   any building or part of a building which is occupied as a dwelling;
      (b)   any caravan, house-boat or structure which is occupied as a dwelling;

and any yard, garden, garage or outhouse belonging to it and occupied with it;]

"education supervision order" has the meaning given in section 36;

"emergency protection order" means an order under section 44;

"family assistance order" has the meaning given in section 16(2);

"family proceedings" has the meaning given by section 8(3);

"functions" includes powers and duties;

"guardian of a child" means a guardian (other than a guardian of the estate of a child) appointed in accordance with the provisions of section 5;

"harm" has the same meaning as in section 31(9) and the question of whether harm is significant shall be determined in accordance with section 31(10);

["Health Authority" means a Health Authority established under section 8 of the National Health Service Act 1977;]

"health service hospital" has the same meaning as in the National Health Service Act 1977;

"hospital" has the same meaning as in the Mental Health Act 1983, except that it does not include a special hospital within the meaning of that Act;

"ill-treatment" has the same meaning as in section 31(9);

["income-based jobseeker's allowance" has the same meaning as in the Jobseekers Act 1995;]

"independent school" has the same meaning as in [the Education Act 1996];

"local authority" means, in relation to England . . ., the council of a county, a metropolitan district, a London Borough or the Common Council of the City of London[, in relation to Wales, the council of a county or a county borough] and, in relation to Scotland, a local authority within the meaning of section 1(2) of the Social Work (Scotland) Act 1968;

"local authority foster parent" has the same meaning as in section 23(3);

"local education authority" has the same meaning as in [the Education Act 1996];

"local housing authority" has the same meaning as in the Housing Act 1985;

"mental nursing home" has the same meaning as in the Registered Homes Act 1984;

"nursing home" has the same meaning as in the Act of 1984;

"parental responsibility" has the meaning given in section 3;

"parental responsibility agreement" has the meaning given in section 4(1);

"prescribed" means prescribed by regulations made under this Act;

"privately fostered child" and "to foster a child privately" have the same meaning as in section 66;

"prohibited steps order" has the meaning given by section 8(1);

"protected child" has the same meaning as in Part III of the Adoption Act 1976;

"registered children's home" has the same meaning as in section 63;

"registered pupil" has the same meaning as in [the Education Act 1996];

"relative", in relation to a child, means a grandparent, brother, sister, uncle or aunt (whether of the full blood or half blood or by affinity) or step-parent;

"residence order" has the meaning given by section 8(1);

"residential care home" has the same meaning as in the Registered Homes Act 1984 [and "small home" has the meaning given by section 1(4A) of that Act];

"responsible person", in relation to a child who is the subject of a supervision order, has the meaning given in paragraph 1 of Schedule 3;

"school" has the same meaning as in [the Education Act 1996] or, in relation to Scotland, in the Education (Scotland) Act 1980;

"service", in relation to any provision made under Part III, includes any facility;

"signed", in relation to any person, includes the making by that person of his mark;

"special educational needs" has the same meaning as in [the Education Act 1996];

["Special Health Authority" means a Special Health Authority established under section 11 of the National Health Service Act 1977;]

"specific issue order" has the meaning given by section 8(1);

"supervision order" has the meaning given by section 31(11);

"supervised child" and "supervisor", in relation to a supervision order or an education supervision order, mean respectively the child who is (or is to be) under supervision and the person under whose supervision he is (or is to be) by virtue of the order;

"upbringing", in relation to any child, includes the care of the child but not his maintenance;

"voluntary home" has the meaning given by section 60;

"voluntary organisation" means a body (other than a public or local authority) whose activities are not carried on for profit.

(2)   References in this Act to a child whose father and mother were, or (as the case may be) were not, married to each other at the time of his birth must be read with section 1 of the Family Law Reform Act 1987 (which extends the meaning of such references).

(3)   References in this Act to—
   (a) a person with whom a child lives, or is to live, as the result of a residence order; or

(b) a person in whose favour a residence order is in force,

shall be construed as references to the person named in the order as the person with whom the child is to live.

(4)   References in this Act to a child who is looked after by a local authority have the same meaning as they have (by virtue of section 22) in Part III.

(5)   References in this Act to accommodation provided by or on behalf of a local authority are references to accommodation so provided in the exercise of functions which stand referred to the social services committee of that or any other local authority under the Local Authority Social Services Act 1970.

(6)   In determining the "ordinary residence" of a child for any purpose of this Act, there shall be disregarded any period in which he lives in any place—
   (a) which is a school or other institution;
   (b) in accordance with the requirements of a supervision order under this Act or an order under section 7(7)(b) of the Children and Young Persons Act 1969; or
   (c) while he is being provided with accommodation by or on behalf of a local authority.

(7)   References in this Act to children who are in need shall be construed in accordance with section 17.

(8)   Any notice or other document required under this Act to be served on any person may be served on him by being delivered personally to him, or being sent by post to him in a registered letter or by the recorded delivery service at his proper address.

(9)   Any such notice or other document required to be served on a body corporate or a firm shall be duly served if it is served on the secretary or clerk of that body or a partner of that firm.

(10)   For the purposes of this section, and of section 7 of the Interpretation Act 1978 in its application to this section, the proper address of a person—
   (a) in the case of a secretary or clerk of a body corporate, shall be that of the registered or principal office of that body;
   (b) in the case of a partner of a firm, shall be that of the principal office of the firm; and
   (c) in any other case, shall be the last known address of the person to be served.

Sub-s (1): definition omitted repealed, and definitions "Health Authority", "Special Health Authority" substituted, by the Health Authorities Act 1995, ss 2(1), 5(1), Sch 1, para 118(10), Sch 3; definition "dwelling-house" inserted by the Family Law Act 1996, s 52, Sch 6, para 5, as from a day to be appointed; definition "income-based jobseeker's allowance" inserted by the Jobseekers Act 1995, s 41(4), Sch 2, para19(4); in definitions "independent school", "local education authority", "registered pupil", "school" and "special educational needs" words in square brackets substituted by the Education Act 1996, s 582(1), Sch37, para 91; in definition "local authority" words omitted repealed, and words in square brackets inserted, by the Local Government (Wales) Act 1994, ss 22(4), 66(8), Sch 10, para 13, Sch 18; in definition, "residential care home" words in square brackets added by the Registered Homes (Amendment) Act 1991, s 2(6).

108 Short title, commencement, extent etc

(1)   This Act may be cited as the Children Act 1989.

(2)–(12)   . . .

NOTES

Sub-ss (2)–(12): outside the scope of this work.

SCHEDULE I
FINANCIAL PROVISION FOR CHILDREN

Section 15(1)

Orders for financial relief against parents

1.—(1)   On an application made by a parent or guardian of a child, or by any person in whose favour a residence order is in force with respect to a child, the court may—
  (a) in the case of an application to the High Court or a county court, make one or more of the orders mentioned in sub-paragraph (2);
  (b) in the case of an application to a magistrates' court, make one or both of the orders mentioned in paragraphs (a) and (c) of that sub-paragraph.

(2)   The orders referred to in sub-paragraph (1) are—
  (a) an order requiring either or both parents of a child—
     (i)   to make to the applicant for the benefit of the child; or
     (ii) to make to the child himself,

such periodical payments, for such term, as may be specified in the order;

  (b) an order requiring either or both parents of a child—

      (i) to secure to the applicant for the benefit of the child; or

     (ii) to secure to the child himself,

such periodical payments, for such term, as may be so specified;

  (c) an order requiring either or both parents of a child—

      (i) to pay to the applicant for the benefit of the child; or

     (ii) to pay to the child himself,

such lump sum as may be so specified;

  (d) an order requiring a settlement to be made for the benefit of the child, and to the satisfaction of the court, of property—

      (i) to which either parent is entitled (either in possession or in reversion); and

     (ii) which is specified in the order;

  (e) an order requiring either or both parents of a child—

      (i) to transfer to the applicant, for the benefit of the child; or

     (ii) to transfer to the child himself,

such property to which the parent is, or the parents are, entitled (either in possession or in reversion) as may be specified in the order.

(3)   The powers conferred by this paragraph may be exercised at any time.

(4)   An order under sub-paragraph (2)(a) or (b) may be varied or discharged by a subsequent order made on the application of any person by or to whom payments were required to be made under the previous order.

(5)   Where a court makes an order under this paragraph—

  (a) it may at any time make a further such order under sub-paragraph (2)(a), (b) or (c) with respect to the child concerned if he has not reached the age of eighteen;

  (b) it may not make more than one order under sub-paragraph (2)(d) or (e) against the same person in respect of the same child.

(6)   On making, varying or discharging a residence order the court may exercise any of its powers under this Schedule even though no application has been made to it under this Schedule.

[(7)   Where a child is a ward of court, the court may exercise any of its powers under this Schedule even though no application has been made to it.]

Orders for financial relief for persons over eighteen

2.—(1)   If, on an application by a person who has reached the age of eighteen, it appears to the court—

    (a) that the applicant is, will be or (if an order were made under this paragraph) would be receiving instruction at an educational establishment or undergoing training for a trade, profession or vocation, whether or not while in gainful employment; or

    (b) that there are special circumstances which justify the making of an order under this paragraph,

the court may make one or both of the orders mentioned in sub-paragraph (2).

(2)   The orders are—

    (a) an order requiring either or both of the applicant's parents to pay to the applicant such periodical payments, for such term, as may be specified in the order;

    (b) an order requiring either or both of the applicant's parents to pay to the applicant such lump sum as may be so specified.

(3)   An application may not be made under this paragraph by any person if, immediately before he reached the age of sixteen, a periodical payments order was in force with respect to him.

(4)   No order shall be made under this paragraph at a time when the parents of the applicant are living with each other in the same household.

(5)   An order under sub-paragraph (2)(a) may be varied or discharged by a subsequent order made on the application of any person by or to whom payments were required to be made under the previous order.

(6)   In sub-paragraph (3) "periodical payments order" means an order made under—

    (a) this Schedule;

    (b) . . .

    (c) section 23 or 27 of the Matrimonial Causes Act 1973;

    (d) Part I of the Domestic Proceedings and Magistrates' Courts Act 1978,

for the making or securing of periodical payments.

(7)   The powers conferred by this paragraph shall be exercisable at any time.

(8)   Where the court makes an order under this paragraph it may from time to time while that order remains in force make a further such order.

Duration of orders for financial relief

3.—(1)   The term to be specified in an order for periodical payments made under paragraph 1(2)(a) or (b) in favour of a child may begin with the date of the making of an application for the order in question or any later date [or a date ascertained in accordance with sub-paragraph (5) or (6)] but—

(a) shall not in the first instance extend beyond the child's seventeenth birthday unless the court thinks it right in the circumstances of the case to specify a later date; and

(b) shall not in any event extend beyond the child's eighteenth birthday.

(2)   Paragraph (b) of sub-paragraph (1) shall not apply in the case of a child if it appears to the court that—

(a) the child is, or will be or (if an order were made without complying with that paragraph) would be receiving instruction at an educational establishment or undergoing training for a trade, profession or vocation, whether or not while in gainful employment; or

(b) there are special circumstances which justify the making of an order without complying with that paragraph.

(3)   An order for periodical payments made under paragraph 1(2)(a) or 2(2)(a) shall, notwithstanding anything in the order, cease to have effect on the death of the person liable to make payments under the order.

(4)   Where an order is made under paragraph 1(2)(a) or (b) requiring periodical payments to be made or secured to the parent of a child, the order shall cease to have effect if—

(a) any parent making or securing the payments; and

(b) any parent to whom the payments are made or secured,

live together for a period of more than six months.

[(5)   Where—

(a) a maintenance assessment ("the current assessment") is in force with respect to a child; and

(b) an application is made for an order under paragraph 1(2)(a) or (b) of this Schedule for periodical payments in favour of that child—

(i) in accordance with section 8 of the Child Support Act 1991; and

(ii) before the end of the period of 6 months beginning with the making of the current assessment,

the term to be specified in any such order made on that application may be expressed to begin on, or at any time after, the earliest permitted date.

(6)   For the purposes of subsection (5) above, "the earliest permitted date" is whichever is the later of—

(a) the date 6 months before the application is made; or

(b) the date on which the current assessment took effect or, where successive maintenance assessments have been continuously in force with respect to a child, on which the first of those assessments took effect.

(7)   Where—

(a) a maintenance assessment ceases to have effect or is cancelled by or under any provision of the Child Support Act 1991, and

(b) an application is made, before the end of the period of 6 months beginning with the relevant date, for an order for periodical payments under paragraph 1(2)(a) or (b) in favour of a child with respect to whom that maintenance assessment was in force immediately before it ceased to have effect or was cancelled,

the term to be specified in any such order, or in any interim order under paragraph 9, made on that application may begin with the date on which that maintenance assessment ceased to have effect or, as the case may be, the date with effect from which it was cancelled, or any later date.

(8)   In sub-paragraph (7)(b)—

(a) where the maintenance assessment ceased to have effect, the relevant date is the date on which it so ceased; and

(b) where the maintenance assessment was cancelled, the relevant date is the later of—

(i)   the date on which the person who cancelled it did so, and

(ii) the date from which the cancellation first had effect.]

Matters to which court is to have regard in making orders for financial relief

4.—(1)   In deciding whether to exercise its powers under paragraph 1 or 2, and if so in what manner, the court shall have regard to all the circumstances including—

(a) the income, earning capacity, property and other financial resources which each person mentioned in sub-paragraph (3) has or is likely to have in the foreseeable future;

(b) the financial needs, obligations and responsibilities which each person mentioned in sub-paragraph (3) has or is likely to have in the foreseeable future;

(c) the financial needs of the child;

(d) the income, earning capacity (if any), property and other financial resources of the child;

(e) any physical or mental disability of the child;

(f) the manner in which the child was being, or was expected to be, educated or trained.

(2) In deciding whether to exercise its powers under paragraph 1 against a person who is not the mother or father of the child, and if so in what manner, the court shall in addition have regard to—

(a) whether that person has assumed responsibility for the maintenance of the child and, if so, the extent to which and basis on which he assumed that responsibility and the length of the period during which he met that responsibility;

(b) whether he did so knowing that the child was not his child;

(c) the liability of any other person to maintain the child.

(3) Where the court makes an order under paragraph 1 against a person who is not the father of the child, it shall record in the order that the order is made on the basis that the person against whom the order is made is not the child's father.

(4) The persons mentioned in sub-paragraph (1) are—

(a) in relation to a decision whether to exercise its powers under paragraph 1, any parent of the child;

(b) in relation to a decision whether to exercise its powers under paragraph 2, the mother and father of the child;

(c) the applicant for the order;

(d) any other person in whose favour the court proposes to make the order.

Provisions relating to lump sums

5.—(1) Without prejudice to the generality of paragraph 1, an order under that paragraph for the payment of a lump sum may be made for the purpose of enabling any liabilities or expenses—

(a) incurred in connection with the birth of the child or in maintaining the child; and

(b) reasonably incurred before the making of the order,

to be met.

(2) The amount of any lump sum required to be paid by an order made by a magistrates' court under paragraph 1 or 2 shall not exceed £1000 or

such larger amount as the [Lord Chancellor] may from time to time by order fix for the purposes of this sub-paragraph.

(3)   The power of the court under paragraph 1 or 2 to vary or discharge an order for the making or securing of periodical payments by a parent shall include power to make an order under that provision for the payment of a lump sum by that parent.

(4)   The amount of any lump sum which a person may be required to pay by virtue of sub-paragraph (3) shall not, in the case of an order made by a magistrates' court, exceed the maximum amount that may at the time of the making of the order be required to be paid under sub-paragraph (2), but a magistrates' court may make an order for the payment of a lump sum not exceeding that amount even though the parent was required to pay a lump sum by a previous order under this Act.

(5)   An order made under paragraph 1 or 2 for the payment of a lump sum may provide for the payment of that sum by instalments.

(6)   Where the court provides for the payment of a lump sum by instalments the court, on an application made either by the person liable to pay or the person entitled to receive that sum, shall have power to vary that order by varying—
    (a) the number of instalments payable;
    (b) the amount of any instalment payable;
    (c) the date on which any instalment becomes payable.

Variation etc of orders for periodical payments

6.—(1)   In exercising its powers under paragraph 1 or 2 to vary or discharge an order for the making or securing of periodical payments the court shall have regard to all the circumstances of the case, including any change in any of the matters to which the court was required to have regard when making the order.

(2)   The power of the court under paragraph 1 or 2 to vary an order for the making or securing of periodical payments shall include power to suspend any provision of the order temporarily and to revive any provision so suspended.

(3)   Where on an application under paragraph 1 or 2 for the variation or discharge of an order for the making or securing of periodical payments

the court varies the payments required to be made under that order, the court may provide that the payments as so varied shall be made from such date as the court may specify, [except that, subject to sub-paragraph (9), the date shall not be] earlier than the date of the making of the application.

(4)   An application for the variation of an order made under paragraph 1 for the making or securing of periodical payments to or for the benefit of a child may, if the child has reached the age of sixteen, be made by the child himself.

(5)   Where an order for the making or securing of periodical payments made under paragraph 1 ceases to have effect on the date on which the child reaches the age of sixteen, or at any time after that date but before or on the date on which he reaches the age of eighteen, the child may apply to the court which made the order for an order for its revival.

(6)   If on such an application it appears to the court that—
   (a)   the child is, will be or (if an order were made under this sub-paragraph) would be receiving instruction at an educational establishment or undergoing training for a trade, profession or vocation, whether or not while in gainful employment; or
   (b)   there are special circumstances which justify the making of an order under this paragraph,

the court shall have power by order to revive the order from such date as the court may specify, not being earlier than the date of the making of the application.

(7)   Any order which is revived by an order under sub-paragraph (5) may be varied or discharged under that provision, on the application of any person by whom or to whom payments are required to be made under the revived order.

(8)   An order for the making or securing of periodical payments made under paragraph 1 may be varied or discharged, after the death of either parent, on the application of a guardian of the child concerned.

[(9)   Where—
   (a)   an order under paragraph 1(2)(a) or (b) for the making or securing of periodical payments in favour of more than one child ("the order") is in force;
   (b)   the order requires payments specified in it to be made to or for the benefit of more than one child without apportioning those payments between them;

(c) a maintenance assessment ("the assessment") is made with respect to one or more, but not all, of the children with respect to whom those payments are to be made; and

(d) an application is made, before the end of the period of 6 months beginning with the date on which the assessment was made, for the variation or discharge of the order,

the court may, in exercise of its powers under paragraph 1 to vary or discharge the order, direct that the variation or discharge shall take effect from the date on which the assessment took effect or any later date.]

[Variation of orders for periodical payments etc made by magistrates' courts

6A.—(1)   Subject to sub-paragraphs (7) and (8), the power of a magistrates' court—

(a) under paragraph 1 or 2 to vary an order for the making of periodical payments, or

(b) under paragraph 5(6) to vary an order for the payment of a lump sum by instalments,

shall include power, if the court is satisfied that payment has not been made in accordance with the order, to exercise one of its powers under paragraphs (a) to (d) of section 59(3) of the Magistrates' Courts Act 1980.

(2)   In any case where—

(a) a magistrates' court has made an order under this Schedule for the making of periodical payments or for the payment of a lump sum by instalments, and

(b) payments under the order are required to be made by any method of payment falling within section 59(6) of the Magistrates' Courts Act 1980 (standing order, etc),

any person entitled to make an application under this Schedule for the variation of the order (in this paragraph referred to as "the applicant") may apply to the clerk to the justices for the petty sessions area for which the court is acting for the order to be varied as mentioned in sub- paragraph (3).

(3)   Subject to sub-paragraph (5), where an application is made under sub-paragraph (2), the clerk, after giving written notice (by post or otherwise) of the application to any interested party and allowing that party, within the period of 14 days beginning with the date of the giving of that notice, an opportunity to make written representations, may vary the order to provide that payments under the order shall be made to the clerk.

(4) The clerk may proceed with an application under sub-paragraph (2) notwithstanding that any such interested party as is referred to in sub-paragraph (3) has not received written notice of the application.

(5) Where an application has been made under sub-paragraph (2), the clerk may, if he considers it inappropriate to exercise his power under sub-paragraph (3), refer the matter to the court which, subject to sub-paragraphs (7) and (8), may vary the order by exercising one of its powers under paragraphs (a) to (d) of section 59(3) of the Magistrates' Courts Act 1980.

(6) Subsection (4) of section 59 of the Magistrates' Courts Act 1980 (power of court to order that account be opened) shall apply for the purposes of sub-paragraphs (1) and (5) as it applies for the purposes of that section.

(7) Before varying the order by exercising one of its powers under paragraphs (a) to (d) of section 59(3) of the Magistrates' Courts Act 1980, the court shall have regard to any representations made by the parties to the application.

(8) If the court does not propose to exercise its power [under paragraph (c), (cc) or (d)] of subsection (3) of section 59 of the Magistrates' Courts Act 1980, the court shall, unless upon representations expressly made in that behalf by the applicant for the order it is satisfied that it is undesirable to do so, exercise its power under paragraph (b) of that subsection.

(9) None of the powers of the court, or of the clerk to the justices, conferred by this paragraph shall be exercisable in relation to an order under this Schedule for the making of periodical payments, or for the payment of a lump sum by instalments, which is not a qualifying maintenance order (within the meaning of section 59 of the Magistrates' Courts Act 1980).

(10) In sub-paragraphs (3) and (4) "interested party", in relation to an application made by the applicant under sub-paragraph (2), means a person who would be entitled to be a party to an application for the variation of the order made by the applicant under any other provision of this Schedule if such an application were made.]

Variation of orders for secured periodical payments after death of parent

7.—(1) Where the parent liable to make payments under a secured periodical payments order has died, the persons who may apply for the variation or discharge of the order shall include the personal representatives of the deceased parent.

(2)   No application for the variation of the order shall, except with the permission of the court, be made after the end of the period of six months from the date on which representation in regard to the estate of that parent is first taken out.

(3)   The personal representatives of a deceased person against whom a secured periodical payments order was made shall not be liable for having distributed any part of the estate of the deceased after the end of the period of six months referred to in sub-paragraph (2) on the ground that they ought to have taken into account the possibility that the court might permit an application for variation to be made after that period by the person entitled to payments under the order.

(4)   Sub-paragraph (3) shall not prejudice any power to recover any part of the estate so distributed arising by virtue of the variation of an order in accordance with this paragraph.

(5)   Where an application to vary a secured periodical payments order is made after the death of the parent liable to make payments under the order, the circumstances to which the court is required to have regard under paragraph 6(1) shall include the changed circumstances resulting from the death of the parent.

(6)   In considering for the purposes of sub-paragraph (2) the question when representation was first taken out, a grant limited to settled land or to trust property shall be left out of account and a grant limited to real estate or to personal estate shall be left out of account unless a grant limited to the remainder of the estate has previously been made or is made at the same time.

(7)   In this paragraph "secured periodical payments order" means an order for secured periodical payments under paragraph 1(2)(b).

Financial relief under other enactments

8.—(1)   This paragraph applies where a residence order is made with respect to a child at a time when there is in force an order ("the financial relief order") made under any enactment other than this Act and requiring a person to contribute to the child's maintenance.

(2)   Where this paragraph applies, the court may, on the application of—
  (a) any person required by the financial relief order to contribute to the child's maintenance; or
  (b) any person in whose favour a residence order with respect to the child is in force,

make an order revoking the financial relief order, or varying it by altering the amount of any sum payable under the order or by substituting the applicant for the person to whom any such sum is otherwise payable under that order.

Interim orders

9.—(1)   Where an application is made under paragraph 1 or 2 the court may, at any time before it disposes of the application, make an interim order—
  (a) requiring either or both parents to make such periodical payments, at such times and for such term as the court thinks fit; and
  (b) giving any direction which the court thinks fit.

(2)   An interim order made under this paragraph may provide for payments to be made from such date as the court may specify, [except that, subject to paragraph 3(5) and (6), the date shall not be] earlier than the date of the making of the application under paragraph 1 or 2.

(3)   An interim order made under this paragraph shall cease to have effect when the application is disposed of or, if earlier, on the date specified for the purposes of this paragraph in the interim order.

(4)   An interim order in which a date has been specified for the purposes of sub-paragraph (3) may be varied by substituting a later date.

Alteration of maintenance agreements

10.—(1)   In this paragraph and in paragraph 11 "maintenance agreement" means any agreement in writing made with respect to a child, whether before or after the commencement of this paragraph, which—
  (a) is or was made between the father and mother of the child; and
  (b) contains provision with respect to the making or securing of payments, or the disposition or use of any property, for the maintenance or education of the child,

and any such provisions are in this paragraph, and paragraph 11, referred to as "financial arrangements".

(2)   Where a maintenance agreement is for the time being subsisting and each of the parties to the agreement is for the time being either domiciled or resident in England and Wales, then, either party may apply to the court for an order under this paragraph.

(3)   If the court to which the application is made is satisfied either—
   (a) that, by reason of a change in the circumstances in the light of which any financial arrangements contained in the agreement were made (including a change foreseen by the parties when making the agreement), the agreement should be altered so as to make different financial arrangements; or
   (b) that the agreement does not contain proper financial arrangements with respect to the child,

then that court may by order make such alterations in the agreement by varying or revoking any financial arrangements contained in it as may appear to it to be just having regard to all the circumstances.

(4)   If the maintenance agreement is altered by an order under this paragraph, the agreement shall have effect thereafter as if the alteration had been made by agreement between the parties and for valuable consideration.

(5)   Where a court decides to make an order under this paragraph altering the maintenance agreement—
   (a) by inserting provision for the making or securing by one of the parties to the agreement of periodical payments for the maintenance of the child; or
   (b) by increasing the rate of periodical payments required to be made or secured by one of the parties for the maintenance of the child,

then, in deciding the term for which under the agreement as altered by the order the payments or (as the case may be) the additional payments attributable to the increase are to be made or secured for the benefit of the child, the court shall apply the provisions of sub-paragraphs (1) and (2) of paragraph 3 as if the order were an order under paragraph 1(2)(a) or (b).

(6)   A magistrates' court shall not entertain an application under sub-paragraph (2) unless both the parties to the agreement are resident in England and Wales and at least one of the parties is resident in the commission area (within the meaning of [the Justices of the Peace Act

1997]) for which the court is appointed, and shall not have power to make any order on such an application except—

   (a) in a case where the agreement contains no provision for periodical payments by either of the parties, an order inserting provision for the making by one of the parties of periodical payments for the maintenance of the child;

   (b) in a case where the agreement includes provision for the making by one of the parties of periodical payments, an order increasing or reducing the rate of, or terminating, any of those payments.

(7)   For the avoidance of doubt it is hereby declared that nothing in this paragraph affects any power of a court before which any proceedings between the parties to a maintenance agreement are brought under any other enactment to make an order containing financial arrangements or any right of either party to apply for such an order in such proceedings.

11.—(1)   Where a maintenance agreement provides for the continuation, after the death of one of the parties, of payments for the maintenance of a child and that party dies domiciled in England and Wales, the surviving party or the personal representatives of the deceased party may apply to the High Court or a county court for an order under paragraph 10.

(2)   If a maintenance agreement is altered by a court on an application under this paragraph, the agreement shall have effect thereafter as if the alteration had been made, immediately before the death, by agreement between the parties and for valuable consideration.

(3)   An application under this paragraph shall not, except with leave of the High Court or a county court, be made after the end of the period of six months beginning with the day on which representation in regard to the estate of the deceased is first taken out.

(4)   In considering for the purposes of sub-paragraph (3) the question when representation was first taken out, a grant limited to settled land or to trust property shall be left out of account and a grant limited to real estate or to personal estate shall be left out of account unless a grant limited to the remainder of the estate has previously been made or is made at the same time.

(5)   A county court shall not entertain an application under this paragraph, or an application for leave to make an application under this paragraph, unless it would have jurisdiction to hear and determine proceedings for an order under section 2 of the Inheritance (Provision for Family and Dependants) Act 1975 in relation to the deceased's estate by virtue of section 25 of the County Courts Act 1984 (jurisdiction under the Act of 1975).

(6)   The provisions of this paragraph shall not render the personal representatives of the deceased liable for having distributed any part of the estate of the deceased after the expiry of the period of six months referred to in sub-paragraph (3) on the ground that they ought to have taken into account the possibility that a court might grant leave for an application by virtue of this paragraph to be made by the surviving party after that period.

(7)   Sub-paragraph (6) shall not prejudice any power to recover any part of the estate so distributed arising by virtue of the making of an order in pursuance of this paragraph.

Enforcement of orders for maintenance

12.—(1)   Any person for the time being under an obligation to make payments in pursuance of any order for the payment of money made by a magistrates' court under this Act shall give notice of any change of address to such person (if any) as may be specified in the order.

(2)   Any person failing without reasonable excuse to give such a notice shall be guilty of an offence and liable on summary conviction to a fine not exceeding level 2 on the standard scale.

(3)   An order for the payment of money made by a magistrates' court under this Act shall be enforceable as a magistrates' court maintenance order within the meaning of section 150(1) of the Magistrates' Courts Act 1980.

Direction for settlement of instrument by conveyancing counsel

13.   Where the High Court or a county court decides to make an order under this Act for the securing of periodical payments or for the transfer or settlement of property, it may direct that the matter be referred to one of the conveyancing counsel of the court to settle a proper instrument to be executed by all necessary parties.

Financial provision for child resident in country outside England and Wales

14.—(1)   Where one parent of a child lives in England and Wales and the child lives outside England and Wales with—

(a) another parent of his;

(b) a guardian of his; or

(c) a person in whose favour a residence order is in force with respect to the child,

the child shall have power, on an application made by any of the persons mentioned in paragraphs (a) to (c), to make one or both of the orders mentioned in paragraph 1(2)(a) and (b) against the parent living in England and Wales.

(2)   Any reference in this Act to the powers of the court under paragraph 1(2) or to an order made under paragraph 1(2) shall include a reference to the powers which the court has by virtue of sub-paragraph (1) or (as the case may be) to an order made by virtue of sub-paragraph (1).

Local authority contribution to child's maintenance

15.—(1)   Where a child lives, or is to live, with a person as the result of a residence order, a local authority may make contributions to that person towards the cost of the accommodation and maintenance of the child.

(2)   Sub-paragraph (1) does not apply where the person with whom the child lives, or is to live, is a parent of the child or the husband or wife of a parent of the child.

Interpretation

16.—(1)   In this Schedule "child" includes, in any case where an application is made under paragraph 2 or 6 in relation to a person who has reached the age of eighteen, that person.

(2)   In this Schedule, except paragraphs 2 and 15, "parent" includes any party to a marriage (whether or not subsisting) in relation to whom the child concerned is a child of the family; and for this purpose any reference to either parent or both parents shall be construed as references to any parent of his and to all of his parents.

[(3)   In this Schedule, "maintenance assessment" has the same meaning as it has in the Child Support Act 1991 by virtue of section 54 of that Act as read with any regulations in force under that section.]

Commencement: 1 April 1992 (para 6A); 14 October 1991 (remainder).

Para 1: sub-para (7) added by the Courts and Legal Services Act 1990, s 116, Sch 16, para 10(2).

Para 2: sub-para (6)(b) repealed by the Child Support Act 1991, s 58(14).

Para 3: words in square brackets in sub-para (1) inserted, and sub-paras (5)–(8) added, by the Maintenance Orders (Backdating) Order 1993, SI 1993/623, art 2, Sch 1, paras 10, 11.

Para 5: words in square brackets in sub-para (2) substituted by the Transfer of Functions (Magistrates' Courts and Family Law) Order 1992, SI 1992/709, art 3(2), Sch 2.

Para 6: words in square brackets in sub-para (3) substituted, and sub-para (9) added, by SI 1993/623, art2, Sch 1, paras 12, 13.

Para 6A: inserted by the Maintenance Enforcement Act 1991, s 6; words in square brackets in sub-para (8) substituted by the Child Support Act 1991 (Consequential Amendments) Order 1994, SI1994/731, art4.

Para 9: words in square brackets in sub-para (2) substituted by the Maintenance Orders (Backdating) Order 1993, SI 1993/623, art 2, Sch 1, para 14.

Para 10: words in square brackets substituted by the Justices of the Peace Act 1997, s 73(2), Sch 5, para 27.

Para 16: sub-para (3) added by SI 1993/623, art 2, Sch 1, para 15.

SCHEDULE 2
LOCAL AUTHORITY SUPPORT FOR CHILDREN AND FAMILIES
Sections 17, 23, 29

PART I
PROVISION OF SERVICES FOR FAMILIES

Identification of children in need and provision of information

1.—(1) Every local authority shall take reasonable steps to identify the extent to which there are children in need within their area.

(2)   Every local authority shall—
  (a) publish information—
    (i) about services provided by them under sections 17, 18, 20 and 24; and
    (ii) where they consider it appropriate, about the provision by others (including, in particular, voluntary organisations) of services which the authority have power to provide under those sections; and
  (b) take such steps as are reasonably practicable to ensure that those who might benefit from the services receive the information relevant to them.

[Children's services plans

1A.—(1)   Every local authority shall, on or before 31st March 1997—
   (a) review their provision of services under sections 17, 20, 21, 23 and 24; and
   (b) having regard to that review and to their most recent review under section 19, prepare and publish a plan for the provision of services under Part III.

(2)   Every local authority—
   (a) shall, from time to time review the plan prepared by them under sub-paragraph (1)(b) (as modified or last substituted under this sub-paragraph), and
   (b) may, having regard to that review and to their most recent review under section 19, prepare and publish—
      (i) modifications (or, as the case may be, further modifications) to the plan reviewed; or
      (ii) a plan in substitution for that plan.

(3)   In carrying out any review under this paragraph and in preparing any plan or modifications to a plan, a local authority shall consult—
   (a) every health authority the whole or any part of whose area lies within the area of the local authority;
   (b) every National Health Service trust which manages a hospital, establishment or facility (within the meaning of the National Health Service and Community Care Act 1990) in the authority's area;
   (c) if the local authority is not itself a local education authority, every local education authority the whole or any part of whose area lies within the area of the local authority;
   (d) any organisation which represents schools in the authority's area which are grant- maintained schools or grant-maintained special schools (within the meaning of the Education Act 1993);
   (e) the governing body of every such school in the authority's area which is not so represented;
   (f) such voluntary organisations as appear to the local authority—
      (i) to represent the interests of persons who use or are likely to use services provided by the local authority under Part III; or
      (ii) to provide services in the area of the local authority which, were they to be provided by the local authority, might be categorised as services provided under that Part;
   (g) the chief constable of the police force for the area;
   (h) the probation committee for the area;
   (i) such other persons as appear to the local authority to be appropriate; and
   (j) such other persons as the Secretary of State may direct.

(4)   Every local authority shall, within 28 days of receiving a written request from the Secretary of State, submit to him a copy of—
  (a) the plan prepared by them under sub-paragraph (1); or
  (b) where that plan has been modified or substituted, the plan as modified or last substituted.]

Maintenance of a register of disabled children

2.—(1)   Every local authority shall open and maintain a register of disabled children within their area.

(2)   The register may be kept by means of a computer.

Assessment of children's needs

3.   Where it appears to a local authority that a child within their area is in need, the authority may assess his needs for the purposes of this Act at the same time as any assessment of his needs is made under—
  (a) the Chronically Sick and Disabled Persons Act 1970;
  (b) [Part IV of the Education Act 1996];
  (c) the Disabled Persons (Services, Consultation and Representation) Act 1986; or
  (d) any other enactment.

Prevention of neglect and abuse

4.—(1)   Every local authority shall take reasonable steps, through the provision of services under Part III of this Act, to prevent children within their area suffering ill-treatment or neglect.

(2)   Where a local authority believe that a child who is at any time within their area—
  (a) is likely to suffer harm; but
  (b) lives or proposes to live in the area of another local authority

they shall inform that other local authority.

(3)   When informing that other local authority they shall specify—
  (a) the harm that they believe he is likely to suffer; and
  (b) (if they can) where the child lives or proposes to live.

Provision of accommodation in order to protect child

5.—(1) Where—
    (a) it appears to a local authority that a child who is living on particular premises is suffering, or is likely to suffer, ill treatment at the hands of another person who is living on those premises; and
    (b) that other person proposes to move from the premises,

the authority may assist that other person to obtain alternative accommodation.

(2)   Assistance given under this paragraph may be in cash.

(3)   Subsections (7) to (9) of section 17 shall apply in relation to assistance given under this paragraph as they apply in relation to assistance given under that section.

Provision for disabled children

6.   Every local authority shall provide services designed—
    (a) to minimise the effect on disabled children within their area of their disabilities; and
    (b) to give such children the opportunity to lead lives which are as normal as possible.

Provision to reduce need for care proceedings etc

7.   Every local authority shall take reasonable steps designed—
    (a) to reduce the need to bring—
        (i) proceedings for care or supervision orders with respect to children within their area;
        (ii) criminal proceedings against such children;
        (iii) any family or other proceedings with respect to such children which might lead to them being placed in the authority's care; or
        (iv) proceedings under the inherent jurisdiction of the High Court with respect to children;
    (b) to encourage children within their area not to commit criminal offences; and
    (c) to avoid the need for children within their area to be placed in secure accommodation.

Provision for children living with their families

8.   Every local authority shall make such provision as they consider appropriate for the following services to be available with respect to children in need within their area while they are living with their families—
  (a) advice, guidance and counselling;
  (b) occupational, social, cultural, or recreational activities;
  (c) home help (which may include laundry facilities);
  (d) facilities for, or assistance with, travelling to and from home for the purpose of taking advantage of any other service provided under this Act or of any similar service;
  (e) assistance to enable the child concerned and his family to have a holiday.

Family centres

9.—(1) Every local authority shall provide such family centres as they consider appropriate in relation to children within their area.

(2)   "Family centre" means a centre at which any of the persons mentioned in sub-paragraph (3) may—
  (a) attend for occupational, social, cultural or recreational activities;
  (b) attend for advice, guidance or counselling; or
  (c) be provided with accommodation while he is receiving advice, guidance or counselling.

(3)   The persons are—
  (a) a child;
  (b) his parents;
  (c) any person who is not a parent of his but who has parental responsibility for him;
  (d) any other person who is looking after him.

Maintenance of the family home

10.   Every local authority shall take such steps as are reasonably practicable, where any child within their area who is in need and whom they are not looking after is living apart from his family—
  (a) to enable him to live with his family; or
  (b) to promote contact between him and his family,

if, in their opinion, it is necessary to do so in order to safeguard or promote his welfare.

Duty to consider racial groups to which children in need belong

11.   Every local authority shall, in making any arrangements—
    (a) for the provision of day care within their area; or
    (b) designed to encourage persons to act as local authority foster parents,

have regard to the different racial groups to which children within their area who are in need belong.

NOTES

Commencement: 1 April 1996 (para 1A); 14 October 1991 (remainder).

Para 1A: inserted by the Children Act 1989 (Amendment) (Children's Services Planning) Order 1996, SI 1996/785, art 2.

Para 3: words in square brackets substituted by the Education Act 1996, s 582(1), Sch 37, Pt I, para 92.

PART II
CHILDREN LOOKED AFTER BY LOCAL AUTHORITIES

Regulations as to placing of children with local authority foster parents

12.   Regulations under section 23(2)(a) may, in particular, make provision—
    (a) with regard to the welfare of children placed with local authority foster parents;
    (b) as to the arrangements to be made by local authorities in connection with the health and education of such children;
    (c) as to the records to be kept by local authorities;
    (d) for securing that a child is not placed with a local authority foster parent unless that person is for the time being approved as a local authority foster parent by such local authority as may be prescribed;
    (e) for securing that where possible the local authority foster parent with whom a child is to be placed is—
        (i)   of the same religious persuasion as the child; or
        (ii) gives an undertaking that the child will be brought up in that religious persuasion;
    (f) for securing that children placed with local authority foster parents, and the premises in which they are accommodated, will be supervised and inspected by a local authority and that the children will be removed from those premises if their welfare appears to require it;
    (g) as to the circumstances in which local authorities may make arrangements for duties imposed on them by the regulations to be discharged, on their behalf.

Regulations as to arrangements under section 23(2)(f)

13.   Regulations under section 23(2)(f) may, in particular, make provisions as to—
- (a) the persons to be notified of any proposed arrangements;
- (b) the opportunities such persons are to have to make representations in relation to the arrangements proposed;
- (c) the persons to be notified of any proposed changes in arrangements;
- (d) the records to be kept by local authorities;
- (e) the supervision by local authorities of any arrangements made.

Regulations as to conditions under which child in care is allowed to live with parent, etc

14.   Regulations under section 23(5) may, in particular, impose requirements on a local authority as to—
- (a) the making of any decision by a local authority to allow a child to live with any person falling within section 23(4) (including requirements as to those who must be consulted before the decision is made, and those who must be notified when it has been made);
- (b) the supervision or medical examination of the child concerned;
- (c) the removal of the child, in such circumstances as may be prescribed, from the care of the person with whom he has been allowed to live;
- [(d) the records to be kept by local authorities.]

Promotion and maintenance of contact between child and family

15.—(1)   Where a child is being looked after by a local authority, the authority shall, unless it is not reasonably practicable or consistent with his welfare, endeavour to promote contact between the child and—
- (a) his parents;
- (b) any person who is not a parent of his but who has parental responsibility for him; and
- (c) any relative, friend or other person connected with him.

(2)   Where a child is being looked after by a local authority—
- (a) the authority shall take such steps as are reasonably practicable to secure that—
  - (i) his parents; and
  - (ii) any person who is not a parent of his but who has parental responsibility for him,

are kept informed of where he is being accommodated; and

(b) every such person shall secure that the authority are kept informed of his or her address.

(3)   Where a local authority ("the receiving authority") take over the provision of accommodation for a child from another local authority ("the transferring authority") under section 20(2)—
  (a) the receiving authority shall (where reasonably practicable) inform—
    (i)   the child's parents; and
    (ii) any person who is not a parent of his but who has parental responsibility for him;
  (b) sub-paragraph (2)(a) shall apply to the transferring authority, as well as the receiving authority, until at least one such person has been informed of the change; and
  (c) sub-paragraph (2)(b) shall not require any person to inform the receiving authority of his address until he has been so informed.

(4)   Nothing in this paragraph requires a local authority to inform any person of the whereabouts of a child if—
  (a) the child is in the care of the authority; and
  (b) the authority has reasonable cause to believe that informing the person would prejudice the child's welfare.

(5)   Any person who fails (without reasonable excuse) to comply with sub-paragraph (2)(b) shall be guilty of an offence and liable on summary conviction to a fine not exceeding level 2 on the standard scale.

(6)   It shall be a defence in any proceedings under sub-paragraph (5) to prove that the defendant was residing at the same address as another person who was the child's parent or had parental responsibility for the child and had reasonable cause to believe that the other person had informed the appropriate authority that both of them were residing at that address.

Visits to or by children: expenses

16.—(1)   This paragraph applies where—
  (a) a child is being looked after by a local authority; and
  (b) the conditions mentioned in sub-paragraph (3) are satisfied.

(2)   The authority may—
  (a) make payments to—
    (i)   a parent of the child;
    (ii) any person who is not a parent of his but who has parental responsibility for him; or

(iii) any relative, friend or other person connected with him,
in respect of travelling, subsistence or other expenses incurred by
that person in visiting the child; or
(b) make payments to the child, or to any person on his behalf, in respect
of travelling, subsistence or other expenses incurred by or on behalf
of the child in his visiting—
    (i) a parent of his;
    (ii) any person who is not a parent of his but who has parental
responsibility for him; or
    (iii) any relative, friend or other person connected with him.

(3) The conditions are that—
    (a) it appears to the authority that the visit in question could not
otherwise be made without undue financial hardship; and
    (b) the circumstances warrant the making of the payments.

Appointment of visitor for child who is not being visited

17.—(1) Where it appears to a local authority in relation to any child that
they are looking after that—
    (a) communication between the child and—
        (i) a parent of his, or
        (ii) any person who is not a parent of his but who has parental
responsibility for him,

has been infrequent; or
    (b) he has not visited or been visited by (or lived with) any such person
during the preceding twelve months,

and that it would be in the child's best interests for an independent person
to be appointed to be his visitor for the purposes of this paragraph, they
shall appoint such a visitor.

(2) A person so appointed shall—
    (a) have the duty of visiting, advising and befriending the child; and
    (b) be entitled to recover from the authority who appointed him any
reasonable expenses incurred by him for the purposes of his functions
under this paragraph.

(3) A person's appointment as a visitor in pursuance of this paragraph
shall be determined if—
    (a) he gives notice in writing to the authority who appointed him that
he resigns the appointment; or

(b) the authority give him notice in writing that they have terminated it.

(4)   The determination of such an appointment shall not prejudice any duty under this paragraph to make a further appointment.

(5)   Where a local authority propose to appoint a visitor for a child under this paragraph, the appointment shall not be made if—
(a) the child objects to it; and
(b) the authority are satisfied that he has sufficient understanding to make an informed decision.

(6)   Where a visitor has been appointed for a child under this paragraph, the local authority shall determine the appointment if—
(a) the child objects to its continuing; and
(b) the authority are satisfied that he has sufficient understanding to make an informed decision.

(7)   The Secretary of State may make regulations as to the circumstances in which a person appointed as a visitor under this paragraph is to be regarded as independent of the local authority appointing him.

Power to guarantee apprenticeship deeds etc

18.—(1)   While a child is being looked after by a local authority, or is a person qualifying for advice and assistance, the authority may undertake any obligation by way of guarantee under any deed of apprenticeship or articles of clerkship which he enters into.

(2)   Where a local authority have undertaken any such obligation under any deed or articles they may at any time (whether or not they are still looking after the person concerned) undertake the like obligation under any supplemental deed or articles.

Arrangements to assist children to live abroad

19.—(1)   A local authority may only arrange for, or assist in arranging for, any child in their care to live outside England and Wales with the approval of the court.

(2)   A local authority may, with the approval of every person who has parental responsibility for the child arrange for, or assist in arranging for, any other child looked after by them to live outside England and Wales.

(3)   The court shall not give its approval under sub-paragraph (1) unless it is satisfied that—
 (a) living outside England and Wales would be in the child's best interests;
 (b) suitable arrangements have been, or will be, made for his reception and welfare in the country in which he will live;
 (c) the child has consented to living in that country; and
 (d) every person who has parental responsibility for the child has consented to his living in that country.

(4)   Where the court is satisfied that the child does not have sufficient understanding to give or withhold his consent, it may disregard sub-paragraph (3)(c) and give its approval if the child is to live in the country concerned with a parent, guardian, or other suitable person.

(5)   Where a person whose consent is required by sub-paragraph (3)(d) fails to give his consent, the court may disregard that provision and give its approval if it is satisfied that that person—
 (a) cannot be found;
 (b) is incapable of consenting; or
 (c) is withholding his consent unreasonably.

(6)   Section 56 of the Adoption Act 1976 (which requires authority for the taking or sending abroad for adoption of a child who is a British subject) shall not apply in the case of any child who is to live outside England and Wales with the approval of the court given under this paragraph.

(7)   Where a court decides to give its approval under this paragraph it may order that its decision is not to have effect during the appeal period.

(8)   In sub-paragraph (7) "the appeal period" means—
 (a) where an appeal is made against the decision, the period between the making of the decision and the determination of the appeal; and
 (b) otherwise, the period during which an appeal may be made against the decision.

Death of children being looked after by local authorities

20.—(1)   If a child who is being looked after by a local authority dies, the authority—
 (a) shall notify the Secretary of State;
 (b) shall, so far as is reasonably practicable, notify the child's parents and every person who is not a parent of his but who has parental responsibility for him;

(c) may, with the consent (so far as it is reasonably practicable to obtain it) of every person who has parental responsibility for the child, arrange for the child's body to be buried or cremated; and

(d) may, if the conditions mentioned in sub-paragraph (2) are satisfied, make payments to any person who has parental responsibility for the child, or any relative, friend or other person connected with the child, in respect of travelling, subsistence or other expenses incurred by that person in attending the child's funeral.

(2)   The conditions are that—
   (a) it appears to the authority that the person concerned could not otherwise attend the child's funeral without undue financial hardship; and
   (b) that the circumstances warrant the making of the payments.

(3)   Sub-paragraph (1) does not authorise cremation where it does not accord with the practice of the child's religious persuasion.

(4)   Where a local authority have exercised their power under sub-paragraph (1)(c) with respect to a child who was under sixteen when he died, they may recover from any parent of the child any expenses incurred by them.

(5)   Any sums so recoverable shall, without prejudice to any other method of recovery, be recoverable summarily as a civil debt.

(6)   Nothing in this paragraph affects any enactment regulating or authorising the burial, cremation or anatomical examination of the body of a deceased person.

NOTES

Para 14: sub-para (d) added by the Courts and Legal Services Act 1990, s 116, Sch 16, para 26.

PART III
CONTRIBUTIONS TOWARDS MAINTENANCE OF CHILDREN LOOKED
AFTER BY LOCAL AUTHORITIES

Liability to contribute

21.—(1)   Where a local authority are looking after a child (other than in the cases mentioned in sub-paragraph (7)) they shall consider whether they should recover contributions towards the child's maintenance from any person liable to contribute ("a contributor").

(2)   An authority may only recover contributions from a contributor if they consider it reasonable to do so.

(3)   The persons liable to contribute are—
   (a) where the child is under sixteen, each of his parents;
   (b) where he has reached the age of sixteen, the child himself.

(4)   A parent is not liable to contribute during any period when he is in receipt of income support[, family credit or disability working allowance] under the [Part VII of the Social Security Contributions and Benefits Act 1992] [or of an income-based jobseeker's allowance].

(5)   A person is not liable to contribute towards the maintenance of a child in the care of a local authority in respect of any period during which the child is allowed by the authority (under section 23(5)) to live with a parent of his.

(6)   A contributor is not obliged to make any contribution towards a child's maintenance except as agreed or determined in accordance with this Part of this Schedule.

(7)   The cases are where the child is looked after by a local authority under—
   (a) section 21;
   (b) an interim care order;
   (c) section 53 of the Children and Young Persons Act 1933.

Agreed contributions

22.—(1) Contributions towards a child's maintenance may only be recovered if the local authority have served a notice ("a contribution notice") on the contributor specifying—
   (a) the weekly sum which they consider that he should contribute; and
   (b) arrangements for payment.

(2)   The contribution notice must be in writing and dated.

(3)   Arrangements for payment shall, in particular, include—
   (a) the date on which liability to contribute begins (which must not be earlier than the date of the notice);

(b) the date on which liability under the notice will end (if the child has not before that date ceased to be looked after by the authority); and

(c) the date on which the first payment is to be made.

(4)   The authority may specify in a contribution notice a weekly sum which is a standard contribution determined by them for all children looked after by them.

(5)   The authority may not specify in a contribution notice a weekly sum greater than that which they consider—

(a) they would normally be prepared to pay if they had placed a similar child with local authority foster parents; and

(b) it is reasonably practicable for the contributor to pay (having regard to his means).

(6)   An authority may at any time withdraw a contribution notice (without prejudice to their power to serve another).

(7)   Where the authority and the contributor agree—

(a) the sum which the contributor is to contribute; and

(b) arrangements for payment,

(whether as specified in the contribution notice or otherwise) and the contributor notifies the authority in writing that he so agrees, the authority may recover summarily as a civil debt any contribution which is overdue and unpaid.

(8)   A contributor may, by serving a notice in writing on the authority, withdraw his agreement in relation to any period of liability falling after the date of service of the notice.

(9)   Sub-paragraph (7) is without prejudice to any other method of recovery.

Contribution orders

23.—(1)   Where a contributor has been served with a contribution notice and has—

(a) failed to reach any agreement with the local authority as mentioned in paragraph 22(7) within the period of one month beginning with the day on which the contribution notice was served; or

(b) served a notice under paragraph 22(8) withdrawing his agreement,

the authority may apply to the court for an order under this paragraph.

(2)   On such an application the court may make an order ("a contribution order") requiring the contributor to contribute a weekly sum towards the child's maintenance in accordance with arrangements for payment specified by the court.

(3)   A contribution order—
  (a) shall not specify a weekly sum greater than that specified in the contribution notice; and
  (b) shall be made with due regard to the contributor's means.

(4)   A contribution order shall not—
  (a) take effect before the date specified in the contribution notice; or
  (b) have effect while the contributor is not liable to contribute (by virtue of paragraph 21); or
  (c) remain in force after the child has ceased to be looked after by the authority who obtained the order.

(5)   An authority may not apply to the court under sub-paragraph (1) in relation to a contribution notice which they have withdrawn.

(6)   Where—
  (a) a contribution order is in force;
  (b) the authority serve another contribution notice; and
  (c) the contributor and the authority reach an agreement under paragraph 22(7) in respect of that other contribution notice,

the effect of the agreement shall be to discharge the order from the date on which it is agreed that the agreement shall take effect.

(7)   Where an agreement is reached under sub-paragraph (6) the authority shall notify the court—
  (a) of the agreement; and
  (b) of the date on which it took effect.

(8)   A contribution order may be varied or revoked on the application of the contributor or the authority.

(9)   In proceedings for the variation of a contribution order, the authority shall specify—
  (a) the weekly sum which, having regard to paragraph 22, they propose that the contributor should contribute under the order as varied; and
  (b) the proposed arrangements for payment.

(10)   Where a contribution order is varied, the order—
  (a) shall not specify a weekly sum greater than that specified by the authority in the proceedings for variation; and
  (b) shall be made with due regard to the contributor's means.

(11)   An appeal shall lie in accordance with rules of court from any order made under this paragraph.

Enforcement of contribution orders etc

24.—(1)   A contribution order made by a magistrates' court shall be enforceable as a magistrates' court maintenance order (within the meaning of section 150(1) of the Magistrates' Courts Act 1980).

(2)   Where a contributor has agreed, or has been ordered, to make contributions to a local authority, any other local authority within whose area the contributor is for the time being living may—
  (a) at the request of the local authority who served the contributions notice; and
  (b) subject to agreement as to any sum to be deducted in respect of services rendered,

collect from the contributor any contributions due on behalf of the authority who served the notice.

(3)   In sub-paragraph (2) the reference to any other local authority includes a reference to—
  (a) a local authority within the meaning of section 1(2) of the Social Work (Scotland) Act 1968; and
  (b) a Health and Social Services Board established under Article 16 of the Health and Personal Social Services (Northern Ireland) Order 1972.

(4)   The power to collect sums under sub-paragraph (2) includes the power to—
  (a) receive and give a discharge for any contributions due; and
  (b) (if necessary) enforce payment of any contributions,

even though those contributions may have fallen due at a time when the contributor was living elsewhere.

(5)   Any contribution collected under sub-paragraph (2) shall be paid (subject to any agreed deduction) to the local authority who served the contribution notice.

(6)   In any proceedings under this paragraph, a document which purports to be—

(a) a copy of an order made by a court under or by virtue of paragraph 23; and

(b) certified as a true copy by the clerk of the court,

shall be evidence of the order.

(7)   In any proceedings under this paragraph, a certificate which—

(a) purports to be signed by the clerk or some other duly authorised officer of the local authority who obtained the contribution order; and

(b) states that any sum due to the authority under the order is overdue and unpaid,

shall be evidence that the sum is overdue and unpaid.

Regulations

25.   The Secretary of State may make regulations—

(a) as to the considerations which a local authority must take into account in deciding—

(i)   whether it is reasonable to recover contributions; and

(ii) what the arrangements for payment should be;

(b) as to the procedures they must follow in reaching agreements with—

(i)   contributors (under paragraphs 22 and 23); and

(ii) any other local authority (under paragraph 23).

NOTES

Para 21: words in first pair of square brackets in sub-para (4) substituted by the Disability Living Allowance and Disability Working Allowance Act 1991, s 7, Sch 3, Pt II, para 15, words in second pair of square brackets substituted by the Social Security (Consequential Provisions) Act 1992, s 4, Sch 2, para 108(c), words in third pair of square brackets added by the Jobseekers Act 1995, s 41(4), Sch 2, para 19(5).

SCHEDULE 3
SUPERVISION ORDERS

Sections 35, 36

PART I
GENERAL

Meaning of "responsible person"

1.   In this Schedule, "the responsible person", in relation to a supervised child, means—
  (a) any person who has parental responsibility for the child; and
  (b) any other person with whom the child is living.

Power of supervisor to give directions to supervised child

2.—(1)   A supervision order may require the supervised child to comply with any directions given from time to time by the supervisor which require him to do all or any of the following things—
  (a) to live at a place or places specified in the directions for a period or periods so specified;
  (b) to present himself to a person or persons specified in the directions at a place or places and on a day or days so specified;
  (c) to participate in activities specified in the directions on a day or days so specified.

(2)   It shall be for the supervisor to decide whether, and to what extent, he exercises his power to give directions and to decide the form of any directions which he gives.

(3)   Sub-paragraph (1) does not confer on a supervisor power to give directions in respect of any medical or psychiatric examination or treatment (which are matters dealt with in paragraphs 4 and 5).

Imposition of obligations on responsible person

3.—(1)   With the consent of any responsible person, a supervision order may include a requirement—
  (a) that he take all reasonable steps to ensure that the supervised child complies with any direction given by the supervisor under paragraph 2;

(b) that he take all reasonable steps to ensure that the supervised child complies with any requirement included in the order under paragraph 4 or 5;

(c) that he comply with any directions given by the supervisor requiring him to attend at a place specified in the directions for the purpose of taking part in activities so specified.

(2)   A direction given under sub-paragraph (1)(c) may specify the time at which the responsible person is to attend and whether or not the supervised child is required to attend with him.

(3)   A supervision order may require any person who is a responsible person in relation to the supervised child to keep the supervisor informed of his address, if it differs from the child's.

Psychiatric and medical examinations

4.—(1) A supervision order may require the supervised child—
(a) to submit to a medical or psychiatric examination; or
(b) to submit to any such examination from time to time as directed by the supervisor.

(2)   Any such examination shall be required to be conducted—
(a) by, or under the direction of, such registered medical practitioner as may be specified in the order;
(b) at a place specified in the order and at which the supervised child is to attend as a non-resident patient; or
(c) at—
(i) a health service hospital; or
(ii) in the case of a psychiatric examination, a hospital or mental nursing home,

at which the child is, or is to attend as, a resident patient.

(3)   A requirement of a kind mentioned in sub-paragraph (2)(c) shall not be included unless the court is satisfied, on the evidence of a registered medical practitioner, that—
(a) the child may be suffering from a physical or mental condition that requires, and may be susceptible to, treatment; and
(b) a period as a resident patient is necessary if the examination is to be carried out properly.

(4)   No court shall include a requirement under this paragraph in a supervision order unless it is satisfied that—

(a) where the child has sufficient understanding to make an informed decision, he consents to its inclusion; and

(b) satisfactory arrangements have been, or can be, made for the examination.

Psychiatric and medical treatment

5.—(1) Where a court which proposes to make or vary a supervision order is satisfied, on the evidence of a registered medical practitioner approved for the purposes of section 12 of the Mental Health Act 1983, that the mental condition of the supervised child—

(a) is such as requires, and may be susceptible to, treatment; but

(b) is not such as to warrant his detention in pursuance of a hospital order under Part III of that Act,

the court may include in the order a requirement that the supervised child shall, for a period specified in the order, submit to such treatment as is so specified.

(2) The treatment specified in accordance with sub-paragraph (1) must be—

(a) by, or under the direction of, such registered medical practitioner as may be specified in the order;

(b) as a non-resident patient at such a place as may be so specified; or

(c) as a resident patient in a hospital or mental nursing home.

(3) Where a court which proposes to make or vary a supervision order is satisfied, on the evidence of a registered medical practitioner, that the physical condition of the supervised child is such as requires, and may be susceptible to, treatment, the court may include in the order a requirement that the supervised child shall, for a period specified in the order, submit to such treatment as is so specified.

(4) The treatment specified in accordance with sub-paragraph (3) must be—

(a) by, or under the direction of, such registered medical practitioner as may be specified in the order;

(b) as a non-resident patient at such place as may be so specified; or

(c) as a resident patient in a health service hospital.

(5) No court shall include a requirement under this paragraph in a supervision order unless it is satisfied—

(a) where the child has sufficient understanding to make an informed decision, that he consents to its inclusion; and

(b) that satisfactory arrangements have been, or can be, made for the treatment.

(6)   If a medical practitioner by whom or under whose direction a supervised person is being treated in pursuance of a requirement included in a supervision order by virtue of this paragraph is unwilling to continue to treat or direct the treatment of the supervised child or is of the opinion that—

   (a) the treatment should be continued beyond the period specified in the order;
   (b) the supervised child needs different treatment;
   (c) he is not susceptible to treatment; or
   (d) he does not require further treatment,

the practitioner shall make a report in writing to that effect to the supervisor.

(7)   On receiving a report under this paragraph the supervisor shall refer it to the court, and on such a reference the court may make an order cancelling or varying the requirement.

PART II
MISCELLANEOUS

Life of supervision order

6.—(1)   Subject to sub-paragraph (2) and section 91, a supervision order shall cease to have effect at the end of the period of one year beginning with the date on which it was made.

(2)   A supervision order shall also cease to have effect if an event mentioned in section 25(1)(a) or (b) of the Child Abduction and Custody Act 1985 (termination of existing orders) occurs with respect to the child.

(3)   Where the supervisor applies to the court to extend, or further extend, a supervision order the court may extend the order for such period as it may specify.

(4)   A supervision order may not be extended so as to run beyond the end of the period of three years beginning with the date on which it was made.

7.   . . .

Information to be given to supervisor etc

8.—(1)   A supervision order may require the supervised child—
   (a) to keep the supervisor informed of any change in his address; and
   (b) to allow the supervisor to visit him at the place where he is living.

(2)   The responsible person in relation to any child with respect to whom a supervision order is made shall—
   (a) if asked by the supervisor, inform him of the child's address (if it is known to him); and
   (b) if he is living with the child, allow the supervisor reasonable contact with the child.

Selection of supervisor

9.—(1)   A supervision order shall not designate a local authority as the supervisor unless—
   (a) the authority agree; or
   (b) the supervised child lives or will live within their area.

(2)   A court shall not place a child under the supervision of a probation officer unless—
   (a) the appropriate authority so request; and
   (b) a probation officer is already exercising or has exercised, in relation to another member of the household to which the child belongs, duties imposed on probation officers—[by section 14, or by rules under section 25(2)(c), of the Probation Service Act 1993.]

(3)   In sub-paragraph (2) "the appropriate authority" means the local authority appearing to the court to be the authority in whose area the supervised child lives or will live.

(4)   Where a supervision order places a person under the supervision of a probation officer, the officer shall be selected in accordance with arrangements made by the probation committee for the area in question.

(5)   If the selected probation officer is unable to carry out his duties, or dies, another probation officer shall be selected in the same manner.

Effect of supervision order on earlier orders

10.   The making of a supervision order with respect to any child brings
to an end any earlier care or supervision order which—
  (a) was made with respect to that child; and
  (b) would otherwise continue in force.

Local authority functions and expenditure

11.—(1)   The Secretary of State may make regulations with respect to the
exercise by a local authority of their functions where a child has been
placed under their supervision by a supervision order.

(2)   Where a supervision order requires compliance with directions given
by virtue of this section, any expenditure incurred by the supervisor for
the purposes of the directions shall be defrayed by the local authority
designated in the order.

NOTES

  Para 7: repealed by the Courts and Legal Services Act 1990, ss 116, 125(7),
Sch 16, para 27, Sch 20.
  Para 9: words in square brackets substituted by the Probation Service Act
1993, s 32, Sch 3, para 9(3).

PART III
EDUCATION SUPERVISION ORDERS

Effect of orders

12.—(1)   Where an education supervision order is in force with respect to
a child, it shall be the duty of the supervisor—
  (a) to advise, assist and befriend, and give directions to—
       (i)   the supervised child; and
       (ii) his parents,

in such a way as will, in the opinion of the supervisor, secure that he is
properly educated;
  (b) where any such directions given to—
       (i)   the supervised child; or
       (ii) a parent of his,

have not been complied with, to consider what further steps to take in the exercise of the supervisor's powers under this Act.

(2)　Before giving any directions under sub-paragraph (1) the supervisor shall, so far as is reasonably practicable, ascertain the wishes and feelings of—

(a)　the child; and

(b)　his parents,

including, in particular, their wishes as to the place at which the child should be educated.

(3)　When settling the terms of any such directions, the supervisor shall give due consideration—

(a)　having regard to the child's age and understanding, to such wishes and feelings of his as the supervisor has been able to ascertain; and

(b)　to such wishes and feelings of the child's parents as he has been able to ascertain.

(4)　Directions may be given under this paragraph at any time while the education supervision order is in force.

13.—(1)　Where an education supervision order is in force with respect to a child, the duties of the child's parents under [sections 7 and 444 of the Education Act 1996 (duties to secure education of children and] to secure regular attendance of registered pupils) shall be superseded by their duty to comply with any directions in force under the education supervision order.

(2)　Where an education supervision order is made with respect to a child—

(a)　any school attendance order—

(i)　made under [section 437 of the Education Act 1996] with respect to the child; and

(ii)　in force immediately before the making of the education supervision order,

shall cease to have effect; and

(b)　while the education supervision order remains in force, the following provisions shall not apply with respect to the child—

(i)　[section 437] of that Act (school attendance orders);

(ii)　[section 9 of that Act] (pupils to be educated in accordance with wishes of their parents);

(iii)　[sections 411 and 423 of that Act] (parental preference and appeals against admission decisions);

(c) a supervision order made with respect to the child in criminal proceedings, while the education supervision order is in force, may not include an education requirement of the kind which could otherwise be included under section 12C of the Children and Young Persons Act 1969;

(d) any education requirement of a kind mentioned in paragraph (c), which was in force with respect to the child immediately before the making of the education supervision order, shall cease to have effect.

Effect where child also subject to supervision order

14.—(1) This paragraph applies where an education supervision order and a supervision order, or order under section 7(7)(b) of the Children and Young Persons Act 1969, are in force at the same time with respect to the same child.

(2) Any failure to comply with a direction given by the supervisor under the education supervision order shall be disregarded if it would not have been reasonably practicable to comply with it without failing to comply with a direction given under the other order.

Duration of orders

15.—(1) An education supervision order shall have effect for a period of one year, beginning with the date on which it is made.

(2) An education supervision order shall not expire if, before it would otherwise have expired, the court has (on the application of the authority in whose favour the order was made) extended the period during which it is in force.

(3) Such an application may not be made earlier than three months before the date on which the order would otherwise expire.

(4) The period during which an education supervision order is in force may be extended under sub-paragraph (2) on more than one occasion.

(5) No one extension may be for a period of more than three years.

(6) An education supervision order shall cease to have effect on—
(a) the child's ceasing to be of compulsory school age; or
(b) the making of a care order with respect to the child;

and sub-paragraphs (1) to (4) are subject to this sub-paragraph.

Information to be given to supervisor etc

16.—(1)   An education supervision order may require the child—
  (a) to keep the supervisor informed of any change in his address; and
  (b) to allow the supervisor to visit him at the place where he is living.

(2)   A person who is the parent of a child with respect to whom an education supervision order has been made shall—
  (a) if asked by the supervisor, inform him of the child's address (if it is known to him); and
  (b) if he is living with the child, allow the supervisor reasonable contact with the child.

Discharge of orders

17.—(1)   The court may discharge any education supervision order on the application of—
  (a) the child concerned;
  (b) a parent of his; or
  (c) the local education authority concerned.

(2)   On discharging an education supervision order, the court may direct the local authority within whose area the child lives, or will live, to investigate the circumstances of the child.

Offences

18.—(1)   If a parent of a child with respect to whom an education supervision order is in force persistently fails to comply with a direction given under the order he shall be guilty of an offence.

(2)   It shall be a defence for any person charged with such an offence to prove that—
  (a) he took all reasonable steps to ensure that the direction was complied with;
  (b) the direction was unreasonable; or
  (c) he had complied with—
    (i)   a requirement included in a supervision order made with respect to the child; or
    (ii) directions given under such a requirement,

and that it was not reasonably practicable to comply both with the direction and with the requirement or directions mentioned in this paragraph.

(3) A person guilty of an offence under this paragraph shall be liable on summary conviction to a fine not exceeding level 3 on the standard scale.

Persistent failure of child to comply with directions

19.—(1) Where a child with respect to whom an education supervision order is in force persistently fails to comply with any direction given under the order, the local education authority concerned shall notify the appropriate local authority.

(2) Where a local authority have been notified under sub-paragraph (1) they shall investigate the circumstances of the child.

(3) In this paragraph "the appropriate local authority" has the same meaning as in section 36.

Miscellaneous

20. The Secretary of State may by regulations make provision modifying, or displacing, the provisions of any enactment about education in relation to any child with respect to whom an education supervision order is in force to such extent as appears to the Secretary of State to be necessary or expedient in consequence of the provision made by this Act with respect to such orders.

Interpretation

21. In this Part of this Schedule "parent" has the same meaning as in [the Education Act 1996].

NOTES

Paras 13, 21: words in square brackets substituted by the Education Act 1996, s 582(1), Sch 37, Pt I, para 93.

Human Fertilisation and Embryology Act 1990

(c 37)

An Act to make provision in connection with human embryos and any subsequent development of such embryos; to prohibit certain practices in connection with embryos and gametes; to establish a Human Fertilisation and Embryology Authority; to make provision about the persons who in certain circumstances are to be treated in law as the parents of a child; and to amend the Surrogacy Arrangements Act 1985

[1 November 1990]

Principal terms used

1 Meaning of "embryo", "gamete" and associated expressions

(1)   In this Act, except where otherwise stated—
  (a)   embryo means a live human embryo where fertilisation is complete, and
  (b)   references to an embryo include an egg in the process of fertilisation,

and, for this purpose, fertilisation is not complete until the appearance of a two cellzygote.

(2)   This Act, so far as it governs bringing about the creation of an embryo, applies only to bringing about the creation of an embryo outside the human body; and in this Act—
  (a)   references to embryos the creation of which was brought about *in vitro* (in their application to those where fertilisation is complete) are to those where fertilisation began outside the human body whether or not it was completed there, and
  (b)   references to embryos taken from a woman do not include embryos whose creation was brought about *in vitro*.

(3)   This Act, so far as it governs the keeping or use of an embryo, applies only to keeping or using an embryo outside the human body.

(4)   References in this Act to gametes, eggs or sperm, except where otherwise stated, are to live human gametes, eggs or sperm but references below in this Act to gametes or eggs do not include eggs in the process of fertilisation.

2   Other terms

(1)   In this Act—

"the Authority" means the Human Fertilisation and Embryology Authority established under section 5 of this Act,

"directions" means directions under section 23 of this Act,

"licence" means a licence under Schedule 2 to this Act and, in relation to a licence, "the person responsible" has the meaning given by section 17 of this Act, and

"treatment services" means medical, surgical or obstetric services provided to the public or a section of the public for the purpose of assisting women to carry children.

(2)   References in this Act to keeping, in relation to embryos or gametes, include keeping while preserved, whether preserved by cryopreservation or in any other way; and embryos or gametes so kept are referred to in this Act as "stored" (and "store" and "storage" are to be interpreted accordingly).

(3)   For the purposes of this Act, a woman is not to be treated as carrying a child until the embryo has become implanted.

Activities governed by the Act

3   Prohibitions in connection with embryos

(1)   No person shall—
(a) bring about the creation of an embryo, or
(b) keep or use an embryo,

except in pursuance of a licence.

(2)   No person shall place in a woman—
(a) a live embryo other than a human embryo, or
(b) any live gametes other than human gametes.

(3)   A licence cannot authorise—
(a) keeping or using an embryo after the appearance of the primitive streak,
(b) placing an embryo in any animal,
(c) keeping or using an embryo in any circumstances in which regulations prohibit its keeping or use, or

(d) replacing a nucleus of a cell of an embryo with a nucleus taken from a cell of any person, embryo or subsequent development of an embryo.

(4)   For the purposes of subsection (3)(a) above, the primitive streak is to be taken to have appeared in an embryo not later than the end of the period of 14 days beginning with the day when the gametes are mixed, not counting any time during which the embryo is stored.

[3A   Prohibition in connection with germ cells

(1)   No person shall, for the purpose of providing fertility services for any woman, use female germ cells taken or derived from an embryo or a foetus or use embryos created by using such cells.

(2)   In this section—
  "female germ cells" means cells of the female germ line and includes such
      cells at any stage of maturity and accordingly includes eggs; and
  "fertility services" means medical, surgical or obstetric services provided
      for the purpose of assisting women to carry children.]

NOTES

Commencement: 10 April 1995.
Inserted by the Criminal Justice and Public Order Act 1994, s 156(1), (2).

4   Prohibitions in connection with gametes

(1)   No person shall—
  (a) store any gametes, or
  (b) in the course of providing treatment services for any woman, use the sperm of any man unless the services are being provided for the woman and the man together or use the eggs of any other woman, or
  (c) mix gametes with the live gametes of any animal,

except in pursuance of a licence.

(2)   A licence cannot authorise storing or using gametes in any circumstances in which regulations prohibit their storage or use.

(3)   No person shall place sperm and eggs in a woman in any circumstances specified in regulations except in pursuance of a licence.

(4)   Regulations made by virtue of subsection (3) above may provide that, in relation to licences only to place sperm and eggs in a woman in such

circumstances, sections 12 to 22 of this Act shall have effect with such modifications as may be specified in the regulations.

(5)   Activities regulated by this section or section 3 of this Act are referred to in this Act as "activities governed by this Act".

The Human Fertilisation and Embryology Authority, its functions and procedure

5   The Human Fertilisation and Embryology Authority

(1)   There shall be a body corporate called the Human Fertilisation and Embryology Authority.

(2)   The Authority shall consist of—
  (a) a chairman and deputy chairman, and
  (b) such number of other members as the Secretary of State appoints.

(3)   Schedule 1 to this Act (which deals with the membership of the Authority, etc) shall have effect.

13   Conditions of licences for treatment

(1)–(4) …

(5)   A woman shall not be provided with treatment services unless account has been taken of the welfare of any child who may be born as a result of the treatment (including the need of that child for a father), and of any other child who may be affected by the birth.

(6)   …

NOTES

Sub-ss (1)–(4), (6): outside the scope of this work.

Status

27   Meaning of "mother"

(1)   The woman who is carrying or has carried a child as a result of the placing in her of an embryo or of sperm and eggs, and no other woman, is to be treated as the mother of the child.

(2)   Subsection (1) above does not apply to any child to the extent that the child is treated by virtue of adoption as not being the child of any person other than the adopter or adopters.

(3)   Subsection (1) above applies whether the woman was in the United Kingdom or elsewhere at the time of the placing in her of the embryo or the sperm and eggs.

28   Meaning of "father"

(1)   This section applies in the case of a child who is being or has been carried by a woman as the result of the placing in her of an embryo or of sperm and eggs or her artificial insemination.

(2)   If—
   (a) at the time of the placing in her of the embryo or the sperm and eggs or of her insemination, the woman was a party to a marriage, and
   (b) the creation of the embryo carried by her was not brought about with the sperm of the other party to the marriage,

then, subject to subsection (5) below, the other party to the marriage shall be treated as the father of the child unless it is shown that he did not consent to the placing in her of the embryo or the sperm and eggs or to her insemination (as the case may be).

(3)   If no man is treated, by virtue of subsection (2) above, as the father of the child but—
   (a) the embryo or the sperm and eggs were placed in the woman, or she was artificially inseminated, in the course of treatment services provided for her and a man together by a person to whom a licence applies, and
   (b) the creation of the embryo carried by her was not brought about with the sperm of that man,

then, subject to subsection (5) below, that man shall be treated as the father of the child.

(4)   Where a person is treated as the father of the child by virtue of subsection (2) or(3) above, no other person is to be treated as the father of the child.

(5)   Subsections (2) and (3) above do not apply—
   (a) in relation to England and Wales and Northern Ireland, to any child who, by virtue of the rules of common law, is treated as the legitimate child of the parties to a marriage,

(b) ...

(c) to any child to the extent that the child is treated by virtue of adoption as not being the child of any person other than the adopter or adopters.

(6) Where—

(a) the sperm of a man who had given such consent as is required by paragraph 5 of Schedule 3 to this Act was used for a purpose for which such consent was required, or

(b) the sperm of a man, or any embryo the creation of which was brought about with his sperm, was used after his death,

he is not to be treated as the father of the child.

(7) The references in subsection (2) above to the parties to a marriage at the time there referred to—

(a) are to the parties to a marriage subsisting at that time, unless a judicial separation was then in force, but

(b) include the parties to a void marriage if either or both of them reasonably believed at that time that the marriage was valid; and for the purposes of this subsection it shall be presumed, unless the contrary is shown, that one of them reasonably believed at that time that the marriage was valid.

(8) This section applies whether the woman was in the United Kingdom or elsewhere at the time of the placing in her of the embryo or the sperm and eggs or her artificial insemination.

(9) In subsection (7)(a) above, "judicial separation" includes a legal separation obtained in a country outside the British Islands and recognised in the United Kingdom.

NOTES

Sub-s (5): para (b) outside the scope of this work.

29 Effect of sections 27 and 28

(1) Where by virtue of section 27 or 28 of this Act a person is to be treated as the mother or father of a child, that person is to be treated in law as the mother or, as the case may be, father of the child for all purposes.

(2) Where by virtue of section 27 or 28 of this Act a person is not to be treated as the mother or father of a child, that person is to be treated in law as not being the mother or, as the case may be, father of the child for any purpose.

(3)   Where subsection (1) or (2) above has effect, references to any relationship between two people in any enactment, deed or other instrument or document (whenever passed or made) are to be read accordingly.

(4)   In relation to England and Wales and Northern Ireland, nothing in the provisions of section 27(1) or 28(2) to (4), read with this section, affects—

   (a)   the succession to any dignity or title of honour or renders any person capable of succeeding to or transmitting a right to succeed to any such dignity or title, or

   (b)   the devolution of any property limited (expressly or not) to devolve (as nearly as the law permits) along with any dignity or title of honour.

(5)   . . .

NOTES

Sub-s (5): outside the scope of this work.

30   Parental orders in favour of gamete donors

(1)   The court may make an order providing for a child to be treated in law as the child of the parties to a marriage (referred to in this section as "the husband" and "the wife") if—

   (a)   the child has been carried by a woman other than the wife as the result of the placing in her of an embryo or sperm and eggs or her artificial insemination,

   (b)   the gametes of the husband or the wife, or both, were used to bring about the creation of the embryo, and

   (c)   the conditions in subsections (2) to (7) below are satisfied.

(2)   The husband and the wife must apply for the order within six months of the birth of the child or, in the case of a child born before the coming into force of this Act, within six months of such coming into force.

(3)   At the time of the application and of the making of the order—

   (a)   the child's home must be with the husband and the wife, and

   (b)   the husband or the wife, of both of them, must be domiciled in a part of the United Kingdom or in the Channel Islands or the Isle of Man.

(4)   At the time of the making of the order both the husband and the wife must have attained the age of eighteen.

(5)   The court must be satisfied that both the father of the child (including a person who is the father by virtue of section 28 of this Act), where he is

not the husband, and the woman who carried the child have freely, and with full understanding of what is involved, agreed unconditionally to the making of the order.

(6)   Subsection (5) above does not require the agreement of a person who cannot be found or is incapable of giving agreement and the agreement of the woman who carried the child is ineffective for the purposes of that subsection if given by her less than six weeks after the child's birth.

(7)   The court must be satisfied that no money or other benefit (other than for expenses reasonably incurred) has been given or received by the husband or the wife for or in consideration of—
   (a) the making of the order,
   (b) any agreement required by subsection (5) above,
   (c) the handing over of the child to the husband and the wife, or
   (d) the making of any arrangements with a view to the making of the order,

unless authorised by the court.

(8)   For the purposes of an application under this section—
   (a) in relation to England and Wales, section 92(7) to (10) of, and Part I of Schedule 11 to, the Children Act 1989 (jurisdiction of courts) shall apply for the purposes of this section to determine the meaning of "the court" as they apply for the purposes of that Act and proceedings on the application shall be "family proceedings" for the purposes of that Act,
   (b) . . .
   (c) in relation to Northern Ireland, "the court" means the High Court or any county court within whose division the child is.

(9)   Regulations may provide—
   (a) for any provision of the enactments about adoption to have effect, with such modifications (if any) as may be specified in the regulations, in relation to orders under this section, and applications for such orders, as it has effect in relation to adoption, and applications for adoption orders, and
   (b) for references in any enactment to adoption, an adopted child or an adoptive relationship to be read (respectively) as references to the effect of an order under this section, a child to whom such an order applies and a relationship arising by virtue of the enactments about adoption, as applied by the regulations, and for similar expressions in connection with adoption to be read accordingly,

and the regulations may include such incidental or supplemental provision as appears to the Secretary of State necessary or desirable in consequence of any provision made by virtue of paragraph (a) or (b) above.

(10)   In this section "the enactments about adoption" means the Adoption Act 1976, the Adoption (Scotland) Act 1978 and the Adoption (Northern Ireland) Order1987.

(11)   Subsection (1)(a) above applies whether the woman was in the United Kingdom or elsewhere at the time of the placing in her of the embryo or the sperm and eggs or her artificial insemination.

NOTES

Commencement: 5 July 1994 (sub-ss (9), (10); 1 November 1994 (remainder). Sub-s (8): para (b) outside the scope of this work.

Information

31   The Authority's register of information

(1)   The Authority shall keep a register which shall contain any information obtained by the Authority which falls within subsection (2) below.

(2)   Information falls within this subsection if it relates to—
(a) the provision of treatment services for any identifiable individual, or
(b) the keeping or use of the gametes of any identifiable individual or of an embryo taken from any identifiable woman,

or if it shows that any identifiable individual was, or may have been, born in consequence of treatment services.

(3)   A person who has attained the age of eighteen ("the applicant") may by notice to the Authority require the Authority to comply with a request under subsection (4) below, and the Authority shall do so if—
(a) the information contained in the register shows that the applicant was, or may have been, born in consequence of treatment services, and
(b) the applicant has been given a suitable opportunity to receive proper counselling about the implications of compliance with the request.

(4)   The applicant may request the Authority to give the applicant notice stating whether or not the information contained in the register shows that a person other than a parent of the applicant would or might, but for sections 27 to 29 of this Act, be a parent of the applicant and, if it does show that—

(a) giving the applicant so much of that information as relates to the person concerned as the Authority is required by regulations to give (but no other information), or

(b) stating whether or not that information shows that, but for sections 27 to 29 of this Act, the applicant, and a person specified in the request as a person whom the applicant proposes to marry, would or might be related.

(5)   Regulations cannot require the Authority to give any information as to the identity of a person whose gametes have been used or from whom an embryo has been taken if a person to whom a licence applied was provided with the information at a time when the Authority could not have been required to give information of the kind in question.

(6)   A person who has not attained the age of eighteen ("the minor") may by notice to the Authority specifying another person ("the intended spouse") as a person whom the minor proposes to marry require the Authority to comply with a request under subsection (7) below, and the Authority shall do so if—

(a) the information contained in the register shows that the minor was, or may have been, born in consequence of treatment services, and

(b) the minor has been given a suitable opportunity to receive proper counselling about the implications of compliance with the request.

(7)   The minor may request the Authority to give the minor notice stating whether or not the information contained in the register shows that, but for sections 27 to 29 of this Act, the minor and the intended spouse would or might be related.

32   Information to be provided to Registrar General

(1)   This section applies where a claim is made before the Registrar General that a man is or is not the father of a child and it is necessary or desirable for the purpose of any function of the Registrar General to determine whether the claim is or may be well-founded.

(2)   The Authority shall comply with any request made by the Registrar General by notice to the Authority to disclose whether any information on the register kept in pursuance of section 31 of this Act tends to show that the man may be the father of the child by virtue of section 28 of this Act and, if it does, disclose that information.

(3)   In this section and section 33 of this Act, "the Registrar General" means the Registrar General for England and Wales, the Registrar General

of Births, Deaths and Marriages for Scotland or the Registrar General for Northern Ireland, as the case may be.

33   Restrictions on disclosure of information

(1)   No person who is or has been a member or employee of the Authority shall disclose any information mentioned in subsection (2) below which he holds or has held as such a member or employee.

(2)   The information referred to in subsection (1) above is—
  (a) any information contained or required to be contained in the register kept in pursuance of section 31 of this Act, and
  (b) any other information obtained by any member or employee of the Authority on terms or in circumstances requiring it to be held in confidence.

(3)   Subsection (1) above does not apply to any disclosure of information mentioned in subsection (2)(a) above made—
  (a) to a person as a member or employee of the Authority,
  (b) to a person to whom a licence applies for the purposes of his functions as such,
  (c) so that no individual to whom the information relates can be identified,
  (d) in pursuance of an order of a court under section 34 or 35 of this Act,
  (e) to the Registrar General in pursuance of a request under section 32 of this Act, or
  (f) in accordance with section 31 of this Act.

(4)   Subsection (1) above does not apply to any disclosure of information mentioned in subsection (2)(b) above—
  (a) made to a person as a member or employee of the Authority,
  (b) made with the consent of the person or persons whose confidence would otherwise be protected, or
  (c) which has been lawfully made available to the public before the disclosure is made.

(5)   No person who is or has been a person to whom a licence applies and no person to whom directions have been given shall disclose any information falling within section 31(2) of this Act which he holds or has held as such a person.

(6)   Subsection (5) above does not apply to any disclosure of information made—
  (a) to a person as a member or employee of the Authority,

(b) to a person to whom a licence applies for the purposes of his functions as such,

(c) so far as it identifies a person who, but for sections 27 to 29 of this Act, would or might be a parent of a person who instituted proceedings under section 1A of the Congenital Disabilities (Civil Liability) Act 1976, but only for the purpose of defending such proceedings, or instituting connected proceedings for compensation against that parent,

(d) so that no individual to whom the information relates can be identified, . . .

(e) in pursuance of directions given by virtue of section 24(5) or (6) of this Act.

[(f) necessarily—
    (i)   for any purpose preliminary to proceedings, or
    (ii) for the purposes of, or in connection with, any proceedings,

(g) for the purpose of establishing, in any proceedings relating to an application for an order under subsection (1) of section 30 of this Act, whether the condition specified in paragraph (a) or (b) of that subsection is met, *or*

(h) under section 3 of the Access to Health Records Act 1990 (right of access to health records).]

[(6A) Paragraph (f) of subsection (6) above, so far as relating to disclosure for the purposes of, or in connection with, any proceedings, does not apply—

(a) to disclosure of information enabling a person to be identified as a person whose gametes were used, in accordance with consent given under paragraph 5 of Schedule 3 to this Act, for the purposes of treatment services in consequence of which an identifiable individual was, or may have been, born, or

(b) to disclosure, in circumstances in which subsection (1) of section 34 of this Act applies, of information relevant to the determination of the question mentioned in that subsection.

(6B) In the case of information relating to the provision of treatment services for any identifiable individual—

(a) where one individual is identifiable, subsection (5) above does not apply to disclosure with the consent of that individual;

(b) where both a woman and a man treated together with her are identifiable, subsection (5) above does not apply—
    (i)   to disclosure with the consent of them both, or
    (ii) if disclosure is made for the purpose of disclosing information about the provision of treatment services for one of them, to disclosure with the consent of that individual.

(6C) For the purposes of subsection (6B) above, consent must be to disclosure to a specific person, except where disclosure is to a person who needs to know—
- (a) in connection with the provision of treatment services, or any other description of medical, surgical or obstetric services, for the individual giving the consent,
- (b) in connection with the carrying out of an audit of clinical practice, or
- (c) in connection with the auditing of accounts.

(6D) For the purposes of subsection (6B) above, consent to disclosure given at the request of another shall be disregarded unless, before it is given, the person requesting it takes reasonable steps to explain to the individual from whom it is requested the implications of compliance with the request.

(6E) In the case of information which relates to the provision of treatment services for any identifiable individual, subsection (5) above does not apply to disclosure in an emergency, that is to say, to disclosure made—
- (a) by a person who is satisfied that it is necessary to make the disclosure to avert an imminent danger to the health of an individual with whose consent the information could be disclosed under subsection (6B) above, and
- (b) in circumstances where it is not reasonably practicable to obtain that individual's consent.

(6F) In the case of information which shows that any identifiable individual was, or may have been, born in consequence of treatment services, subsection (5) above does not apply to any disclosure which is necessarily incidental to disclosure under subsection (6B) or (6E) above.

(6G) Regulations may provide for additional exceptions from subsection (5) above, but no exception may be made under this subsection—
- (a) for disclosure of a kind mentioned in paragraph (a) or (b) of subsection (6A) above, or
- (b) for disclosure, in circumstances in which section 32 of this Act applies, of information having the tendency mentioned in subsection (2) of that section.]

(7) This section does not apply to the disclosure to any individual of information which—
- (a) falls within section 31(2) of this Act by virtue of paragraph (a) or (b) of that subsection, and

(b) relates only to that individual or, in the case of an individual treated together with another, only to that individual and that other.

(8) . . .

[(9) In subsection (6)(f) above, references to proceedings include any formal procedure for dealing with a complaint.]

NOTES

Sub-s (6): word omitted from para (d) repealed and paras (f)–(h) added by the Human Fertilisation and Embryology (Disclosure of Information) Act 1992, s 1, in relation to information obtained before, as well as in relation to information obtained after, the passing of the 1992 Act (16 July 1992); the word "or" at the end of para (g) is repealed, and para (i) is added, by the Access to Health Records (Northern Ireland) Order 1993, SI 1993/1250, art 13, under art 1(2) of that order, as from a day to be appointed, as follows—
"or
(i) under Article 5 of the Access to Health Records (Northern Ireland) Order 1993 (right of access to health records).".
Sub-ss (6A)–(6G): inserted by the Human Fertilisation and Embryology (Disclosure of Information) Act 1992, s 1, in relation to information obtained before, as well as in relation to information obtained after, the passing of the 1992 Act (16 July 1992).
Sub-s (8): outside the scope of this work.
Sub-s (9): added by the Human Fertilisation and Embryology (Disclosure of Information) Act 1992, s1, in relation to information obtained before, as well as in relation to information obtained after, the passing of the 1992 Act (16 July 1992).

34 Disclosure in interests of justice

(1) Where in any proceedings before a court the question whether a person is or is not the parent of a child by virtue of sections 27 to 29 of this Act falls to be determined, the court may on the application of any party to the proceedings make an order requiring the Authority—
(a) to disclose whether or not any information relevant to that question is contained in the register kept in pursuance of section 31 of this Act, and
(b) if it is, to disclose so much of it as is specified in the order,

but such an order may not require the Authority to disclose any information falling within section 31(2)(b) of this Act.

(2) The court must not make an order under subsection (1) above unless it is satisfied that the interests of justice require it to do so, taking into account—

(a) any representations made by any individual who may be affected by the disclosure, and

(b) the welfare of the child, if under 18 years old, and of any other person under that age who may be affected by the disclosure.

(3)   If the proceedings before the court are civil proceedings, it—

(a) may direct that the whole or any part of the proceedings on the application for an order under subsection (2) above shall be heard in camera, and

(b) if it makes such an order, may then or later direct that the whole or any part of any later stage of the proceedings shall be heard in camera.

(4)   An application for a direction under subsection (3) above shall be heard in camera unless the court otherwise directs.

35 Disclosure in interests of justice: congenital disabilities, etc

(1)   Where for the purpose of instituting proceedings under section 1 of the Congenital Disabilities (Civil Liability) Act 1976 (civil liability to child born disabled) it is necessary to identify a person who would or might be the parent of a child but for sections 27 to 29 of this Act, the court may, on the application of the child, make an order requiring the Authority to disclose any information contained in the register kept in pursuance of section 31 of this Act identifying that person.

(2)   . . .

(3)   Subsections (2) to (4) of section 34 of this Act apply for the purposes of this section as they apply for the purposes of that.

(4)   . . .

NOTES

Sub-ss (2), (4): outside the scope of this work.

Offences

41 Offences

(1)   A person who—

(a) contravenes section 3(2)[, 3A] or 4(1)(c) of this Act, or

(b) does anything which, by virtue of section 3(3) of this Act, cannot be authorised by a licence,

is guilty of an offence and liable on conviction on indictment to imprisonment for a term not exceeding ten years or a fine or both.

(2) A person who—
    (a) contravenes section 3(1) of this Act, otherwise than by doing something which, by virtue of section 3(3) of this Act, cannot be authorised by a licence,
    (b) keeps or uses any gametes in contravention of section 4(1)(a) or (b) of this Act,
    (c) contravenes section 4(3) of this Act, or
    (d) fails to comply with any directions given by virtue of section 24(7)(a) of this Act,

is guilty of an offence.

(3) If a person—
    (a) provides any information for the purposes of the grant of a licence, being information which is false or misleading in a material particular, and
    (b) either he knows the information to be false or misleading in a material particular or he provides the information recklessly,

he is guilty of an offence.

(4) A person guilty of an offence under subsection (2) or (3) above is liable—
    (a) on conviction on indictment, to imprisonment for a term not exceeding two years or a fine or both, and
    (b) on summary conviction, to imprisonment for a term not exceeding six months or a fine not exceeding the statutory maximum or both.

(5) A person who discloses any information in contravention of section 33 of this Act is guilty of an offence and liable—
    (a) on conviction on indictment, to imprisonment for a term not exceeding two years or a fine or both, and
    (b) on summary conviction, to imprisonment for a term not exceeding six months or a fine not exceeding the statutory maximum or both.

(6) A person who—
    (a) fails to comply with a requirement made by virtue of section 39(1)(b) or (2)(b) or 40(2)(b)(ii) or (5)(b) of this Act, or
    (b) intentionally obstructs the exercise of any rights conferred by a warrant issued under section 40 of this Act,

is guilty of an offence.

(7)   A person who without reasonable excuse fails to comply with a requirement imposed by regulations made by virtue of section 10(2)(a) of this Act is guilty of an offence.

(8)   Where a person to whom a licence applies or the nominal licensee gives or receives any money or other benefit, not authorised by directions, in respect of any supply of gametes or embryos, he is guilty of an offence.

(9)   A person guilty of an offence under subsection (6), (7) or (8) above is liable on summary conviction to imprisonment for a term not exceeding six months or a fine not exceeding level five on the standard scale or both.

(10)   It is a defence for a person ("the defendant") charged with an offence of doing anything which, under section 3(1) or 4(1) of this Act, cannot be done except in pursuance of a licence to prove—
  (a) that the defendant was acting under the direction of another, and
  (b) that the defendant believed on reasonable grounds—
    (i)   that the other person was at the material time the person responsible under a licence, a person designated by virtue of section 17(2)(b) of this Act as a person to whom a licence applied, or a person to whom directions had been given by virtue of section 24(9) of this Act, and
    (ii) that the defendant was authorised by virtue of the licence or directions to do the thing in question.

(11)   It is a defence for a person charged with an offence under this Act to prove—
  (a) that at the material time he was a person to whom a licence applied or to whom directions had been given, and
  (b) that he took all such steps as were reasonable and exercised all due diligence to avoid committing the offence.

NOTES

Sub-s (1): number in square brackets in para (a) inserted by the Criminal Justice and Public Order Act 1994, s 156(1), (3).

42 Consent to prosecution

No proceedings for an offence under this Act shall be instituted—

(a) in England and Wales, except by or with the consent of the Director of Public Prosecutions, and

(b) in Northern Ireland, except by or with the consent of the Director of Public Prosecutions for Northern Ireland.

49 Short title, commencement, etc

(1) This Act may be cited as the Human Fertilisation and Embryology Act 1990.

(2) This Act shall come into force on such day as the Secretary of State may by order made by statutory instrument appoint and different days may be appointed for different provisions and for different purposes.

(3) Sections 27 to 29 of this Act shall have effect only in relation to children carried by women as a result of the placing in them of embryos or of sperm and eggs, or of their artificial insemination (as the case may be), after the commencement of those sections.

(4) Section 27 of the Family Law Reform Act 1987 (artificial insemination) does not have effect in relation to children carried by women as the result of their artificial insemination after the commencement of sections 27 to 29 of this Act.

(5)–(7) . . .

NOTES

Sub-ss (5)–(7): outside the scope of this work.

Child Support Act 1991

(c 48)

An Act to make provision for the assessment, collection and enforcement of periodical maintenance payable by certain parents with respect to children of theirs who are not in their care; for the collection and enforcement of certain other kinds of maintenance; and for connected purposes
[25 July 1991]

The basic principles

1 The duty to maintain

(1) For the purposes of this Act, each parent of a qualifying child is responsible for maintaining him.

(2) For the purposes of this Act, an absent parent shall be taken to have met his responsibility to maintain any qualifying child of his by making periodical payments of maintenance with respect to the child of such amount, and at such intervals, as may be determined in accordance with the provisions of this Act.

(3) Where a maintenance assessment made under this Act requires the making of periodical payments, it shall be the duty of the absent parent with respect to whom the assessment was made to make those payments.

2 Welfare of children: the general principle

Where, in any case which falls to be dealt with under this Act, the Secretary of State . . . is considering the exercise of any discretionary power conferred by this Act, he shall have regard to the welfare of any child likely to be affected by his decision.

NOTES

Words omitted repealed by the Social Security Act 1998, s 86(1), (2), Sch 7, para 18, Sch 8.

3 Meaning of certain terms used in this Act

(1) A child is a "qualifying child" if—
   (a) one of his parents is, in relation to him, an absent parent; or
   (b) both of his parents are, in relation to him, absent parents.

(2) The parent of any child is an "absent parent", in relation to him, if—
   (a) that parent is not living in the same household with the child; and
   (b) the child has his home with a person who is, in relation to him, a person with care.

(3)   A person is a "person with care", in relation to any child, if he is a person—
  (a) with whom the child has his home;
  (b) who usually provides day to day care for the child (whether exclusively or in conjunction with any other person); and
  (c) who does not fall within a prescribed category of person.

(4)   The Secretary of State shall not, under subsection (3)(c), prescribe as a category—
  (a) parents;
  (b) guardians;
  (c) persons in whose favour residence orders under section 8 of the Children Act 1989 are in force;
  (d) in Scotland, persons [with whom a child is to live by virtue of a residence order under section 11 of the Children (Scotland) Act 1995.]

(5)   For the purposes of this Act there may be more than one person with care in relation to the same qualifying child.

(6)   Periodical payments which are required to be paid in accordance with a maintenance assessment are referred to in this Act as "child support maintenance".

(7)   Expressions are defined in this section only for the purposes of this Act.

NOTES

Sub-s (4): words in square brackets in para (d) substituted by the Children (Scotland) Act 1995, s 105(4), Sch 4, para 52(2).

4   Child support maintenance

(1)   A person who is, in relation to any qualifying child or any qualifying children, either the person with care or the absent parent may apply to the Secretary of State for a maintenance assessment to be made under this Act with respect to that child, or any of those children.

(2)   Where a maintenance assessment has been made in response to an application under this section the Secretary of State may, if the person with care or absent parent with respect to whom the assessment was made applies to him under this subsection, arrange for—
  (a) the collection of the child support maintenance payable in accordance with the assessment;

(b) the enforcement of the obligation to pay child support maintenance in accordance with the assessment.

(3)   Where an application under subsection (2) for the enforcement of the obligation mentioned in subsection (2)(b) authorises the Secretary of State to take steps to enforce that obligation whenever he considers it necessary to do so, the Secretary of State may act accordingly.

(4)   A person who applies to the Secretary of State under this section shall, so far as that person reasonably can, comply with such regulations as may be made by the Secretary of State with a view to the Secretary of State . . . being provided with the information which is required to enable—
(a) the absent parent to be traced (where that is necessary);
(b) the amount of child support maintenance payable by the absent parent to be assessed; and
(c) that amount to be recovered from the absent parent.

(5)   Any person who has applied to the Secretary of State under this section may at any time request him to cease acting under this section.

(6)   It shall be the duty of the Secretary of State to comply with any request made under subsection (5) (but subject to any regulations made under subsection (8)).

(7)   The obligation to provide information which is imposed by subsection (4)—
(a) shall not apply in such circumstances as may be prescribed; and
(b) may, in such circumstances as may be prescribed, be waived by the Secretary of State.

(8)   The Secretary of State may by regulations make such incidental, supplemental or transitional provision as he thinks appropriate with respect to cases in which he is requested to cease to act under this section.

(9)   No application may be made under this section if there is in force with respect to the person with care and absent parent in question a maintenance assessment made in response to an application under section 6.

[(10)   No application may be made at any time under this section with respect to a qualifying child or any qualifying children if—
(a) there is in force a written maintenance agreement made before 5th April 1993, or a maintenance order, in respect of that child or those children and the person who is, at that time, the absent parent; or

(b) benefit is being paid to, or in respect of, a parent with care of that child or those children.

(11) In subsection (10) "benefit" means any benefit which is mentioned in, or prescribed by regulations under, section 6(1).]

NOTES

Sub-s (4): words omitted repealed by the Social Security Act 1998, s 86(1), (2), Sch 7, para 19, Sch 8.

Sub-ss (10), (11): added by the Child Support Act 1995, s 18(1), subject to savings in s 18(6) thereof.

5 Child support maintenance: supplemental provisions

(1) Where—
  (a) there is more than one person with care of a qualifying child; and
  (b) one or more, but not all, of them have parental responsibility for ... the child;

no application may be made for a maintenance assessment with respect to the child by any of those persons who do not have parental responsibility for . . . the child.

(2) Where more than one application for a maintenance assessment is made with respect to the child concerned, only one of them may be proceeded with.

(3) The Secretary of State may by regulations make provision as to which of two or more applications for a maintenance assessment with respect to the same child is to be proceeded with.

NOTES

Sub-s (1): words omitted repealed by the Children (Scotland) Act 1995, s 105(4), (5), Sch 4, para 52(3), Sch 5.

6 Applications by those receiving benefit

(1) Where income support, [an income-based jobseeker's allowance,] family credit or any other benefit of a prescribed kind is claimed by or in respect of, or paid to or in respect of, the parent of a qualifying child she shall, if—

   (a) she is a person with care of the child; and

   (b) she is required to do so by the Secretary of State,

authorise the Secretary of State to take action under this Act to recover child support maintenance from the absent parent.

(2)   The Secretary of State shall not require a person ("the parent") to give him the authorisation mentioned in subsection (1) if he considers that there are reasonable grounds for believing that—

   (a) if the parent were to be required to give that authorisation; or

   (b) if she were to give it,

there would be a risk of her, or of any child living with her, suffering harm or undue distress as a result.

(3)   Subsection (2) shall not apply if the parent requests the Secretary of State to disregard it.

(4)   The authorisation mentioned in subsection (1) shall extend to all children of the absent parent in relation to whom the parent first mentioned in subsection (1) is a person with care.

(5)   That authorisation shall be given, without unreasonable delay, by completing and returning to the Secretary of State an application—

   (a) for the making of a maintenance assessment with respect to the qualifying child or qualifying children; and

   (b) for the Secretary of State to take action under this Act to recover, on her behalf, the amount of child support maintenance so assessed.

(6)   Such an application shall be made on a form ("a maintenance application form") provided by the Secretary of State.

(7)   A maintenance application form shall indicate in general terms the effect of completing and returning it.

(8)   Subsection (1) has effect regardless of whether any of the benefits mentioned there is payable with respect to any qualifying child.

(9)   A person who is under the duty imposed by subsection (1) shall, so far as she reasonably can, comply with such regulations as may be made by the Secretary of State with a view to the Secretary of State . . . being provided with the information which is required to enable—

    (a) the absent parent to be traced;

    (b) the amount of child support maintenance payable by the absent parent to be assessed; and

    (c) that amount to be recovered from the absent parent.

(10)   The obligation to provide information which is imposed by subsection (9)—

    (a) shall not apply in such circumstances as may be prescribed; and

    (b) may, in such circumstances as may be prescribed, be waived by the Secretary of State.

(11)   A person with care who has authorised the Secretary of State under subsection (1) but who subsequently ceases to fall within that subsection may request the Secretary of State to cease acting under this section.

(12)   It shall be the duty of the Secretary of State to comply with any request made under subsection (11) (but subject to any regulations made under subsection (13)).

(13)   The Secretary of State may by regulations make such incidental or transitional provision as he thinks appropriate with respect to cases in which he is requested under subsection (11) to cease to act under this section.

(14)   The fact that a maintenance assessment is in force with respect to a person with care shall not prevent the making of a new maintenance assessment with respect to her in response to an application under this section.

NOTES

Sub-s (1): words in square brackets inserted by the Jobseekers Act 1995, s 41(4), Sch 2, para 20(2).

Sub-s (9): words omitted repealed by the Social Security Act 1998, s 86(1), (2), Sch 7, para 20, Sch 8.

8 Role of the courts with respect to maintenance for children

(1)   This subsection applies in any case where [the Secretary of State] would have jurisdiction to make a maintenance assessment with respect to a qualifying child and an absent parent of his on an application duly made by a person entitled to apply for such an assessment with respect to that child.

(2)   Subsection (1) applies even though the circumstances of the case are such that [the Secretary of State] would not make an assessment if it were applied for.

(3)   In any case where subsection (1) applies, no court shall exercise any power which it would otherwise have to make, vary or revive any maintenance order in relation to the child and absent parent concerned.

[(3A) In any case in which section 4(10) or 7(10) prevents the making of an application for a maintenance assessment, and—
   (a) no application has been made for a maintenance assessment under section 6, or
   (b) such an application has been made but no maintenance assessment has been made in response to it,

subsection (3) shall have effect with the omission of the word "vary".]

(4)   Subsection (3) does not prevent a court from revoking a maintenance order.

(5)   The Lord Chancellor or in relation to Scotland the Lord Advocate may by order provide that, in such circumstances as may be specified by the order, this section shall not prevent a court from exercising any power which it has to make a maintenance order in relation to a child if—
   (a) a written agreement (whether or not enforceable) provides for the making, or securing, by an absent parent of the child of periodical payments to or for the benefit of the child; and
   (b) the maintenance order which the court makes is, in all material respects, in the same terms as that agreement.

(6)   This section shall not prevent a court from exercising any power which it has to make a maintenance order in relation to a child if—
   (a) a maintenance assessment is in force with respect to the child;
   (b) the amount of the child support maintenance payable in accordance with the assessment was determined by reference to the alternative formula mentioned in paragraph 4(3) of Schedule 1; and
   (c) the court is satisfied that the circumstances of the case make it appropriate for the absent parent to make or secure the making of periodical payments under a maintenance order in addition to the child support maintenance payable by him in accordance with the maintenance assessment.

(7)   This section shall not prevent a court from exercising any power which it has to make a maintenance order in relation to a child if—

(a) the child is, will be or (if the order were to be made) would be receiving instruction at an educational establishment or undergoing training for a trade, profession or vocation (whether or not while in gainful employment); and

(b) the order is made solely for the purposes of requiring the person making or securing the making of periodical payments fixed by the order to meet some or all of the expenses incurred in connection with the provision of the instruction or training.

(8)   This section shall not prevent a court from exercising any power which it has to make a maintenance order in relation to a child if—

(a) a disability living allowance is paid to or in respect of him; or

(b) no such allowance is paid but he is disabled,

and the order is made solely for the purpose of requiring the person making or securing the making of periodical payments fixed by the order to meet some or all of any expenses attributable to the child's disability.

(9)   For the purposes of subsection (8), a child is disabled if he is blind, deaf or dumb or is substantially and permanently handicapped by illness, injury, mental disorder or congenital deformity or such other disability as may be prescribed.

(10)   This section shall not prevent a court from exercising any power which it has to make a maintenance order in relation to a child if the order is made against a person with care of the child.

(11)   In this Act "maintenance order", in relation to any child, means an order which requires the making or securing of periodical payments to or for the benefit of the child and which is made under—

(a) Part II of the Matrimonial Causes Act 1973;

(b) the Domestic Proceedings and Magistrates' Courts Act 1978;

(c) Part III of the Matrimonial and Family Proceedings Act 1984;

(d) the Family Law (Scotland) Act 1985;

(e) Schedule 1 to the Children Act 1989; or

(f) any other prescribed enactment,

and includes any order varying or reviving such an order.

NOTES

Sub-ss (1), (2): words in square brackets substituted by the Social Security Act 1998, s 86(1), Sch 7, para 22.

Sub-s (3A): inserted by the Child Support Act 1995, s 18(3).

9 Agreements about maintenance

(1)   In this section "maintenance agreement" means any agreement for the making, or for securing the making, of periodical payments by way of maintenance, or in Scotland aliment, to or for the benefit of any child.

(2)   Nothing in this Act shall be taken to prevent any person from entering into a maintenance agreement.

(3)   [Subject to section 4(10)(a) and section 7(10),] the existence of a maintenance agreement shall not prevent any party to the agreement, or any other person, from applying for a maintenance assessment with respect to any child to or for whose benefit periodical payments are to be made or secured under the agreement.

(4)   Where any agreement contains a provision which purports to restrict the right of any person to apply for a maintenance assessment, that provision shall be void.

(5)   Where section 8 would prevent any court from making a maintenance order in relation to a child and an absent parent of his, no court shall exercise any power that it has to vary any agreement so as—
   (a) to insert a provision requiring that absent parent to make or secure the making of periodical payments by way of maintenance, or in Scotland aliment, to or for the benefit of that child; or
   (b) to increase the amount payable under such a provision.

[(6)   In any case in which section 4(10) or 7(10) prevents the making of an application for a maintenance assessment, and—
   (a) no application has been made for a maintenance assessment under section 6, or
   (b) such an application has been made but no maintenance assessment has been made in response to it,

subsection (5) shall have effect with the omission of paragraph (b).]

NOTES

Sub-s (3): words in square brackets inserted by the Child Support Act 1995, s 18(4).
Sub-s (6): added by the Child Support Act 1995, s 18(4).

10 Relationship between maintenance assessments and certain court orders and related matters

(1) Where an order of a kind prescribed for the purposes of this subsection is in force with respect to any qualifying child with respect to whom a maintenance assessment is made, the order—
    (a) shall, so far as it relates to the making or securing of periodical payments, cease to have effect to such extent as may be determined in accordance with regulations made by the Secretary of State; or
    (b) where the regulations so provide, shall, so far as it so relates, have effect subject to such modifications as may be so determined.

(2) Where an agreement of a kind prescribed for the purposes of this subsection is in force with respect to any qualifying child with respect to whom a maintenance assessment is made, the agreement—
    (a) shall, so far as it relates to the making or securing of periodical payments, be unenforceable to such extent as may be determined in accordance with regulations made by the Secretary of State; or
    (b) where the regulations so provide, shall, so far as it so relates, have effect subject to such modifications as may be so determined.

(3) Any regulations under this section may, in particular, make such provision with respect to—
    (a) any case where any person with respect to whom an order or agreement of a kind prescribed for the purposes of subsection (1) or (2) has effect applies to the prescribed court, before the end of the prescribed period, for the order or agreement to be varied in the light of the maintenance assessment and of the provisions of this Act;
    (b) the recovery of any arrears under the order or agreement which fell due before the coming into force of the maintenance assessment,

as the Secretary of State considers appropriate and may provide that, in prescribed circumstances, an application to any court which is made with respect to an order of a prescribed kind relating to the making or securing of periodical payments to or for the benefit of a child shall be treated by the court as an application for the order to be revoked.

(4) The Secretary of State may by regulations make provision for—
    (a) notification to be given by [the Secretary of State] to the prescribed person in any case where [he] considers that the making of a maintenance assessment has affected, or is likely to affect, any order of a kind prescribed for the purposes of this subsection;

(b) notification to be given by the prescribed person to the Secretary of State in any case where a court makes an order which it considers has affected, or is likely to affect, a maintenance assessment.

(5) Rules may be made under section 144 of the Magistrates' Courts Act 1980 (rules of procedure) requiring any person who, in prescribed circumstances, makes an application to a magistrates' court for a maintenance order to furnish the court with a statement in a prescribed form, and signed by [an officer of the Secretary of State], as to whether or not, at the time when the statement is made, there is a maintenance assessment in force with respect to that person or the child concerned.

In this subsection—
"maintenance order" means an order of a prescribed kind for the making or securing of periodical payments to or for the benefit of a child; and
"prescribed" means prescribed by the rules.

NOTES

Sub-ss (4), (5): words in square brackets substituted by the Social Security Act 1998, s 86(1), Sch 7, para 23.

Maintenance assessments

11 Maintenance assessments

(1) Any application for a maintenance assessment made to the Secretary of State shall be [dealt with by him] in accordance with the provision made by or under this Act.

[(1A) Where—
 (a) an application for a maintenance assessment is made under section 6, but
 (b) the Secretary of State becomes aware, [before determining the application], that the claim mentioned in subsection (1) of that section has been disallowed or withdrawn,

he shall, subject to subsection (1B), treat the application as if it had not been made.

(1B) If it appears to the Secretary of State that subsection (10) of section 4 would not have prevented the parent with care concerned from making an application for a maintenance assessment under that section he shall—

(a) notify her of the effect of this subsection, and

(b) if, before the end of the period of 28 days beginning with the day on which notice was sent to her, she asks him to do so, treat the application for a maintenance assessment under section 6 but under section 4.

(1C) Where the application is not preserved under subsection (1B) (and so is treated as not having been made) the Secretary of State shall notify—

(a) the parent with care concerned; and

(b) the absent parent (or alleged absent parent), where it appears to him that that person is aware of the application.]

(2) The amount of child support maintenance to be fixed by any maintenance assessment shall be determined in accordance with the provisions of Part I of Schedule 1.

(3) Part II of Schedule 1 makes further provision with respect to maintenance assessments.

NOTES

Sub-s (1): words in square brackets substituted by the Social Security Act 1998, s 86(1), Sch 7, para 24(1).

Sub-s (1A): inserted by the Child Support Act 1995, s 19; words in square brackets substituted by the Social Security Act 1998, s 86(1), Sch 7, para 24(2).

Sub-ss (1B), (1C): inserted by the Child Support Act 1995, s 19.

12   Interim maintenance assessments

[(1) Where the Secretary of State—

(a) is required to make a maintenance assessment; or

(b) is proposing to make a decision under section 16 or 17,

and (in either case) it appears to him that he does not have sufficient information to enable him to do so, he may make an interim maintenance assessment.]

(2) The Secretary of State may by regulations make provision as to interim maintenance assessments.

(3)   The regulations may, in particular, make provision as to—
  (a) the procedure to be followed in making an interim maintenance assessment; and
  (b) the basis on which the amount of child support maintenance fixed by an interim assessment is to be calculated.

(4)   Before making any interim assessment [the Secretary of State] shall, if it is reasonably practicable to do so, give written notice of his intention to make such an assessment to—
  (a) the absent parent concerned;
  (b) the person with care concerned; and
  (c) where the application for a maintenance assessment was made under section 7, the child concerned.

(5)   Where [the Secretary of State] serves notice under subsection (4), he shall not make the proposed interim assessment before the end of such period as may be prescribed.

NOTES

Sub-s (1): substituted by the Social Security Act 1998, s 86(1), Sch 7, para 25(1).
Sub-ss (4), (5): words in square brackets substituted by the Social Security Act 1998, s 86(1), Sch 7, para 25(2).

Information

14   Information required by Secretary of State

(1)   The Secretary of State may make regulations requiring any information or evidence needed for the determination of any application under this Act, or any question arising in connection with such an application, or needed in connection with the collection or enforcement of child support or other maintenance under this Act, to be furnished—
  (a) by such persons as may be determined in accordance with regulations made by the Secretary of State; and
  (b) in accordance with the regulations.

[(1A) Regulations under subsection (1) may make provision for notifying any person who is required to furnish any information or evidence under the regulations of the possible consequences of failing to do so.]

(2)   . . .

[(2A) ...]

(3)   The Secretary of State may by regulations make provision authorising the disclosure by him . . . , in such circumstances as may be prescribed, of such information held by [him] for purposes of this Act as may be prescribed.

(4)   The provisions of Schedule 2 (which relate to information which is held for purposes other than those of this Act but which is required by the Secretary of State) shall have effect.

NOTES

Sub-ss (1A): inserted by the Child Support Act 1995, s 30(5), Sch 3, para 3.

Sub-s (2): repealed by the Social Security Act 1998, s 86(1), (2), Sch 7, para 27(a), Sch 8.

Sub-s (2A): inserted by the Child Support Act 1995, s 30(5), Sch 3, para 3; repealed by the Social Security Act 1998, s 86(1), (2), Sch 7, para 27(a), Sch 8.

Sub-s (3): words omitted repealed and words in square brackets substituted by the Social Security Act 1998, s 86(1), (2), Sch 7, para 27(b), Sch 8.

15   Powers of inspectors

(1)   Where, in a particular case, the Secretary of State considers it appropriate to do so for the purpose of acquiring information which he . . . requires for purposes of this Act, he may appoint a person to act as an inspector under this section.

(2)   Every inspector shall be furnished with a certificate of his appointment.

(3)   Without prejudice to his being appointed to act in relation to any other case, or being appointed to act for a further period in relation to the case in question, an inspector's appointment shall cease at the end of such period as may be specified.

(4)   An inspector shall have power—
    (a) to enter at all reasonable times—
       (i)   any specified premises, other than premises used solely as a dwelling- house; and
      (ii)   any premises which are not specified but which are used by any specified person for the purpose of carrying on any trade, profession, vocation or business; and

(b) to make such examination and enquiry there as he considers appropriate.

(5)   An inspector exercising his powers may question any person aged 18 or over whom he finds on the premises.

(6)   If required to do so by an inspector exercising his powers, any person who is or has been—
    (a) an occupier of the premises in question;
    (b) an employer or an employee working at or from those premises;
    (c) carrying on at or from those premises any trade, profession, vocation or business;
    (d) an employee or agent of any person mentioned in paragraphs (a) to (c),

shall furnish to the inspector all such information and documents as the inspector may reasonably require.

(7)   No person shall be required under this section to answer any question or to give any evidence tending to incriminate himself or, in the case of a person who is married, his or her spouse.

(8)   On applying for admission to any premises in the exercise of his powers, an inspector shall, if so required, produce his certificate.

(9)   If any person—
    (a) intentionally delays or obstructs any inspector exercising his powers; or
    (b) without reasonable excuse, refuses or neglects to answer any question or furnish any information or to produce any document when required to do so under this section,

he shall be guilty of an offence and liable on summary conviction to a fine not exceeding level 3 on the standard scale.

(10)   In this section—
    "certificate" means a certificate of appointment issued under this section;
    "inspector" means an inspector appointed under this section;
    "powers" means powers conferred by this section; and
    "specified" means specified in the certificate in question.

NOTES

Sub-s (1): words omitted repealed by the Social Security Act 1998, s 86(1), (2), Sch 7, para 28, Sch 8.

[16 Revision of decisions

(1) Any decision of the Secretary of State under section 11, 12 or 17 may be revised by the Secretary of State—

    (a) either within the prescribed period or in prescribed cases or circumstances; and

    (b) either on an application made for the purpose or on his own initiative;

and regulations may prescribe the procedure by which a decision of the Secretary of State may be so revised.

(2) In making a decision under subsection (1), the Secretary of State need not consider any issue that is not raised by the application or, as the case may be, did not cause him to act on his own initiative.

(3) Subject to subsections (4) and (5) and section 28ZC, a revision under this section shall take effect as from the date on which the original decision took (or was to take) effect.

(4) Regulations may provide that, in prescribed cases or circumstances, a revision under this section shall take effect as from such other date as may be prescribed.

(5) Where a decision is revised under this section, for the purpose of any rule as to the time allowed for bringing an appeal, the decision shall be regarded as made on the date on which it is so revised.

(6) Except in prescribed circumstances, an appeal against a decision of the Secretary of State shall lapse if the decision is revised under this section before the appeal is determined.]

NOTES

Commencement: 16 November 1998 (so far as it introduces provision authorising the making of regulations) (subject to transitional provisions and savings (SI 1998/2780)); 7 December 1998 (otherwise) (subject to transitional provisions and savings (SI 1998/2780)).

Substituted by the Social Security Act 1998, s 40.

[17 Decisions superseding earlier decisions

(1)   Subject to subsection (2), the following, namely—
  (a) any decision of the Secretary of State under section 11 or 12 or this section, whether as originally made or as revised under section 16;
  (b) any decision of an appeal tribunal under section 20; and
  (c) any decision of a Child Support Commissioner on an appeal from such a decision as is mentioned in paragraph (b),

may be superseded by a decision made by the Secretary of State, either on an application made for the purpose or on his own initiative.

(2)   In making a decision under subsection (1), the Secretary of State need not consider any issue that is not raised by the application or, as the case may be, did not cause him to act on his own initiative.

(3)   Regulations may prescribe the cases and circumstances in which, and the procedure by which, a decision may be made under this section.

(4)   Subject to subsection (5) and section 28ZC, a decision under this section shall take effect as from the date on which it is made or, where applicable, the date on which the application was made.

(5)   Regulations may provide that, in prescribed cases or circumstances, a decision under this section shall take effect as from such other date as may be prescribed.]

NOTES

Commencement: 4 March 1999 (so far as authorising the making of regulations and in so far as substitutes Child Support Act 1991, s 17(3), (5)) (SI 1999/528); 1 June 1999 (otherwise) (SI 1999/1510).

Substituted for original ss 17–19 by the Social Security Act 1998, s 41.

[20 Appeals to appeal tribunals

(1)   Where an application for a maintenance assessment is refused, the person who made that application shall have a right of appeal to an appeal tribunal against the refusal.

(2)   Where a maintenance assessment is in force—

(a) the absent parent or person with care with respect to whom it was made; or

(b) where the application for the assessment was made under section 7, either of them or the child concerned,

shall have a right of appeal to an appeal tribunal against the amount of the assessment or the date from which the assessment takes effect.

(3) Where a maintenance assessment is cancelled, or an application for the cancellation of a maintenance assessment is refused—

(a) the absent parent or person with care with respect to whom the maintenance assessment in question was, or remains, in force; or

(b) where the application for that assessment was made under section 7, either of them or the child concerned,

shall have a right of appeal to an appeal tribunal against the cancellation or refusal.

(4) A person with a right of appeal under this section shall be given such notice of that right and, in the case of a right conferred by subsection (1) or (3), such notice of the decision as may be prescribed.

(5) Regulations may make—

(a) provision as to the manner in which, and the time within which, appeals are to be brought; and

(b) such provision with respect to proceedings before appeal tribunals as the Secretary of State considers appropriate.

(6) The regulations may in particular make any provision of a kind mentioned in Schedule 5 to the Social Security Act 1998.

(7) In deciding an appeal under this section, an appeal tribunal—

(a) need not consider any issue that is not raised by the appeal; and

(b) shall not take into account any circumstances not obtaining at the time when the decision or assessment appealed against was made.]

NOTES

Commencement: 4 March 1999 (so far as authorising the making of regulations and in so far as substitutes Child Support Act 1991, s 17(3), (5)) (SI 1999/528); 1 June 1999 (otherwise) (SI 1999/1510).

Substituted for original ss 20, 20A (s 20A as inserted by the Child Support Act 1995, s 16), 21, by the Social Security Act 1998, s 42.

22 Child Support Commissioners

(1)   Her Majesty may from time to time appoint a Chief Child Support Commissioner and such number of other Child Support Commissioners as she may think fit.

(2)   The Chief Child Support Commissioner and the other Child Support Commissioners shall be appointed from among persons who—
(a) have a 10 year general qualification; or
(b) are advocates or solicitors in Scotland of 10 years' standing.

(3)   The Lord Chancellor, after consulting the Lord Advocate, may make such regulations with respect to proceedings before Child Support Commissioners as he considers appropriate.

(4)   The regulations—
(a) may, in particular, make any provision of a kind mentioned in [Schedule 5 to the Social Security Act 1998]; and
(b) shall provide that any hearing before a Child Support Commissioner shall be in public except in so far as the Commissioner for special reasons directs otherwise.

(5)   Schedule 4 shall have effect with respect to Child Support Commissioners.

NOTES

Sub-s (4): repealed by the Northern Ireland Act 1998, s 100(2), Sch 15, as from a day to be appointed; words in square brackets substituted by the Social Security Act 1998, s 86(1), Sch 7, para 29.

Sub-s (5): repealed by the Northern Ireland Act 1998, s 100(2), Sch 15, as from a day to be appointed.

24 Appeal to Child Support Commissioner

(1)   Any person who is aggrieved by a decision of [an appeal tribunal, and the Secretary of State], may appeal to a Child Support Commissioner on a question of law.

[(1A) . . .]

(2)   Where, on an appeal under this section, a Child Support Commissioner holds that the decision appealed against was wrong in law he shall set it aside.

(3)   Where a decision is set aside under subsection (2), the Child Support Commissioner may—

    (a) if he can do so without making fresh or further findings of fact, give the decision which he considers should have been given by [the appeal tribunal];

    (b) if he considers it expedient, make such findings and give such decision as he considers appropriate in the light of those findings; or

    [(c) on an appeal by the Secretary of State, refer the case to [an appeal tribunal] with directions for its determination; or

    (d) on any other appeal, refer the case to [the Secretary of State] or, if he considers it appropriate, to [an appeal tribunal] with directions for its determination.]

[(4)   The reference under subsection (3) to the Secretary of State shall, subject to any direction of the Child Support Commissioner, be to an officer of his, or a person providing him with services, who has taken no part in the decision originally appealed against.]

(5)   On a reference under subsection (3) to [an appeal tribunal], the tribunal shall, subject to any direction of the Child Support Commissioner, consist of persons who were not members of the tribunal which gave the decision which has been appealed against.

(6)   No appeal lies under this section without the leave—

    (a) of the person [who constituted, or was the chairman of, the appeal tribunal] when the decision appealed against was given or of [such other person] as may be determined in accordance with regulations made by the Lord Chancellor; or

    (b) subject to and in accordance with regulations so made, of a Child Support Commissioner.

(7)   The Lord Chancellor may by regulations make provision as to the manner in which, and the time within which, appeals under this section are to be brought and applications for leave under this section are to be made.

(8)   Where a question which would otherwise fall to be determined by [the Secretary of State] first arises in the course of an appeal to a Child Support Commissioner, he may, if he thinks fit, determine it even though it has not been considered by [the Secretary of State].

(9)   Before making any regulations under subsection (6) or (7), the Lord Chancellor shall consult the Lord Advocate.

NOTES

Sub-ss (1), (5), (6), (8): words in square brackets substituted by the Social Security Act 1998, s 86(1), Sch 7, para 30(1), (5)–(7).

Sub-s (1A): inserted by the Child Support Act 1995, s 30(5), Sch 3, para 7(2); repealed by the Social Security Act 1998, s 86(1), (2), Sch 7, para 30(2), Sch 8.

Sub-s (3): words in square brackets in para (a) substituted by the Social Security Act 1998, s 86(1), Sch 7, para 30(3)(a); paras (c), (d) substituted for para (c) as originally enacted by the Child Support Act 1995, s 30(5), Sch 3, para 7(3), words in square brackets in paras (c), (d) substituted by the Social Security Act 1998, s 86(1), Sch 7, para 30(3)(b), (c).

Sub-s (4): substituted by the Social Security Act 1998, s 86(1), Sch 7, para 30(4).

25 Appeal from Child Support Commissioner on question of law

(1)　　An appeal on a question of law shall lie to the appropriate court from any decision of a Child Support Commissioner.

(2)　　No such appeal may be brought except—
  (a) with leave of the Child Support Commissioner who gave the decision or, where regulations made by the Lord Chancellor so provide, of a Child Support Commissioner selected in accordance with the regulations; or
  (b) if the Child Support Commissioner refuses leave, with the leave of the appropriate court.

(3)　　An application for leave to appeal under this section against a decision of a Child Support Commissioner ("the appeal decision") may only be made by—
  (a) a person who was a party to the proceedings in which the original decision, or appeal decision, was given;
  (b) the Secretary of State; or
  (c) any other person who is authorised to do so by regulations made by the Lord Chancellor.

[(3A)　The Child Support Commissioner to whom an application for leave to appeal under this section is made shall specify as the appropriate court either the Court of Appeal or the Court of Session.

(3B)　In determining the appropriate court, the Child Support Commissioner shall have regard to the circumstances of the case, and in particular the convenience of the persons who may be parties to the appeal.]

(4)   In this section—

"appropriate court"[, except in subsections (3A) and (3B), means the court specified in accordance with those subsections]; and

"original decision" means the decision to which the appeal decision in question relates.

(5)   The Lord Chancellor may by regulations make provision with respect to—

(a) the manner in which and the time within which applications must be made to a Child Support Commissioner for leave under this section; and

(b) the procedure for dealing with such applications.

(6)   Before making any regulations under subsection (2), (3) or (5), the Lord Chancellor shall consult the Lord Advocate.

NOTES

Sub-ss (3A), (3B): inserted by the Child Support Act 1995, s 30(5), Sch 3, para 8(1).

Sub-s (4): in definition "appropriate court" words in square brackets substituted by the Child Support Act 1995, s 30(5), Sch 3, para 8(2).

26 Disputes about parentage

(1)   Where a person who is alleged to be a parent of the child with respect to whom an application for a maintenance assessment has been made ("the alleged parent") denies that he is one of the child's parents, [the Secretary of State] shall not make a maintenance assessment on the assumption that the alleged parent is one of the child's parents unless the case falls within one of those set out in subsection (2).

(2)   The Cases are—

CASE A

Where the alleged parent is a parent of the child in question by virtue of having adopted him.

CASE B

Where the alleged parent is a parent of the child in question by virtue of an order under section 30 of the Human Fertilisation and Embryology Act 1990 (parental orders in favour of gamete donors).

CASE C

Where—
  (a) either—
    (i) a declaration that the alleged parent is a parent of the child in question (or a declaration which has that effect) is in force under section 56 of the Family Law Act 1986 [or Article 32 of the Matrimonial and Family Proceedings (Northern Ireland) Order 1989] (declarations of parentage); or
    (ii) a declarator by a court in Scotland that the alleged parent is a parent of the child in question (or a declarator which has that effect) is in force; and
  (b) the child has not subsequently been adopted.

CASE D

Where—
  (a) a declaration to the effect that the alleged parent is one of the parents of the child in question has been made under section 27; and
  (b) the child has not subsequently been adopted.

CASE E

Where—
  (a) the child is habitually resident in Scotland;
  (b) [the Secretary of State] is satisfied that one or other of the presumptions set out in section 5(1) of the Law Reform (Parent and Child) (Scotland) Act 1986 applies; and
  (c) the child has not subsequently been adopted.

CASE F

Where—
  (a) the alleged parent has been found, or adjudged, to be the father of the child in question—
    (i) in proceedings before any court in England and Wales which are relevant proceedings for the purposes of section 12 of the Civil Evidence Act 1968 [or in proceedings before any court in Northern Ireland which are relevant proceedings for the purposes of section 8 of the Civil Evidence Act (Northern Ireland) 1971]; or
    (ii) in affiliation proceedings before any court in the United Kingdom,

(whether or not he offered any defence to the allegation of paternity) and that finding or adjudication still subsists; and
    (b) the child has not subsequently been adopted.

(3)   In this section—
    "adopted" means adopted within the meaning of Part IV of the Adoption Act 1976 or, in relation to Scotland, Part IV of the Adoption (Scotland) Act 1978; and
    "affiliation proceedings", in relation to Scotland, means any action of affiliation and aliment.

NOTES

Sub-s (1): words in square brackets substituted by the Social Security Act 1998, s 86(1), Sch 7, para 31(1).

Sub-s (2): words in square brackets in Case C, Case F inserted by the Children (Northern Ireland Consequential Amendments) Order 1995, SI 1995/756, art 13; words in square brackets in Case E substituted by the Social Security Act 1998, s 86(1), Sch 7, para 31(2).

27 Reference to court for declaration of parentage

[(1)   Subsection (1A) applies in any case where—
    (a) an application for a maintenance assessment has been made, or a maintenance assessment is in force, with respect to a person ("the alleged parent") who denies that he is a parent of a child with respect to whom the application or assessment was made; and
    (b) [the Secretary of State] is not satisfied that the case falls within one of those set out in section 26(2).

(1A) In any case where this subsection applies, the Secretary of State or the person with care may apply to the court for a declaration as to whether or not the alleged parent is one of the child's parents.]

(2)   If, on hearing any application under subsection [(1A)], the court is satisfied that the alleged parent is, or is not, a parent of the child in question it shall make a declaration to that effect.

[(3)   A declaration under this section shall have effect only for the purposes of—
    (a) this Act; and
    (b) proceedings in which a court is considering whether to make a maintenance order in the circumstances mentioned in subsection (6), (7) or (8) of section 8.]

(4)   In this section "court" means, subject to any provision made under Schedule 11 to the Children Act 1989 (jurisdiction of courts with respect to certain proceedings relating to children) the High Court, a county court or a magistrates' court.

(5)   . . .

(6)   This section does not apply to Scotland.

NOTES

Sub-ss (1): substituted, together with sub-s (1A), for sub-s (1) as originally enacted by the Child Support Act 1995, s 20(2); words in square brackets substituted by the Social Security Act 1998, s 86(1), Sch 7, para 32.

Sub-s (1A): substituted, together with sub-s (1), for sub-s (1) as originally enacted, by the Child Support Act 1995, s 20(2).

Sub-s (2): number in square brackets substituted by the Child Support Act 1995, s 20(3).

Sub-s (3): substituted by the Child Support Act 1995, s 20(4).

Sub-s (5): amends the Civil Evidence Act 1968, s 12(5).

[27A   Recovery of fees for scientific tests

(1)   This section applies in any case where—
  (a) an application for a maintenance assessment has been made or a maintenance assessment is in force;
  (b) scientific tests have been carried out (otherwise than under a direction or in response to a request) in relation to bodily samples obtained from a person who is alleged to be a parent of a child with respect to whom the application or assessment is made;
  (c) the results of the tests do not exclude the alleged parent from being one of the child's parents; and
  (d) one of the conditions set out in subsection (2) is satisfied.

(2)   The conditions are that—
  (a) the alleged parent does not deny that he is one of the child's parents;
  (b) in proceedings under section 27, a court has made a declaration that the alleged parent is a parent of the child in question; or
  (c) in an action under section 7 of the Law Reform (Parent and Child) (Scotland) Act 1986, brought by the Secretary of State by virtue of section 28, a court has granted a decree of declarator of parentage to the effect that the alleged parent is a parent of the child in question.

(3)   In any case to which this section applies, any fee paid by the Secretary of State in connection with scientific tests may be recovered by him from the alleged parent as a debt due to the Crown.

(4)   In this section—
"bodily sample" means a sample of bodily fluid or bodily tissue taken for the purpose of scientific tests;
"direction" means a direction given by a court under section 20 of the Family Law Reform Act 1969 (tests to determine paternity);
"request" means a request made by a court under section 70 of the Law Reform (Miscellaneous Provisions) (Scotland) Act 1990 (blood and other samples in civil proceedings); and
"scientific tests" means scientific tests made with the object of ascertaining the inheritable characteristics of bodily fluids or bodily tissue.

(5)   Any sum recovered by the Secretary of State under this section shall be paid by him into the Consolidated Fund.]

NOTES

Commencement: 4 September 1995.
Inserted by the Child Support Act 1995, s 21.

[*Departure from usual rules for determining maintenance assessments*

28A   Application for a departure direction

(1)   Where a maintenance assessment ("the current assessment") is in force—
   (a) the person with care, or absent parent, with respect to whom it was made, or
   (b) where the application for the current assessment was made under section 7, either of those persons or the child concerned,

may apply to the Secretary of State for a direction under section 28F (a "departure direction").

(2)   An application for a departure direction shall state in writing the grounds on which it is made and shall, in particular, state whether it is based on—

(a) the effect of the current assessment; or

(b) a material change in the circumstances of the case since the current assessment was made.

(3)   In other respects, an application for a departure direction shall be made in such manner as may be prescribed.

[(4)   An application may be made under this section even though an application has been made under section 16(1) or 17(1) with respect to the current assessment.]

(5)   If the Secretary of State considers it appropriate to do so, he may by regulations provide for the question whether a change of circumstances is material to be determined in accordance with the regulations.

(6)   Schedule 4A has effect in relation to departure directions.]

NOTES

Commencement: 1 June 1999 (sub-s (4)); 14 October 1996 (sub-ss (1)–(3), (5), (6) for certain purposes); 2 December 1996 ((sub-ss (1)–(3), (5), (6) otherwise).
Inserted, together with the cross-heading, by the Child Support Act 1995, s 1(1).
Sub-s (4): substituted by the Social Security Act 1998, s 86(1), Sch 7, para 34.

[28C   Imposition of a regular payments condition

(1)   Where an application for a departure direction is made by an absent parent, the Secretary of State may impose on him one of the conditions mentioned in subsection (2) ("a regular payments condition").

(2)   The conditions are that—
  (a) the applicant must make the payments of child support maintenance fixed by the current assessment;
  (b) the applicant must make such reduced payments of child support maintenance as may be determined in accordance with regulations made by the Secretary of State.

(3)–(5)   . . .

(6)   Where an absent parent has failed to comply with a regular payments condition—

    (a) the Secretary of State may refuse to consider the application; and

    (b) in prescribed circumstances the application shall lapse.

(7), (8)   . . .]

NOTES

    Commencement: 14 October 1996 (for certain purposes); 2 December 1996 (otherwise).

    Inserted by the Child Support Act 1995, s 3.

    Sub-ss (3)–(5), (7), (8): outside the scope of this work.

[28E Matters to be taken into account

(1)   In determining any application for a departure direction, the Secretary of State shall have regard both to the general principles set out in subsection (2) and to such other considerations as may be prescribed.

(2)   The general principles are that—
    (a) parents should be responsible for maintaining their children whenever they can afford to do so;
    (b) where a parent has more than one child, his obligation to maintain any one of them should be no less of an obligation than his obligation to maintain any other of them.

(3)   In determining any application for a departure direction, the Secretary of State shall take into account any representations made to him—
    (a) by the person with care or absent parent concerned; or
    (b) where the application for the current assessment was made under section 7, by either of them or the child concerned.

(4)   In determining any application for a departure direction, no account shall be taken of the fact that—
    (a) any part of the income of the person with care concerned is, or would be if a departure direction were made, derived from any benefit; or
    (b) some or all of any child support maintenance might be taken into account in any manner in relation to any entitlement to benefit.

(5)   In this section "benefit" has such meaning as may be prescribed.]

NOTES

Commencement: 14 October 1996 (for certain purposes); 2 December 1996 (otherwise).

Inserted by the Child Support Act 1995, s 5.

[28F Departure directions

(1)   The Secretary of State may give a departure direction if—
  (a) he is satisfied that the case is one which falls within one or more of the cases set out in Part I of Schedule 4B or in regulations made under that Part; and
  (b) it is his opinion that, in all the circumstances of the case, it would be just and equitable to give a departure direction.

(2)   In considering whether it would be just and equitable in any case to give a departure direction, the Secretary of State shall have regard, in particular, to—
  (a) the financial circumstances of the absent parent concerned,
  (b) the financial circumstances of the person with care concerned, and
  (c) the welfare of any child likely to be affected by the direction.

(3)   The Secretary of State may by regulations make provision—
  (a) for factors which are to be taken into account in determining whether it would be just and equitable to give a departure direction in any case;
  (b) for factors which are not to be taken into account in determining such a question.

(4)   The Secretary of State shall not give a departure direction if he is satisfied that the difference between the current amount and the revised amount is less than an amount to be calculated in accordance with regulations made by the Secretary of State for the purposes of this subsection and section 28B(2).

(5)   In subsection (4)—
  "the current amount" means the amount of the child support maintenance fixed by the current assessment, and
  "the revised amount" means the amount of child support maintenance which would be fixed if a fresh maintenance assessment were to be made as a result of the departure direction which the Secretary of State would give in response to the application but for subsection (4).

(6)–(8) . . .]

NOTES
Commencement: 14 October 1996 (for certain purposes); 2 December 1996 (otherwise).
Inserted by the Child Support Act 1995, s 6(1).
Sub-ss (6)–(8): outside the scope of this work.

29 Collection of child support maintenance

(1)   The Secretary of State may arrange for the collection of any child support maintenance payable in accordance with a maintenance assessment where—

(a) the assessment is made by virtue of section 6; or

(b) an application has been made to the Secretary of State under section 4(2) or 7(3) for him to arrange for its collection.

(2)   Where a maintenance assessment is made under this Act, payments of child support maintenance under the assessment shall be made in accordance with regulations made by the Secretary of State.

(3)   The regulations may, in particular, make provision—

(a) for payments of child support maintenance to be made—

(i)   to the person caring for the child or children in question;

(ii) to, or through, the Secretary of State; or

(iii) to, or through, such other person as the Secretary of State may, from time to time, specify;

(b) as to the method by which payments of child support maintenance are to be made;

(c) as to the intervals at which such payments are to be made;

(d) as to the method and timing of the transmission of payments which are made, to or through the Secretary of State or any other person, in accordance with the regulations;

(e) empowering the Secretary of State to direct any person liable to make payments in accordance with the assessment—

(i)   to make them by standing order or by any other method which requires one person to give his authority for payments to be made from an account of his to an account of another's on specific dates during the period for which the authority is in force and without the need for any further authority from him;

(ii) to open an account from which payments under the assessment may be made in accordance with the method of payment which that person is obliged to adopt;

(f) providing for the making of representations with respect to matters with which the regulations are concerned.

30 Collection and enforcement of other forms of maintenance

(1)   Where the Secretary of State is arranging for the collection of any payments under section 29 or subsection (2), he may also arrange for the collection of any periodical payments, or secured periodical payments, of a prescribed kind which are payable to or for the benefit of any person who falls within a prescribed category.

(2)   The Secretary of State may arrange for the collection of any periodical payments or secured periodical payments of a prescribed kind which are payable for the benefit of a child even though he is not arranging for the collection of child support maintenance with respect to that child.

(3)   Where—
   (a) the Secretary of State is arranging, under this Act, for the collection of different payments ("the payments") from the same absent parent;
   (b) an amount is collected by the Secretary of State from the absent parent which is less than the total amount due in respect of the payments; and
   (c) the absent parent has not stipulated how that amount is to be allocated by the Secretary of State as between the payments,

the Secretary of State may allocate that amount as he sees fit.

(4)   In relation to England and Wales, the Secretary of State may by regulations make provision for sections 29 and 31 to 40 to apply, with such modifications (if any) as he considers necessary or expedient, for the purpose of enabling him to enforce any obligation to pay any amount which he is authorised to collect under this section.

(5)   In relation to Scotland, the Secretary of State may by regulations make provision for the purpose of enabling him to enforce any obligation to pay any amount which he is authorised to collect under this section—
   (a) empowering him to bring any proceedings or take any other steps (other than diligence against earnings) which could have been brought or taken by or on behalf of the person to whom the periodical payments are payable;
   (b) applying sections 29, 31 and 32 with such modifications (if any) as he considers necessary or expedient.

[(5A) Regulations made under subsection (1) or (2) prescribing payments which may be collected by the Secretary of State may make provision for the payment to him by such person or persons as may be prescribed of such fees as may be prescribed.]

Sub-s (5A): added by the Child Support Act 1995, s 30(5), Sch 3, para 9, as from a day to be appointed.

31 Deduction from earnings orders

(1)   This section applies where any person ("the liable person") is liable to make payments of child support maintenance.

(2)   The Secretary of State may make an order ("a deduction from earnings order") against a liable person to secure the payment of any amount due under the maintenance assessment in question.

(3)   A deduction from earnings order may be made so as to secure the payment of—
   (a) arrears of child support maintenance payable under the assessment;
   (b) amounts of child support maintenance which will become due under the assessment; or
   (c) both such arrears and such future amounts.

(4)   A deduction from earnings order—
   (a) shall be expressed to be directed at a person ("the employer") who has the liable person in his employment; and
   (b) shall have effect from such date as may be specified in the order.

(5)   A deduction from earnings order shall operate as an instruction to the employer to—
   (a) make deductions from the liable person's earnings; and
   (b) pay the amounts deducted to the Secretary of State.

(6)   The Secretary of State shall serve a copy of any deduction from earnings order which he makes under this section on—
   (a) the person who appears to the Secretary of State to have the liable person in question in his employment; and
   (b) the liable person.

(7)   Where—
   (a) a deduction from earnings order has been made; and
   (b) a copy of the order has been served on the liable person's employer,

it shall be the duty of that employer to comply with the order; but he shall not be under any liability for non-compliance before the end of the period of seven days beginning with the date on which the copy was served on him.

(8) In this section and in section 32 "earnings" has such meaning as may be prescribed.

32 Regulations about deduction from earnings orders

(1) The Secretary of State may by regulations make provision with respect to deduction from earnings orders.

(2) The regulations may, in particular, make provision—
  (a) as to the circumstances in which one person is to be treated as employed by another;
  (b) requiring any deduction from earnings under an order to be made in the prescribed manner;
  (c) requiring an order to specify the amount or amounts to which the order relates and the amount or amounts which are to be deducted from the liable person's earnings in order to meet his liabilities under the maintenance assessment in question;
  (d) requiring the intervals between deductions to be made under an order to be specified in the order;
  (e) as to the payment of sums deducted under an order to the Secretary of State;
  (f) allowing the person who deducts and pays any amount under an order to deduct from the liable person's earnings a prescribed sum towards his administrative costs;
  (g) with respect to the notification to be given to the liable person of amounts deducted, and amounts paid, under the order;
  (h) requiring any person on whom a copy of an order is served to notify the Secretary of State in the prescribed manner and within a prescribed period if he does not have the liable person in his employment or if the liable person ceases to be in his employment;
  (i) as to the operation of an order where the liable person is in the employment of the Crown;
  (j) for the variation of orders;
  (k) similar to that made by section 31(7), in relation to any variation of an order;
  (l) for an order to lapse when the employer concerned ceases to have the liable person in his employment;
  (m) as to the revival of an order in such circumstances as may be prescribed;
  (n) allowing or requiring an order to be discharged;
  (o) as to the giving of notice by the Secretary of State to the employer concerned that an order has lapsed or has ceased to have effect.

(3)   The regulations may include provision that while a deduction from earnings order is in force—

(a) the liable person shall from time to time notify the Secretary of State, in the prescribed manner and within a prescribed period, of each occasion on which he leaves any employment or becomes employed, or re-employed, and shall include in such a notification a statement of his earnings and expected earnings from the employment concerned and of such other matters as may be prescribed;

(b) any person who becomes the liable person's employer and knows that the order is in force shall notify the Secretary of State, in the prescribed manner and within a prescribed period, that he is the liable person's employer, and shall include in such a notification a statement of the liable person's earnings and expected earnings from the employment concerned and of such other matters as may be prescribed.

(4)   The regulations may include provision with respect to the priority as between a deduction from earnings order and—

(a) any other deduction from earnings order;

(b) any order under any other enactment relating to England and Wales which provides for deductions from the liable person's earnings;

(c) any diligence against earnings.

(5)   The regulations may include a provision that a liable person may appeal to a magistrates' court (or in Scotland to the sheriff) if he is aggrieved by the making of a deduction from earnings order against him, or by the terms of any such order, or there is a dispute as to whether payments constitute earnings or as to any other prescribed matter relating to the order.

(6)   On an appeal under subsection (5) the court or (as the case may be) the sheriff shall not question the maintenance assessment by reference to which the deduction from earnings order was made.

(7)   Regulations made by virtue of subsection (5) may include provision as to the powers of a magistrates' court, or in Scotland of the sheriff, in relation to an appeal (which may include provision as to the quashing of a deduction from earnings order or the variation of the terms of such an order).

(8)   If any person fails to comply with the requirements of a deduction from earnings order, or with any regulation under this section which is designated for the purposes of this subsection, he shall be guilty of an offence.

(9)   In subsection (8) "designated" means designated by the regulations.

(10)   It shall be a defence for a person charged with an offence under subsection (8) to prove that he took all reasonable steps to comply with the requirements in question.

(11)   Any person guilty of an offence under subsection (8) shall be liable on summary conviction to a fine not exceeding level two on the standard scale.

33   Liability orders

(1)   This section applies where—
  (a) a person who is liable to make payments of child support maintenance ("the liable person") fails to make one or more of those payments; and
  (b) it appears to the Secretary of State that—
    (i) it is inappropriate to make a deduction from earnings order against him (because, for example, he is not employed); or
    (ii) although such an order has been made against him, it has proved ineffective as a means of securing that payments are made in accordance with the maintenance assessment in question.

(2)   The Secretary of State may apply to a magistrates' court or, in Scotland, to the sheriff for an order ("a liability order") against the liable person.

(3)   Where the Secretary of State applies for a liability order, the magistrates' court or (as the case may be) sheriff shall make the order if satisfied that the payments in question have become payable by the liable person and have not been paid.

(4)   On an application under subsection (2), the court or (as the case may be) the sheriff shall not question the maintenance assessment under which the payments of child support maintenance fell to be made.

[(5)   If the Secretary of State designates a liability order for the purposes of this subsection it shall be treated as a judgment entered in a county court for the purposes of section 73 of the County Courts Act 1984 (register of judgments and orders).]

NOTES

Sub-s (5): added by the Child Support Act 1995, s 30(5), Sch 3, para 10.

34 Regulations about liability orders

(1)   The Secretary of State may make regulations in relation to England and Wales
    (a) prescribing the procedure to be followed in dealing with an application by the Secretary of State for a liability order;
    (b) prescribing the form and contents of a liability order; and
    (c) providing that where a magistrates' court has made a liability order, the person against whom it is made shall, during such time as the amount in respect of which the order was made remains wholly or partly unpaid, be under a duty to supply relevant information to the Secretary of State.

(2)   In subsection (1) "relevant information" means any information of a prescribed description which is in the possession of the liable person and which the Secretary of State has asked him to supply.

NOTES

Commencement: 17 June 1992 (sub-s (1)); to be appointed (remainder).

35 Enforcement of liability orders by distress

(1)   Where a liability order has been made against a person ("the liable person"), the Secretary of State may levy the appropriate amount by distress and sale of the liable person's goods.

(2)   In subsection (1), "the appropriate amount" means the aggregate of—
    (a) the amount in respect of which the order was made, to the extent that it remains unpaid; and
    (b) an amount, determined in such manner as may be prescribed, in respect of the charges connected with the distress.

(3)   The Secretary of State may, in exercising his powers under subsection (1) against the liable person's goods, seize—
    (a) any of the liable person's goods except—
        (i)   such tools, books, vehicles and other items of equipment as are necessary to him for use personally by him in his employment, business or vocation;
        (ii) such clothing, bedding, furniture, household equipment and provisions as are necessary for satisfying his basic domestic needs; and

(b) any money, banknotes, bills of exchange, promissory notes, bonds, specialties or securities for money belonging to the liable person.

(4) For the purposes of subsection (3), the liable person's domestic needs shall be taken to include those of any member of his family with whom he resides.

(5) No person levying a distress under this section shall be taken to be a trespasser—
(a) on that account; or
(b) from the beginning, on account of any subsequent irregularity in levying the distress.

(6) A person sustaining special damage by reason of any irregularity in levying a distress under this section may recover full satisfaction for the damage (and no more) by proceedings in trespass or otherwise.

(7) The Secretary of State may make regulations supplementing the provisions of this section.

(8) The regulations may, in particular—
(a) provide that a distress under this section may be levied anywhere in England and Wales;
(b) provide that such a distress shall not be deemed unlawful on account of any defect or want of form in the liability order;
(c) provide for an appeal to a magistrates' court by any person aggrieved by the levying of, or an attempt to levy, a distress under this section;
(d) make provision as to the powers of the court on an appeal (which may include provision as to the discharge of goods distrained or the payment of compensation in respect of goods distrained and sold).

36 Enforcement in county courts

(1) Where a liability order has been made against a person, the amount in respect of which the order was made, to the extent that it remains unpaid, shall, if a county court so orders, be recoverable by means of garnishee proceedings or a charging order, as if it were payable under a county court order.

(2) In subsection (1) "charging order" has the same meaning as in section 1 of the Charging Orders Act 1979.

39 Liability orders: enforcement throughout United Kingdom

(1)   The Secretary of State may by regulations provide for—
  (a) any liability order made by a court in England and Wales; or
  (b) any corresponding order made by a court in Northern Ireland,

to be enforced in Scotland as if it had been made by the sheriff.

(2)   The power conferred on the Court of Session by section 32 of the Sheriff Courts (Scotland) Act 1971 (power of Court of Session to regulate civil procedure in the sheriff court) shall extend to making provision for the registration in the sheriff court for enforcement of any such order as is referred to in subsection (1).

(3)   The Secretary of State may by regulations make provision for, or in connection with, the enforcement in England and Wales of—
  (a) any liability order made by the sheriff in Scotland; or
  (b) any corresponding order made by a court in Northern Ireland,

as if it had been made by a magistrates' court in England and Wales.

(4)   Regulations under subsection (3) may, in particular, make provision for the registration of any such order as is referred to in that subsection in connection with its enforcement in England and Wales.

40 Commitment to prison

(1)   Where the Secretary of State has sought—
  (a) to levy an amount by distress under this Act; or
  (b) to recover an amount by virtue of section 36,

and that amount, or any portion of it, remains unpaid he may apply to a magistrates' court for the issue of a warrant committing the liable person to prison.

(2)   On any such application the court shall (in the presence of the liable person) inquire as to—
  (a) the liable person's means; and
  (b) whether there has been wilful refusal or culpable neglect on his part.

(3)   If, but only if, the court is of the opinion that there has been wilful refusal or culpable neglect on the part of the liable person it may—

    (a) issue a warrant of commitment against him; or

    (b) fix a term of imprisonment and postpone the issue of the warrant until such time and on such conditions (if any) as it thinks just.

(4)   Any such warrant—

    (a) shall be made in respect of an amount equal to the aggregate of—

        (i) the amount mentioned in section 35(1) or so much of it as remains outstanding; and

       (ii) an amount (determined in accordance with regulations made by the Secretary of State) in respect of the costs of commitment; and

    (b) shall state that amount.

(5)   No warrant may be issued under this section against a person who is under the age of 18.

(6)   A warrant issued under this section shall order the liable person—

    (a) to be imprisoned for a specified period; but

    (b) to be released (unless he is in custody for some other reason) on payment of the amount stated in the warrant.

(7)   The maximum period of imprisonment which may be imposed by virtue of subsection (6) shall be calculated in accordance with Schedule 4 to the Magistrates' Courts Act 1980 (maximum periods of imprisonment in default of payment) but shall not exceed six weeks.

(8)   The Secretary of State may by regulations make provision for the period of imprisonment specified in any warrant issued under this section to be reduced where there is part payment of the amount in respect of which the warrant was issued.

(9)   A warrant issued under this section may be directed to such person or persons as the court issuing it thinks fit.

(10)   Section 80 of the Magistrates' Courts Act 1980 (application of money found on defaulter) shall apply in relation to a warrant issued under this section against a liable person as it applies in relation to the enforcement of a sum mentioned in subsection (1) of that section.

(11)   The Secretary of State may by regulations make provision—

    (a) as to the form of any warrant issued under this section;

    (b) allowing an application under this section to be renewed where no warrant is issued or term of imprisonment is fixed;

(c) that a statement in writing to the effect that wages of any amount have been paid to the liable person during any period, purporting to be signed by or on behalf of his employer, shall be evidence of the facts stated;

(d) that, for the purposes of enabling an inquiry to be made as to the liable person's conduct and means, a justice of the peace may issue a summons to him to appear before a magistrates' court and (if he does not obey) may issue a warrant for his arrest;

(e) that for the purpose of enabling such an inquiry, a justice of the peace may issue a warrant for the liable person's arrest without issuing a summons;

(f) as to the execution of a warrant for arrest.

(12) Subsections (1) to (11) do not apply to Scotland.

(13) For the avoidance of doubt, it is declared that a sum payable under a liability order is a sum decerned for aliment for the purposes of the Debtors (Scotland) Act 1880 and the Civil Imprisonment (Scotland) Act 1882.

(14) Where a liability order has been made, the Secretary of State (and he alone) shall be regarded as, and may exercise all the powers of, the creditor for the purposes of section 4 (imprisonment for failure to obey decree for alimentary debt) of the Civil Imprisonment (Scotland) Act 1882.

41 Arrears of child support maintenance

(1) This section applies where—
(a) the Secretary of State is authorised under section 4, 6 or 7 to recover child support maintenance payable by an absent parent in accordance with a maintenance assessment; and
(b) the absent parent has failed to make one or more payments of child support maintenance due from him in accordance with that assessment.

[(2) Where the Secretary of State recovers any such arrears he may, in such circumstances as may be prescribed and to such extent as may be prescribed, retain them if he is satisfied that the amount of any benefit paid to or in respect of the person with care of the child or children in question would have been less had the absent parent made the payment or payments of child support maintenance in question.

(2A) In determining for the purposes of subsection (2) whether the amount of any benefit paid would have been less at any time than the amount which was paid at that time, in a case where the maintenance assessment had effect from a date earlier than that on which it was made, the assessment shall be taken to have been in force at that time.]

(3)   In such circumstances as may be prescribed, the absent parent shall be liable to make such payments of interest with respect to the arrears of child support maintenance as may be prescribed.

(4)   The Secretary of State may by regulations make provision—
  (a) as to the rate of interest payable by virtue of subsection (3);
  (b) as to the time at which, and person to whom, any such interest shall be payable;
  (c) as to the circumstances in which, in a case where the Secretary of State has been acting under section 6, any such interest may be retained by him;
  (d) for the Secretary of State, in a case where he has been acting under section 6 and in such circumstances as may be prescribed, to waive any such interest (or part of any such interest).

(5)   The provisions of this Act with respect to—
  (a) the collection of child support maintenance;
  (b) the enforcement of any obligation to pay child support maintenance,

shall apply equally to interest payable by virtue of this section.

(6)   Any sums retained by the Secretary of State by virtue of this section shall be paid by him into the Consolidated Fund.

NOTES

Sub-ss (2), (2A): substituted for sub-s (2) as originally enacted by the Child Support Act 1995, s 30(5), Sch 3, para 11.

[41A Arrears: alternative to interest payments

(1)   The Secretary of State may by regulations make provision for the payment by absent parents who are in arrears with payments of child support maintenance of sums determined in accordance with the regulations.

(2)   A sum payable under any such regulations is referred to in this section as an "additional sum".

(3)   Any liability of an absent parent to pay an additional sum shall not affect any liability of his to pay the arrears of child support maintenance concerned.

(4)   The Secretary of State shall exercise his powers under this section and those under section 41(3) in such a way as to ensure that no absent parent is liable to pay both interest and an additional sum in respect of the same period (except by reference to different maintenance assessments).

(5)–(7) . . .]

NOTES

Inserted by the Child Support Act 1995, s 22, as from a day to be appointed. Sub-ss (5)–(7): outside the scope of this work.

[41B Repayment of overpaid child support maintenance

(1)   This section applies where it appears to the Secretary of State that an absent parent has made a payment by way of child support maintenance which amounts to an overpayment by him of that maintenance and that—
   (a) it would not be possible for the absent parent to recover the amount of the overpayment by way of an adjustment of the amount payable under a maintenance assessment; or
   (b) it would be inappropriate to rely on an adjustment of the amount payable under a maintenance assessment as the means of enabling the absent parent to recover the amount of the overpayment.

(2)   The Secretary of State may make such payment to the absent parent by way of reimbursement, or partial reimbursement, of the overpayment as the Secretary of State considers appropriate.

(3)   Where the Secretary of State has made a payment under this section he may, in such circumstances as may be prescribed, require the relevant person to pay to him the whole, or a specified proportion, of the amount of that payment.

(4)–(7) . . .

(8)   In this section "relevant person", in relation to an overpayment, means the person with care to whom the overpayment was made.

(9) . . .]

NOTES
Commencement: 1 October 1995 (sub-ss (3), (8)); 4 September 1995 (remainder).
Inserted by the Child Support Act 1995, s 23.
Sub-ss (4)–(7), (9): outside the scope of this work.

Special cases

42 Special cases

(1)   The Secretary of State may by regulations provide that in prescribed circumstances a case is to be treated as a special case for the purposes of this Act.

(2)   Those regulations may, for example, provide for the following to be special cases—
  (a) each parent of a child is an absent parent in relation to the child;
  (b) there is more than one person who is a person with care in relation to the same child;
  (c) there is more than one qualifying child in relation to the same absent parent but the person who is the person with care in relation to one of those children is not the person who is the person with care in relation to all of them;
  (d) a person is an absent parent in relation to more than one child and the other parent of each of those children is not the same person;
  (e) the person with care has care of more than one qualifying child and there is more than one absent parent in relation to those children;
  (f) a qualifying child has his home in two or more separate households.

(3)   The Secretary of State may by regulations make provision with respect to special cases.

(4)   Regulations made under subsection (3) may, in particular—
  (a) modify any provision made by or under this Act, in its application to any special case or any special case falling within a prescribed category;
  (b) make new provision for any such case; or
  (c) provide for any prescribed provision made by or under this Act not to apply to any such case.

43 Contribution to maintenance by deduction from benefit

(1)   This section applies where—
    (a) by virtue of paragraph 5(4) of Schedule 1, an absent parent is taken for the purposes of that Schedule to have no assessable income; and
    (b) such conditions as may be prescribed for the purposes of this section are satisfied.

(2)   The power of the Secretary of State to make regulations under [section 5 of the Social Security Administration Act 1992 by virtue of subsection (1)(t),] (deductions from benefits) may be exercised in relation to cases to which this section applies with a view to securing that—
    (a) payments of prescribed amounts are made with respect to qualifying children in place of payments of child support maintenance; and
    (b) arrears of child support maintenance are recovered.

[(3)   Schedule 4C shall have effect for applying sections [16, 17, 20 and 28ZA to 28ZC to any decision with respect to a person's liability under this section, that is to say, his liability to make payments under regulations made by virtue of this section.]

NOTES

Sub-s (2): words in square brackets substituted by the Social Security (Consequential Provisions) Act 1992, s 4, Sch 2, para 113.
Sub-s (3): added by the Social Security Act 1998, s 86(1), Sch 7, para 40.

Jurisdiction

44 Jurisdiction

(1)   [The Secretary of State] shall have jurisdiction to make a maintenance assessment with respect to a person who is—
    (a) a person with care;
    (b) an absent parent; or
    (c) a qualifying child,

only if that person is habitually resident in the United Kingdom.

(2)   Where the person with care is not an individual, subsection (1) shall have effect as if paragraph (a) were omitted.

(3)   The Secretary of State may by regulations make provision for the cancellation of any maintenance assessment where—

(a)   the person with care, absent parent or qualifying child with respect to whom it was made ceases to be habitually resident in the United Kingdom;

(b)   in a case falling within subsection (2), the absent parent or qualifying child with respect to whom it was made ceases to be habitually resident in the United Kingdom; or

(c)   in such circumstances as may be prescribed, a maintenance order of a prescribed kind is made with respect to any qualifying child with respect to whom the maintenance assessment was made.

NOTES

Sub-s (1): words in square brackets substituted by the Social Security Act 1998, s 86(1), Sch 7, para 41.

45   Jurisdiction of courts in certain proceedings under this Act

(1)   The Lord Chancellor or, in relation to Scotland, the Lord Advocate may by order make such provision as he considers necessary to secure that appeals, or such class of appeals as may be specified in the order—

(a)   shall be made to a court instead of being made to [an appeal tribunal]; or

(b)   shall be so made in such circumstances as may be so specified.

(2)   In subsection (1), "court" means

(a)   in relation to England and Wales and subject to any provision made under Schedule 11 to the Children Act 1989 (jurisdiction of courts with respect to certain proceedings relating to children) the High Court, a county court or a magistrates' court; and

(b)   in relation to Scotland, the Court of Session or the sheriff.

(3)   Schedule 11 to the Act of 1989 shall be amended in accordance with subsections (4) and (5).

(4), (5)   . . .

(6)   Where the effect of any order under subsection (1) is that there are no longer any appeals which fall to be dealt with by [appeal tribunals], the Lord Chancellor after consultation with the Lord Advocate may by order provide for the abolition of those tribunals.

(7)   Any order under subsection (1) or (6) may make—
   (a) such modifications of any provision of this Act or of any other enactment; and
   (b) such transitional provision,

as the Minister making the order considers appropriate in consequence of any provision made by the order.

NOTES

Sub-ss (1), (6): words in square brackets substituted by the Social Security Act 1998, s 86(1), Sch 7, para 42.
Sub-ss (4), (5): outside the scope of this work.

Miscellaneous and supplemental

46   Failure to comply with obligations imposed by section 6

(1)   This section applies where any person ("the parent")—
   (a) fails to comply with a requirement imposed on her by the Secretary of State under section 6(1); or
   (b) fails to comply with any regulation made under section 6(9).

(2)   [The Secretary of State] may serve written notice on the parent requiring her, before the end of the specified period, either to comply or to give him her reasons for failing to do so.

(3)   When the specified period has expired, [the Secretary of State] shall consider whether, having regard to any reasons given by the parent, there are reasonable grounds for believing that, if she were to be required to comply, there would be a risk of her or of any children living with her suffering harm or undue distress as a result of complying.

(4)   If [the Secretary of State] considers that there are such reasonable grounds, he shall—
   (a) take no further action under this section in relation to the failure in question; and
   (b) notify the parent, in writing, accordingly.

(5)   If [the Secretary of State] considers that there are no such reasonable grounds, he may[, except in prescribed circumstances,] give a reduced benefit direction with respect to the parent.

(6)   Where [the Secretary of State] gives a reduced benefit direction he shall send a copy of it to the parent.

[(7)   Schedule 4C shall have effect for applying sections 16, 17, 20 and 28ZA to 28ZC to decisions with respect to reduced benefit directions.]

(9)   A reduced benefit direction shall take effect on such date as may be specified in the direction.

(10)   Reasons given in response to a notice under subsection (2) may be given either in writing or orally.

(11)   In this section—
"comply" means to comply with the requirement or with the regulation in question; and "complied" and "complying" shall be construed accordingly;
"reduced benefit direction" means a direction . . . that the amount payable by way of any relevant benefit to, or in respect of, the parent concerned be reduced by such amount, and for such period, as may be prescribed;
"relevant benefit" means income support, [an income-based jobseeker's allowance,] family credit or any other benefit of a kind prescribed for the purposes of section 6; and
"specified", in relation to any notice served under this section, means specified in the notice; and the period to be specified shall be determined in accordance with regulations made by the Secretary of State.

NOTES

Sub-ss (2)–(4), (6): words in square brackets substituted by the Social Security Act 1998, s 86(1), Sch 7, para 43(1), (2).

Sub-s (5): words in first pair of square brackets substituted by the Social Security Act 1998, s 86(1), Sch 7, para 43(2): words in second pair of square brackets inserted by the Child Support Act 1995, s 30(5), Sch 3, para 12.

Sub-s (7): substituted for sub-ss (7), (8) as originally enacted by the Social Security Act 1998, s 86(1), Sch 7, para 43(3).

Sub-s (11): in definition "reduced benefit direction" words omitted repealed by the Social Security Act 1998, s 86(1), (2), Sch 7, para 43(4), Sch 8; in definition "relevant benefit" words in square brackets inserted by the Jobseekers Act 1995, s 41(4), Sch 2, para 20(4).

[46A   Finality of decisions

(1)   Subject to the provisions of this Act, any decision of the Secretary of State or an appeal tribunal made in accordance with the foregoing provisions of this Act shall be final.

(2)   If and to the extent that regulations so provide, any finding of fact or other determination embodied in or necessary to such a decision, or on which such a decision is based, shall be conclusive for the purposes of—

(a) further such decisions;

(b) decisions made in accordance with sections 8 to 16 of the Social Security Act 1998, or with regulations under section 11 of that Act; and

(c) decisions made under the Vaccine Damage Payments Act 1979.]

NOTES

Commencement: 4 March 1999 (so far as authorising the making of regulations, and in so far as relates to the insertions of the Child Support Act 1991, ss 46A(2) and 46B); 1 June 1999 (otherwise).

Inserted, together with s 46B by the Social Security Act 1998, s 86(1), Sch 7, para 44.

[46B   Matters arising as respects decisions

(1)   Regulations may make provision as respects matters arising pending—

(a) any decision of the Secretary of State under section 11, 12 or 17;

(b) any decision of an appeal tribunal under section 20; or

(c) any decision of a Child Support Commissioner under section 24.

(2)   Regulations may also make provision as respects matters arising out of the revision under section 16, or on appeal, of any such decision as is mentioned in subsection (1).

(3)   Any reference in this section to section 16, 17 or 20 includes a reference to that section as extended by Schedule 4C."

NOTES

Commencement: 4 March 1999 (so far as authorising the making of regulations, and in so far as relates to the insertions of the Child Support Act 1991, ss 46A(2) and 46B); 1 June 1999 (otherwise).

Inserted as noted to s 46A.

47   Fees

(1)   The Secretary of State may by regulations provide for the payment, by the absent parent or the person with care (or by both), of such fees as

may be prescribed in cases where the Secretary of State takes[, or proposes to take,] any action under section 4 or 6.

(2)   The Secretary of State may by regulations provide for the payment, by the absent parent, the person with care or the child concerned (or by any or all of them), of such fees as may be prescribed in cases where the Secretary of State takes[, or proposes to take,] any action under section 7.

(3)   Regulations made under this section—
(a) may require any information which is needed for the purpose of determining the amount of any such fee to be furnished, in accordance with the regulations, by such person as may be prescribed;
(b) shall provide that no such fees shall be payable by any person to or in respect of whom income support, [an income-based jobseeker's allowance,] family credit or any other benefit of a prescribed kind is paid; and
(c) may, in particular, make provision with respect to the recovery by the Secretary of State of any fees payable under the regulations.

NOTES

Sub-ss (1), (2): words in square brackets inserted by the Child Support Act 1995, s 30(5), Sch 3, para 13, as from a day to be appointed.

Sub-s (3): words in square brackets in para (b) inserted by the Jobseekers Act 1995, s 41(4), Sch 2, para 20(5).

48   Right of audience

(1)   Any [officer of the Secretary of State who is authorised] by the Secretary of State for the purposes of this section shall have, in relation to any proceedings under this Act before a magistrates' court, a right of audience and the right to conduct litigation.

(2)   In this section "right of audience" and "right to conduct litigation" have the same meaning as in section 119 of the Courts and Legal Services Act 1990.

NOTES

Sub-s (1): words in square brackets substituted by the Child Support Act 1995, s 30(5), Sch 3, para 14.

50   Unauthorised disclosure of information

(1)   Any person who is, or has been, employed in employment to which this section applies is guilty of an offence if, without lawful authority, he discloses any information which—
   (a) was acquired by him in the course of that employment; and
   (b) relates to a particular person.

(2)   It is not an offence under this section—
   (a) to disclose information in the form of a summary or collection of information so framed as not to enable information relating to any particular person to be ascertained from it; or
   (b) to disclose information which has previously been disclosed to the public with lawful authority.

(3)   It is a defence for a person charged with an offence under this section to prove that at the time of the alleged offence—
   (a) he believed that he was making the disclosure in question with lawful authority and had no reasonable cause to believe otherwise; or
   (b) he believed that the information in question had previously been disclosed to the public with lawful authority and had no reasonable cause to believe otherwise.

(4)   A person guilty of an offence under this section shall be liable—
   (a) on conviction on indictment, to imprisonment for a term not exceeding two years or a fine or both; or
   (b) on summary conviction, to imprisonment for a term not exceeding six months or a fine not exceeding the statutory maximum or both.

(5)   This section applies to employment as—
   (a) the Chief Child Support Officer;
   (b) any other child support officer;
   (c) any clerk to, or other officer of, [an appeal tribunal or] a child support appeal tribunal;
   (d) any member of the staff of such a tribunal;
   (e) a civil servant in connection with the carrying out of any functions under this Act,

and to employment of any other kind which is prescribed for the purposes of this section.

(6)   For the purposes of this section a disclosure is to be regarded as made with lawful authority if, and only if, it is made—
   (a) by a civil servant in accordance with his official duty; or

(b) by any other person either—
    (i) for the purposes of the function in the exercise of which he holds the information and without contravening any restriction duly imposed by the responsible person; or
    (ii) to, or in accordance with an authorisation duly given by, the responsible person;
(c) in accordance with any enactment or order of a court;
(d) for the purpose of instituting, or otherwise for the purposes of, any proceedings before a court or before any tribunal or other body or person mentioned in this Act; or
(e) with the consent of the appropriate person.

(7) "The responsible person" means—
(a) the Lord Chancellor;
(b) the Secretary of State;
(c) any person authorised by the Lord Chancellor, or Secretary of State, for the purposes of this subsection; or
(d) any other prescribed person, or person falling within a prescribed category.

(8) "The appropriate person" means the person to whom the information in question relates, except that if the affairs of that person are being dealt with—
(a) under a power of attorney;
(b) by a receiver appointed under section 99 of the Mental Health Act 1983;
(c) by a Scottish mental health custodian, that is to say—
    (i) a curator bonis, tutor or judicial factor; or
    (ii) the managers of a hospital acting on behalf of that person under section 94 of the Mental Health (Scotland) Act 1984; or
(d) by a mental health appointee, that is to say—
    (i) a person directed or authorised as mentioned in sub-paragraph (a) of rule 41(1) of the Court of Protection Rules 1984; or
    (ii) a receiver ad interim appointed under sub-paragraph (b) of that rule;

the appropriate person is the attorney, receiver, custodian or appointee (as the case may be) or, in a case falling within paragraph (a), the person to whom the information relates.

NOTES

Sub-s (5): words in square brackets inserted by the Social Security Act 1998, s 86(1), Sch 7, para 45.

51 Supplementary powers to make regulations

(1)   The Secretary of State may by regulations make such incidental, supplemental and transitional provision as he considers appropriate in connection with any provision made by or under this Act.

(2)   The regulations may, in particular, make provision—
  (a) as to the procedure to be followed with respect to—
      (i)   the making of applications for maintenance assessments;
      (ii) the making, cancellation or refusal to make maintenance assessments;
    [(iii) the making of decisions under section 16 or 17;]
  (b) extending the categories of case to which [Schedule 4C] applies;
  (c) as to the date on which an application for a maintenance assessment is to be treated as having been made;
  (d) for attributing payments made under maintenance assessments to the payment of arrears;
  (e) for the adjustment, for the purpose of taking account of the retrospective effect of a maintenance assessment, of amounts payable under the assessment;
  (f) for the adjustment, for the purpose of taking account of overpayments or under-payments of child support maintenance, of amounts payable under a maintenance assessment;
  (g) as to the evidence which is to be required in connection with such matters as may be prescribed;
  (h) as to the circumstances in which any official record or certificate is to be conclusive (or in Scotland, sufficient) evidence;
  (i) with respect to the giving of notices or other documents;
  (j) for the rounding up or down of any amounts calculated, estimated or otherwise arrived at in applying any provision made by or under this Act.

(3)   No power to make regulations conferred by any other provision of this Act shall be taken to limit the powers given to the Secretary of State by this section.

NOTES

Sub-s (2): words in square brackets substituted by the Social Security Act 1998, s 86(1), Sch 7, para 46.

52 Regulations and orders

(1)   Any power conferred on the Lord Chancellor, the Lord Advocate or the Secretary of State by this Act to make regulations or orders (other than a deduction from earnings order) shall be exercisable by statutory instrument.

(2)   No statutory instrument containing (whether alone or with other provisions) regulations made under section 4(7), 5(3), 6(1), (9) or (10), 7(8), 12(2), [28C(2)(b), 28F(3), 30(5A)], 41(2), (3) or (4), [41A, 41B(6)], 42, 43(1), 46 or 47 or under Part I of Schedule 1 [or under Schedule 4B], or an order made under section 45(1) or (6), shall be made unless a draft of the instrument has been laid before Parliament and approved by a resolution of each House of Parliament.

(3)   Any other statutory instrument made under this Act (except an order made under section 58(2)) shall be subject to annulment in pursuance of a resolution of either House of Parliament.

(4)   Any power of a kind mentioned in subsection (1) may be exercised—
  (a)   in relation to all cases to which it extends, in relation to those cases but subject to specified exceptions or in relation to any specified cases or classes of case;
  (b)   so as to make, as respects the cases in relation to which it is exercised—
    (i)   the full provision to which it extends or any lesser provision (whether by way of exception or otherwise);
    (ii)   the same provision for all cases, different provision for different cases or classes of case or different provision as respects the same case or class of case but for different purposes of this Act;
    (iii) provision which is either unconditional or is subject to any specified condition;
  (c)   so to provide for a person to exercise a discretion in dealing with any matter.

NOTES

Sub-s (2): words in square brackets inserted by the Child Support Act 1995, s 30(5), Sch 3, para 15.

53 Financial provisions

Any expenses of the Lord Chancellor or the Secretary State under this Act shall be payable out of money provided by Parliament.

54   Interpretation

In this Act—

"absent parent", has the meaning given in section 3(2);

"adjudication officer" has the same meaning as in the benefit Acts;

["application for a departure direction" means an application under section 28A;]

["appeal tribunal" means an appeal tribunal constituted under Chapter I of Part I of the Social Security Act 1998;]

"assessable income" has the meaning given in paragraph 5 of Schedule 1;

"benefit Acts" means the [Social Security Contributions and Benefits Act 1992 and the Social Security Administration Act 1992];

"Chief Adjudication Officer" has the same meaning as in the benefit Acts;

"child benefit" has the same meaning as in the Child Benefit Act 1975;

"child support maintenance" has the meaning given in section 3(6);

["current assessment", in relation to an application for a departure direction, means (subject to any regulations made under paragraph 10 of Schedule 4A) the maintenance assessment with respect to which the application is made;]

"deduction from earnings order" has the meaning given in section 31(2);

["departure direction" has the meaning given in section 28A; and]

"disability living allowance" has the same meaning as in the [benefit Acts];

"family credit" has the same meaning as in the benefit Acts;

"general qualification" shall be construed in accordance with section 71 of the Courts and Legal Services Act 1990 (qualification for judicial appointments);

"income support" has the same meaning as in the benefit Acts;

["income-based jobseeker's allowance" has the same meaning as in the Jobseekers Act 1995;]

"interim maintenance assessment" has the meaning given in section 12;

"liability order" has the meaning given in section 33(2);

"maintenance agreement" has the meaning given in section 9(1);

"maintenance assessment" means an assessment of maintenance made under this Act and, except in prescribed circumstances, includes an interim maintenance assessment;

"maintenance order" has the meaning given in section 8(11);

"maintenance requirement" means the amount calculated in accordance with paragraph 1 of Schedule 1;

"parent", in relation to any child, means any person who is in law the mother or father of the child;

["parental responsibility", in the application of this Act—

    (a) to England and Wales, has the same meaning as in the Children Act 1989; and

    (b) to Scotland, shall be construed as a reference to "parental responsibilities" within the meaning given by section 1(3) of the Children (Scotland) Act 1995;]

. . . . .

["parent with care" means a person who is, in relation to a child, both a parent and a person with care."]

"person with care" has the meaning given in section 3(3);

"prescribed" means prescribed by regulations made by the Secretary of State;

"qualifying child" has the meaning given in section 3(1).

NOTES

Definitions "adjudication officer" and "Chief Adjudication Officer" repealed as from a day to be appointed, and definitions omitted in the first, second and third places repealed, definition "appeal tribunal" inserted by the Social Security Act 1998, s 86(1), (2), Sch 7, para 47, Sch 8; definitions "application for a departure direction", "current assessment", "departure direction" and "parent with care" inserted by the Child Support Act 1995, s 30(5), Sch 3, para 16; in definitions "benefit Acts" and "disability living allowance", words in square brackets substituted by the Social Security (Consequential Provisions) Act 1992, s 4, Sch 2, para 114; definition "income-based jobseeker's allowance" inserted by the Jobseekers Act 1995, s 41(4), Sch 2, para 20(6); definition "parental responsibility" substituted, and definition omitted in the final place repealed, by the Children (Scotland) Act 1995, s 105(4), (5), Sch 4, para 52(4), Sch 5.

55 Meaning of "child"

(1)   For the purposes of this Act a person is a child if—

  (a) he is under the age of 16;

  (b) he is under the age of 19 and receiving full-time education (which is not advanced education)—

    (i) by attendance at a recognised educational establishment; or

    (ii) elsewhere, if the education is recognised by the Secretary of State; or

  (c) he does not fall within paragraph (a) or (b) but—

    (i) he is under the age of 18, and

    (ii) prescribed conditions are satisfied with respect to him.

(2)   A person is not a child for the purposes of this Act if he—

  (a) is or has been married;

(b) has celebrated a marriage which is void; or

(c) has celebrated a marriage in respect of which a decree of nullity has been granted.

(3)   In this section—

"advanced education" means education of a prescribed description; and

"recognised educational establishment" means an establishment recognised by the Secretary of State for the purposes of this section as being, or as comparable to, a university, college or school.

(4)   Where a person has reached the age of 16, the Secretary of State may recognise education provided for him otherwise than at a recognised educational establishment only if the Secretary of State is satisfied that education was being so provided for him immediately before he reached the age of 16.

(5)   The Secretary of State may provide that in prescribed circumstances education is or is not to be treated for the purposes of this section as being full-time.

(6)   In determining whether a person falls within subsection (1)(b), no account shall be taken of such interruptions in his education as may be prescribed.

(7)   The Secretary of State may by regulations provide that a person who ceases to fall within subsection (1) shall be treated as continuing to fall within that subsection for a prescribed period.

(8)   No person shall be treated as continuing to fall within subsection (1) by virtue of regulations made under subsection (7) after the end of the week in which he reaches the age of 19.

57 Application to Crown

(1)   The power of the Secretary of State to make regulations under section 14 requiring prescribed persons to furnish information may be exercised so as to require information to be furnished by persons employed in the service of the Crown or otherwise in the discharge of Crown functions.

(2)   In such circumstances, and subject to such conditions, as may be prescribed, an inspector appointed under section 15 may enter any Crown premises for the purpose of exercising any powers conferred on him by that section.

(3)   Where such an inspector duly enters any Crown premises for those purposes, section 15 shall apply in relation to persons employed in the service of the Crown or otherwise in the discharge of Crown functions as it applies in relation to other persons.

(4)   Where a liable person is in the employment of the Crown, a deduction from earnings order may be made under section 31 in relation to that person; but in such a case subsection (8) of section 32 shall apply only in relation to the failure of that person to comply with any requirement imposed on him by regulations made under section 32.

58   Short title, commencement and extent, etc

(1)   This Act may be cited as the Child Support Act 1991.

(2)   Section 56(1) and subsections (1) to (11) and (14) of this section shall come into force on the passing of this Act but otherwise this Act shall come into force on such date as may be appointed by order made by the Lord Chancellor, the Secretary of State or Lord Advocate, or by any of them acting jointly.

(3)   Different dates may be appointed for different provisions of this Act and for different purposes (including, in particular, for different cases or categories of case).

(4)   An order under subsection (2) may make such supplemental, incidental or transitional provision as appears to the person making the order to be necessary or expedient in connection with the provisions brought into force by the order, including such adaptations or modifications of—
  (a) the provisions so brought into force;
  (b) any provisions of this Act then in force; or
  (c) any provision of any other enactment,

as appear to him to be necessary or expedient.

(5)   Different provision may be made by virtue of subsection (4) with respect to different periods.

(6)   Any provision made by virtue of subsection (4) may, in particular, include provision for—
  (a) the enforcement of a maintenance assessment (including the collection of sums payable under the assessment) as if the assessment were a court order of a prescribed kind;

(b) the registration of maintenance assessments with the appropriate court in connection with any provision of a kind mentioned in paragraph (a);

(c) the variation, on application made to a court, of the provisions of a maintenance assessment relating to the method of making payments fixed by the assessment or the intervals at which such payments are to be made;

(d) a maintenance assessment, or an order of a prescribed kind relating to one or more children, to be deemed, in prescribed circumstances, to have been validly made for all purposes or for such purposes as may be prescribed.

In paragraph (c) "court" includes a single justice.

(7)   The Lord Chancellor, the Secretary of State or the Lord Advocate may by order make such amendments or repeals in, or such modifications of, such enactments as may be specified in the order, as appear to him to be necessary or expedient in consequence of any provision made by or under this Act (including any provision made by virtue of subsection (4)).

(8)–(14)   . . .

NOTES

Sub-ss (8)–(13): outside the scope of this work.
Sub-s (14): repeals the Children Act 1989, Sch 1, para 2(6).

SCHEDULE I

Section 11

MAINTENANCE ASSESSMENTS

PART I
CALCULATION OF CHILD SUPPORT MAINTENANCE

The maintenance requirement

1.—(1)   In this Schedule "the maintenance requirement" means the amount, calculated in accordance with the formula set out in sub-paragraph (2), which is to be taken as the minimum amount necessary for the maintenance of the qualifying child or, where there is more than one qualifying child, all of them.

(2)   The formula is—

$$MR = AG - CB$$

where—

MR is the amount of the maintenance requirement;

AG is the aggregate of the amounts to be taken into account under sub-paragraph (3); and

CB is the amount payable by way of child benefit (or which would be so payable if the person with care of the qualifying child were an individual) or, where there is more than one qualifying child, the aggregate of the amounts so payable with respect to each of them.

(3)   The amounts to be taken into account for the purpose of calculating AG are—

(a) such amount or amounts (if any), with respect to each qualifying child, as may be prescribed;

(b) such amount or amounts (if any), with respect to the person with care of the qualifying child or qualifying children, as may be prescribed; and

(c) such further amount or amounts (if any) as may be prescribed.

(4)   For the purposes of calculating CB it shall be assumed that child benefit is payable with respect to any qualifying child at the basic rate.

(5)   In sub-paragraph (4) "basic rate" has the meaning for the time being prescribed.

The general rule

2.—(1)   In order to determine the amount of any maintenance assessment, first calculate—

$$(A+C) \times P$$

where—

A is the absent parent's assessable income;

C is the assessable income of the other parent, where that parent is the person with care, and otherwise has such value (if any) as may be prescribed; and

P is such number greater than zero but less than 1 as may be prescribed.

(2)   Where the result of the calculation made under sub-paragraph (1) is an amount which is equal to, or less than, the amount of the maintenance requirement for the qualifying child or qualifying children, the amount of maintenance payable by the absent parent for that child or those children shall be an amount equal to—

$$A \times P$$

where A and P have the same values as in the calculation made under sub-paragraph (1).

(3)   Where the result of the calculation made under sub-paragraph (1) is an amount which exceeds the amount of the maintenance requirement for the qualifying child or qualifying children, the amount of maintenance payable by the absent parent for that child or those children shall consist of—

(a)   a basic element calculated in accordance with the provisions of paragraph 3; and

(b)   an additional element calculated in accordance with the provisions of paragraph 4.

The basic element

3.—(1)   The basic element shall be calculated by applying the formula—

$$BE = A \times G \times P$$

where—

BE is the amount of the basic element;

A and P have the same values as in the calculation made under paragraph 2(1); and

G has the value determined under sub-paragraph (2).

(2)   The value of G shall be determined by applying the formula

$$G = \frac{MR}{(A + C) \times P}$$

where—

MR is the amount of the maintenance requirement for the qualifying child or qualifying children; and

A, C and P have the same values as in the calculation made under paragraph 2(1).

The additional element

4.—(1)   Subject to sub-paragraph (2), the additional element shall be calculated by applying the formula—

$$AE = (1 - G) \times A \times R$$

where—
AE is the amount of the additional element;
A has the same value as in the calculation made under paragraph 2(1);
G has the value determined under paragraph 3(2); and
R is such number greater than zero but less than 1 as may be prescribed.

(2)   Where applying the alternative formula set out in sub-paragraph (3) would result in a lower amount for the additional element, that formula shall be applied in place of the formula set out in sub-paragraph (1).

(3)   The alternative formula is—

$$AE = Z \times Q \times \left(\frac{A}{A + C} \right)$$

where—
A and C have the same values as in the calculation made under paragraph 2(1);
Z is such number as may be prescribed; and
Q is the aggregate of—
   (a) any amount taken into account by virtue of paragraph 1(3)(a) in calculating the maintenance requirement; and
   (b) any amount which is both taken into account by virtue of paragraph 1(3)(c) in making that calculation and is an amount prescribed for the purposes of this paragraph.

Assessable income

5.—(1)   The assessable income of an absent parent shall be calculated by applying the formula—

$$A = N - E$$

where—
A is the amount of that parent's assessable income;
N is the amount of that parent's net income, calculated or estimated in accordance with regulations made by the Secretary of State for the purposes of this sub-paragraph; and

E is the amount of that parent's exempt income, calculated or estimated in accordance with regulations made by the Secretary of State for those purposes.

(2)   The assessable income of a parent who is a person with care of the qualifying child or children shall be calculated by applying the formula—

$$C = M - F$$

where—

C is the amount of that parent's assessable income;

M is the amount of that parent's net income, calculated or estimated in accordance with regulations made by the Secretary of State for the purposes of this sub-paragraph; and

F is the amount of that parent's exempt income, calculated or estimated in accordance with regulations made by the Secretary of State for those purposes.

(3)   Where the preceding provisions of this paragraph would otherwise result in a person's assessable income being taken to be a negative amount his assessable income shall be taken to be nil.

(4)   Where income support[, an income-based jobseeker's allowance] or any other benefit of a prescribed kind is paid to or in respect of a parent who is an absent parent or a person with care that parent shall, for the purposes of this Schedule, be taken to have no assessable income.

Protected income

6.—(1)   This paragraph applies where—
(a) one or more maintenance assessments have been made with respect to an absent parent; and
(b) payment by him of the amount, or the aggregate of the amounts, so assessed would otherwise reduce his disposable income below his protected income level.

(2)   The amount of the assessment, or (as the case may be) of each assessment, shall be adjusted in accordance with such provisions as may be prescribed with a view to securing so far as is reasonably practicable that payment by the absent parent of the amount, or (as the case may be) aggregate of the amounts, so assessed will not reduce his disposable income below his protected income level.

(3)   Regulations made under sub-paragraph (2) shall secure that, where the prescribed minimum amount fixed by regulations made under paragraph 7 applies, no maintenance assessment is adjusted so as to provide for the amount payable by an absent parent in accordance with that assessment to be less than that amount.

(4)   The amount which is to be taken for the purposes of this paragraph as an absent parent's disposable income shall be calculated, or estimated, in accordance with regulations made by the Secretary of State.

(5)   Regulations made under sub-paragraph (4) may, in particular, provide that, in such circumstances and to such extent as may be prescribed—
   (a) income of any child who is living in the same household with the absent parent; and
   (b) where the absent parent is living together in the same household with another adult of the opposite sex (regardless of whether or not they are married), income of that other adult,

is to be treated as the absent parent's income for the purposes of calculating his disposable income.

(6)   In this paragraph the "protected income level" of a particular absent parent means an amount of income calculated, by reference to the circumstances of that parent, in accordance with regulations made by the Secretary of State.

The minimum amount of child support maintenance

7.—(1)   The Secretary of State may prescribe a minimum amount for the purposes of this paragraph.

(2)   Where the amount of child support maintenance which would be fixed by a maintenance assessment but for this paragraph is nil, or less than the prescribed minimum amount, the amount to be fixed by the assessment shall be the prescribed minimum amount.

(3)   In any case to which section 43 applies, and in such other cases (if any) as may be prescribed, sub-paragraph (2) shall not apply.

Housing costs

8.   Where regulations under this Schedule require [the Secretary of State] to take account of the housing costs of any person in calculating, or

estimating, his assessable income or disposable income, those regulations may make provision—

    (a) as to the costs which are to be treated as housing costs for the purpose of the regulations;

    (b) for the apportionment of housing costs; and

    (c) for the amount of housing costs to be taken into account for prescribed purposes not to exceed such amount (if any) as may be prescribed by, or determined in accordance with, the regulations.

Regulations about income and capital

9. The Secretary of State may by regulations provide that, in such circumstances and to such extent as may be prescribed—

    (a) income of a child shall be treated as income of a parent of his;

    (b) where [the Secretary of State] is satisfied that a person has intentionally deprived himself of a source of income with a view to reducing the amount of his assessable income, his net income shall be taken to include income from that source of an amount estimated by [the Secretary of State];

    (c) a person is to be treated as possessing capital or income which he does not possess;

    (d) capital or income which a person does possess is to be disregarded;

    (e) income is to be treated as capital;

    (f) capital is to be treated as income.

References to qualifying children

10.   References in this Part of this Schedule to "qualifying children" are to those qualifying children with respect to whom the maintenance assessment falls to be made.

NOTES

Para 5: words in square brackets in sub-para (4) inserted by the Jobseekers Act 1995, s 41(4), Sch 2, para 20(7).

Paras 8, 9: words in square brackets substituted by the Social Security Act 1998, s 86(1), Sch 7, para 48(1), (2).

PART II
GENERAL PROVISIONS ABOUT MAINTENANCE ASSESSMENTS

Effective date of assessment

11.—(1) A maintenance assessment shall take effect on such date as may be determined in accordance with regulations made by the Secretary of State.

(2) That date may be earlier than the date on which the assessment is made.

Form of assessment

12. Every maintenance assessment shall be made in such form and contain such information as the Secretary of State may direct.

Assessments where amount of child support is nil

13. [The Secretary of State] shall not decline to make a maintenance assessment only on the ground that the amount of the assessment is nil.

Consolidated applications and assessments

14. The Secretary of State may by regulations provide—
  (a) for two or more applications for maintenance assessments to be treated, in prescribed circumstances, as a single application; and
  (b) for the replacement, in prescribed circumstances, of a maintenance assessment made on the application of one person by a later maintenance assessment made on the application of that or any other person.

Separate assessments for different periods

15. Where [the Secretary of State] is satisfied that the circumstances of a case require different amounts of child support maintenance to be assessed in respect of different periods, he may make separate maintenance assessments each expressed to have effect in relation to a different specified period.

Termination of assessments

16.—(1)   A maintenance assessment shall cease to have effect—

(a)   on the death of the absent parent, or of the person with care, with respect to whom it was made;

(b)   on there no longer being any qualifying child with respect to whom it would have effect;

(c)   on the absent parent with respect to whom it was made ceasing to be a parent of—

(i)   the qualifying child with respect to whom it was made; or

(ii)   where it was made with respect to more than one qualifying child, all of the qualifying children with respect to whom it was made;

(d)   where the absent parent and the person with care with respect to whom it was made have been living together for a continuous period of six months;

(e)   where a new maintenance assessment is made with respect to any qualifying child with respect to whom the assessment in question was in force immediately before the making of the new assessment.

(2)   A maintenance assessment made in response to an application under section 4 or 7 shall be cancelled by [the Secretary of State] if the person on whose application the assessment was made asks him to do so.

(3)   A maintenance assessment made in response to an application under section 6 shall be cancelled by [the Secretary of State] if—

(a)   the person on whose application the assessment was made ("the applicant") asks him to do so; and

(b)   he is satisfied that the applicant has ceased to fall within subsection (1) of that section.

(4)   Where [the Secretary of State] is satisfied that the person with care with respect to whom a maintenance assessment was made has ceased to be a person with care in relation to the qualifying child, or any of the qualifying children, with respect to whom the assessment was made, he may cancel the assessment with effect from the date on which, in his opinion, the change of circumstances took place.

[(4A)   A maintenance assessment may be cancelled by [the Secretary of State] if he is [proposing to make a decision under section 16 or 17] and it appears to him—

(a)   that the person with care with respect to whom the maintenance assessment in question was made has failed to provide him with sufficient information to enable him to [make the decision]; and

    (b) where the maintenance assessment in question was made in response to an application under section 6, that the person with care with respect to whom the assessment was made has ceased to fall within subsection (1) of that section.]

(5)   Where—
    (a) at any time a maintenance assessment is in force but [the Secretary of State] would no longer have jurisdiction to make it if it were to be applied for at that time; and
    (b) the assessment has not been cancelled, or has not ceased to have effect, under or by virtue of any other provision made by or under this Act,

it shall be taken to have continuing effect unless cancelled by [the Secretary of State] in accordance with such prescribed provision (including provision as to the effective date of cancellation) as the Secretary of State considers it appropriate to make.

(6)   Where both the absent parent and the person with care with respect to whom a maintenance assessment was made request [the Secretary of State] to cancel the assessment, he may do so if he is satisfied that they are living together.

(7)   Any cancellation of a maintenance assessment under sub-paragraph [(4A),] (5) or (6) shall have effect from such date as may be determined by [the Secretary of State].

(8)   Where [the Secretary of State] cancels a maintenance assessment, he shall immediately notify the absent parent and person with care, so far as that is reasonably practicable.

(9)   Any notice under sub-paragraph (8) shall specify the date with effect from which the cancellation took effect.

(10)   A person with care with respect to whom a maintenance assessment is in force shall provide the Secretary of State with such information, in such circumstances, as may be prescribed, with a view to assisting the Secretary of State . . . in determining whether the assessment has ceased to have effect, or should be cancelled.

(11)   The Secretary of State may by regulations make such supplemental, incidental or transitional provision as he thinks necessary or expedient in consequence of the provisions of this paragraph.

NOTES

Paras 13, 15: words in square brackets substituted by the Social Security Act 1998, s 86(1), Sch 7, para 48(3), (4).

Para 16: sub-para (4A) and number in square brackets in sub-para (7) inserted by the Child Support Act 1995, s 14(2), (3); remaining words in square brackets substituted and words omitted repealed by the Social Security Act 1998, s 86(1), Sch 7, para 48(5).

SCHEDULE 2
PROVISION OF INFORMATION TO SECRETARY OF STATE

Section 14(4)

Inland Revenue records

1.—(1) This paragraph applies where the Secretary of State or the Department of Health and Social Services for Northern Ireland requires information for the purpose of tracing—

(a) the current address of an absent parent; or

(b) the current employer of an absent parent.

(2) In such a case, no obligation as to secrecy imposed by statute or otherwise on a person employed in relation to the Inland Revenue shall prevent any information obtained or held in connection with the assessment or collection of income tax from being disclosed to—

(a) the Secretary of State;

(b) the Department of Health and Social Services for Northern Ireland; or

(c) an officer of either of them authorised to receive such information in connection with the operation of this Act or of any corresponding Northern Ireland legislation.

(3) This paragraph extends only to disclosure by or under the authority of the Commissioners of Inland Revenue.

(4) Information which is the subject of disclosure to any person by virtue of this paragraph shall not be further disclosed to any person except where the further disclosure is made—

(a) to a person to whom disclosure could be made by virtue of sub-paragraph (2); or

(b) for the purposes of any proceedings (civil or criminal) in connection with the operation of this Act or of any corresponding Northern Ireland legislation.

2. . . .

NOTES
Para 2: repealed by the Social Security Act 1998, s 86(1), (2), Sch 7, para 49, Sch 8.

[SCHEDULE 4B
DEPARTURE DIRECTIONS: THE CASES AND CONTROLS

Section 6(2)

PART I
THE CASES

General

1.—(1)   The cases in which a departure direction may be given are those set out in this Part of this Schedule or in regulations made under this Part.

(2)   In this Schedule "applicant" means the person whose application for a departure direction is being considered.

Special expenses

2.—(1)   A departure direction may be given with respect to special expenses of the applicant which were not, and could not have been, taken into account in determining the current assessment in accordance with the provisions of, or made under, Part I of Schedule 1.

(2)   In this paragraph "special expenses" means the whole, or any prescribed part, of expenses which fall within a prescribed description of expenses.

(3)   In prescribing descriptions of expenses for the purposes of this paragraph, the Secretary of State may, in particular, make provision with respect to—
   (a) costs incurred in travelling to work;
   (b) costs incurred by an absent parent in maintaining contact with the child, or with any of the children, with respect to whom he is liable to pay child support maintenance under the current assessment;
   (c) costs attributable to a long-term illness or disability of the applicant or of a dependant of the applicant;
   (d) debts incurred, before the absent parent became an absent parent in relation to a child with respect to whom the current assessment was made—

(i)　for the joint benefit of both parents;

(ii)　for the benefit of any child with respect to whom the current assessment was made; or

(iii)　for the benefit of any other child falling within a prescribed category;

(e)　pre-1993 financial commitments from which it is impossible for the parent concerned to withdraw or from which it would be unreasonable to expect that parent to have to withdraw;

(f)　costs incurred by a parent in supporting a child who is not his child but who is part of his family.

(4)　For the purposes of sub-paragraph (3)(c)—

(a)　the question whether one person is a dependant of another shall be determined in accordance with regulations made by the Secretary of State;

(b)　"disability" and "illness" have such meaning as may be prescribed; and

(c)　the question whether an illness or disability is long-term shall be determined in accordance with regulations made by the Secretary of State.

(5)　For the purposes of sub-paragraph (3)(e), "pre-1993 financial commitments" means financial commitments of a prescribed kind entered into before 5th April 1993 in any case where—

(a)　a court order of a prescribed kind was in force with respect to the absent parent and the person with care concerned at the time when they were entered into; or

(b)　an agreement between them of a prescribed kind was in force at that time.

(6)　For the purposes of sub-paragraph (3)(f), a child who is not the child of a particular person is a part of that person's family in such circumstances as may be prescribed.

Property or capital transfers

3.—(1)　A departure direction may be given if—

(a)　before 5th April 1993—

(i)　a court order of a prescribed kind was in force with respect to the absent parent and either the person with care with respect to whom the current assessment was made or the child, or any of the children, with respect to whom that assessment was made, or

(ii)　an agreement of a prescribed kind between the absent parent and any of those persons was in force;

   (b) in consequence of one or more transfers of property of a prescribed kind—
      (i) the amount payable by the absent parent by way of maintenance was less than would have been the case had that transfer or those transfers not been made; or
     (ii) no amount was payable by the absent parent by way of maintenance; and
   (c) the effect of that transfer, or those transfers, is not properly reflected in the current assessment.

(2)   For the purposes of sub-paragraph (1)(b), "maintenance" means periodical payments of maintenance made (otherwise than under this Act) with respect to the child, or any of the children, with respect to whom the current assessment was made.

(3)   For the purposes of sub-paragraph (1)(c), the question whether the effect of one or more transfers of property is properly reflected in the current assessment shall be determined in accordance with regulations made by the Secretary of State.

4.—(1)   A departure direction may be given if—
   (a) before 5th April 1993—
      (i) a court order of a prescribed kind was in force with respect to the absent parent and either the person with care with respect to whom the current assessment was made or the child, or any of the children, with respect to whom that assessment was made, or
     (ii) an agreement of a prescribed kind between the absent parent and any of those persons was in force;
   (b) in pursuance of the court order or agreement, the absent parent has made one or more transfers of property of a prescribed kind;
   (c) the amount payable by the absent parent by way of maintenance was not reduced as a result of that transfer or those transfers;
   (d) the amount payable by the absent parent by way of child support maintenance under the current assessment has been reduced as a result of that transfer or those transfers, in accordance with provisions of or made under this Act; and
   (e) it is nevertheless inappropriate, having regard to the purposes for which the transfer or transfers was or were made, for that reduction to have been made.

(2)   For the purposes of sub-paragraph (1)(c), "maintenance" means periodical payments of maintenance made (otherwise than under this Act) with respect to the child, or any of the children, with respect to whom the current assessment was made.

Additional cases

5.—(1)   The Secretary of State may by regulations prescribe other cases in which a departure direction may be given.

(2)   Regulations under this paragraph may, for example, make provision with respect to cases where—
  (a)   assets which do not produce income are capable of producing income;
  (b)   a person's life-style is inconsistent with the level of his income;
  (c)   housing costs are unreasonably high;
  (d)   housing costs are in part attributable to housing persons whose circumstances are such as to justify disregarding a part of those costs;
  (e)   travel costs are unreasonably high; or
  (f)   travel costs should be disregarded.]

NOTES

Commencement: 14 October 1996 (for certain purposes); 2 December 1996 (otherwise). Inserted by the Child Support Act 1995, s 6(2), Sch 2.

Criminal Justice Act 1991

(c 53)

An Act to make further provision with respect to the treatment of offenders and the position of children and young persons and persons having responsibility for them; to make provision with respect to certain services provided or proposed to be provided for purposes connected with the administration of justice or the treatment of offenders; to make financial and other provision with respect to that administration; and for connected purposes

[25 July 1991]

PART III
CHILDREN AND YOUNG PERSONS

Responsibilities of parent or guardian

58   Binding over of parent or guardian

(1)   Where a child or young person ("the relevant minor") is convicted of an offence, the powers conferred by this section shall be exercisable by the

court by which he is sentenced for that offence; and it shall be the duty of the court, in a case where the relevant minor has not attained the age of 16 years—

    (a) to exercise those powers if it is satisfied, having regard to the circumstances of the case, that their exercise would be desirable in the interests of preventing the commission by him of further offences; and

    (b) where it does not exercise them, to state in open court that it is not satisfied as mentioned in paragraph (a) above and why it is not so satisfied.

(2)   The powers conferred by this section are as follows—

    (a) with the consent of the relevant minor's parent or guardian, to order the parent or guardian to enter into a recognisance to take proper care of him and exercise proper control over him; and

    (b) if the parent or guardian refuses consent and the court considers the refusal unreasonable, to order the parent or guardian to pay a fine not exceeding £1,000.

[Where the court has passed on the relevant minor a community sentence (within the meaning of section 6 above) it may include in the recognisance a provision that the minor's parent or guardian ensure that the minor complies with the requirements of that sentence.]

(3)   An order under this section shall not require the parent or guardian to enter into a recognisance—

    (a) for an amount exceeding £1,000; or

    (b) for a period exceeding three years or, where the relevant minor will attain the age of 18 years in a period shorter than three years, for a period exceeding that shorter period;

and section 120 of the 1980 Act (which relates to the forfeiture of recognisances) shall apply in relation to a recognisance entered into in pursuance of such an order as it applies to a recognisance to keep the peace.

[(4)   A fine imposed under subsection (2)(b) above shall be deemed, for the purposes of any enactment, to be a sum adjudged to be paid by a conviction.]

(5)   In fixing the amount of a recognisance under this section, the court shall take into account among other things the means of the parent or guardian so far as they appear or are known to the court; and this subsection applies whether taking into account the means of the parent or guardian has the effect of increasing or reducing the amount of the recognisance.

(6)   A parent or guardian may appeal to the Crown Court against an order under this section made by a magistrates' court.

(7)   A parent or guardian may appeal to the Court of Appeal against an order under this section made by the Crown Court, as if he had been convicted on indictment and the order were a sentence passed on his conviction.

(8)   A court may vary or revoke an order made by it under this section if, on the application of the parent or guardian, it appears to the court, having regard to any change in the circumstances since the order was made, to be in the interests of justice to do so.

[(9)   For the purposes of this section—
    (a) "guardian" has the same meaning as in the 1993 Act; and
    (b) taking "care" of a person includes giving him protection and guidance and "control" includes discipline.]

NOTES

Sub-s (2): words in square brackets added by the Criminal Justice and Public Order Act 1994, s 168(1), Sch 9, para 50.

Sub-s (4): substituted by the Criminal Justice Act 1993, s 65(3), (4), Sch 3, para 6(6).

Sub-s (9): added by the Crime and Disorder Act 1998, s 106, Sch 7, para 45.

1980 Act: Magistrates' Courts Act 1980.

PART VI
SUPPLEMENTAL

102   Short title, commencement and extent

(1)   This Act may be cited as the Criminal Justice Act 1991.

(2)   This Act shall come into force on such day as the Secretary of State may by order made by statutory instrument appoint, and different days may be appointed for different provisions or for different purposes.

(3)   Without prejudice to the provisions of Schedule 12 to this Act, an order under subsection (2) above may make such transitional provisions and savings as appear to the Secretary of State necessary or expedient in connection with any provision brought into force by the order.

(4)   Subject to subsections (5) to (8) below, this Act extends to England and Wales only.

(5)–(8)   . . .

NOTES

Sub-ss (5)–(8): outside the scope of this work.

Social Security Contributions and Benefits Act 1992

(c 4)

An Act to consolidate certain enactments relating to social security contributions and benefits with amendments to give effect to recommendations of the Law Commission and the Scottish Law Commission

[13 February 1992]

PART VII
INCOME-RELATED BENEFITS

Income support

124   Income support

(1)   A person in Great Britain is entitled to income support if—
   [(a) he is of or over the age of 16;]
   (b) he has no income or his income does not exceed the applicable amount;
   (c) he is not engaged in remunerative work and, if he is a member of a married or unmarried couple, the other member is not so engaged;
       . . .
   [(d) except in such circumstances as may be prescribed, he is not receiving relevant education;]
   [(e) he falls within a prescribed category of person; and
    (f) he is not entitled to a jobseeker's allowance and, if he is a member of a married or unmarried couple, the other member of the couple is not entitled to an income-based jobseeker's allowance.]

(2), (3) . . .

(4)   Subject to subsection (5) below, where a person is entitled to income support, then—
  (a) if he has no income, the amount shall be the applicable amount; and
  (b) if he has income, the amount shall be the difference between his income and the applicable amount.

(5)   Where a person is entitled to income support for a period to which this subsection applies, the amount payable for that period shall be calculated in such manner as may be prescribed.

(6)   Subsection (5) above applies—
  (a) to a period of less than a week which is the whole period for which income support is payable; and
  (b) to any other period of less than a week for which it is payable.

NOTES

Sub-s (1): paras (a), (d) substituted, word omitted from para (c) repealed, and paras (e), (f) added, by the Jobseekers Act 1995, s 41(4), (5), Sch 2, para 30, Sch 3.
Sub-ss (2), (3): repealed by the Jobseekers Act 1995, s 41(5), Sch 3.

Family credit

128 Family credit

(1)   Subject to regulations under section 5(1)(a) of the Administration Act, a person in Great Britain is entitled to family credit if, when the claim for it is made or is treated as made—
  (a) his income—
    (i)   does not exceed the amount which is the applicable amount at such date as may be prescribed; or
    (ii) exceeds it, but only by such an amount that there is an amount remaining if the deduction for which subsection (2)(b) below provides is made;
  (b) he or, if he is a member of a married or unmarried couple, he or the other member of the couple, is engaged and normally engaged in remunerative work;
  (c) except in such circumstances as may be prescribed, neither he nor any member of his family is entitled to a disability working allowance; and

(d) he or, if he is a member of a married or unmarried couple, he or the other member, is responsible for a member of the same household who is a child or a person of a prescribed description.

(2) Where a person is entitled to family credit, then—
(a) if his income does not exceed the amount which is the applicable amount at the date prescribed under subsection (1)(a)(i) above, the amount of the family credit shall be the amount which is the appropriate maximum family credit in his case; and
(b) if his income exceeds the amount which is the applicable amount at that date, the amount of the family credit shall be what remains after the deduction from the appropriate maximum family credit of a prescribed percentage of the excess of his income over the applicable amount.

(3) Family credit shall be payable for a period of 26 weeks or such other period as may be prescribed and, subject to regulations, an award of family credit and the rate at which it is payable shall not be affected by any change of circumstances during that period or by any order under section 150 of the Administration Act.

(4)–(6) . . .

NOTES

Sub-ss (4)–(6): outside the scope of this work.
Administration Act: Social Security Administration Act 1992.

Housing benefit

130 Housing benefit

(1) A person is entitled to housing benefit if—
(a) he is liable to make payments in respect of a dwelling in Great Britain which he occupies as his home;
(b) there is an appropriate maximum housing benefit in his case; and
(c) either—
(i) he has no income or his income does not exceed the applicable amount; or
(ii) his income exceeds that amount, but only by so much that there is an amount remaining if the deduction for which subsection (3)(b) below provides is made.

(2)   In subsection (1) above "payments in respect of a dwelling" means such payments as may be prescribed, but the power to prescribe payments does not include power to prescribe

[(a) payments to a billing or [local authority in Scotland] in respect of council tax; or

(b) mortgage payments, or, in relation to Scotland, payments under heritable securities].

(3)   Where a person is entitled to housing benefit, then—

(a) if he has no income or his income does not exceed the applicable amount, the amount of the housing benefit shall be the amount which is the appropriate maximum housing benefit in his case; and

(b) if his income exceeds the applicable amount, the amount of the housing benefit shall be what remains after the deduction from the appropriate maximum housing benefit of prescribed percentages of the excess of his income over the applicable amount.

(4)   Regulations shall prescribe the manner in which the appropriate maximum housing benefit is to be determined in any case.

(5)   . . .

NOTES

Sub-s (2): words in first pair of square brackets substituted by the Local Government Finance Act 1992, s 103, Sch 9, para 3; words in square brackets in para (a) substituted by the Local Government etc (Scotland) Act 1994, s 180(1), Sch 13, para 174(4).

Sub-s (5): outside the scope of this work.

[Council tax benefit

131   Council tax benefit

(1)   A person is entitled to council tax benefit in respect of a particular day falling after 31st March 1993 if the following are fulfilled, namely, the condition set out in subsection (3) below and either—

(a) each of the two conditions set out in subsections (4) and (5) below; or

(b) the condition set out in subsection (6) below.

(2)   Council tax benefit—

(a) shall not be allowed to a person in respect of any day falling before the day on which his entitlement is to be regarded as commencing for that purpose by virtue of paragraph (l) of section 6(1) of the Administration Act; but

  (b) may be allowed to him in respect of not more than 6 days immediately following the day on which his period of entitlement would otherwise come to an end, if his entitlement is to be regarded by virtue of that paragraph as not having ended for that purpose.

(3)   The main condition for the purposes of subsection (1) above is that the person concerned—

  (a) is for the day liable to pay council tax in respect of a dwelling of which he is a resident; and

  (b) is not a prescribed person or a person of a prescribed class.

(4)   The first condition for the purposes of subsection (1)(a) above is that there is an appropriate maximum council tax benefit in the case of the person concerned.

(5)   The second condition for the purposes of subsection (1)(a) above is that—

  (a) the day falls within a week in respect of which the person concerned has no income;

  (b) the day falls within a week in respect of which his income does not exceed the applicable amount; or

  (c) neither paragraph (a) nor paragraph (b) above is fulfilled in his case but amount A exceeds amount B where—

     (i) amount A is the appropriate maximum council tax benefit in his case; and

    (ii) amount B is a prescribed percentage of the difference between his income in respect of the week in which the day falls and the applicable amount.

(6)   The condition for the purposes of subsection (1)(b) above is that—

  (a) no other resident of the dwelling is liable to pay rent to the person concerned in respect of the dwelling; and

  (b) there is an alternative maximum council tax benefit in the case of that person which is derived from the income or aggregate incomes of one or more residents to whom this subsection applies.

(7)   Subsection (6) above applies to any other resident of the dwelling who—

  (a) is not a person who, in accordance with Schedule 1 to the Local Government Finance Act 1992, falls to be disregarded for the purposes of discount; and

  (b) is not a prescribed person or a person of a prescribed class.

(8)   Subject to subsection (9) below, where a person is entitled to council tax benefit in respect of a day, the amount to which he is entitled shall be—
  (a) if subsection (5)(a) or (b) above applies, the amount which is the appropriate maximum council tax benefit in his case;
  (b) if subsection (5)(c) above applies, the amount found by deducting amount B from amount A, where "amount A" and "amount B" have the meanings given by that subsection; and
  (c) if subsection (6) above applies, the amount which is the alternative maximum council tax benefit in his case.

(9)   Where a person is entitled to council tax benefit in respect of a day, and both subsection (5) and subsection (6) above apply, the amount to which he is entitled shall be whichever is the greater of—
  (a) the amount given by paragraph (a) or, as the case may be, paragraph (b) of subsection (8) above; and
  (b) the amount given by paragraph (c) of that subsection.

(10)   Regulations shall prescribe the manner in which—
  (a) the appropriate maximum council tax benefit;
  (b) the alternative maximum council tax benefit,

are to be determined in any case.

(11)   In this section "dwelling" and "resident" have the same meanings as in Part I or II of the Local Government Finance Act 1992.]

NOTES

Substituted, together with the cross-heading, by the Local Government Finance Act 1992, s 103, Sch 9, para 4.
Administration Act: Social Security Administration Act 1992.

PART VIII
THE SOCIAL FUND

138   Payments out of the social fund

[(1)   There may be made out of the social fund, in accordance with this Part of this Act—
  (a) payments of prescribed amounts, whether in respect of prescribed items or otherwise, to meet, in prescribed circumstances, maternity expenses and funeral expenses; and

(b)   payments by way of community care grant, crisis loan or budgeting loan to meet other needs in accordance with directions given or guidance issued by the Secretary of State.]

(2)   Payments may also be made out of that fund, in accordance with this Part of this Act, of a prescribed amount or a number of prescribed amounts to prescribed descriptions of persons, in prescribed circumstances to meet expenses for heating which appear to the Secretary of State to have been or to be likely to be incurred in cold weather.

(3)   The power to make a payment out of the social fund such as is mentioned in subsection (1)(b) above may be exercised by making a payment to a third party with a view to the third party providing, or arranging for the provision of, goods or services for the applicant.

(4)   In this section "prescribed" means specified in or determined in accordance with regulations.

[(5)   In this Part—
    "budgeting loan" means a loan awarded in circumstances specified in directions issued by the Secretary of State for the purpose of defraying an intermittent expense;
    "community care grant" means a grant awarded in circumstances so specified for the purpose of meeting a need for community care;
    "crisis loan" means a loan awarded in circumstances so specified for the purpose of meeting an immediate short term need;

and any reference in this subsection to meeting a need or defraying an expense includes a reference to helping to meet the need or to defray the expense.]

NOTES

Sub-s (1): substituted by the Social Security Act 1998, s 70(1).
Sub-s (5): added by the Social Security Act 1998, s 70(2).

139   Awards by social fund officers

(1)   The questions whether a payment such as is mentioned in section 138(1)(b) above is to be awarded and how much it is to be shall be determined by a social fund officer.

(2)   A social fund officer may determine that an award shall be payable in specified instalments at specified times.

(3) . . .

(4)   An award [of a crisis loan or a budgeting loan] shall be repayable upon such terms and conditions as before the award is paid the Secretary of State notifies to the person by or on behalf of whom the application for it was made.

(5)   Payment of an award shall be made to the applicant unless *the social fund officer* determines otherwise.

NOTES

Sub-s (1): substituted by the Social Security Act 1998, s 86(1), Sch 7, para 72(1), as from a day to be appointed, as follows—

"(1) Whether a payment mentioned in section 138(1)(b) above is to be awarded, and how much it is to be, shall be determined by an appropriate officer, that is to say, an officer of the Secretary of State who, acting under his authority, is exercising functions of the Secretary of State in relation to payments so mentioned."

Sub-ss (2): for the words in italics there are substituted the words "An appropriate officer" by the Social Security Act 1998, s 86(1), Sch 7, para 72(2), as from a day to be appointed.

Sub-s (3): repealed by the Social Security Act 1998, s 86(1), (2), Sch 7, para 72(3), Sch 8.

Sub-s (4): words in square brackets substituted by the Social Security Act 1998, s 86(1), Sch 7, para 72(4).

Sub-s (5): for the words in italics there are substituted the words "the appropriate officer" by the Social Security Act 1998, s 86(1), Sch 7, para 72(5), as from a day to be appointed.

140   Principles of determination

(1)   In determining whether to make an award [of a community care grant or a crisis loan] to the applicant or the amount or value to be awarded *a social fund officer* shall have regard, subject to subsection (2) below, to all the circumstances of the case and, in particular—

  (a) the nature, extent and urgency of the need;
  (b) the existence of resources from which the need may be met;
  (c) the possibility that some other person or body may wholly or partly meet it;
  (d) where the payment is repayable, the likelihood of repayment and the time within which repayment is likely;
  (e) any relevant allocation under section 168(1) to (4) of the Administration Act.

[(1A) Subject to subsection (2) below, in determining whether to make an award of a budgeting loan to the applicant, or the amount or value to be awarded, an appropriate officer shall have regard to—

    (a) such of the applicant's personal circumstances as are of a description specified in directions issued by the Secretary of State; and

    (b) the criteria specified in paragraphs (b) to (e) of subsection (1) above;

but where the criterion mentioned in paragraph (a) above would preclude the award of such a loan, the appropriate officer shall have regard instead to such other criterion as may be specified in directions so issued.]

(2)   *A social fund officer* shall determine any question in accordance with any general directions issued by the Secretary of State and in determining any question shall take account of any general guidance issued by him.

(3)–(5) . . .

NOTES

Sub-s (1): words in square brackets inserted by the Social Security Act 1998, s 71(1), and for the words in italics there are substituted the words "an appropriate officer" by the Social Security Act 1998, s 86(1), Sch 7, para 73(1), as from a day to be appointed.

Sub-s (1A): inserted by the Social Security Act 1998, s 71(2), Sch 7, para 73(1). Note: until the coming into force of Sch 7, para 73 of the 1998 Act, this section shall have effect as if the references to "an appropriate officer" and "the appropriate officer" were references respectively to "a social fund officer" and "the social fund officer".

Sub-s (2): for the words in italics there are substituted the words "An appropriate officer" by the Social Security Act 1998, s 86(1), Sch 7, para 73(2), as from a day to be appointed.

Sub-ss (3)–(5): outside the scope of this work.

Administration Act: Social Security Administration Act 1992,

PART IX
CHILD BENEFIT

141 Child benefit

A person who is responsible for one or more children in any week shall be entitled, subject to the provisions of this Part of this Act, to a benefit (to be known as "child benefit") for that week in respect of the child or each of the children for whom he is responsible.

142 Meaning of "child"

(1)   For the purposes of this Part of this Act a person shall be treated as a child for any week in which—

(a) he is under the age of 16; or

(b) he is under the age of 18 and not receiving full-time education and prescribed conditions are satisfied in relation to him; or

(c) he is under the age of 19 and receiving full-time education either by attendance at a recognised educational establishment or, if the education is recognised by the Secretary of State, elsewhere.

(2)   The Secretary of State may recognise education provided otherwise than at a recognised educational establishment for a person who, in the opinion of the Secretary of State, could reasonably be expected to attend such an establishment only if the Secretary of State is satisfied that education was being so provided for that person immediately before he attained the age of 16.

(3)   Regulations may prescribe the circumstances in which education is or is not to be treated for the purposes of this Part of this Act as full-time.

(4)   In determining for the purposes of paragraph (c) of subsection (1) above whether a person is receiving full-time education as mentioned in that paragraph, no account shall be taken of such interruptions as may be prescribed.

(5)   Regulations may provide that a person who in any week ceases to fall within subsection (1) above shall be treated as continuing to do so for a prescribed period; but no person shall by virtue of any such regulations be treated as continuing to fall within that subsection for any week after that in which he attains the age of 19.

143 Meaning of "person responsible for child"

(1)   For the purposes of this Part of this Act a person shall be treated as responsible for a child in any week if—

(a) he has the child living with him in that week; or

(b) he is contributing to the cost of providing for the child at a weekly rate which is not less than the weekly rate of child benefit payable in respect of the child for that week.

(2)   Where a person has had a child living with him at some time before a particular week he shall be treated for the purposes of this section as

having the child living with him in that week notwithstanding their absence from one another unless, in the 16 weeks preceding that week, they were absent from one another for more than 56 days not counting any day which is to be disregarded under subsection (3) below.

(3)   Subject to subsection (4) below, a day of absence shall be disregarded for the purposes of subsection (2) above if it is due solely to the child's—

(a) receiving full-time education by attendance at a recognised educational establishment;

(b) undergoing medical or other treatment as an in-patient in a hospital or similar institution; or

(c) being, in such circumstances as may be prescribed, in residential accommodation pursuant to arrangements made under—

    (i) *section 21 of the National Assistance Act 1948;*

    (ii) *the Children Act 1989; or*

    (iii) *the Social Work (Scotland) Act 1968.*

(4)   The number of days that may be disregarded by virtue of subsection (3)(b) or (c) above in the case of any child shall not exceed such number as may be prescribed unless the person claiming to be responsible for the child regularly incurs expenditure in respect of the child.

(5)   Regulations may prescribe the circumstances in which a person is or is not to be treated—

(a) as contributing to the cost of providing for a child as required by subsection (1)(b) above; or

(b) as regularly incurring expenditure in respect of a child as required by subsection (4) above;

and such regulations may in particular make provision whereby a contribution made or expenditure incurred by two or more persons is to be treated as made or incurred by one of them or whereby a contribution made or expenditure incurred by one of two spouses residing together is to be treated as made or incurred by the other.

NOTES

Sub-s (3): words in italics in para (c) temporarily substituted by the Social Security (Consequential Provisions) Act 1992, s 6, Sch 4, para 5, until a day appointed under Sch 4, para 1(3) thereof, as follows—

"(i) paragraph 2 of Schedule 8 to the National Health Service Act 1977;

(ii) the Children Act 1989; or

(iii) section 37 of the National Health Service (Scotland) Act 1978.".

145   Rate of child benefit

(1)   Child benefit shall be payable at such weekly rate as may be prescribed.

(2)   Different rates may be prescribed in relation to different cases, whether by reference to the age of the child in respect of whom the benefit is payable or otherwise.

(3)–(7) . . .

NOTES

Sub-ss (3)–(7): outside the scope of this work.

147   Interpretation of Part IX and supplementary provisions

(1)   In this Part of this Act—
   "prescribed" means prescribed by regulations;
   "recognised educational establishment" means an establishment recognised by the Secretary of State as being, or as comparable to, a university, college or school;
   "voluntary organisation" means a body, other than a public or local authority, the activities of which are carried on otherwise than for profit; and
   "week" means a period of 7 days beginning with a Monday.

(2)   Subject to any provision made by regulations, references in this Part of this Act to any condition being satisfied or any facts existing in a week shall be construed as references to the condition being satisfied or the facts existing at the beginning of that week.

(3)   References in this Part of this Act to a parent, father or mother of a child shall be construed as including references to a step-parent, step-father or step-mother.

(4)   Regulations may prescribe the circumstances in which persons are or are not to be treated for the purposes of this Part of this Act as residing together.

(5)   Regulations may make provision as to the circumstances in which [a marriage during the subsistence of which a party to it is at any time married

to more than one person is to be treated for the purposes of this Part of this Act as having, or not having, the same consequences as any other marriage.]

(6)   Nothing in this Part of this Act shall be construed as conferring a right to child benefit on any body corporate; but regulations may confer such a right on voluntary organisations and for that purpose may make such modifications as the Secretary of State thinks fit—

(a) of any provision of this Part of this Act; or

(b) of any provision of the Administration Act relating to child benefit.

NOTES

Sub-s (5): words in square brackets substituted by the Private International Law (Miscellaneous Provisions) Act 1995, s 8(2), Schedule, para 4(3).
Administration Act: Social Security Administration Act 1992.

PART XIII
GENERAL

Short title, commencement and extent

177   Short title, commencement and extent

(1)   This Act may be cited as the Social Security Contributions and Benefits Act 1992.

(2)   This Act is to be read, where appropriate, with the Administration Act and the Consequential Provisions Act.

(3)–(6) . . .

NOTES

Sub-ss (3)–(6): outside the scope of this work.

Social Security Administration Act 1992

(c 5)

An Act to consolidate certain enactments relating to the administration of social security and related matters with amendments to give effect to recommendations of the Law Commission and the Scottish Law Commission

[13 February 1992]

PART III
OVERPAYMENTS AND ADJUSTMENTS OF BENEFIT

Adjustments of benefit

[74A Payment of benefit where maintenance payments collected by Secretary of State

(1)   This section applies where—
   (a) a person ("the claimant") is entitled to a benefit to which this section applies;
   (b) the Secretary of State is collecting periodical payments of child or spousal maintenance made in respect of the claimant or a member of the claimant's family; and
   (c) the inclusion of any such periodical payment in the claimant's relevant income would, apart from this section, have the effect of reducing the amount of the benefit to which the claimant is entitled.

(2)   The Secretary of State may, to such extent as he considers appropriate, treat any such periodical payment as not being relevant income for the purposes of calculating the amount of benefit to which the claimant is entitled.

(3)   The Secretary of State may, to the extent that any periodical payment collected by him is treated as not being relevant income for those purposes, retain the whole or any part of that payment.

(4)   Any sum retained by the Secretary of State under subsection (3) shall be paid by him into the Consolidated Fund.

(5)   In this section—
"child" means a person under the age of 16;
"child maintenance", "spousal maintenance" and "relevant income" have
such meaning as may be prescribed;
"family" means—
(a) a married or unmarried couple;
(b) a married or unmarried couple and a member of the same
household for whom one of them is, or both are, responsible and
who is a child or a person of a prescribed description;
(c) except in prescribed circumstances, a person who is not a
member of a married or unmarried couple and a member of the
same household for whom that person is responsible and who is
a child or a person of a prescribed description;
"married couple" means a man and woman who are married to each
other and are members of the same household; and
"unmarried couple" means a man and woman who are not married to
each other but are living together as husband and wife otherwise
than in prescribed circumstances.

(6)   For the purposes of this section, the Secretary of State may by
regulations make provision as to the circumstances in which—
(a) persons are to be treated as being or not being members of the
same household;
(b) one person is to be treated as responsible or not responsible for
another.

(7)   The benefits to which this section applies are income support, an income-
based jobseeker's allowance and such other benefits (if any) as may be prescribed.]

NOTES

Commencement: 1 October 1995.
Inserted by the Child Support Act 1995, s 25.

Social fund awards

78   Recovery of social fund awards

(1)   A social fund award which is repayable shall be recoverable by the
Secretary of State.

(2)   Without prejudice to any other method of recovery, the Secretary of
State may recover an award by deduction from prescribed benefits.

(3)   The Secretary of State may recover an award—
  (a) from the person to or for the benefit of whom it was made;
  (b) where that person is a member of a married or unmarried couple, from the other member of the couple;
  (c) from a person who is liable to maintain the person by or on behalf of whom the application for the award was made or any person in relation to whose needs the award was made.

(3A)–(4)   . . .

(5)   In this section—
  "married couple" means a man and woman who are married to each other and are members of the same household;
  "unmarried couple" means a man and woman who are not married to each other but are living together as husband and wife otherwise than in circumstances prescribed under section 132 of the Contributions and Benefits Act.

(6)   For the purposes of this section—
  (a) a man shall be liable to maintain his wife and any children of whom he is the father;
  (b) a woman shall be liable to maintain her husband and any children of whom she is the mother;
  (c) a person shall be liable to maintain another person throughout any period in respect of which the first-mentioned person has, on or after 23rd May 1980 (the date of the passing of the Social Security Act 1980) and either alone or jointly with a further person, given an undertaking in writing in pursuance of immigration rules within the meaning of the Immigration Act 1971 to be responsible for the maintenance and accommodation of the other person; and
  (d) "child" includes a person who has attained the age of 16 but not the age of 19 and in respect of whom either parent, or some person acting in the place of either parent, is receiving income support [or an income-based jobseeker's allowance].

(7)   Any reference in subsection (6) above to children of whom the man or the woman is the father or the mother shall be construed in accordance with section 1 of the Family Law Reform Act 1987.

(8), (9)   . . .

NOTES

Sub-ss (3A)–(4), (8), (9): outside the scope of this work.
Sub-s (6): words in square brackets in para (d) added by the Jobseekers Act 1995, s 41(4), Sch 2, para 51.

PART V
INCOME SUPPORT AND THE DUTY TO MAINTAIN

105 Failure to maintain–general

(1)   If—
   (a) any person persistently refuses or neglects to maintain himself or
        any person whom he is liable to maintain; and
   (b) in consequence of his refusal or neglect income support [or an
        income- based jobseeker's allowance] is paid to or in respect of him
        or such a person,

he shall be guilty of an offence and liable on summary conviction to
imprisonment for a term not exceeding 3 months or to a fine of an amount
not exceeding level 4 on the standard scale or to both.

(2)   For the purposes of subsection (1) above a person shall not be
taken to refuse or neglect to maintain himself or any other person by
reason only of anything done or omitted in furtherance of a trade
dispute.

(3)   [Subject to subsection (4) below,] subsections (6) to (9) of section 78
above shall have effect for the purposes of this Part of this Act as they have
effect for the purposes of that section.

[(4)   For the purposes of this section, in its application to an income-
based jobseeker's allowance, a person is liable to maintain another if that
other person is his or her spouse.]

NOTES

   Sub-ss (1), (3): words in square brackets inserted by the Jobseekers Act 1995,
s 41(4), Sch 2, para 53(2), (3).
   Sub-s (4): added by the Jobseekers Act 1995, s 41(4), Sch 2, para 52(4).

106 Recovery of expenditure on benefit from person liable for maintenance

(1)   Subject to the following provisions of this section, if income support
is claimed by or in respect of a person whom another person is liable to
maintain or paid to or in respect of such a person, the Secretary of State
may make a complaint against the liable person to a magistrates' court for
an order under this section.

(2)   On the hearing of a complaint under this section the court shall have regard to all the circumstances and, in particular, to the income of the liable person, and may order him to pay such sum, weekly or otherwise, as it may consider appropriate, except that in a case falling within section 78(6)(c) above that sum shall not include any amount which is not attributable to income support (whether paid before or after the making of the order).

(3)   In determining whether to order any payments to be made in respect of income support for any period before the complaint was made, or the amount of any such payments, the court shall disregard any amount by which the liable person's income exceeds the income which was his during that period.

(4)   Any payments ordered to be made under this section shall be made—
    (a) to the Secretary of State in so far as they are attributable to any income support (whether paid before or after the making of the order);
    (b) to the person claiming income support or (if different) the dependant; or
    (c) to such other person as appears to the court expedient in the interests of the dependant.

(5)   An order under this section shall be enforceable as a magistrates' court maintenance order within the meaning of section 150(1) of the Magistrates' Courts Act 1980.

(6)   In the application of this section to Scotland, subsection (5) above shall be omitted and for the references to a complaint and to a magistrates' court there shall be substituted respectively references to an application and to the sheriff.

(7)   On an application under subsection (1) above a court in Scotland may make a finding as to the parentage of a child for the purpose of establishing whether a person is, for the purposes of section 105 above and this section, liable to maintain him.

107 Recovery of expenditure on income support: additional amounts and transfer of orders

(1)   In any case where—
    (a) the claim for income support referred to in section 106(1) above is or was made by the parent of one or more children in respect of both himself and those children; and

(b) the other parent is liable to maintain those children but, by virtue of not being the claimant's husband or wife, is not liable to maintain the claimant,

the sum which the court may order that other parent to pay under subsection (2) of that section may include an amount, determined in accordance with regulations, in respect of any income support paid to or for the claimant by virtue of such provisions as may be prescribed.

(2)–(14)   . . .

(15)   In this section—
"child" means a person under the age of 16, notwithstanding section 78(6)(d) above;
"court" shall be construed in accordance with section 106 above;
"maintenance order"—
(a) in England and Wales, means—
   (i) any order for the making of periodical payments or for the payment of a lump sum which is, or has at any time been, a maintenance order within the meaning of the Attachment of Earnings Act 1971;
   (ii) any order under Part III of the Matrimonial and Family Proceedings Act 1984 (overseas divorce) for the making of periodical payments or for the payment of a lump sum;
(b) in Scotland, has the meaning assigned by section 106 of the Debtors (Scotland) Act 1987, but disregarding paragraph (h) (alimentary bond or agreement);
"the relevant rights", in relation to an order under section 106(2) above, means the right to bring any proceedings, take any steps or do any other thing under or in relation to the order which the Secretary of State could have brought, taken or done apart from any transfer under this section.

NOTES

Sub-ss (2)–(14): outside the scope of this work.

Child Support Act 1995

(c 34)

An Act to make provision with respect to child support maintenance and other maintenance; and to provide for a child maintenance bonus
[19 July 1995]

10 The child maintenance bonus

(1) The Secretary of State may by regulations make provision for the payment, in prescribed circumstances, of sums to persons—
   (a) who are or have been in receipt of child maintenance; and
   (b) to or in respect of whom income support or a jobseeker's allowance is or has been paid.

(2) A sum payable under the regulations shall be known as "a child maintenance bonus".

(3) A child maintenance bonus shall be treated for all purposes as payable by way of income support or (as the case may be) a jobseeker's allowance.

(4) Subsection (3) is subject to section 617 of the Income and Corporation Taxes Act 1988 (which, as amended by paragraph 1 of Schedule 3, provides for a child maintenance bonus not to be taxable).

(5) The regulations may, in particular, provide for—
   (a) a child maintenance bonus to be payable only on the occurrence of a prescribed event;
   (b) a bonus not to be payable unless a claim is made before the end of the prescribed period;
   (c) the amount of a bonus (subject to any maximum prescribed by virtue of paragraph (f)) to be determined in accordance with the regulations;
   (d) enabling amounts to be calculated by reference to periods of entitlement to income support and periods of entitlement to a jobseeker's allowance;
   (e) treating a bonus as payable wholly by way of a jobseeker's allowance or wholly by way of income support, in a case where amounts have been calculated in accordance with provision made by virtue of paragraph (d);
   (f) the amount of a bonus not to exceed a prescribed maximum;
   (g) a bonus not to be payable if the amount of the bonus which would otherwise be payable is less than the prescribed minimum;
   (h) prescribed periods to be disregarded for prescribed purposes;
   (i) a bonus which has been paid to a person to be treated, in prescribed circumstances and for prescribed purposes, as income or capital of hers or of any other member of her family;

(j) treating the whole or a prescribed part of an amount which has accrued towards a person's bonus—
  (i) as not having accrued towards her bonus; but
  (ii) as having accrued towards the bonus of another person.

(6) The Secretary of State may by regulations provide—
  (a) for the whole or a prescribed part of a child maintenance bonus to be paid in such circumstances as may be prescribed to such person, other than the person who is or had been in receipt of child maintenance, as may be determined in accordance with the regulations;
  (b) for any payments of a prescribed kind which have been collected by the Secretary of State, and retained by him, to be treated for the purposes of this section as having been received by the appropriate person as payments of child maintenance.

(7) In this section—
  "appropriate person" has such meaning as may be prescribed;
  "child" means a person under the age of 16;
  "child maintenance" has such meaning as may be prescribed;
  "family" means—
    (a) a married or unmarried couple;
    (b) a married or unmarried couple and a member of the same household for whom one of them is, or both are, responsible and who is a child or a person of a prescribed description;
    (c) except in prescribed circumstances, a person who is not a member of a married or unmarried couple and a member of the same household for whom that person is responsible and who is a child or a person of a prescribed description;
  "married couple" means a man and woman who are married to each other and are members of the same household; and
  "unmarried couple" means a man and woman who are not married to each other but are living together as husband and wife otherwise than in prescribed circumstances.

(8) For the purposes of this section, the Secretary of State may by regulations make provision as to the circumstances in which—
  (a) persons are to be treated as being or not being members of the same household;
  (b) one person is to be treated as responsible or not responsible for another.

24 Compensation payments

(1)   The Secretary of State may by regulations make provision for the payment by him, in prescribed circumstances and to or in respect of qualifying persons, of sums by way of compensation or partial compensation for any reduction which is attributable to one or more prescribed changes in child support legislation.

(2)–(4) . . .

NOTES

Commencement: to be appointed.
Sub-ss (2)–(4): outside the scope of this work.

27 Interpretation

(1)   In this Act "the 1991 Act" means the Child Support Act 1991.

(2)   Expressions in this Act which are used in the 1991 Act have the same meaning in this Act as they have in that Act.

NOTES

Commencement: 1 October 1995.

Family Law Act 1996

(c 27)

An Act to make provision with respect to: divorce and separation; legal aid in connection with mediation in disputes relating to family matters; proceedings in cases where marriages have broken down; rights of occupation of certain domestic premises; prevention of molestation; the inclusion in certain orders under the Children Act 1989 of provisions about the occupation of a dwelling-house; the transfer of tenancies between spouses and persons who have lived together as husband and wife; and for connected purposes

[4 July 1996]

PART I
PRINCIPLES OF PARTS II AND III

1 The general principles underlying Parts II and III

The court and any person, in exercising functions under or in consequence of Parts II and III, shall have regard to the following general principles—
  (a) that the institution of marriage is to be supported;
  (b) that the parties to a marriage which may have broken down are to be encouraged to take all practicable steps, whether by marriage counselling or otherwise, to save the marriage;
  (c) that a marriage which has irretrievably broken down and is being brought to an end should be brought to an end—
      (i)   with minimum distress to the parties and to the children affected;
      (ii) with questions dealt with in a manner designed to promote as good a continuing relationship between the parties and any children affected as is possible in the circumstances; and
      (iii) without costs being unreasonably incurred in connection with the procedures to be followed in bringing the marriage to an end; and
  (d) that any risk to one of the parties to a marriage, and to any children, of violence from the other party should, so far as reasonably practicable, be removed or diminished.

NOTES

Commencement: 21 March 1997.

PART II
DIVORCE AND SEPARATION

Court orders

2 Divorce and separation

(1) The court may—
  (a) by making an order (to be known as a divorce order), dissolve a marriage; or
  (b) by making an order (to be known as a separation order), provide for the separation of the parties to a marriage.

(2) Any such order comes into force on being made.

(3)   A separation order remains in force—
  (a) while the marriage continues; or
  (b) until cancelled by the court on the joint application of the parties.

NOTES

Commencement: to be appointed.

3   Circumstances in which orders are made

(1)   If an application for a divorce order or for a separation order is made to the court under this section by one or both of the parties to a marriage, the court shall make the order applied for if (but only if)—
  (a) the marriage has broken down irretrievably;
  (b) the requirements of section 8 about information meetings are satisfied;
  (c) the requirements of section 9 about the parties' arrangements for the future are satisfied; and
  (d) the application has not been withdrawn.

(2)   A divorce order may not be made if an order preventing divorce is in force under section 10.

(3)   If the court is considering an application for a divorce order and an application for a separation order in respect of the same marriage it shall proceed as if it were considering only the application for a divorce order unless—
  (a) an order preventing divorce is in force with respect to the marriage;
  (b) the court makes an order preventing divorce; or
  (c) section 7(6) or (13) applies.

NOTES

Commencement: to be appointed.

4   Conversion of separation order into divorce order

(1)   A separation order which is made before the second anniversary of the marriage may not be converted into a divorce order under this section until after that anniversary.

(2)   A separation order may not be converted into a divorce order under this section at any time while—
  (a) an order preventing divorce is in force under section 10; or
  (b) subsection (4) applies.

(3)   Otherwise, if a separation order is in force and an application for a divorce order—
   (a) is made under this section by either or both of the parties to the marriage, and
   (b) is not withdrawn,

the court shall grant the application once the requirements of section 11 have been satisfied.

(4)   Subject to subsection (5), this subsection applies if—
   (a) there is a child of the family who is under the age of sixteen when the application under this section is made; or
   (b) the application under this section is made by one party and the other party applies to the court, before the end of such period as may be prescribed by rules of court, for time for further reflection.

(5)   Subsection (4)—
   (a) does not apply if, at the time when the application under this section is made, there is an occupation order or a non-molestation order in force in favour of the applicant, or of a child of the family, made against the other party;
   (b) does not apply if the court is satisfied that delaying the making of a divorce order would be significantly detrimental to the welfare of any child of the family;
   (c) ceases to apply—
       (i) at the end of the period of six months beginning with the end of the period for reflection and consideration by reference to which the separation order was made; or
       (ii) if earlier, on there ceasing to be any children of the family to whom subsection (4)(a) applied.

NOTES

Commencement: to be appointed.

Marital breakdown

5   Marital breakdown

(1)   A marriage is to be taken to have broken down irretrievably if (but only if)—
   (a) a statement has been made by one (or both) of the parties that the maker of the statement (or each of them) believes that the marriage has broken down;

(b) the statement complies with the requirements of section 6;

(c) the period for reflection and consideration fixed by section 7 has ended; and

(d) the application under section 3 is accompanied by a declaration by the party making the application that—

   (i)   having reflected on the breakdown, and

   (ii) having considered the requirements of this Part as to the parties' arrangements for the future,

the applicant believes that the marriage cannot be saved.

(2)   The statement and the application under section 3 do not have to be made by the same party.

(3)   An application may not be made under section 3 by reference to a particular statement if—

(a) the parties have jointly given notice (in accordance with rules of court) withdrawing the statement; or

(b) a period of one year ("the specified period") has passed since the end of the period for reflection and consideration.

(4)   Any period during which an order preventing divorce is in force is not to count towards the specified period mentioned in subsection (3)(b).

(5)   Subsection (6) applies if, before the end of the specified period, the parties jointly give notice to the court that they are attempting reconciliation but require additional time.

(6)   The specified period—

(a) stops running on the day on which the notice is received by the court; but

(b) resumes running on the day on which either of the parties gives notice to the court that the attempted reconciliation has been unsuccessful.

(7)   If the specified period is interrupted by a continuous period of more than 18 months, any application by either of the parties for a divorce order or for a separation order must be by reference to a new statement received by the court at any time after the end of the 18 months.

(8)   The Lord Chancellor may by order amend subsection (3)(b) by varying the specified period.

Commencement: to be appointed.

6 Statement of marital breakdown

(1)   A statement under section 5(1)(a) is to be known as a statement of marital breakdown; but in this Part it is generally referred to as "a statement".

(2)   If a statement is made by one party it must also state that that party—
  (a) is aware of the purpose of the period for reflection and consideration as described in section 7; and
  (b) wishes to make arrangements for the future.

(3)   If a statement is made by both parties it must also state that each of them—
  (a) is aware of the purpose of the period for reflection and consideration as described in section 7; and
  (b) wishes to make arrangements for the future.

(4)   A statement must be given to the court in accordance with the requirements of rules made under section 12.

(5)   A statement must also satisfy any other requirements imposed by rules made under that section.

(6)   A statement made at a time when the circumstances of the case include any of those mentioned in subsection (7) is ineffective for the purposes of this Part.

(7)   The circumstances are—
  (a) that a statement has previously been made with respect to the marriage and it is, or will become, possible—
    (i)   for an application for a divorce order, or
    (ii) for an application for a separation order,

  to be made by reference to the previous statement;
  (b) that such an application has been made in relation to the marriage and has not been withdrawn;
  (c) that a separation order is in force.

Commencement: to be appointed.

Reflection and consideration

7 Period for reflection and consideration

(1)   Where a statement has been made, a period for the parties—
   (a) to reflect on whether the marriage can be saved and to have an opportunity to effect a reconciliation, and
   (b) to consider what arrangements should be made for the future,

must pass before an application for a divorce order or for a separation order may be made by reference to that statement.

(2)   That period is to be known as the period for reflection and consideration.

(3)   The period for reflection and consideration is nine months beginning with the fourteenth day after the day on which the statement is received by the court.

(4)   Where—
   (a) the statement has been made by one party,
   (b) rules made under section 12 require the court to serve a copy of the statement on the other party, and
   (c) failure to comply with the rules causes inordinate delay in service,

the court may, on the application of that other party, extend the period for reflection and consideration.

(5)   An extension under subsection (4) may be for any period not exceeding the time between—
   (a) the beginning of the period for reflection and consideration; and
   (b) the time when service is effected.

(6)   A statement which is made before the first anniversary of the marriage to which it relates is ineffective for the purposes of any application for a divorce order.

(7)   Subsection (8) applies if, at any time during the period for reflection and consideration, the parties jointly give notice to the court that they are attempting a reconciliation but require additional time.

(8)   The period for reflection and consideration—
   (a) stops running on the day on which the notice is received by the court; but

(b) resumes running on the day on which either of the parties gives notice to the court that the attempted reconciliation has been unsuccessful.

(9) If the period for reflection and consideration is interrupted under sub-section (8) by a continuous period of more than 18 months, any application by either of the parties for a divorce order or for a separation order must be by reference to a new statement received by the court at any time after the end of the 18 months.

(10) Where an application for a divorce order is made by one party, subsection (13) applies if—
(a) the other party applies to the court, within the prescribed period, for time for further reflection; and
(b) the requirements of section 9 (except any imposed under section 9(3)) are satisfied.

(11) Where any application for a divorce order is made, subsection (13) also applies if there is a child of the family who is under the age of sixteen when the application is made.

(12) Subsection (13) does not apply if—
(a) at the time when the application for a divorce order is made, there is an occupation order or a non-molestation order in force in favour of the applicant, or of a child of the family, made against the other party; or
(b) the court is satisfied that delaying the making of a divorce order would be significantly detrimental to the welfare of any child of the family.

(13) If this subsection applies, the period for reflection and consideration is extended by a period of six months, but—
(a) only in relation to the application for a divorce order in respect of which the application under subsection (10) was made; and
(b) without invalidating that application for a divorce order.

(14) A period for reflection and consideration which is extended under sub-section (13), and which has not otherwise come to an end, comes to an end on there ceasing to be any children of the family to whom subsection (11) applied.

NOTES

Commencement: to be appointed.

8 Attendance at information meetings

(1) The requirements about information meetings are as follows.

(2) A party making a statement must (except in prescribed circumstances) have attended an information meeting not less than three months before making the statement.

(3) Different information meetings must be arranged with respect to different marriages.

(4) In the case of a statement made by both parties, the parties may attend separate meetings or the same meeting.

(5) Where one party has made a statement, the other party must (except in prescribed circumstances) attend an information meeting before—
    (a) making any application to the court—
        (i) with respect to a child of the family; or
        (ii) of a prescribed description relating to property or financial matters; or
    (b) contesting any such application.

(6) In this section "information meeting" means a meeting organised, in accordance with prescribed provisions for the purpose—
    (a) of providing, in accordance with prescribed provisions, relevant information to the party or parties attending about matters which may arise in connection with the provisions of, or made under, this Part or Part III; and
    (b) of giving the party or parties attending the information meeting the opportunity of having a meeting with a marriage counsellor and of encouraging that party or those parties to attend that meeting.

(7) An information meeting must be conducted by a person who—
    (a) is qualified and appointed in accordance with prescribed provisions; and
    (b) will have no financial or other interest in any marital proceedings between the parties.

(8) Regulations made under this section may, in particular, make provision—
    (a) about the places and times at which information meetings are to be held;
    (b) for written information to be given to persons attending them;

(c) for the giving of information to parties (otherwise than at information meetings) in cases in which the requirement to attend such meetings does not apply;

(d) for information of a prescribed kind to be given only with the approval of the Lord Chancellor or only by a person or by persons approved by him; and

(e) for information to be given, in prescribed circumstances, only with the approval of the Lord Chancellor or only by a person, or by persons, approved by him.

(9) Regulations made under subsection (6) must, in particular, make provision with respect to the giving of information about—

(a) marriage counselling and other marriage support services;

(b) the importance to be attached to the welfare, wishes and feelings of children;

(c) how the parties may acquire a better understanding of the ways in which children can be helped to cope with the breakdown of a marriage;

(d) the nature of the financial questions that may arise on divorce or separation, and services which are available to help the parties;

(e) protection available against violence, and how to obtain support and assistance;

(f) mediation;

(g) the availability to each of the parties of independent legal advice and representation;

(h) the principles of legal aid and where the parties can get advice about obtaining legal aid;

(i) the divorce and separation process.

(10) Before making any regulations under subsection (6), the Lord Chancellor must consult such persons concerned with the provision of relevant information as he considers appropriate.

(11) A meeting with a marriage counsellor arranged under this section—

(a) must be held in accordance with prescribed provisions; and

(b) must be with a person qualified and appointed in accordance with prescribed provisions.

(12) A person who would not be required to make any contribution towards mediation provided for him under Part IIIA of the Legal Aid Act 1988 shall not be required to make any contribution towards the cost of a meeting with a marriage counsellor arranged for him under this section.

(13)   In this section "prescribed" means prescribed by regulations made by the Lord Chancellor.

Commencement: to be appointed.

9   Arrangements for the future

(1)   The requirements as to the parties' arrangements for the future are as follows.

(2)   One of the following must be produced to the court—
  (a)   a court order (made by consent or otherwise) dealing with their financial arrangements;
  (b)   a negotiated agreement as to their financial arrangements;
  (c)   a declaration by both parties that they have made their financial arrangements;
  (d)   a declaration by one of the parties (to which no objection has been notified to the court by the other party) that—
    (i)   he has no significant assets and does not intend to make an application for financial provision;
    (ii)   he believes that the other party has no significant assets and does not intend to make an application for financial provision; and
    (iii)   there are therefore no financial arrangements to be made.

(3)   If the parties—
  (a)   were married to each other in accordance with usages of a kind mentioned in section 26(1) of the Marriage Act 1949 (marriages which may be solemnized on authority of superintendent registrar's certificate), and
  (b)   are required to co-operate if the marriage is to be dissolved in accordance with those usages,

the court may, on the application of either party, direct that there must also be produced to the court a declaration by both parties that they have taken such steps as are required to dissolve the marriage in accordance with those usages.

(4)   A direction under subsection (3)—
  (a)   may be given only if the court is satisfied that in all the circumstances of the case it is just and reasonable to give it; and

(b) may be revoked by the court at any time.

(5)   The requirements of section 11 must have been satisfied.

(6)   Schedule 1 supplements the provisions of this section.

(7)   If the court is satisfied, on an application made by one of the parties after the end of the period for reflection and consideration, that the circumstances of the case are—
  (a) those set out in paragraph 1 of Schedule 1,
  (b) those set out in paragraph 2 of that Schedule,
  (c) those set out in paragraph 3 of that Schedule, or
  (d) those set out in paragraph 4 of that Schedule,

it may make a divorce order or a separation order even though the requirements of subsection (2) have not been satisfied.

(8)   If the parties' arrangements for the future include a division of pension assets or rights under section 25B of the 1973 Act or section 10 of the Family Law (Scotland) Act 1985, any declaration under subsection (2) must be a statutory declaration.

NOTES

Commencement: to be appointed.

Orders preventing divorce

10 Hardship: orders preventing divorce

(1)   If an application for a divorce order has been made by one of the parties to a marriage, the court may, on the application of the other party, order that the marriage is not to be dissolved.

(2)   Such an order (an "order preventing divorce") may be made only if the court is satisfied—
  (a) that dissolution of the marriage would result in substantial financial or other hardship to the other party or to a child of the family; and
  (b) that it would be wrong, in all the circumstances (including the conduct of the parties and the interests of any child of the family), for the marriage to be dissolved.

(3)   If an application for the cancellation of an order preventing divorce is made by one or both of the parties, the court shall cancel the order unless it is still satisfied—

    (a) that dissolution of the marriage would result in substantial financial or other hardship to the party in whose favour the order was made or to a child of the family; and

    (b) that it would be wrong, in all the circumstances (including the conduct of the parties and the interests of any child of the family), for the marriage to be dissolved.

(4)   If an order preventing a divorce is cancelled, the court may make a divorce order in respect of the marriage only if an application is made under section 3 or 4(3) after the cancellation.

(5)   An order preventing divorce may include conditions which must be satisfied before an application for cancellation may be made under subsection (3).

(6)   In this section "hardship" includes the loss of a chance to obtain a future benefit (as well as the loss of an existing benefit).

NOTES

Commencement: to be appointed.

Welfare of children

11 Welfare of children

(1)   In any proceedings for a divorce order or a separation order, the court shall consider—

    (a) whether there are any children of the family to whom this section applies; and

    (b) where there are any such children, whether (in the light of the arrangements which have been, or are proposed to be, made for their upbringing and welfare) it should exercise any of its powers under the Children Act 1989 with respect to any of them.

(2)   Where, in any case to which this section applies, it appears to the court that—

(a) the circumstances of the case require it, or are likely to require it, to exercise any of its powers under the Children Act 1989 with respect to any such child,

(b) it is not in a position to exercise the power, or (as the case may be) those powers, without giving further consideration to the case, and

(c) there are exceptional circumstances which make it desirable in the interests of the child that the court should give a direction under this section,

it may direct that the divorce order or separation order is not to be made until the court orders otherwise.

(3)   In deciding whether the circumstances are as mentioned in subsection (2)(a), the court shall treat the welfare of the child as paramount.

(4)   In making that decision, the court shall also have particular regard, on the evidence before it, to—

(a) the wishes and feelings of the child considered in the light of his age and understanding and the circumstances in which those wishes were expressed;

(b) the conduct of the parties in relation to the upbringing of the child;

(c) the general principle that, in the absence of evidence to the contrary, the welfare of the child will be best served by—

(i) his having regular contact with those who have parental responsibility for him and with other members of his family; and

(ii) the maintenance of as good a continuing relationship with his parents as is possible; and

(d) any risk to the child attributable to—

(i) where the person with whom the child will reside is living or proposes to live;

(ii) any person with whom that person is living or with whom he proposes to live; or

(iii) any other arrangements for his care and upbringing.

(5)   This section applies to—

(a) any child of the family who has not reached the age of sixteen at the date when the court considers the case in accordance with the requirements of this section; and

(b) any child of the family who has reached that age at that date and in relation to whom the court directs that this section shall apply.

NOTES

Commencement: to be appointed.

Supplementary

12 Lord Chancellor's rules

(1) The Lord Chancellor may make rules—

(a) as to the form in which a statement is to be made and what information must accompany it;

(b) requiring the person making the statement to state whether or not, since satisfying the requirements of section 8, he has made any attempt at reconciliation;

(c) as to the way in which a statement is to be given to the court;

(d) requiring a copy of a statement made by one party to be served by the court on the other party;

(e) as to circumstances in which such service may be dispensed with or may be effected otherwise than by delivery to the party;

(f) requiring a party who has made a statement to provide the court with information about the arrangements that need to be made in consequence of the breakdown;

(g) as to the time, manner and (where attendance in person is required) place at which such information is to be given;

(h) where a statement has been made, requiring either or both of the parties—

    (i) to prepare and produce such other documents, and

    (ii) to attend in person at such places and for such purposes,

as may be specified;

(i) as to the information and assistance which is to be given to the parties and the way in which it is to be given;

(j) requiring the parties to be given, in such manner as may be specified, copies of such statements and other documents as may be specified.

(2) The Lord Chancellor may make rules requiring a person who is the legal representative of a party to a marriage with respect to which a statement has been, or is proposed to be, made—

(a) to inform that party, at such time or times as may be specified—

    (i) about the availability to the parties of marriage support services;

    (ii) about the availability to them of mediation; and

    (iii) where there are children of the family, that in relation to the arrangements to be made for any child the parties should consider the child's welfare, wishes and feelings;

(b) to give that party, at such time or times as may be specified, names and addresses of persons qualified to help—

      (i)   to effect a reconciliation; or

      (ii) in connection with mediation; and

  (c) to certify, at such time or times as may be specified—

      (i)   whether he has complied with the provision made in the rules by virtue of paragraphs (a) and (b);

      (ii) whether he has discussed with that party any of the matters mentioned in paragraph (a) or the possibility of reconciliation; and

     (iii) which, if any, of those matters they have discussed.

(3)   In subsections (1) and (2) "specified" means determined under or described in the rules.

(4)   This section does not affect any power to make rules of court for the purposes of this Act.

NOTES

Commencement: to be appointed.

Resolution of disputes

13 Directions with respect to mediation

(1)   After the court has received a statement, it may give a direction requiring each party to attend a meeting arranged in accordance with the direction for the purpose—

  (a) of enabling an explanation to be given of the facilities available to the parties for mediation in relation to disputes between them; and

  (b) of providing an opportunity for each party to agree to take advantage of those facilities.

(2)   A direction may be given at any time, including in the course of proceedings connected with the breakdown of the marriage (as to which see section 25).

(3)   A direction may be given on the application of either of the parties or on the initiative of the court.

(4)   The parties are to be required to attend the same meeting unless—

  (a) one of them asks, or both of them ask, for separate meetings; or

  (b) the court considers separate meetings to be more appropriate.

(5)   A direction shall—
   (a) specify a person chosen by the court (with that person's agreement) to arrange and conduct the meeting or meetings; and
   (b) require such person as may be specified in the direction to produce to the court, at such time as the court may direct, a report stating—
      (i) whether the parties have complied with the direction; and
      (ii) if they have, whether they have agreed to take part in any mediation.

NOTES

Commencement: to be appointed.

14   Adjournments

(1)   The court's power to adjourn any proceedings connected with the breakdown of a marriage includes power to adjourn—
   (a) for the purpose of allowing the parties to comply with a direction under section 13; or
   (b) for the purpose of enabling disputes to be resolved amicably.

(2)   In determining whether to adjourn for either purpose, the court shall have regard in particular to the need to protect the interests of any child of the family.

(3)   If the court adjourns any proceedings connected with the breakdown of a marriage for either purpose, the period of the adjournment must not exceed the maximum period prescribed by rules of court.

(4)   Unless the only purpose of the adjournment is to allow the parties to comply with a direction under section 13, the court shall order one or both of them to produce to the court a report as to—
   (a) whether they have taken part in mediation during the adjournment;
   (b) whether, as a result, any agreement has been reached between them;
   (c) the extent to which any dispute between them has been resolved as a result of any such agreement;
   (d) the need for further mediation; and
   (e) how likely it is that further mediation will be successful.

NOTES

Commencement: to be appointed.

Financial provision

15 Financial arrangements

(1)   Schedule 2 amends the 1973 Act.

(2)   The main object of Schedule 2 is—
  (a) to provide that, in the case of divorce or separation, an order about financial provision may be made under that Act before a divorce order or separation order is made; but
  (b) to retain (with minor changes) the position under that Act where marriages are annulled.

(3)   Schedule 2 also makes minor and consequential amendments of the 1973 Act connected with the changes mentioned in subsection (1).

Commencement: to be appointed.

Jurisdiction and commencement of proceedings

19 Jurisdiction in relation to divorce and separation

(1)   In this section "the court's jurisdiction" means—
  (a) the jurisdiction of the court under this Part to entertain marital proceedings; and
  (b) any other jurisdiction conferred on the court under this Part, or any other enactment, in consequence of the making of a statement.

(2)   The court's jurisdiction is exercisable only if—
  (a) at least one of the parties was domiciled in England and Wales on the statement date;
  (b) at least one of the parties was habitually resident in England and Wales throughout the period of one year ending with the statement date; or
  (c) nullity proceedings are pending in relation to the marriage when the marital proceedings commence.

(3)–(7) . . .

NOTES

Commencement: to be appointed.
Sub-ss (3)–(7): outside the scope of this work.

20 Time when proceedings for divorce or separation begin

(1)   The receipt by the court of a statement is to be treated as the commencement of proceedings.

(2)   The proceedings are to be known as marital proceedings.

(3)–(6) . . .

NOTES

Commencement: to be appointed.
Sub-ss (3)–(6): outside the scope of this work.

Intestacy

21 Intestacy: effect of separation

Where—
    (a) a separation order is in force, and
    (b) while the parties to the marriage remain separated, one of them
        dies intestate as respects any real or personal property,

that property devolves as if the other had died before the intestacy occurred.

NOTES

Commencement: to be appointed.

Marriage support services

22 Funding for marriage support services

(1)   The Lord Chancellor may, with the approval of the Treasury, make grants in connection with—

(a)   the provision of marriage support services;
(b)   research into the causes of marital breakdown;
(c)   research into ways of preventing marital breakdown.

(2)   Any grant under this section may be made subject to such conditions as the Lord Chancellor considers appropriate.

(3)   In exercising his power to make grants in connection with the provision of marriage support services, the Lord Chancellor is to have regard, in particular, to the desirability of services of that kind being available when they are first needed.

NOTES

Commencement: 21 March 1997.

23   Provision of marriage counselling

(1)   The Lord Chancellor or a person appointed by him may secure the provision, in accordance with regulations made by the Lord Chancellor, of marriage counselling.

(2)   Marriage counselling may only be provided under this section at a time when a period for reflection and consideration—
(a)   is running in relation to the marriage; or
(b)   is interrupted under section 7(8) (but not for a continuous period of more than 18 months).

(3)   Marriage counselling may only be provided under this section for persons who would not be required to make any contribution towards the cost of mediation provided for them under Part IIIA of the Legal Aid Act 1988.

(4)   Persons for whom marriage counselling is provided under this section are not to be required to make any contribution towards the cost of the counselling.

(5)–(9) . . .

NOTES

Commencement: to be appointed.
Sub-ss (5)–(9): outside the scope of this work.

24 Interpretation of Part II etc

(1)   In this Part—
"the 1973 Act" means the Matrimonial Causes Act 1973;
"child of the family" and "the court" have the same meaning as in the
    1973 Act;
"divorce order" has the meaning given in section 2(1)(a);
"divorce proceedings" is to be read with section 20;
"marital proceedings" has the meaning given in section 20;
"non-molestation order" has the meaning given by section 42(1);
"occupation order" has the meaning given by section 39;
"order preventing divorce" has the meaning given in section 10(2);
"party", in relation to a marriage, means one of the parties to the
    marriage;
"period for reflection and consideration" has the meaning given in section 7;
"separation order" has the meaning given in section 2(1)(b);
"separation proceedings" is to be read with section 20;
"statement" means a statement of marital breakdown;
"statement of marital breakdown" has the meaning given in section 6(1).

(2)–(3) . . .

NOTES

Commencement: to be appointed.
Sub-ss (2), (3): outside the scope of this work.

25 Connected proceedings

(1)   For the purposes of this Part, proceedings are connected with the
breakdown of a marriage if they fall within subsection (2) and, at the time
of the proceedings—
  (a) a statement has been received by the court with respect to the
      marriage and it is or may become possible for an application for a
      divorce order or separation order to be made by reference to that
      statement;
  (b) such an application in relation to the marriage has been made and
      not withdrawn; or
  (c) a divorce order has been made, or a separation order is in force, in
      relation to the marriage.

(2)   The proceedings are any under Parts I to V of the Children Act 1989 with respect to a child of the family or any proceedings resulting from an application—

    (a) for, or for the cancellation of, an order preventing divorce in relation to the marriage;

    (b) by either party to the marriage for an order under Part IV;

    (c) for the exercise, in relation to a party to the marriage or child of the family, of any of the court's powers under Part II of the 1973 Act;

    (d) made otherwise to the court with respect to, or in connection with, any proceedings connected with the breakdown of the marriage.

NOTES

Commencement: to be appointed.

PART IV
FAMILY HOMES AND DOMESTIC VIOLENCE

Rights to occupy matrimonial home

30 Rights concerning matrimonial home where one spouse has no estate, etc

(1)   This section applies if—

    (a) one spouse is entitled to occupy a dwelling-house by virtue of—

        (i) a beneficial estate or interest or contract; or

        (ii) any enactment giving that spouse the right to remain in occupation; and

    (b) the other spouse is not so entitled.

(2)   Subject to the provisions of this Part, the spouse not so entitled has the following rights ("matrimonial home rights")—

    (a) if in occupation, a right not to be evicted or excluded from the dwelling- house or any part of it by the other spouse except with the leave of the court given by an order under section 33;

    (b) if not in occupation, a right with the leave of the court so given to enter into and occupy the dwelling-house.

(3)   If a spouse is entitled under this section to occupy a dwelling-house or any part of a dwelling-house, any payment or tender made or other thing done by that spouse in or towards satisfaction of any liability of the

other spouse in respect of rent, mortgage payments or other outgoings affecting the dwelling-house is, whether or not it is made or done in pursuance of an order under section 40, as good as if made or done by the other spouse.

(4)   A spouse's occupation by virtue of this section—
    (a) is to be treated, for the purposes of the Rent (Agriculture) Act 1976 and the Rent Act 1977 (other than Part V and sections 103 to 106 of that Act), as occupation by the other spouse as the other spouse's residence, and
    (b) if the spouse occupies the dwelling-house as that spouse's only or principal home, is to be treated, for the purposes of the Housing Act 1985[, Part I of the Housing Act 1988 and Chapter I of Part V of the Housing Act 1996], as occupation by the other spouse as the other spouse's only or principal home.

(5)   If a spouse ("the first spouse")—
    (a) is entitled under this section to occupy a dwelling-house or any part of a dwelling-house, and
    (b) makes any payment in or towards satisfaction of any liability of the other spouse ("the second spouse") in respect of mortgage payments affecting the dwelling-house,

the person to whom the payment is made may treat it as having been made by the second spouse, but the fact that that person has treated any such payment as having been so made does not affect any claim of the first spouse against the second spouse to an interest in the dwelling-house by virtue of the payment.

(6)   If a spouse is entitled under this section to occupy a dwelling-house or part of a dwelling-house by reason of an interest of the other spouse under a trust, all the provisions of subsections (3) to (5) apply in relation to the trustees as they apply in relation to the other spouse.

(7)   This section does not apply to a dwelling-house which has at no time been, and which was at no time intended by the spouses to be, a matrimonial home of theirs.

(8)   A spouse's matrimonial home rights continue—
    (a) only so long as the marriage subsists, except to the extent that an order under section 33(5) otherwise provides; and
    (b) only so long as the other spouse is entitled as mentioned in subsection (1) to occupy the dwelling-house, except where provision

is made by section 31 for those rights to be a charge on an estate or interest in the dwelling-house.

(9)   It is hereby declared that a spouse—
  (a) who has an equitable interest in a dwelling-house or in its proceeds of sale, but
  (b) is not a spouse in whom there is vested (whether solely or as joint tenant) a legal estate in fee simple or a legal term of years absolute in the dwelling-house,

is to be treated, only for the purpose of determining whether he has matrimonial home rights, as not being entitled to occupy the dwelling-house by virtue of that interest.

NOTES

Commencement: 1 October 1997.

Sub-s (4): words in square brackets substituted by the Housing Act 1996 (Consequential Amendments) Order 1997, SI 1997/74, art 2, Schedule, para 10(a).

31 Effect of matrimonial home rights as charge on dwelling-house

(1)   Subsections (2) and (3) apply if, at any time during a marriage, one spouse is entitled to occupy a dwelling-house by virtue of a beneficial estate or interest.

(2)   The other spouse's matrimonial home rights are a charge on the estate or interest.

(3)   The charge created by subsection (2) has the same priority as if it were an equitable interest created at whichever is the latest of the following dates—
  (a) the date on which the spouse so entitled acquires the estate or interest;
  (b) the date of the marriage; and
  (c) 1st January 1968 (the commencement date of the Matrimonial Homes Act 1967).

(4)   Subsections (5) and (6) apply if, at any time when a spouse's matrimonial home rights are a charge on an interest of the other spouse under a trust, there are, apart from either of the spouses, no persons, living or unborn, who are or could become beneficiaries under the trust.

(5)   The rights are a charge also on the estate or interest of the trustees for the other spouse.

(6)   The charge created by subsection (5) has the same priority as if it were an equitable interest created (under powers overriding the trusts) on the date when it arises.

(7)   In determining for the purposes of subsection (4) whether there are any persons who are not, but could become, beneficiaries under the trust, there is to be disregarded any potential exercise of a general power of appointment exercisable by either or both of the spouses alone (whether or not the exercise of it requires the consent of another person).

(8)   Even though a spouse's matrimonial home rights are a charge on an estate or interest in the dwelling-house, those rights are brought to an end by—
    (a) the death of the other spouse, or
    (b) the termination (otherwise than by death) of the marriage,

unless the court directs otherwise by an order made under section 33(5).

(9)   If—
    (a) a spouse's matrimonial home rights are a charge on an estate or interest in the dwelling-house, and
    (b) that estate or interest is surrendered to merge in some other estate or interest expectant on it in such circumstances that, but for the merger, the person taking the estate or interest would be bound by the charge,

the surrender has effect subject to the charge and the persons thereafter entitled to the other estate or interest are, for so long as the estate or interest surrendered would have endured if not so surrendered, to be treated for all purposes of this Part as deriving title to the other estate or interest under the other spouse or, as the case may be, under the trustees for the other spouse, by virtue of the surrender.

(10)   If the title to the legal estate by virtue of which a spouse is entitled to occupy a dwelling-house (including any legal estate held by trustees for that spouse) is registered under the Land Registration Act 1925 or any enactment replaced by that Act—
    (a) registration of a land charge affecting the dwelling-house by virtue of this Part is to be effected by registering a notice under that Act; and

    (b) a spouse's matrimonial home rights are not an overriding interest within the meaning of that Act affecting the dwelling-house even though the spouse is in actual occupation of the dwelling-house.

(11)   A spouse's matrimonial home rights (whether or not constituting a charge) do not entitle that spouse to lodge a caution under section 54 of the Land Registration Act 1925.

(12)   If—
    (a) a spouse's matrimonial home rights are a charge on the estate of the other spouse or of trustees of the other spouse, and
    (b) that estate is the subject of a mortgage,

then if, after the date of the creation of the mortgage ("the first mortgage"), the charge is registered under section 2 of the Land Charges Act 1972, the charge is, for the purposes of section 94 of the Law of Property Act 1925 (which regulates the rights of mortgagees to make further advances ranking in priority to subsequent mortgages), to be deemed to be a mortgage subsequent in date to the first mortgage.

(13)   It is hereby declared that a charge under subsection (2) or (5) is not registrable under subsection (10) or under section 2 of the Land Charges Act 1972 unless it is a charge on a legal estate.

NOTES

Commencement: 1 October 1997.

33 Occupation orders where applicant has estate or interest etc or has matrimonial home rights

(1)   If—
    (a) a person ("the person entitled")—
        (i) is entitled to occupy a dwelling-house by virtue of a beneficial estate or interest or contract or by virtue of any enactment giving him the right to remain in occupation, or
        (ii) has matrimonial home rights in relation to a dwelling-house, and
    (b) the dwelling-house—
        (i) is or at any time has been the home of the person entitled and of another person with whom he is associated, or
        (ii) was at any time intended by the person entitled and any such other person to be their home,

the person entitled may apply to the court for an order containing any of the provisions specified in subsections (3), (4) and (5).

(2)   If an agreement to marry is terminated, no application under this section may be made by virtue of section 62(3)(e) by reference to that agreement after the end of the period of three years beginning with the day on which it is terminated.

(3)   An order under this section may—
  (a) enforce the applicant's entitlement to remain in occupation as against the other person ("the respondent");
  (b) require the respondent to permit the applicant to enter and remain in the dwelling-house or part of the dwelling-house;
  (c) regulate the occupation of the dwelling-house by either or both parties;
  (d) if the respondent is entitled as mentioned in subsection (1)(a)(i), prohibit, suspend or restrict the exercise by him of his right to occupy the dwelling- house;
  (e) if the respondent has matrimonial home rights in relation to the dwelling-house and the applicant is the other spouse, restrict or terminate those rights;
  (f) require the respondent to leave the dwelling-house or part of the dwelling-house; or
  (g) exclude the respondent from a defined area in which the dwelling-house is included.

(4)   An order under this section may declare that the applicant is entitled as mentioned in subsection (1)(a)(i) or has matrimonial home rights.

(5)   If the applicant has matrimonial home rights and the respondent is the other spouse, an order under this section made during the marriage may provide that those rights are not brought to an end by—
  (a) the death of the other spouse; or
  (b) the termination (otherwise than by death) of the marriage.

(6)   In deciding whether to exercise its powers under subsection (3) and (if so) in what manner, the court shall have regard to all the circumstances including—
  (a) the housing needs and housing resources of each of the parties and of any relevant child;
  (b) the financial resources of each of the parties;
  (c) the likely effect of any order, or of any decision by the court not to exercise its powers under subsection (3), on the health, safety or well-being of the parties and of any relevant child; and
  (d) the conduct of the parties in relation to each other and otherwise.

(7)   If it appears to the court that the applicant or any relevant child is likely to suffer significant harm attributable to conduct of the respondent if an order under this section containing one or more of the provisions mentioned in subsection (3) is not made, the court shall make the order unless it appears to it that—

(a) the respondent or any relevant child is likely to suffer significant harm if the order is made; and

(b) the harm likely to be suffered by the respondent or child in that event is as great as, or greater than, the harm attributable to conduct of the respondent which is likely to be suffered by the applicant or child if the order is not made.

(8)   The court may exercise its powers under subsection (5) in any case where it considers that in all the circumstances it is just and reasonable to do so.

(9)   An order under this section—

(a) may not be made after the death of either of the parties mentioned in subsection (1); and

(b) except in the case of an order made by virtue of subsection (5)(a), ceases to have effect on the death of either party.

(10)   An order under this section may, in so far as it has continuing effect, be made for a specified period, until the occurrence of a specified event or until further order.

NOTES

Commencement: 1 October 1997.

34   Effect of order under s 33 where rights are charge on dwelling-house

(1)   If a spouse's matrimonial home rights are a charge on the estate or interest of the other spouse or of trustees for the other spouse—

(a) an order under section 33 against the other spouse has, except so far as a contrary intention appears, the same effect against house. persons deriving title under the other spouse or under the trustees and affected by the charge, and

(b) sections 33(1), (3), (4) and (10) and 30(3) to (6) apply in relation to any person deriving title under the other spouse or under the trustees and affected by the charge as they apply in relation to the other spouse.

(2)   The court may make an order under section 33 by virtue of subsection (1)(b) if it considers that in all the circumstances it is just and reasonable to do so.

NOTES

Commencement: 1 October 1997.

35   One former spouse with no existing right to occupy

(1)   This section applies if—
- (a) one former spouse is entitled to occupy a dwelling-house by virtue of a beneficial estate or interest or contract, or by virtue of any enactment giving him the right to remain in occupation;
- (b) the other former spouse is not so entitled; and
- (c) the dwelling-house was at any time their matrimonial home or was at any time intended by them to be their matrimonial home.

(2)   The former spouse not so entitled may apply to the court for an order under this section against the other former spouse ("the respondent").

(3)   If the applicant is in occupation, an order under this section must contain provision—
- (a) giving the applicant the right not to be evicted or excluded from the dwelling-house or any part of it by the respondent for the period specified in the order; and
- (b) prohibiting the respondent from evicting or excluding the applicant during that period.

(4)   If the applicant is not in occupation, an order under this section must contain provision—
- (a) giving the applicant the right to enter into and occupy the dwelling-house for the period specified in the order; and
- (b) requiring the respondent to permit the exercise of that right.

(5)   An order under this section may also—
- (a) regulate the occupation of the dwelling-house by either or both of the parties;
- (b) prohibit, suspend or restrict the exercise by the respondent of his right to occupy the dwelling-house;
- (c) require the respondent to leave the dwelling-house or part of the dwelling- house; or

(d) exclude the respondent from a defined area in which the dwelling-house is included.

(6) In deciding whether to make an order under this section containing provision of the kind mentioned in subsection (3) or (4) and (if so) in what manner, the court shall have regard to all the circumstances including—
(a) the housing needs and housing resources of each of the parties and of any relevant child;
(b) the financial resources of each of the parties;
(c) the likely effect of any order, or of any decision by the court not to exercise its powers under subsection (3) or (4), on the health, safety or well-being of the parties and of any relevant child;
(d) the conduct of the parties in relation to each other and otherwise;
(e) the length of time that has elapsed since the parties ceased to live together;
(f) the length of time that has elapsed since the marriage was dissolved or annulled; and
(g) the existence of any pending proceedings between the parties—
   (i) for an order under section 23A or 24 of the Matrimonial Causes Act 1973 (property adjustment orders in connection with divorce proceedings etc);
   (ii) for an order under paragraph 1(2)(d) or (e) of Schedule 1 to the Children Act 1989 (orders for financial relief against parents); or
   (iii) relating to the legal or beneficial ownership of the dwelling-house.

(7) In deciding whether to exercise its power to include one or more of the provisions referred to in subsection (5) ("a subsection (5) provision") and (if so) in what manner, the court shall have regard to all the circumstances including the matters mentioned in subsection (6)(a) to (e).

(8) If the court decides to make an order under this section and it appears to it that, if the order does not include a subsection (5) provision, the applicant or any relevant child is likely to suffer significant harm attributable to conduct of the respondent, the court shall include the subsection (5) provision in the order unless it appears to the court that—
(a) the respondent or any relevant child is likely to suffer significant harm if the provision is included in the order; and
(b) the harm likely to be suffered by the respondent or child in that event is as great as or greater than the harm attributable to conduct of the respondent which is likely to be suffered by the applicant or child if the provision is not included.

(9)   An order under this section—
(a) may not be made after the death of either of the former spouses; and
(b) ceases to have effect on the death of either of them.

(10)   An order under this section must be limited so as to have effect for a specified period not exceeding six months, but may be extended on one or more occasions for a further specified period not exceeding six months.

(11)   A former spouse who has an equitable interest in the dwelling-house or in the proceeds of sale of the dwelling-house but in whom there is not vested (whether solely or as joint tenant) a legal estate in fee simple or a legal term of years absolute in the dwelling-house is to be treated (but only for the purpose of determining whether he is eligible to apply under this section) as not being entitled to occupy the dwelling-house by virtue of that interest.

(12)   Subsection (11) does not prejudice any right of such a former spouse to apply for an order under section 33.

(13)   So long as an order under this section remains in force, subsections (3) to (6) of section 30 apply in relation to the applicant—
(a) as if he were the spouse entitled to occupy the dwelling-house by virtue of that section; and
(b) as if the respondent were the other spouse.

NOTES

Commencement: 1 October 1997.

36   One cohabitant or former cohabitant with no existing right to occupy

(1)   This section applies if—
(a) one cohabitant or former cohabitant is entitled to occupy a dwelling-house by virtue of a beneficial estate or interest or contract or by virtue of any enactment giving him the right to remain in occupation;
(b) the other cohabitant or former cohabitant is not so entitled; and
(c) that dwelling-house is the home in which they live together as husband and wife or a home in which they at any time so lived together or intended so to live together.

(2)   The cohabitant or former cohabitant not so entitled may apply to the court for an order under this section against the other cohabitant or former cohabitant ("the respondent").

(3)   If the applicant is in occupation, an order under this section must contain provision—

(a) giving the applicant the right not to be evicted or excluded from the dwelling-house or any part of it by the respondent for the period specified in the order; and

(b) prohibiting the respondent from evicting or excluding the applicant during that period.

(4)   If the applicant is not in occupation, an order under this section must contain provision—

(a) giving the applicant the right to enter into and occupy the dwelling-house for the period specified in the order; and

(b) requiring the respondent to permit the exercise of that right.

(5)   An order under this section may also—

(a) regulate the occupation of the dwelling-house by either or both of the parties;

(b) prohibit, suspend or restrict the exercise by the respondent of his right to occupy the dwelling-house;

(c) require the respondent to leave the dwelling-house or part of the dwelling- house; or

(d) exclude the respondent from a defined area in which the dwelling-house is included.

(6)   In deciding whether to make an order under this section containing provision of the kind mentioned in subsection (3) or (4) and (if so) in what manner, the court shall have regard to all the circumstances including—

(a) the housing needs and housing-resources of each of the parties and of any relevant child;

(b) the financial resources of each of the parties;

(c) the likely effect of any order, or of any decision by the court not to exercise its powers under subsection (3) or (4), on the health, safety or well-being of the parties and of any relevant child;

(d) the conduct of the parties in relation to each other and otherwise;

(e) the nature of the parties' relationship;

(f) the length of time during which they have lived together as husband and wife;

(g) whether there are or have been any children who are children of both parties or for whom both parties have or have had parental responsibility;

(h) the length of time that has elapsed since the parties ceased to live together; and

(i) the existence of any pending proceedings between the parties—

     (i) for an order under paragraph 1 (2)(d) or (e) of Schedule to the Children Act 1989 (orders for financial relief against parents); or

    (ii) relating to the legal or beneficial ownership of the dwelling-house.

(7)   In deciding whether to exercise its powers to include one or more of the provisions referred to in subsection (5) ("a subsection (5) provision") and (if so) in what manner, the court shall have regard to all the circumstances including—

  (a) the matters mentioned in subsection (6)(a) to (d); and

  (b) the questions mentioned in subsection (8).

(8)   The questions are—

  (a) whether the applicant or any relevant child is likely to suffer significant harm attributable to conduct of the respondent if the subsection (5) provision is not included in the order; and

  (b) whether the harm likely to be suffered by the respondent or child if the provision is included is as great as or greater than the harm attributable to conduct of the respondent which is likely to be suffered by the applicant or child if the provision is not included.

(9)   An order under this section—

  (a) may not be made after the death of either of the parties; and

  (b) ceases to have effect on the death of either of them.

(10)   An order under this section must be limited so as to have effect for a specified period not exceeding six months, but may be extended on one occasion for a further specified period not exceeding six months.

(11)   A person who has an equitable interest in the dwelling-house or in the proceeds of sale of the dwelling-house but in whom there is not vested (whether solely or as joint tenant) a legal estate in fee simple or a legal term of years absolute in the dwelling-house is to be treated (but only for the purpose of determining whether he is eligible to apply under this section) as not being entitled to occupy the dwelling- house by virtue of that interest.

(12)   Subsection (11) does not prejudice any right of such a person to apply for an order under section 33.

(13)   So long as the order remains in force, subsections (3) to (6) of section 30 apply in relation to the applicant—

(a) as if he were a spouse entitled to occupy the dwelling-house by virtue of that section; and

(b) as if the respondent were the other spouse.

NOTES

Commencement: 1 October 1997.

37 Neither spouse entitled to occupy

(1)   This section applies if—
  (a) one spouse or former spouse and the other spouse or former spouse occupy a dwelling-house which is or was the matrimonial home; but
  (b) neither of them is entitled to remain in occupation—
    (i)   by virtue of a beneficial estate or interest or contract; or
    (ii) by virtue of any enactment giving him the right to remain in occupation.

(2)   Either of the parties may apply to the court for an order against the other under this section.

(3)   An order under this section may—
  (a) require the respondent to permit the applicant to enter and remain in the dwelling-house or part of the dwelling-house;
  (b) regulate the occupation of the dwelling-house by either or both of the spouses;
  (c) require the respondent to leave the dwelling-house or part of the dwelling- house; or
  (d) exclude the respondent from a defined area in which the dwelling-house is included.

(4)   Subsections (6) and (7) of section 33 apply to the exercise by the court of its powers under this section as they apply to the exercise by the court of its powers under subsection (3) of that section.

(5)   An order under this section must be limited so as to have effect for a specified period not exceeding six months, but may be extended on one or more occasions for a further specified period not exceeding six months.

NOTES

Commencement: 1 October 1997.

38 Neither cohabitant or former cohabitant entitled to occupy

(1)   This section applies if—
- (a) one cohabitant or former cohabitant and the other cohabitant or former cohabitant occupy a dwelling-house which is the home in which they live or lived together as husband and wife; but
- (b) neither of them is entitled to remain in occupation—
  - (i) by virtue of a beneficial estate or interest or contract; or
  - (ii) by virtue of any enactment giving him the right to remain in occupation.

(2)   Either of the parties may apply to the court for an order against the other under this section.

(3)   An order under this section may—
- (a) require the respondent to permit the applicant to enter and remain in the dwelling-house or part of the dwelling-house;
- (b) regulate the occupation of the dwelling-house by either or both of the parties;
- (c) require the respondent to leave the dwelling-house or part of the dwelling- house; or
- (d) exclude the respondent from a defined area in which the dwelling-house is included.

(4)   In deciding whether to exercise its powers to include one or more of the provisions referred to in subsection (3) ("a subsection (3) provision") and (if so) in what manner, the court shall have regard to all the circumstances including—
- (a) the housing needs and housing resources of each of the parties and of any relevant child;
- (b) the financial resources of each of the parties;
- (c) the likely effect of any order, or of any decision by the court not to exercise its powers under subsection (3), on the health, safety or well-being of the parties and of any relevant child;
- (d) the conduct of the parties in relation to each other and otherwise; and
- (e) the questions mentioned in subsection (5).

(5)   The questions are—
- (a) whether the applicant or any relevant child is likely to suffer significant harm attributable to conduct of the respondent if the subsection (3) provision is not included in the order; and
- (b) whether the harm likely to be suffered by the respondent or child if the provision is included is as great as or greater than the harm

attributable to conduct of the respondent which is likely to be suffered by the applicant or child if the provision is not included.

(6)   An order under this section shall be limited so as to have effect for a specified period not exceeding six months, but may be extended on one occasion for a further specified period not exceeding six months.

NOTES

Commencement: 1 October 1997.

39   Supplementary provisions

(1)   In this Part an "occupation order" means an order under section 33, 35, 36, 37 or 38.

(2)   An application for an occupation order may be made in other family proceedings or without any other family proceedings being instituted.

(3)   If—
  (a)   an application for an occupation order is made under section 33, 35, 36, 37 or 38, and
  (b)   the court considers that it has no power to make the order under the section concerned, but that it has power to make an order under one of the other sections,

the court may make an order under that other section.

(4)   The fact that a person has applied for an occupation order under sections 35 to 38, or that an occupation order has been made, does not affect the right of any person to claim a legal or equitable interest in any property in any subsequent proceedings (including subsequent proceedings under this Part).

NOTES

Commencement: 1 October 1997.

40   Additional provisions that may be included in certain occupation orders

(1)   The court may on, or at any time after, making an occupation order under section 33, 35 or 36—

    (a) impose on either party obligations as to—
        (i) the repair and maintenance of the dwelling-house; or
       (ii) the discharge of rent, mortgage payments or other outgoings affecting the dwelling-house;
    (b) order a party occupying the dwelling-house or any part of it (including a party who is entitled to do so by virtue of a beneficial estate or interest or contract or by virtue of any enactment giving him the right to remain in occupation) to make periodical payments to the other party in respect of the accommodation, if the other party would (but for the order) be entitled to occupy the dwelling-house by virtue of a beneficial estate or interest or contract or by virtue of any such enactment;
    (c) grant either party possession or use of furniture or other contents of the dwelling-house;
    (d) order either party to take reasonable care of any furniture or other contents of the dwelling-house;
    (e) order either party to take reasonable steps to keep the dwelling-house and any furniture or other contents secure.

(2)   In deciding whether and, if so, how to exercise its powers under this section, the court shall have regard to all the circumstances of the case including—
    (a) the financial needs and financial resources of the parties; and
    (b) the financial obligations which they have, or are likely to have in the foreseeable future, including financial obligations to each other and to any relevant child.

(3)   An order under this section ceases to have effect when the occupation order to which it relates ceases to have effect.

NOTES

Commencement: 1 October 1997.

41   Additional considerations if parties are cohabitants or former cohabitants

(1)   This section applies if the parties are cohabitants or former cohabitants.

(2)   Where the court is required to consider the nature of the parties' relationship, it is to have regard to the fact that they have not given each other the commitment involved in marriage.

NOTES

Commencement: 1 October 1997.

Non-molestation orders

42   Non-molestation orders

(1)   In this Part a "non-molestation order" means an order containing either or both of the following provisions—
  (a) provision prohibiting a person ("the respondent") from molesting another person who is associated with the respondent;
  (b) provision prohibiting the respondent from molesting a relevant child.

(2)   The court may make a non-molestation order—
  (a) if an application for the order has been made (whether in other family proceedings or without any other family proceedings being instituted) by a person who is associated with the respondent; or
  (b) if in any family proceedings to which the respondent is a party the court considers that the order should be made for the benefit of any other party to the proceedings or any relevant child even though no such application has been made.

(3)   In subsection (2) "family proceedings" includes proceedings in which the court has made an emergency protection order under section 44 of the Children Act 1989 which includes an exclusion requirement (as defined in section 44A(3) of that Act).

(4)   Where an agreement to marry is terminated, no application under subsection (2)(a) may be made by virtue of section 62(3)(e) by reference to that agreement after the end of the period of three years beginning with the day on which it is terminated.

(5)   In deciding whether to exercise its powers under this section and, if so, in what manner, the court shall have regard to all the circumstances including the need to secure the health, safety and well-being—
  (a) of the applicant or, in a case falling within subsection (2)(b), the person for whose benefit the order would be made; and
  (b) of any relevant child.

(6)   A non-molestation order may be expressed so as to refer to molestation in general, to particular acts of molestation, or to both.

(7)   A non-molestation order may be made for a specified period or until further order.

(8)   A non-molestation order which is made in other family proceedings ceases to have effect if those proceedings are withdrawn or dismissed.

NOTES

Commencement: 1 October 1997.

Further provisions relating to occupation and non-molestation orders

43   Leave of court required for applications by children under sixteen

(1)   A child under the age of sixteen may not apply for an occupation order or a non-molestation order except with the leave of the court.

(2)   The court may grant leave for the purposes of subsection (1) only if it is satisfied that the child has sufficient understanding to make the proposed application for the occupation order or non-molestation order.

NOTES

Commencement: 1 October 1997.

44   Evidence of agreement to marry

(1)   Subject to subsection (2), the court shall not make an order under section 33 or 42 by virtue of section 62(3)(e) unless there is produced to it evidence in writing of the existence of the agreement to marry.

(2)   Subsection (1) does not apply if the court is satisfied that the agreement to marry was evidenced by—
    (a) the gift of an engagement ring by one party to the agreement to the other in contemplation of their marriage, or
    (b) a ceremony entered into by the parties in the presence of one or more other persons assembled for the purpose of witnessing the ceremony.

NOTES
Commencement: 1 October 1997.

45 Ex parte orders

(1) The court may, in any case where it considers that it is just and convenient to do so, make an occupation order or a non-molestation order even though the respondent has not been given such notice of the proceedings as would otherwise be required by rules of court.

(2) In determining whether to exercise its powers under subsection (1), the court shall have regard to all the circumstances including—

(a) any risk of significant harm to the applicant or a relevant child, attributable to conduct of the respondent, if the order is not made immediately;

(b) whether it is likely that the applicant will be deterred or prevented from pursuing the application if an order is not made immediately; and

(c) whether there is reason to believe that the respondent is aware of the proceedings but is deliberately evading service and that the applicant or a relevant child will be seriously prejudiced by the delay involved—

(i) where the court is a magistrates' court, in effecting service of proceedings; or

(ii) in any other case, in effecting substituted service.

(3) If the court makes an order by virtue of subsection (1) it must afford the respondent an opportunity to make representations relating to the order as soon as just and convenient at a full hearing.

(4) If, at a full hearing, the court makes an occupation order ("the full order"), then—

(a) for the purposes of calculating the maximum period for which the full order may be made to have effect, the relevant section is to apply as if the period for which the full order will have effect began on the date on which the initial order first had effect; and

(b) the provisions of section 36(10) or 38(6) as to the extension of orders are to apply as if the full order and the initial order were a single order.

(5) In this section—
"full hearing" means a hearing of which notice has been given to all the parties in accordance with rules of court;

"initial order" means an occupation order made by virtue of subsection (1); and "relevant section" means section 33(10), 35(10), 36(10), 37(5) or 38(6).

NOTES

Commencement: 1 October 1997.

46 Undertakings

(1)   In any case where the court has power to make an occupation order or non- molestation order, the court may accept an undertaking from any party to the proceedings.

(2)   No power of arrest may be attached to any undertaking given under subsection (1).

(3)   The court shall not accept an undertaking under subsection (1) in any case where apart from this section a power of arrest would be attached to the order.

(4)   An undertaking given to a court under subsection (1) is enforceable as if it were an order of the court.

(5)   This section has effect without prejudice to the powers of the High Court and the county court apart from this section.

NOTES

Commencement: 1 October 1997.

47 Arrest for breach of order

(1)   In this section "a relevant order" means an occupation order or a non-molestation order.

(2)   If—
  (a) the court makes a relevant order; and
  (b) it appears to the court that the respondent has used or threatened violence against the applicant or a relevant child,

it shall attach a power of arrest to one or more provisions of the order unless satisfied that in all the circumstances of the case the applicant or child will be adequately protected without such a power of arrest.

(3)   Subsection (2) does not apply in any case where the relevant order is made by virtue of section 45(1), but in such a case the court may attach a power of arrest to one or more provisions of the order if it appears to it—

(a) that the respondent has used or threatened violence against the applicant or a relevant child; and

(b) that there is a risk of significant harm to the applicant or child, attributable to conduct of the respondent, if the power of arrest is not attached to those provisions immediately.

(4)   If, by virtue of subsection (3), the court attaches a power of arrest to any provisions of a relevant order, it may provide that the power of arrest is to have effect for a shorter period than the other provisions of the order.

(5)   Any period specified for the purposes of subsection (4) may be extended by the court (on one or more occasions) on an application to vary or discharge the relevant order.

(6)   If, by virtue of subsection (2) or (3), a power of arrest is attached to certain provisions of an order, a constable may arrest without warrant a person whom he has reasonable cause for suspecting to be in breach of any such provision.

(7)   If a power of arrest is attached under subsection (2) or (3) to certain provisions of the order and the respondent is arrested under subsection (6)—

(a) he must be brought before the relevant judicial authority within the period of 24 hours beginning at the time of his arrest; and

(b) if the matter is not then disposed of forthwith, the relevant judicial authority before whom he is brought may remand him.

In reckoning for the purposes of this subsection any period of 24 hours, no account is to be taken of Christmas Day, Good Friday or any Sunday.

(8)   If the court has made a relevant order but—

(a) has not attached a power of arrest under subsection (2) or (3) to any provisions of the order, or

(b) has attached that power only to certain provisions of the order,

then, if at any time the applicant considers that the respondent has failed to comply with the order, he may apply to the relevant judicial authority for the issue of a warrant for the arrest of the respondent.

(9)   The relevant judicial authority shall not issue a warrant on an application under subsection (8) unless—

(a) the application is substantiated on oath; and

(b) the relevant judicial authority has reasonable grounds for believing that the respondent has failed to comply with the order.

(10)   If a person is brought before a court by virtue of a warrant issued under subsection (9) and the court does not dispose of the matter forthwith, the court may remand him.

(11)   Schedule 5 (which makes provision corresponding to that applying in magistrates' courts in civil cases under sections 128 and 129 of the Magistrates' Courts Act 1980) has effect in relation to the powers of the High Court and a county court to remand a person by virtue of this section.

(12)   If a person remanded under this section is granted bail (whether in the High Court or a county court under Schedule 5 or in a magistrates' court under section 128 or 129 of the Magistrates' Courts Act 1980), he may be required by the relevant judicial authority to comply, before release on bail or later, with such requirements as appear to that authority to be necessary to secure that he does not interfere with witnesses or otherwise obstruct the course of justice.

NOTES

Commencement: 1 October 1997.

49 Variation and discharge of orders

(1)   An occupation order or non-molestation order may be varied or discharged by the court on an application by—
   (a) the respondent, or
   (b) the person on whose application the order was made.

(2)   In the case of a non-molestation order made by virtue of section 42(2)(b), the order may be varied or discharged by the court even though no such application has been made.

(3)   If a spouse's matrimonial home rights are a charge on the estate or interest of the other spouse or of trustees for the other spouse, an order under section 33 against the other spouse may also be varied or discharged by the court on an application by any person deriving title under the other spouse or under the trustees and affected by the charge.

(4)   If, by virtue of section 47(3), a power of arrest has been attached to certain provisions of an occupation order or non-molestation order, the court may vary or discharge the order under subsection (1) in so far as it confers a power of arrest (whether or not any application has been made to vary or discharge any other provision of the order).

NOTES

Commencement: 1 October 1997.

Transfer of tenancies

53   Transfer of certain tenancies

Schedule 7 makes provision in relation to the transfer of certain tenancies on divorce etc or on separation of cohabitants.

NOTES

Commencement: 1 October 1997.

General

62   Meaning of "cohabitants", "relevant child" and "associated persons"

(1)   For the purposes of this Part—
  (a) "cohabitants" are a man and a woman who, although not married to each other, are living together as husband and wife; and
  (b) "former cohabitants" is to be read accordingly, but does not include cohabitants who have subsequently married each other.

(2)   In this Part, "relevant child", in relation to any proceedings under this Part, means—
  (a) any child who is living with or might reasonably be expected to live with either party to the proceedings;
  (b) any child in relation to whom an order under the Adoption Act 1976 or the Children Act 1989 is in question in the proceedings; and
  (c) any other child whose interests the court considers relevant.

(3)   For the purposes of this Part, a person is associated with another person if—
(a) they are or have been married to each other;
(b) they are cohabitants or former cohabitants;
(c) they live or have lived in the same household, otherwise than merely by reason of one of them being the other's employee, tenant, lodger or boarder;
(d) they are relatives;
(e) they have agreed to marry one another (whether or not that agreement has been terminated);
(f) in relation to any child, they are both persons falling within subsection (4); or
(g) they are parties to the same family proceedings (other than proceedings under this Part).

(4)   A person falls within this subsection in relation to a child if—
(a) he is a parent of the child; or
(b) he has or has had parental responsibility for the child.

(5)   If a child has been adopted or has been freed for adoption by virtue of any of the enactments mentioned in section 16(1) of the Adoption Act 1976, two persons are also associated with each other for the purposes of this Part if—
(a) one is a natural parent of the child or a parent of such a natural parent; and
(b) the other is the child or any person—
(i)   who has become a parent of the child by virtue of an adoption order or has applied for an adoption order, or
(ii) with whom the child has at any time been placed for adoption.

(6)   A body corporate and another person are not, by virtue of subsection (3)(f) or (g), to be regarded for the purposes of this Part as associated with each other.

NOTES

Commencement: 1 October 1997.

63   Interpretation of Part IV

(1)   In this Part—
"adoption order" has the meaning given by section 72(1) of the Adoption Act 1976;

"associated", in relation to a person, is to be read with section 62(3) to (6);

"child" means a person under the age of eighteen years;

"cohabitant" and "former cohabitant" have the meaning given by section 62(1);

"the court" is to be read with section 57;

"development" means physical, intellectual, emotional, social or behavioural development;

"dwelling-house" includes (subject to subsection (4))—

   (a) any building or part of a building which is occupied as a dwelling,

   (b) any caravan, house-boat or structure which is occupied as a dwelling,

and any yard, garden, garage or outhouse belonging to it and occupied with it;

"family proceedings" means any proceedings—

   (a) under the inherent jurisdiction of the High Court in relation to children; or

   (b) under the enactments mentioned in subsection (2);

"harm"—

   (a) in relation to a person who has reached the age of eighteen years, means ill-treatment or the impairment of health; and

   (b) in relation to a child, means ill-treatment or the impairment of health or development;

"health" includes physical or mental health;

"ill-treatment" includes forms of ill-treatment which are not physical and, in relation to a child, includes sexual abuse;

"matrimonial home rights" has the meaning given by section 30;

"mortgage", "mortgagor" and "mortgagee" have the same meaning as in the Law of Property Act 1925;

"mortgage payments" includes any payments which, under the terms of the mortgage, the mortgagor is required to make to any person;

"non-molestation order" has the meaning given by section 42(1);

"occupation order" has the meaning given by section 39;

"parental responsibility" has the same meaning as in the Children Act 1989;

"relative", in relation to a person, means—

   (a) the father, mother, stepfather, stepmother, son, daughter, stepson, stepdaughter, grandmother, grandfather, grandson or granddaughter of that person or of that person's spouse or former spouse, or

(b)   the brother, sister, uncle, aunt, niece or nephew (whether of the full blood or of the half blood or by affinity) of that person or of that person's spouse or former spouse,

and includes, in relation to a person who is living or has lived with another person as husband and wife, any person who would fall within paragraph (a) or (b) if the parties were married to each other;

"relevant child", in relation to any proceedings under this Part, has the meaning given by section 62(2);

. . . . .

(2)   The enactments referred to in the definition of "family proceedings" are—

(a)   Part II;

(b)   this Part;

(c)   the Matrimonial Causes Act 1973;

(d)   the Adoption Act 1976;

(e)   the Domestic Proceedings and Magistrates' Courts Act 1978;

(f)   Part III of the Matrimonial and Family Proceedings Act 1984;

(g)   Parts I, II and IV of the Children Act 1989;

(h)   section 30 of the Human Fertilisation and Embryology Act 1990.

(3)   Where the question of whether harm suffered by a child is significant turns on the child's health or development, his health or development shall be compared with that which could reasonably be expected of a similar child.

(4)   For the purposes of sections 31, 32, 53 and 54 and such other provisions of this Part (if any) as may be prescribed, this Part is to have effect as if paragraph (b) of the definition of "dwelling-house" were omitted.

(5)   It is hereby declared that this Part applies as between the parties to a marriage even though either of them is, or has at any time during the marriage been, married to more than one person.

NOTES

Commencement: 1 October 1997.

Sub-s (1): definition omitted outside the scope of this work.

PART V

Supplemental

64   Provision for separate representation for children

(1)   The Lord Chancellor may by regulations provide for the separate representation of children in proceedings in England and Wales for which relate to any matter in respect of which a question has arisen, or may arise, under—
   (a)   Part II;
   (b)   Part IV;
   (c)   the 1973 Act; or
   (d)   the Domestic Proceedings and Magistrates' Courts Act 1978.

(2)   The regulations may provide for such representation only in specified circumstances.

NOTES

Commencement: to be appointed.

67   Short title, commencement and extent

(1)   This Act may be cited as the Family Law Act 1996.

(2)   Section 65 and this section come into force on the passing of this Act.

(3)   The other provisions of this Act come into force on such day as the Lord Chancellor may by order appoint; and different days may be appointed for different purposes.

(4)   . . .

NOTES

Sub-s (4): outside the scope of this work.

SCHEDULES

SCHEDULE 1

Section 9(6)

ARRANGEMENTS FOR THE FUTURE

The first exemption

1.   The circumstances referred to in section 9(7)(a) are that—
   (a) the requirements of section 11 have been satisfied;
   (b) the applicant has, during the period for reflection and consideration, taken such steps as are reasonably practicable to try to reach agreement about the parties' financial arrangements; and
   (c) the applicant has made an application to the court for financial relief and has complied with all requirements of the court in relation to proceedings for financial relief but—
      (i)   the other party has delayed in complying with requirements of the court or has otherwise been obstructive; or
      (ii) for reasons which are beyond the control of the applicant, or of the other party, the court has been prevented from obtaining the information which it requires to determine the financial position of the parties.

The second exemption

2.   The circumstances referred to in section 9(7)(b) are that—
   (a) the requirements of section 11 have been satisfied;
   (b) the applicant has, during the period for reflection and consideration, taken such steps as are reasonably practicable to try to reach agreement about the parties' financial arrangements;
   (c) because of
      (i)   the ill health or disability of the applicant, the other party or a child of the family (whether physical or mental), or
      (ii) an injury suffered by the applicant, the other party or a child of the family,

the applicant has not been able to reach agreement with the other party about those arrangements and is unlikely to be able to do so in the foreseeable future; and

(d) a delay in making the order applied for under section 3—
    (i) would be significantly detrimental to the welfare of any child of the family; or
    (ii) would be seriously prejudicial to the applicant.

The third exemption

3.   The circumstances referred to in section 9(7)(c) are that—
  (a) the requirements of section 11 have been satisfied;
  (b) the applicant has found it impossible to contact the other party; and
  (c) as a result, it has been impossible for the applicant to reach agreement with the other party about their financial arrangements.

The fourth exemption

4.   The circumstances referred to in section 9(7)(d) are that—
  (a) the requirements of section 11 have been satisfied;
  (b) an occupation order or a non-molestation order is in force in favour of the applicant or a child of the family, made against the other party;
  (c) the applicant has, during the period for reflection and consideration, taken such steps as are reasonably practicable to try to reach agreement about the parties' financial arrangements;
  (d) the applicant has not been able to reach agreement with the other party about those arrangements and is unlikely to be able to do so in the foreseeable future; and
  (e) a delay in making the order applied for under section 3—
    (i) would be significantly detrimental to the welfare of any child of the family; or
    (ii) would be seriously prejudicial to the applicant.

5.–9. . . .

NOTES

Paras 5–9: outside the scope of this work.

SCHEDULE 7

Section 53

TRANSFER OF CERTAIN TENANCIES ON DIVORCE ETC OR ON SEPARATION OF COHABITANTS

PART I
GENERAL

Interpretation

1.   In this Schedule—
"cohabitant", except in paragraph 3, includes (where the context requires) former cohabitant;
"the court" does not include a magistrates' court,
"landlord" includes—
    (a) any person from time to time deriving title under the original landlord; and
    (b) in relation to any dwelling-house, any person other than the tenant who is, or (but for Part VII of the Rent Act 1977 or Part II of the Rent (Agriculture) Act 1976) would be, entitled to possession of the dwelling-house;
"Part II order" means an order under Part II of this Schedule;
"a relevant tenancy" means—
    (a) a protected tenancy or statutory tenancy within the meaning of the Rent Act 1977;
    (b) a statutory tenancy within the meaning of the Rent (Agriculture) Act 1976;
    (c) a secure tenancy within the meaning of section 79 of the Housing Act 1985; . . .
    (d) an assured tenancy or assured agricultural occupancy within the meaning of Part I of the Housing Act 1988; [or
    (e) an introductory tenancy within the meaning of Chapter I of Part V of the Housing Act 1996;]
"spouse", except in paragraph 2, includes (where the context requires) former spouse; and
"tenancy" includes sub-tenancy.

Cases in which the court may make an order

2.—(1) This paragraph applies if one spouse is entitled, either in his own right or jointly with the other spouse, to occupy a dwelling-house by virtue of a relevant tenancy.

(2) At any time when it has power to make a property adjustment order under section 23A (divorce or separation) or 24 (nullity) of the Matrimonial Causes Act 1973 with respect to the marriage, the court may make a Part II order.

3.—(1) This paragraph applies if one cohabitant is entitled, either in his own right or jointly with the other cohabitant, to occupy a dwelling-house by virtue of a relevant tenancy.

(2) If the cohabitants cease to live together as husband and wife, the court may make a Part II order.

4. The court shall not make a Part II order unless the dwelling-house is or was—
   (a) in the case of spouses, a matrimonial home; or
   (b) in the case of cohabitants, a home in which they lived together as husband and wife.

Matters to which the court must have regard

5. In determining whether to exercise its powers under Part II of this Schedule and, if so, in what manner, the court shall have regard to all the circumstances of the case including—
   (a) the circumstances in which the tenancy was granted to either or both of the spouses or cohabitants or, as the case requires, the circumstances in which either or both of them became tenant under the tenancy;
   (b) the matters mentioned in section 33(6)(a), (b) and (c) and, where the parties are cohabitants and only one of them is entitled to occupy the dwelling-house by virtue of the relevant tenancy, the further matters mentioned in section 36(6)(e), (f), (g) and (h); and
   (c) the suitability of the parties as tenants.

NOTES

Para 1: in definition "a relevant tenancy" word omitted from para (c) repealed and para (e) and word immediately preceding it added by the Housing Act 1996 (Consequential Amendments) Order 1997, SI 1997/74, art 2, Schedule, para 10(1)(b).

PART II
ORDERS THAT MAY BE MADE

References to entitlement to occupy

6.   References in this Part of this Schedule to a spouse or a cohabitant being entitled to occupy a dwelling-house by virtue of a relevant tenancy apply whether that entitlement is in his own right or jointly with the other spouse or cohabitant.

Protected, secure or assured tenancy or assured agricultural occupancy

7.—(1)   If a spouse or cohabitant is entitled to occupy the dwelling-house by virtue of a protected tenancy within the meaning of the Rent Act 1977, a secure tenancy within the meaning of the Housing Act 1985[, an assured tenancy] or assured agricultural occupancy within the meaning of Part I of the Housing Act 1988 [or an introductory tenancy within the meaning of Chapter I of Part V of the Housing Act 1996], the court may by order direct that, as from such date as may be specified in the order, there shall, by virtue of the order and without further assurance, be transferred to, and vested in, the other spouse or cohabitant—

(a)   the estate or interest which the spouse or cohabitant so entitled had in the dwelling-house immediately before that date by virtue of the lease or agreement creating the tenancy and any assignment of that lease or agreement, with all rights, privileges and appurtenances attaching to that estate or interest but subject to all covenants, obligations, liabilities and incumbrances to which it is subject; and

(b)   where the spouse or cohabitant so entitled is an assignee of such lease or agreement, the liability of that spouse or cohabitant under any covenant of indemnity by the assignee express or implied in the assignment of the lease or agreement to that spouse or cohabitant.

(2)   If an order is made under this paragraph, any liability or obligation to which the spouse or cohabitant so entitled is subject under any covenant having reference to the dwelling-house in the lease or agreement, being a liability or obligation falling due to be discharged or performed on or after the date so specified, shall not be enforceable against that spouse or cohabitant.

(3)   If the spouse so entitled is a successor within the meaning of Part IV of the Housing Act 1985, his former spouse or former cohabitant (or, if a separation order is in force, his spouse) shall be deemed also to be a successor within the meaning of that Part.

[(3A) If the Spouse or cohabitant so entitled is a successor within the meaning of section 132 of the Housing Act 1996, his former spouse or former cohabitant (or, if a separation order is in force, his spouse) shall be deemed also to be a successor within the meaning of that section.]

(4)   If the spouse or cohabitant so entitled is for the purpose of section 17 of the Housing Act 1988 a successor in relation to the tenancy or occupancy, his former spouse or former cohabitant (or, if a separation order is in force, his spouse) is to be deemed to be a successor in relation to the tenancy or occupancy for the purposes of that section.

(5)   If the transfer under sub-paragraph (1) is of an assured agricultural occupancy, then, for the purposes of Chapter III of Part I of the Housing Act 1988—
   (a) the agricultural worker condition is fulfilled with respect to the dwelling-house while the spouse or cohabitant to whom the assured agricultural occupancy is transferred continues to be the occupier under that occupancy, and
   (b) that condition is to be treated as so fulfilled by virtue of the same paragraph of Schedule 3 to the Housing Act 1988 as was applicable before the transfer.

(6)   In this paragraph, references to a separation order being in force include references to there being a judicial separation in force.

Statutory tenancy within the meaning of the Rent Act 1977

8.—(1)   This paragraph applies if the spouse or cohabitant is entitled to occupy the dwelling- house by virtue of a statutory tenancy within the meaning of the Rent Act 1977.

(2)   The court may by order direct that, as from the date specified in the order—
   (a) that spouse or cohabitant is to cease to be entitled to occupy the dwelling-house; and
   (b) the other spouse or cohabitant is to be deemed to be the tenant or, as the case may be, the sole tenant under that statutory tenancy.

(3)   The question whether the provisions of paragraphs 1 to 3, or (as the case may be) paragraphs 5 to 7 of Schedule l to the Rent Act 1977, as to the succession by the surviving spouse of a deceased tenant, or by a member of the deceased tenant's family, to the right to retain possession are capable of having effect in the event of the death of the person deemed by an order

under this paragraph to be the tenant or sole tenant under the statutory tenancy is to be determined according as those provisions have or have not already had effect in relation to the statutory tenancy.

Statutory tenancy within the meaning of the Rent (Agriculture) Act 1976

9.—(1)   This paragraph applies if the spouse or cohabitant is entitled to occupy the dwelling- house by virtue of a statutory tenancy within the meaning of the Rent (Agriculture) Act 1976.

(2)   The court may by order direct that, as from such date as may be specified in the order—
- (a)   that spouse or cohabitant is to cease to be entitled to occupy the dwelling-house; and
- (b)   the other spouse or cohabitant is to be deemed to be the tenant or, as the case may be, the sole tenant under that statutory tenancy.

(3)   A spouse or cohabitant who is deemed under this paragraph to be the tenant under a statutory tenancy is (within the meaning of that Act) a statutory tenant in his own right, or a statutory tenant by succession, according as the other spouse or cohabitant was a statutory tenant in his own right or a statutory tenant by succession.

NOTES

Para 7: in sub-para (1) words in first pair of square brackets substituted and words in second pair of square brackets inserted, sub-para (3) inserted, by the Housing Act 1996 (Consequential Amendments) Order 1997, SI 1997/74, art 2, Schedule, para 10(b)(ii), (iii).

PART III
SUPPLEMENTARY PROVISIONS

Compensation

10.—(1)   If the court makes a Part II order, it may by the order direct the making of a payment by the spouse or cohabitant to whom the tenancy is transferred ("the transferee") to the other spouse or cohabitant ("the transferor").

(2)   Without prejudice to that, the court may, on making an order by virtue of sub- paragraph (1) for the payment of a sum—

(a) direct that payment of that sum or any part of it is to be deferred until a specified date or until the occurrence of a specified event, or

(b) direct that that sum or any part of it is to be paid by instalments.

(3) Where an order has been made by virtue of sub-paragraph (1), the court may, on the application of the transferee or the transferor—

(a) exercise its powers under sub-paragraph (2), or

(b) vary any direction previously given under that sub-paragraph,

at any time before the sum whose payment is required by the order is paid in full.

(4) In deciding whether to exercise its powers under this paragraph and, if so, in what manner, the court shall have regard to all the circumstances including—

(a) the financial loss that would otherwise be suffered by the transferor as a result of the order;

(b) the financial needs and financial resources of the parties; and

(c) the financial obligations which the parties have, or are likely to have in the foreseeable future, including financial obligations to each other and to any relevant child.

(5) The court shall not give any direction under sub-paragraph (2) unless it appears to it that immediate payment of the sum required by the order would cause the transferee financial hardship which is greater than any financial hardship that would be caused to the transferor if the direction were given.

Liabilities and obligations in respect of the dwelling-house

11.—(1) If the court makes a Part II order, it may by the order direct that both spouses or cohabitants are to be jointly and severally liable to discharge or perform any or all of the liabilities and obligations in respect of the dwelling-house (whether arising under the tenancy or otherwise) which—

(a) have at the date of the order fallen due to be discharged or performed by one only of them; or

(b) but for the direction, would before the date specified as the date on which the order is to take effect fall due to be discharged or performed by one only of them.

(2) If the court gives such a direction, it may further direct that either spouse or cohabitant is to be liable to indemnify the other in whole or in part against any payment made or expenses incurred by the other in discharging or performing any such liability or obligation.

Date when order made between spouses is to take effect

12.—(1)   In the case of a decree of nullity of marriage, the date specified in a Part II order as the date on which the order is to take effect must not be earlier than the date on which the decree is made absolute.

(2)   In the case of divorce proceedings or separation proceedings, the date specified in a Part II order as the date on which the order is to take effect is to be determined as if the court were making a property adjustment order under section 23A of the Matrimonial Causes Act 1973 (regard being had to the restrictions imposed by section 23B of that Act).

Remarriage of either spouse

13.—(1)   If after the making of a divorce order or the grant of a decree annulling a marriage either spouse remarries, that spouse is not entitled to apply, by reference to the making of that order or the grant of that decree, for a Part II order.

(2)   For the avoidance of doubt it is hereby declared that the reference in sub-paragraph (1) to remarriage includes a reference to a marriage which is by law void or voidable.

Rules of court

14.—(1)   Rules of court shall be made requiring the court, before it makes an order under this Schedule, to give the landlord of the dwelling-house to which the order will relate an opportunity of being heard.

(2)   Rules of court may provide that an application for a Part II order by reference to an order or decree may not, without the leave of the court by which that order was made or decree was granted, be made after the expiration of such period from the order or grant as may be prescribed by the rules.

Saving for other provisions of Act

15.—(1)   If a spouse is entitled to occupy a dwelling-house by virtue of a tenancy, this Schedule does not affect the operation of sections 30 and 31 in relation to the other spouse's matrimonial home rights.

(2)   If a spouse or cohabitant is entitled to occupy a dwelling-house by virtue of a tenancy, the court's powers to make orders under this Schedule are additional to those conferred by sections 33, 35 and 36.

Private International Law (Miscellaneous Provisions) Act 1995

(1995 c 42)

An Act to make provision about interest on judgment debts and arbitral awards expressed in a currency other than sterling; to make further provision as to marriages entered into by unmarried persons under a law which permits polygamy; to make provision for choice of law rules in tort and delict; and for connected purposes

[8 November 1995]

PART II
VALIDITY OF MARRIAGES UNDER A LAW WHICH PERMITS POLYGAMY

5   Validity in English law of potentially polygamous marriages

(1)   A marriage entered into outside England and Wales between parties neither of whom is already married is not void under the law of England and Wales on the ground that it is entered into under a law which permits polygamy and that either party is domiciled in England and Wales.

(2)   This section does not affect the determination of the validity of a marriage by reference to the law of another country to the extent that it falls to be so determined in accordance with the rules of private international law.

NOTES

Commencement: 8 January 1996.

6   Application of section 5 to prior marriages

(1)   Section 5 above shall be deemed to apply, and always to have applied, to any marriage entered into before commencement which is not excluded by subsection (2) or (3) below.

(2)   That section does not apply to a marriage a party to which has (before commencement) entered into a later marriage which either—

(a) is valid apart from this section but would be void if section 5 above applied to the earlier marriage; or

(b) is valid by virtue of this section.

(3)   That section does not apply to a marriage which has been annulled before commencement, whether by a decree granted in England and Wales or by an annulment obtained elsewhere and recognised in England and Wales at commencement.

(4)   An annulment of a marriage resulting from legal proceedings begun before commencement shall be treated for the purposes of subsection (3) above as having taken effect before that time.

(5)   For the purposes of subsections (3) and (4) above a marriage which has been declared to be invalid by a court of competent jurisdiction in any proceedings concerning either the validity of the marriage or any right dependent on its validity shall be treated as having been annulled.

(6)   Nothing in section 5 above, in its application to marriages entered into before commencement—

(a) gives or affects any entitlement to an interest—

(i)   under the will or codicil of, or on the intestacy of, a person who died before commencement; or

(ii) under a settlement or other disposition of property made before that time (otherwise than by will or codicil);

(b) gives or affects any entitlement to a benefit, allowance, pension or other payment—

(i)   payable before, or in respect of a period before, commencement; or

(ii) payable in respect of the death of a person before that time;

(c) affects tax in respect of a period or event before commencement; or

(d) affects the succession to any dignity or title of honour.

(7)   In this section "commencement" means the commencement of this Part.

NOTES

Commencement: 8 January 1996.

8   Part II: supplemental

(1)   Nothing in this Part affects any law or custom relating to the marriage of members of the Royal Family.

(2)   The enactments specified in the Schedule to this Act (which contains consequential amendments and amendments removing unnecessary references to potentially polygamous marriages) are amended in accordance with that Schedule.

(3)   Nothing in that Schedule affects either the generality of any enactment empowering the making of subordinate legislation or any such legislation made before the commencement of this Part.

NOTES

Commencement: 8 January 1996.

Trusts of Land and Appointment of Trustees Act 1996

(c 47)

An Act to make new provision about trusts of land including provision phasing out the Settled Land Act 1925, abolishing the doctrine of conversion and otherwise amending the law about trusts for sale of land; to amend the law about the appointment and retirement of trustees of any trust; and for connected purposes.

[24 July 1996]

PART I
TRUSTS OF LAND

Powers of court

14   Applications for order

(1)   Any person who is a trustee of land or has an interest in a property subject to a trust of land may make an application to the court for an order under this section.

(2)   On an application for an order under this section the court may make any such order—

(a) relating to the exercise by the trustees of any of their functions (including an order relieving them of any obligation to obtain the consent of, or to consult, any person in connection with the exercise of any of their functions), or

(b) declaring the nature or extent of a person's interest in property subject to the trust,

as the court thinks fit.

(3) The court may not under this section make any order as to the appointment or removal of trustees.

(4) The powers conferred on the court by this section are exercisable on an application whether it is made before or after the commencement of this Act.

NOTES

Commencement: 1 January 1997.

15 Matters relevant in determining applications

(1) The matters to which the court is to have regard in determining an application for an order under section 14 include—

(a) the intentions of the person or persons (if any) who created the trust,

(b) the purposes for which the property subject to the trust is held,

(c) the welfare of any minor who occupies or might reasonably be expected to occupy any land subject to the trust as his home, and

(d) the interests of any secured creditor of any beneficiary.

(2) In the case of an application relating to the exercise in relation to any land of the powers conferred on the trustees by section 13, the matters to which the court is to have regard also include the circumstances and wishes of each of the beneficiaries who is (or apart from any previous exercise by the trustees of those powers would be) entitled to occupy the land under section 12.

(3) In the case of any other application, other than one relating to the exercise of the power mentioned in section 6(2), the matters to which the court is to have regard also include the circumstances and wishes of any

beneficiaries of full age and entitled to an interest in possession in property subject to the trust or (in case of dispute) of the majority (according to the value of their combined interests).

(4)   This section does not apply to an application if section 335A of the Insolvency Act 1986 (which is inserted by Schedule 3 and relates to applications by a trustee of a bankrupt) applies to it.

NOTES

Commencement: 1 January 1997.

PART III
SUPPLEMENTARY

27   Short title, commencement and extent

(1)   This Act may be cited as the Trusts of Land and Appointment of Trustees Act 1996.

(2)   This Act comes into force on such day as the Lord Chancellor appoints by order made by statutory instrument.

(3), (4)   . . .

NOTES

Commencement: 1 January 1997.
Sub-ss (3), (4): outside the scope of this work.

Housing Act 1996

(1996 c 52)

An Act to make provision about housing, including provision about the social rented sector, houses in multiple occupation, landlord and tenant matters, the administration of housing benefit, the conduct of tenants, the allocation of housing accommodation by local housing authorities and homelessness; and for connected purposes

[24 July 1996]

PART V
CONDUCT OF TENANTS

CHAPTER I
INTRODUCTORY TENANCIES

General provisions

124 Introductory tenancies

(1)   A local housing authority or a housing action trust may elect to operate an introductory tenancy regime.

(2)   When such an election is in force, every periodic tenancy of a dwelling-house entered into or adopted by the authority or trust shall, if it would otherwise be a secure tenancy, be an introductory tenancy, unless immediately before the tenancy was entered into or adopted the tenant or, in the case of joint tenants, one or more of them was—

    (a) a secure tenant of the same or another dwelling-house, or

    (b) an assured tenant of a registered social landlord (otherwise than under an assured shorthold tenancy) in respect of the same or another dwelling-house.

(3)   Subsection (2) does not apply to a tenancy entered into or adopted in pursuance of a contract made before the election was made.

(4)   For the purposes of this Chapter a periodic tenancy is adopted by a person if that person becomes the landlord under the tenancy, whether on a disposal or surrender of the interest of the former landlord.

(5)   An election under this section may be revoked at any time, without prejudice to the making of a further election.

NOTES

Commencement: 12 February 1997.

Succession on death of tenant

131 Persons qualified to succeed tenant

A person is qualified to succeed the tenant under an introductory tenancy if he occupies the dwelling-house as his only or principal home at the time of the tenant's death and either—

   (a) he is the tenant's spouse, or

   (b) he is another member of the tenant's family and has resided with the tenant throughout the period of twelve months ending with the tenant's death;

unless, in either case, the tenant was himself a successor, as defined in section 132.

NOTES

Commencement: 12 February 1997.

132 Cases where the tenant is a successor

(1)   The tenant is himself a successor if—

   (a) the tenancy vested in him by virtue of section 133 (succession to introductory tenancy),

   (b) he was a joint tenant and has become the sole tenant,

   (c) he became the tenant on the tenancy being assigned to him (but subject to subsections (2) and (3)), or

   (d) he became the tenant on the tenancy being vested in him on the death of the previous tenant.

(2)   A tenant to whom the tenancy was assigned in pursuance of an order under section 24 of the Matrimonial Causes Act 1973 (property adjustment orders in connection with matrimonial proceedings) or section 17(1) of the Matrimonial and Family Proceedings Act 1984 (property adjustment orders after overseas divorce, &c) is a successor only if the other party to the marriage was a successor.

(3)   Where within six months of the coming to an end of an introductory tenancy ("the former tenancy") the tenant becomes a tenant under another introductory tenancy, and—

(a) the tenant was a successor in relation to the former tenancy, and

(b) under the other tenancy either the dwelling-house or the landlord, or both, are the same as under the former tenancy,

the tenant is also a successor in relation to the other tenancy unless the agreement creating that tenancy otherwise provides.

NOTES

Commencement: 12 February 1997.

133 Succession to introductory tenancy

(1) This section applies where a tenant under an introductory tenancy dies.

(2) Where there is a person qualified to succeed the tenant, the tenancy vests by virtue of this section in that person, or if there is more than one such person in the one to be preferred in accordance with the following rules—

(a) the tenant's spouse is to be preferred to another member of the tenant's family;

(b) of two or more other members of the tenant's family such of them is to be preferred as may be agreed between them or as may, where there is no such agreement, be selected by the landlord.

(3) Where there is no person qualified to succeed the tenant, the tenancy ceases to be an introductory tenancy—

(a) when it is vested or otherwise disposed of in the course of the administration of the tenant's estate, unless the vesting or other disposal is in pursuance of an order made under—

(i) section 24 of the Matrimonial Causes Act 1973 (property adjustment orders made in connection with matrimonial proceedings),

(ii) section 17(1) of the Matrimonial and Family Proceedings Act 1984 (property adjustment orders after overseas divorce, &c), or

(iii) paragraph 1 of Schedule 1 to the Children Act 1989 (orders for financial relief against parents); or

(b) when it is known that when the tenancy is so vested or disposed of it will not be in pursuance of such an order.

NOTES

Commencement: 12 February 1997.

Assignment

134 Assignment in general prohibited

(1)   An introductory tenancy is not capable of being assigned except in the cases mentioned in subsection (2).

(2)   The exceptions are—
  (a) an assignment in pursuance of an order made under—
    (i)   section 24 of the Matrimonial Causes Act 1973 (property adjustment orders in connection with matrimonial proceedings),
    (ii) section 17(1) of the Matrimonial and Family Proceedings Act 1984 (property adjustment orders after overseas divorce, &c), or
    (iii) paragraph 1 of Schedule 1 to the Children Act 1989 (orders for financial relief against parents);
  (b) an assignment to a person who would be qualified to succeed the tenant if the tenant died immediately before the assignment.

(3)   Subsection (1) also applies to a tenancy which is not an introductory tenancy but would be if the tenant, or where the tenancy is a joint tenancy, at least one of the tenants, were occupying or continuing to occupy the dwelling-house as his only or principal home.

NOTES

Commencement: 12 February 1997.

Supplementary

140 Members of a person's family: Chapter I

(1)   A person is a member of another's family within the meaning of this Chapter if—
  (a) he is the spouse of that person, or he and that person live together as husband and wife, or
  (b) he is that person's parent, grandparent, child, grandchild, brother, sister, uncle, aunt, nephew or niece.

(2)   For the purpose of subsection (1)(b)—

(a) a relationship by marriage shall be treated as a relationship by blood,

(b) a relationship of the half-blood shall be treated as a relationship of the whole blood, and

(c) the stepchild of a person shall be treated as his child.

NOTES

Commencement: 1 October 1996.

PART VII
HOMELESSNESS

Homelessness and threatened homelessness

175 Homelessness and threatened homelessness

(1)   A person is homeless if he has no accommodation available for his occupation, in the United Kingdom or elsewhere, which he—

(a) is entitled to occupy by virtue of an interest in it or by virtue of an order of a court,

(b) has an express or implied licence to occupy, or

(c) occupies as a residence by virtue of any enactment or rule of law giving him the right to remain in occupation or restricting the right of another person to recover possession.

(2)   A person is also homeless if he has accommodation but—

(a) he cannot secure entry to it, or

(b) it consists of a moveable structure, vehicle or vessel designed or adapted for human habitation and there is no place where he is entitled or permitted both to place it and to reside in it.

(3)   A person shall not be treated as having accommodation unless it is accommodation which it would be reasonable for him to continue to occupy.

(4)   A person is threatened with homelessness if it is likely that he will become homeless within 28 days.

NOTES

Commencement: 20 January 1997.

176 Meaning of accommodation available for occupation

Accommodation shall be regarded as available for a person's occupation only if it is available for occupation by him together with—
  (a) any other person who normally resides with him as a member of his family, or
  (b) any other person who might reasonably be expected to reside with him.

References in this Part to securing that accommodation is available for a person's occupation shall be construed accordingly.

NOTES

Commencement: 20 January 1997.

177 Whether it is reasonable to continue to occupy accommodation

(1)   It is not reasonable for a person to continue to occupy accommodation if it is probable that this will lead to domestic violence against him, or against—
  (a) a person who normally resides with him as a member of his family, or
  (b) any other person who might reasonably be expected to reside with him.

For this purpose "domestic violence", in relation to a person, means violence from a person with whom he is associated, or threats of violence from such a person which are likely to be carried out.

(2)   In determining whether it would be, or would have been, reasonable for a person to continue to occupy accommodation, regard may be had to the general circumstances prevailing in relation to housing in the district of the local housing authority to whom he has applied for accommodation or for assistance in obtaining accommodation.

(3)   The Secretary of State may by order specify—
  (a) other circumstances in which it is to be regarded as reasonable or not reasonable for a person to continue to occupy accommodation, and
  (b) other matters to be taken into account or disregarded in determining whether it would be, or would have been, reasonable for a person to continue to occupy accommodation.

NOTES
Commencement: 20 January 1997 (sub-ss (1), (2)); 1 October 1996 (remainder).

178 Meaning of associated person

(1)   For the purposes of this Part, a person is associated with another person if—

(a) they are or have been married to each other;

(b) they are cohabitants or former cohabitants;

(c) they live or have lived in the same household;

(d) they are relatives;

(e) they have agreed to marry one another (whether or not that agreement has been terminated);

(f) in relation to a child, each of them is a parent of the child or has, or has had, parental responsibility for the child.

(2)   If a child has been adopted or has been freed for adoption by virtue of any of the enactments mentioned in section 16(1) of the Adoption Act 1976, two persons are also associated with each other for the purposes of this Part if—

(a) one is a natural parent of the child or a parent of such a natural parent, and

(b) the other is the child or a person—

(i)   who has become a parent of the child by virtue of an adoption order or who has applied for an adoption order, or

(ii)   with whom the child has at any time been placed for adoption.

(3)   In this section—

"adoption order" has the meaning given by section 72(1) of the Adoption Act 1976;

"child" means a person under the age of 18 years;

"cohabitants" means a man and a woman who, although not married to each other, are living together as husband and wife, and "former cohabitants" shall be construed accordingly;

"parental responsibility" has the same meaning as in the Children Act 1989; and

"relative", in relation to a person, means—

(a) the father, mother, stepfather, stepmother, son, daughter, stepson, stepdaughter, grandmother, grandfather, grandson or granddaughter of that person or of that person's spouse or former spouse, or

(b) the brother, sister, uncle, aunt, niece or nephew (whether of the full blood or of the half blood or by affinity) of that person or of that person's spouse or former spouse, and includes, in relation to a person who is living or has lived with another person as husband and wife, a person who would fall within paragraph (a) or (b) if the parties were married to each other.

NOTES

Commencement: 20 January 1997.

Interim duty to accommodate

188 Interim duty to accommodate in case of apparent priority need

(1)   If the local housing authority have reason to believe that an applicant may be homeless, eligible for assistance and have a priority need, they shall secure that accommodation is available for his occupation pending a decision as to the duty (if any) owed to him under the following provisions of this Part.

(2)   The duty under this section arises irrespective of any possibility of the referral of the applicant's case to another local housing authority (see sections 198 to 200).

(3)   The duty ceases when the authority's decision is notified to the applicant, even if the applicant requests a review of the decision (see section 202).

The authority may continue to secure that accommodation is available for the applicant's occupation pending a decision on a review.

NOTES

Commencement: 20 January 1997.

189 Priority need for accommodation

(1)   The following have a priority need for accommodation—
(a) a pregnant woman or a person with whom she resides or might reasonably be expected to reside;
(b) a person with whom dependent children reside or might reasonably be expected to reside;

(c) a person who is vulnerable as a result of old age, mental illness or handicap or physical disability or other special reason, or with whom such a person resides or might reasonably be expected to reside;

(d) a person who is homeless or threatened with homelessness as a result of an emergency such as flood, fire or other disaster.

(2)   The Secretary of State may by order—
(a) specify further descriptions of persons as having a priority need for accommodation, and
(b) amend or repeal any part of subsection (1).

(3)   Before making such an order the Secretary of State shall consult such associations representing relevant authorities, and such other persons, as he considers appropriate.

(4)   No such order shall be made unless a draft of it has been approved by resolution of each House of Parliament.

NOTES

Commencement: 20 January 1997 (sub-s (1)); 1 October 1996 (remainder).

Duties to persons found to be homeless or threatened with homelessness

190   Duties to persons becoming homeless intentionally

(1)   This section applies where the local housing authority are satisfied that an applicant is homeless and is eligible for assistance but are also satisfied that he became homeless intentionally.

(2)   If the authority are satisfied that the applicant has a priority need, they shall—
(a) secure that accommodation is available for his occupation for such period as they consider will give him a reasonable opportunity of securing accommodation for his occupation, and
(b) provide him with advice and such assistance as they consider appropriate in the circumstances in any attempts he may make to secure that accommodation becomes available for his occupation.

(3)   If they are not satisfied that he has a priority need, they shall provide him with advice and such assistance as they consider appropriate in the

circumstances in any attempts he may make to secure that accommodation becomes available for his occupation.

NOTES

Commencement: 20 January 1997.

191   Becoming homeless intentionally

(1)   A person becomes homeless intentionally if he deliberately does or fails to do anything in consequence of which he ceases to occupy accommodation which is available for his occupation and which it would have been reasonable for him to continue to occupy.

(2)   For the purposes of subsection (1) an act or omission in good faith on the part of a person who was unaware of any relevant fact shall not be treated as deliberate.

(3)   A person shall be treated as becoming homeless intentionally if—
  (a) he enters into an arrangement under which he is required to cease to occupy accommodation which it would have been reasonable for him to continue to occupy, and
  (b) the purpose of the arrangement is to enable him to become entitled to assistance under this Part,

and there is no other good reason why he is homeless.

(4)   A person who is given advice or assistance under section 197 (duty where other suitable alternative accommodation available), but fails to secure suitable accommodation in circumstances in which it was reasonably to be expected that he would do so, shall, if he makes a further application under this Part, be treated as having become homeless intentionally.

NOTES

Commencement: 20 January 1997.

192   Duty to persons not in priority need who are not homeless intentionally

(1)   This section applies where the local housing authority—
  (a) are satisfied that an applicant is homeless and eligible for assistance, and

(b) are not satisfied that he became homeless intentionally,

but are not satisfied that he has a priority need.

(2)   The authority shall provide the applicant with advice and such assistance as they consider appropriate in the circumstances in any attempts he may make to secure that accommodation becomes available for his occupation.

NOTES

Commencement: 20 January 1997.

193   Duty to persons with priority need who are not homeless intentionally

(1)   This section applies where the local housing authority are satisfied that an applicant is homeless, eligible for assistance and has a priority need, and are not satisfied that he became homeless intentionally.

This section has effect subject to section 197 (duty where other suitable accommodation available).

(2)   Unless the authority refer the application to another local housing authority (see section 198), they shall secure that accommodation is available for occupation by the applicant.

(3)   The authority are subject to the duty under this section for a period of two years ("the minimum period"), subject to the following provisions of this section.

After the end of that period the authority may continue to secure that accommodation is available for occupation by the applicant, but are not obliged to do so (see section 194).

(4)   The minimum period begins with—
   (a) if the applicant was occupying accommodation made available under section 188 (interim duty to accommodate), the day on which he was notified of the authority's decision that the duty under this section was owed to him;
   (b) if the applicant was occupying accommodation made available to him under section 200(3) (interim duty where case considered for referral but not referred), the date on which he was notified under

subsection (2) of that section of the decision that the conditions for referral were not met;

(c) in any other case, the day on which accommodation was first made available to him in pursuance of the duty under this section.

(5) The local housing authority shall cease to be subject to the duty under this section if the applicant, having been informed by the authority of the possible consequence of refusal, refuses an offer of accommodation which the authority are satisfied is suitable for him and the authority notify him that they regard themselves as having discharged their duty under this section.

(6) The local housing authority shall cease to be subject to the duty under this section if the applicant—

(a) ceases to be eligible for assistance,

(b) becomes homeless intentionally from the accommodation made available for his occupation,

(c) accepts an offer of accommodation under Part VI (allocation of housing), or

(d) otherwise voluntarily ceases to occupy as his only or principal home the accommodation made available for his occupation.

(7) The local housing authority shall also cease to be subject to the duty under this section if—

(a) the applicant, having been informed of the possible consequence of refusal, refuses an offer of accommodation under Part VI, and

(b) the authority are satisfied that the accommodation was suitable for him and that it was reasonable for him to accept it and notify him accordingly within 21 days of the refusal.

(8) For the purposes of subsection (7) an applicant may reasonably be expected to accept an offer of accommodation under Part VI even though he is under contractual or other obligations in respect of his existing accommodation, provided he is able to bring those obligations to an end before he is required to take up the offer.

(9) A person who ceases to be owed the duty under this section may make a fresh application to the authority for accommodation or assistance in obtaining accommodation.

NOTES

Commencement: 20 January 1997.

194   Power exercisable after minimum period of duty under s 193

(1)   Where a local housing authority have been subject to the duty under section 193 in relation to a person until the end of the minimum period, they may continue to secure that accommodation is available for his occupation.

(2)   They shall not do so unless they are satisfied on a review under this section that—
   (a) he has a priority need,
   (b) there is no other suitable accommodation available for occupation by him in their district, and
   (c) he wishes the authority to continue securing that accommodation is available for his occupation;

and they shall not continue to do so for more than two years at a time unless they are satisfied on a further review under this section as to those matters.

The review shall be carried out towards the end of the minimum period, or subsequent two year period, with a view to enabling the authority to make an assessment of the likely situation at the end of that period.

(3)   They shall cease to do so if events occur such that, by virtue of section 193(6) or (7), they would cease to be subject to any duty under that section.

(4)   Where an authority carry out a review under this section they shall make such inquiries as they consider appropriate to determine—
   (a) whether they are satisfied as to the matters mentioned in subsection (2)(a) to (c), and
   (b) whether any of the events referred to in subsection (3) has occurred;

and on completing the review they shall notify the applicant of their determination and of whether they propose to exercise, or continue to exercise, their power under this section.

(5)   The authority may at any time, whether in consequence of a review or otherwise, give notice to the person concerned that they propose to cease exercising their power under this section in his case.

(6)   The notice must specify—
   (a) the day on which they will cease exercising their power under this section, and

(b) any action that they intend to take as a result,

and must be given not less than the prescribed period before the day so specified.

NOTES

Commencement: 20 January 1997 (sub-ss (1)–(5)); 1 October 1996 (remainder).

195 Duties in case of threatened homelessness

(1)   This section applies where the local housing authority are satisfied that an applicant is threatened with homelessness and is eligible for assistance.

(2)   If the authority—
   (a) are satisfied that he has a priority need, and
   (b) are not satisfied that he became threatened with homelessness intentionally,

they shall take reasonable steps to secure that accommodation does not cease to be available for his occupation.

This subsection has effect subject to section 197 (duty where other suitable accommodation available).

(3)   Subsection (2) does not affect any right of the authority, whether by virtue of a contract, enactment or rule of law, to secure vacant possession of any accommodation.

(4)   Where in pursuance of the duty under subsection (2) the authority secure that accommodation other than that occupied by the applicant when he made his application is available for occupation by him, the provisions of section 193(3) to (9) (period for which duty owed) and section 194 (power exercisable after minimum period of duty) apply, with any necessary modifications, in relation to the duty under this section as they apply in relation to the duty under section 193.

(5)   If the authority—
   (a) are not satisfied that the applicant has a priority need, or
   (b) are satisfied that he has a priority need but are also satisfied that he became threatened with homelessness intentionally,

they shall furnish him with advice and such assistance as they consider appropriate in the circumstances in any attempts he may make to secure that accommodation does not cease to be available for his occupation.

NOTES

Commencement: 20 January 1997.

196 Becoming threatened with homelessness intentionally

(1)   A person becomes threatened with homelessness intentionally if he deliberately does or fails to do anything the likely result of which is that he will be forced to leave accommodation which is available for his occupation and which it would have been reasonable for him to continue to occupy.

(2)   For the purposes of subsection (1) an act or omission in good faith on the part of a person who was unaware of any relevant fact shall not be treated as deliberate.

(3)   A person shall be treated as becoming threatened with homelessness intentionally if—
  (a) he enters into an arrangement under which he is required to cease to occupy accommodation which it would have been reasonable for him to continue to occupy, and
  (b) the purpose of the arrangement is to enable him to become entitled to assistance under this Part,

and there is no other good reason why he is threatened with homelessness.

(4)   A person who is given advice or assistance under section 197 (duty where other suitable alternative accommodation available), but fails to secure suitable accommodation in circumstances in which it was reasonably to be expected that he would do so, shall, if he makes a further application under this Part, be treated as having become threatened with homelessness intentionally.

NOTES

Commencement: 20 January 1997.

Protection from Harassment Act 1997

(1997 c 40)

An Act to make provision for protecting persons from harassment and similar conduct

[21 March 1997]

England and Wales

1 Prohibition of harassment

(1) A person must not pursue a course of conduct—
  (a) which amounts to harassment of another, and
  (b) which he knows or ought to know amounts to harassment of the other.

(2) For the purposes of this section, the person whose course of conduct is in question ought to know that it amounts to harassment of another if a reasonable person in possession of the same information would think the course of conduct amounted to harassment of the other.

(3) Subsection (1) does not apply to a course of conduct if the person who pursued it shows—
  (a) that it was pursued for the purpose of preventing or detecting crime,
  (b) that it was pursued under any enactment or rule of law or to comply with any condition or requirement imposed by any person under any enactment, or
  (c) that in the particular circumstances the pursuit of the course of conduct was reasonable.

NOTES

Commencement: 16 June 1997.

2 Offence of harassment

(1) A person who pursues a course of conduct in breach of section 1 is guilty of an offence.

(2)   A person guilty of an offence under this section is liable on summary conviction to imprisonment for a term not exceeding six months, or a fine not exceeding level 5 on the standard scale, or both.

(3)   In section 24(2) of the Police and Criminal Evidence Act 1984 (arrestable offences), after paragraph (m) there is inserted—
> "(n) an offence under section 2 of the Protection from Harassment Act 1997 (harassment).".

Commencement: 16 June 1997.

3   Civil remedy

(1)   An actual or apprehended breach of section 1 may be the subject of a claim in civil proceedings by the person who is or may be the victim of the course of conduct in question.

(2)   On such a claim, damages may be awarded for (among other things) any anxiety caused by the harassment and any financial loss resulting from the harassment.

(3)   Where—
   (a) in such proceedings the High Court or a county court grants an injunction for the purpose of restraining the defendant from pursuing any conduct which amounts to harassment, and
   (b) the plaintiff considers that the defendant has done anything which he is prohibited from doing by the injunction,

the plaintiff may apply for the issue of a warrant for the arrest of the defendant.

(4)   An application under subsection (3) may be made—
   (a) where the injunction was granted by the High Court, to a judge of that court, and
   (b) where the injunction was granted by a county court, to a judge or district judge of that or any other county court.

(5)   The judge or district judge to whom an application under subsection (3) is made may only issue a warrant if—
   (a) the application is substantiated on oath, and
   (b) the judge or district judge has reasonable grounds for believing that

the defendant has done anything which he is prohibited from doing by the injunction.

(6)   Where—
   (a)   the High Court or a county court grants an injunction for the purpose mentioned in subsection (3)(a), and
   (b)   without reasonable excuse the defendant does anything which he is prohibited from doing by the injunction,

he is guilty of an offence.

(7)   Where a person is convicted of an offence under subsection (6) in respect of any conduct, that conduct is not punishable as a contempt of court.

(8)   A person cannot be convicted of an offence under subsection (6) in respect of any conduct which has been punished as a contempt of court.

(9)   A person guilty of an offence under subsection (6) is liable—
   (a)   on conviction on indictment, to imprisonment for a term not exceeding five years, or a fine, or both, or
   (b)   on summary conviction, to imprisonment for a term not exceeding six months, or a fine not exceeding the statutory maximum, or both.

NOTES

Commencement: 1 September 1998 (sub-ss (3)–(9)); 16 June 1997 (remainder).

4   Putting people in fear of violence

(1)   A person whose course of conduct causes another to fear, on at least two occasions, that violence will be used against him is guilty of an offence if he knows or ought to know that his course of conduct will cause the other so to fear on each of those occasions.

(2)   For the purposes of this section, the person whose course of conduct is in question ought to know that it will cause another to fear that violence will be used against him on any occasion if a reasonable person in possession of the same information would think the course of conduct would cause the other so to fear on that occasion.

(3)   It is a defence for a person charged with an offence under this section to show that—

(a) his course of conduct was pursued for the purpose of preventing or detecting crime,

(b) his course of conduct was pursued under any enactment or rule of law or to comply with any condition or requirement imposed by any person under any enactment, or

(c) the pursuit of his course of conduct was reasonable for the protection of himself or another or for the protection of his or another's property.

(4)   A person guilty of an offence under this section is liable—

(a) on conviction on indictment, to imprisonment for a term not exceeding five years, or a fine, or both, or

(b) on summary conviction, to imprisonment for a term not exceeding six months, or a fine not exceeding the statutory maximum, or both.

(5)   If on the trial on indictment of a person charged with an offence under this section the jury find him not guilty of the offence charged, they may find him guilty of an offence under section 2.

(6)   The Crown Court has the same powers and duties in relation to a person who is by virtue of subsection (5) convicted before it of an offence under section 2 as a magistrates' court would have on convicting him of the offence.

NOTES

Commencement: 16 June 1997.

5   Restraining orders

(1)   A court sentencing or otherwise dealing with a person ("the defendant") convicted of an offence under section 2 or 4 may (as well as sentencing him or dealing with him in any other way) make an order under this section.

(2)   The order may, for the purpose of protecting the victim of the offence, or any other person mentioned in the order, from further conduct which—

(a) amounts to harassment, or

(b) will cause a fear of violence,

prohibit the defendant from doing anything described in the order.

(3)   The order may have effect for a specified period or until further order.

(4)   The prosecutor, the defendant or any other person mentioned in the order may apply to the court which made the order for it to be varied or discharged by a further order.

(5)   If without reasonable excuse the defendant does anything which he is prohibited from doing by an order under this section, he is guilty of an offence.

(6)   A person guilty of an offence under this section is liable—
  (a) on conviction on indictment, to imprisonment for a term not exceeding five years, or a fine, or both, or
  (b) on summary conviction, to imprisonment for a term not exceeding six months, or a fine not exceeding the statutory maximum, or both.

NOTES

Commencement: 16 June 1997.

7   Interpretation of this group of sections

(1)   This section applies for the interpretation of sections 1 to 5.

(2)   References to harassing a person include alarming the person or causing the person distress.

(3)   A "course of conduct" must involve conduct on at least two occasions.

(4)   "Conduct" includes speech.

NOTES

Commencement: 16 June 1997.

General

16   Short title

This Act may be cited as the Protection from Harassment Act 1997.

NOTES

Commencement: 21 March 1997.

The European Convention for the Protection of Human Rights and Fundamental Freedoms (1950)

SECTION I
RIGHTS AND FREEDOMS

Article 6

Right to a fair trial

1.   In the determination of his civil rights and obligations or of any criminal charge against him, everyone is entitled to a fair and public hearing within a reasonable time by an independent and impartial tribunal established by law. Judgment shall be pronounced publicly but the press and public may be excluded from all or part of the trial in the interests of morals, public order or national security in a democratic society, where the interests of juveniles or the protection of the private life of the parties so require, or to the extent strictly necessary in the opinion of the court in special circumstances where publicity would prejudice the interests of justice.

2.   Everyone charged with a criminal offence shall be presumed innocent until proved guilty according to law.

3.   Everyone charged with a criminal offence has the following minimum rights:
   (a) to be informed promptly, in a language which he understands and in detail, of the nature and cause of the accusation against him;
   (b) to have adequate time and facilities for the preparation of his defence;
   (c) to defend himself in person or through legal assistance of his own choosing or, if he has not sufficient means to pay for legal assistance, to be given it free when the interests of justice so require;
   (d) to examine or have examined witnesses against him and to obtain the attendance and examination of witnesses on his behalf under the same conditions as witnesses against him;
   (e) to have the free assistance of an interpreter if he cannot understand or speak the language used in court.

Article 8

Right to respect for private and family life

1.   Everyone has the right to respect for his private and family life, his home and his correspondence.

2.   There shall be no interference by a public authority with the exercise of this right except such as is in accordance with the law and is necessary in a democratic society in the interests of national security, public safety or the economic well-being of the country, for the prevention of disorder or crime, for the protection of health or morals, or for the protection of the rights and freedoms of others.

Article 12

Right to marry

Men and women of marriageable age have the right to marry and to found a family, according to the national laws governing the exercise of this right.

Article 14

Prohibition of discrimination

The enjoyment of the rights and freedoms set forth in this Convention shall be secured without discrimination on any ground such as sex, race, colour, language, religion, political or other opinion, national or social origin, association with a national minority, property, birth or other status.

United Nations Convention on the Rights of the Child (1989)

Article 1

For the purposes of the present Convention, a child means every human being below the age of eighteen years unless, under the law applicable to the child, majority is attained earlier.

Article 2

1.   States Parties shall respect and ensure the rights set forth in the present Convention to each child within their jurisdiction without discrimination of any kind, irrespective of the child's or his or her parent's or legal guardian's race, colour, sex, language, religion, political or other opinion, national, ethnic or social origin, property, disability, birth or other status.

2.   States Parties shall take all appropriate measures to ensure that the child is protected against all forms of discrimination or punishment on the basis of the status, activities, expressed opinions, or beliefs of the child's parents, legal guardians, or family members.

Article 3

1.   In all actions concerning children, whether undertaken by public or private social welfare institutions, courts of law, administrative authorities or legislative bodies, the best interests of the child shall be a primary consideration.

2.   States Parties undertake to ensure the child such protection and care as is necessary for his or her well-being, taking into account the rights and duties of his or her parents, legal guardians, or other individuals legally responsible for him or her, and to this end, shall take all appropriate legislative and administrative measures.

3.   States Parties shall ensure that the institutions, services and facilities responsible for the care or protection of children shall conform with the standards established by competent authorities, particularly in the areas of safety, health, in the number and suitability of their staff, as well as competent supervision.

Article 6

1.   States Parties recognise that every child has the inherent right to life.

2.   States Parties shall ensure to the maximum extent possible the survival and development of the child.

Article 7

1.   The child shall be registered immediately after birth and shall have the right from birth to a name, the right to acquire a nationality

and, as far as possible, the right to know and be cared for by his or her parents.

2.   States Parties shall ensure the implementation of these rights in accordance with their national law and their obligations under the relevant international instruments in this field, in particular where the child would otherwise be stateless.

Article 9

1.   States Parties shall ensure that a child shall not be separated from his or her parents against their will, except when competent authorities subject to judicial review determine, in accordance with applicable law and procedures, that such separation is necessary for the best interests of the child. Such determination may be necessary in a particular case such as one involving abuse or neglect of the child by the parents, or one where the parents are living separately and a decision must be made as to the child's place of residence.

2.   In any proceedings pursuant to paragraph 1 of the present article, all interested parties shall be given the opportunity to participate in the proceedings and make their views known.

3.   States Parties shall respect the right of the child who is separated from one or both parents to maintain personal relations and direct contact with both parents on a regular basis, except if it is contrary to the child's best interests.

4.   Where such separation results from any action initiated by a State Party, such as the detention, imprisonment, exile, deportation or death (including death arising from any cause while the person is in the custody of the State) of one or both parents or of the child, that State Party shall, upon request, provide the parents, the child or, if appropriate, another member of the family with the essential information concerning the whereabouts of the absent member(s) of the family unless the provision of the information would be detrimental to the well-being of the child. States Parties shall further ensure that the submission of such a request shall of itself entail no adverse consequences for the person(s) concerned.

Article 10

1.   In accordance with the obligation of States Parties under article 9, paragraph 1, applications by a child or his or her parents to enter or leave

a State Party for the purposes of family reunification shall be dealt with by States Parties in a positive, humane and expeditious manner. States Parties shall further ensure that the submission of such a request shall entail no adverse consequences for the applicants and for the members of their family.

2.   A child whose parents reside in different States shall have the right to maintain on a regular basis, save in exceptional circumstances personal relations and direct contacts with both parents. Towards that end and in accordance with the obligation of States Parties under article 9, paragraph 1, States Parties shall respect the right of the child and his or her parents to leave any country, including their own, and to enter their own country. The right to leave any country shall be subject only to such restrictions as are prescribed by law and which are necessary to protect the national security, public order *(ordre public)*, public health or morals or the rights and freedoms of others and are consistent with the other rights recognised in the present Convention.

Article 12

1.   States Parties shall assure to the child who is capable of forming his or her own views the right to express those views freely in all matters affecting the child, the views of the child being given due weight in accordance with the age and maturity of the child.

2.   For this purpose, the child shall in particular be provided the opportunity to be heard in any judicial and administrative proceedings affecting the child, either directly, or through a representative or an appropriate body, in a manner consistent with the procedural rules of national law.

Article 18

1.   States Parties shall use their best efforts to ensure recognition of the principle that both parents have common responsibilities for the upbringing and development of the child. Parents or, as the case may be, legal guardians, have the primary responsibility for the upbringing and development of the child. The best interests of the child will be their basic concern.

2.   For the purpose of guaranteeing and promoting the rights set forth in the present Convention, States Parties shall render appropriate assistance to parents and legal guardians in the performance of their child-rearing responsibilities and shall ensure the development of institutions, facilities and services for the care of children.

3.   States Parties shall take all appropriate measures to ensure that children of working parents have the right to benefit from child-care services and facilities for which they are eligible.

Article 22

1.   States Parties shall take appropriate measures to ensure that a child who is seeking refugee status or who is considered a refugee in accordance with applicable international or domestic law and procedures shall, whether unaccompanied or accompanied by his or her parents or by any other person, receive appropriate protection and humanitarian assistance in the enjoyment of applicable rights set forth in the present convention and in other international human rights or humanitarian instruments to which the said States are Parties.

2.   For this purpose, States Parties shall provide, as they consider appropriate, co- operation in any efforts by the United Nations and other competent intergovernmental organisations or non-governmental organisations co-operating with the United Nations to protect and assist such a child and to trace the parents or other members of the family of any refugee child in order to obtain information necessary for reunification with his or her family. In cases where no parents or other members of the family can be found, the child shall be accorded the same protection as any other child permanently or temporarily deprived of his or her family environment for any reason, as set forth in the present Convention.

Article 40

1.   States Parties recognise the right of every child alleged as, accused of, or recognised as having infringed the penal law to be treated in a manner consistent with the promotion of the child's sense of dignity and worth, which reinforces the child's respect for the human rights and fundamental freedoms of others and which takes into account the child's age and the desirability of promoting the child's reintegration and the child's assuming a constructive role in society.

2.   To this end, and having regard to the relevant provisions of international instruments, States Parties shall, in particular, ensure that:
    (a) No child shall be alleged as, be accused of, or recognised as having infringed the penal law by reason of acts or omissions that were not prohibited by national or international law at the time they were committed;

(b) Every child alleged as or accused of having infringed the penal law has at least the following guarantees:

  (i) To be presumed innocent until proven guilty according to law;

  (ii) To be informed promptly and directly of the charges against him or her, and, if appropriate, through his or her parents or legal guardians, and to have legal or other appropriate assistance in the preparation and presentation of his or her defence;

  (iii) To have the matter determined without delay by a competent, independent and impartial authority or judicial body in a fair hearing according to law, in the presence of legal or other appropriate assistance and, unless it is considered not to be in the best interest of the child, in particular, taking into account his or her age or situation, his or her parents or legal guardians;

  (iv) Not to be compelled to give testimony or to confess guilt; to examine or have examined adverse witnesses and to obtain the participation and examination of witnesses on his or her behalf under conditions of equality;

  (v) If considered to have infringed the penal law, to have this decision and any measures imposed in consequence thereof reviewed by a higher competent, independent and impartial authority or judicial body according to law;

  (vi) To have the free assistance of an interpreter if the child cannot understand or speak the language used;

  (vii) To have his or her privacy fully respected at all stages of the proceedings.

3.   States Parties shall seek to promote the establishment of laws, procedures, authorities and institutions specifically applicable to children alleged as, accused of, or recognised as having infringed the penal law, and, in particular:

(a) The establishment of a minimum age below which children shall be presumed not to have the capacity to infringe the penal law;

(b) Whenever appropriate and desirable, measures for dealing with such children without resorting to judicial proceedings, providing that human rights and legal safeguards are fully respected.

4.   A variety of dispositions, such as care, guidance and supervision orders; counselling; probation; foster care; education and vocational training programmes and other alternatives to institutional care shall be available to ensure that children are dealt with in a manner appropriate to their well-being and proportionate both to their circumstances and the offence.

ALSO OF INTEREST FROM XPL

Networked Communications and Compliance with the Law
Stephen Mason, Barrister

Stephen Mason's new book has evolved from the leading UK guide about Email and the Internet at Work to cover all **Networked Communications** – and is your simple-to-use guide to the law and compliance for your network. Communications from email, to Voice over Internet and messaging are covered. The steps compliance officers and their advisers must take are clearly laid out and examples from cases amply illustrate the point.

ISBN 1 85811 356 3   £44   New in 2005

Law for IT Professionals
Paul Brennan, Former General Counsel of the Federation Against Software Theft (FAST)

IT professionals should be concentrating on delivery IT. Now, however, professionals in every position or role are faced with a legion of complex legal issues from the internet to data protection, to copyright to EU Directives.They need something short to give them the bottom line. This book does that. The idea is to identify the key laws which are needed and describe them as briefly as possible (in a readable way), covering the essentials andhighlighting the pitfalls to avoid.

ISBN 1 85811 322 9   £19.95   2003

Legal Protection of Software
Richard Morgan, Consultant, Cornwell Affiliates and Kit Burden, Partner, Barlow Lyde & Gilbert

By covering the life of a software product, the book provides all the individual or company would need. Like all the books Richard Morgan and Kit Burden have written, this title is legally authoritative and will be of great use to lawyers working in the area – especially commercial lawyers without expertise in IT. Full of checklists and flowcharts and other useful tools, it will prove invaluable to advisers and data users alike. Far more than just a law book, it will have a wide sale to business and their professional advisers.

ISBN 1 85811 294 X   £38

Intellectual Property and Information Technology Law
David Bainbridge BSc, LLB, PhD, CEng, MICE, MBCS, Reader in Law, University of Aston

Intellectual Property and Information Technology Law is a paper and electronic journal covering key developments in each of the major areas of Intellectual Property: *Trade Marks *Copyright *Patents *Designs *Licensing and *Computer Software. Essential developments in intellectual property law and procedure in the UK, Europe and worldwide are covered in an accessible and concise way. In-depth articles also cover issues of particular concern. Contact us for subscription details at the address below.

To order:
**xpl publishing, 99 hatfield road, st albans, AL1 4EG
tel 0870 143 2569   fax 0845 456 6385   web: www.xplpublishing.com**

DATA PROTECTION

Second Edition

D1745112

DATA PROTECTION

Second Edition

David Bainbridge, BSc, LLB, PhD, CEng, MICE, MBCS, CITP

Barrister of Lincoln's Inn

Professor of Business Law, Aston Business School, University of Aston

xpl

© Author 2005

Published by

xpl publishing
99 Hatfield Road
St Albans AL1 4JL
www.xplpublishing.com

ISBN 185811 342 3

Typeset by Saxon Graphics Ltd, Derby

Printed in Great Britain by Lighting Source